MACV
The Joint Command in the Years of Escalation, 1962–1967

United States Army in Vietnam

MACV
The Joint Command in the Years of Escalation, 1962–1967

by

Graham A. Cosmas

Center of Military History
United States Army
Washington, D.C., 2006

Library of Congress Cataloging-in-Publication Data

Cosmas, Graham A.
    MACV : the joint command in the years of escalation, 1962–1967 / by Graham A. Cosmas.
       p. cm. — (United States Army in Vietnam)
    Includes bibliographical references and index.
  1. Vietnamese Conflict, 1961–1975—United States. 2. United States. Military Assistance Command, Vietnam—History. I. Title. II. Series.

    DS558.C68 2006
    959.704'340973—dc22

                                                    2005025726

CMH Pub 91–6–1

First Printing

For sale by the Superintendent of Documents, U.S. Government Printing Office
Internet: bookstore.gpo.gov   Phone: toll free (866) 512-1800;   DC area (202) 512-1800
Fax: (202) 512-2250 Mail: Stop SSOP, Washington, DC 20402-0001

United States Army in Vietnam

Jeffrey J. Clarke, General Editor

Advisory Committee
(As of August 2005)

Jon T. Sumida
University of Maryland

Eric M. Bergerud
Lincoln University

Lt. Gen. Anthony R. Jones
U.S. Army Training and Doctrine
Command

Brig. Gen. Daniel J. Kaufman
U.S. Military Academy

Adrian R. Lewis
University of North Texas

Brian M. Linn
Texas A&M University

Howard P. Lowell
National Archives and Records
Administration

Col. Craig Madden
U.S. Army War College

John H. Morrow, Jr.
University of Georgia

Reina J. Pennington
Norwich University

Sandy R. Riley
Administrative Assistant to the
Secretary of the Army

Ronald H. Spector
George Washington University

Brig. Gen. Volney Warner
U.S. Army Command and General Staff College

U.S. Army Center of Military History

Brig. Gen. (Ret.) John S. Brown, Chief of Military History

Chief Historian
Chief, Histories Division
Acting Editor in Chief

Jeffrey J. Clarke
Richard W. Stewart
Keith R. Tidman

. . . to Those Who Served

Foreword

MACV: The Joint Command in the Years of Escalation, 1962–1967, is the first of two volumes that examine the Vietnam conflict from the perspective of the theater commander and his headquarters. It traces the story of the Military Assistance Command, Vietnam (MACV), from its establishment in February 1962 to the climax of American escalation at the end of 1967. It deals with theater-level command relationships, strategy, and operations and supplements detailed studies in the Center of Military History's United States Army in Vietnam series covering combat operations, the advisory effort, and relations with the media.

MACV: The Joint Command recounts how the MACV commander and his staff viewed the war at various periods and how and why they arrived at their decisions. It analyzes the interservice politics of organizing and managing a joint command; MACV's relationships with Pacific Command, the Joint Chiefs of Staff, and the secretary of defense; and the evolution of the command's dealings with its South Vietnamese and third country allies. Perhaps most important, it traces the commander's role in developing and executing U.S. policy in Vietnam, a role that extended beyond military operations to encompass diplomacy and pacification. As an experiment—not entirely successful—in nation-building, the story of the Military Assistance Command contains many parallels to more recent Army engagements and so serves as a potential source of important lessons.

This is the ninth volume published in the Unites States Army in Vietnam series. Its appearance constitutes another step in the fulfillment of the Center of Military History's commitment to produce an authoritative history of Army participation in the Vietnam War.

Washington, D.C.
30 September 2005

JOHN S. BROWN
Brigadier General, USA (Ret.)
Chief of Military History

The Author

Graham A. Cosmas was born in Weehawken, New Jersey, and received his education from the schools of Leonia, New Jersey, and from Columbia University, Oberlin College, and the University of Wisconsin. After teaching at the University of Texas (Austin) and the University of Guam, he joined the staff of the U.S. Marine Corps History and Museums Division in December 1973. Dr. Cosmas moved to the U.S. Army Center of Military History in 1979 and remained there until 2001, when he became deputy director of the Joint History Office of the Joint Chiefs of Staff. Dr. Cosmas is the author of *An Army for Empire: The U.S. Army in the Spanish-American War, 1898–1899*, and coauthor of *U.S. Marines in Vietnam: Vietnamization and Redeployment, 1970–1971* and *The Medical Department: Medical Service in the European Theater of Operations*, a volume in the United States Army in World War II series. He served in 1984–85 as the Harold K. Johnson Visiting Professor of Military History at the U.S. Army Military History Institute, Carlisle Barracks, Pennsylvania. He has published numerous articles and book reviews.

Preface

MACV: The Joint Command in the Years of Escalation describes the evolution of the command during the period of gradual expansion of the American effort in South Vietnam. From its establishment in February 1962 as a small, temporary organization to administer an assistance program, the Military Assistance Command, Vietnam, grew by late 1967 into a large, permanent headquarters that directed more than half a million American soldiers, sailors, airmen, and marines in a wide range of combat and pacification operations.

This volume tells the story of MACV's development as an organization and of the command's role in making and implementing American national policy in Southeast Asia. Hence, it treats both national-level decisions and military operations from the perspective of the theater joint commander. In relation to the United States Army in Vietnam series, this volume and its sequel, dealing with the later period of the conflict, will provide a general overview of aspects of the war that are covered in much greater detail in the other works. The inclusion of this study of a joint command in a series devoted principally to the activities of a single service results from two circumstances: that MACV throughout its existence was an Army-dominated headquarters and that upon the command's disestablishment its records were placed in the custody of the Army's Office of the Adjutant General.

The preparation of a work of this scope was possible only with the assistance and support of a great many other people. Throughout the years, my colleagues in the Southeast Asia Branch of Histories Division at the Center of Military History guided me through the sources, read and critiqued drafts of chapters, and through many hours of conversation broadened and deepened my understanding of the war. Vincent H. Demma helped me get started through his encyclopedic knowledge of the Center of Military History's documents on the Vietnam War. Charles R. Anderson, Dale W. Andrade, William M. Hammond, Richard A. Hunt, George L. MacGarrigle, Joel D. Meyerson, and Adrian G. Traas generously permitted me to draw upon their work, which made an imprint on mine.

Others at the Center of Military History contributed to this book. The Historical Resources and Organizational History Branches were always responsive to my requests for books, documents, and information, and members of the Production Services Division edited and proofread the manuscript, designed the maps and charts, and chose the illustrations.

As chief of the Southeast Asia Branch, John Schlight guided my early steps on this volume and ensured that I gave due attention to the role of air power in MACV's war. I am grateful to a succession of division chiefs who supervised this project over its lengthy gestation—Lt. Col. Richard O. Perry; Cols. Robert H. Sholly, William T. Bowers, and Clyde L. Jonas; and Richard W. Stewart. Several Chiefs of Military History supervised and supported this work. Brig. Gen. Douglas Kinnard initiated the project and set its direction. Brig. Gens. William A. Stofft, Harold W. Nelson, John W. Mountcastle, and John S. Brown all helped it on its way. I owe a special debt of thanks to my current supervisor, Brig. Gen. David A. Armstrong (U.S. Army, Ret.), director of the Joint History Office, Joint Chiefs of Staff, for allowing me time after leaving the Center's employ to finish this volume.

The review panel, chaired by Jeffrey J. Clarke, the Center's chief historian, provided useful comments and recommendations. I am grateful to panel members—General William A. Knowlton (U.S. Army, Ret.), Brig. Gen. Douglas Kinnard, Larry Berman, Robert Buzzanco, Paul Miles, William Hammond, John Elsberg, and Cody Phillips. My special thanks go to General William B. Rosson, who provided detailed written comments on the manuscript.

As appropriate for a volume on a joint command, members of other service historical offices helped me with advice and access to sources. They include William Heimdahl and Wayne Thompson of the Office of Air Force History; Edward J. Marolda of the U.S. Naval Historical Center; and Jack Shulimson, formerly of the History and Museums Division, U.S. Marine Corps. Walter Poole of the Joint History Office, Joint Chiefs of Staff, read and criticized a draft of the manuscript.

Like all historians, I could have accomplished little without the assistance of the staffs of records repositories. David C. Humphrey and Gary Gallagher, both of whom have since moved on to other positions, were of great help at the Lyndon B. Johnson Library. At the U.S. Army Military History Institute, Richard J. Sommers, David A. Keogh, Randy Rakers, and John J. Slonaker guided me through the institute's extensive Vietnam collections. Members of the National Defense University Library staff provided me with access to the papers of Maxwell D. Taylor. Richard L. Boylan and the staff of the National Archives and Records Administration were responsive to all my requests.

Three participants in the events described in this volume graciously consented to be interviewed on their experiences. Paul E. Suplizio, formerly of the MACV J3 office, discussed with me the transition from the guerrilla to the big-unit war. George Allen of the Central Intelligence Agency provided insight into the order of battle controversy and other aspects of intelligence in Vietnam and also shared with me his teaching notes on the subject. James M. Loome recounted his experiences in the Analysis Division of CORDS.

Finally, I would like to thank Daniel and Lindy Mings of Austin, Texas, for their hospitality during my two visits to the Lyndon B. Johnson Library.

It remains only to note that the conclusions and interpretations in this book are mine alone and that I am solely responsible for any errors.

Washington, D.C. GRAHAM A. COSMAS
30 September 2005

Contents

Chapter   *Page*

1. **A Deepening Commitment and a New Command** . . . 3
    Beginnings of United States Involvement 5
    Toward the Second Indochina War 8
    The United States Responds to the New Threat 15
    Creating the Command 21

2. **A Joint Command: Complications and Conflicts, 1962–1963** 35
    MACV and the Pacific Chain of Command 36
    MACV and the MAAG 42
    Formation of MACV Headquarters 44
    The Component Commands 53
    The Debate over Control of Air Power 56
    A Small But Complicated Command 60

3. **From Hope to Frustration** 71
    The Enemy 71
    Developing an Allied Strategy 75
    The Campaign Falls Apart 85
    MACV and the Coup Against Diem 95

4. **Reorganizing and Reviving Pacification** 117
    United States Policy: Picking Up the Pieces 117
    Hanoi Prepares for a Larger War 120
    A New MACV Commander 122
    Headquarters Reorganization and Expansion 125
    MACV: Executive Agent for Pacification? 139
    Struggling for Stability 144

5. **The Beginning of Escalation** 157
    Widening the War 157
    OPLAN 34A 159
    Air and Ground Operations in Laos 161
    Early Planning for the Air War 164
    After Tonkin Gulf: Reinforcing the South 167
    Air War in the North: Planning and Command 172
    The Marines Land at Da Nang 176

Chapter	Page

6. Beginnings of the Ground Troop Commitment, January–June 1965 187
    Plans and Proposals, 1954–1964 187
    Collapse of the CHIEN THANG Plan 190
    A Limited Response 195
    Three Proposals for Sending Troops 200
    Edging into the Ground War 206
    Questions of Command and the Concept of Operations . . 212
    Where the Question Stood, June 1965 218

7. The Fateful Decisions, June 1965–February 1966 . . . 227
    South Vietnam in Peril 227
    Air Power Holds Back the Enemy 230
    Decisions for an American Ground War 232
    Implementing Phase I 245
    Planning Phase II 252
    Decisions at Honolulu 256

8. MACV Headquarters: The Years of Expansion, 1965–1967 267
    Enlarging the Headquarters 267
    Planning and Control of Operations 275
    Combined Intelligence 284
    The Advisory Mission 288
    Reporting, Research, and Analysis 290
    How Joint the Command? 295

9. Controlling U.S. Forces 307
    Military Assistance Command, Pacific Command, and the JCS 307
    Naval Forces, Vietnam 310
    U.S. Army, Vietnam: A Question of Roles 314
    The Seventh Air Force: A Multiplicity of Masters 320
    The Air War in the South: A Single Manager? 323
    The Field Forces and the III Marine Amphibious Force . . . 331

10. The Allies and Pacification 343
    The Allies 343
    The South Vietnamese: Cooperation and Coordination . . 348
    Pacification and Saigon Politics 353
    CORDS: A Single Manager at Last 357

11. The Wider Theater 371
    Fragmentation of Command 371

Chapter	Page

    The Ho Chi Minh Trail and the Plain of Jars 373
    Cambodia 379
    MACV and Rolling Thunder 382
    A Tangled Chain of Command 389

12. An Evolving Strategy 395
    Basic Questions 395
    The Initial Concept 397
    Problems of Implementation 405
    More Troops or a New Strategy? 411
    Incremental Adjustments 420

13. An Autumn of Uncertainty 439
    The Public Relations War 441
    The Order of Battle Controversy 446
    President Johnson Moves To Level Off the War 461
    The Enemy Plans an Offensive 466

14. Conclusion: The Years of Escalation 477

Bibliographical Note 495

Glossary 509

Military Map Symbols 512

Index 513

Table

MACV Principal Officers at Activation. 48

Charts

No.

    1. U.S. Military Assistance Command, Vietnam, 1964 61
    2. U.S. Military Assistance Command, Vietnam,
        31 December 1964 133
    3. Organization of MACV Headquarters, May 1967 276
    4. Pacific Command Relationships, 1967. 319

Maps

No.		Page
1.	Indochina, 1961	4
2.	South Vietnam Corps Areas, 1963	84
3.	Major U.S. and Allied Forces, South Vietnam, 1966	235
4.	Saigon, 1967	269
5.	Interdiction Areas, Laos, 1965–1967	384
6.	ROLLING THUNDER Route Packages, North Vietnam, 1967	387
7.	Strong Point Obstacle System, 1967	424

Illustrations

General Paul D. Harkins	3
Ho Chi Minh	5
Prime Minister Ngo Dinh Diem	9
Walt W. Rostow	19
Lt. Gen. Lionel C. McGarr with U.S. Ambassador to Vietnam Frederick E. Nolting	23
Generals Lyman L. Lemnitzer and Maxwell D. Taylor, Secretary of Defense Robert S. McNamara, and President John F. Kennedy, 1961	25
General Harkins, Admiral Harry D. Felt, and Ambassador Nolting	27
Secretary of Defense McNamara	36
Admiral Felt	37
MACV Headquarters, 137 Pasteur Street	46
Maj. Gen. Richard G. Weede, USMC	47
The MACV Staff	49
Brig. Gen. Rollen H. Anthis, USAF	55
Vietnamese T–28 Fighter-Bombers	58
U.S. B–26 Light Bomber	58
H–21 "Flying Banana"	60
Viet Cong Patrol a Canal	74
Self-immolation of a Buddhist Priest	89
Brig. Gen. Robert H. York, Lt. Col. John P. Vann, and Capt. William R. Johnson	93
Maj. Gen. Duong Van Minh and Nguyen Ngoc	96
Ambassador Henry Cabot Lodge with President Diem	99
Secretary McNamara with South Vietnamese Premier Nguyen Khanh and General Taylor	118
General William C. Westmoreland	124
PACAF Chief, General Hunter Harris, USAF, with General Westmoreland and Lt. Gen. Joseph Moore, USAF	132
Admiral Ulysses S. G. Sharp	134
Ambassador Maxwell D. Taylor with Secretary McNamara	142

Page

U.S. Adviser with a Montagnard Strike Force	147
Aftermath of a Mortar Attack at Bien Hoa Air Base	159
U.S. Ambassador to Laos William H. Sullivan	163
President Lyndon B. Johnson with Secretary of Defense McNamara and Ambassador Taylor	166
McGeorge Bundy with General Westmoreland	173
Military Dependents Depart South Vietnam	177
Marines in Defensive Positions After Landing at Da Nang	180
A Viet Cong Soldier Wielding an AK–47 Rifle	193
U.S. Army Helicopters Cover South Vietnamese Marines near Binh Gia, December 1964	194
F–4B Phantom II Aircraft	199
General Harold K. Johnson	201
The Joint Chiefs of Staff	207
Secretary of Defense McNamara with Nguyen Van Thieu, South Vietnamese Chief of State	212
Marines Wading Across a River	213
Chief of State Thieu	229
Air Vice Marshal Nguyen Cao Ky	229
A B–52 Arc Light Bombing Mission	232
General Earle G. Wheeler	233
Ambassdor-Designate Henry Cabot Lodge, Secretary of Defense McNamara, Chief of State Thieu, and Premier Ky	242
1st Cavalry Division (Airmobile) Soldiers Arrive at Qui Nhon	246
Aerial View of the Cam Ranh Bay Complex	247
Maj. Gen. Stanley R. Larsen	248
General Wheeler, Secretary of State Dean Rusk, and President Johnson at the February 1966 Honolulu Conference	257
MACV Headquarters at Tan Son Nhut	270
General Westmoreland receives the Boy Scout Silver Buffalo Award for Distinguished Service as Generals Harold Johnson and Creighton W. Abrams, Jr., Look On	274
General Abrams	277
Lt. Gen. John R. Chaisson	279
Maj. Gen. Joseph A. McChristian	285
Admiral Ulysses S. G. Sharp	309
Rear Adm. Norvell G. Ward	311
A Vessel of the Riverine Force Patrols the Mekong Delta Waters	313
Brig. Gen. John Norton	316
USARV Headquarters at Long Binh	317
General John P. McConnell	322
Lt. Gen. William W. Momyer Receives His Fourth Star from Generals Westmoreland and Abrams	326
Maj. Gen. Lewis W. Walt	333

	Page
Brig. Gen. Edward H. de Saussure, with Korean Maj. Gen. Chae Myung Shin	346
South Korean Troops Inspect a Dead Viet Cong Guerrilla	347
Lt. Gen. Le Nghen Khan, General Cao Van Vien, and Lt. Col. Ted Gordiner	350
Lt. Gen. Nguyen Chanh Thi	355
Generals Westmoreland and Wheeler with Ambassador Ellsworth Bunker	360
Brig. Gen. Donald D. Blackburn	376
Prince Souvanna Phouma	377
Prince Norodom Sihanouk with President Kennedy	380
Ambassador Bunker and General Westmoreland Greet Secretary of Defense McNamara on Arrival in Saigon	388
Lt. Gen. Victor H. Krulak	403
General Westmoreland Tours III Marine Amphibious Force Headquarters	409
Dr. Alain Enthoven	418
Armored Vehicles of the 11th Armored Cavalry Advance During Operation JUNCTION CITY	421
General Westmoreland with Barry Zorthian	440
Antiwar Protesters at the Pentagon, October 1967	442
General Westmoreland Addresses a Joint Session of Congress, April 1967	444
CIA Director Richard Helms	451
Maj. Gen. Phillip B. Davidson	453
Col. Daniel O. Graham	453

MACV
The Joint Command
in the
Years of Escalation, 1962–1967

1

A Deepening Commitment and a New Command

On 13 February 1962, a tall, gray-haired, athletic-looking United States Army officer stepped off an airplane at Saigon's Tan Son Nhut Air Base. He was General Paul Donal Harkins, commander of the United States Military Assistance Command, Vietnam (MACV), the headquarters newly organized to direct expanding American participation in the war between the Republic of Vietnam and its Communist-led insurgent adversaries, popularly known as the Viet Cong. Harkins, a principal staff officer under General George S. Patton in World War II and most recently deputy commander in chief of the U.S. Army, Pacific (USARPAC), came to Vietnam with a solid record as a military planner and administrator and with a reputation for tact and diplomatic finesse. In a brief arrival statement, he expressed "admiration" for the Vietnamese people and declared that he regarded his Vietnam assignment as "a great challenge," which he accepted with "determination and humility."[1]

General Harkins (NARA)

As General Harkins prepared to assume his duties, his command already included almost 5,000 American military personnel. Some were engaged in advising and assisting the Armed Forces of the Republic of Vietnam (RVNAF); others, in increasing numbers, served in Army, Air Force, Navy, and Marine units providing direct combat and logistical support to the Vietnamese or, in the case of the Navy, patrolling Indochinese coastal waters. These Americans, especially advisers and helicopter crews, were beginning to come under, and return, Viet Cong fire. Back in the United States, there was talk of an undeclared war in Southeast Asia, coupled with public demands that the administra-

MAP 1

A Deepening Commitment and a New Command

Ho Chi Minh
(Time Life Pictures/Getty Images)

tion of President John F. Kennedy explain candidly to the American people its plans and purposes in intensifying U.S. involvement in the Vietnamese conflict.[2]

Beginnings of United States Involvement

The struggle in which General Harkins and his command were engaged had been in progress since the end of World War II. Its initial antagonists were France and the Communist-controlled Viet Minh (more formally, the Vietnamese Independence League, or *Viet Nam Doc Lap Dong Minh Hoi)*.[3] As the principal Vietnamese nationalist organization, the Viet Minh owed its survival and success in large part to the skill and determination of its founder and principal leader, Ho Chi Minh. *(Map 1)* Ho, a dedicated Vietnamese nationalist, became a Communist while living in France in the early 1920s and was trained in Moscow as an agent of the Comintern (the Communist International whose aim was to overthrow the "international bourgeoisie").

By the outbreak of World War II, he had recruited a party cadre of young intellectuals and had outlined a revolutionary strategy calling for an alliance of urban workers, peasants, and bourgeois nationalists in a broad patriotic front covertly dominated by a Communist hard core. The front's mission was to employ guerrilla warfare in the countryside and propaganda and subversion in the cities to destroy French authority in a protracted conflict and to establish an independent Vietnam governed according to Marxist-Leninist principles.

Ho and the Viet Minh exploited to the full the near-anarchy created in much of Vietnam by the Japanese occupation, which coexisted with a weakened, discredited French colonial administration. By V-J Day, the Viet Minh possessed significant military forces equipped with captured Japanese and French weapons. Their clandestine village and hamlet People's Revolutionary Committees exercised effective political control of much of the countryside, especially in northern and central Vietnam. In August 1945, as the Japanese surrendered and the Nationalist Chinese prepared to occupy northern Indochina (with the British in the south), the Viet Minh assumed political authority over most of northern Vietnam, including the capital city of Hanoi. There, early in September, Ho proclaimed Vietnamese independence and established the Democratic Republic of Vietnam (DRV). Meanwhile the French, with British assistance, took control of most of southern Vietnam, including the southern capital, Saigon.[4]

During 1946 war broke out between France and the Viet Minh. The French enjoyed initial military success. They drove the Viet Minh out of Hanoi and most other towns in northern and central Vietnam and inflicted heavy casualties. But the Viet Minh proved resilient. Exploiting popular nationalism and their own organizational and propaganda skills, they kept clandestine control of most of the rural population. Their local guerrillas continually harassed French troops and terrorized pro-French Vietnamese; and their regular forces, who increased steadily in numbers, evaded French offensives and counterattacked where they had the advantage. In a belated effort to counter Viet Minh political appeal, the French in March 1949 created a client Vietnamese state under Emperor Bao Dai, a surviving member of Vietnam's precolonial imperial dynasty. The regime was intended as a rallying point for the considerable number of Vietnamese nationalists who opposed Ho's Communists, but the French granted it so little real sovereignty that it never became a viable political alternative to the Viet Minh.

By mid-1950 the war was going badly for the French. The Viet Minh, with advisers and heavy weapons provided by the newly victorious Chinese Communists, fielded a regular force of about 120,000 men, organized into divisions. With at least an equal number of guerrillas and village militia at their disposal, they began winning victories over French forces. The government in Paris, with military and financial exhaustion looming and with home public opinion turning against an apparently futile colonial struggle, directed increasingly urgent appeals for aid to the United States.

The administration of President Harry S. Truman initially kept its distance from the Indochina war, which many American officials viewed as a losing French effort to preserve outmoded colonialism. However, the U.S. association with France under the North Atlantic Treaty, coupled with mounting concern over Viet Minh ties to the Soviet Union and to the Communist People's Republic of China, both of which recognized the DRV in January 1950, led the administration to extend to French Indochina a policy of containment. The State Department and the Joint Chiefs of Staff both concluded that the fall of Indochina to the Viet Minh would open all Southeast Asia to Communist aggression and subversion.

A Deepening Commitment and a New Command

Accepting this assessment, President Truman, on 4 February 1950, formally recognized pro-French regimes in Laos, Cambodia, and Vietnam, known collectively as the Associated States of Indochina. A month later, he approved $15 million in military aid for the French forces there. The outbreak of the Korean War in June merely added urgency to a commitment already made and induced a doubling of the amount of aid. At the end of the year, after the French signed a treaty increasing the Associated States' control over their own affairs, and after they agreed with Bao Dai to form a Vietnamese National Army to fight alongside the French expeditionary force, the United States joined with France and the Associated States in a mutual assistance pact. Under it, the United States promised aid to the other signatories, to be administered by an American military assistance advisory group (MAAG). By these decisions, the Truman administration committed the United States to a long, tortuous struggle against Vietnamese communism.

In August 1950, even before the assistance pact was signed, the Indochina MAAG began work in Saigon, the seat of the Bao Dai government and the French military headquarters. Gradually expanded from its initial 128 officers and enlisted men to over 300, the group spent most of its time attempting to validate French aid requests and monitoring the turnover and use of American-supplied equipment, standard tasks of such U.S. advisory groups around the world.[5]

During the ensuing three years, a massive infusion of American aircraft, artillery, vehicles, infantry weapons, and munitions enabled the French to stave off defeat—but not much more. In a grim attritional struggle, the Viet Minh bled the French expeditionary force in large-unit battles in northern and central Vietnam and kept up guerrilla activity and subversion everywhere. To the frustration of the Americans, the French refused to accept tactical advice and obstructed U.S. efforts to develop the indigenous anti-Communist political and military forces. As 1953 came to an end, a war-weary French government was edging toward a negotiated settlement. The Viet Minh also were feeling the strain of the long, increasingly violent struggle. Their principal foreign backers, the Soviet Union and the People's Republic of China, for their own reasons, wanted an early end to hostilities—the Soviets to gain a respite to deal with the aftermath of Joseph Stalin's death; the Chinese Communists to recover from the Korean War and consolidate their newly won control of their country.[6]

Early in 1954 the United States, the Soviet Union, and their principal allies agreed to hold an Indochina peace conference at Geneva in May. To strengthen their negotiating position, the Viet Minh launched a final offensive. In March 1954, 35,000 Communist regulars, well equipped with artillery, laid siege to 15,000 French Union troops at Dien Bien Phu in western Tonkin. During the ensuing weeks, they slowly but surely overcame the French defenders. The garrison surrendered on 7 May, the opening day of the Geneva Conference. After considering and rejecting proposals for U.S. military intervention to save Dien Bien Phu, President Dwight D. Eisenhower and Secretary of State John Foster Dulles resigned themselves to a distasteful negotiated settlement. They set in motion efforts to supplant France in shoring up whatever was left of the anti-Communist position in Indochina and began planning for a Southeast Asia collective defense organization.[7]

In July, after prolonged negotiations, the contending parties in Indochina and the concerned outside powers—the United States, Britain, the Soviet Union, and the People's Republic of China—arrived at a compromise settlement. The French and Viet Minh agreed to a cease-fire under international supervision and to a temporary partition of Vietnam along the 17th Parallel, which was to be a demilitarized zone. French forces were to regroup south of the parallel and the Viet Minh to its north. Neither side was to introduce new troops or equipment except as replacements. Separate from the cease-fire agreement, all participants in the conference except the United States and Bao Dai's government signed a declaration calling for nationwide elections in 1956 to choose a government for a unified Vietnam. Under still other agreements, Laos and Cambodia became independent, neutral states under non-Communist regimes. In Laos, the Viet Minh–sponsored insurgents, the Pathet Lao, received a regroupment zone of two provinces. The United States made no secret of its disgust at the surrender of half of Vietnam but pledged not to disrupt the agreements.

Far from establishing peace, the diplomats at Geneva drew the lines for the next stage of the conflict. In effect, the Viet Minh had accepted half a loaf at the insistence of their Russian and Chinese comrades. Their revolution was politically and militarily well developed and had made itself a state in the northern half of Vietnam. In the south, a strong political underground and guerrilla forces were poised to resume the liberation struggle when circumstances permitted. By contrast, the Vietnamese anti-Communists, grouped around Bao Dai's regime, were fragmented and discredited by their association with France. For their part, the Americans had no intention of writing off Indochina. U.S. civilian and military leaders believed that French mistakes, in particular failure to support Indochina's anti-Communist nationalists, had caused the defeat of 1954. Confident that they could do better, the Americans were bent on trying to save at least South Vietnam from communism.

Toward the Second Indochina War

Although the Geneva declaration implied only a temporary partition of Vietnam, both sides organized their halves of the country as separate states. In the north, the Viet Minh established a thoroughgoing Marxist-Leninist regime, with the title Democratic Republic of Vietnam. In the south, the French, the Americans, and the anti-Com-

A Deepening Commitment and a New Command

Prime Minister Diem (NARA)

munist regime that the French had set up under Emperor Bao Dai also tried to organize a functioning state. They faced an almost impossible task. The Bao Dai government exercised little political authority outside Saigon, the southern capital; its 170,000-man army was an aggregation of poorly armed and trained small units rather than an integrated, cohesive force. Saigon's police were controlled by a gangster syndicate, the Binh Xuyen, which had its own private army and was a longtime ally of the French. Outside the capital, two political-religious sects, the Hoa Hao and Cao Dai, also with armies of their own, dominated portions of the countryside. The Viet Minh underground was still present in much of the rest. As if these adversities were not enough, South Vietnam faced the problem of resettling over 800,000 Catholic refugees from the north who had fled the prospect of life under communism. Bao Dai's prime minister, Ngo Dinh Diem, who took office in June 1954, was a proud, reclusive Catholic intellectual, disliked about equally by the French, the Vietnamese army commander, the Binh Xuyen, and the sects.[8]

In spite of these unpromising circumstances, President Dwight D. Eisenhower committed his administration to preserving South Vietnam and the other non-Communist Indochinese states. The administration in mid-August 1954 expanded the mission of the Indochina Military Assistance Advisory Group, which had supported the French military effort, to include reorganizing and training the armed forces of South Vietnam, Laos, and Cambodia. Besides assigning the training mission to the advisory group, President Eisenhower on 20 August approved a National Security Council policy statement pledging the United States to "make every possible effort, not openly inconsistent with . . . the [Geneva] armistice agreements, to defeat Communist subversion and influence and to maintain and support friendly non-Communist governments" in Indochina. The following month, the United States joined Great Britain, France, New Zealand, Australia, Pakistan, the Philippines, and Thailand in signing a collective security pact for Southeast Asia and forming a loose regional defense organization, the Southeast Asia Treaty Organization (SEATO). Its members pledged united action if any of them was attacked; in a separate protocol they extended their protection to the Indochinese states.

The year following these decisions witnessed what seemed at the time to be a political near miracle in South Vietnam. Prime Minister Diem, whose chances of survival most observers had rated minimal at best, displayed unexpected determination and staying power. With American help (and money), Diem first secured control of the South Vietnamese armed forces. He then defeated or bought off the Binh Xuyen, Cao Dai, and Hoa Hao. In October 1955 he staged a referendum in which South Vietnamese voters deposed Bao Dai as head of state and elected Diem president of a new Republic of Vietnam. The following year the French withdrew their last military advisers, their remaining expeditionary troops, and their high commissioner from South Vietnam. They left the United States with a clear field for its attempt to create an anti-Communist bastion in Indochina.

For three or four years after the tumultuous events of 1955, it seemed that the United States, through Diem, was achieving its goal. Bolstered by some $190 million a year in American military and economic aid, Diem enforced at least a degree of governmental authority throughout South Vietnam. His regime resettled the refugees, achieved a measure of economic prosperity, and promulgated what was, on paper, a progressive land reform policy. By means of a series of harsh and indiscriminate but effective anti-Communist "denunciation" campaigns, Diem made progress in destroying the remaining Viet Minh organization in the countryside. His troops kept the surviving sect and Communist guerrillas on the run, and his government attempted to establish mass organizations of its own to control and indoctrinate the people.[9] In 1956 Diem refused to hold, or even discuss, the all-Vietnam elections called for in the Geneva declaration. The Communist bloc acquiesced with only minimal protest. Diem's regime received diplomatic recognition from most non-Communist nations.

With the departure of the French and the consolidation of Diem's power, the U.S. Military Assistance Advisory Group took on the task of organizing, training, and advising the armed forces of the Republic of Vietnam. In November 1955 the Indochina MAAG became the Mili-

A Deepening Commitment and a New Command

tary Assistance Advisory Group, Vietnam, in acknowledgment of the separation of Vietnam from the other independent Associated States. The United States subsequently set up separate military assistance organizations for Cambodia and Laos.

In South Vietnam, the MAAG constituted a component of the United States country team headed by the American ambassador. Militarily, it was a joint entity under the commander in chief of U.S. forces in the Pacific (CINCPAC). The advisory group, which grew from an initial strength of 342 officers and enlisted men in 1954 to 685 in 1960, included sections in charge of support for the Vietnamese Army, Navy, Marine Corps, and Air Force, as well as small general and special staffs. It assigned advisers to Vietnamese corps and division headquarters, the armed forces schools and training centers, and major logistic installations. MAAG officers also worked with the Ministry of Defense and with the Joint General Staff (JGS), South Vietnam's highest military command element.[10]

Both MAAG chiefs of the early Diem era, Lt. Gen. John W. ("Iron Mike") O'Daniel (April 1954–November 1955) and Lt. Gen. Samuel T. ("Hanging Sam") Williams (November 1955–August 1960), concentrated on preparing South Vietnam to resist a conventional invasion across the 17th Parallel. Their objective was to build a lightly equipped regular ground force that, supported by a small air force and a coastal navy, could delay a North Vietnamese or Chinese incursion until U.S. or SEATO reinforcements arrived. Both commanders assumed the same units could readily counter any guerrilla challenge to the regime. Neither O'Daniel nor Williams envisioned that internal rebellion alone would bring South Vietnam to the verge of collapse.

By 1959 the advisory group, through hard, persistent work, had brought the South Vietnamese armed forces a long way from the ragtag collection of disparate units that the French had left behind three years before. The Army of the Republic of Vietnam (ARVN), the largest component of the 150,000-man force, consisted of seven infantry divisions patterned on those of the U.S. Army in World War II: four separate armored battalions, an airborne brigade, a marine group, and a helicopter squadron. Its chain of command ran from the Joint General Staff through corps and military regions to the divisions. South Vietnam possessed a modest air force of fighter-bombers, transports, and light observation planes and a small navy of subchasers, minesweepers, and amphibious craft. With American assistance, the armed forces had developed a well-conceived system of schools and training centers; many South Vietnamese officers had undergone additional military schooling in the United States. On the surface, the RVNAF seemed to be the "crack, combat-ready force" described by one optimistic American journalist. Most U.S. officials considered it more than adequate to ensure internal security and to hold back any drive from the north pending U.S. and SEATO intervention.

MACV: The Years of Escalation, 1962–1967

Sadly, the truth was different. The Vietnamese armed forces had severe weaknesses rooted in their nation's politics and society. Jealous of his power and determined not to allow a rival to concentrate armed force against him, President Diem divided military authority wherever possible, totally disrupting the formal chain of command. The entire officer corps was riddled with corruption and political favoritism; promotion went to men subservient to Diem rather than to those of proven professional competence, who were few enough in any case. Weak leadership, the social gulf between urban upper- and middle-class officers and peasant soldiers, and the absence of basic amenities and services for the enlisted men undermined morale. Operational commitments, especially as the Communist insurgency revived, forced curtailment of individual and unit training—even basic training.

MAAG advisers tried to remedy these failings—with at best limited success. The Vietnamese simply ignored American advice that did not suit them. Advisers, serving eleven-month tours, usually lacked proficiency in the Vietnamese language and familiarity with Vietnamese politics and culture; most had difficulty finding out what was going on in their units, not to mention influencing their counterparts. Making matters worse were an inadequate readiness reporting system and a tendency—especially under General Williams—to discourage adverse adviser reports on Vietnamese units that might reflect unfavorably on MAAG leadership and work to the detriment of the allies' morale. Thus, for a long time, the advisory group headquarters remained unaware of the extent of the dry rot.[11]

The armed forces reflected the state of Diem's regime as a whole: an impressive facade with fundamental weaknesses behind it. The regime's deficiencies grew worse with time. At the top President Diem, suspicious of everyone including the Americans, increasingly concentrated all political power in his own hands and in those of a shrinking circle of family members and sycophantic retainers. The closed, autocratic nature of the regime, and its ruthless suppression of all dissent, alienated a widening spectrum of non-Communist Vietnamese. In the countryside, the remnants of the Cao Dai and Hoa Hao were hostile to Diem. His anti-Communist campaigns, while gravely damaging the party organization in the villages, also inflicted injury and injustice on innocent peasants, making more enemies for the government. Diem's land reform program became bogged down in administrative inefficiency and corruption; in practice, it did little to improve the lot of the rural poor. In the Central Highlands, Diem's policy of settling ethnic Vietnamese on the land of the indigenous tribes, the so-called Montagnards, further turned those people—ever suspicious of the Vietnamese—against Saigon. By the late 1950s, the Diem regime owed its continued survival more to inaction by its enemies than to its own successes—and enemy inaction was coming to an end.

A Deepening Commitment and a New Command

Ho Chi Minh and his colleagues accepted the Geneva settlement as a temporary necessity but never abandoned their ultimate objective: a unified, Communist-ruled Vietnam dominating the rest of Indochina. Under the cease-fire agreement, they withdrew from South Vietnam to the north perhaps 100,000 troops and political cadres while leaving another 10,000 in the south to maintain the core of their movement. Initially, a number of constraints prevented their use of these forces, and of the battle-hardened DRV regular army, to finish off the shaky southern state. In the immediate post-Geneva years, Hanoi had all it could do to rebuild the war-shattered economy of North Vietnam while at the same time restructuring society along Marxist-Leninist lines. North Vietnam's international sponsors, the Soviet Union and China, were not disposed to support an assault on the south, especially at the risk of a direct military confrontation with the United States. In addition, the Hanoi leaders and their allies with good reason doubted the political viability of South Vietnam and probably expected it to collapse of its own accord. Hence, North Vietnam and its allies let pass Diem's refusal to hold the 1956 elections. Under instructions from the party in Hanoi, the Viet Minh cadres in the south confined their activities to political agitation and party and front-group organization. In the main, they adhered to these directives even as Diem's army and police uprooted their organizations and arrested and killed their members.[12]

Between 1957 and 1961 Hanoi, with the acquiescence and limited support of the Soviet Union and China, launched a new revolutionary war in the south, aimed at overthrowing the Diem regime. Ostensibly, the uprising was an indigenous southern response to an oppressive government, without visible connection to North Vietnam, Vietnamese communism, or the Viet Minh. In fact, it was organized and directed by a unified national Communist party headquartered in Hanoi that received a clandestine and unacknowledged but growing amount of manpower and materiel assistance from North Vietnam. Early in 1957, responding to Diem's inroads against the southern infrastructure, the northern party endorsed a campaign of assassination and terrorism against local officials of the Saigon regime, already begun by activists in parts of the south. Additionally, it directed accelerated party organization and the formation of small military units. Two years later, in January 1959, the Fifteenth Plenum of the Communist Party Central Committee, meeting in Hanoi, secretly ordered the launching of an armed struggle aimed at using the "political force of the masses" in concert with military action to bring down Diem. In the same year the North Vietnamese began sending back south the trained military and political functionaries who had regrouped north of the 17th Parallel in 1954, along with a growing amount of specialized equipment. These infiltrators, some 2,000 per year during 1959 and 1960, traveled by junk down the coast or by a land route through eastern Laos that became known as the Ho Chi Minh Trail. In May 1959, North Vietnam set up a special military command to improve the trail and manage traffic along it.

Other decisions and organizational steps followed. In September 1960 a national congress of the Vietnam Workers' Party (the official name of the Communist Party) declared liberation of the south and national reunification to be of equal importance with completing the socialist revolution in the north. Three months later, repeating the broad-front tactics of the Viet Minh, the party created the National Front for the Liberation of South Vietnam (NLF), a coalition of southern social, religious, and political groups that ostensibly directed the growing resistance to Diem and that in turn was run by a Communist inner core. To strengthen its own political and military command and control in the south, early in 1961 Hanoi reactivated the *Central Office for South Vietnam (COSVN)*, a southern branch of the party Central Committee that had directed operations in the region during the French war and had been disbanded in 1954. About the same time the party issued orders for still greater intensification of the struggle, emphasizing expansion of the military effort.[13]

In the south, the insurrection, once unleashed, made rapid progress. The stay-behind Viet Minh cadres, soon reinforced from the north, put in motion a threefold campaign of terrorism, rural and urban political agitation, and military action. To break down Diem's grass-roots authority, agents and guerrilla squads kidnapped or killed village, hamlet, and district officials; the number of victims increased each year, amounting to over 2,000 in 1960 alone. Armed propaganda teams moved into the villages. They recruited adherents by exploiting the many popular grievances against Diem and where possible set up local shadow governments.

Starting as early as 1957–1958 in a few places, and more generally after 1959, the insurgents raised military forces on the pattern of the war with the French: hamlet militia, local guerrillas, and mobile main force units, all formally known as the *People's Liberation Armed Forces (PLAF)*. The Diem regime quickly coined another name for them: "Viet Cong," a derogatory term for Vietnamese Communists, which became their common designation among South Vietnamese and Americans. In platoon, company, and occasionally battalion strength, and in escalating intensity year by year, the *PLAF* ambushed government units and raided small, isolated outposts, often to capture arms and ammunition. Under the test of combat, weak ARVN leadership, training deficiencies, and lackluster morale produced an embarrassingly high rate of weapon losses in small engagements and an all too common failure by large units even to find the Viet Cong, let alone engage and destroy them. By the end of 1960, the *PLAF*, counting all categories of its forces, had an estimated 15,000 men under arms; the Saigon government's authority in portions of rural South Vietnam had all but ceased to exist. What came to be called the Second Indochina War was well under way.[14]

A Deepening Commitment and a New Command

The United States Responds to the New Threat

In its early stages, the revived insurgency largely escaped the attention of both the United States country team and the Diem regime. The Americans had no intelligence network of their own in rural Vietnam, where most of the enemy activity occurred. Both they and the South Vietnamese government relied on the fragmented, poorly managed intelligence services. Those agencies, run by people mainly interested in keeping in favor with Diem, were slow to report bad news, thereby denying the allies early warning of the developing threat. Only in late 1959 and early 1960, as Viet Cong military activity intensified, did both the country team and the Central Intelligence Agency (CIA) begin reporting that a nationwide insurgency was under way and receiving significant support from North Vietnam. They also called attention to increasing disaffection with the Diem regime among otherwise anti-Communist elements. An abortive military coup against Diem in November 1960 demonstrated that discontent existed even within the armed forces themselves.[15]

As early as 1955 a CIA estimate had declared that "should the Viet Minh initiate large-scale guerrilla operations supported by substantial infiltration from the north, the South Vietnamese government would be hard-pressed" and probably would require outside military assistance to survive. Nevertheless, during the late 1950s American contingency plans for Southeast Asia, prepared by the U.S. Pacific Command (PACOM), concentrated on deployment of American and SEATO forces to counter a conventional North Vietnamese and Chinese offensive across the Demilitarized Zone and down the Mekong valley. MAAG defense plans, supporting those of the Pacific Command, also were directed toward a Korea-style conflict. The advisory group did recognize the need for local paramilitary forces to keep order in rural districts. However, it and the U.S. Operations Mission (USOM), the civilian foreign economic aid agency, engaged in a prolonged jurisdictional wrangle over responsibility for training and assisting the Diem government's several overlapping rural militias. This dispute, which also involved disagreements over the organization and missions of the local units, prevented development of what should have been the government's first line of defense against the Viet Cong.[16]

During 1960, as the new threat became apparent, the United States began increasing its assistance to South Vietnam. It sent additional arms and equipment to Saigon's forces, including more modern field radios and helicopters. When President Diem decided to organize counter-guerrilla ranger units, the United States provided Army Special Forces officers and enlisted men to help train the new companies. Various agencies, including the MAAG, began making comprehensive civil-military counterinsurgency plans for South Vietnam. Late in the year, at joint State and Defense Department direction, the Saigon country team assembled an overall plan for U.S. support of a South Vietnamese "national emergency effort" to defeat the Viet Cong and pacify the country. This Counterinsurgency Plan, which the team dispatched to Washington in January 1961, called for a U.S.-financed increase of 20,000 men in the RVNAF and for additional American military and training aid to the paramilitary forces. Partly resolving the MAAG-USOM jurisdictional dispute, the plan recommended transfer of one paramilitary component, the Civil Guard, from the USOM-advised Interior Ministry to the MAAG-advised Defense Ministry. In return for this increased American assistance, President Diem was to broaden the political base of his regime, reduce corruption, restore a coherent military chain of command, unify his intelligence effort, and improve civic action and psychological warfare programs.

The Counterinsurgency Plan fit in well with the thinking of newly inaugurated President John F. Kennedy. Much impressed by the threat to fragile developing countries of Communist-supported insurgencies, Kennedy and his national security advisers from their first days in office began prodding the government to develop a comprehensive response to this new challenge. Under White House urging, interagency coordinating bodies and study groups proliferated, as did new civilian and military staffs and training programs concerned with preventing or defeating insurgencies. The Office of the Secretary of Defense, for example, created an Office of Special Assistant for Counterinsurgency and Special Activities (SACSA) within the Joint Staff. Similarly, the Army appointed a special assistant to the chief of staff for special warfare activities. The other armed services took comparable steps. Counterinsurgency-oriented Army elements, notably the green beret–wearing Special Forces, enjoyed increased official interest, resources, and public visibility. The long-term effectiveness of the Kennedy team in redirecting the government toward meeting the unique requirements of counterinsurgency is debatable; but the president's interest in the subject generated much activity and made all but inevitable a deeper U.S. commitment to beleaguered South Vietnam.[17]

The administration's counterinsurgency theorists, most notably White House Deputy Special Assistant for National Security Affairs Walt W. Rostow, approached the challenge of Communist-influenced uprisings in Asia, Africa, and Latin America on the assumption that those movements were rooted in social injustice and economic underdevelopment. Local Communists exploited the resulting legitimate grievances, especially those of the peasants, to build revolutionary movements aimed at the seizure by force of national power. To defeat these efforts, the United States, while providing military assistance and advice to threatened allies, also had to persuade established regimes to promote economic growth and to regain the allegiance of their people by making necessary political and social changes. This combination of military action with development and reform was the essence of what Kennedy and his advisers called counterinsurgency.

Where armed revolt was in progress, as in South Vietnam, counterinsurgency received practical implementation in the process known as pacification. A term that originated in nineteenth century French wars of conquest in North Africa, pacification denoted efforts both to recapture territory from insurgents and to win the allegiance of the territory's inhabitants. Pacification began with military operations to expel rebel armed forces from selected areas. In the wake of the soldiers would come government police to uproot the insurgent political underground and officials to reestablish local administration and public services. Then would follow measures to improve the lives of the people: new schools, clinics, and roads, as well as redistribution of land to the poor. These good works sought to win the peasants' allegiance to the central government. As a final step, participating local governments would be established at the hamlet and village levels, organized for self-government and armed to prevent the return of the insurgents. Critical to the success of pacification was the closest possible coordination of military and civilian activity at every level from the national capital to the rural hamlet.[18]

At the outset, Vietnam's neighboring state, Laos, posed a more urgent problem for Kennedy than did Vietnam, and one that seemed more like a civil war between conventional armies than a true guerrilla insurgency. The Geneva settlement had established in Laos a three-way balance of power between the Communist Pathet Lao, which controlled territory bordering on North Vietnam; a neutralist government under Prince Souvanna Phouma; and a military-based anti-Communist faction led by Prince Boun Oum and General Phoumi Nosavan. Since the Geneva Agreements permitted Laos to accept foreign military assistance for its own defense, the United States financed, equipped, and trained the 25,000-man Royal Laotian Army by means of a thinly disguised advisory group called the Programs Evaluation Office. It also conducted a variety of covert anti-Communist paramilitary activities. As a result, by the end of the Eisenhower administration the United States had secured the overthrow of Souvanna Phouma and the installation of a more overtly pro-American regime under Boun Oum and Phoumi Nosavan. Fighting broke out between the Royal Laotian Army and the Pathet Lao, whose forces received arms and equipment from the Soviet Union and troops and advisers from the North Vietnamese. With this backing, the Pathet Lao soon gained the advantage over the government.

After a careful review of the situation in Laos, Kennedy decided that U.S. armed intervention was neither militarily nor politically feasible. Instead he sought a cease-fire and return to neutralization. In March 1961 he accepted a British proposal for a new Geneva conference to reneutralize Laos. The following year, after lengthy negotiations and a major U.S. force deployment to Thailand to deter the Pathet

Lao from continuing their offensive, the interested powers agreed to restore Souvanna as head of a nonaligned coalition regime without American military assistance. In practice, the settlement turned into a de facto partitioning of Laos, especially after fighting resumed between a new coalition of Souvanna and the Phoumi forces on one side and the Pathet Lao and North Vietnamese on the other. The Communists gained control of eastern Laos, thereby securing the Ho Chi Minh Trail infiltration route, and the neutralists and anti-Communists held the western region and the Mekong valley cities. Kennedy's retreat in Laos both increased the vulnerability of South Vietnam and intensified the administration's determination to hold the line there as a demonstration of will and of its ability to contain an externally assisted Communist insurgency.[19]

South Vietnam became perforce the testing ground for the Kennedy administration's counterinsurgency doctrines and programs. During the first half of 1961, the new president received a series of discouraging reports on the country from special emissaries and from the Military Assistance Advisory Group, describing continuing political and military deterioration. The cumulative weight of this information led Kennedy to remark to an aide, "This is the worst one we've got, isn't it?" Nevertheless, South Vietnam—if only because it was more accessible geographically than land-locked Laos and seemed to have a functioning government—looked like the place to make a stand.

Kennedy therefore endorsed most of the recommendations in the country team's counterinsurgency plan, including American support for a 20,000-man increase in Diem's armed forces. He also sought additional measures to reinforce and revitalize the campaign against the Viet Cong. In April 1961 he established a special interagency task force to evaluate the Communist threat and to recommend actions to combat it. The following month, he approved National Security Action Memorandum (NSAM) 52, which reaffirmed that the U.S. objective was to "prevent communist domination of South Vietnam; to create in that country a viable and increasingly democratic society; and to initiate, on an accelerated basis, a series of mutually supporting actions to achieve this objective." These actions included dispatch of 400 Special Forces troops to South Vietnam and authorization of covert sabotage and harassment missions against the DRV. In October, after President Diem formally requested American assistance in adding 100,000 men to his armed forces to meet the increasing Viet Cong threat, Kennedy sent General Maxwell D. Taylor, his special military representative, and Walt Rostow, his deputy special assistant for national security affairs, to South Vietnam. He instructed them to evaluate the entire military and political situation and to recommend a comprehensive course of American remedial action.[20]

Both Taylor and Rostow were active proponents of the administration's emphasis on counterinsurgency. Accompanied by a large civil-

A Deepening Commitment and a New Command

ian-military entourage, they spent the last half of October 1961 touring South Vietnam and consulting with officials of the American mission and the Diem government. Early on, the group concluded that South Vietnam was in serious trouble. Viet Cong military strength and activity were increasing steadily, and the enemy seemed to be assembling large reserve striking forces northwest of Saigon and in the Central Highlands. South Vietnamese forces operated with little effectiveness due to lack of mobility, poor intelligence, and Diem's constant disruption of the chain of command. In the society as a whole, the Taylor mission found a crisis of confidence driven by alienation from Diem, despair at continued Viet Cong successes, and doubts about U.S. steadfastness stemming from Kennedy's compromise in Laos. The heavily populated Mekong Delta south of Saigon also had been devastated by the worst flood in decades. Taylor and his colleagues, nevertheless, believed that South Vietnam possessed underlying advantages, including a large armed force and a "surprisingly resiliant" economy, which would enable it to prevail if they could be mobilized. On the assumption, as Taylor later put it, that the "question was how to change a losing game and begin to win, not how to call it off," the group concentrated its deliberations on what additional American support was needed to save South Vietnam.

Walt Rostow (NARA)

On 1 November, Taylor cabled to Washington the unanimous recommendations of his group. After summarizing the threat to South Vietnam and relating it to general Communist-bloc efforts to outflank containment by means of revolutionary wars-by-proxy, he proposed that the United States and South Vietnam enter into a "massive joint effort" to defeat the Viet Cong. Taylor recommended that the United States move beyond its advisory role to active participation in government administration, military planning and operations, and intelligence activities. This would entail sending more advisers and deploying them down to the lowest levels of civil and military organization. Taylor further advocated that the United States send military units of its own to perform needed tasks beyond South Vietnamese capabilities, such as provision of helicopter lift, aerial reconnaissance, coordination of air and ground operations, and coastal and river surveillance.

In what became his most controversial proposal, Taylor called for insertion into the Mekong Delta of an American ground force of about 8,000 troops, predominately engineers and logistic personnel but including some combat elements. This force, he said, could assist in flood relief, provide various kinds of support to the RVNAF, and act as a final reserve in the event of a major Viet Cong offensive. Most important, its presence would constitute tangible evidence of American determination to see through the struggle alongside the Vietnamese. Going further, the military members of Taylor's group declared that only full-scale intervention by major U.S. and SEATO combat forces could save South Vietnam.[21]

In mid-November, after considerable discussion within the administration (most of it concerning the question of a ground troop commitment), President Kennedy adopted the bulk of Taylor's recommendations. He directed that the advisory effort be reinforced substantially, and he ordered deployment of fixed- and rotary-wing air units and a variety of other specialized American military elements. In return, Kennedy expected President Diem to give "concrete demonstrations" of willingness to work in an orderly way with subordinates and to broaden his political base. Kennedy by omission rejected Taylor's proposal for an 8,000-man American ground force. He was concerned that direct U.S. intervention on that scale might upset the Laos negotiations then in progress. Also, he accepted the opinion of Secretary of State Dean Rusk and Secretary of Defense Robert S. McNamara that such a contingent was too small to affect the situation decisively but large enough to draw the United States into serious difficulties. The president did not entirely foreclose the possibility of sending American troops; he instructed the Defense Department to plan for such a contingency. Nevertheless, he clearly hoped that the more limited measures he had authorized would suffice to save South Vietnam.[22]

Kennedy's November decisions entailed a drastic enlargement of the number of American military people in South Vietnam and an expansion of their range of activities. The enhanced American participation in the war far exceeded both the normal mission and the command capabilities of a military assistance advisory group. Recognizing this fact, the Taylor mission called for "a change in the charter, the spirit, and the organization of the MAAG in South Vietnam . . . from an advisory group to something nearer—but not quite—an operational headquarters in a theater of war." As part of his acceptance of Taylor's recommendations, Kennedy announced that the United States would provide "such new terms of reference, reorganization and additional personnel" for its command in Vietnam as were required for increased military assistance, "operational collaboration" with the Vietnamese, and "operational direction" of U.S. forces. A new American headquarters would be needed to conduct what was rapidly becoming a new American war.[23]

Creating the Command

The Defense Department, with Secretary McNamara taking personal charge of the details of the effort, rapidly put into effect the military part of President Kennedy's Vietnam program. Before the end of 1961, an Air Force counterinsurgency tactical air unit was establishing itself in South Vietnam, as were two Army helicopter companies. Navy minesweepers meanwhile took up coastal patrol stations just below the 17th Parallel. Army and Air Force specialists began building and manning communications and tactical air control systems. Still other Americans arrived to improve and expand South Vietnamese government military intelligence. The Military Assistance Advisory Group enlarged its intelligence activities and, following a mid-December directive from McNamara, prepared to deploy battalion and province advisers to help the Vietnamese plan and conduct combat and pacification operations.[24]

Formation of a new headquarters to control these forces took longer than expected and required extended negotiations between the State and Defense Departments. At issue was the relationship of the proposed military command to the U.S. ambassador to South Vietnam and to the other agencies of his country team. Was the commander to be subordinate to or independent of the ambassador, and how much authority was he to have over the counterinsurgency activities of agencies such as the CIA, the U.S. Agency for International Development (USAID), and the U.S. Information Agency (USIA)? Beyond these issues loomed the fundamental question of the balance between military and nonmilitary elements in counterinsurgency. Was the struggle against the Viet Cong an essentially military enterprise with other programs in an auxiliary role, or was the military to be only one element, and not necessarily the dominant one, in a comprehensive effort—the view held in principle by President Kennedy and his counterinsurgency advisers?[25]

During the long era of the Military Assistance Advisory Group, American civilian-military relations in Saigon had been less than harmonious. General Williams, the advisory group chief during the late 1950s, had conducted the MAAG's affairs largely independently of Ambassador Elbridge Durbrow, with whom Williams had occasional loud arguments in country team meetings. Williams' successor as MAAG chief, Lt. Gen. Lionel C. McGarr, did little better. A reclusive man, preoccupied with drafting lengthy treatises on counterinsurgency doctrine, McGarr managed to alienate not only the country team but also President Diem and Admiral Harry D. Felt, the PACOM commander. Coordination of the Vietnam effort also had been lacking in Washington. The State and Defense Departments competed for overall control and the Central Intelligence Agency, the Agency for International Development, and the U.S. Information Agency independently made and executed policy in their own fields.[26]

Early in his administration, President Kennedy unintentionally compounded his own difficulties in resolving the civil-military conflict in Saigon. On 29 May 1961, in a letter of instructions to American ambassadors around the world, Kennedy reaffirmed their authority, as heads of their respective country teams, over all U.S. government agencies represented in their missions, including military assistance and advisory groups. The president, however, exempted from ambassadorial control "United States military forces operating in the field . . . under the command of a United States area commander." This category appeared to include the proposed new headquarters in South Vietnam, which would have operating units under it and perform at least some functions of a field command. The commander of such a force, under Kennedy's instructions, was to keep the ambassador informed about military activities and consult with him on policy matters, but he was not under the ambassador's orders; the two were to refer any persistent disagreements through their respective chains of command to Washington for adjudication.[27]

Such a collegial arrangement, intended for countries where large American conventional forces were deployed, seemed unlikely to produce the close civilian-military coordination required for effective direction of counterinsurgency operations. Nevertheless, Secretary McNamara and the Joint Chiefs of Staff used it as guidance in developing their plan for the new Vietnam command. On 13 November, as preparations for expansion of the American effort were just getting under way, McNamara directed the Joint Chiefs of Staff to develop a proposal for a U.S. military command in South Vietnam. Following instructions from President Kennedy, McNamara went beyond the Taylor mission's recommendation for a simple enlargement of the MAAG's strength, authority, and functions. Instead, he called for establishment of an entirely new headquarters. The Kennedy administration believed that such action would demonstrate forcefully to both friends and enemies the American commitment to victory over the Viet Cong. In addition, a full-fledged military command would be better suited than an advisory group to control major ground combat units in Vietnam, and perhaps Laos, if the United States should decide to commit them. McNamara told the Joint Chiefs that the projected headquarters should be responsible for all counterinsurgency military activities in South Vietnam. Further emphasizing the importance of the organization, the defense secretary wanted its commander to report directly to him through the JCS, bypassing the Pacific Command.[28]

The Joint Chiefs expressed doubt that a fundamental change in the U.S. command in South Vietnam was necessary or desirable in the absence of a major combat troop commitment. Nevertheless, they complied with McNamara's directive. On 22 November they proposed creation within the existing Pacific Command structure of a subordinate unified (multiservice) command, to be entitled United States

Forces, Vietnam (USFV). The new command's objective would be to increase American economic and military assistance to the Republic of Vietnam, "short of introduction of combat forces," and to participate in the direction and control of South Vietnamese counterinsurgency operations. To this end, the command was to "draw together, under single command and control, all those U.S. activities in Vietnam, including intelligence operations, MAAG . . . , and economic aid, which are related to the counter insurgency effort." The Joint Chiefs proposed to give the USFV commander, in addition to command over all U.S. military forces in South Vietnam, "full control" of all American intelligence efforts and the right to "supervise and direct" counterinsurgency-related civilian economic aid programs. The commander was to act as "principal US military advisor" to the commander in chief of the South Vietnamese armed forces. He was to be "co-equal" with the American ambassador and was to possess the independent military authority spelled out in Kennedy's 29 May 1961 letter, to which the Joint Chiefs explicitly referred and which they attached as an annex to their memorandum.[29]

General McGarr with Ambassador Nolting
(Time Life Pictures/Getty Images)

McNamara promptly approved the Joint Chiefs' proposal in principle, but the State Department and other agencies registered objections. Secretary of State Rusk, supported by General Taylor, argued that retitling the U.S. military commander was unnecessary and would convey to the world a degree of commitment to South Vietnam that the administration had not yet made. Rusk and Taylor favored instead a simple enlargement of the mission and authority of the MAAG chief. Significantly, however, Rusk did not object to the commander's co-equal status with the ambassador. Predictably, AID and the CIA both sought to keep their own programs out of the military commander's control, preferring the existing system of coordination through the country team.[30]

In response, on 7 December McNamara and the Joint Chiefs modified their proposal to eliminate the USFV commander's authority over intelligence and economic aid activities. Although acknowledging the ambassador's primacy in "political and basic policy matters," McNamara declared that enhancement of the status of the senior U.S. military leader in Saigon was essential "if we are to give full impact to the increased efforts we are now making" and if the commander was to "move into a new and more active role." The State Department in effect bowed to McNamara's wishes. It held out only for acknowledgment of the ambassador's preeminence in general policy matters and urged that the title of the command be changed to "Military Assistance Command, Vietnam," to denote the continued advice-and-support character of American military activity in South Vietnam.[31]

After a mid-December meeting in Honolulu attended by Rusk, McNamara, Ambassador to South Vietnam Frederick E. Nolting, and General McGarr, the two departments reached agreement on the main issues. Defense accepted State's proposed title for the headquarters, which henceforth was to be known as Military Assistance Command, Vietnam (MACV). The commander of the Military Assistance Command (COMUSMACV) was to direct U.S. military activities and advise the Saigon government on internal security and on the organization, deployment, and operations of the armed forces. For this purpose, he could hold discussions with President Diem and "the leaders of his government." On the commander's relationship to the ambassador, the departments repeated the principles of Kennedy's letter. The general was to keep the ambassador fully informed about his high-level contacts with Diem's government and to "consult" with him on "political and basic policy matters," for which the ambassador had final responsibility. In case of irreconcilable disagreements, each was free to request a decision from Washington through his department's channels. The departments thus envisioned something approaching a coequal relationship between the ambassador and the MACV commander, with the ambassador implicitly *primus inter pares* on questions of high policy. Secretary McNamara transmitted this agreement to President Kennedy on 22 December, along with his nomination of General Paul Harkins as MACV commander. Kennedy early in January approved both the terms of reference and the selection of Harkins.[32]

This agreement met with strong protests from the senior American military and political officials in Saigon, General McGarr and Ambassador Nolting. McGarr objected bitterly to General Lyman W. Lemnitzer, chairman of the Joint Chiefs of Staff, at the proposal to disregard his and the MAAG's experience and achievements and to supersede them with a new headquarters and presumably a new commander. However, as noted previously, McGarr had made himself thoroughly unpopular

*Generals Lemnitzer and Taylor, Secretary McNamara,
and President Kennedy, 1961* (© Bettman/CORBIS)

in Saigon and Washington. The Taylor mission had snubbed the advisory group chief during its pivotal tour of South Vietnam, and many of President Kennedy's advisers believed that he was not the man to lead the expanded counterinsurgency effort. Indeed, it appears that getting rid of McGarr was, for some in the administration, a secondary reason for establishing a new U.S. command in Vietnam. Lemnitzer, therefore, could do little but commiserate with McGarr, reassure him of the Joint Chiefs' esteem for him and appreciation of his efforts, and urge him to accept the situation like the good soldier he was.[33]

Ambassador Nolting, an experienced foreign service officer and the administration's choice to head the Saigon mission, was not so easily dismissed. From the start, Nolting opposed the enlargement of the military command on two main grounds. He argued that giving the military commander nearly equal status with the ambassador would weaken the mission in dealing with the South Vietnamese, who would play off the two heads of the American team against each other. "There should clearly be one US spokesman in V[iet] N[am]," he said, "otherwise we shall get the run-around." Nolting had no objection to the commander's dealing directly with Diem on strictly military matters; but he urged that, however the command was reorganized, the top military man should remain subordinate to the ambassador as head of the country team. From a broader perspective, Nolting argued that enlargement of the command in Saigon would overbalance the anti–Viet Cong campaign in favor of the military. "I am profoundly convinced," he told Secretary Rusk, "that the problem cannot be solved on a military basis (although military force is an indispensable element)." Yet enhancement of the Saigon command would "almost inevitably build into our effort a disproportionate emphasis, in resources and planning as well as appearance, on a military solution" and would encourage the Diem regime's already pronounced tendency to do the same. "Our counterinsurgency effort," Nolting emphasized, must be "well balanced and flexible otherwise we are likely either to lose the fight or to throw this country into another Korean-type war."[34]

With support from Rusk, Nolting urged that language be added to Harkins' directive to the effect that the ambassador remained the senior American representative in Saigon with the military commander a subordinate member of the country team. Nolting received support on this point from President Diem, who declared his preference for dealing with a single American team, headed by a civilian, to reduce the credibility of Viet Cong charges that the Americans were taking over direction of the war. But while willing to acknowledge the ambassador's primacy, McNamara would not agree to formal subordination of the commander to the country team, for fear of diluting responsibility for the military program. In addition, he told Nolting, the Joint Chiefs insisted that "no four-star general is going to be under an Ambassador."[35]

In the end, Secretaries Rusk and McNamara settled the issue by informal agreement. McNamara directed General Harkins to defer to Nolting on all policy matters and, for practical purposes, to consider himself subordinate to the ambassador. The defense secretary went so far as to tell the prospective MACV commander to treat his written terms of reference as modified to that effect, even though the two secretaries decided to attempt no change in the formal wording. A face-to-face meeting between Nolting and Harkins at another of the periodic Honolulu policy conferences in January further cleared the air. On 23 February Rusk reassured Nolting that "if actual problems arise which require more formal general statement of relationships than those you now have, I will of course go into it." Publicly, administration spokesmen emphasized to the press that the ambassador remained in sole charge of American programs in South Vietnam.[36]

Even before these final understandings were completed, the Military Assistance Command, Vietnam, went into operation. At the peremp-

General Harkins, Admiral Felt, and Ambassador Nolting, Saigon, 1962 (NARA)

tory direction of the State Department, Ambassador Nolting obtained President Diem's consent to the American military reorganization on 3 February 1962. Five days later, Admiral Felt, commander in chief, Pacific (CINCPAC), formally activated the command. Within less than a week, General Harkins arrived in Saigon to take up his duties. Harkins' formal statement of authority from the Joint Chiefs of Staff reiterated the terms of the earlier State-Defense agreement. As COMUSMACV, he was to work directly with President Diem and his commanders on military affairs, consult with the ambassador on "US political and basic policy matters," keep the ambassador fully informed on his contacts with the South Vietnamese, and refer unresolved disagreements to Washington through the military chain of command.[37]

Harkins' instructions appeared to place him, as he later said, "practically . . . on the same level as the Ambassador" in dealing with President Diem; President Kennedy gave the general the same impression during a brief, perfunctory interview before the MACV commander left for Saigon. Nevertheless, due partly to the informal accord between McNamara and Rusk and perhaps more to personal rapport between Nolting and Harkins, the division of authority did not disrupt the country team. Harkins followed Nolting's lead on overall policy toward Diem, and the two men maintained full communication and a good working relationship. Harkins' participation in country team meetings was a potentially contentious issue, since McNamara had wanted the MACV commander to maintain his separation from the team. Initially, General Lemnitzer, the JCS chairman, had expected Harkins to stay away. In practice, McGarr's successor as MAAG chief, Maj. Gen. Charles Timmes, sat in as the full military country team member. General Harkins, or his representative, took part as an invited additional participant, a legalistic distinction that maintained the formality of the MACV commander's independence of the ambassador but had little practical significance.[38]

The State and Defense Departments, through an unwritten agreement between their secretaries and through cordial personal relations between their senior representatives in Saigon, seemed to have ensured subordination of the military to the political element in the direction of the counterinsurgency struggle. Yet coordination rested on fragile foundations. Unity of effort within the American mission depended finally on personal rapport between the ambassador and the MACV commander and on "treaty arrangements . . . arrived at in the Country Team meetings." In the making of those arrangements, the military command predominated through sheer weight of resources and administrative vigor, however much General Harkins formally deferred to Ambassador Nolting. Nolting, with comparatively weak backing from his own department and lacking any political constituency of his own, would have found it difficult to impose constraints on the military even if he had desired to do so; on most day-to-day policy issues, he appeared disinclined to challenge the soldiers. The result, however, was not a unified effort under the military. Harkins possessed neither authority over the civilian elements of the country team nor responsibility for their counterinsurgency programs. Hence, he and they tended to go their separate ways in combating the Viet Cong, although with unequal resources and therefore unequal and at times mutually frustrating effect.[39]

The same lack of a single directing authority and imbalance of power in favor of the military prevailed in Washington. President Kennedy neglected to provide for continuing, authoritative interagency oversight of the expanded effort in Vietnam, and what direction was provided came largely from the Department of Defense. When he took office, Kennedy abolished the elaborate national security policy-making machinery he had inherited from Eisenhower and instead relied on informal groups of trusted associates and ad hoc task forces to deal with particular problems. The system depended heavily on Kennedy's personal interest and intervention. But preoccupied as he was during these years with full-blown crises in Berlin and Cuba, the president gave relatively little attention to Vietnam and took only the most per-

A Deepening Commitment and a New Command

functory part in the deliberations over the creation of MACV. He never acted upon the suggestion of several of his counterinsurgency experts that he establish a superdepartmental agency in Washington, with a parallel organization in Saigon, to direct the entire anti–Viet Cong effort. A Defense-chaired Vietnam task force during 1961 and a high-level interdepartmental Special Group (Counterinsurgency) the following year proved to be inadequate substitutes for such a superagency.

In the event, Vietnam policy-making fell largely to Secretary of State Rusk and Secretary of Defense McNamara, who worked together on this issue, as on most others, in a partnership based on mutual confidence and respect. In the case of Vietnam, however, Defense clearly predominated. McNamara commanded more resources than did Rusk and from the beginning of the Kennedy administration pushed himself to the forefront of the Vietnam effort. The defense secretary, for example, instituted and largely controlled the periodic Honolulu strategy conferences. Rusk seemed content to let leadership on Vietnam go to Defense by default. Ambassador Nolting later complained that "I never could get him [Rusk] to focus on our problems while I was in Vietnam."[40]

The Kennedy administration, in creating the Military Assistance Command, Vietnam, thus committed itself to solving, in General McGarr's words, a "very unconventional situation in a basically conventional manner."[41] It set up an ambassador–field commander coalition of a standardized type that was related only tangentially to the requirements of counterinsurgency warfare. In the interdepartmental compromises that established the Military Assistance Command's charter of responsibility and relationship to the rest of the country team, Defense gained more than it gave up, but the result still left MACV short of control of the entire counterinsurgency effort. If this handicap were not enough, in its purely military sphere MACV labored under complex command relationships and had to thread its way through intractable interservice conflicts over fine points of organization, staffing, and doctrine.

MACV: The Years of Escalation, 1962–1967

Notes

[1] *New York Times*, 14 Feb 62, p. 6.

[2] Ibid., pp. 1, 6, 34; see also ibid.,10 Feb 62, p. 3.

[3] Unless otherwise indicated, this section is based on Ronald H. Spector, *Advice and Support: The Early Years, 1941–1960*, United States Army in Vietnam (Washington, D.C.: U.S. Army Center of Military History, 1983), chs. 1–11.

[4] For a summary of the rise of Vietnamese nationalism and communism, see William J. Duiker, *The Communist Road to Power in Vietnam* (Boulder, Colo.: Westview Press, 1981), esp. chs. 2–4. The postwar occupation of Indochina is covered in Duiker, *Road to Power*; Spector, *Early Years*; and George C. Herring, *America's Longest War: The United States and Vietnam, 1950–1975* (New York: Wiley, 1979), pp. 3–7.

[5] For formation of the MAAG, see Maj. Gen. George S. Eckhardt, *Command and Control*. Vietnam Studies (Washington, D.C.: Department of the Army, 1974), pp. 7–20.

[6] The Communist maneuvers surrounding Geneva and Soviet assessments that the Viet Minh were close to military exhaustion are discussed in Douglas Pike, *Vietnam and the Soviet Union: Anatomy of an Alliance* (Boulder, Colo.: Westview Press, 1987), pp. 39–42. See also Janos Radvanyi, "Dien Bien Phu: Thirty Years After," *Parameters* 15 (Summer 1985):63–97.

[7] Spector, *Early Years*, ch. 11, gives details of the intervention debate. See also Herring, *Longest War*, pp. 28–36; and George C. Herring and Richard H. Immerman, "Eisenhower, Dulles and Dien Bien Phu: 'The Day We Didn't Go to War' Revisited," *Journal of American History* 71 (September 1984), passim.

[8] Unless otherwise noted, this section is based on Spector, *Early Years*, chs. 12–18.

[9] On the effectiveness of Diem's campaigns, see William J. Duiker, *The Communist Road to Power in Vietnam* (Boulder, Colo.: Westview Press, 1981), pp. 174–78.

[10] For organization and evolution of MAAGV, see Spector, *Early Years*, ch.15 and pp. 360–61; and Eckhardt, Command and Control, pp. 7–21.

[11] Spector, *Early Years*, pp. 294–95.

[12] Duiker, *Road to Power*, pp. 169–74. For the international Communist maneuvering after Geneva, see R. B. Smith, *An International History of the Vietnam War*, vol. 1, *Revolution versus Containment, 1955–1961* (New York: St. Martin's Press, 1983), chs. 2 and 4.

[13] For the evolution of Hanoi policy and strategy, see Duiker, *Road to Power*, ch. 8; and Smith, *Revolution versus Containment*, chs. 6–10 and 12–13.

[14] The early development of the insurgency is well covered in Spector, *Early Years*, chs.16–18; Duiker, *Road to Power*, chs. 8 and 9; and Admiral U. S. G. Sharp and General W. C. Westmoreland, *Report on the War in Vietnam (as of 30 June 1968)* (hereafter cited as *Report on the War*) (Washington, D.C.: Government Printing Office, 1968), pp. 78–79.

[15] Unless otherwise noted, this section is based on Spector, *Early Years*, chs. 16–18. On the intelligence problem, see Maxwell D. Taylor, *Swords and Ploughshares* (New York: Norton, 1972), pp. 237–38.

[16] For discussion of the impasse over internal security forces, see General William B. Rosson, USA (Ret.), "Four Periods of American Involvement in Vietnam: Development and Implementation of Policy, Strategy and Programs, Described and Analyzed on the Basis of Service Experience at Progressively Senior Levels" (Ph.D. diss., New College, Oxford, England, 1979), pp. 244–47.

[17] For an overview of Kennedy administration counterinsurgency activity, see Douglas S. Blaufarb, *The Counterinsurgency Era: U.S. Doctrine and Performance, 1950 to the Present* (New York: Free Press, 1977), ch. 3. Rosson, "Involvement in Vietnam," pp.

A Deepening Commitment and a New Command

98–115, 137; and Interv, Senior Officer Oral History Program with Gen William B. Rosson, 1981, pp. 270–88, U.S. Army Military History Institute, (MHI), Carlisle, Pa., describe Army Staff efforts at counterinsurgency planning.

[18] For a convenient summary of counterinsurgency and pacification theory, see Andrew J. Birtle, "U.S. Army Counterinsurgency and Contingency Operations Doctrine, 1942–1976" (MS, U.S. Army Center of Military History), ch. 6.

[19] For the Laotian crisis, see Spector, *Early Years*, pp. 357–58; Taylor, *Swords and Ploughshares*, pp. 216–19; and Smith, *Revolution versus Containment*, pp. 244–52. Kennedy's policy is analyzed and defended in Roger Hilsman, *To Move a Nation: The Politics of Foreign Policy in the Administration of John F. Kennedy* (Garden City, N.Y.: Doubleday, 1967), chs. 10–12.

[20] For a sampling of the many analyses of Kennedy's Vietnam policy, see: Herring, *Longest War*, pp. 73–80; Taylor, *Swords and Ploughshares*, pp. 220–24; Smith, *Revolution versus Containment*, pp. 252–61; Larry Berman, *Planning a Tragedy: The Americanization of the War in Vietnam* (New York: Norton, 1982), pp. 18–20; and Leslie H. Gelb and Richard K. Betts, *The Irony of Vietnam: The System Worked* (Washington, D.C.: Brookings Institution, 1979), pp. 69–73.

[21] Taylor-Rostow Mission, Oct–Nov 61, Taylor Report, 1 Nov 61, Historians files, CMH. For accounts of the mission and its recommendations, see Taylor, *Swords and Ploughshares*, pp. 224–44; and Berman, *Planning*, pp. 20–21.

[22] National Security Action Memo (NSAM) 111, 22 Nov 61, in Gareth Porter, ed., *Vietnam: The Definitive Documentation of Human Decisions*, 2 vols. (Stanfordville, N.Y.: Earl M. Coleman Enterprises, 1979), 2:146–48; Msg, SecState to Amb Nolting, 15 Nov 61, Historians files, CMH. For comment and interpretation, see Berman, *Planning a Tragedy*, pp. 21–23, 29; Taylor, *Swords and Ploughshares*, pp. 245–48; Rosson, "Involvement in Vietnam," pp. 107–08; and Gelb and Betts, *Irony of Vietnam*, pp. 75–79.

[23] The first quote is from Taylor, tab C. The second is from Porter, *Vietnam Documentation*, 2:147. See also Eckhardt, *Command and Control*, p. 22.

[24] For details of the Vietnam buildup, see *United States–Vietnam Relations 1954–1967. Study Prepared by the Department of Defense*, 12 vols. (Washington, D.C.: Government Printing Office, 1971), sec. 4.B.1, pp. 147–48; ibid., sec. 5 B.4, pp. 428–39; MS, Charles von Luttichau, "The U.S. Army Role in the Conflict in Vietnam," 1964, ch. 6, pp. 19–20, 22–24, CMH files; Robert F. Futrell, The United States Air Force in Southeast Asia *The Advisory Years to 1965*, (Washington, D.C.: Office of Air Force History, 1981), pp. 79–84; and Edward J. Marolda and Oscar P. Fitzgerald, *From Military Assistance to Combat, 1959–1965*, United States Navy and the Vietnam Conflict (Washington, D.C: Naval Historical Center, 1986), 2:169–171.

[25] Kennedy administration counterinsurgency doctrine is summarized in Blaufarb, *Counterinsurgency Era*, pp. 66–67.

[26] Spector, *Early Years*, pp. 276–78, 316–20, describes Williams' difficulties. For McGarr's troubles, see Memo, Col Thomas A. Ware, sub: Political/Military Situation in South Vietnam, 11 Jan 62, Historians files, CMH; and Ltrs, Ernest J. Murray to Lt Gen Samuel T. Williams, 28 July 62 and 28 Sep 62, Samuel T. Williams Papers, Hoover Institution on War, Revolution and Peace, Palo Alto, Calif.

[27] The Kennedy letter is summarized in *U.S.–Vietnam Relations*, sec. 4.B.3, pp. 19–20. This instruction grew in part from a State Department–CIA dispute; see Hilsman, *To Move a Nation*, pp. 77, 81.

[28] Memo, SecDef for Chairman, Joint Chiefs of Staff (CJCS), 13 Nov 61, sub: Command Structure for South Vietnam, in U.S. Department of State, *Foreign Relations of the United States, 1961–1963*, vol. 1, *Vietnam 1961* (Washington, D.C.: Government Printing Office, 1988), pp. 589–590 hereafter cited as State, *Foreign Relations: Vietnam 1961*.

Memo, SecDef for Gen Lyman L. Lemnitzer, 14 Nov 61, sub: Command Structure for South Vietnam, copy in William P. Bundy Chronological Files —1961, John F. Kennedy Library (JFKL), Boston, Mass.

[29] Memo, Joint Chiefs of Staff (JCS) JCSM–812–61 to SecDef, 22 Nov 61, sub: South Vietnam, in State, *Foreign Relations: Vietnam 1961*, pp. 652–55.

[30] Memo, William P. Bundy for SecDef, 25 Nov 61, sub: Command Arrangements for Vietnam; Memo, Bundy for U. A. Johnson, et al., 28 Nov 61, sub: Command Arrangements for Vietnam, Historians files, CMH. Memo, Taylor for President, 27 Nov 61, sub: Possible Command Relationships in South Vietnam; Memo, Bundy for SecDef, 1 Dec 61, sub: Vietnam Command Arrangements. Both in State, *Foreign Relations: Vietnam 1961*, pp. 673–74, 702–03.

[31] Ltr, Robert S. McNamara to Dean Rusk, 7 Dec 61; Msg, George W. Ball to SecState, 12 Dec 61; both in State, *Foreign Relations: Vietnam 1961*, pp. 720–21, 728–30. McNamara quotes are in first document cited.

[32] State, *Foreign Relations: Vietnam 1961*, pp. 742–46, 756. Language quoted is from Paper, 19 Dec 61, sub: State-Defense Agreement, Maxwell D. Taylor Papers, National Defense University (NDU), Washington, D.C.; Memorandum for Record (MFR), Dep SecDef, sub: President's Meeting with JCS on January 3, 1962, box 55, 65A3501, Record Group (RG) 330, National Archives and Records Administration (NARA), Washington, D.C.

[33] McGarr protests are in Msgs to CJCS, 20 and 27 Dec 61, State, *Foreign Relations: Vietnam 1961*, pp. 749–50, 765. In same volume, see pp. 687–89, 719, 758–60. Other comments on McGarr's difficulties: Memo, Col T. A. Ware, 11 Jan 62, sub: Political/Military Situation in South Vietnam, Historians files, CMH; Ltrs, Ernest J. Murray to Williams, 28 July 62 and 28 Sep 62, Williams Papers, Hoover Institution.

[34] Quotes are from Msgs, Frederick Nolting to Dept of State, 13 and 19 Dec 61, in State, *Foreign Relations: Vietnam, 1961*, pp. 731–732, 747–49. In same volume, see Ltr, Political Adviser (POLAD) to CINCPAC to Dir, Vietnam Task Force, 18 Dec 61, pp. 742–44.

[35] Hilsman, *To Move a Nation*, p.442. Msg, Nolting to SecState, 20 Jan 62; Msgs, Nolting Saigon 980 to SecState, 27 Jan 62 and Saigon 1008 to SecState, 3 Feb 62; Historians files, CMH. Nolting quote is from 20 Jan 62 message. Memo, Rusk for McNamara, 19 Jan 62; Memo, Taylor, 13 Jan 62, sub: Points at Issue with Regard to the Command Structure in South Vietnam; and Nolting Draft, sub: Terms of Reference for the Senior U.S. Military Commander in South Vietnam, 8J and 62, attached to copy of Memo, McNamara for President, 22 Dec 61. All in Taylor Papers, NDU. Frederick Nolting, *From Trust to Tragedy: The Political Memoirs of Frederick Nolting, Kennedy's Ambassador to Diem's Vietnam* (New York: Praeger, 1988), pp. 50–52. Quote concerning the Joint Chiefs is from p. 52.

[36] Quote is from Msg, SecState 1015 to Nolting, 23 Feb 62, Historians files, CMH. *New York Times*, 11 Feb 62, p. 16, is an example of administration press statements. Nolting, *Trust to Tragedy*, p. 52, describes his meeting with Harkins.

[37] Memo, Taylor for McNamara,1 Feb 62, Taylor Papers, NDU. Msg, JCS to CINCPAC, 7 Feb 62; Msg, CINCPAC to Pacific Commands, 8 Feb 62. Both in Table of Distribution Files (1963), box 1, 69A702, RG 334, NARA. For Diem's consent see Msg, Amb Nolting Saigon 1008 to SecState, 3 Feb 62, Historians files, CMH. On Harkins' arrival see *New York Times*, 14 Feb 62, p. 6.

[38] Quote is from Ltr, Harkins to Lt Gen Don H. Cowles, 29 Aug 79, Historians files, CMH. The account of his meeting with Kennedy is from Interv, USAF Project CORONA HARVEST with Harkins, 23 Feb 72, p. 17, AFCHO; see also p. 24. Interv, Senior Officers Debriefing Program with Harkins, Apr 74, p. 49, MHI; see also p. 62. For Nolting's view,

see *Trust to Tragedy*, pp. 52–53, and Interv, USAF Project Corona Harvest with Nolting, 9 Nov 71, pp. 28–29, 43–44, 54–56, AFCHO. Memo, Bundy for SecDef, 12 Feb 62, sub: State-Defense Relationships re Vietnam, Historians files, CMH. Interv, USAF Project Corona Harvest with Lt Col Franklin L. Smith, USMC, 1 Feb 64, pp. 25–28, AFCHO.

[39] Quote is from Memo, Roger Hilsman and Michael Forrestal for the President, 25 Jan 63, sub: A Report on South Vietnam, Historian's files, CMH. Memo, W. H. Sullivan, ca. late 1963, sub: Divergent Attitudes in U.S. Official Community, Historians files, CMH, discusses civilian complaints that Nolting deferred excessively to Harkins' policy views. Nolting, a former Navy officer, had joined the Foreign Service immediately after World War II. Most of his previous assignments had been in Europe, most recently as deputy chief of the U.S. Mission to NATO; see Nolting, *Trust to Tragedy*, pp. 11–12.

[40] This discussion is based on: Blaufarb, *Counterinsurgency Era*, pp. 66–75, 86; Eckhardt, *Command and Control*, pp. 21–22; *U.S.–Vietnam Relations*, sec. 4.B.3, pp. 18–19; Hilsman, *To Move a Nation*, pp. 23–60; Jeffrey G. Barlow, "President John F. Kennedy and His Joint Chiefs of Staff" (Ph.D. diss., University of South Carolina, 1981), pp. 127–32; and Robert W. Komer, *Bureaucracy Does Its Thing: Institutional Constraints on U.S.–GVN Performance in Vietnam* (Washington, D.C.: Rand Corporation, 1973), pp. 79–81. Nolting quote is from *Trust to Tragedy*, p. 129; see also pp. 12–13.

[41] Msg, McGarr to Lemnitzer, 27 Dec 61, in State, *Foreign Relations: Vietnam 1961*, p. 765.

2

A Joint Command: Complications and Conflicts, 1962–1963

As the Military Assistance Command went into operation, General Harkins' task, as defined in terms of reference issued by the Joint Chiefs of Staff and in a mission statement from Admiral Felt, his immediate superior, was twofold. As senior United States military commander in South Vietnam, he had "direct responsibility for all US military policy, operations and assistance in that country." In that capacity, he was to exercise "operational command" of all U.S. military forces and agencies assigned to him, including the military assistance group. He was to plan and conduct American military operations, coordinate American military intelligence in South Vietnam, and serve as "CINCPAC's single U.S. spokesman in South Vietnam for U.S. military policy, planning and contemplated force employment." At the same time, as head of an assistance command, Harkins was to advise the Saigon government on "all matters relative to . . . maintaining internal security in South Vietnam and to the organization and employment of the RVNAF and of counterinsurgency and other paramilitary forces." He was to "assist and support the Government of Vietnam in its efforts to provide for its internal security, defeat Communist insurgency, and resist overt aggression." [1]

The Military Assistance Command, Vietnam, thus functioned in two separate but interrelated capacities. First, as a U.S. military headquarters and a subordinate unified command under CINCPAC, it controlled units and personnel in South Vietnam as part of a complex, worldwide command structure. Second, MACV existed to advise and assist the government and the armed forces of its host country and to cooperate with the rest of the American country team in formulating, and persuading the Vietnamese to carry out, a comprehensive program aimed simultaneously at rooting out the Viet Cong insurgents and reforming and modernizing the nation. In each of these roles, the headquarters, from the planning stage, was enmeshed in complex institutional relationships and conflicts.

Many of the controversies that affected MACV in its capacity as an American military headquarters originated in the upheavals created in the defense establishment by the Kennedy administration's reorientation of U.S. military strategy and the aggressive management style of Secretary McNamara. During the period of MACV's creation, the Kennedy administration discarded the so-called Massive Retaliation strategy, based on air power and nuclear weapons in favor of a posture of Flexible Response, which accorded increased importance (and funding) to nonnuclear forces, limited war, and counterinsurgency. At the same time, McNamara dramatically enlarged his office's influence over all aspects of military policy, planning, and budgeting. In the process, he invaded realms formerly the exclusive preserve of the uniformed services and of the Joint Chiefs, whose judgment the secretary's civilian "whiz kids" from industry and the universities frequently challenged. In this changing political and strategic context, the services struggled with McNamara and with each other over a wide range of issues. Under these circumstances, few questions of military organization and command in Vietnam could be decided solely on their merits in relation to the conflict at hand.[2]

Secretary of Defense McNamara (NARA)

MACV and the Pacific Chain of Command

Since the establishment of the Department of Defense in the late 1940s, most U.S. Army, Navy, Air Force, and Marine Corps units had been assigned to the operational control of unified commands staffed by officers of all services and responsible for particular geographical theaters of operations. Under each such headquarters, component commanders exercised tactical and administrative control over the assigned units of their respective services. As the system had evolved by the early 1960s, deployed forces had a dual chain of command: for operations from their component commander to their unified commander, who then reported via the secretary of defense to the president; and for administration from their component commander to their service department and thence to the secretary of defense and the president.

A Joint Command: Complications and Conflicts, 1962–1963

A unified command might have under it subordinate unified commands, each with its own component commanders who in turn were subordinate to the overall theater component commanders.[3]

Interservice politics affected the JCS deliberations over MACV's place in the existing joint command structure in the Pacific. From the start, the Joint Chiefs looked askance at McNamara's proposal that the assistance command report directly to him. That arrangement would encroach upon the jurisdiction of Pacific Command (PACOM), the unified headquarters that directed American military operations throughout the vast expanse of land and water stretching from the Aleutians to the Indian Ocean. The officer in charge of that region, Commander in Chief, Pacific (CINCPAC), Admiral Harry D. Felt, had all of mainland Southeast Asia within his domain. Headquartered in Honolulu, he controlled U.S. forces operating in that area and oversaw contingency planning for both conventional defense and counterinsurgency. During the recurring Laotian crises, Felt directed American preparations for military intervention. The Military Assistance Advisory Group in South Vietnam constituted a subordinate unified command under Admiral Felt.[4]

Admiral Felt (NARA)

McNamara's proposal for a headquarters in South Vietnam outside CINCPAC's control would upset this entire command arrangement and require revision of a long list of American unilateral and allied Southeast Asia Treaty Organization contingency plans. In addition, Navy leaders feared that it might provide an opening wedge for establishment of a new version of the Army-dominated Far East Command that had directed joint operations in Japan, Korea, north China, and the Ryukyus during and immediately after the Korean conflict. Existence of that unified command had caused an awkward division of control over the Pacific Fleet. Hence, the Navy had welcomed its disestablishment on 1 July 1957 and its replacement with a unified air and naval theater in the form of the Pacific Command. Army leaders, on the other hand, had opposed disestablishment of the Far East Command and favored a separate command for operations on the Asian mainland, at least in situations involving limited wars.[5]

Not surprisingly, then, Admiral Felt and the Chief of Naval Operations, Admiral George W. Anderson, Jr., strongly objected to McNamara's plan. They instead advocated establishment of a subordinate unified command for Vietnam under CINCPAC. Anderson and Felt pointed out that the American forces to be deployed in South Vietnam were not large enough to justify a separate theater command and that Vietnam was geographically and strategically inseparable from the rest of mainland Southeast Asia, which would remain a CINCPAC responsibility.

The Joint Chiefs deferred to the Navy argument. In their initial proposal to McNamara on 22 November 1961, they recommended that the "Commander, United States Forces in Vietnam" (his original working title), should head a subordinate unified headquarters under CINCPAC, complete with joint staff and service component commands. Besides reiterating the Navy arguments for such a command structure, the Joint Chiefs added that it would conform to those for American forces in Taiwan, South Korea, and Japan. Secretary McNamara accepted the chiefs' recommendation, choosing not to make an issue of the command relationship. In practice, he intended to exercise close personal control of activities in Vietnam through periodic face-to-face conferences with both the PACOM and MACV commanders.[6]

By nominating Lt. Gen. Paul D. Harkins to head MACV, the Joint Chiefs reinforced that headquarters' close relationship with Pacific Command. Harkins, an affable 57-year-old West Pointer who received his fourth star when President Kennedy confirmed his new assignment, had made his career as a staff officer, operational planner, and military diplomat. At the time of his selection, he was serving as deputy commander of U.S. Army, Pacific (USARPAC), PACOM's Army component headquarters. Harkins possessed neither formal training nor operational experience in counterinsurgency. However, as an Army planner in the Pentagon, he had worked with the State Department and become familiar with America's worldwide military assistance programs. Commanding North Atlantic Treaty Organization land forces in southeastern Europe, his last assignment before joining USARPAC, he had acquired experience in dealing with sometimes fractious allies. Having served under General Taylor in a succession of important assignments, Harkins enjoyed the confidence of Taylor, who would soon become chairman of the Joint Chiefs of Staff. Taylor evidently had the USARPAC deputy commander in mind for the Vietnam position from the time of his October 1961 trip to Saigon. During a Honolulu stopover on his way back to report to Kennedy, Taylor told Harkins: "Paul, you better be ready to get your fist in the dike, there is going to be a flood over there."[7]

Whatever his career background and influential support, Harkins' principal qualification for the Military Assistance Command assignment was his extensive involvement, as deputy U.S. Army, Pacific, commander, with Southeast Asia operations and contingency planning. During the 1961 Laotian crisis, Harkins, on additional duty as commander of SEATO Field Forces, spent several months on Okinawa and in the Philippines directing preparations for allied military inter-

A Joint Command: Complications and Conflicts, 1962–1963

vention. In the capacity of commander-designate of both U.S. and SEATO ground forces, he continued working on regional contingency plans after inactivation of the Field Force headquarters. On various assignments, Harkins had studied South Vietnam and its problems; and he had paid several visits to the country, the earliest while the French still were fighting there. In sum, Harkins, while not a counterinsurgency specialist, had a broad general knowledge of regional conditions and the diplomatic skills to get along with the Diem regime. He could be counted on to incorporate his new headquarters smoothly into the Pacific Command.[8]

General Harkins' position in the Pacific Command structure underwent further elaboration within three months of the activation of MACV. The occasion was a new high point in the persistent Laotian crisis. In May 1962, with negotiations for a tripartite coalition government temporarily deadlocked, President Kennedy marshaled U.S. air, naval, and land forces to deter the Lao Communists from further military advances and to reassure Thailand, Laos' neighbor, of continued United States defense support. To this end, he deployed to northern Thailand brigade-size Army and Marine ground units, plus air and supporting elements, and ordered contingency planning for American occupation and defense of portions of southern and western Laos.[9]

To command the deployed American forces in whatever action became necessary, Kennedy ordered creation of a new headquarters in Thailand, designated U.S. Military Assistance Command, Thailand (USMACTHAI), and appointed General Harkins its commander in addition to his duties as COMUSMACV. Activated on 15 May 1962, Harkins' Thai command consisted of the existing Joint U.S. Military Assistance Group (JUSMAG) in that country, plus the American air and ground units. Harkins directed the latter forces through an intermediate headquarters, Joint Task Force (JTF) 116, which Pacific Command maintained for the contingency of major troop deployments to Southeast Asia.[10]

With the agreement on a coalition government in June and the signing of the new Geneva Accords the following month, the Laotian crisis soon passed. However, American command arrangements for Southeast Asia remained the subject of debate even as the forces in Thailand prepared to leave. On 30 May, Admiral Felt proposed that the Defense Department consolidate the positions of COMUSMACV and COMUSMACTHAI into a single office named Commander, U.S. Military Assistance Command, Thailand/Vietnam. Presumably, General Harkins would fill the job, with a deputy commander, staff, and component commands under him in each country. This would make Harkins, in effect, a Southeast Asia regional military commander. The Joint Chiefs of Staff endorsed Felt's recommendation, but political objections from the State Department blocked its implementation. Argument then continued over the fate of MACTHAI and over the respective roles of that headquarters, Joint Task Force 116, and MACV in contingency planning and command arrangements. General Harkins favored enlargement of his regional role, whereas Admiral Felt preferred to keep MACV's jurisdiction limited to South Vietnam.[11]

Secretary McNamara resolved the question. At a conference in Honolulu on 8 October, he directed Harkins to retain his position as COMUSMACTHAI and in fact changed the general's title to COMUSMAC, Vietnam/Thailand. The chief of the Military Assistance Group in Thailand was to serve as Harkins' deputy for advice and support in that country and for control of any American troops deployed there. MACV's Air Force component command was to exercise operational control over all activities of its service in Southeast Asia, but the other service components were to confine their attention to South Vietnam. The Pacific Command, through its component headquarters, was to support American forces in Thailand. McNamara vested in Harkins planning responsibility for Southeast Asia and gave him a small staff in Bangkok for that purpose. From then on, Harkins, as COMUSMACV/THAI and commander-designate of U.S. and SEATO field forces, supervised the drafting and periodic revision of Pacific Command and SEATO plans for resisting North Vietnamese and Chinese attacks on Laos, South Vietnam, and Thailand, in contingencies ranging from intensified insurgency to a full-scale onslaught by massed Chinese armies. In addition, Harkins participated in preparations for American military operations in Thailand as the fragile Laotian peace began to disintegrate.[12]

The Military Assistance Command's place in the chain of command between Washington and Saigon came under periodic but inconclusive scrutiny. The chain was a complicated one which allowed many different agencies and individuals to dabble in MACV's affairs. Secretary McNamara, the Joint Chiefs of Staff—both in their collective capacity and as chiefs of their respective services—and Admiral Felt all watched MACV's activities closely and intervened to promote particular policies or service interests. Members of the JCS regularly visited General Harkins in Saigon. All the Defense Department principals, and often the ambassador to South Vietnam and other State Department and White House officials, assembled in Hawaii roughly once a month for conferences convened by McNamara. Harkins found these conferences and visits helpful in resolving disputes and securing support for his endeavors; but he also later complained that "the personal feelings of many senior U.S. officials found their way into directives received in Saigon. . . . The whole setup of command and control," he concluded, "was too complicated."[13]

As a side effect of the complicated chain of command, General Harkins and his staff were at times all but overrun by visitors from both the executive branch and Congress. Most came to assess the progress of the counterinsurgency campaign, but many had ulterior political purposes

A Joint Command: Complications and Conflicts, 1962–1963

as well. Within a single month in the fall of 1962, the Military Assistance Command accommodated over 200 guests from the Defense Department alone. Each delegation had to be housed, briefed, entertained, and—usually—escorted into the countryside to observe the "real" war at the cost of lost working time to the MACV staff and the diversion of vehicles and helicopters from their assigned tasks. Trying to ease the burden on the command, General Taylor, now chairman of the Joint Chiefs of Staff, in October 1962 directed Defense Department agencies to "reduce the number of visitors to South Vietnam and Thailand to those having actual business of pressing interest." His directive, the first of many on this subject, only temporarily checked the influx.[14]

Throughout the Military Assistance Command's first two years of operation, Admiral Felt kept the Saigon headquarters on a tight rein. He lost no opportunity to demonstrate that MACV, however unique its mission and circumstances, was merely another subordinate unified command under CINCPAC. For example, when Harkins requested authority to convene general courts-martial in Vietnam to speed up the administration of justice among his widely dispersed troops, Felt turned him down and left the task to the PACOM service component commanders. The admiral also interjected himself repeatedly into questions of internal Military Assistance Command organization, including the relationship between MACV and the military advisory group. He intervened as well in operational planning, at one point pressing General Harkins to give high priority to clearing out the Viet Cong's War Zone D base area north of Saigon and suggesting tactics for doing so.[15]

Admiral Felt's constant interventions led several presidential advisers early in 1963 to reopen the question of whether Harkins should report directly to Secretary McNamara and the Joint Chiefs. President Kennedy himself raised the issue with the chiefs at a meeting on 28 February 1963, requesting their views on whether Felt had Harkins "on a leash" so tight that the commander found it difficult to cooperate effectively with the rest of the country team. General Taylor and the other chiefs defended the existing arrangement. Taylor did so, he recalled later, "because I felt at that stage [that] Saigon as a headquarters had a very limited capacity" and that a great deal of support was available from Honolulu to reinforce "this small theater of operations which was just starting to emerge." When queried by his military superiors, General Harkins made no request for a change in his chain of command. He pointed out in retrospect that he had to rely on CINCPAC for "supply and support" regardless of whether or not he had a direct line to the JCS. Deferring to military opinion, the administration early in April accepted a recommendation from Taylor that the existing arrangement continue. It did so, however, only after Taylor, in a personal conference with Admiral Felt, informally instructed the Pacific commander to allow more latitude where Harkins and his area of responsibility were concerned.[16]

41

MACV and the MAAG

If the Military Assistance Command's relationships up the chain of command to CINCPAC and beyond were at issue, so were its relationships downward, in particular those with its predecessor in Saigon, the Military Assistance Advisory Group. Early in the planning for MACV, the Joint Chiefs of Staff had decided that the MAAG should remain in existence as a separate subordinate command under the new headquarters. The group, under the MACV commander's direction, was to continue its advisory and training missions and its management of the Military Assistance Program (MAP) under which the United States financed and equipped its ally's armed forces. By retaining these functions, the Joint Chiefs and Admiral Felt believed, the group could give MACV the benefit of its years of experience and its established contacts in Vietnam while relieving the assistance command of burdensome, complex administrative tasks. In practice, however, this division of labor soon began to break down. Thus, within a year of MACV's activation, General Harkins would recommend dissolution of the MAAG and reassignment of its functions to the MACV staff and component commands.[17]

At the time of MACV's activation, the 200-man MAAG headquarters consisted of a small joint staff, a Military Assistance Program Division, a development and testing center, and Army, Navy, and Air Force sections that oversaw and supported American advisers with the Vietnamese services. Largest in size, the Army section played the key role in guiding the Vietnamese armed forces by assigning advisers to the Joint General Staff (JGS), the ARVN high command, and the corps, divisions, training centers, schools, and territorial force headquarters under them. By early 1962 this modest establishment was reaching the limit of its command and control capabilities. After eight years of stability, the group's manpower had grown in a few months from 685 officers and enlisted men to almost 3,000 advisers deployed down to the province and battalion levels. Until MACV went into operation, the group took operational control of arriving American units and furnished them administrative and logistical support. It also assumed what were for it the new tasks of directly assisting the South Vietnamese in intelligence and operational planning. In the end, a Joint Staff officer could report after a visit to Vietnam in February 1962 only that the MAAG "appears to lack organizational purpose and direction."[18]

The Military Assistance Command was supposed to relieve the advisory group of the additional tasks it had assumed during the Kennedy buildup; but Admiral Felt was determined to keep the new headquarters away from those aspects of the advisory, training, and military assistance programs that were the MAAG's established areas of responsibility. MACV's final terms of reference, which Felt promulgated on 7 April 1962, firmly placed the MAAG chief under General Harkins for all matters but emphasized that the nuts and bolts of Military Assistance

Program budgeting, planning, and accounting should be left to the MAAG with only "minimal" supervisory involvement by the MACV staff. In substance, the MAAG chief was to be COMUSMACV's representative and agent for managing military assistance to the South Vietnamese and administering routine aspects of his advisory and training role. The admiral summed up his view of the relationship between the two American headquarters in a personal letter to Harkins:

> ChMAAG is your representative with respect to MAP. . . . Specific responsibilities and functions in regard to MAP include making recommendations and submitting Military Assistance plans and programs to CINCPAC. We tried to spell this out quite carefully in order to relieve you of the administrative burden of actually performing voluminous chores related to MAP, while at the same time recognizing that the MAAG has been in operation for a long time and is best equipped to absorb the policies dictated by DOD and CINCPAC and such other directives that may be issued by SECDEF, the Military Departments and you. . . . The key to the problem is for you to provide strategic guidance in respect to defense problems of SVN and for the ChMAAG to do the laborious work of carrying out MAP administrative procedures.[19]

As the Military Assistance Command went into full operation during 1962, Admiral Felt and General Harkins during that year reorganized the MAAG headquarters to reflect the group's more circumscribed functions. They eliminated the MAAG general staff sections and reduced the rank structure—the most visible change being the MAAG chief's position, when Maj. Gen. Charles J. Timmes replaced General McGarr in July 1962. General Harkins considered reducing overall MAAG strength by about 160 headquarters people supposedly rendered surplus by the shift of functions to MACV, but General Timmes persuaded Harkins that a modest increase in the advisory group was long overdue. Timmes pointed out that the group's field advisory activities and reporting responsibilities were expanding and that the MAAG headquarters never had been adequately manned for the tasks MACV had assumed. In the end, both commanders agreed to recommend a modest increase in the MAAG to 3,250 officers and enlisted men, the approximate strength of the group through 1963. In a limited consolidation of activities, the MAAG's Army section handled all Army personnel actions for both headquarters while MACV assumed responsibility for all intelligence and legal functions.[20]

Although Admiral Felt was constrained to respect Harkins' areas of responsibility, the division of labor between the MACV and the MAAG headquarters evolved along some of the lines he desired. The Military Assistance Command took over the drafting and revision of PACOM contingency plans; in cooperation with the South Vietnamese Joint General Staff, it drew up the annual government plan of campaign; it prepared estimates of South Vietnamese force increases required by that plan; and it assumed the increasingly heavy burden of reporting to CINCPAC, the Joint Chiefs, and the secretary of defense on the progress of the American effort. Liaison officers from MACV staff sections replaced those from the MAAG as advisers to the Joint General Staff and other top-level South Vietnamese defense agencies. MACV also issued orders to the MAAG field advisers on matters of intelligence and operational planning and advice. For its part, the Military Assistance Advisory Group worked out the detailed training, construction, and materiel requirements of the Vietnamese forces specified by MACV; established unit activation schedules; and drafted requests and justifications for MAP funding and equipment. The MAAG also continued to administer and support the field advisers and to direct their work with the Vietnamese on training and logistics.

Despite these arrangements, the spheres of interest of MACV and the MAAG inevitably overlapped in practice, creating confusion and duplication of effort for both. In Saigon, the MACV staff intervened in the MAAG's detailed planning of the Vietnamese force structure and also became involved in other aspects of the Military Assistance Program's administration, such as ammunition procurement, which directly affected field operations. In the field, meanwhile, advisers served two masters. The line between MACV's area of concern—intelligence and operations—and the training and logistical interests of the MAAG was often faint at best. Both the advisory group and the developing MACV service commands became involved in the administration and supply of the advisory teams.[21]

General Harkins lost little time in concluding that the advisory group constituted an unnecessary complication in his command structure. As early as September 1962, he proposed that all MAAG functions except administration of the Military Assistance Program should come under the MACV component commands and that the remainder of the advisory group's headquarters should become a staff division within MACV. A JCS delegation that visited Vietnam in January 1963 supported Harkins' recommendation, on the grounds that the assistance command and the advisory group were using the same personnel in the field to perform overlapping tasks. Admiral Felt, however, continued to argue against eliminating the MAAG. He insisted that MACV must avoid becoming "bogged down" in advisory and military assistance details. The question remained unresolved through the end of 1963, with General Harkins continuing to press for consolidation of the two headquarters.[22]

Formation of MACV Headquarters

If MACV command relationships were influenced by interservice politics, even more so was the formation of its headquarters and subordinate elements. Battles over distribution of staff billets, assignment of important functions, and command and control of American forces punctuated the fleshing out of the command's structure.

A Joint Command: Complications and Conflicts, 1962–1963

MACV headquarters had a small, improvised beginning. After a brief meeting with President Kennedy and the Joint Chiefs at Palm Beach, Florida, on 6 January, General Harkins traveled to Saigon to confer with General McGarr, who was less than enthusiastic at being supplanted by the new commander and headquarters. Both officers then attended McNamara's January Honolulu conference. Harkins returned to Saigon to take over his command on 13 February and began work in earnest a week later, after a final Honolulu planning session. At that time, the Military Assistance Command headquarters consisted of Harkins, his aide, his chief of staff, the chief of staff's assistant, and two enlisted clerks on loan from the MAAG, which also provided office space, communications, and staff support. The MACV staff expanded slowly at first, through arrivals from outside the country and more numerous transfers of people from functions within the advisory group to equivalent MACV slots. To avoid disruption of group operations, most of the latter personnel remained temporarily at their MAAG desks, doing their MACV jobs as an additional duty. A member of the early MACV staff described the resulting difficulties:

> You had a mixed-up situation of certain officers and enlisted men in the J–3 at MAAG who would get a task given to them by the Chief of Staff at MACV, at the same time having to work for their own boss . . . , who was the J–3 of MAAG. This existed throughout the MAAG staff and it made a very difficult time for both MACV and for MAAG. . . . We were ultimately able to segregate portions of our staff from the MAAG staff in the old MAAG conference building. But that building just wasn't large enough to take them all and make any kind of operating staff divisions. . . . The MAAG classified mail and records section was attempting to file MACV traffic and letters separate from MAAG, some of which were addressed to both. As a result some of this traffic-correspondence is missing from one or the other files. I really think they did a real fine job in an awkward situation.[23]

The new headquarters grew rapidly. In mid-May, it separated physically from the MAAG, occupying its own leased office building at 137 Pasteur Street in downtown Saigon and subsequently at other locations as well. The staff quickly attained its authorized strength of 216 officers and enlisted men, nearly two-thirds of them transfers from the MAAG. General Harkins soon found this complement insufficient to perform all the tasks his office had assumed from the advisory group and in August he asked the Joint Chiefs of Staff for an increase in headquarters strength to 352. The JCS approved the request in early 1963.[24]

As the size of its staff expanded, the Military Assistance Command early standardized its people's tours of duty. Initially, the personnel of each military service served in Vietnam for different lengths of time, depending on whether or not they were accompanied by their families and whether they were stationed in Saigon or in the provinces. By early 1963, after much negotiation, the services had agreed upon and were implementing a common tour of twelve months unaccompanied and twenty-four months accompanied for all personnel in Vietnam, regardless of whether they served in the capital or outside it. For

MACV headquarters people, many of whom had their families with them, living conditions in Saigon were far from austere. Quartered in villas and hotels, they could take advantage of the amenities of a city that offered a mixture of European elegance and Oriental exoticism as yet largely unscarred by the war and its attendant afflictions.[25]

The command's headquarters organization followed conventional military lines. The joint staff included the traditional numbered general sections for personnel (J1), intelligence (J2), operations (J3), logistics (J4), planning (J5), and communications/electronics (J6), as well as special sections for protocol, the comptroller, the judge advocate, public information, inspector general, surgeon, chaplain, provost marshal, and civil affairs. An additional special staff element, combining an Advanced Research Projects Agency field unit and a Joint Operational Evaluation Group, conducted counterinsurgency research and development as well as field tests of equipment and tactical concepts. These headquarters subdivisions for the most part performed their standard tasks, but with variations arising from the command's special mission. Each general and special staff office, for example, advised and assisted a counterpart agency within the South Vietnamese Joint General Staff. Many also participated in MACV's Southeast Asia contingency planning, and the J5 office included an entire branch for that purpose. The command maintained its own small combat operations center in the operations section and a message center staffed by the communications/electronics office.[26]

MACV Headquarters, 137 Pasteur Street (NARA)

From the beginning, the services engaged in a tug-of-war over distribution of the senior MACV staff positions. Maneuvering got under way in November 1961, when Admiral Felt prepared an organization and staffing plan, or Joint Table of Distribution (JTD), for the projected headquarters. Felt's plan called for a joint staff with an Army general in command and Army personnel predominant in numbers, but with strong balancing representation from the other services. Air Force officers, in particular, would occupy the positions of chief of staff and of the assistant chiefs of staff for intelligence (J2) and plans (J5). At General Harkins' request, the JCS switched the chief of staff billet from the Air Force to the Marine Corps to accommodate Harkins' personal choice for the job, Maj. Gen. Richard G. Weede, USMC. In return, the Air Force

A Joint Command: Complications and Conflicts, 1962–1963

General Weede (NARA)

received the assistant chief of staff for operations (J3) slot. Harkins accepted this arrangement—even though it would give an aviator responsibility for directing what was primarily a ground war—because he expected to "guide the G-3 [sic] business" himself.[27]

The Chief of Staff of the Army, General George W. Decker, objected to Air Force control of the intelligence and operations offices. While expressing confidence in the Air Force's ability to provide competent high-level staff officers, Decker declared that "it seems inappropriate to put them . . . where they will exert so much influence on what is basically a ground operation, and where the great preponderance of U.S. personnel involved will be Army." Privately, Decker told Harkins that the Army, more than any other service, was "on the spot" in South Vietnam and that "any failure will be placed directly on our doorstep." Hence, he wanted Army officers in the positions that could determine success or failure. Decker wanted Harkins, whose preferences as commander-designate carried great weight in determining the composition of the staff, to press the Army's case with Admiral Felt and Secretary McNamara.[28]

How strongly Harkins advocated the Army position in discussions of the MACV organizational structure is not recorded. However, General Decker did receive support from Secretary McNamara, who also viewed the Vietnam conflict as essentially a ground war. In February 1962, over the objections of Air Force Chief of Staff General Curtis E. LeMay, McNamara awarded the operations, logistics, and communications billets to the Army. The Marine Corps kept the chief of staff position, while the Air Force had to settle for the intelligence and planning offices and the Navy for the chief of personnel. All the special staff section heads were from the Army except the comptroller (Navy) and the public information officer (Air Force). *(Table)*

Of the initial headquarters complement of 216 officers and enlisted men, 113 came from the Army, 35 from the Navy, 18 from the Marine Corps, and 50 from the Air Force. This distribution of senior staff positions and proportional manpower strength remained largely unchanged as MACV headquarters expanded.[29]

The outcome of this maneuvering left Air Force leaders convinced that their service had been shortchanged—in rank, offices, and num-

47

MACV: The Years of Escalation, 1962–1967

bers—at MACV headquarters, to the detriment of the effective use of air power in Vietnam. They had grounds for their frustration. The MACV J3, an Army officer, quickly edged the Air Force J5 out of the planning for operations within South Vietnam. To make matters worse, as the headquarters expanded, the J5 office was shunted aside into a separate building away from the rest of the senior staff. The commander of MACV's Air Force component, whose headquarters came into being late in 1962, also reported that he had difficulty in obtaining regular, timely access to General Harkins.

TABLE—MACV PRINCIPAL OFFICERS AT ACTIVATION

Commander	General Paul D. Harkins, USA
Chief of Staff	Maj. Gen. Richard G. Weede, USMC
AC/S, J1	Capt. Joseph A. Tvedt, USN
AC/S, J2	Col. James M. Winterbottom, USAF
AC/S, J3	Brig. Gen. Gerald C. Kelleher, USA
AC/S, J4	Brig. Gen. Frank A. Osmanski, USA
AC/S, J5	Brig. Gen. John A. Dunning, USAF
AC/S, J6	Col. Philip S. Pomeroy, Jr., USA

Source: CINCPAC Command History, 1962

Seeking to remedy what he considered an injustice to his service and a hindrance to effective prosecution of the war, LeMay campaigned forcefully, and not always tactfully, for a larger, higher-ranking Air Force contingent at MACV headquarters. After a visit to Saigon early in 1962, LeMay angered General Harkins by alleging before the Joint Chiefs of Staff that MACV was ignorant of and unconcerned with proper air support. Harkins responded with a strong defense of his own and of General Weede's expertise in air matters. In an effort to gain more influence at the top level of the Military Assistance Command, Air Force leaders at various times during the next two years urged creation of a deputy MACV commander's position, to be filled by a three-star Air Force general. They also pushed for transfer of the chief of staff billet from the Marine Corps to the Air Force at the end of General Weede's tour of duty. Neither campaign achieved its goal, in good measure because Secretary McNamara persisted in regarding the Vietnam conflict as a ground war over which the Army should properly have charge.[30]

Aside from the persistent arguments over Air Force representation, which originated as much outside Vietnam as within it, the Military Assistance Command's senior staff formed a relatively harmonious team. "We were all acquainted with each other," General Weede, the chief of staff, recalled, "and were used to working together." General Harkins

A Joint Command: Complications and Conflicts, 1962–1963

MACV staff members
(Photo courtesy of Maj. Gen. Carl A. Youngdale, USMC (Ret.))

and most of his principal subordinates came to MACV from previous assignments in the Pacific Command. General Weede, for example, had commanded the 1st Marine Brigade at Kaneohe, Hawaii, for three years before joining MACV. His chief assistant had been a Pacific Command staff member in charge of "monitoring, then taking the actions necessary to execute" PACOM contingency plans for Southeast Asia. The chief of staff, along with the J4, Brig. Gen. Frank A. Osmanski, and the J6, Col. Philip S. Pomeroy, Jr., as well as other members of the staff, had served under Harkins the year before in the SEATO Field Forces headquarters activated for the Laotian crisis. Weede had been Harkins' chief of staff in that command. He, Osmanski, and Pomeroy all were personal selections of Harkins for the MACV staff.[31]

Harkins maintained a rather distant relationship with his staff section chiefs. He spent much of his time traveling outside Saigon and held only brief daily staff meetings, relying largely on Weede for communication with the rest of the headquarters. For his part, Weede jealously guarded his position as principal channel to and from the commander. According to the secretary of the MACV Joint Staff, he "didn't like anybody to deal directly with Gen H[arkins]. He was a great one for wanting the C[hief] of S[taff] to be the way of getting through to the commander."[32]

One comparatively small element of the Military Assistance Command headquarters, concerned with counterinsurgency research, development, and testing, absorbed a disproportionate amount of command attention from General Harkins and his superiors. For the Kennedy administration and its armed forces, South Vietnam afforded a potential laboratory for trying out counterinsurgency technologies and techniques in active warfare. Unfortunately, this effort became an interagency, interservice battleground. At issue, the MACV Air Force component commander declared, was "who was going to control [the program] and who was going to end up with whatever was developed as . . . a part of their service's roles and missions."[33]

Testing and evaluation agencies proliferated in Vietnam. Before MACV was organized, the Advanced Research Projects Agency (ARPA) of Secretary McNamara's office in August 1961 established a field unit to advise and cooperate with a Combat Development and Test Center (CDTC) formed by the Vietnamese Joint General Staff.[34] Charged with aiding the Vietnamese in developing new devices and techniques for combating the Viet Cong, the ARPA unit was responsible neither to CINCPAC nor to his subordinate unified commanders. Instead, it reported directly to the director of defense for research and engineering and obtained experimental equipment through its own procurement channels. To secure a testing agency more closely controlled by the uniformed services, the Joint Chiefs of Staff in July 1962 set up the Joint Operational Evaluation Group–Vietnam (JOEG-V). This group, under General Harkins' control, was to coordinate service testing of concepts, tactics, techniques, and materiel. It also was to ensure that such trials did not interfere with operations against the Viet Cong and to make its own evaluations of tests that were likely to have results of interest to more than one service. To carry out its own counterinsurgency experiments, the Army lost no time in establishing an Army Concept Team in Vietnam (ACTIV) under the joint evaluation group. This unit had as its initial mission the trial in combat of Army aircraft and airmobile tactics. Not to be left behind by its rival, the Air Force early in 1963 formed a twelve-man test unit of its own within its Vietnam component command, the 2d Air Division.[35]

Admiral Felt viewed this multiplication of testing agencies with displeasure. He worked continuously to limit their size and to ensure that their activities supported rather than interfered with prosecution of the counterinsurgency campaign. In February 1962 he secured agreement from ARPA representatives that all projects undertaken by their agency in Southeast Asia would require concurrence from the host government, the appropriate military commands, and the ARPA field unit. Similarly, Felt postponed deployment of half of the Army Concept Team in Vietnam, with its ninety-nine personnel and its aircraft test units, until the Army reduced the team's permanently assigned manpower by one-third. The admiral also insisted that the

A Joint Command: Complications and Conflicts, 1962–1963

Army permit him and General Harkins to review and amend proposals for new tests at an early stage in their development and to rewrite the test plans as necessary to bring them into line with operational needs in Vietnam.[36]

In spite these efforts, in November 1962 Felt told the Joint Chiefs that he was "becoming concerned that desire to use [South Vietnam] as a US test bed is beclouding CINCPAC and COMUSMACV primary objective of advising [the government of Vietnam] how to fight and assisting them to win their war." Organizations and tests continued to proliferate. The Combat Development Test Center and the ARPA field unit alone soon had some fifty projects under way, including experiments with chemical defoliation of Viet Cong hideouts and food-growing areas, employment of patrol dogs and ground surveillance radar, and the use of special grenades to splash fluorescent paint on guerrillas during engagements. Duplication of effort inevitably followed, especially between the ARPA unit and the service agencies, which regarded the ARPA unit with distrust. "ARPA has shown tendency to get into combat developments field (doctrine, troop tests) which is service responsibility," an Army information brief declared early in 1963. "ARPA also jealously guards its responsibility for [South Vietnamese testing activities]" and "may try to block R&D or perhaps troop testing Army may want to do in VN. . . . ARPA is in influential position to block Army if it desires."[37]

The Joint Chiefs of Staff, seconded by Admiral Felt and General Harkins, campaigned for placement of all testing and research agencies in Vietnam under the Military Assistance Command, to ensure unity of effort and to keep the activities subordinate to the prosecution of the war. However, Dr. Harold Brown, the director of defense research and engineering, and his staff insisted on keeping the ARPA field unit out of the military chain of command and procurement system. Secretary McNamara supported them. In a partial concession to the Joint Chiefs, McNamara in August 1962 appointed a single director, Brig. Gen. Robert H. York, a member of Dr. Brown's Pentagon staff, for both the ARPA field unit and the Joint Operational Evaluation Group. Under the terms of reference issued by Admiral Felt in December, General York was to oversee and evaluate all military research, development, and testing in South Vietnam. He was to report to ARPA on matters of research and development and tests of equipment and systems and to the MACV commander, CINCPAC, and the Joint Chiefs on the evaluation of military operations and tests of materiel by troops in the field.[38]

York's appointment satisfied neither General Harkins nor the Joint Chiefs of Staff. Harkins complained to Admiral Felt that the "entire subject of Research Development Test and Evaluation structure, scope of authority and relationship of the numerous agencies becomes more confusing as time passes." Early in 1963, the same JCS inspection team that recommended the merger of MACV and the MAAG also concluded that Harkins should have authority over all U.S. military research and development within his command, so that he could review each project's usefulness to the war effort and eliminate those he deemed superfluous.[39]

Armed with this recommendation, the Joint Chiefs secured Secretary McNamara's agreement, at least in principle, to MACV control of all testing. At JCS direction, Admiral Felt and General Harkins drafted a plan for a Research and Evaluation Division of the MACV staff that would incorporate all the testing organizations, including the ARPA field unit, as separate branches. Harkins then would supervise all military testing within South Vietnam, assigning responsibility for trials of interest to more than one service and recommending to the secretary of defense discontinuation of any projects that he deemed would interfere with operations or that could be done outside Vietnam. This plan became mired in disputes within the defense establishment. The Air Force demanded that the position of MACV director of research and evaluation rotate among the services; the Army claimed permanent possession of the slot because of the predominance in Vietnam of tests of concern to it. Both the Advanced Research Projects Agency and the Army wanted to retain a measure of autonomy for their respective testing units. These issues remained unresolved through the end of 1963. In the meantime, the various testing and development agencies went their separate ways, loosely coordinated by General York, with frequent intervention by Admiral Felt.[40]

In contrast to the command attention devoted to research and testing, a more important element of MACV headquarters—its intelligence section—suffered from neglect. As a result of he interservice jockeying for key staff positions, the first two assistant chiefs of staff for intelligence were Air Force colonels, specialists in strategic reconnaissance and Soviet missiles rather than in counterinsurgency. With a limited staff and few American resources in South Vietnam upon which to draw, the MACV J2 concentrated on providing technical advice to its Saigon government counterparts and relied on them for most of the data on which it based its own reports. The South Vietnamese intelligence services were ill trained, organizationally fragmented, and inclined to shape their output to please President Diem. They furnished MACV with what was at best incomplete, inaccurate, and biased information on such vital matters as the enemy order of battle, conditions in the countryside, and the internal politics of the regime. Since effective intelligence is an indispensable element in a counterinsurgency campaign, MACV was thus handicapped from the outset. The weakness of its intelligence arm was to have damaging effects as the military and political situation in South Vietnam began to deteriorate.[41]

As the Military Assistance Command and other American headquarters grew, their requirements for supplies, facilities, and medical and other support overwhelmed the MAAG's rudimentary logistical

A Joint Command: Complications and Conflicts, 1962–1963

arrangements. Creation of a new support agency, however, involved considerations of interservice politics as well as military efficiency. Under a Department of Defense directive dating back to the late 1950s, the Navy Department was to provide administrative and logistical support for unified commands in the Pacific even when, as with MACV, they consisted largely of non-Navy forces. With the formation of MACV in prospect, Admiral John H. Sides, Commander in Chief, Pacific Fleet (CINCPACFLT), whose forces would perform the support mission, objected to Navy personnel's having to act as "janitors" for a predominantly Army command, especially since the Navy was not then supporting the Army in Japan, Korea, and Okinawa. The Chief of Naval Operations, Admiral George W. Anderson, Jr., and Admiral Felt overruled Sides on the bluntly stated grounds that "command implications" were involved, specifically strengthening the Navy's case for subordination of MACV to Pacific Command and forestalling an Army bid to take the position of CINCPAC away from the Navy. The fleet must support MACV, Anderson told Felt, "despite the price we must pay in personnel and Navy dollars."

So directed, the Navy took on the support mission. Under plans developed by Pacific Fleet, Headquarters Support Activity, Saigon (HSAS), went into operation on 1 July 1962 with a joint complement that eventually included over 400 personnel, most of them Navy with a sprinkling from the Army and Air Force. Under interservice agreements, HSAS furnished common supply, fiscal, public works, medical, commissary, exchange, and special services support to the MACV and MAAG headquarters and to U.S. Army and Air Force commands in the vicinity of the Vietnamese capital. By early 1963, at General Harkins' request, the activity was preparing to expand its cargo-handling and storage operations to outlying ports as well, the better to support American units and advisers in the field. However, HSAS did not begin upcountry port operations until mid-1964, due to unresolved disagreements between the services about their respective contributions to the effort of manpower, funds, and materiel.[42]

The Component Commands

General Harkins was to direct his American forces in South Vietnam through Army, Navy, and Air Force service component commands. Those commands developed only slowly and unevenly, however, during MACV's first two years in operation. Their halting growth resulted from the small size of the American forces committed, the peculiarities of their mission, and diplomatic and political complications.

The Navy in fact got along at first without a service component command headquarters. Its section of the Military Assistance Advisory Group administered its modest contingent advising the Vietnamese Navy. Headquarters Support Activity, Saigon, was under MACV's operational control and for all other purposes answered to the commander, U.S. Naval Forces, Philippines.[43]

With the largest number of men and units deployed, the Army developed its component command most fully. In December 1961, General James F. Collins, Commanding General, U.S. Army, Pacific, established a provisional logistical group to support the Army helicopter companies then arriving in Vietnam. This 300-man group constituted an advance element of U.S. Army, Ryukyu Islands (USARYIS), on Okinawa, from which it drew personnel and supplies. In March 1962, at Admiral Felt's direction, Collins redesignated this provisional element as U.S. Army Support Group, Vietnam (USASGV). He assigned most Army units in Vietnam to its operational control and made the group responsible for the units' administrative and logistical support. At the same time, he placed USASGV under the operational command of General Harkins, giving it at least the implied status of a MACV Army component command. Further to clarify command relationships between USARPAC, USARYIS, MACV, USASGV, and the Army forces in South Vietnam, General Collins on 20 April designated the commander of USASGV as Army component commander under COMUSMACV. The support group, however, remained under the administrative control of the Army command on Okinawa.

In practice, the U.S. Army Support Group, Vietnam, performed the logistical and administrative—but not tactical—functions of a component command. General Harkins exercised direct operational control over most Army units in Vietnam, delegating command of the helicopter companies to the MAAG and its corps senior advisers. In effect, Harkins acted as his own Army component commander and employed the USASGV commander as his deputy for Army logistical and administrative matters. In August 1963, U.S. Army, Pacific, formally acknowledged this practice by designating Harkins as Army component commander in Vietnam and the U.S. Army Support Group commander as his deputy. This dual role of the military assistance commander met with criticism, especially from the Air Force, as violating the customary prohibition against a unified commander personally commanding a component force and as imposing too much purely Army business on the MACV joint staff. However, the arrangement conformed to the practice in other unified commands in which Army elements predominated, and Pacific Command contingency plans for Southeast Asia called for such a command structure there if major American combat forces were committed. In Vietnam, the arrangement permitted MACV headquarters to parallel in functions the South Vietnamese Joint General Staff, which had direct operational control over that nation's army. For those reasons, COMUSMACV was to retain his Army component "hat" throughout the life of his command.[44]

Creation of an Air Force component command was delayed until October 1962. The delay was due in large measure to the Kennedy

A Joint Command: Complications and Conflicts, 1962–1963

administration's desire to avoid acknowledging publicly the fact that the FARM GATE counterinsurgency unit of piston-engine fighters, light bombers, and transports was flying combat missions in South Vietnam, under Vietnamese insignia and carrying Vietnamese crewmen, ostensibly for training. As early as 20 November 1961, Pacific Air Forces, with Admiral Felt's permission, established a headquarters in Saigon, the 2d Advance Echelon (2d ADVON), Thirteenth Air Force, under Brig. Gen. Rollen H. Anthis, USAF, to direct FARM GATE's combat operations. At the same time, the MAAG's Air Force section, also under General Anthis, oversaw the unit in its other mission of training the South Vietnamese Air Force. However, in deference to the wishes of Ambassador Nolting, the 2d ADVON's real title and functions remained covert. Known simply as Detachment 7, Anthis and his tiny staff of temporary duty personnel were hidden in the MAAG offices.[45]

General Anthis (U.S. Air Force)

This was an unsatisfactory arrangement for the Air Force, especially from the logistics standpoint. Therefore, as soon as the Military Assistance Command went into operation, Pacific Air Forces, supported by General LeMay, launched a campaign for reorganization of the 2d ADVON into a full-fledged air division. Admiral Felt agreed in principle to this action on 21 March 1962, but he stipulated that the change would take place only "at such time as COMUSMACV organization and operations become regularized and attention of news media to U.S. military operations in S[outh] V[ietnam] slackens." Although media attention to American operations did not in fact lessen, the advance unit gradually evolved into a true component command. During May and June the Air Force secured open designation of the section as a command to which people could be assigned and formed regular base squadrons at Tan Son Nhut, Bien Hoa, Nha Trang, and Da Nang air bases. In July, Ambassador Nolting withdrew his objection to creation of an Air Force headquarters, although he continued to urge minimum publicity for the change.[46]

Final action on the Air Force component command accompanied the designation of General Harkins as U.S. commander for both South Vietnam and Thailand. On 8 October, Pacific Air Forces discontinued the 2d ADVON and activated the 2d Air Division under General Anthis, with headquarters at Tan Son Nhut. Under the agreements reached at

55

the 8 October Honolulu conference, the division, under a chain of command running from CINCPAC through COMUSMACV and COMUSMACTHAI, exercised operational control over all Air Force activities in Southeast Asia except those advisory groups in South Vietnam and Thailand. Its commander was responsible to Harkins for operational matters and to Pacific Air Forces through the Thirteenth Air Force for administration and logistics.[47]

The Debate over Control of Air Power

As commander of the 2d Air Division, General Anthis also functioned as the commander of MACV's Air Force component and principal air adviser to General Harkins. In those capacities, backed by his Air Force superiors, he became embroiled with Harkins in a bitter, unresolved dispute over the command and control of aviation in Vietnam. Stemming from fundamental Army–Air Force disagreements over air doctrine, the argument took place against the background of the Army's acquisition in the late fifties of its own helicopters and airplanes and its development of a concept of airmobile operations that employed Army infantry and artillery units with their own organic aviation. In this context, both sides assumed that the outcome of the argument in Vietnam would set vital precedents for the future of their services and of American air power in general. "It may be improper to say we are at war with the Army," the air staff director of plans avowed at the time. "However, we believe that if the Army efforts are successful, they may have a long term adverse effect in the U.S. military posture that could be more important than the battle presently being waged with the Viet Cong."[48]

Both services built up their aviation strength in South Vietnam during the Military Assistance Command's first two years. Besides adding aircraft to its FARM GATE unit, the Air Force introduced squadrons of short takeoff and landing transports and light observation planes. The Army brought in troop-carrying and gunship helicopters, as well as its own fixed-wing transports and reconnaissance craft, and the marines established their presence with a helicopter squadron. By the end of 1963, 325 Army, 117 Air Force, and 20 Marine aircraft were operating in South Vietnam, alongside the 219 airplanes and helicopters of the Vietnamese Air Force (VNAF). The functions of many of these aircraft overlapped, leading to competition for roles and missions and some duplication of services, a circumstance not unwelcome to ground commanders who could then select the air support provider most responsive to their needs.[49]

At Military Assistance Command headquarters, service partisanship became intense and at times disruptive. Maj. Gen. Edward L. Rowney, first chief of the Army Concept Team in Vietnam, used the team's testing programs to introduce Army aircraft into combat under the most

A Joint Command: Complications and Conflicts, 1962–1963

favorable circumstances for validating his service's airmobility doctrine. ACTIV, he boasted at the end of his tour, had allowed

> air mobile operations to function without being fettered by Air Force controls. While we seem slow to adopt new methods for fighting guerrillas, the Army is nonetheless considerably ahead of the Air Force. They insist on applying the wrong tools in the wrong way. It is my conviction that by providing the assets and protecting them from being hampered we can squeeze many of the Air Force artificialities and anomalies out of the field of counterinsurgency.[50]

General Anthis was equally zealous in upholding the Air Force's position. He referred privately to the Army as "a customer that is also a competitor" and suggested that it would be desirable for "the Army concept of close air support" to be discredited early by minor reverses in Vietnam rather than by "the ultimate catastrophe their concept must lead us to at a time and place where we will not have the elasticity we presently enjoy." Observing the infighting between Anthis and Rowney at MACV headquarters and the general "dirty work of selling our service product at the expense of others," the J5, Maj. Gen. Milton B. Adams, himself an Air Force general, wondered for a while "who the principal enemy was, the VC or the Army or the Air Force."[51]

The competition for missions largely resolved itself, because the intensifying war created more than enough work for aircraft of every type and service. The Army–Air Force doctrinal dispute over command and control, on the other hand, proved intractable. Each service set up a version of its preferred control system. Pacific Air Forces, even before MACV went into operation, obtained authorization from Secretary McNamara to establish an Air Force–type tactical air control system (TACS) in South Vietnam. By late 1962 that system, although plagued by equipment shortages and communications problems, was in place and operating. It consisted of a Joint Air Operations Center (JAOC) at Tan Son Nhut with a subordinate operations center at each ARVN corps headquarters. Manned by American and South Vietnamese personnel, this system assigned missions to and controlled the flights of both American and South Vietnamese Air Force aircraft, although each service remained under the command of its own national authorities. A separate Southeast Asia Airlift System, built around a combat cargo group under the 2d Air Division and a Joint Airlift Allocation Board in the MACV J4 section, controlled operations of U.S. Air Force and VNAF transport planes and set priorities for fulfilling airlift requests.[52]

General Harkins took the Army's side on most aviation issues, including command and control. He had sought to promote the interests of Army aviation while deputy commander of USARPAC, and he continued doing so as MACV commander. Accordingly, Harkins pressed for introduction into Vietnam of the maximum number of Army aircraft, so that, in the Air Force view, he much too readily ac-

FARM GATE aircraft: left, *South Vietnamese T–28 fighter-bombers;*
right, *U.S. Air Force B–26 light bomber* (NARA)

quiesced in Army encroachment on Air Force missions. Worst of all in Air Force eyes, he kept all the Army and Marine helicopters and most Army fixed-wing aircraft (except for a few token CV–2 Caribou transports assigned to the Southeast Asia Airlift System) out of the centralized control structure. He gave operational control of the Army and Marine craft to his corps senior advisers, who dispatched them on missions with little reference to the Joint Air Operations Center, and he advised the Joint General Staff members to follow suit by distributing their own helicopters and observation planes rather than employing them within the Air Force system.[53]

Harkins thus had under him two separate air command and control systems which, between them, controlled four separate air organizations. His Air Force component commander, in conjunction with the Joint General Staff and using a common tactical air control system, managed the U.S. and Vietnamese Air Forces as a pool of centrally allocated air power. The Army corps senior advisers, working with the ARVN corps headquarters, disposed of a much larger force of U.S. Army and Marine aircraft over which, for practical purposes, General Anthis had no authority and which advisers and ground commanders preferred for its greater responsiveness to their requirements. This bifurcation of control seemingly violated a CINCPAC instruction of 6 June 1962, which gave the Air Force component commander coordinating authority over all air organizations operating within his area of responsibility. However, General Harkins chose to interpret "coordinating authority" his own way, as little more than air traffic control. He also made the most of the fact that the instruction did nothing to require assignment of non–Air Force aircraft to the operational control of the Air Force component commander. In day-to-day operations, the men in the field meshed the two systems after a fashion, but Air Force leaders objected bitterly to what they felt was subversion by MACV of the principles of unified command and warned that MACV's divided tactical air control system would sooner or later lead to disaster.[54]

A Joint Command: Complications and Conflicts, 1962–1963

Harkins, who considered himself an expert on close air support as a result of his World War II experience on General Patton's staff, argued uncompromisingly for decentralized control. He claimed that "there is no air battle in Vietnam, and there are no indications that one will develop. There is an extensive utilization of air power in support of the ground battle." The "geographical extent" of South Vietnam and limited communications facilities "unequivocally" ruled out centralized management of air support by the Joint Air Operations Center, which should confine its functions to redistributing of aircraft among the corps and to following and controlling missions once they were airborne. The air units themselves, Harkins affirmed, must fly from fields close to the areas of ground operations; they must be assigned "the mission of direct support of the Corps"; and they must be "under the direct control of the A[ir] S[upport] O[perations] C[enters] . . . and in direct response to the requirements established by the supported commander." So as to leave no doubt where he stood, Harkins issued a MACV directive on 8 July that placed his Army J3 in charge of allocating Army and Marine Corps aircraft. He also set up an aviation headquarters in each corps, through which the senior adviser as his representative could command the aircraft that flew in support of that corps' units and operations. In practice these included all but a handful of the Army and Marine aircraft in Vietnam. General Anthis argued against adoption of this plan, but to no avail.[55]

Admiral Felt deplored the service partisanship on both sides of the air controversy and attempted to mediate the dispute. He leaned, however, toward the Army side by agreeing that Harkins had the authority to withhold from his Air Force component commander operational control of Army and Marine aviation units. In that event, Felt said, the units withheld were to receive mission assignments from the commanders they supported, but should report to the tactical air control system for control of their flight operations. Felt repeatedly urged Harkins to place his Army helicopters and light observation planes under the TACS and his Caribous under the Southeast Asia airlift system, but he took no action when Harkins responded with only temporary token compliance. The Pacific commander accepted on a "provisional" basis Harkins' establishment of separate corps-level headquarters for Army and Marine aviation. Late in 1963 he convened a special interservice board to attempt to resolve the aviation command dispute, but the board's report drew fire from Pacific Air Forces as overly diluting the authority of the Air Force component commander.[56]

At the end of 1963, as an Air Force study aptly summed up, "resolution of the unfortunate doctrinal controversy seemed as remote as the successful culmination of the struggle against communist insurgency in Vietnam." General Harkins still commanded two separate air arms, one centrally directed by his Air Force component commander, the other parceled out among and controlled by the corps senior advisers.

MACV: The Years of Escalation, 1962–1967

H–21 "Flying Banana" (U.S. Army)

At that stage of the war, this probably was an acceptable compromise. The MACV Joint Operational Evaluation Group, reviewing the results of tests of Army aircraft and airmobile tactics, concluded in mid-1963 that a "flexible" system with some aircraft under central control and others distributed among the corps and divisions best met the requirements of the counterinsurgency campaign. General York, the evaluation group's director, vainly urged the services to adapt doctrine to Vietnam rather than Vietnam to doctrine and to "maintain an open mind and a willingness to consider new concepts." The soldiers and airmen fighting the battle acted in the spirit of York's words; but their superiors, driven by service considerations reaching far beyond Vietnam, frequently did not. The struggle over command and control of air power was to continue throughout most of the Military Assistance Command's existence, increasing in complexity in step with air operations in Southeast Asia.[57]

A Small But Complicated Command

Secretary of Defense McNamara's late 1961 initiative to create a new military organization to assist the South Vietnamese government brought into being a small unified headquarters carrying a heavy burden of command relationships, a growing load of additional missions, and interservice conflicts. *(Chart 1)* The Military Assistance Command, Vietnam, from the start was enmeshed in a complex, unified command structure

CHART 1—U.S. MILITARY ASSISTANCE COMMAND, VIETNAM, 1964
SAIGON, VIETNAM

- COMUSMACV—MACJOO
  - DEPCOMUSMACV—MACJ01
  - CHIEF OF STAFF—MACJ02
  - SECRETARY, JOINT STAFF—MACJ03
  - INSPECTOR GENERAL—MACIG
  - COMBINED STUDIES
  - OFFICE OF INFORMATION—MACO1 COMMAND INFORMATION BR
    - DODSPECREP
  - ASST. CHIEF OF STAFF FOR PERSONNEL—MACJ 1
    - ADJUTANT GENERAL—MACAG
    - JOINT RESEARCH & TEST ACT—JRATA
  - ASST. CHIEF OF STAFF FOR INTEL—MACJ 2
    - HEADQUARTERS COMMANDANT—MACHC
    - MAP DIRECTORATE—MACMAP
  - ASST. CHIEF OF STAFF FOR OPERATIONS—MACJ 3
    - COMPTROLLER—MACCO
    - DIR OF ARMY MAP LOGISTICS—MACLOG
  - ASST. CHIEF OF STAFF FOR LOGISTICS—MACJ 4
    - SURGEON—MACMD
    - OFFICE OF SECTOR—MACSA AFFAIRS
  - ASST. CHIEF OF STAFF FOR PLANS—MACJ 5
    - STAFF JUDGE ADVOCATE—MACJA
    - DIR FOR ORG. AND TRAINING—MACOT
  - ASST. CHIEF OF STAFF FOR COMM—ELECT—MACJ 6
    - PROVOST MARSHAL—MACPM
    - CHAPLAIN—MACCH
  - STUDIES AND OBSERVATIONS GROUP—MACSOG
    - HOP TAC SECRETARIAT

- ARMY ADV GP—I CORPS
- ARMY ADV GP—II CORPS
- ARMY ADV GP—III CORPS
- ARMY ADV GP—IV CORPS
- AIRBORNE BRIGADE ADV DET
- PR–PF ADVISORY DETACHMENT
- CAPITAL MILITARY DISTRICT

- US ARMY SUPPORT COMMAND—USASCV
- HEADQUARTERS SUPPORT ACTIVITY SAIGON—HEDSUPPACT
- RAILWAY SECURITY ADV DET
- NAVAL ADVISORY GROUP
- COMMANDER TASK ELEMENT 79.3.3.6
- SECOND AIR DIVISION
- AIR FORCE ADVISORY GROUP

- AUSTRALIAN ARMY TRAINING TEAM VIETNAM (AATTV)
- NEW ZEALAND ARMY DETACHMENT VIETNAM (NEW Z ADV)
- PHILIPPINE CONTINGENT VIETNAM (PHILCON)
- MIL ADV GP REPUBLIC OF CHINA TO RVN
- KOREA MIL ASST. GP. VN.

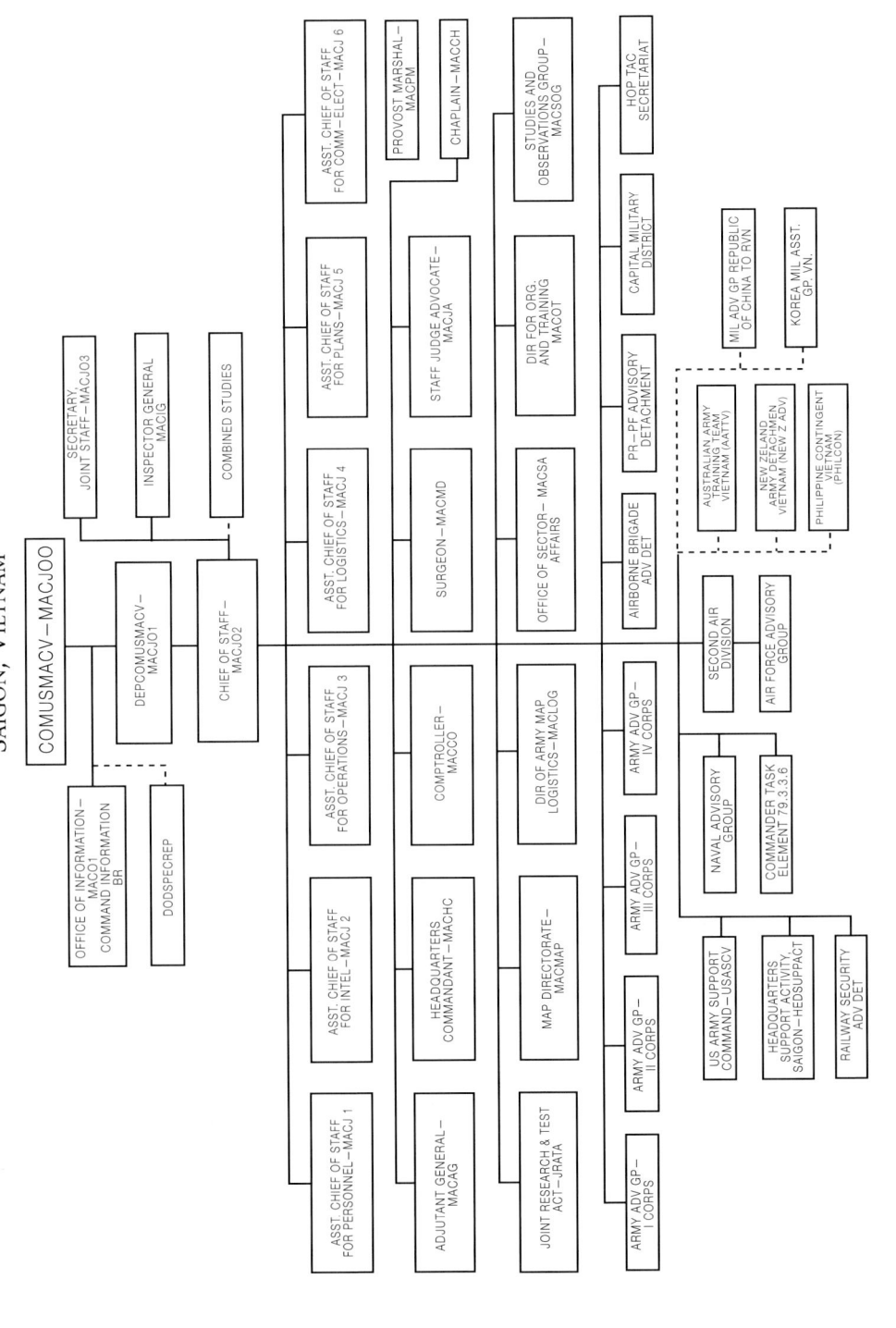

oriented primarily toward theater- and regional-wide conventional warfare. Besides its task in Vietnam, MACV acquired responsibility for U.S. forces and military assistance in Thailand, for military activity in support of American policy in Laos, and for contingency planning for most of mainland Southeast Asia. Its commander and principal staff officers at the outset were far better prepared by experience for their missions outside Vietnam than for their primary task.

Unresolved issues of American military organization—the overlapping of functions with the Military Assistance Advisory Group; the inability to unify multiple research, development, and combat testing agencies; and the Army–Air Force deadlock over command and control of aviation—persisted throughout the command's first two years of existence. As the air power dispute demonstrated, the command at times served as a battleground for doctrinal and policy conflicts which originated outside its area of responsibility and in which the contending parties were only partially, if at all, concerned with the immediate situation in Vietnam. Its commander's initiative and independence in carrying out his missions seemed likely to be quite circumscribed, given the penchant of his superiors for interfering in every detail of MACV organization and activity.

Simply as an American military command, then, the Military Assistance Command labored from the outset under complicated, difficult conditions. At the same time, in its advisory and assistance capacity, the headquarters struggled with another set of tangled relationships and intractable conflicts. The Military Assistance Command had to cooperate with other American agencies and with the regime of President Ngo Dinh Diem in a politico-military campaign against a tenacious, resourceful enemy of steadily increasing strength. In that campaign, progress was to prove difficult to measure and even more difficult to achieve.

A Joint Command: Complications and Conflicts, 1962–1963

Notes

[1] Msgs, JCS to CINCPAC, 7 Feb 62; CINCPAC to Pacific Cmds, 8 Feb 62; both in file 204–58 (205–19), Table of Distribution Files (1963), box 1, 69A702, RG 334, NARA.

[2] For a summary of McNamara's effect on the DOD, see Douglas Kinnard, *The Secretary of Defense* (Lexington: University Press of Kentucky, 1980), ch. 3. A convenient precis of the change in defense strategy can be found in Allen R. Millett and Peter Maslowski, *For the Common Defense: A Military History of the United States of America* (New York: The Free Press, 1984), ch. 16. On the general evolution of U.S. Cold War strategy, see John L. Gaddis, *Strategies of Containment: A Critical Appraisal of Postwar American National Security Policy* (New York: Oxford University Press, 1982).

[3] For a summary of this system, see Eckhardt, *Command and Control*, pp. 3–5; and *JCS Publication 2: United Action Armed Forces*. "Operational control" was defined as those command functions involving the composition of subordinate forces, the assignment of tasks, the designation of objectives, and "the authoritative direction necessary to accomplish the mission." "Administrative control" denoted authority in respect to such matters as personnel management, supply, internal organization, and unit training. *JCS Publication 1: Dictionary of United States Military Terms for Joint Usage*, 1 Feb 62, pp. 3, 160.

[4] For Felt's and PACOM's role in the Laos crises and in early counterinsurgency planning for Southeast Asia, see Marolda and Fitzgerald, *Assistance to Combat*, pp. 6–7, 59–76, 88–95. See also Futrell, *Advisory Years*, p. 94.

[5] Edwin B. Hooper, Dean C. Allard, and Oscar P. Fitzgerald, *The Setting of the Stage to 1959*, The United States Navy and the Vietnam Conflict, (Washington, D.C.: Naval History Division, 1976), 1: 274, 355; hereafter cited as Hooper et al., *Setting of the Stage*. Ronald H. Cole, Walter S. Poole, James F. Schnabel, Robert J. Watson, and Willard J. Webb, *The History of the Unified Command Plan, 1946–1993* (Washington, D.C.: Joint History Office, Office of the Chairman of the Joint Chiefs of Staff, Feb 95), pp. 25–27. General Bruce Palmer, Jr., *The 25-Year War: America's Military Role in Vietnam* (Lexington: University Press of Kentucky, 1984), pp. 29–30.

[6] Marolda and Fitzgerald, *Assistance to Combat*, pp. 219–20, 252–53. Eckhardt, *Command and Control*, pp. 26–27, 30–31. Memo, Ch, Plans Div, G–3 USARPAC, for Ch, MH Div, G–3 USARPAC, sub: History of Development of SEA Contingency Command Structure for PACOM with Encl., Study, Lt Col Adrian St. John, 21 Nov 63, sub: Command Structure, Historians files, CMH. Memo, William P. Bundy for SecDef, 14 Nov 61, File I–19319/61; Note, Bundy for SecDef, 17 Nov 61, sub: Re the Vietnam Command Problem, File I–19334/61; JCSM 812–61, 22 Nov 61, sub: South Vietnam, File I–19358/61; memo, Bundy for SecDef, 25 Nov 61, sub: Command Arrangements for Vietnam, File I–19366/61; and memo, Bundy for U. Alexis Johnson et al., 28 Nov 61, sub: Command Arrangements for Vietnam, File I–19381/61. All in box 54, 64A2382, RG 330, NARA.

[7] MFR, Dep SecDef, sub: President's Meeting with JCS on January 3, 1962, File 25048/62, ISA 337, box 55, 65A3501, RG 330, NARA. Taylor Interv, sess. 4, p. 41. Harkins' career and relationship with Taylor are related in U.S. Army Military History Institute (USAMHI) Senior Officer Debriefing Program, Conversation between Gen Paul D. Harkins and Maj Jacob B. Couch, Jr., transcript, passim.; Taylor quote is on pp. 32–34 of this transcript. See also Interv, USAF Oral History Program with Gen Paul D. Harkins, 23 Feb 72, (AFCHO), pp. 21–23.

[8] For history of SEATO Field Force headquarters, see CINCPAC Command History, 1961, pt. 1, pp. 138–224; pt. 2, pp. 135, 141; and Interv, Marine Corps Historical Center (MCHC) with Lt Gen Richard G. Weede, USMC, 23 Jul 73, pp. 1–3, MCHC. Harkins' selec-

tion came under much retrospective criticism because of his lack of counterinsurgency background. See, for example, David Halberstam, *The Best and the Brightest* (New York: Random House, 1969), pp. 183–88 (a portrait etched in vitriol); and Hilsman, *To Move a Nation*, pp. 426–27, 580. Hilsman's view of Harkins in 1962 was more favorable; see MFR, Hilsman, 19 Mar 62, sub: Visit with Gen Paul Harkins and Amb Nolting . . . ; and Memo, Hilsman for Gen Taylor, 31 Mar 62, sub: (1) Report on Meeting with Gen Harkins. . . . Both in Box 3, VN 3/1/62–7/27/62, Folder 8, Roger Hilsman Papers, JFKL.

[9] Msg, JCS 4551 to CINCPAC, 15 May 62, National Security File (NSF) 134 Laos Cables 5/14/62, JFKL. For an overview of U.S. military actions, see Marolda and Fitzgerald, *Assistance to Combat*, pp. 76–83. Kennedy's orders on contingency planning are in NSAM 157, 29 May 62, sub: Presidential Meeting on Laos, May 24, 1962, in *U.S.–Vietnam Relations*, sec. 5.B.4, pp. 467–68.

[10] Marolda and Fitzgerald, *Assistance to Combat*, p. 79. Eckhardt, *Command and Control*, p. 30. Msg, SecState 2575 to AmEmb Bangkok, 12 May 62; NSF Laos Cables 5/12/62, JFKL. Msg, JCS 4528 to CINCPAC, 12 May 62, NSF134 Laos Cables 5/12/61, JFKL. Msg, CINCPAC to COMUSMACV et al., 15 May 62, File 204–58 (201–45) Org. Planning Files—Functions, Missions and Command Relationships (1963), box 1, 69A702, RG 334, NARA. Harkins' formal terms of reference as COMUSMACTHAI, not issued until early March 1963, were identical to those he worked under as COMUSMACV; see Ltr, Cmdr, US Military Assistance Command, to Distribution, 7 Mar 63, sub: Command Relationships in Thailand, loc. cit.

[11] The command argument is summarized in USARPAC, CINC's Booklet for 8 Oct SecDef Meeting, 5 Oct 62, item IV–A, Historians files, CMH. JCSM 444–62, sub: Command Arrangements—Southeast Asia; Memo, William P. Bundy for SecDef, 26 Jun 62, sub: JCS Proposal for Change in Command Arrangements in Thailand and Vietnam, 7 Jul 62. Both in File I–25670/62, ISA 323.3 SEA, box 59, 65A3501 RG 330, NARA. Eckhardt, *Command and Control*, pp. 33–35.

[12] Msgs, Taylor to JCS, 9 Oct 62; CINCPAC to COMUSMACTHAI, 14 Oct 62; CINCPAC to JCS, 19 Oct 62; JCS 7332 to CINCPAC, 9 Nov 62. All in Taylor Papers, National Defense University (NDU), Washington, D.C. Eckhardt, *Command and Control*, pp. 28–29, 34–35. JCSM 825–62, 30 Oct 62, sub: Command Arrangements—Southeast Asia, File I–21091/62, ISA 320.2 SEA, box 36, 65A3501, RG 330, NARA. An 85-man COMUSMACTHAI headquarters in Bangkok was authorized in August 1962; see Msg, Bangkok 192 to SecState, 3 Aug 62, NSF 104 Thai Vol. IV 8/1/62–8/15/62, JFKL. Harkins' responsibilities are summarized in USARPAC Notebook, Jun–Jul 63, tabs 4, 5, and 6, Historians files, CMH.

[13] Quote is from Ltr, Harkins to Cowles, 29 Aug 79, Historians files, CMH. Harkins Interv, 23 Feb 72, pp. 25, 77–78. For details of McNamara's intervention in Vietnam, see Hist Div, JCS, *JCS and Vietnam*, 1960–68, ch. 3, p. 12. For Honolulu conferences, see Rpt, McGarr, Ch, MAAG, Vietnam, for Period 2 September 1961 to 8 February 1962, 8 Feb 62, p. 3, Historians files, CMH. For typical list of attendees, see MFR, sub: Trip to Hawaii—Third Secretary of Defense Conference on Vietnam, 19 February 1962, HQ, CINCPAC, Historians files, CMH.

[14] Harkins Interv, 23 Feb 72, p. 78. Memo, Taylor for Joint Chiefs of Staff and Joint Commanders, 9 Oct 62, sub: Reduction in the Number of Visitors to South Vietnam and Thailand, Historians files, CMH.

[15] Ltrs, Harkins to SecDef via CINCPAC, sub: General Court-Martial Jurisdiction for COMUSMACV; CINCPAC to COMUSMACV, sub: General Court-Martial Jurisdiction for COMUSMACV, 26 Apr 62. Both in box 2, 72A6939, RG 334, NARA. Msg, CINCPAC to COMUSMACV, 12 Sep 62, Historians files, CMH. MFR, n.d., sub: Conversation with Maj Gen Edward J. Rowney. VN Hilsman Trip File, Box 3, Hilsman Papers, JFKL.

A Joint Command: Complications and Conflicts, 1962–1963

[16] Memos, Forrestal for the President, 28 Jan 63, sub: South Vietnam; Forrestal for the President, 1 Feb 63; Forrestal for the President, 4 Feb 63. All in NSF 197/VN Jan 63 and Feb–Mar 63, JFKL. Memo of Conference with the President, February 28, 1963—5:25 to 6:45 pm., NSF 345; Chester V. Clifton, Conf with the Pres: 1/63–11/63, JFKL. Taylor quote is from Interv, Senior Officer Debriefing Program with General Maxwell D. Taylor, 16 Feb 73, sess. 4, pp. 46–47, MHI. Copy in CMH. Report of Visit by JCS Team to South Vietnam, Jan 63, pp. 17–18, Historians files, CMH. Memo of Conversation, Taylor and W. Averell Harriman, 2 Apr 63, sub: Command Relationships, Pacific, Historians files, CMH. Harkins' retrospective view is in Harkins Interv, 23 Feb 72, p. 25.

[17] For planning for the MAAG's role, see USARPAC Command Study, 21 Nov 63. See also Eckhardt, *Command and Control*, pp. 30–31.

[18] Memo, Maj Gen Charles J. Timmes for CINCPAC via COMUSMACV, 9 Aug 62, sub: Reorganization Military Assistance Advisory Group, Vietnam, File 204–58 (201–45) Organization Planning Files (1963), box 1, 69A702, RG 334, NARA. Ltr, McGarr to Adm Harry D. Felt, 8 Aug 61; and Chart, 3 Aug 61, Organization MAAG–V, Aug 61, Historians files, CMH. On expansion, see *U.S.–Vietnam Relations*, sec. 4.B.3, pp. 29–32; Von Luttichau, "U.S. Army Role," ch. 6, pp. 24–25, 47–48; Eckhardt, *Command and Control*, pp. 23, 25. Msg, CINCPAC to ChMAAG Vietnam, 20 Jan 62, Historians files, CMH. Quote is from memo, Col H. F. Queenin for Dir of Ops, DCSOPS, 26 Feb 62, sub: Joint Staff Visit to CINCPAC, and MAAGs and JUSMAG Vietnam, Laos, and Thailand, box 82, 66A3138, RG 319, NARA.

[19] Ltr, Felt to Harkins, 27 Nov 62, box 1, 72A6939, RG 334, NARA. Memo, CINCPAC for COMUSMACV and ChMAAG, 7 Apr 62, sub: Terms of Reference for U.S. Military Assistance Advisory Group, Vietnam, File 204–58 (201–45) Org. Planning Files—Functions, Missions and Command Relationships (1963), box 1, 69A702, RG 334, NARA.

[20] JCSM 262–62, 6 Apr 62, sub: Grade of Chief, MAAG, Vietnam; Memo, Palmer for CJCS, 11 Apr 62, sub: Grade of Chief, MAAG, Vietnam, File I–16258/62, ISA 200 VN, box 51, 65A3501, RG 330, NARA. Memos, Timmes for CINCPAC via COMUSMACV, 9 Aug 62, sub: Reorganization Military Assistance Advisory Group Vietnam; Maj Gen Richard G. Weede for ChMAAGV, 25 Aug 62, same sub; Harkins for CINCPAC, 30 Aug 62, same sub; Msg, CINCPAC to JCS, 25 Apr 63. All in File 204–58 (201–45) Organization Planning Files (1963), box 1, 69A702; Memo, MACV J4 to Distribution, 19 Jan 63, sub: Projected Buildup of U.S. Forces in SVN, box 2, 69A702; RG 334, NARA.

[21] MACV Summary 62–63, p. 1. Smith Interv, 1 Feb 64, pp. 20–21, 30–31. Colonel Smith was administrative assistant to the first MACV chief of staff. Ltr, Harkins to ChMAAGV, 8 Sep 62, sub: Comprehensive Plan for SVN, File 204–58 (1418–03) MAP Files (1963), box 2, 69A702; Msg, PACAF to CINCPAC, 17 Apr 63 and 4 May 63, File 204–58 (201–45) Organization Planning Files (1963), box 1, 69A702; RG 334, NARA. Memo, CINCPAC for COMUSMACV and ChMAAGV, 27 Aug 63, sub: CINCPAC MAP Inspection of Military Assistance to the Republic of Vietnam; Report of PACOM MAAG Chiefs' Conference, 1963, 13 Jun 63, pp. 8, 14. Both in Historians files, CMH. Von Luttichau, "U.S. Army Role," ch. 7, pp. 10–11. Eckhardt, *Command and Control*, pp. 33, 38–39.

[22] Eckhardt, *Command and Control*, pp. 39–41. Report of Visit by JCS Team to South Vietnam, Jan 63, pp. 16–17, 25, 28, Historians files, CMH. Talking Paper, 30 Nov 63, sub: Additional Actions Which Could Be Taken to Facilitate Attainment of U.S. Objectives in SVN, in tab 1–E, Westmoreland Historical (Hist) File 2 (Jan 64–4 Feb 64), William C. Westmoreland Papers, CMH.

[23] Quote is from Smith Interv, 1 Feb 64, pp. 10–13. Harkins describes his meeting with Kennedy in Harkins Interv, 23 Feb 72, p. 17. McGarr's reception of Harkins is recounted in Ltr, Ernest J. Murray to Lt Gen Samuel T. Williams, 28 Jul 62, Williams Papers, Hoover Institution.

²⁴ MACV Summary 62–63, p. 5. Smith Interv, 1 Feb 64, p. 12. Von Luttichau, "U.S. Army Role," ch. 7, p. 8. Memo, MACV J4 for Distribution, 19 Jan 63, sub: Projected Buildup of U.S. Forces in SVN, box 2, 69A702, RG 334, NARA. Ltrs, Harkins to JCS via CINCPAC, 29 Aug 62, sub: Joint Table of Distribution . . . for Military Assistance Command, Vietnam; CINCPAC to JCS, 29 Oct 62, sub: Proposed 10 August 1962 JTD for USMAC Vietnam; Memo, CINCPAC for JCS, 15 Feb 63, sub: Proposed 1 July 1963 JTD for USMAC Vietnam. All in box 1, 72A6939, RG 334, NARA. Ltr, Murray to Williams, 28 Jul 62, Williams Papers, Hoover Institution.

²⁵ On duty tours, see MACV Summary 62–63, p. 6. Memo, Dir of Manpower, ODCSPER, sub: Personnel Support of MAAG Vietnam and MACV, Historians files, CMH. On facilities and housing see Memo, Weede for CINCPAC, 22 Aug 62, sub: Physical Security of U.S. Personnel, SVN, File 204–58 (510–02) Physical Security Instruction Files (1963), box 2, 69A702, RG 334, NARA. CINCPAC Command History, 1962, pp. 159–60. For an impression of Saigon at this time, see David Halberstam, *The Making of a Quagmire* (New York: Random House, 1964), pp. 125–35.

²⁶ This description is based on Joint Table of Distribution, U.S. Military Assistance Command, Vietnam, 1 Jul 63, Historians files, CMH. For advice to JGS, see MACV Summary 62–63, p. 1.

²⁷ Msgs, JCS 2964 to CINCPAC, 19 Jan 62; JCS 3110 to CINCPAC, 31 Jan 62; Harkins to Gen G. H. Decker, 15 Feb 62. All in File 204–58 (205–19) Table of Distribution Files (1963), box 1, 69A702, RG 334, NARA. Harkins Interv, 23 Feb 72, pp. 28–29. Weede Interv, 23 Jul 73, pp. 3–4. Futrell, *Advisory Years*, p. 94.

²⁸ Decker quote is from Msg, Decker WDC 1669 to Harkins, 14 Feb 62; Harkins quote is from Msg, Harkins to Decker, 15 Feb 62; see also Msg, Decker WDC 1004, to Harkins, 19 Feb 62. All in File 204–58 (205–19) Table of Distribution Files (1963), box 1, 69A702, RG 334, NARA.

²⁹ CINCPAC Command History, 1962, p. 154. Von Luttichau, "U.S. Army Role," ch. 7, pp. 5–8. USAF Project CHECO Southeast Asia Report, pt. 4, *Command Structure/ Relationships, Oct 61–Dec 63*, May 64, pp. 38–39, copy in CMH files. Futrell, *Advisory Years*, p. 97. Marolda and Fitzgerald, *Assistance to Combat*, p. 220.

³⁰ Futrell, *Advisory Years*, pp. 101–02. Robert F. Futrell, "The United States Air Force in Southeast Asia: The Advisory Years, 1950–1965" (Comment Edition. Washington, D.C.: AFCHO, 1971), p. 183; USAF, CHECO Rpt, *Command Structure*, pp. 21–23, 42–44. Harkins Interv, 23 Feb 72, pp. 26–28. For component commander's view, see Interv, Project CORONA HARVEST with Maj Gen Rollen Anthis, USAF, 17 Nov 69, AFCHO, pp. 41–43, 46, AFCHO.

³¹ First quote is from Weede Interv, 23 Jul 73, pp. 5–6; see also pp. 4–5. Second is from Smith Interv, 1 Feb 64, p. 1. On Osmanski and Pomeroy, see Msgs, Harkins to Decker, 15 Feb 62; Decker WDC 1004 to Harkins, 19 Feb 62. Both in File 204–58 (205–19) Table of Distribution Files (1963), box 1, 69A702, RG 334, NARA.

³² Quote is from Greene Interv, 6 Jun 65, pp. 24–25; see also pp. 1–2, 9–11, 22–27. Harkins comments on his frequent field trips in Interv, 23 Feb 72, p. 64. See also Interv, MACV Historian's Office with Maj Gen Richard G. Stilwell, 11 Jul 65, p. 2, Historian's files, CMH.

³³ Anthis Interv, 17 Nov 69, pp. 149–50.

³⁴ The ARPA was a division of the Office of the Deputy for Defense Research and Engineering (DDR&E). Headed by a civilian scientist or engineer who worked directly for the secretary of defense, the director's office was created by the 1958 DOD reorganization act to provide central management for all research and engineering in the department, with the aim of reducing interservice rivalry and duplication of effort. Under DDR&E, ARPA conducted basic and applied research using facilities and

A Joint Command: Complications and Conflicts, 1962–1963

resources of the military services, other government agencies, and private firms and institutions as appropriate. See C. W. Borklund, *The Department of Defense* (New York: Praeger, 1968), pp. 74–75, 83–84.

[35] CINCPAC Command History, 1961, p. 183; ibid., 1962, pp. 167–70; ibid.,1963, p. 223. Von Luttichau, "U.S. Army Role," ch. 6, pp. 64–65; ch. 10, pp. 34–36. Msg, CINCPAC to COMUSMACV, 25 Jul 62, File 204–58 (201–47) Activation and Deactivation Files (1963), box 1, 69A702, RG 334, NARA. Memos, SecArmy Cyrus R. Vance for Chief of Staff, 11 Aug 62, sub: Field Testing in Vietnam, and Decker for Vance, sub: Field Testing in Vietnam, 23 Aug 62. Both in File Ops 250/10 VN, box 1, 65A3314, RG 335, NARA.

[36] Memo, CINCPAC for COMUSMACV, CHMAAGV, and CHJUSMAG Thailand, 19 Feb 62, sub: Memo of Understanding for the Implementation of Project AGILE in PACOM Area, Historians files, CMH. Von Luttichau, "U.S. Army Role," ch. 10, pp. 36–38. Ltr, CINCPAC to COMUSMACV, 1 Sep 62, sub: Army Tests to be Conducted in South Vietnam, box 2, 72A6935, RG 334, NARA; Memo, ODCSOPS for Chief of Staff, 30 Nov 62, sub: Theater Clearance for ACTIV Personnel, box 1, 65A3314, RG 319; NARA. Msgs, CINCPAC to COMUSMACV, 12 Dec 62; CINCPAC to DA, 22 Dec 62; CINCPAC to DA, 7 Jan 63; Info Brief, Dir, Combat Developments, ODCSOPS, 11 Jan 63, sub: Rowney Group (ACTIV) TD and Test Processing Procedure Changes; Msg, CINCPAC to DA, 20 Jan 63. All in Historians files, CMH.

[37] Felt quote is from USAF, CHECO Rpt, *Command Structure*, p. 55. Second is from Info Brief, Special Warfare Office, OCRD, 9 Jan 63, sub: Research and Development Activities in Vietnam; see also Memo, Col E. H. Almquist for Lt Gen Theodore W. Parker, 15 Jan 63, sub: Coordination between DA and ARPA. Both in Historians files, CMH. USAF, CHECO Rpt, *Command Structure*, pp. 18–19. For number and types of test, see CINCPAC Command History, 1961, p. 183; ibid., 1963, pp. 226–27; ARPA hamlet defense proposal is in ibid., pp. 225–26. For another ARPA intrusion into tactics, see Draft MS, Futrell, "Advisory Years," pp. 230–31.

[38] CINCPAC Command History, 1962, pp. 168–69. Ltr, CINCPAC to COMUSMACV, sub: Terms of Reference, 12 Dec 62, Historians files, CMH. USAF, CHECO Rpt, *Command Structure*, p. 18. For arguments against putting the ARPA unit under MACV, see memo, Lt Col E. T. Sage for A. P. Tower, 9 Mar 62, sub: Proposal to Put CDTCV under COMUSMACV, and Defense Development Exchange Program Survey Team, Report of Visit to Far East (11 Feb–11 Apr 62), 13 Jun 62. Both in File I–18421/62, ISA333FE, box 40, 65A3501, RG 330, NARA.

[39] Harkins quote is from USAF, CHECO Rpt, *Command Structure*, pp. 55–56. Report of Visit by JCS Team to South Vietnam, Jan 63, pp. 26–28, Historians files, CMH.

[40] CINCPAC Command History, 1962, p. 170; ibid., 1963, pp. 223–24. Von Luttichau, "U.S. Army Role," ch. 10, p. 38. Msgs, JCS to CINCPAC, 7 Mar 63; COMUSMACV to CINCPAC, 13 Mar 63. Both in Historians files, CMH. Msg, JCS 9743 to CINCPAC, 3 May 63; Telecon, Rear Adm Henry L. Miller, J5 CINCPAC, et al., with Brig Gen Robert H. York et al., 27 May 63, sub: R and D Command Relationships; File 204–58 (201–45) Organization Planning Files—Functions, Missions, and Command Relationships 1963), box 1, 69A702, RG 334; Memo, Lt Gen Ben Harrell, 2 Jul 63, sub: A Single Organization for All CD and RDT&E Activities in RVN, File 201–45 VN ODCSOPS 63, box 4, 66A3140, 319, NARA.

[41] George Allen, Course Notes on Intelligence in Vietnam, Historians files, CMH. Memo, Capt J. B. Drachnik, USN, for Vice Chief of Naval Operations, 13 Mar 64, sub: Experiences as Chief of Navy Section, MAAG Vietnam, Dec 61–Jan 64, Box 575, COMNAVFORV Records, Navy Historical Center (NHC), Washington, D.C.

[42] Marolda and Fitzgerald, *Assistance to Combat*, pp. 252–55, 259–61. Memo, Cmdr,

MACV: The Years of Escalation, 1962–1967

US Naval Forces Philippines, for CINCPACFLT, USARPAC, and CINCPACAF, 9 May 63, sub: Proposed Agreement for Logistics Support of U.S. Forces in the Republic of Vietnam, File 204–58 (201–45) Org. Planning File—Functions, Missions and Command Relationships (1963), box 1, 69A702, RG 334, NARA.

[43] Eckhardt, *Command and Control*, p. 29. Marolda and Fitzgerald, *Assistance to Combat*, pp. 253–54.

[44] Msgs, CINCPAC to CINCUSARPAC, PACAF, CINCPACFLT, and COMUSMACV, 21 Mar 62; CINCPAC to CG USARYIS et al., 31 Mar 62; COMUSMACV to CINCPAC, 6 Apr 62; Ltr, CINCUSARPAC to CG USARYIS and CG USASGV, 20 Apr 62, sub: Letter of Instructions (LOI). All in File 204–58 (201–45) Org. Planning Files—Functions, Missions and Command Relationships (1963), box 1, 69A702, RG 334, NARA. USARPAC LOI, 16 Aug 63, sub: Current Roles and Missions of USASGV, Historians files, CMH. Eckhardt, *Command and Control*, pp. 26–27, 31–33, 36, 48–49. Futrell, *Advisory Years*, p. 98.

[45] Quote is from Futrell, *Advisory Years*, pp. 95–96. Draft MS, Futrell, "Advisory Years" p. 182. Interv, Project CORONA HARVEST with Maj Gen Rollen H. Anthis, 30 Aug 63, Transcript in AFCHO, describes early facilities of 2d ADVON. Anthis had been vice commander of Thirteenth Air Force before taking over 2d ADVON.

[46] Futrell, *Advisory Years*, pp. 98–101. Eckhardt, *Command and Control*, p. 35. Pacific Air Forces, History of the Thirteenth Air Force, 1 January – 31 December 1962, ch. 1, pp. 23–25, AFCHO. Quote is from Msg, CINCPAC to CINCUSARPAC, CINCPACAF, CINCPACFLT, and COMUSMACV, 21 Mar 62, File 204–58 (201–45) Org. Planning Files—Functions, Missions and Command Relationships (1963), box 1, 69A702, RG 334, NARA.

[47] Msgs Taylor to JCS, 9 Oct 62; JCS 7332 to CINCPAC, 9 Nov 62. Both in Taylor Papers, NDU.

[48] Quote is from Futrell, *Advisory Years*, p. 148. The airmobility issue came to a head in April 1962, when an Army board headed by Lt Gen Hamilton H. Howze, working under Secretary McNamara's direction, produced a proposal for an airmobile division with its own aviation for both combat and logistical support. An Air Force board, chaired by Lt Gen Gabriel P. Disosway, responded with a critique and alternative recommendations, in particular challenging both the capacity of Army aviation to sustain airmobile operations and the validity of the Army practice of apportioning aircraft among ground commands. Vietnam was to be the first testing ground for many Army airmobility concepts. For accounts of the development of the airmobility concept and controversy, see: Lt Gen John J. Tolson, *Airmobility, 1961–1971, Vietnam Studies* (Washington, D.C.: Department of the Army, 1973), ch. 1. See also Ray L. Bowers, *Tactical Airlift*, The United States Air Force in Southeast Asia (Washington, D.C.: Office of Air Force History, 1983), 108–09.

[49] As one example of duplication, the Army CV–2 Caribou and the Air Force C–123 Provider twin–engine transports both were designed to haul men and supplies in and out of underdeveloped airfields with short runways. Figures are from CHECO Rpt, *Command Structure*, pp. 9–10; see also pp. 6, 47–49, 51–52. For buildup and roles and missions rivalries, see Futrell, *Advisory Years*, pp. 148, 167, 171–72; Bowers, *Airlift*, pp. 91–92, 95–103, 109–11, 128–37; Tolson, *Airmobility*, pp. 11–13, 29–32, 40–44, 46–47; and Von Luttichau, "U.S. Army Role," ch. 8, pp. 10–12, 17–19; ch. 10, p. 13.

[50] Quote is from Memo, Rowney for CSA via AC/S FD, sub: ACTIV Progress as of 1 June 1963, Historians files, CMH. For an Air Force objection to Rowney's actions and attitudes, see Ltr, Gen Emmett O'Donnell, Jr., USAF, to Harkins, 8 Mar 63, Historians files, CMH. See also MFR, sub: Conversation with Maj Gen Edward L. Rowney, in VN Hilsman Trip File, Hilsman Papers, box 3, JFKL; and Info Brief by Dir, Combat Developments, ODCSOPS, 11 Jan 63, sub: Rowney Group (ACTIV) Testing . . . , Historians files, CMH. Rowney had been a member of the Howze Board.

[51] First quote is from Ltr, Anthis to Gen Jacob E. Smart, 25 Nov 63, in Futrell,

A Joint Command: Complications and Conflicts, 1962–1963

Advisory Years, p. 160. Second is from Interv, MACV Historian's Office with Maj Gen Milton B. Adams, USAF, pp. 10, 24–25, Historians files, CMH. Memo, Queenin for Dir Ops, DCSOPS, 26 Feb 62, sub: Joint Staff Visit to CINCPAC and MAAGs and JUSMAG Vietnam, Laos, and Thailand, box 82, 66A3138, RG 319, NARA, warns of Air Force and Marine intrigues against the Army in Southeast Asia.

[52] Futrell, *Advisory Years*, pp. 105–12. Bowers, *Airlift*, pp. 86, 103–08. USAF, CHECO Rpt, *Command Structure*, pp. 11–14. Von Luttichau, "U.S. Army Role," ch. 8, p. 58; ch. 10, pp. 18–21.

[53] For Harkins' interest in aviation as deputy USARPAC commander, see Ltrs, Harkins to Lt Gen Barksdale Hamlett, 8 Nov 61; and Hamlett to Harkins, 27 Nov 61, Historians files, CMH. For Harkins' air policies as COMUSMACV, see Von Luttichau, "U.S. Army Role," ch. 8, pp. 19–20; ch. 10, pp. 18–21. Futrell, *Advisory Years*, pp. 107, 110–11, 155–56, 167, 181–82. Bowers, *Airlift*, pp. 121–22, 150–53. USAF, CHECO Rpt, *Command Structure*, pp. 35–37, 44–45, 52–54, 58–64. Ltr, Weede to Sr Adviser, IV Corps Advisory Detachment, 13 May 63, sub: Request for Additional Aviation Support; memo, Weede for Cmdr, 2d Air Div, 16 Aug 63, sub: US Army Armed UH–1B Helicopter Incidents. Both in File 204–58 (201–45) Organization Planning Files (1963), box 1, 69A702, RG 334, NARA.

[54] Draft MS, Futrell, "Advisory Years," pp. 210–11; USAF, CHECO Rpt, *Command Structure*, pp. 4–5, 45. Anthis Interv, 17 Nov 69, pp. 46–49, 113–14, recalls the frustrations of MACV's Air Force component commander. Admiral Felt attempts to clarify his 6 Jun 62 instruction in Ltr, Felt to Harkins, 20 May 63, Historians files, CMH.

[55] Harkins quotes are from Ltr to O'Donnell, 22 Mar 63; see also Ltrs, Harkins to Felt, 20 Mar 63 and 21 Jun 63, Historians files, CMH. On 8 July directive, see USAF, CHECO Rpt, *Command Structure*, pp. 37–38; Draft MS, Futrell, "Advisory Years," pp. 316–17. Harkins discusses his own close air support coordination qualifications in Harkins Interv, 23 Feb 72, pp. 27, 29–30.

[56] Msg, Felt to Harkins, 11 Mar 63; Ltr, Felt to Harkins and O'Donnell, 20 May 63; Msgs, CINCPAC to CINCPACAF, 30 Mar 63, and Felt to Harkins, 21 Jul 63. USAF, CHECO Rpt, *Command Structure*, pp. 35, 46, 98–99, 102–05.

[57] First quote is from USAF, CHECO Rpt, *Command Structure*, p. 105; see also pp. 97–98. The JOEG–V conclusions are in Memo, CINCPAC for JCS, 26 Aug 63, sub: Evaluation of Test Results of the Employment of OV–1 (Mohawk) Aircraft in Support of Counterinsurgency Operations, Historians files, CMH.

3

From Hope to Frustration

The Military Assistance Command played a major part in the intensified American–South Vietnamese campaign against the Viet Cong that accompanied its founding in 1962. Responsible for training, equipping, supporting, and advising the South Vietnamese armed forces, MACV sought in every way to mesh its activities with the nonmilitary portion of the allied effort while participating in the development of an effective counterinsurgency strategy. Despite its best efforts, however, and those of General Harkins—who pressed President Diem to make the sort of changes in the nation's military effort that would lead to success against the Viet Cong—the performance of the South Vietnamese government and armed forces fell far short of what was needed for victory.

The Enemy

By the time of the Military Assistance Command's establishment, the Viet Cong insurgency was highly organized and had attained formidable military and political proportions.[1] The National Liberation Front *(NLF)* and its Communist directing inner core, the People's Revolutionary Party (PRP), the renamed southern branch of the ruling Lao Dong (Communist) Party of North Vietnam, conducted the insurgency in South Vietnam through a hierarchy of front and party committees. At the top was the *Central Office for South Vietnam (COSVN)*, its existence not yet confirmed by the allies in early 1962. That headquarters transmitted to the southern forces the policy directives of the Lao Dong Central Committee and Politburo in Hanoi, of which *COSVN*'s senior civilian and military officials were members. Under *COSVN*'s direction but exercising considerable local tactical initiative, regional, provincial, district, and village committees carried on the day-to-day work of political agitation and guerrilla warfare. They used NLF mass organizations for farmers, youth, women, students, and other groups to mobilize rural and urban Vietnamese for the struggle.

The Communists were committed in principle to the "people's war" strategy articulated in China by Mao Tse Tung and in Vietnam by Vo Nguyen Giap. However, in early 1962 they were still in the initial guerrilla warfare stage of the struggle's progression toward large-scale military campaigns and widespread popular uprisings. They were preoccupied with building their political and military strength in South Vietnam. While Viet Cong strategy directives continually stressed the equal importance of the political and military struggles, the military side by early 1962 was receiving increased emphasis. The Lao Dong politburo in Hanoi proclaimed in February the necessity of "consolidating and expanding the base areas and strengthening the people's forces in all respects . . . in order to advance to building a large, strong armed force which can, along with all the people, defeat the enemy troops and win ultimate victory." [2]

Thanks to effective village- and hamlet-level organization, skillful appeals to peasant aspirations and grievances, and selective use of assassination and terrorism, by early 1962 the insurgency had gained a worrisome, if difficult-to-measure, degree of control over much of South Vietnam's rural population, especially in the flat, wet, fertile, and thickly settled Mekong Delta south of Saigon. The U.S. Defense Intelligence Agency (DIA) estimated in February that the Viet Cong openly ruled about 10 percent of Vietnam's hamlets and exercised influence or partial control over another 60 percent, and that they had access to at least a quarter of the nation's men of military age. In the cities, however, the Viet Cong organization remained underdeveloped. Most of the growing urban opposition to Diem persistently eluded the National Liberation Front's control. In the countryside, Catholic, Cao Dai, and Hoa Hao villages resisted the NLF. The Montagnard tribes of the Central Highlands, long oppressed by the Vietnamese, held themselves aloof from both Saigon and the Viet Cong. The Viet Cong devoted much effort to enlarging their military establishment, which they had formally unified in February 1961 under the title *People's Liberation Armed Forces (PLAF)*. Those forces grew rapidly, from about 4,000 full-time fighters in early 1960 to over 20,000 two years later, organized into as many as 20 battalions, 80 separate companies, and perhaps 100 platoons of widely varying personnel strength. As of early 1962, a majority of the units and the bulk of the manpower were concentrated in the Mekong Delta and the area immediately surrounding Saigon; but the Communists were forming new units, and increasing their military activity, in the northern two-thirds of South Vietnam.

Following the military doctrine established during the French war, the Viet Cong forces consisted of three elements. The main forces—full-time soldiers well armed with light infantry weapons brought from the north or, more often, captured from the South Vietnamese Army—operated under the command of *COSVN* and its subordinate regional headquarters and were carefully conserved for major attacks Next down in the hierarchy came the provincial and district units, a mixture of guerrillas and organized companies and battalions. At the bottom, not part of the estimated 20,000 combat troops counted by the allies, were the part-time village and hamlet guerrillas and militiamen. Usually operating in platoons or smaller formations under the orders of district and village front committees, these forces, armed with primitive, frequently homemade, weapons, guarded leaders and cadres, enforced revolutionary authority among the people, and engaged in assassinations and small-scale raids and ambushes. They also furnished intelligence, logistic support, and partially trained recruits and replacements for the provincial and main forces.

All three categories of troops drew upon the countryside and the civilian economy for food, clothing, and medical supplies. Weapons and equipment came from captures, infiltration, and the insurgents' own small workshops. In early 1962 the Viet Cong were building up their base areas, sections of rough, remote country rarely penetrated by government forces; the areas contained headquarters, supply dumps, arms workshops, medical facilities, training areas, and semi-permanent camps. The most important of these were the U Minh Forest and the Plain of Reeds, both located in the western part of the Mekong Delta along the Cambodian border, and War Zones C and D in the heavily forested region north of Saigon. The enemy had also begun establishing similar bases in the Central Highlands and elsewhere in northern South Vietnam.

The revolutionary organizations, both political and military, owed their capacity for rapid expansion in good part to a steady flow of infiltrators from North Vietnam. As early as May 1959, the Hanoi government had created an organization, *Group 559*, to shuttle people and supplies through western Laos down the network of mountain paths that the allies had nicknamed the Ho Chi Minh Trail, a route safeguarded by Pathet Lao troops and by the de facto partition of Laos under the 1962 Geneva Agreement. While *Group 559* handled primarily personnel reinforcements, another organization, *Group 759*, also created in 1959, was establishing a coastal route for bulky cargo to be carried in small vessels. Its first ship would sail in September 1962.

The reinforcements who made the arduous trek down the Ho Chi Minh Trail during *Group 559*'s first three years of existence were mostly southerners by birth, selected from among the 100,000 or so Viet Minh soldiers and civilians who had moved north after the 1954 armistice and found places in North Vietnam's armed forces and civil service. Including a large proportion of full Lao Dong Party members, the infiltrators underwent intensive political and military training and indoctrination at special centers. Then they were organized into temporary detachments for the march down the trail to base areas in South Vietnam, from which they dispersed to assignments with the Viet Cong. According to later MACV estimates, they entered South Vietnam at a rate of 500–1,000 men a month during most of 1961 and early 1962. The infiltrators provided the expanding southern revolution with an indispensable hard core of skilled, ideologically reliable military com-

MACV: The Years of Escalation, 1962–1967

A Viet Cong patrol moves along a canal in sampans. (AP photo)

manders, technical specialists, and party and front committee members. At the highest ranks, they constituted the military command and staff of *COSVN*; and they may have furnished one-fourth or more of the lower-ranking *PLAF* officers. With such men as leavening, the National Liberation Front could readily expand into new areas, and it could organize and indoctrinate rapidly its large mass of politically unsophisticated southern recruits.

As MACV went into operation, the Military Assistance Advisory Group, the country team, CINCPAC, and U.S. national intelligence agencies all shared a common assessment of the situation, capabilities, and probable intentions of the enemy. They noted that throughout South Vietnam, combat of all sorts was increasing in intensity, as indicated by a doubling of government casualties in 1961 over 1960. Ominously, Communist losses, while larger, were increasing at a lower rate. The agencies agreed that the Viet Cong, while retaining and expanding their areas of control in the Mekong Delta and their war zones just north of Saigon, now were building up forces and intensifying both political and military activity in the northern coastal provinces and the Central Highlands; they expected the enemy to make those areas, especially the highlands, the theater of their eventual big-unit campaign of annihilation against the South Vietnamese Army.

Although American analysts credited the Viet Cong with the ability to launch multiple 1,000-man attacks simultaneously at widely separated places and took note of a temporary upsurge of such actions during the early fall of 1961, they doubted that the insurgents were yet ready to move from the guerrilla stage of the conflict to the stage of sustained major engagements. Instead, the Americans expected that the Viet Cong during 1962, while continuing to enlarge and improve their main forces, would concentrate on "intensive but relatively small-scale" warfare aimed at wearing down Saigon's local administration and territorial forces through ambushes and hit-and-run attacks on small units, outposts, and progovernment hamlets. This pattern of action, a MAAG briefer declared, "has the advantage to the Communists of hitting President Diem's government at its weakest points while avoiding damaging conflict between a limited VC offensive force and a much more numerous ARVN." The Americans believed that the South Vietnamese forces were doing little more than holding their own and that the key to eventual allied success lay in weaning the peasants away from the Viet Cong by political and social, as well as security, measures. Admiral Felt stated the matter bluntly: "VC cannot be defeated by purely military means. . . . Final success will come only when people can be alienated away from Viet Cong and given adequate protection/security."[3]

Developing an Allied Strategy

When the Military Assistance Command, Vietnam, went into operation, it inherited a strategic concept that had evolved during 1961 out of two sets of plans, one developed by the American country team and the Military Assistance Advisory Group and the other advanced by British advisers and favored by Diem. The American contribution took the form of two documents: the country team's Counterinsurgency Plan, issued in January 1961, and the MAAG's Geographically Phased National Level Operation Plan for Counterinsurgency, promulgated nine months later. Both plans emphasized the necessity of a coordinated military-political attack on both the enemy's armed forces and his administrative and political bases in the villages.

The more detailed of the two, the MAAG plan called for a three-phase offensive involving the military and all government ministries and coordinated by President Diem through a National Internal Security Council and subordinate regional, province, district, and village security committees. Under the plan, government forces were to concentrate on clearing and holding areas according to geographical priorities, beginning with six provinces around Saigon and a section of the Central Highlands. In each area, a preparatory phase of intelligence gathering, training, and preliminary operations was to be followed by a military phase, in which South Vietnamese Army regulars expelled the organized insurgent forces; territorials, police, and civilian agencies would then uproot the Viet Cong rural administration and substitute a progovernment one. Last would come a security phase, during which, in the plan's words, "the populace is reoriented, civilian political control established, social and economic programs initiated, law and order established, [and] intelligence net perfected." Meanwhile, government forces outside the priority areas were to attack enemy units, so as to wear down the Viet Cong forces and keep them off balance. The MAAG planners wanted to begin the entire campaign with such a spoiling attack, a large-scale sweep of the War Zone D base area north of Saigon, aimed both at protecting the capital and enhancing ARVN self-confidence.[4]

The author of the second source of early allied counterinsurgency strategy, Sir Robert G. K. Thompson of the British Advisory Mission, had come to South Vietnam with five other officials, all veterans of the Malayan "emergency," at President Diem's invitation to give the president the benefit of their country's experience in defeating a rural Communist rebellion. In agreement with the MAAG, Thompson urged the government to employ combined military and civil operations to clear the enemy's armed forces and political underground from selected areas, beginning where Diem's regime already was strong and gradually working outward into Viet Cong–controlled territory. Thompson's particular contribution was his proposal to consolidate government control by regrouping the peasants into what came to be called strategic hamlets, an expedient the British had used successfully in Malaya. Essentially, these hamlets would be the same communities in which the people already lived, but they would be surrounded with simple fortifications that the inhabitants, won to the government side by social and economic benefits and organized and armed for their own defense, would man themselves. In this way, the countryside could be closed progressively to Viet Cong political and military penetration, and the insurgency would wither and die for lack of peasant manpower, food, and intelligence. In late 1961 Thompson urged Diem to begin implementing this plan in the Mekong Delta, South Vietnam's most heavily populated and Viet Cong–infested region.[5]

The British adviser's plan, especially its strategic hamlet element, won rapid acceptance from President Diem and his brother and principal adviser, Ngo Dinh Nhu, who had been experimenting since 1959 (not very successfully) with similar programs for protecting and controlling the rural population. With an eye to suppressing Communist subversion, creating a new agrarian power base for his regime, and displaying independence from the Americans by adopting a British scheme, Diem declared early in February 1962 that the delta plan should be executed without delay. He created an Interministerial Committee for Strategic Hamlets overseen by Nhu to direct the plan's implementation.

Thompson's approach also won favor with General Taylor, who learned of it during his October 1961 visit to Saigon. It impressed President Kennedy and his counterinsurgency-minded advisers as well. In

Saigon, after initial objections to Thompson's independent dealings with Diem and to details of his proposal, the U.S. Mission worked out what amounted to a merger of the British and American plans that drew upon their fundamental similarity in principle. Secretary McNamara, for his part, rejected General McGarr's recommendation for an early offensive against War Zone D and instead approved a plan for a pilot project featuring strategic hamlets in Binh Duong Province northwest of Saigon. The South Vietnamese had already begun a major pacification campaign in that province, and General McGarr favored operations there because they would protect an important highway and sever communications between two Viet Cong base areas.[6]

As a result of these decisions, the Military Assistance Command, Vietnam, when activated in February, had the task of refining and implementing a strategy already decided upon. General Harkins participated in McNamara's Honolulu conferences of January and February, but he allowed the MAAG representative to brief the conferees on the Binh Duong plan, code named Operation SUNRISE. Harkins and other American officials had doubts about the suitability of Binh Duong as an initial strategic hamlet project, since the province lay between concentrations of Viet Cong strength and would require constant commitment of regular troops to prevent enemy main forces from overrunning and destroying the hamlets. Nevertheless, the MACV commander felt compelled to continue with the operation because his predecessor, General McGarr, had helped develop it and the South Vietnamese were committed to it.[7]

The Military Assistance Command and the rest of the country team spent much of 1962 struggling to impose order on the burgeoning strategic hamlet program. Operation SUNRISE, which began in late March with a sweep by elements of the ARVN 5th Division followed by construction of several strategic hamlets, got off to a slow start, with few Viet Cong killed or captured and many sullen peasants forcibly herded from their homes into the new settlements. Notwithstanding this unpromising beginning, Diem and Nhu, apparently hoping to preempt the Viet Cong organization throughout the countryside, pushed the province chiefs to form strategic hamlets wherever possible, using primarily their local resources and without regard to geographical priorities or coordination with military operations. The resulting nationwide burst of activity produced much progress on paper but few strategic hamlets really capable of the military and civil roles Thompson intended for them. While this hit-or-miss effort went on, the country team employed persuasion—and the selective provision of U.S. military and civilian aid money and supplies—to secure concentration of effort in accord with the priorities of the MAAG's geographically phased plan. Representatives from both MACV and the MAAG sat on the mission's Interagency Committee on Province Rehabilitation, the American counterpart to Nhu's Interministerial Committee; and General Harkins directed his military advisers throughout the South Vietnamese chain of command to promote orderly planning and development of hamlets.

American persuasion and pressure gradually achieved results. During July and August, Diem instituted division tactical area and province strategic hamlet committees to promote unified planning and action by ARVN commanders and province chiefs. He also issued a national strategic hamlet plan that called for concentration of military and civilian resources successively in four priority areas, beginning with eleven provinces around Saigon, then moving to the central coast and the border regions. Within this overall plan, the division and province authorities, working closely with American military and civilian advisers, prepared comprehensive province pacification plans integrating offensives against Viet Cong units with the expansion outward from secure areas of the strategic hamlet system. The U.S. Mission channeled Military Assistance Program and U.S. Operations Mission resources as well as a special piaster fund to those province projects highest on the national priority list and to well-planned and -executed lower priority efforts. By late 1962 the Vietnamese had completed, and the American province rehabilitation committee had approved for U.S. support, plans for 27 of South Vietnam's 40 provinces. At that point, operations were under way, on varying scales, in 16 provinces with approved plans.[8]

Besides working with the rest of the mission on the strategic hamlet program, the Military Assistance Command during 1962 and 1963 devoted much command and staff attention to three subjects: transfer of the CIA's Civilian Irregular Defense Group (CIDG) program to military control; preparation of a long-range plan for completing the South Vietnamese force buildup and concurrently reducing American forces and assistance; and development of a comprehensive South Vietnamese national counterinsurgency campaign plan.

During late 1961, the Central Intelligence Agency had begun employing U.S. Army Special Forces teams to organize and train Montagnard tribesmen in the Central Highlands and Catholic and other minorities in the Mekong Delta and elsewhere for defense of their own villages and also for offensive antiguerrilla operations and border surveillance. The operation was controlled, funded, and supplied by the agency separately from the Military Assistance Program and conducted on the Saigon government side by Diem's Presidential Survey Office, his personal clandestine-activity agency, which commanded the South Vietnamese Special Forces. After initial experiments showed promise, early in 1962 the CIA proposed to enlarge the U.S. Special Forces contingent to thirty-nine detachments and a group headquarters and to train, arm, and equip a projected 100,000 irregulars. Both the Military Assistance and Pacific Commands expressed interest in bringing this expanding, militarily significant program under their control. Such action would conform to a ruling President Kennedy made after the Bay of Pigs debacle that large-scale, overt paramilitary operations should be conducted by the Defense Department rather than the CIA. At the outset, under a May 1962 agreement with MACV, the CIA's Saigon station nevertheless retained both operational control and logistical support responsibility for the civilian irregulars, while the Military Assistance Command supervised their activities through a Special Warfare Branch of its operations staff section.[9]

Secretary McNamara, however, lost no time in bringing the CIDG program under the Defense Department. After obtaining agreement from CIA Director John A. McCone, McNamara announced at a July conference in Honolulu that the Defense Department, with the Army as its agent, would assume the task of training and supporting the Civilian Irregular Defense Groups. Following an outline plan, code-named Operation SWITCHBACK, and proposed by the Department of the Army, representatives of the Army staff, the Army Special Warfare Center, the CIA, and the interested Pacific commands, the group then worked out the complicated administrative and logistical details of the transfer. Execution of the program took until 1 July 1963 to complete, in part because congressional action was required to authorize Army use of covert CIA budget procedures and funds. At the end of the transition, the Military Assistance Command exercised operational control of the Special Forces teams through Headquarters, U.S. Army Special Forces (Provisional), Vietnam, a subordinate element of its Army component command. MACV now had under its purview all the major armed elements fighting the Viet Cong and, it was hoped, would be able to integrate their efforts into a concerted national campaign.[10]

In addition to ordering the transfer of the Civilian Irregular Defense Program to MACV, McNamara at the July 1962 conference also instructed the Military Assistance Command to prepare plans for working itself out of a job. The defense secretary was impressed by General Harkins' optimistic reports on the progress of the expanded assistance program. At the same time, he knew that the administration faced more urgent crises in Berlin and Cuba and that the American public's tolerance for this Asian combat involvement had its limits. Therefore, he was determined to restrict the scale and duration of American engagement in Vietnam. To that end, he asked his subordinates to stop "concentrating on short-term crash-type actions" and "look ahead to a carefully conceived long-range program for training and equipping RVNAF and phase out of major US combat, advisory and logistics support activities." He ordered development of a schedule for preparing South Vietnamese forces to replace the American helicopter, communications, and other units then operating in Vietnam and for withdrawing those units as rapidly as the Vietnamese could take over their tasks. This process was to run concurrently with an intensified American–South Vietnamese campaign against the Viet Cong and should take no more than three years to complete, an allowance of time that McNamara considered "conservative." At the end of it, the South Vietnamese on their own, assisted only by an advisory group, should be able to finish off the remnants of the insurgency.[11]

Elaborating on this guidance, the Joint Chiefs of Staff on 26 July directed Harkins to develop a Comprehensive Plan for South Vietnam designed to bring that country's armed forces, by the end of calendar year 1965, to "the strength necessary to exercise permanent and continued sovereignty over that part of Vietnam which lies below the demarcation line without the need for continued US special military assistance." Specifically, Felt told Harkins a month later, the Military Assistance Command's plan should cover such subjects as the recommended size and structure of the Republic of Vietnam Armed Forces by the end of 1965, including additional units, manpower, and equipment needed to replace the withdrawing Americans; a schedule for removing American forces; and a summary of Military Assistance Program costs by year.[12]

During the remainder of 1962, the Military Assistance Command worked out the complex details of the Comprehensive Plan. The final version, which Harkins issued on 19 January 1963 and which Felt promptly endorsed, was aimed at giving the South Vietnamese armed forces "the capability to defeat the current insurgency with US special military assistance; defeat any new insurgency threat which may arise after phase down and withdrawal of US special assistance; and provide an initial defense against overt invasion until outside forces can be introduced."

To achieve this objective, the Military Assistance Command's planners wanted to expand South Vietnamese forces to a peak strength of 458,500 men by mid-1964, including a regular establishment of almost 240,000, the bulk of them in a 9-division army. Thereafter, with the Viet Cong presumably going down in defeat, the RVNAF was to decline gradually to 368,400 men in mid-1968, primarily through demobilizing the territorials and Civilian Irregular Defense Groups. MACV envisioned that the regular force would level off at 224,400, that it would possess such sophisticated weapons as jet fighters, and that it would remain at that strength indefinitely to deter conventional North Vietnamese attacks. This force would cost the United States a total of $978 million in Military Assistance Program (MAP) funds during fiscal years 1963 through 1968 (mid-1963 through mid-1968), a substantial increase over previous MAP projections for those years, but one that MACV considered justified to obtain more rapid RVNAF expansion and, until 1965, to support an intensified counterinsurgency campaign. As the South Vietnamese buildup progressed, the Military Assistance Command and its service components were to reduce strength from 12,200 personnel in mid-1965 to 1,500 in mid-1968. MACV headquarters itself was to go out of existence by 1 July 1966, leaving the MAAG again in charge of the remaining advisory and training effort.[13]

The Joint Chiefs of Staff promptly accepted MACV's Comprehensive Plan, but Secretary McNamara rejected it. At his Honolulu conference in May 1963, McNamara declared the plan unsatisfactory in that it called for a post-1965 South Vietnamese force too large and too lavishly equipped for a small, poor nation to support. Its MAP spending levels for the entire period were at least $270 million too high, and its projected pace for the American withdrawal was too slow. Upon his return from Honolulu, the defense secretary put his own office, the Joint Chiefs, CINCPAC, and MACV to work on reducing the post-1965 projected size and MAP cost of the South Vietnamese forces and developing a more rapid American withdrawal schedule, to include removal of 1,000 troops before the end of 1963.[14]

Working within McNamara's guidelines, the Military Assistance Command, in late July, produced its own "Model M" version of the Comprehensive Plan. By such expedients as replacing the territorials with a civilian National Police Force funded by foreign aid and by reducing regular force manpower to 80 percent of authorized strength after the end of the insurgency, the command was able to project a postwar RVNAF of 120,000 at a MAP cost of $400 million during fiscal years 1965–1969. The force included an army of four divisions and four "mobile brigades" which General Harkins deemed sufficient for guarding the Demilitarized Zone and cleaning up the last Viet Cong units and base areas. McNamara accepted the model M plan. Then, after a late-September visit to Saigon and more optimistic progress reports from Harkins, he ordered further modification of the plan to reduce South Vietnamese forces more rapidly in the northern part of the country, where government operations seemed to be going well, and to reinforce them in the Mekong Delta, where the strategic hamlet program was in severe difficulty. Harkins submitted the "Accelerated Model Plan" on 8 November, barely a week after the overthrow of President Diem rendered invalid most of the assumptions upon which it was based.[15]

Concurrently with work on the Comprehensive Plan, the Pacific and Military Assistance Commands prepared plans for the first 1,000-man American withdrawal. McNamara and his staff initially demanded that the personnel involved be withdrawn from operating units that could be replaced by the improving South Vietnamese forces. They settled, however, for a withdrawal composed largely of those individuals most easily spared from throughout the assistance command. In the end, the required number of Americans, almost all from the Army and Air Force, left the country in four increments during the last two months of 1963. In the light of the collapse of the Diem regime, their departure seemed more like an empty public relations gesture than the start of a genuine American disengagement. General Weede, the MACV chief of staff, later called the withdrawal "a political gimmick" and declared that "the situation wasn't such that this was a wise move at that time."[16]

The Military Assistance Command's third major planning effort was the most ambitious: development in conjunction with the South Vietnamese of a comprehensive National Campaign Plan. During the fall of 1962, Harkins and his staff proposed plans to President Diem for strengthening the South Vietnamese military chain of command and for launching a "nationwide offensive campaign" that would unite the armed forces and "all . . . loyal citizens" in an "integrated campaign to destroy the VC and restore control of the country to the duly constituted government." In General Harkins' view, the Vietnamese needed such a plan to tie together all the various anti–Viet Cong efforts then getting under way. In addition, the plan would stimulate the Saigon government to make maximum use of the forces being trained and equipped by the United States. At the outset, Harkins grandiloquently labeled his proposal the Explosion Plan, implying an eruption of government offensive activity. Later he toned down his rhetoric, declaring that he had really meant a "hotter fire" rather than a "great detonation" and envisioned essentially a more systematic and intensive implementation of existing programs. Both he and Ambassador Nolting saw the national plan above all as a device for pushing the South Vietnamese into continuous, concerted offensive action.[17]

In the view of General Harkins and the rest of the U.S. Mission, rationalization of the South Vietnamese military chain of command was a prerequisite for the preparation and execution of a national counterinsurgency plan. Under American pressure, Diem in April 1961 had established a ground forces chain of command that ran in theory from the Joint General Staff, which functioned as the supreme command of both the armed forces and the army, through an Army Field Command to three regional corps headquarters, each of which controlled several divisions. Each division was responsible for a tactical zone that encompassed one or more provinces, the chiefs of which, themselves usually soldiers, were to be subordinate to the divisions for counterinsurgency operations.

In practice, concerned with keeping his armed men divided lest they ovethrow him, Diem subverted this structure as he had earlier ones. He ignored the Field Command because he considered its commander, the able and popular Maj. Gen. Duong Van Minh, politically unreliable and sent orders to the army directly through the Joint General Staff. Diem kept the Vietnamese Special Forces outside the army command structure. He left control of the Civil Guard and Self-Defense Corps, which conducted most day-to-day antiguerrilla operations, in the hands of the province chiefs who also commanded ARVN units operating within their boundaries; and he upheld the province chiefs in their frequent disregard of orders from the divisions. Further to disrupt the chain of command, Diem often issued orders directly from Saigon to province chiefs and regimental and battalion commanders in the field.[18]

Late in 1962, MACV and the mission persuaded Diem to endorse another American-drafted reform of the chain of command, designed to unify all government military components in support of a national campaign. The rearrangement, which Diem set in motion on 26 November, served one of his political purposes by placing the Joint General Staff in direct charge of the ARVN corps and abolishing General Minh's Field Command. Minh received the honorific post of special military adviser to the president, with few duties and no command of troops. At that time also, Diem established a new IV Corps to control forces in the Mekong Delta south of Saigon, thereby allowing III Corps to concentrate on the difficult areas immediately around and north of the capital, and adjusted the boundaries of the other corps areas for better control of operations in the Central Highlands. *(Map 2)* In an effort to unify direction of all armed elements, Diem created new commands for the army, navy, air force, Special Forces, and Civil Guard/Self-Defense Corps, each directly subordinate to the Joint General Staff. He also reaffirmed that province chiefs were to be subordinate for military operations to the division tactical zones, a clarification of authority that, Americans hoped, would end divided command at the level most crucial to the conduct of the counterinsurgency campaign. In connection with this reorganization, the Military Assistance Command in December helped the Joint General Staff set up a Joint Operations Center to monitor and direct nationwide military activity. This 130-man agency, located in the JGS compound, included a contingent of twenty-five MACV advisers, through whom General Harkins hoped to strengthen his influence upon South Vietnamese plans and operations.[19]

The Joint General Staff's General Offensive Campaign Plan, promulgated late in February 1963 and based on a concept developed by MACV and approved by Diem, bore more than a passing family resemblance to the MAAG's geographically phased plan. It called for South Vietnamese military and civil agencies to cooperate in a nationwide attack upon both the Viet Cong's organized armed forces and its village infrastructure, with the objective of restoring government control over the people and reestablishing popular allegiance to the government. The offensive was to have three phases, each made up of many small local actions and conducted according to geographical priorities. Besides continuing military operations and strategic hamlet programs already under way, the first included reorganization and training of the forces, collection of intelligence, and preparation of national, corps, division, and province plans. This phase was supposed to end with completion of two-thirds of the already-planned strategic hamlets, putting the greater part of the population under government control. During the second phase, the actual offensive, government forces throughout the country would attack enemy troops and base areas in a multitude of operations that would continue until the enemy had been "killed, pacified, or driven from the Republic of Vietnam." The third phase, which could run concurrently with the second in areas free of organized Viet Cong units, was to be one of consolidation, during which civilian agencies would follow up military success with good works aimed at cementing the loyalty of the people to the government.

MAP 2

From Hope to Frustration

The plan prescribed basic missions for the armed forces, to be executed as appropriate during the different stages of the offensive. In government-dominated regions, territorial troops, under the province and district chiefs, were to concentrate on protecting the people and eliminating the Viet Cong underground. In contested areas, regular units were to drive out organized enemy forces, paving the way for the formation of strategic hamlets, then gradually to transfer security responsibilities to the territorials and eventually to hamlet militias. In both contested and Viet Cong–controlled regions, the South Vietnamese Amy was to seek out and destroy insurgent armed elements, headquarters, supplies, and equipment so as to weaken the opposing armed forces and forestall enemy interference with pacification. For each corps, the plan established relative priorities between pursuing Viet Cong forces and clearing and holding territory, and it specified for each the most important provinces to be cleared and held. The Military Assistance Command and the Joint General Staff assumed that Phase I of the plan was already being implemented, in the form of the operations and province strategic-hamlet planning then going on. General Harkins initially spoke of a D-day for Phase II late in February 1963; but as that date approached, with implementing arrangements for the general offensive campaign still not completed, he ceased predicting when the climactic phase would start.[20]

By late 1963, the allies had seemingly assembled a comprehensive program for prosecuting the war and ultimately reducing American involvement in it. They had defined their military and political objectives and had committed themselves to general strategy and tactics for their attainment. At least on paper, they had reorganized South Vietnam's military command so as to ensure unified action by all the armed forces under the national campaign plan. The Military Assistance Command possessed firm goals for its own effort to develop the South Vietnamese forces, as well as a deadline for finishing the job. Ambassador Nolting and General Harkins appreciated that Vietnamese plans had to be taken at less than face value. Nevertheless, they believed that they had prevailed upon their ally to begin moving, however haltingly, in a direction that would lead toward victory. Unfortunately, even as the allies completed their planning, both the extent of the achievements already made and the prospects for further advancement became increasingly uncertain.

The Campaign Falls Apart

During 1962 and early 1963, the South Vietnamese armed forces showed the beneficial effects of expanded American advice and assistance. Regular and paramilitary strength grew by more than 100,000 men, including two new army divisions. Under the Military Assistance Command's supervision, U.S. advisers and an expanding cadre of trained Vietnamese specialists dramatically improved the government's collection and use of military intelligence. Other Americans installed and manned new radio, teletype, and telephone systems, giving South Vietnam for the first time a modern, reliable, nationwide military communications network. Additional weapons and armored personnel carriers enhanced ARVN mobility and firepower even as intensified training, the participation of American advisers at all echelons, and the availability of American helicopter and fixed-wing air support improved the army's tactical effectiveness. ARVN units launched airmobile assaults on hitherto untouched Viet Cong base areas and increased the frequency of both large- and small-unit offensive operations in all regions. Viet Cong casualties rose, the number of their battalion-size attacks declined, and captured documents spoke of territorial and manpower losses and unit demoralization.[21]

Yet these improvements, as the American senior adviser to IV Corps pointed out, had to be "measured against an armed force that was poorly organized, poorly trained, poorly equipped and poorly led." Major deficiencies persisted. Diem still selected and promoted commanders for political loyalty and reliability rather than military competence, and he continued to disregard the chain of command. To avoid contributing to the rise of a battlefield hero who might challenge his regime, Diem pressed his generals to minimize casualties. Under that influence, ARVN commanders often maneuvered to avoid contact with the enemy. When combat did occur, they relied excessively on artillery and air support and hesitated to use their infantry to close with and destroy the Viet Cong. Many regular army battalions remained idle on static defensive missions while the ill-trained and poorly equipped Civil Guard and Self-Defense Corps, frequently scattered in small, vulnerable outposts, tried to carry on the battle in the countryside and suffered the majority of government casualties.[22]

The engagement at Ap Bac in the Mekong Delta on 2 January 1963 epitomized the military inadequacies that persisted. On that occasion, elements of the 7th ARVN Division and provincial troops, acting on good intelligence in a well-planned operation, trapped a small Viet Cong main-force battalion and several lesser formations. Then, in a monumental display of command-level cowardice and incompetence, these forces allowed the enemy to slip away after a day of confused, desultory fighting during which the Viet Cong killed 63 government troops and 3 American advisers, wounded over 100 government soldiers, and shot down 5 American helicopters.[23]

As 1963 went on, the South Vietnamese had better fortune in other small engagements. Nevertheless, the great preponderance of their offensive operations produced no enemy contact; and when government troops did encounter the Viet Cong, they often faced stubborn, effective resistance by units better trained and armed than in the past. Ratios between government and Viet Cong casualties and weapons losses gradually shifted in favor of the insurgents. Viet Cong military strength inexorably increased in spite of ARVN claims of heavy enemy casualties. By mid-June, when the Joint General Staff proclaimed the start of Phase II of the National Campaign Plan, the Military Assistance Command estimated that the enemy's full-time fighting force had grown to 22,000–25,000 men.[24]

Like the military half of the effort, the strategic hamlet program also fell short of its objectives. The effort, under both its scatter-shot South Vietnamese version and its concentrated American-supported one, produced much activity and impressive results on paper. By April 1963, according to Ambassador Nolting, the South Vietnamese had established about 6,000 hamlets out of a planned 11,000, incorporating perhaps 60 percent of the rural population. The Viet Cong's *Central Office for South Vietnam*, in assessments captured much later by U.S. forces, acknowledged that the program was "shrewder, bolder, and more widespread" than previous government pacification efforts; had cost them people and territory; and constituted a major threat to their political and military control of rural South Vietnam.[25]

Nevertheless, the South Vietnamese government lacked the administrative talent to carry out the program effectively on the scale contemplated. Many province chiefs, under pressure from Diem and Nhu to show progress, did little more than build fences around hamlets, often using labor and materials extorted from the peasants. By American assessment, in fact, only a small proportion of the hamlets reported as organized met the military, political, and social criteria for completion. These deficiencies were less prevalent in the central coastal provinces of I and II Corps, where ARVN commanders and province chiefs, cooperating closely with American advisers, combined strategic hamlet construction in relatively secure areas with well-conceived military operations to clear and hold additional territory. In the Mekong Delta, however, the program floundered, due to greater population dispersal (which forced much unpopular relocation of farmers), obstructionism and maladministration by local commanders and province chiefs, and the military and political strength of the Viet Cong. By late 1963, the delta's strategic hamlets, strung out along major highways and waterways because organization was easier there, had become little more than vulnerable targets for the guerrilla and main-force enemy units that maneuvered freely through the rest of the countryside.[26]

In the view of an increasing number of Americans, the source of most of these failures lay in the governing methods of President Ngo Dinh Diem. Increasingly under the influence of his arrogant, abrasive brother, Ngo Dinh Nhu and disregarding American pressure and persuasion, Diem persisted in all his bad administrative and military practices, which he considered essential to his own and his regime's survival, and he stubbornly tried to confine power, position, and privilege in government and society to his family and to a favored and loyal

Catholic minority. In a February 1963 assessment, the United States intelligence community summed up the effect of Diem's method of rule on the counterinsurgency effort:

> Although there is no doubt that President Diem and his family are dedicated to Vietnamese independence, they are also deeply committed to maintaining themselves in power. In order to prevent the rise of serious contenders for political power, they have conducted the business of government in a fashion which has reduced its effectiveness. They have driven into the opposition or into exile many whose talents are sorely needed. Above all, they have been insensitive to popular interests, needs, and grievances, and have therefore failed to win the positive loyalty of the people. We believe it unlikely that US involvement can be substantially curtailed or that there will be a material and lasting reduction in the Communist threat so long as present political conditions persist.[27]

To his critics, Diem's confrontation with his country's Buddhists exemplified his inability to unify his nation. The Buddhists long had resented Diem's legal and political discrimination in favor of his own coreligionists, and a group of radical young monks sought dominant political influence for their own faith. Open conflict erupted in May 1963, after nine people were killed by military gunfire during a Buddhist protest demonstration in Hue. Buddhist demonstrations then spread to most major South Vietnamese cities, coordinated by the Buddhists' General Association. Skilled propagandists, the Buddhists early won the sympathetic attention of resident American journalists, who kept their cause before the eyes of the world, especially after monks and nuns began burning themselves to death in public places to protest alleged government religious persecution. Other anti-Diem elements gradually rallied around the Buddhists, whose demands escalated from religious issues toward drastic modification or overthrow of the regime.

From the beginning, Diem viewed the Buddhist movement as a political attack on his government. Under American pressure, he made some conciliatory gestures and, on paper at least, granted many Buddhist demands. However, Nhu at the same time kept up harsh police repression and strident anti-Buddhist propaganda. The confrontation dragged on into the summer, with more demonstrations, riots, and self-immolations, and with younger, politically ambitious monks, notably the skilled agitator Thich Tri Quang, assuming leadership of the movement. The regime responded with more repression. On 21 August, police and Special Forces units under Nhu's personal command made a violent assault on Buddhist pagodas in Saigon, Hue, and other major cities. This action, taken under a martial-law decree issued by Diem at the instigation of a group of senior generals, resulted only in more demonstrations, for the first time involving thousands of university and high school students, children of South Vietnam's urban upper and middle classes. High government officials, including the foreign minister, resigned in protest, and Diem's relations with the United States deteriorated further.[28]

A Buddhist self-immolation (©Bettman/CORBIS)

The American side of the allied effort also did not go altogether smoothly. In spite of counterinsurgency plans calling for unified civilian and military action and in spite of Ambassador Nolting's efforts at coordination, each American agency had its own interpretation of the common strategy and too often went its own way in implementing it. An Australian adviser in Vietnam declared that the Americans seemed to be trying to wage three campaigns at once—a MACV military one; a U.S. Operations Mission (USOM) civilian foreign-aid one; and a CIA paramilitary one. Notwithstanding General Harkins' harmonious relationship with Ambassador Nolting, and perhaps because of it, the military campaign overwhelmed the others. As the ambassador had warned it would, the Military Assistance Command, by sheer size and wealth of resources and by virtue of the fact that it controlled more pieces of the pacification program than any other agency, dominated the advisory and support effort and often the counsels of the country team—in the civilian view often to the detriment of the effort to win the people's allegiance for the government.[29]

For example, over State Department objections, and over the dissent of some Army advisers, Nolting and Harkins persistently endorsed FARM GATE and Vietnamese Air Force bombing and napalm strikes in populated areas, both in aid of ground operations and in "interdiction" raids on targets identified only by questionable South Vietnamese intelligence. The ambassador and the MACV commander, although strictly controlling air operations in order to minimize civilian casualties, insisted that the military advantages of these tactics outweighed the political and propaganda use the Viet Cong might make of the inevitable bombing errors. Similarly, the military view prevailed, within the mission and in Washington, on experimental use of commercial weed killers to clear fields of fire and destroy Viet Cong food supplies, again overriding civilian concern that the tactic would alienate peasants whose crops were damaged and allow the Communists to charge the United States with employing chemical warfare. Military-civilian cooperation in the field continued in spite of these high-level disagreements. However, as a State Department official put it, there persisted within the civilian agencies "a number of nagging doubts about the qualitative effect of the effort in which they were engaged"; and "a certain head of emotional pressure built up in the Embassy." In Washington, members of President Kennedy's staff began urging him to strengthen the civilian leadership of the Saigon mission.[30]

Throughout these months, General Harkins, in common with Ambassador Nolting, continued to express confidence in Diem and conviction that the war effort was moving forward. While fully aware of the regime's many deficiencies, Nolting and Harkins considered Diem the only leader who had any real chance of holding South Vietnam together and eventually defeating the Viet Cong. Both were committed to the Kennedy administration's policy of trying to reform Diem through friendly persuasion and patient encouragement. They were convinced that, by tactful, persistent effort, they were moving Diem, albeit slowly, toward the correct policies and that American advice and assistance gradually were improving his regime's execution of them. In July, as the Buddhist crisis intensified, Nolting insisted that "our best bet still lies in encouraging and prodding and helping [Diem] to accept and follow through on policies that look reasonably good."[31]

In dealing with President Diem and other high Vietnamese officials, General Harkins maintained a consistent tone of encouragement. He told Diem in February 1963 that "we have taken the military, psychological, economical and political initiative away from the enemy." Yet he also was cognizant, from advisers' reports and from his own frequent visits to the field, of the military inadequacies of the government forces. That awareness was reflected in his advice to the Vietnamese leaders.[32]

Repeatedly, often at the price of enduring the president's interminable chain-smoking monologues until he could break in for a word, Harkins urged Diem to release the South Vietnamese Army from static defense and deploy it into the countryside against the Viet Cong. He advocated the conduct of many company- and battalion-size operations, both day and night, rather than the usually futile multibattalion sweeps much favored by the Vietnamese. Harkins continually urged Diem to respect his own chain of command. He exhorted the president and his senior defense aides on such subjects as elimination of small, vulnerable outposts, improved officer and NCO training and promotion, more effective employment of Rangers and Special Forces in border surveillance, more rapid reinforcement and rehabilitation of strategic hamlets attacked by the Viet Cong, and removal of incompetent or insubordinate local commanders. The MACV commander used his control of Military Assistance Program funding to dissuade the Vietnamese from creating units such as additional artillery and anti-aircraft elements that were not needed for fighting guerrillas. Aware early in 1963 that the strategic hamlet program in the Mekong Delta was being mismanaged, Harkins tried to persuade Diem and his commanders to coordinate military offensives there more closely with hamlet construction and to consolidate areas already partially under government control before extending operations into additional territory. He also prevailed upon Diem, during the last weeks of his regime, to reinforce IV Corps with another division and to rearrange its boundary with III Corps for better control of operations around Saigon and in the delta.[33]

At the same time, in official reports and public statements, Harkins emphasized the positive, to the point where he rewrote or played down assessments from the field that contradicted the MACV line. Within six months of taking command in Saigon, he had committed himself to an optimistic estimate of the probable duration of American involvement in the struggle. From then on, he held stubbornly to the view that the war was being won, albeit more rapidly in some parts of South Vietnam than in others. Harkins' optimism had various sources. Impressed with the apparent success of his own command in its specific mission of improving the equipment, training, and operations of the South Vietnamese armed forces, he rationalized away contrary reports as reflecting only localized failures rather than the big picture, and he largely discounted civilian reservations about the political and social effects of military activity. An optimist by temperament (he later admitted, "I always think of the bright side of things"), he also felt compelled by policy to maintain publicly that the campaign was going well. Harkins, according to his executive assistant, "always used to say, if I am not optimistic, and I don't go around saying that we can win, we are going ahead, and it comes out in the press, a stat[e]ment of Gen Harkins saying that we are losing . . . and the [South Vietnamese] can't fight, it would have a disastrous effect."[34]

As setbacks multiplied, Harkins attempted to put the best possible face on them. After the ARVN failure at Ap Bac, Harkins was on the ground early, heard a full briefing on the action from indignant American advisers, and reported to Admiral Felt that South Vietnamese commanders had let slip away a chance to destroy an enemy main-force unit. Publicly, however, he vehemently denied American news media claims that the South Vietnamese had been defeated and denounced those who questioned the fighting quality of Saigon's forces as "doing a disservice to thousands of gallant and courageous men who are fighting so well in defense of their country." When American reporters publicized the difficulties of the strategic hamlet program in the delta, Harkins in response admitted the setbacks but insisted that overall the situation was improving and that the government and the American mission were correcting the mistakes that had been made. In the face of official and media skepticism, he affirmed that the National Campaign Plan was proceeding on schedule into its second phase, although he acknowledged that the campaign would develop at a different rate in different areas, depending on the local balance of forces. Even after the pagoda raids, Harkins reported that the urban conflict between the regime and the Buddhists was not affecting counterinsurgency operations in the countryside. He told General Taylor late in August: "Our programs are completed. We have accomplished our part of everything we set out to do after your visit in the fall of '61—all except ending the war, and that is not far off if things continue at present pace." American programs, he continued, "at least the military," were "paying off. . . . All that is needed to end the conflict is the will and determination of the Vietnamese to win."[35]

In retrospect, Harkins' optimistic reports appeared to be at best the products of self-delusion and at worst deliberate efforts to deceive the U.S. government and the American public concerning the state of the war. At the time, however, the facts were not so clear-cut. In a war without fronts and decisive battles, success and failure were difficult to define and measure, especially when political and social intangibles played so large a part. The Military Assistance Command, like other American agencies, relied heavily on statistical indicators to measure progress—numbers of troops equipped and trained, strategic hamlets organized, sacks of fertilizer and rolls of barbed wire distributed, Viet Cong killed, weapons lost and captured, the size and frequency of Viet Cong attacks, and many others. Most of the statistics were of Vietnamese origin and doubtful reliability, since the officials who furnished them commonly adjusted the figures to please and placate their superiors. Then, too, the numbers' meanings were often ambiguous. For example, fewer Viet Cong attacks on strategic hamlets could indicate success in pacification, but they also could mean that the Viet Cong had subverted the hamlets so completely that they had no need to attack them. Harkins, Nolting, and their subordinates all realized that Vietnamese reports and statistics had to be discounted, but they differed over which information to discount and by how much. From this plethora of amorphous data, one could select evidence to document General Harkins' and Ambassador Nolting's belief in progress; one could build a case equally well for the other side, and an increasing number of Americans began to do so.[36]

Until mid-1963, most U.S. agencies in Saigon and Washington concurred, although with qualifications and reservations in some cases,

From Hope to Frustration

in their general assessment of the situation in South Vietnam. They agreed that the American buildup had produced improvements in South Vietnamese performance, especially in military operations. A consensus also existed that the government had stopped losing the war and, in the northern provinces, actually might be gaining ground against the Viet Cong. As the Buddhist crisis intensified, the consensus broke down, with the civilians taking the occasion to express their long-held doubts about the effectiveness of the American effort. Although with exceptions, representatives of the State Department, the CIA, the Operations Mission, and the U.S. Information Agency—both in South Vietnam and in the United States—began to take the view that whatever military and pacification progress had been made was being nullified by Diem's failure to conciliate his non-Communist opposition and in particular by his inability to reach terms with the Buddhists. Taking its cue from General Harkins, the Defense Department countered that the Buddhist upheaval was having little impact on civilian and military attitudes in the countryside, where the war was being fought; that the army still was carrying the fight to the Viet Cong; and that, except possibly in the Mekong Delta, the strategic hamlet program was continuing to move forward. President Kennedy, disturbed by these conflicting assessments, dispatched a succession of high-level fact-finding missions to Vietnam. Those missions returned with reports that reflected, rather than resolved, the dispute.[37]

Colonel Vann, center, with Brig. Gen. Robert H. York and Capt. William R. Johnson (NARA)

In Vietnam, the civilian and military sides were not monolithic. Among the civilians, Ambassador Nolting and CIA station chief John

MACV: The Years of Escalation, 1962–1967

Richardson shared General Harkins' optimism and sympathy for Diem, to the frustration of many of their subordinates. On the military side, advisers in the field, notably Lt. Col. John P. Vann, senior adviser to the 7th ARVN Division in the Ap Bac engagement, minced no words in detailing South Vietnamese deficiencies. Vann insisted that the government forces possessed the men and equipment to destroy the organized Viet Cong units throughout the country in six months to a year, but were being prevented from doing so by corrupt, incompetent leadership at the higher levels. His outspokenness, especially within earshot of reporters, displeased General Harkins, and Vann left Vietnam under a cloud. He resigned from the Army late in 1963 after the Joint Chiefs of Staff, at the last moment, canceled a briefing at which he was to air his views.[38]

Lacking the ear of their superiors, lower-ranking members of the American mission, whether civilian or military, found a ready audience for their complaints among the American newsmen in Saigon. Young, able, and ambitious, the resident reporters generally agreed with U.S. goals in Vietnam. However, they resented the mission's lack of candor about many aspects of the American role in the war, for example, the combat involvement of advisers and airmen, and they considered the embassy insufficiently vigorous in defending press freedom against the Diem regime, which treated foreign newsmen with unremitting hostility. The journalists sympathized with the Buddhists in their conflict with Diem. Increasingly, they sided with those Americans who believed the war was going badly and favored either drastic changes in the government or its overthrow. The correspondents cultivated outspoken field advisers like Colonel Vann, from whom they drew much of their view of military operations. For the reporters, Vann and others like him were the heroes of a morality play in which Harkins was the villain, the embodiment of self-delusion and dishonesty. The MACV staff, at State and Defense Department direction, devoted much time and effort to attempting to refute adverse media stories about the course and conduct of the war. General Harkins himself in retrospect bitterly denounced the Saigon reporters, claiming they were to blame for the fall of Diem. On the other side, David Halberstam of the *New York Times* allegedly drove past Harkins' quarters, shook his fist, and vowed, "I'll get you, Paul Harkins." Whatever the excesses on both sides, by late 1963 print and television journalists were becoming major actors in the Vietnam drama. In spite of the best efforts of Harkins and other defenders of U.S. friendship toward Diem, the newsmen's view of the situation—which reflected that of many official participants—was beginning to dominate both American public opinion and Kennedy administration policy-making.[39]

MACV and the Coup Against Diem

A military conspiracy against Diem brought the internal American policy conflict to a head. South Vietnam's officer corps had long resented Diem's favoritism in promotions and his meddling in operations, and a growing number of commanders also feared that the president was leading them to defeat at the hands of the Viet Cong. As early as November 1960, a military-civilian conspiracy backed by several battalions of paratroopers came near to overthrowing the regime. Again, in February 1962, under the eyes of newly arrived General Harkins, dissident Vietnamese Air Force pilots bombed the presidential palace in Saigon in an attempt to assassinate Diem and Nhu.[40]

The conspiracy that finally succeeded began taking shape in mid-1963 under the leadership of Maj. Gens. Duong Van Minh, Tran Van Don, and several other senior generals, all located at the Joint General Staff and other Saigon headquarters. These officers wanted Nhu out of the government at minimum and were willing to oust Diem as well if he remained adamant against reform of his regime. The inner group gradually added other commanders, including those of three of the four corps, to their conspiracy. Knowing that non-Communist South Vietnam could not survive prolonged internecine fighting, they delayed action until they were sure of the virtually unanimous support of the armed forces and enough civilian backing to make their action appear to represent the will of the nation. To strengthen their position, the conspirators persuaded Diem to issue his martial law decree of 20 August, only to have Nhu turn it to his advantage with the pagoda raids, for which the army initially took the blame. Minh and his group, in self-defense and because they needed American support in any event, then contacted the U.S. Mission, using a CIA officer and other intermediaries. They informed the Americans that the armed forces had not conducted the attack on the Buddhists and asked what the American reaction would be to a forcible change of government.[41]

The generals' feeler reached the U.S. Mission during a change of ambassadors. Nolting had requested relief for family reasons, and Kennedy had selected Henry Cabot Lodge to replace him. Kennedy appointed Lodge, a former senator who had run for vice president on the Republican ticket in 1960 and had served as chief U.S. representative at the United Nations, both to strengthen civilian leadership in the Saigon embassy and to give the administration's Vietnam policy an aura of bipartisanship.[42]

Arriving in Saigon immediately after the August pagoda raids, Lodge received the generals' overture and reported it to Washington with a request for instructions. His report precipitated a hasty administration policy decision followed by an increasingly bitter internal debate. As early as 1960, American officials, notably Nolting's predecessor, Elbridge Durbrow, had raised the possibility of U.S. action to

Maj. Gen. Duong Van "Big" Minh with Nguyen Ngoc (AP photo)

replace Diem if he persisted in his self-destructive policies. For lack of an obvious alternative, Kennedy had continued trying to work with Diem; but a growing faction among his advisers, centered in the State Department, became convinced that Diem's removal was essential to allied victory. The Buddhist crisis solidified this group's resolve and intensified its sense of urgency. Lodge's request for guidance gave the anti-Diem faction its occasion for action.

On 24 August, while Kennedy, Rusk, McNamara, and CIA Chief McCone all were out of Washington, a group of mid-level State Department and White House officials led by Assistant Secretary of State for Far Eastern Affairs Roger Hilsman and Under Secretary for Political Affairs W. Averell Harriman took action. Harriman and Hilsman drafted a cable to Lodge, secured the president's clearance for it with the aid of Michael Forrestal, a member of the White House staff, and dispatched it without concurrence of the Defense Department, the Joint Chiefs of Staff, or the CIA. Establishing what amounted to a new American policy toward Diem, the instructions declared that the United States no longer could tolerate Nhu's dominance of Diem's government. Diem, the cable declared, "must be given chance to rid himself of Nhu and his coterie and replace them with best military and political personalities available." If Diem failed to do so, "then we must face the possibility that Diem himself cannot be preserved." Lodge was to issue public statements absolving the armed forces from complicity in the pagoda raids and placing blame on Nhu, and he was to demand that Diem free the monks and nuns arrested in the raids. The ambassador was to inform the generals that American military and economic aid could continue only if the government ended its anti-Buddhist campaign, which would require removal of Nhu, and that the United States would furnish the armed forces "direct support in any interim period of breakdown [of] central government." Concurrently with these actions, "Ambassador and country team should urgently examine all possible alternative leadership and make detailed plans as to how we might bring about Diem's replacement if this should become necessary."[43]

This cable went out over a weekend. When President Kennedy and his senior officials returned to work on Monday, many were dismayed by the implications of the action taken in their absence. For the better part of the week, Kennedy and his senior national security advisers, with Ambassador Nolting also sitting in, argued over the merits of promoting Diem's overthrow. The State Department people, except for Nolting, who passionately took the opposing side, defended the policy set by the cable. McNamara, General Taylor (now chairman of the Joint Chiefs of Staff), and McCone expressed outrage that the policy change had been initiated behind their backs and pointed out that the government was proposing to support an alternative leadership, the composition and even the existence of which were at best highly uncertain. Nevertheless, when directly polled by Kennedy, none of the senior officials favored countermanding Lodge's instructions. The policy set in the 24 August cable remained in effect.[44]

The instructions affected the Military Assistance Command as well as the embassy. Harkins' command already had dissociated itself from Diem's anti-Buddhist activities. On 5 June, MACV had ordered its personnel to "stand aloof" from the controversy and avoid statements and actions supporting either side. American advisers were not to accompany Vietnamese units operating against demonstrators or rioters, and the command was to withhold equipment and American air transport from such units. After the 24 August cable, the command moved beyond neutrality. On 25 August, Admiral Felt, who had been in telephone communication with the drafters of the controversial cable and agreed with their views, directed General Harkins to assist Ambassador Lodge in carrying out the new policy. Harkins was to help Lodge especially in contacts with the generals, with whom Harkins was well acquainted and Lodge as yet was not.[45]

The ambassador and the MACV commander began implementing the new policy in general harmony of views. Both men favored American repudiation of the pagoda raids. They agreed that Nhu must leave the government and that the United States should assure the generals of support in the event they moved against the regime. They differed only on whether to deliver a final ultimatum to Diem before approaching the generals. Harkins favored such a demarche while Lodge argued that it would accomplish nothing and might demoralize the coup planners. Harkins contributed a generally accurate lineup of pro- and anti-regime commanders, on the basis of which he expressed doubt that the conspirators yet controlled enough troops in the Saigon area to give them a chance for quick victory. He added that, in the event of prolonged fighting between pro- and anti-Diem forces, his command could assist the rebels with military advice and could furnish unarmed American aircraft for troop transport, supply, reconnaissance, and liaison while withholding such aid from the loyalists. Initially, he and Lodge left contacts with the generals to the CIA so that the "American official hand should not show." However, as the days passed and the generals showed no signs of acting, under Lodge's instructions, Harkins on 31 August sought a direct conference with General Minh so as to add his voice to American reassurance of the plotters. Harkins learned from intermediaries that Minh's group was suspending activities because it still lacked the necessary preponderance of military force. He and Lodge then concurrently reported that no military move against Diem and Nhu was in immediate prospect.[46]

During the tense last week of August and over the following two months, the Military Assistance Command prepared for the possible consequences of governmental overthrow and civil strife. In conjunction with the embassy, the command reviewed long-standing plans for evacuating the approximately 4,500 American noncombatants from South Vietnam, modifying its procedures to allow for the contingency that a friendly regime might not be in control. To support the evacuation and to protect American forces and installations, the Pacific Command on 26 August dispatched an amphibious task group with an embarked Marine battalion, as well as a carrier task group, from the Philippines to cruise in the South China Sea within short steaming distance of Saigon. If needed, the marines could be flown by helicopter directly from their ships to Tan Son Nhut Air Base and be reinforced by two additional battalions airlifted from Okinawa, where they were on alert. These forces dispersed early in September but deployed again in late October when a coup once more seemed imminent. Also in October, as rumors spread in Saigon that pro-Diem mobs might attack the American embassy, MACV prepared plans for dispatching military police and a provisional infantry battalion formed from personnel of U.S. Army Support Group, Vietnam, to protect American facilities. It also arranged for helicopter evacuation of people from the embassy roof, a precaution that foreshadowed what was to happen twelve years later.[47]

In the wake of the seeming failure of the coup, a divided Kennedy administration struggled to develop an alternative policy. The debate over the wisdom of trying to oust Diem, which had begun after the 24 August telegram, continued with ever greater intensity in the pres-

Ambassador Lodge with President Diem
(©Bettman/CORBIS)

ident's councils in Washington, in the mission in Saigon, and in the American press, which enthusiastically broadcast the Kennedy administration's internal differences. The argument became entwined with the civilian-military dispute over how the war was going. Civilian pessimists generally favored a forceful anti-Diem policy while military optimists insisted that the political crisis had not yet damaged a winning war effort and that the United States should not scrap a functioning government, no matter how objectionable some of its policies might be.

After a major fact-finding mission to Vietnam in late September led by Secretary McNamara and General Taylor and including representatives of all the contending departments, the administration at last chose a course of action. In public statements, President Kennedy reaffirmed that the military campaign was making progress and announced plans gradually to reduce American forces in accord with the Comprehensive Plan. At the same time, Kennedy publicly deplored Diem's treatment of the Buddhists and declared that political reconciliation between the regime and its foes was essential to final victory over the Viet Cong. Privately, the president authorized Lodge to suspend most nonmilitary aid to the regime, as well as American support to the Vietnamese Special Forces, which Nhu had used in attacking the pagodas. In a separate action, early in October, the administration recalled Saigon CIA Station Chief John Richardson, a long-time friend of Nhu. Kennedy and his advisers made these moves with mixed motives. Some members of the administration hoped that the diplomatic and economic pressure would elicit concessions from Diem; others expected that this show of American firmness would revive South Vietnamese efforts to overthrow the government.[48]

In the event, the initiatives had the latter effect. On 2 October, General Don, chief of the Joint General Staff and a leading member of Minh's conspiracy, reestablished communication with the mission through a CIA officer who also had figured in the maneuvering that had accompanied the abortive August coup. In subsequent clandestine meetings, Don and Minh indicated that they now possessed enough military support to guarantee success but wanted assurances from the United States that it would not oppose them and that it would continue military and economic aid to a new regime. After hearing of the new feeler from the generals, the administration instructed Lodge to do nothing to thwart a revolt and promised that the United States would continue to aid a new regime that appeared capable of accelerating the military campaign, winning popular support, and improving working relations with its allies. By then a vigorous proponent of a change of government, Lodge kept in touch with the plotters through the CIA contact. Perturbed by Lodge's inability to learn details of the coup plan and fearing entanglement in another Bay of Pigs fiasco, Kennedy and his advisers reluctantly drifted along with events while urging Lodge to minimize overt American involvement and to dissuade the generals from moving if he thought they might fail. Their reluctance, however, did nothing to halt the unfolding of the final act of Diem's tragedy. Neither did conciliatory overtures to Lodge from Diem during the last days of October.[49]

As they had in August, Lodge and Harkins initially worked together to implement the administration's October policy of pressure on Diem. The Military Assistance Command pressed ahead with drafting an accelerated Comprehensive Plan for reduction of American forces, continued preparing for the first 1,000-man withdrawal, and arranged for South Vietnamese reinforcement of the Mekong Delta. As part of the administration's punitive reduction of economic and military assistance, Harkins in mid-October notified Diem that MACV, in coordination with the Central Intelligence Agency, was cutting off funds to the ten South Vietnamese Special Forces companies stationed in Saigon that had conducted the pagoda raids. The Americans would resume support of these units only when Diem placed them under command of the Joint General Staff, in accord with the 1962 RVNAF reorganization decrees, and committed them to the counterinsurgency operations for which they had been organized and trained. On 26 October, Harkins learned from General Don that the Joint General Staff was preparing to dispatch the Special Forces companies from Saigon to I and II Corps. Neither Harkins nor the Vietnamese Special Forces commander, a Diem loyalist, knew that this was a preliminary to an imminent military coup.[50]

The ambassador and the MACV commander also were in concert in their initial response to Don's renewed coup overtures. Lodge informed Harkins of Don's approach to the CIA officer, and the two men concurred in recommending that the United States refrain from thwarting the revived conspiracy and guarantee aid to a new regime—the policy soon embodied in administration instructions to Lodge. From that point, however, communication between the two men concerning the coup, and indeed their entire working relationship, began to break down.[51]

Lodge and Harkins, both natives of Massachusetts, had been acquainted for many years and in Saigon maintained outwardly cordial social and official relations. Nevertheless, as General Taylor later put it, "they just didn't click as a team." Kennedy had appointed Lodge in the hope that he would possess the reputation and force of personality to dominate the Vietnam country team. Lodge in fact did so. He also established good relations with the American reporters in Saigon, who welcomed his accessibility and candor. With these advantages, Lodge shifted the balance of power in the mission against General Harkins. Unlike Nolting, Lodge treated Harkins more as an adviser and subordinate than as a colleague, rarely consulting or informing the general on major policy matters outside the purely military sphere and often sending his own military assessments to Washington without first showing them to Harkins. The latter practice especially annoyed Harkins because Lodge, in contrast to his predecessor, agreed with the civilian pessimists in the mission that the war was going against South Vietnam and so reported to the State Department.[52]

Most important, Lodge and Harkins disagreed about the desirability of Diem's overthrow. Soon after his selection to replace Nolting, Lodge allied himself with the anti-Diem faction in the State Department and the White House. He maintained regular communication with them after his arrival in Saigon. The ambassador early concluded that Diem could not reform and strongly favored promoting any likely Vietnamese effort to oust him. Harkins agreed that Nhu should be removed from power and supported U.S. pressure on Diem, including aid reductions or cutoffs, to bring about that and other needed changes in the regime. However, to the end, he insisted that the United States should seek to save the president, whom Harkins regarded as a dedicated patriot, who "knew more about his country than anybody I knew and . . . was doing a lot of good." On the basis of his experience in dealing with the Vietnamese generals, Harkins doubted that they possessed the character and ability to head a successful government. He declared of General Minh, for example, that "he has contributed nothing to the war effort. In fact, he has done nothing but complain to me about the government and the way it is handled ever since I have been here." Summing up his position, on 30 October Harkins urged that the United States "not try to change horses too quickly," but instead "continue to take persuasive actions that will make the horses change their course and methods of action." "After all," he concluded, "rightly or wrongly we have backed Diem for eight long, hard years. To me it seems incongruous now to get him down, kick him around, and get rid of him."[53]

In support of his position, General Harkins and the Defense Department officials he briefed claimed persistently that the Buddhist protests and the declaration of martial law in August had done nothing to damage the morale of the South Vietnamese armed forces or to weaken their loyalty to the regime. This questionable assessment was the product of a lack of information, which the Military Assistance Command had brought upon itself. A year before the Buddhist crisis began, MACV had directed its advisers and other military personnel to avoid discussing U.S. and Vietnamese politics with their counterparts because the Vietnamese tended to confuse individual Americans' opinions with statements of official U.S. policy. Aware of these strictures and often under similar directives from their own commanders, Vietnamese officers in turn all but ceased communicating with their counterparts on political matters as the governmental crisis approached its climax. As a result, when American advisers received instructions to assess Vietnamese military attitudes toward the regime, they could furnish little solid information beyond noting that sentiment seemed to be running against the Nhus and in favor of some sort of change in government. At the highest levels of command, the conspiring generals and their civilian allies distrusted Harkins for his known friendliness to Diem. They either did not confide in him at all or dissembled. The Military Assistance Command's effort to remain outside Vietnamese politics thus had ensured only that when the command unavoidably did become involved, it would operate half blind and partially deaf.[54]

During the final phase of the generals' coup preparations, coordination between Ambassador Lodge and General Harkins all but collapsed, to the embarrassment of both men, the distress of the Vietnamese conspirators, and the annoyance of President Kennedy. Lodge excluded Harkins from his contacts with the plotters, conducted almost entirely through the CIA officer; and, under State Department instructions, the ambassador reported on them to Washington through Central Intelligence Agency channels. Uninformed about Lodge's relations with the generals, Harkins interpreted the "not thwart" principle of the administration's instructions more negatively than did the ambassador. At one point, he nearly scotched the plot. On 22 October he told General Don privately that this was no time for a coup because the war was going well. Concluding that the U.S. government had turned against a coup, a disconcerted Don sought reassurance from Lodge through the CIA contact. Harkins, for his part, claimed that until this point he had no idea the generals still were planning action against Diem. Reflecting continuing administration policy disagreements, the Joint Chiefs of Staff retrospectively endorsed Harkins' posture of noninvolvement with the coup. Indicative of Lodge's tenuous communications with Harkins, at the height of this mini-crisis the ambassador thought the general had left Saigon for Bangkok when in fact Harkins was on a field trip to the Mekong Delta.[55]

This incident led to temporary reestablishment of coordination between the ambassador and the MACV commander, but the improvement was short-lived. During the final days before the coup, in the interests of "maximum security," Lodge restricted all information on

From Hope to Frustration

contacts with the plotters to the minimum number of Americans, a group that did not include Harkins. Accordingly, on 30 October, Admiral Felt's precautionary deployment of amphibious and carrier task groups came as a surprise to the MACV commander, who had not realized the crisis was imminent. In response to a cue from General Taylor, who had become concerned over the lack of MACV content in Lodge's cables, Harkins forwarded a list of important messages from Washington that had not been passed to him when they were received and declared that Lodge had been submitting estimates of the military situation without consulting him. He professed ignorance of the most recent Don-CIA contacts and declared that he and Lodge were "certainly in touch with each other but whether the communications between us are effective is something else."[56]

President Kennedy was irritated at the lack of concerted action by the two principal officials of his Vietnam country team. On 29 and 30 October, he instructed Lodge to include Harkins as well as the CIA station chief in supervision of the American agent's contacts with the rebels. Since Lodge was scheduled to return to Washington for consultations at the end of October, Kennedy ruled that, in the ambassador's absence from Saigon, Deputy Chief of Mission William Trueheart was to head the country team and issue all instructions to the CIA operative, but only after consultation with Harkins and the CIA chief, "so that all three know what is said to [the operative]." If the three men could not agree on what to say, they should refer the matter to Washington for resolution "when time permits." Over Lodge's objections, the president specified further that, if the uprising occurred while the ambassador was away, General Harkins, the "most senior officer with experience of military decisions" on the scene, was to assume leadership of the mission. Whoever was in charge when the coup began, all U.S. agencies were to maintain strict neutrality, although the mission could offer good offices if the fighting was indecisive and asylum to the perpetrators if the coup failed. These restrictions notwithstanding, the president emphasized, once a revolt under "responsible leadership" began, "it is in the interest of the US Government that it should succeed."[57]

Lodge was still in Saigon on 1 November, when the generals finally acted. Hence, during the coup, the Military Assistance Command was largely a spectator. General Harkins spent the morning of the fatal day accompanying Admiral Felt, who was making a previously planned visit to Saigon, and Ambassador Lodge in a courtesy call on President Diem. Around midday, he saw the admiral off at Tan Son Nhut Air Base. General Don, who was with the Americans throughout the morning, seemed nervous; he declined Harkins' invitation to lunch, claiming he had to attend to other business. At 1345, Don telephoned the Military Assistance Command J3, Brig. Gen. Richard G. Stilwell. He asked Stilwell to inform General Harkins at once that the South Vietnamese generals were assembled at Joint General Staff headquarters, next door

103

to Tan Son Nhut, and were initiating a coup. By that time, the conspirators had arrested the senior officers still loyal to Diem. Meanwhile, troops of the marine and airborne brigades, the Quang Trung Training Center, and the 5th Infantry Division had seized largely unopposed key military and civil installations throughout Saigon and had closed in on Gia Long Palace, where Diem's 1,500-man Presidential Guard brigade offered the only serious resistance.

The Military Assistance Command broadcast over the Armed Forces Radio station orders to all American military personnel and civilians to stay off the streets and to avoid any action in support of either side. It also alerted American forces against possible Viet Cong efforts to exploit the situation, but none occurred. From then on, the command simply observed events, drawing much information from the Americans who remained on the job at the Joint Operations Center and reporting it to Pacific Command and the Joint Chiefs of Staff. By late afternoon on the first, MACV had determined that all division and corps commanders throughout the country had declared for the coup and that Diem and Nhu were isolated and under siege in Gia Long Palace. The command also reported that, in spite of the collapse of Diem's police and the presence of thousands of jubilant, riotous citizens in the streets, no Americans were in danger. However, a few MACV officers' families endured tense hours when their homes came under cross-fire or their children were away on school outings when the coup began.

The end of the Diem regime came early on the 2d, with the surrender of the palace garrison, the attempted flight and arrest of Diem and Nhu, and their murder by their military escort, most probably at the order of General Minh and the leading plotters. Besides the president of the republic and his brother, some 20 Vietnamese, including 4 civilians, died in the fighting in Saigon and 248 were wounded. The conspirators had achieved their purpose: a swift, relatively bloodless overthrow of the regime, carried out with overwhelming military force and popular support and with American acquiescence.[58]

During the week following the coup, the generals dissolved Diem's cabinet and National Assembly and suspended the 1956 constitution. On 4 November they formally established a provisional regime consisting of a Military Revolutionary Council of generals headed by Minh as chief of state and a mixed civilian-military cabinet with Diem's former vice president, Nguyen Ngoc Tho, as premier and General Don as minister of defense. The Revolutionary Council in fact held the real power, since it had charge of government finance and national security. The Kennedy administration recognized the new government on 8 November, notwithstanding the revulsion of the American president and public at the executions of Diem and Nhu. The Viet Cong reacted to the coup with a flurry of minor attacks, which accomplished little and soon abated. By the 8th, most of the troops brought into Saigon for the coup were returning to their regular stations and government forces throughout the country were resuming their normal pattern of operations. The military regime shook up the officer corps with a wave of promotions and command changes and began systematically purging Diem's province chiefs and other local officials. Americans, both civilian and military, enjoyed the applause of celebrating crowds in Saigon and other cities. General Harkins reported a "surge of cooperativeness" toward MACV personnel at Joint General Staff headquarters and in the field, with Vietnamese counterparts associating more freely with advisers and providing "increased spontaneity of information."[59]

General Harkins quickly established relations with the new military leaders. He planned to press the new regime for the same reforms he had urged on Diem: adherence to the chain of command; an end to the division of military authority between province chiefs and division commanders; improved troop training, especially of hamlet militia; and more efficient, aggressive employment of all elements of the armed forces. General Don called on Harkins the morning of the 5th, their first meeting since the coup, to bring him up to date on RVNAF command changes and reorganizations. Don promised that the new government would be ready soon for more vigorous prosecution of the war. Harkins, in reply, pointedly "reminded Don that the courage and determination showed by the coup's battalions in overcoming the Presidential Brigade of 1,500 men, if displayed in fighting a VC battalion of three to four hundred men, would make short order of the remaining VC" in South Vietnam.[60]

Yet even in the period of good feeling following the coup, the discord of the previous months persisted within the American mission. Ambassador Lodge exuded optimism about the prospects of the new government. Harkins, on the other hand, on 13 November in his first press interview after the coup, declared that "the Diem government had a good national campaign plan," that the war was "moving along," and that it would take the new government some time to establish the same degree of momentum. The American reporters in Saigon were quick to interpret the coup as a defeat for General Harkins. They claimed Harkins had disregarded timely warnings of the coup from his staff and that the ruling generals lacked confidence in the MACV commander, whom they considered "a left-over symbol of the former American policy of all-out support for the Diem family." These reports, which the administration suspected of originating within the Saigon mission, led Secretary Rusk to enjoin Lodge to take "corrective measures" to "stop this kind of talk with newsmen which only creates internal difficulties within U.S. Government and friction with GVN." The talk and the stories continued, however, as did the personal and policy conflicts underlying them.[61]

Following the war, General Harkins would harshly criticize the American officials who helped bring down Diem. "It was a shame," he declared in 1974, "to have Diem go when things were going so well.

... It wasn't worth the price, period." Whether the war had been going as well before Diem's overthrow as Harkins claimed was debatable, but his adverse judgment of the consequences of the coup of 1 November 1963 proved to be all too accurate. Initial American optimism notwithstanding, the elimination of Diem did nothing to remedy the fundamental political, social, and institutional deficiencies of South Vietnam. Instead, the fall of the government simply swept away most of what administrative machinery the nation had. At the same time, the Kennedy administration, by associating itself publicly with the anti-Diem forces, left the U.S. government deeply implicated in both the murders of Diem and Nhu and the failings of subsequent regimes. The Military Assistance Command and the rest of the country team at the end of 1963 had to pick up the pieces of the counterinsurgency struggle and start over again. They were to do so in the aftermath of the assassination of an American president, as well as a Vietnamese one, and in the context of important strategic decisions by both North Vietnam and the United States.[62]

Notes

[1] Unless otherwise noted, the rest of this section is based on *U.S.–Vietnam Relations*, sec. 4.A.5, tabs 2, 3, and 4; sec. 5.B.4, pp. 428–39, 487–521; Duiker, *Road to Power*, pp. 193–99, 204–14; War Experiences Recapitulation Committee of the High-Level Military Institute, Vietnam, *The Anti-U.S. Resistance War for National Salvation 1954–1975: Military Events* (hereafter cited as *Resistance War*) (Hanoi: People's Army Publishing House, 1980) trans. Joint Publications Research Service (JPRS), doc. 80968, 3 Jun 82. All citations are from the JPRS translation, pp. 30–32, 45–52; "A Party Account of the Revolutionary Movement in South Vietnam from 1954 to 1963, and a Summary of the Situation in the South from 1962 to mid–1963" (Document captured by allied forces in Operation Crimp, early 1966, copy in Historians files, CMH), pp. 8–9, 12–28.

[2] Quoted in *Resistance War*, pp. 48–49.

[3] Quotes from MFR, HQ MAAGV, sub: Briefing for Mr Bundy . . . , 1 Mar 62; and Msg, CINCPAC to JCS, 23 Feb 62. Threat is summarized in HQ USARPAC, USARPAC Intelligence Bulletin, Jan 62, p. 17; and USARYIS Intelligence Digest, 2–62, 29 Jan 62. All in Historians files, CMH.

[4] MAAG, Vietnam, Geographically Phased National Level Operation Plan for Counterinsurgency, 15 Sep 61, Historians files, CMH; quotes from pp. A–1, A–4. McGarr, Report of Chief, MAAG, Vietnam, for Period 2 September 1961 to 8 February 1962, 8 Feb 62, pp. 5–6, Historians files, CMH; *U.S.–Vietnam Relations*, sec. 4.A.5, tab 4, pp. 83–94; sec. 4.B.2, pp. 7–9. Von Luttichau, "U.S. Army Role," ch. 5, pp. 15–18. Rosson, "Involvement in Vietnam," pp. 119–20. Blaufarb, *Counterinsurgency Era*, pp. 101–03.

[5] Thompson's proposals are summarized in *U.S.–Vietnam Relations*, sec. 4.B.2, pp. i, 11–12; and Rosson, "Involvement in Vietnam," pp. 116–17. Blaufarb, *Counterinsurgency Era*, pp. 44–49, points out that the strategic hamlets were far from the most important ingredient in British success in Malaya; see also his evaluation of the Thompson plan, pp. 103–04. For a later succinct, idealized description of a strategic hamlet, see State Research Memo, George C. Denny, Jr., for Actg SecState, 1 Jul 63, sub: Strategic Hamlets, in box 23: SEA: VN 1963 General, 4/63–9/63, Thompson Papers, JFKL.

[6] For mission criticism of Thompson plan, see: Msgs, Nolting to SecState, 5 and 30 Nov 61; and Ltr, McGarr to McNamara, 27 Nov 61. All in Historians files, CMH. The process of U.S. assimilation of Thompson's ideas can be traced in *U.S.–Vietnam Relations*, sec. 4.B.2, pp. 1–19; Von Luttichau, "U.S. Army Role," ch. 6, pp. 20–22, 26–28; McGarr Rpt, Feb 62, pp. 3–5; MFR, HQ MAAGV, 1 Mar 62, sub: Briefing for Mr. Bundy . . ., Historians files, CMH; Blaufarb, *Counterinsurgency Era*, pp. 104–07; Hilsman, *To Move a Nation*, pp. 438–39; and Rosson, "Involvement in Vietnam," pp. 118–21, 135.

[7] MFR, Brig Gen William B. Rosson, 23 Feb 62, sub: Trip to Hawaii—Third Secretary of Defense Conference on Vietnam, 19 February 1962, HQ CINCPAC, Historians files, CMH; McGarr Rpt, Feb 62, pp. 6–7; Rosson, "Involvement in Vietnam," pp. 104–05. For doubts about Operation Sunrise, see MFR, Hilsman, 19 Mar 62, sub: Visit with General Paul Harkins and Ambassador Nolting, 17 March 1962, and Memo, Hilsman for Taylor, sub: (1) Report on Meeting with General Harkins . . . , (2) Doubts on Operation Sunrise, 31 Mar 62. Both in VN 3/1/62–7/27/62, Fldr 8, Box 3, Hilsman Papers, JFKL. For results of Operation Sunrise, see *U.S.–Vietnam Relations*, sec. 4.B.2, pp. 22–24.

[8] CM 117–62, sub: Viet Cong Attacks on Strategic Hamlets, 17 Nov 62, File I–21605/62, ISA 092 VN, box 51, 65A3501, RG 330, NARA. USMACV, Summary of Highlights, 8 Feb 62–7 Feb 63, pp. 97–98; Msgs, Nolting Saigon 84 to SecState, 20 Jul 62; COMUSMACV MAC J-3 2495 to AIG 924, 8 Sep 62. Record of Sixth SecDef Conference,

23 July 1962, HQ CINCPAC . . . , 26 Jul 62, p. 3–1. All in Historians files, CMH. *U.S.–Vietnam Relations*, sec. 4.B.2, pp. 20–21, 24; sec. 4.B.4, pp. 469–80, 503–04. Diem gives his rationale for a scattergun program in Ltr, Frederick W. Flott to Harkins, 2 Oct 63, with att. Memo of Conversation with Diem, 29 Sep 63, File 204–58, Policy and Precedent Files (1963), box 1, 69A702, RG 334, NARA.

[9] Supply for the Special Forces and CIDGs came through U.S. Army Support Group, Vietnam, and U.S. Army, Ryukyus. For origins of the CIDG program and its initial relationship to MACV, see Col Francis J. Kelly, *U.S. Army Special Forces, 1961–1971*, Vietnam Studies (Washington, D.C.: Department of the Army, 1973), pp. 19–28. For Kennedy decisions on paramilitary activities, see Hilsman, *To Move a Nation*, pp. 78–79; NSAM 57, Jun 61, quoted in Memo, S. A. Loftus, Jr., for Gen Wood, 7 Dec 62, sub: Operation SWITCHBACK, File I–26540/62, ISA 354.2 SWITCHBACK, box 55, 65A350, RG 330, NARA.

[10] SecDef Conf, 23 Jul 62, pp. 7–1, 7–2. Memo, Sec Army Cyrus R. Vance for SecDef, 19 Jul 62, sub: DOD/CIA Responsibilities in South Vietnam, File I–25751/62, ISA 092 VN, box 62, 65A3501, RG 330, NARA. Info Brief, Dir, Special Warfare, ODCSOPS, 10 Jan 63, sub: Special Forces Operations in South Vietnam, Historians files, CMH. Rosson, "Involvement in Vietnam," pp. 124–26, 150–55. Von Luttichau, "U.S. Army Role," ch. 7, pp. 41–49; ch. 10, p. 28.

[11] SecDef Conf, 23 Jul 62, sec. 1, pp. 1–2, and sec. 2, pp. 1, 4; quotes are from the latter section. *U.S.–Vietnam Relations*, sec. 4.B.4, pp. i–iii, 1–4. For comment on the origins of the plan and its relationship to McNamara's management style, see Rosson, "Involvement in Vietnam," pp. 139–44, 179.

[12] Quote is from USMACV Summary 62–63, p. 102. Msg, CINCPAC to COMUSMACV, 29 Aug 62, Historians files, CMH; *U.S.–Vietnam Relations*, sec. 4.B.4, pp. 3–5.

[13] Quote is from Memo, Harkins for CINCPAC, 19 Jan 63, sub: Comprehensive Plan for South Vietnam; Memo, Adams, USAF, for Distribution, 22 Jun 63, sub: Phaseout of U.S. Forces, File 204–58 (201–45) Organization Planning File (1963), box 1; Ltr, Harkins to ChMAAGV, 8 Sep 62, sub: Comprehensive Plan for SVN, File 204–58 (1418–03) MAP Files (1963), box 2, 69A702, RG 334, NARA. USMACV Summary 62–63, pp. 102–09; Memo, CINCPAC for JCS, 25 Jan 63, sub: Comprehensive Plan for South Vietnam. Both in Historians files, CMH. *U.S.–Vietnam Relations*, sec. 4.B.4, pp. 6–10.

[14] *U.S.–Vietnam Relations*, sec. 4.B.4, pp. 11–15; Rosson, "Involvement in Vietnam," pp. 144–50.

[15] Memo, CINCPAC for JCS, 18 Jul 63, sub: Transmittal of FY65–69 Alternate MA Plans for Republic of Vietnam, box 2, 71A226; Memo, Weede for ChMAAGV, 30 Sep 63, sub: Revision of MAP Model Plan, 1965–1969, File 204–58 (201–10) Joint Strategic Objectives Plans Files (1963), box 1, 69A702; Ltr, Harkins to CINCPAC, 8 Nov 63, sub: Transmittal of FY 65–69 Accelerated Model Plan (CPSVN) for RVN, File 204–58 (1418–03) MAP Files (1963), box 2, 69A702; all in RG 334, NARA. Memo, JCS JCSM–640–63 for SecDef, 27 Aug 63, sub: Comparison and Analysis of FY 1965–69 Alternate MAP Plans for the Republic of Vietnam, USARPAC Notebook, Jun–Jul 63, tab 33, Historians files, CMH.

[16] Quote is from Weede Interv, 23 Jul 73, p. 37. *U.S.–Vietnam Relations*, sec. 4.B.4, pp. 13, 15–16; Msg, COMUSMACV MACJ–1–8667 to ChMAAG and Cmdr, 2d Air Div, 7 Nov 63, File 204–58 (201–45) Organization Planning Files (1963), box 1, 69A702, RG 334, NARA; Von Luttichau, "U.S. Army Role," ch. 9, p. 38.

[17] Quotes are from Chairman, JCS memo (CM) 178–62, 4 Jan 63, sub: Honolulu Conference, with att.: Discussions on Vietnam at Pacific Command Headquarters, 17–18 December 1962, File I–20722/63, ISA 337 Hawaii, box 7, 67A4564, RG 330, NARA; and USMACV Summary 62–63, p. 94. Msg, CINCPAC to COMUSMACV, 19 Sep 62, Historians files,

From Hope to Frustration

CMH, indicates Admiral Felt's belief the Vietnamese needed a national plan. Rosson, "Involvement in Vietnam," p. 167; *U.S.–Vietnam Relations*, 4.B.4, pp. 5–6. Nolting gives his view in Msg Saigon 604 to SecState, 19 Dec 62. Harkins' view of the plan's purpose is in Memo for CINCPAC, 19 Jan 63, sub: Comprehensive Plan for South Vietnam; and MACV briefing, untitled. Both in Historians files, CMH.

[18] The South Vietnamese command problem is summarized in: *U.S.–Vietnam Relations*, sec 4.A.5, tab 4, p. 82, and sec. 4.B.2, pp. 3–4; Taylor, *Swords and Plowshares*, p. 234; Memo, Maj Gen Andrew J. Boyle for CofS, USARPAC, 24 Jan 63, sub: USARPAC Analysis of Counterinsurgency Operations in Vietnam, pt. 2, pp. 1–2; and Memo, Col Hugh F. Queenin, for Dir of Ops, ODCSOPS, 26 Feb 62, sub: Joint Staff Visit to CINCPAC, and MAAGs and JUSMAG Vietnam, Laos, and Thailand; both in Historians files, CMH.

[19] USMACV Summary 62–63, pp. 95–96, 114–15. Msgs, CINCUSARPAC to AIG 731, ACSI DA, et al., 29 Nov 62 and 14 Dec 62; PACAF to Distribution, 1 Dec 62; OUSARMY Saigon to DEPTAR, Washington, 10 Dec 62; Nolting Saigon 597 and 648 to SecState, 15 Dec 62 and 5 Jan 63. All in Historians files, CMH. National Campaign Plan–Briefing, box 1, 67A4604, RG 334, NARA.

[20] USMACV Summary 62–63, pp. 94–96. National Campaign Plan–Briefing; MACV Briefing, untitled, box 1, 67A4604, RG 334, NARA; ODCSOPS Fact Sheet for CSA, 9 Jan 63, sub: National Campaign Plan for South Vietnam, USARPAC Notebook, Jun–Jul 63, tab 34, Historians files, CMH. Harkins' unwillingness to specify a D-day is recounted in HQ, CINCPAC, Verbatim Transcript of JCS Team (Wheeler Group) Debrief of Trip to South Vietnam, 28 Jan 63, copy in Historians files, CMH.

[21] For a general summary of progress during 1962, see USMACV Summary 62–63, passim, and Ltr, Harkins to Diem, 15 May 63, File 204-58 (206-05) Command Reporting Files 2 (1963), box 1, 69A702, RG 334, NARA. See also (CM 178–62, 4 Jan 63, sub: Honolulu Conference, with att: Discussions on Vietnam at Pacific Command Headquarters, 17–18 December 1962, I–20722/63, ISA 337 Hawaii, box 7, 67A4564, RG 330, NARA. Von Luttichau, "U.S. Army Role," ch. 7, p. 17; ch. 8, pp. 38–41. For Viet Cong views, see "Party Account of the Revolutionary Movement," pp. 29–33 and Msg, Nolting Saigon 668 to SecState, 12 Jan 63, MACV J–2, Translation of VC Document on Ap Bac Battle 2 Jan 63 (hereafter cited as VC Ap Bac AAR). Both in Historians files, CMH.

[22] Quote is from CofS, MAAGV, info CSA, 21 Jan 63, encl. 5, *U.S.–Vietnam Relations*, sec. 4.B.3, p. 34; MFR, sub: Conversation with Maj Gen Edward J. Rowny, in VN Hilsman Trip File, Box 3, Hilsman Papers, JFKL; Memo, Col F. P. Serong, 14 Mar 63, sub: Strategic Review, File 1 (30 Mar 62–Nov 63), tab 29, CMH. Memo, CIA, 25 Feb 63, sub: NIE 53–63, Prospects in South Vietnam, Historians files, CMH. Memo, Lt Col John P. Vann for Ch, US Army Sec, MAAGV, 1 Apr 63, sub: Senior Adviser's Final Report; Interv, Charles V. P. von Luttichau with Lt Col John P. Vann, 22 Jul 63, pp. 1–18, 35, 39–40, 53; and Vann, JCS Briefing, 8 Jul 63, sub: Observations of the Senior Adviser to the Vietnamese Seventh Infantry Division, pp. 4–6. All in Historians files, CMH.

[23] Ltr, Sr Adviser, 7th Inf Div, to Ch, US Army Sec, MAAGV, 9 Jan 63, sub: After Action Report, Opn Duc Thang 1/TC; Msg, Sr Adviser, 7th Inf Div, to Sr Adviser, IV CTZ, 8 Jan 63; Memo, Sr Adviser, IV Corps for Ch, US Army Sec, MAAGV, 16 Jan 63, sub: After Action Report . . . ; VC Ap Bac AAR. All in Historians files, CMH. Vann Interv, 22 Jul 63, pp. 11–13, 44–51. For a detailed account of this battle, and the meanings that both sides attached to it, see David M. Toczek, *The Battle of Ap Bac, Vietnam: They Did Everything but Learn from It* (Westport, Conn.: Greenwood Press, 2001).

[24] *U.S.–Vietnam Relations*, sec. 4.B.5, pp. 38–39. Von Luttichau, "U.S. Army Role," ch. 9, pp. 13–14, 21–25. Msg, Nolting Saigon 174 to SecState, 4 Aug 63; National Cam-

paign Plan–Briefing. Both in Historians files, CMH. Msg, PACAF to Distribution, 4 Apr 63; DIA Intell Bull Supp, Republic of Vietnam,18 Jul 63; CIA Info Rpt, 1 Aug 63, sub: Assessment of the Progress of the War against the Viet Cong . . . during the First Half of 1963; All in Historians files, CMH. Enemy assessment: "A Party Account of the Revolutionary Movement," p. 36; *COSVN* Standing Committee Directive Discussing the Tasks for the Last Six Months of 1963, Sep 63 (Trans. of doc captured in Phuoc Long Prov, 29 Apr 69), pp. 1–4, copy in Historians files, CMH.

[25] Msg, Nolting Saigon 981 to SecState, 4 May 63; CofS, MAAGV, Info Paper, 21 Jan 62, encl. 5. Both in Historians files, CMH. MFR, Rufus C. Phillips, 30 Apr 63, sub: Financing and the Future of the Counterinsurgency Effort in Vietnam, Lansdale-Phillips Correspondence, Hoover Institution. For Communist view, see "Party Account of the Revolutionary Movement," pp. 33–35, 45–46; and *COSVN* Directive, Sep 63.

[26] For samples of the extensive documentation on the difficulties of the strategic hamlet program, see the following, all in Historians files, CMH: Memo, CIA, 25 Feb 63, sub: NIE 53–63, Prospects in South Vietnam; Msg, Nolting Saigon 981 to SecState, 4 May 63; CIA Info Rpt, 1 Aug 63; Msgs, Lodge Saigon 510 and 572 to SecState,14 Sep 63 and 21 Sep 63. Memo, Col F. P. Serong, 14 Mar 63, sub: Strategic Review, Westmoreland Hist File 1 (30 Mar 62–Nov 63), tab 29; and Memo, Phillips for Joseph L. Brent, 1 May 63, sub: An Evaluation of Progress in the Strategic Hamlet-Provincial Rehabilitation Program, in Lansdale-Phillips Correspondence, Hoover Institution. For an example of success in II Corps, see Progress Rpt, 25th Inf Div, Operation Trung Nghia . . . ,16 Jul 63, Historians files, CMH.

[27] Quote is from CIA Memo, 25 Feb 63, Historians files, CMH. Spector, *Early Years*, pp. 224–25, sketches Diem's character. *U.S.–Vietnam Relations*, sec. 4.A.5, tab 2, pp. 13–45, describes Diem's regime; see also sec. 4.B.1, pp. i–ii, sec. 4.B.2, p. 19, sec. 4.B.4, pp. 469–80, 487–21. Douglas Pike, *Viet Cong: The Organization and Techniques of the National Liberation Front of South Vietnam* (Cambridge: Massachusetts Institute of Technology Press, 1966), pp. 71–73, presents a chronology of Diem's alienation of Vietnamese society. Memo, Thomas L. Hughes for SecState, sub: The Problem of Nhu, 15 Sep 63, Historians files, CMH.

[28] *U.S.–Vietnam Relations*, sec. 4.B.5, pp. 4–17, outlines the course of the crisis. Ellen J. Hammer, *A Death in November: America in Vietnam* (New York: Dutton, 1987), pp. 83–84, 103–16, 138–43, 146, 154–55, 165–68, takes Diem's side of the story. William M. Hammond, *Public Affairs: The Military and the Media, 1962–1968*, United States Army in Vietnam (Washington, D.C.: U.S. Army Center of Military History, 1988), chs. 1 and 2, describes the important role of the American press. The August crisis is reflected in Msgs, Trueheart CRITIC to DA, Washington, DC, 20 Aug 63 and PACAF to Distribution, 22 Aug 63. Both in Historians files, CMH.

[29] Taylor, *Swords and Plowshares*, pp. 249–50, comments on the differing military and civilian buildup rates. On weak civilian–military operational coordination, see Blaufarb, *Counterinsurgency Era*, pp. 64–65, 116–19; Memo, William H. Sullivan, sub: Divergent Attitudes in U.S. Official Community, Historians files, CMH; Hilsman, *To Move a Nation*, p. 442; Memo, Hilsman and Forrestal for the President 25 Jan 63, sub: A Report on South Vietnam, NSF VN Hilsman File, LBJL; and Msg, CIA to White House Situation Room, 15 Jan 63, NSF 320, NSC Staff Memoranda, Mr. Forrestal 12/62–11/63, JFKL. Australian comment: Memo, Col F. P. Serong, 14 Mar 63, sub: Strategic Review, Westmoreland Hist File 1 (30 Mar 62–Nov 63), tab 29, CMH.

[30] Quote is from Memo, Sullivan, sub: Divergent Attitudes in U.S. Official Community, Historians files, CMH. State Department doubts about air strikes, napalm, and defoliants are summed up in Hilsman, *To Move a Nation*, pp. 442–44, 453–54, 578; and Futrell, "Advisory Years" (comment edition), pp. 198–200, 202–08; Msg, CINCPAC to JCS,

9 Mar 63, Hilsman, Box 3, VN: Hilsman Trip 12/62–1/63, Fldr 12, JFKL. Msg, State to AmEmb Saigon, 22 Mar 63; Msg, Nolting to Harriman and Hilsman, 25 Apr 63. Both in Historians files, CMH. For White House staff discontent with civilian leadership in Saigon, see Memo, Forrestal for the President,10 May 63, NSF 197/Apr–May 63, JFKL.

[31] Quote is from Msg, Nolting Saigon 117 to SecState, 20 Jul 63, NSF 198 VN 7/1–7/20/63, JFKL. Nolting outlines his approach to Diem in Msg to SecState, 7 Nov 61, Historians files, CMH. In same files, see Msg, Nolting Saigon 1036 to SecState, 17 May 63. Overviews of administration policy are in *U.S.–Vietnam Relations*, sec. 4.B.1, pp. 138–48, sec. 4.B.2, p. 35, sec. 4.B.5, pp. 7–8. Rosson, "Involvement in Vietnam," pp. 133–34. Hilsman, *To Move a Nation*, p. 453.

[32] Quote is from Ltr, Harkins to Diem, 23 Feb 63, file 204–58 (206–05), Command Reporting Files 1 (1963). An example of advisers' reports reaching Harkins is Memo, Lt Col Bryce F. Denno for Harkins, 25 Apr 63, sub: Morale in I Corps, file 204–58 (206–05) Command Reporting Files 2 (1963); both in box 1, 69A702, RG 334, NARA. For Harkins' retrospective views of the South Vietnamese, see Harkins Intervs, Apr 74, pp. 50–51, 58–59; and, 23 Feb 72, pp. 36–37; and Ltr, Harkins to Cowles, 29 Aug 79, Historians files, CMH. HQ,CINCPAC, Verbatim Transcript of JCS Team (Wheeler Group) Debrief of Trip to South Vietnam, 28 Jan 63, pp. 13–14, contains observations on Harkins' relationship to the South Vietnamese leaders. Copy in Historians files, CMH.

[33] An early example of Harkins' advice to Diem is in MFR, 31 Jul 62, sub: Conversation between COMUSMACV and President Diem . . . , 18 July 1962, OASD/ISA Files 092 Vietnam, box 51, 65A3501, RG 330, NARA. Other examples are in MACV Agenda Items for Conference with President Diem, 1–2 Aug 63, Historians files, CMH. See also correspondence files in boxes 1 and 2, 69A702, RG 334, NARA. For delta reorganization, in addition to material in the above, see Von Luttichau, "U.S. Army Role," ch. 9, pp. 11–12.

[34] Rosson, "Involvement in Vietnam," pp. 179–80; see also pp. 155–60. First quote is from Harkins Interv, Apr 74, pp. 60–61; see also pp. 50, 52–53. Second is from Greene Interv, 6 Jun 65, p. 17. Hilsman, *To Move a Nation*, p. 453, considers Harkins' optimism at least partially justified.

[35] For an overview of MACV optimism, see *U.S.–Vietnam Relations*, sec. 4.B.4, pp. 11–12; and sec. 4.B.5, p. 10. Ap Bac: Sr Adviser, Ap Bac AAR, ann. B, p. 9. Telecon, CINCPAC and MACV, 2 Jan 63, box 1, 69A702, RG 334, NARA. Msgs, Harkins to Gen Charles G. Dodge, 4 Jan 63 and Harkins MAC J74 0188 to Taylor, 10 Jan 63. Both in Historians files, CMH. First quote is from last msg. Delta: Msg, Trueheart Saigon 261 to SecState, 19 Aug 63, Historians files, CMH. National Campaign: Memo, Harkins for Trueheart, 6 Jul 63, sub: TF Saigon Monthly Wrap-Up Report for June 1963, File 204–58 (201–29) Special Warfare Planning File (1963), box 2, 69A702, RG 334, NARA. Final quote: Msg, Harkins to Taylor, 23 Aug 63, NSF 198 VN 8/21–23/63, JFKL

[36] The delusion-deception view is advocated in Halberstam, *Best and Brightest*, pp. 183–88. *U.S.–Vietnam Relations*, sec. 4.A.5, tab 4, p. 52; sec. 4.B.2, pp. i–ii, 20, 30–35; sec. 4.B.3, p. 35; sec. 4.C.1, pp. 10–12, analyzes the difficulty of assessing the course of the war. Memo, Sullivan, sub: Divergent Attitudes in U.S. Official Community, Historians files, CMH, outlines the different perspectives from which civilians and military usually approached the "facts." Msg, Nolting Saigon 376 to SecState, 3 Oct 62, Historians files, CMH, gives the ambassador's view on the reliability of Vietnamese statistics.

[37] *U.S.–Vietnam Relations*, sec. 4.B.4, pp. 17–18, 24; sec. 4.B.5, pp. 25–26; and sec. 5.B.4, pp. 554–73, 579–89, summarize the shifting assessments. CIA Memo, 25 Feb 63; CIA Info Rpt, 1 Aug 63; Historians Files, CMH. Memo, Forrestal for SecDef, sub: Vietnam, 20 Sep 63, with att.: USOM RA, Second Informal Appreciation of the Status of the Strategic Hamlet Program,1 Sep 63, box 18, 67A4564, RG 330, NARA. Msg, Lodge

Saigon 447 to SecState, 9 Sep 63, NSF 199 VN, vol. 15, 1–10 Sep 63, State Cables (B), JFKL. Memo to Sr Adviser I Corps, 30 Sep 63, sub: Special Evaluation Team Report, File 204–08 (206–05) Command Reporting File 2 (1963), box 1, 69A702, RG 334, NARA.

[38] For Vann's views, see Vann Final, Apr 63; Rpt, von Luttichau-Vann Interv, 22 Jul 63; and Vann Briefing, Jul 63 (the text of his abortive briefing to the JCS); see also Interv, *U.S. News and World Report* with Lt Col John P. Vann, 16 Sep 63, copy in Westmoreland Hist File 2 (Jan 64–4 Feb 64), tab B–2, CMH. Palmer, *The 25-Year War*, pp. 21–23; and Rosson, "Involvement in Vietnam," pp. 165–66, discuss Vann's conflict with Harkins and the abortive JCS briefing, generally in terms sympathetic to Vann. Rosson, pp. 123–24, 161–66, 177–78, and 180, notes other instances of field dissent from MACV assessments.

[39] Hammond, *Military and Media, 1962–1968*, chs. 1 and 2, details the deterioration of government-press relations; Halberstam quote is from p. 37. Taylor, *Swords and Plowshares*, pp. 257–58, 300, comments unfavorably on the U.S. press in Saigon. See also *U.S.–Vietnam Relations*, sec. 4.C.1, pp. 9–10. Halberstam's views are expressed in *Best and Brightest*, passim; see especially p. 183. A MACV staff officer criticizes the press in Adams Interv, pp. 13–14. On Harkins' views, see Greene Interv, 6 Jun 65, p. 17; Harkins Interv, Apr 74, pp. 53, 60–61; and Ltr, Harkins to Cowles, 29 Aug 79, Historians files, CMH.

[40] Harkins' description of the palace bombing is quoted in Memo, Taylor for the President, 8 Mar 62, Taylor Papers, NDU. See also Msg, COMUSMACV to CINCPAC, 27 Feb 62, Historians files, CMH. William J. Rust and the Editors of *U.S. News* Books, *Kennedy in Vietnam* (New York: Charles Scribner's Sons, 1985), ch. 1 describes the November 1960 coup attempt.

[41] *U.S.–Vietnam Relations*, sec. 4.B.5, pp. 6–7, 13–14, 52–55. Hammer, *Death in November*, pp. 124–26, 133. Rust, *Kennedy in Vietnam*, pp. 109–11. Tran Van Don, *Our Endless War: Inside Vietnam* (San Rafael, Calif.: Presidio Press, 1978), pp. 84–91, describes events from the viewpoint of a key conspirator. For initial contacts with the CIA, see Chronology, sub: Contacts with Vietnamese Generals, 23 August through 23 October 1963, 23 Oct 63, DSDOF/Hilsman (VN–Diem 63/2), LBJL. Msg, no sender or addressee, 24 Aug 63, NSF VN vol. 14, 24–31 Aug 63, M & Misc, box 198, JFKL.

[42] Rust, *Kennedy in Vietnam*, pp. 108–09; Hilsman, *To Move a Nation*, pp. 478–79, 514–15; Hammer, *Death in November*, pp. 169–71; and Memo of Conv, 4 July 63, Hilsman, Memos and Correspondence, Jul 63, box 6, Hilsman Papers, JFKL.

[43] Kennedy cleared the cable by telephone from his vacation home in Hyannisport, Massachusetts. The drafting of the cable is recounted in *U.S.–Vietnam Relations*, sec. 4.B.5, pp. 10–16; Rust, *Kennedy in Vietnam*, pp. 111–16; Hilsman, *To Move a Nation*, ch. 31; and Barlow, "JFK and JCS," pp. 139–43. See also Taylor, *Swords and Plowshares*, pp. 289–93. Text of the cable is quoted from Msg, State 243 to AmEmb Saigon, 24 Aug 63, in *U.S.–Vietnam Relations*, sec. 5.B.4, pp. 536–37; see ibid., sec. 4.A.5, tab 4, pp. 57–58, 64–65, for Durbrow's earlier warnings about Diem.

[44] *U.S.–Vietnam Relations*, sec. 4.B.5, pp. 19–21. Rust, *Kennedy in Vietnam*, pp. 119–21. Taylor, *Swords and Plowshares*, pp. 291–95.

[45] MACV and Buddhist controversy: Msg, COMUSMACV to CINCPAC, 6 Jun 63, Historians files, CMH. Von Luttichau, "U.S. Army Role," ch. 9, p. 8. Felt's orders to Harkins are quoted in Msg, JCS to SecState, 28 Aug 63, NSF/CO/VN/198, JFKL.

[46] Lodge's and Harkins' views and actions can be traced in the following, all in JFKL: Msgs, Lodge to Rusk and Hilsman, 25 Aug 63; Saigon to Washington, 26 Aug 63; CIA to Dept of State, 27 Aug 63; Harkins to Taylor, 27 Aug 63; in NSF VN 8/24–31/63, box 198. Msgs, Taylor JCS 3385–63 to Harkins, 29 Aug 63; Lodge Saigon 375 to SecState,

29 Aug 63; Harkins MAC 1566 to Taylor, 29 Aug 63; Harkins MAC 1583 to Taylor, 31 Aug 63; Lodge Saigon 391 to SecState, 31 Aug 63; NSF/CO/VN/198. Also Msg, Lodge Saigon 364 to SecState, 28 Aug 63, Historians files, CMH. Harkins Interv, Apr 74, pp. 62–64. *U.S.–Vietnam Relations*, sec. 4.B.5, pp. 16–21; and Rust, *Kennedy in Vietnam*, pp. 118–27, give a general narrative of events.

[47] Msg, Harkins to Taylor, 27 Aug 63, NSF 198 VN 8/24–31/63; Msg, CINCPAC to SecState, 26 Aug 63, NSF 198 VN 8/24–31/63; Msg, CINCPAC to SecState, 2 Sep 63, NSF 199 VN vol. 9/1–10/63 Def Cables; Msg, Lodge Saigon 692 to SecState,12 Oct 63, NSF 200 VN vol. 19 6–14 Oct 63, State Cables. All in JFKL. Msg, JCS 3301 to CINCPAC, 29 Oct 63, Historians files, CMH. Von Luttichau, "U.S. Army Role," ch. 9, pp. 9–11. For naval preparations, see Marolda and Fitzgerald, *Assistance to Combat*, pp. 269–72.

[48] *U.S.–Vietnam Relations*, sec. 4.B.4, pp. 18–24; sec. 4.B.5, pp. 21–40; sec. 5.B.4, pp. 54–73. Rust, *Kennedy in Vietnam*, pp. 140–41. Hammer, *Death in November*, pp. 158–59, 204, 230–32, 252–60, 268–70. Hilsman, *To Move a Nation*, pp. 496–99, 511–12, 515. Taylor, *Swords and Plowshares*, pp. 295–301. Examples of administration disagreements on facts and policy are in Ltrs, Paul M. Kattenburg to Lodge, 7 and 16 Sep 63; Memo of Conversation, Dept of State, 10 Sep 63, 10:30 AM, sub: Vietnam; Ltr, Hilsman to Lodge, 23 Sep 63; all in Hilsman Papers, box 4, JFKL. Memo, Forrestal for Bundy, 16 Sep 63, sub: South Vietnam; NSF 199 VN, vols. 15 1–10 Sep 63 and 16 11–17 Sep 63, JFKL.

[49] *U.S.–Vietnam Relations*, sec. 5.B.4, p. 574; see also sec. 4.B.5, pp. 45–49, and sec. 5.B.4, p. 590. Rust, *Kennedy in Vietnam*, pp. 146–52. Msg, CIA Saigon to White House, 3 Oct 63, NSF VN, Oct 63, box 204, tab C, JFKL. Msgs, McGeorge Bundy CAP 63590 to Lodge and Harkins via CIA Channel, 25 Oct 63; Lodge Saigon 1964 to McGeorge Bundy, 25 Oct 63. Both in Porter, *Vietnam Documentation*, 2:210–12. Hammer, *Death in November*, pp. 266–68, 278–79, 282–84, sympathetically describes Diem's last-minute efforts to resume discussions with Lodge.

[50] *U.S.–Vietnam Relations*, sec. 4.B.4, pp. 21–22; sec. 4.B.5, p. 38; sec. 5.B.4, pp. 554–73. Msg, CJCS JCS 279 to CINCPAC, 5 Oct 63; Msgs, State 570 to AmEmb Saigon,12 Oct 63; AmEmb Saigon 731 to State, 18 Oct 63; COMUSMACV MAC J-3 8399 to CINCPAC, 26 Oct 63; Harkins MAC 2006 to Taylor, 26 Oct 63. All in Historians files, CMH. Ltr, Harkins to Diem, 19 Oct 63, File 004–58 (201–45) Organization Planning File (1963), box 1, 69A702, RG 334, NARA. Msg, Harkins MAC 8250 to Taylor and Felt, 19 Oct 63, NSF 201 VN, vol. 20 15–26 Oct 63, Defense Cables, JFKL.

[51] Msg, Lodge CIA cable to SecState, 5 Oct 63, Porter, *Vietnam Documentation*, 2: 205–06.

[52] Quote is from Taylor Interv, sess. 5, pp. 2–3. Memo, Sullivan, [late Sep 63], sub: Divergent Attitudes in U.S. Official Community, Historians files, CMH. For other comments on Lodge-Harkins relations, see Harkins Interv, Apr 74, pp. 62–64; ibid., 23 Feb 72, p. 46. Ltr, Harkins to Cowles, 29 Aug 79, Historians files, CMH. Greene Interv, 6 Jun 65, p. 3. Taylor, *Swords and Plowshares*, pp. 299–300. For Lodge's military assessments, see: Msgs, Lodge Saigon 478 to SecState, 11 Sep 63, NSF 199 VN vol. 16 11–17 Sep 63, State Cables; Lodge Saigon 768 to SecState, 23 Oct 63, NSF 201 VN, vol. 20 15–28 Oct 63, State Cables; Harkins MAC 2033 to Taylor, 30 Oct 63, NSF 201 VN, vol. 21 State/Def Cables 29–31 Oct 63. All in JFKL.

[53] For general views of the Lodge-Harkins disagreement, see *U.S.–Vietnam Relations*, sec. 4.B.5, pp. 28, 47–48. Hammer, *Death in November*, pp. 170–71. Taylor, *Swords and Plowshares*, p. 294. For an example of Lodge's contacts with mid-level State Department officials, see Ltr, Paul. M. Kattenburg to Lodge, 16 Sep 63, RH/4/VN 11–20 Sep 63, vol. 3, JFKL. First Harkins quote is from Harkins Interv, Apr 1974, p. 52; see also p. 54. Second is in Msg, Harkins MAC 7585 to Felt and Taylor, 20 Sep 63, NSF VN, Box 200, VN

MACV: The Years of Escalation, 1962–1967

vol. 17 18–22 Sep 63, Defense Cables, JFKL. Third is from Msg, Harkins MAC 2028 to Taylor, 30 Oct 63, in Porter, *Vietnam Documentation*, 2:216–18.

[54] Ltr, Weede to ChMAAGV; Cmdr, 2d ADVON; Cmdr, USASGV; CO, HSAS; and CO, USMC Helicopter Unit, 27 Jun 62 sub: Discussions and Statements by US Personnel, File 204–58 (403–03) Public Info Instruction Files (1963), box 1, 69A702, RG 334, NARA. Dept of State, Memo of Conversation, 10 Sep 63 sub: Vietnam, 10:30 AM, Hilsman, box 4; Msg, State 445 to AmEmb Saigon, 20 Sep 63, NSF 200 VN vol. 17. Both in JFKL. Memo, Brig Gen Delk M. Oden for COMUSMACV, 9 Sep 63, sub: Evaluation of Attitudes of Selected Vietnamese Officials; Memo, Lt Col R. L. Powell for COMUSMACV, 9 Sep 63, sub: Evaluation of Attitudes. Both in File 204–58 (501–08) Intel Rpt File no. 2 (1963), box 1, 69A702, RG 334, NARA.

[55] *U.S.–Vietnam Relations*, sec. 4.B.5, pp. 44–45. Rust, *Kennedy in Vietnam*, pp. 152–53. Gen Don gives his version of this incident in *Endless War*, pp. 96–98. Msgs, Harkins MAC 1991 and 1993 to Taylor, 24 Oct 63; Taylor JCS 4137–63 to Harkins, 24 Oct 63. All in Historians files, CMH. Msgs, Lodge Saigon 1896 and 1906 to SecState, 23 Oct 63; and CIA Saigon to CIA, 25 Oct 63. All in NSF 204 VN TS Cables (A), tab C, Oct 63, JFKL.

[56] Quote is from Msg, Harkins MAC 2028 to Taylor, 30 Oct 63, in Porter, *Vietnam Documentation*, 2:216–18. Msg, Taylor JCS 4188–63 to Harkins, 29 Oct 63, Historians files, CMH. Msgs, Lodge Saigon 2003 to SecState, 28 Oct 63, NSF 204 VN, TS Cables (A), tab C, Oct 63; and Harkins MAC 2034 to Taylor, 30 Oct 63, NSF 201 VN vol. 21, State/Def Cables 29–31 Oct 63. Both in JFKL.

[57] Quotes are from Msg, Bundy CIA cable to Lodge, [31 Oct 63], in Porter, *Vietnam Documentation*, 2:218–19; in same source, 2:212–16, see Msg, Bundy CIA cable to Lodge, 30 Oct 63, with draft, 29 Oct 63; and Msg, Lodge CIA cable to SecState, 30 Oct 63. Memo of Conference with the President October 29, 1963, 4:20 PM, sub: Vietnam, NSF 317, Mtngs on VN, 29 Oct 63, JFKL. *U.S.–Vietnam Relations*, sec. 4.B.5, pp. 47–51; sec. 5.B.4, p. 604.

[58] Narrative of events is based on *U.S.–Vietnam Relations*, sec. 4.B.5, pp. 55–59; Rust, *Kennedy in Vietnam*, ch. 10; and Von Luttichau, "U.S. Army Role," ch. 11, pp. 5–6. MACV's first report of the coup is Msg, MACV CRITIC to DIRNSA, 1 Nov 63, box 64, 66A3106, RG 319, NARA. All other information on MACV's actions is drawn from the MACV Coup Notebook and from Coup d'Etat, November 1963–MACV File, in Historians files, CMH. Msg, Harkins MAC 8512 to Taylor, 1 Nov 63, NSFVN box 201, VN 1–2 Nov 63, Defense Cables, JFKL. Greene Interv, 6 Jun 65, pp. 32–33. Coup casualties: Msg, COMUSMACV MAC J3 8632 to JCS, 5 Nov 63, Historians files, CMH.

[59] Harkins quotes are from Msg, COMUSMACV MAC J3 8607 to JCS, 4 Nov 63; see also Msg, COMUSMACV MAC J3 8587 to JCS, 03 Nov 63. Both in NSF VN box 201 VN 3–5 Nov 63, Defense Cables, JFKL. On the post-coup military situation, see Msgs, COMUSMACV MAC J3 8632 and 8681 to JCS, 5 and 8 Nov 63; and Lodge Saigon 986 to SecState, 9 Nov 63. All in Historians files, CMH. A general description of new government is in *U.S.–Vietnam Relations*, sec. 4.B.5, pp. 59–62. Von Luttichau, "U.S. Army Role," ch. 11, pp. 8–9.

[60] Msg, Harkins MAC 8556 to Taylor and Felt, 2 Nov 63, NSF VN 201, Defense Cables, 1–2 Nov 63, JFKL. Quote is from Msg, Harkins MAC 8625 to Taylor, 5 Nov 63; see also Msg, Harkins MAC 2081 to Taylor, 3 Nov 63. Both in NSF 201 VN vol. 23, Defense Cables, 3–5 Nov 63, JFKL.

[61] Lodge optimism: Msg, Lodge Saigon 949 to SecState, 6 Nov 63, NSF VN 202, vol. 24, 6–15 Nov 63, State Cables, JFKL. Harkins interview is summarized in Msg, COMUSMACV MAC J74 8807 to OASD/PA, 14 Nov 63, MACV Coup Notebook, Historians files, CMH. Adverse reports: Msg, PIO MACV to PIO CINCPAC, 13 Nov 63; Msg,

COMUSMACV MAC J74 87764 to OASD/PA, CINCPAC, 12 Nov 63. Both in MACV Coup Notebook, Historians files, CMH. See also UPI Dispatch, 13 Nov 63, copy in Coup d'Etat, November 1963–MACV File, Historians files, CMH. Rusk quote is from Msg, State 784 to Lodge, 13 Nov 63, NSF 202 VN vol. 24, 6–15 Nov 63, State Cables, JFKL.

[62] Harkins quotation is from Interv, Apr 74, p. 58. Taylor, *Swords and Plowshares*, pp. 301–02, 407, retrospectively regrets the U.S. role. For typical historical assessments, see: *U.S.–Vietnam Relations*, sec. 4.B.5, p. 60; Rust, *Kennedy in Vietnam*, pp. 179–82; and Gelb and Betts, *Irony of Vietnam*, pp. 91–92.

4

Reorganizing and Reviving Pacification

During the year following the deaths of Presidents Kennedy and Diem, the Military Assistance Command's activities and responsibilities expanded steadily. The command itself underwent reorganization and reinforcement. No longer a temporary headquarters expected to work itself out of a job within two years, the Military Assistance Command, under a new commander and a new ambassador, settled in for the duration of what clearly was to be a prolonged and increasingly severe struggle. MACV, with partial success, sought to become the American mission's lead agency in attempts to revive the pacification campaign. Its commander assisted the ambassador in vain efforts to promote a stable, efficient, popular South Vietnamese government and shared in the general American frustration when continued instability stalled the war against the Viet Cong. By the end of 1964, MACV, like the rest of the mission and the administration in Washington, had begun to look outside South Vietnam for a solution to the conflict.

United States Policy: Picking Up the Pieces

After Diem's fall, the pessimists within the U.S. government rapidly gained the upper hand in assessing the situation in South Vietnam. As appointees of the Minh regime replaced those of Diem and took control of operational and pacification reporting, evidence of the mismanagement and failure of the strategic hamlet program, of the ineffectiveness of government military operations, and of Viet Cong gains in population control and armed strength became overwhelming. Most U.S. agencies had concluded by the end of 1963 that the Saigon government's position had been deteriorating for at least six months before Diem's fall and that prospects for early improvement were slim at best. Some officials foresaw outright allied defeat. After a late December visit to South Vietnam, Secretary McNamara declared, "Current trends, unless reversed in the next 2–3 months, will lead to neutralization at best and more likely to a Communist-controlled state."[1]

McNamara's projection, like many others that envisioned South Vietnam's imminent collapse, proved wrong. The adverse trends were not really reversed, but the southern republic neither fell to the Com-

MACV: The Years of Escalation, 1962–1967

General Khanh, center, with Secretary of Defense McNamara and General Taylor
(Time Life Pictures/Getty Images)

munists nor went neutralist. Nevertheless, the post-Diem military government proved ineffectual and short-lived. General Minh and his colleagues began encouragingly, with promises to revive the pacification program and to carry out military actions such as reinforcement of the delta that MACV had long advocated. The new regime's purge of Diem's appointees, however, temporarily paralyzed civil and military administration. Political unrest continued. Buddhists, Catholics, intellectuals, labor unions, the non-Communist political parties, and factions within the officer corps all jockeyed for position in the new order. Although patriotic and popular, Chief of State Minh proved an indecisive, indolent leader. Like Diem before them, he and his associates resisted direct American participation in provincial and district affairs. Partly from sheer inefficiency and partly, perhaps, from desire to seek an accommodation with non-Communist elements of the National Liberation Front, they delayed the resumption of aggressive military and pacification programs. Rumors spread that the Minh government actually was plotting to neutralize South Vietnam along lines recently proposed by French President Charles de Gaulle. For all these reasons, Minh's regime rapidly lost the confidence of the U.S. Mission.[2]

Whatever the regime's intentions may have been, it had not long to pursue them. In the early hours of 30 January 1964, Maj. Gen. Nguyen Khanh, commanding general of II Corps, seized power in a bloodless coup, which Khanh claimed was necessary to forestall a proneutralist

Reorganizing and Reviving Pacification

takeover by other officers. An adherent of the anti-Diem coup but an outspoken critic of the Minh government, Khanh had the support of Maj. Gen. Tran Thien Khiem, commander of III Corps, who furnished the troops for the venture, as well as other officers disaffected from the Minh group. Retaining Minh as figurehead chief of state, Khanh assumed the offices of premier and head of the Military Revolutionary Council that dominated the government.[3]

Khanh acted with at least the acquiescence of Ambassador Lodge and General Harkins. Warned in advance of the impending coup, at Lodge's decision, the two delayed notifying Washington until the very last moment and never warned Minh at all. The Americans regarded the ebullient 33-year-old Khanh as an effective military commander and a staunch anti-Communist but were uncertain of his relationship to the various South Vietnamese political factions. Claiming that Khanh's *putsch* took them by surprise, Lodge, Harkins, and their Washington superiors accepted the change of government as an accomplished fact. The administration of President Lyndon B. Johnson soon proclaimed its full support of Khanh and, in cooperation with him, sought to revive the struggle against the Viet Cong. In spite of a promising early demonstration of administrative vigor and political skill, however, Khanh soon became enmeshed in difficulties of his own with the many contending South Vietnamese factions, much to the detriment of the Saigon government, which remained essentially feeble and disorganized.[4]

Amid these unpromising circumstances, Johnson and the national security team he had inherited from Kennedy adopted essentially a two-track approach to Vietnam. The first track concentrated on reviving the pacification effort. The second, at the outset largely a matter of contingency planning, involved direct American and South Vietnamese attacks on North Vietnam aimed at compelling the Hanoi regime to cease its support of the Viet Cong.

President Johnson's first major Vietnam policy directive, NSAM 288, issued on 17 March 1964, included elements of both approaches. It reiterated the U.S. commitment to help South Vietnam defeat the Viet Cong and promised unequivocal support to General Khanh's regime. Endorsing Khanh's newly announced plan for national mobilization, the memorandum promised American subsidies for a 50,000-man expansion of Saigon's military establishment. It called for provision of additional equipment including more powerful aircraft, and for American help to the South Vietnamese in building a civil administration corps and in strengthening their paramilitary forces. Edging onto the second track, the United States and South Vietnam were to undertake small-scale reconnaissance operations in Laos against the Ho Chi Minh Trail and to begin making plans and preparations for both retaliatory actions and "graduated overt military pressures" against North Vietnam.[5]

MACV: The Years of Escalation, 1962–1967

Of especial importance to the Military Assistance Command, Vietnam, NSAM 288 effectively put an end to plans for an early withdrawal of American forces. On 27 March, Secretary McNamara instructed Admiral Felt and General Harkins to abandon the Model Plan with its extended projections of American troop reductions. Instead, they were to plan no farther ahead than the end of fiscal year 1966 and to work on the assumption that the United States would "furnish assistance and support of South Vietnam for as long as is required to bring communist aggression and terrorism under control." MACV had already begun revising its Model Plan to slow the withdrawal of American aviation and other units. In response to McNamara's order, the command early in April adopted new planning assumptions—that its own headquarters and all U.S. aviation and support units would remain at least through FY 1966 and that the American advisory effort would continue at its existing level through the end of the insurgency. The command added a second assumption that would prove incorrect: that the character of the insurgency and the scope of enemy activity would remain "essentially the same" through the next couple of years.[6]

Hanoi Prepares for a Larger War

Although the Americans and South Vietnamese did not know it at the time, 1963 was a period of change for the Vietnamese Communists. During the year, the Viet Cong destroyed or took over a growing number of the government's strategic hamlets, steadily increasing the proportion of the rural population under their effective control. At the same time, they continued building up their main forces, which reached a strength of 22,000–25,000 men by the end of the year. The Military Assistance Command during 1963 confirmed the existence of fifteen new Viet Cong battalions and five regiments. The Viet Cong regulars carried more formidable armament, including Communist bloc–manufactured recoilless rifles, mortars, and heavy machine guns. When they chose to engage the South Vietnamese Army, they fought with greater effectiveness than ever before.[7]

The Communists, however, also had their difficulties and shortcomings. Their armed forces still could not challenge the South Vietnamese on anything approaching even terms. Indeed, possibly in response to improved South Vietnamese training and firepower, the insurgents reduced the frequency of their company- and larger-size attacks on government regulars and concentrated on small territorial posts and strategic hamlets. In some rural areas and in all the cities, party and front organizations remained underdeveloped, with inadequately motivated and indoctrinated leadership. Diem's removal from power both benefited and damaged the insurgency. The collapse of the former regime's political and administrative apparatus in the countryside facilitated the expansion of Viet Cong control. However, with Diem and his hated family gone, the National Liberation Front lost a major source of its appeal to non-Communist South Vietnamese, among whom the military government initially enjoyed considerable popularity. Some groups, notably the Cao Dai and Hoa Hao, which had sided with the Viet Cong out of hostility to Diem, sought accommodation with the new Saigon regime. With the prospect of finishing off South Vietnam through political agitation and organization thus becoming more remote, the advocates of intensified armed struggle gained in influence within the Hanoi government and the Communist Party.[8]

The promoters of an enlarged military campaign secured the upper hand in December 1963, at a general meeting (the Ninth Plenum) of the Central Committee of the Vietnam Workers' (Communist) Party in Hanoi. After prolonged debate, the Central Committee adopted a secret directive to the party, north and south, calling for an accelerated buildup of the *PLAF*, especially the main forces, in preparation for an effort to destroy the South Vietnamese armed forces on the battlefield. The resolution acknowledged the continued importance of political action and guerrilla operations, especially in breaking up strategic hamlets, but declared that because the South Vietnamese Army was "the primary enemy force," the main objective of the armed struggle must be "to attack, destroy, and defeat the army of the lackey administration. Only in this manner can the revolution win decisive victory." Equally important, the party committed the full resources of North Vietnam to support of the southern revolution, abandoning its earlier position that the north should concentrate on building socialism while the south liberated itself primarily through mobilization of its own strength. Implicitly at least, the North Vietnamese leaders expressed willingness to press ahead with the southern campaign even at the risk of direct U.S. military intervention: "If the U.S. imperialists throw into South Vietnam an additional 50,000 to 100,000 troops, the total, people's and protracted war must strongly develop and cause them to become bogged down and gradually defeated."[9]

The resolution of the Ninth Plenum seemed to point toward escalation of the Viet Cong's military campaign from purely guerrilla operations toward the "big-unit" or "mobile" phase of revolutionary warfare, in which units of regimental and larger size would mount sustained attacks aimed at destroying comparable formations of Saigon's regulars. However, the elaboration of its principles and their practical application in South Vietnam took place only gradually. Dissent in Hanoi from prominent Communists who continued to favor a primarily political campaign in the south, reinforced with guerrilla operations, complicated and perhaps delayed the resolution's implementation. In addition, Hanoi had to maneuver carefully through the worsening Soviet-Chinese feud within the world Communist movement so as to obtain maximum diplomatic and military assistance from both major powers at minimum sacrifice of freedom of action. By late 1964, especially after the ouster in October of Soviet Premier Nikita S. Khruschev, who had been reluctant to intensify the conflict in Southeast Asia, the North Vietnamese were assured of the economic aid and military materiel, especially for air defense, that they deemed essential to their expanding war effort. Even before then, North Vietnam had begun organizing and training its people for defense against both air raids and invasion. In April it started preparing regular regiments of the *People's Army of Vietnam (PAVN)*, for dispatch to the south over the Ho Chi Minh Trail. The first regiment began its long march in October, with others soon to follow. By that time, individual North Vietnamese already had appeared, along with regrouped southerners, among infiltrators captured by the allies in South Vietnam.[10]

The full extent of Hanoi's preparations for escalation, however, remained unknown to the Americans and South Vietnamese until early 1965. MACV and other allied agencies expected the enemy to continue his guerrilla and subversive campaign with only gradually increasing intensity and with no fundamental change in tactics. On that assumption, the American command during 1964 reorganized itself and tried to press ahead with the antiguerrilla war.[11]

A New MACV Commander

General Harkins' working relationship with Ambassador Lodge steadily deteriorated after the November 1963 coup. "Lodge has virtually no official contact with Harkins," Secretary McNamara reported in December. "Lodge sends in reports with major military implications without showing them to Harkins, and does not show Harkins important incoming traffic." The two men responded in concert to Khanh's seizure of power, but that episode proved to be only an interlude in the progressive decline of mutual confidence. Late in April, Lodge ordered all U.S. agency heads in Saigon to secure embassy permission before arranging conferences with General Khanh and other officials. Harkins, who had established friendly working relations with Khanh, at once protested that the order violated his terms of reference, which entitled him to confer at will with the Vietnamese so long as he kept the ambassador informed of his contacts. Secretary of State Rusk, on behalf of the administration, upheld Lodge's authority, but he also vainly urged the ambassador to respect the special character of Harkins' position and to coordinate activities more closely with him. Privately, McGeorge Bundy declared, "the whole business between Lodge and Harkins is childish."[12]

Early in 1964 the president and his advisers began looking for a way to replace Harkins. Secretary McNamara and other officials had lost confidence in the general for his persistent optimism and apparent lack of appreciation for the nonmilitary aspects of the conflict, and it was obvious that Harkins could not work effectively with the

Reorganizing and Reviving Pacification

ambassador. Michael Forrestal of the White House staff declared, "If Lodge must remain, the military commander must be changed." Even so, McNamara and the Joint Chiefs of Staff balked at summary relief of Harkins, both because they wanted to spare the general a humiliation unwarranted by any personal misconduct and because Harkins' relationship with Khanh might be of value in the first months of the shaky new regime. Harkins was due for relief and retirement in late 1964 at any event. The administration compromised by dispatching Harkins' intended replacement, Lt. Gen. William C. Westmoreland, to Saigon late in January as deputy commander of MACV, a position in which Westmoreland could prepare for his coming promotion and help mediate between the Military Assistance Command and the rest of the country team. On 25 April, President Johnson announced that Harkins would step down and retire on 1 August and that Westmoreland was to succeed him.[13]

Continuing personality conflicts between Lodge and Harkins appear to have hastened the MACV commander's departure. On 28 May the president abruptly ordered Harkins to return to the United States in time to receive a decoration at the White House on 24 June. After that, he was to remain in Washington for the rest of his active duty to "counsel" the president on Vietnam. This order dismayed and embittered Harkins, who viewed it as a thinly disguised dismissal. In late June, after several awkward weeks during which Lodge increasingly took counsel with Westmoreland rather than Harkins, the retiring commander left Saigon. Westmoreland then served as acting COMUSMACV until his predecessor retired. He formally assumed command on 1 August, at the same time as he received his fourth star.[14]

A fifty-year-old West Pointer, Westmoreland had been selected for his position in December of the previous year, after extensive deliberations involving the president, Secretary McNamara, General Taylor, and other high officials. Handsome, impeccable in military appearance, affable if somewhat reserved in manner, Westmoreland had seemed destined for leadership since his days as First Captain of Cadets at West Point. During World War II he distinguished himself as an artillery battalion commander and division chief of staff in North Africa, the Mediterranean, and Northwest Europe. Senior officers, including General Taylor, marked him as deserving of rapid advancement. Transferring to the airborne forces after the war, Westmoreland performed effectively in a succession of challenging assignments. He served as secretary of the Army General Staff, commander of the 101st Airborne Division, superintendent of the U.S. Military Academy, and commander of the XVIII Airborne Corps—his final post before going to Saigon. Ambitious and politically astute, he associated himself with the fashionable military trends of the 1960s, espousing efficient, scientific management in the McNamara style (as a brigadier general, he took an advanced management course at the Harvard Graduate School of Business) and intro-

General Westmoreland (NARA)

ducing counterinsurgency into the West Point curriculum.[15]

According to Maj. Gen. Bruce Palmer, Jr., of the Army Staff, Westmoreland was to provide in Saigon "a senior experienced strong and tough leader to get behind the advisory effort while General Harkins can devote his main attention to the politico-military sphere." In practice, as Harkins' deputy, Westmoreland spent much of his time mediating between the embassy and the military command. Michael Forrestal reported in late May that "such coordination between U.S. [military and civilian] agencies as there is takes place because of the efforts of General Westmoreland." To gain Lodge's confidence, according to Forrestal, Westmoreland went out of his way to emphasize the essentially political nature of the war and his receptivity to political guidance.[16]

Westmoreland had not long to work with Lodge. The ambassador resigned in June to take part in the American election campaign. To replace him, President Johnson selected the recently retired chairman of the Joint Chiefs, General Maxwell D. Taylor, who assumed his duties early in July. Under Taylor, Westmoreland became a full but definitely subordinate member of the ambassador's country team. Taylor arrived in Saigon armed with a directive from President Johnson that he would exercise "full responsibility" for U.S. activities in South Vietnam, including "the whole military effort," over which Taylor was to exert "the degree of command and control that you consider appropriate." Reinforcing this presidential grant of authority, Taylor, as Westmoreland's military senior, inevitably elicited a certain deference from the younger general, the more so since he had been an important sponsor of Westmoreland's rise in the Army. "There was never a question as to my relationship with Ambassador Taylor," Westmoreland would later recall. "He was the boss."[17]

For practical purposes, the MACV commander functioned as Taylor's deputy ambassador for military affairs. At Taylor's direction, Westmoreland cleared with the ambassador all significant MACV messages to CINCPAC and the Joint Chiefs. Taylor routinely included Westmoreland in his negotiations with the Khanh government and before assuming his post solicited the MACV commander's views as to which embassy civilians he should retain or remove. Taylor also employed the MACV staff as an extension of his own; he called on it regularly for studies, reports, and briefings much as he had upon the Joint Staff in the Pentagon.[18]

Headquarters Reorganization and Expansion

When Westmoreland assumed command, MACV was in the final stages of abolishing the Military Assistance Advisory Group and taking over its functions and most of its personnel. General Harkins had proposed such action as early as September 1962, to eliminate division of authority over the field advisers and duplication of many administrative and logistical activities. However, by mid-February 1964, he had changed his mind. When the Joint Chiefs of Staff revived consideration of the issue at that time, he joined Admiral Felt in recommending against any change. The existing arrangement was working satisfactorily, the two argued. Reorganization could only disrupt operations and confuse the South Vietnamese in a time of governmental instability. In addition, Harkins assumed that under the Model Plan, then still in effect, MACV sooner or later was to go out of existence, leaving the Military Assistance Advisory Group as the senior U.S. headquarters in South Vietnam. Supporting Harkins, Felt repeated an objection he had made earlier that the move would merely burden the MACV commander and his staff with the details of administering the Military Assistance Program.[19]

Nevertheless, elimination of the MAAG had strong support within MACV and Pacific Command, particularly among the Army contingent. Once he arrived in Saigon, General Westmoreland became an active advocate of the proposal. Most important, Secretary McNamara indicated interest in eliminating the MAAG as a means of increasing American military efficiency in South Vietnam. In preparation for a visit by the secretary in early March, a MACV staff group began work on a combined plan and feasibility study for the reorganization. McNamara received a preliminary briefing on the results while in Saigon. On the basis of it, he directed General Harkins to submit a full reorganization plan for concurrent consideration by CINCPAC and the Joint Chiefs of Staff.[20]

The final proposal, submitted over General Harkins' signature on 12 March, called for abolition of the MAAG headquarters and the incorporation of a number of its divisions—notably those for ARVN organization and training, MAP administration, and strategic hamlet support—within MACV as special staff sections. The group's Air Force, Navy, and Army advisory sections would cease to function. Command and control of the advisers, as well as their administrative and logistical support, would go to the service components under MACV and in the case of the Army advisers to MACV headquarters itself. This rearrangement, according to the study, would simplify command by making advisers responsible for all purposes to a single headquarters and would improve efficiency by eliminating the MAAG's role in administration and supply of the advisory teams. Personnel savings would result from consolidation of MACV and MAAG special staff agencies, such as the adjutant general's and public information offices.[21]

The plan met with opposition from Admiral Felt and the Navy, Air Force, and Marine service chiefs. Felt and his supporters argued that abolition of the MAAG would complicate rather than simplify the existing command structure by adding to the number of advisory detachments and staff agencies under the MACV commander's direct control and entangling him and his staff in the intricacies of MAP programming and administration. Admiral Felt questioned the wisdom of disrupting American organization at a time when the South Vietnamese were struggling to restore stable government. In the event of full-scale war in Southeast Asia, he added, a reorganized Military Assistance Command would have difficulty in shifting to its intended role of directing U.S. and allied forces in conventional combat.[22]

On 8 April the chief of staff of the Air Force, the chief of naval operations, and the commandant of the Marine Corps recommended against reorganization. General Taylor, then still chairman, supported by Army Chief of Staff General Earle G. Wheeler, upheld COMUSMACV's prerogative to organize his headquarters as he saw fit. They endorsed the proposed restructuring as "clean-cut" and eliminating dual channels of American military authority in South Vietnam. McNamara accepted the latter view. At his direction, the Joint Chiefs on 10 April authorized MACV to absorb the MAAG.[23]

The change took effect on 15 May, as did an amendment to the MACV commander's terms of reference to include responsibility for all aspects of the Military Assistance Program. Due to thorough planning by the MACV and MAAG staffs, the reorganization caused no major disruption of headquarters operations. It also, however, did not solve all the problems it was intended to. The Army advisers still found themselves answering to a multitude of masters in the form of the different MACV staff sections. Two separate MAAG agencies, the MAP Directorate and the Army MAP Logistics Directorate, had to be retained to manage the Military Assistance Program. In addition, the MACV chief of staff, the heads of the general staff sections, and other key officers became involved in detailed review and approval of the South Vietnamese defense budget.[24]

Largely as a result of further expansion of the advisory effort and of other MACV activities during 1964, the reorganized headquarters, far from reducing manpower, required additional personnel. A revised organization table, submitted the same day the headquarters merged, called for enlargement of the staff by 140 people, to a strength of over 1,000.[25] Another revision, on 1 September, increased the MACV headquarters complement to 1,128, with further growth sure to come.[26]

The reorganized Military Assistance Command headquarters included a Joint Research and Testing Activity, which represented the resolution of another long-standing organizational controversy. Although Secretary McNamara had approved consolidation of the various research units into a single agency under MACV, disagreements among the services over staffing and composition of such an agency delayed implementation of the directive. The duplication of efforts continued until February 1964, when the Joint Chiefs of Staff ordered the establishment of the Joint Research and Testing Activity, a MACV staff agency to be headed by an Army brigadier general with an Air Force colonel as his deputy. The new agency replaced the Joint Operational Evaluation Group—Vietnam and incorporated the Advanced Research Projects Agency (ARPA) field unit, Army Concept Team in Vietnam (ACTIV), and the Air Force Test Unit. Its director served as the MACV commander's principal staff adviser on research and development and also advised and assisted the South Vietnamese in those fields. Under guidance from Admiral Felt, General Harkins directed in April that testing in Vietnam should be confined to projects that would enhance directly the counterinsurgency capability of allied forces, with issues of long-term impact on U.S. forces and doctrine and questions of service roles and missions to be settled elsewhere.[27]

As a result of the expansion of American military activity in Southeast Asia and of the merger of the two headquarters, MACV reorganized and enlarged some of its general and special staff agencies and added new ones. A few staff divisions, notably the personnel and logistics sections, changed little. On the other hand, the operations section, primarily responsible for overseeing the advisory effort and pacification programs in South Vietnam and for keeping track of operations in Laos and North Vietnam, continually enlarged and rearranged its branches. Supplementing its Combat Operations Center, which monitored operations within South Vietnam, the section added a War Room concerned with activities elsewhere in Southeast Asia. It also created a new Operations Analysis Section and a Pacification Planning and Operations Branch. The long-range planning (J5) section, besides planning for operations against North Vietnam, also took on supervision of the MAP Directorate and of an International Military Assistance Office (IMAO) designed to support forces sent by other non-Communist countries to assist South Vietnam. The office also supervised the Studies and Observations Group (SOG), a mixed military-civilian staff established under MACV in early 1964 that conducted clandestine operations against the Ho Chi Minh Trail and North Vietnam.[28]

Two MACV headquarters agencies—the intelligence (J2) section and the Public Information Office—underwent major enlargement and reorganization. The intelligence buildup resulted from the dissatisfaction of President Johnson and his advisers with the inaccurate, conflicting information the government had received during Diem's final crisis. At

Harkins' request, the Joint Chiefs of Staff in January 1964 increased the rank of MACV's chief of intelligence from colonel to brigadier general and shifted the billet from the Air Force to the Marine Corps in order to place a ground officer in the job. During a visit to Saigon in March, Secretary McNamara then instructed MACV to double the size of its intelligence directorate and to enhance the capacity of American field advisers to collect, report, and verify military information.[29]

As a result of McNamara's decisions, during 1964 the new MACV J2, Brig. Gen. Carl A. Youngdale, presided over the expansion of his section from 76 officers and enlisted men to 135. To its existing five branches (Collection, Counterintelligence and Security, Production, Reconnaissance and Photo Intelligence, and J2 High Command Advisory), he added a sixth, the Current Intelligence and Indications Center, to keep track of events in Southeast Asia outside South Vietnam and to help prepare lists of air strike targets in North Vietnam and Laos.[30]

Youngdale placed increased emphasis on intelligence collection, an area in which he believed his office had been weak. Through publication of MACV's first formal Intelligence Collection Plan and issuance of a new guide and operating procedures, he attempted to involve American intelligence advisers more regularly in information gathering and reporting. To exploit more fully data from American technical intelligence sources and aerial photography and observation, Youngdale late in the year began work on a unified MACV nationwide reconnaissance program. He also set up a Target Research and Analysis Center, manned by both Americans and Vietnamese, which was to locate enemy positions in remote areas for ground reconnaissance and air attack. To unify American counterintelligence planning, operations, and reporting, he organized a Counterintelligence Advisory Committee with representation from all U.S. agencies in that field. General Youngdale also established closer cooperation with the U.S. Operations Mission (USOM) and U.S. Information Service (USIS), both of which had access to sources of military information not directly available to MACV.[31]

In one area, however, MACV during 1964 narrowed the range of its contacts. The command secured abolition of the separate defense attaché offices in the American embassy and transfer of their duties to the Collection Branch of J2. The Army's assistant chief of staff for intelligence protested, claiming that during the 1963 crisis the Army staff received more complete and timely information on the political situation and on dissidence within the RVNAF from the attachés than it did from the MACV commander. The action was nevertheless implemented, effectively eliminating the military's access to certain diplomatic sources of information and closing down a channel for intelligence reporting and evaluation independent of the Military Assistance Command.[32]

However much MACV expanded and systematized its own collection efforts, in the absence of large American forces in the field, the command still had to rely upon the South Vietnamese for most of its data on the war in the countryside and on the enemy. Hence, General Youngdale and his section devoted much effort to improving their allies' collection and use of intelligence. There was much to be done. South Vietnamese military intelligence had long lacked effective high-level direction, unity of effort, and qualified personnel; the administrative upheaval following Diem's overthrow had exacerbated all these deficiencies. During 1964 MACV prevailed upon the Joint General Staff to reorganize its Directorate of Intelligence on an American instead of a French pattern, thereby facilitating cooperation between the allied counterpart agencies. In the process, it persuaded the Vietnamese to issue, if not always follow, basic manuals (drafted by American advisers in most cases) on such matters as processing captured documents and treatment and interrogation of prisoners. It also assisted in expansion of Vietnamese military intelligence schools and arranged for more Vietnamese intelligence personnel to be trained in the United States. Through the network of American intelligence advisers that eventually reached down to battalion and district level, Youngdale's directorate worked with some success to expedite the upward flow of information from all sources, notably captured enemy documents and prisoner interrogation reports. In spite of these efforts, MACV at the end of 1964 still lacked complete, timely, and reliable operational and tactical intelligence. After two years of collating and analyzing every scrap of obtainable data, the command's estimates of the enemy order of battle and of the rate of infiltration through Laos remained imprecise and, especially in the latter case, were up to half a year out of date.[33]

The Military Assistance Command's relations with the American news media had been embittered by the correspondents' feud with Harkins at the same time as the command's information effort was crippled by personnel shortages and the absence, in General Westmoreland's words, of a "long range, objective, conceptual program." To alleviate these deficiencies and in hopes of obtaining more favorable coverage of U.S. and South Vietnamese activities, Westmoreland, as soon as he became acting commander early in June, reorganized and enlarged the MACV Public Information Office. Working in cooperation with Barry Zorthian, the mission's chief public affairs officer, and with Col. Roger Bankson of the Office of the Assistant Secretary of Defense for Public Affairs, Westmoreland retitled the agency the MACV Office of Information (MACCOI) and enlarged its staff from nineteen officers and enlisted men to fifty-nine.

The restructured office had three divisions. Troop Information oversaw the command newspaper, the Armed Forces Radio station, and orientation of newly arrived personnel. Press Relations, the sole American release point in South Vietnam for news on military operations, conducted press briefings, issued releases, answered reporters' questions, and monitored South Vietnamese public information activities. The third division, Special Projects and Liaison, was to be the "catalyst" in developing a "vitalized, objective" MACV information program. This division, which cooperated closely with the embassy and the U.S. Information Service, had the task of finding stories that presented allied efforts in a favorable light and guiding correspondents to them. With Caribou transports and helicopters at its disposal, the division made arrangements for reporters' trips to the field; it supervised the work of MACV information officers in the corps areas; and it collaborated with South Vietnamese government information agencies. Its staff also prepared news stories, radio programs, and film clips for transmission to the media. This intensification of MACV's information effort underscored the degree to which the news media had become a major, and influential, participant in the war. In the short run, the command improved its public relations; but it nonetheless also became a participant in the Johnson administration's campaign to manipulate public opinion in support of its Vietnam policy.[34]

By the time General Westmoreland took charge, the Military Assistance Command was bearing an increasingly heavy burden of military and pacification reporting, both to the embassy and to higher authorities. MACV since 1962 had been assembling village-by-village estimates of government and Viet Cong control of the countryside, based on information obtained from the province chiefs by American intelligence advisers and, to a limited extent, verified by them. As South Vietnam's situation deteriorated during 1963, the Kennedy administration demanded more and more information, as though the accumulation of enough facts would resolve its internal policy disagreements. In response, MACV in October 1963 established an Information and Reports Working Group under the Operations Directorate's supervision to recommend improvements in the command's counterinsurgency reporting. The command at the same time began furnishing combat information to the Pacific Command for incorporation in its automated Republic of Vietnam Statistical Data Base, an early effort to employ computers for the storage, retrieval, and analysis of data on the war. In November, as part of the American reassessment of pacification following Diem's fall, MACV instituted a Province Studies Working Group, coordinated by the intelligence directorate, to oversee preparation of detailed studies of every one of South Vietnam's forty-five provinces. These studies were to establish a more accurate picture of what actually was happening in the countryside and to constitute the basis for measuring subsequent counterinsurgency progress by the new government.[35]

During early 1964, a joint Defense, State Department, and CIA team reviewed pacification reporting by the entire U.S. Mission. Building on the findings of MACV's Information and Reports Working Group, the team made recommendations for a series of mission weekly and monthly reports to Washington that would incorporate submissions from all agencies, including MACV. As a result, by mid-1964 MACV was producing regular daily and weekly military situation reports, a monthly military evaluation, and a quarterly review of counterinsurgency progress. Information from these documents, which contained both statistical summaries and more impressionistic evaluations, went into corresponding mission reports. Ambassador Lodge used MACV as the mission's principal collecting point for information about the provinces. The better to perform that role, General Harkins in May established a Province Reports Center, located in the South Vietnamese High Command compound, which was to provide pacification data and analyses to all U.S. agencies. At the end of the year, MACV combined this organization and the former MAAG Office of Sector Affairs into the Pacification Planning and Operations Branch under its J3 section, constituting what one staff officer called "a [combat operations center] for pacification."[36]

MACV had other reporting responsibilities as well. At Defense Department direction, the command furnished CINCPAC and the Joint Chiefs with a Senior Adviser's Monthly Evaluation Report on the personnel, equipment, and combat effectiveness (as evaluated by American advisers) of every South Vietnamese unit down to battalion size. It made still more periodic reports to CINCPAC in connection with the Military Assistance Program and psychological warfare operations. In September, General Westmoreland began giving Ambassador Taylor his personal weekly and monthly military estimates for incorporation into similar reports demanded of Taylor by Secretary Rusk. As if that were not enough, each visit by Secretary McNamara and each Honolulu policy conference produced calls for comprehensive information—what General Stilwell characterized as "impossible (but salute and comply dammit) requirements"—on a long list of subjects. This demand by higher authority for growing quantities of information, much of it in statistical form, as well as a never-resolved debate over the most meaningful indicators of counterinsurgency progress, was to continue as the war expanded.[37]

As the Military Assistance Command headquarters reorganized and expanded, the Army gained increased ascendancy within it. Both Harkins and Westmoreland supported greater Army representation in the belief that the Vietnam conflict was "predominantly a land campaign and therefore senior commanders should be prepared by experience and orientation primarily to deal with problems involving ground operations." In addition, they argued that because MACV staff procedures were those of the Army, only officers of that service could work effectively in most billets. Over objections from CINCPAC and the Air Force, General Westmoreland selected another Army officer, Lt. Gen. John L. Throckmorton, as his deputy commander. As the tours of duty of other members of the original MACV staff came to an end, the Joint Chiefs, at Westmoreland's recommendation, transferred the positions of many of them to the Army. Thus General Weede, the Marine chief of staff, was replaced by Army Maj. Gen. Richard G. Stilwell, formerly

MACV: The Years of Escalation, 1962–1967

General Moore (shown as a Lieutenant General), right, *with Pacific Air Forces Commander, General Hunter Harris,* left, *and General Westmoreland.*
(Time Life Pictures/Getty Images)

MACV's director of operations. The Navy relinquished the personnel directorate to the Army. As part of the public information reorganization, Westmoreland attempted to obtain an Army colonel to head the new MACV Office of Information. Air Force opposition, however, delayed achievement of this goal until early 1965. Under the Joint Table of Distribution of 15 May, adopted immediately after abolition of the MAAG, only the intelligence and long-range planning sections did not have Army chiefs, and even then the Army staff was pressing for control of the intelligence slot. At the same time, in the May Joint Table of Distribution and others that followed, an increasing proportion of deputy and branch chief slots were shifted from the other services to the Army. By late 1964 as a result, about 80 percent of the personnel in the general staff sections were from that service. The secretary of the MACV joint staff declared that the command was really "an Army staff with some A[ir] F[orce] and Navy officers on it. All the paperwork and procedures are Army procedures."[38] *(Chart 2)*

The Air Force, especially its chief of staff, General LeMay, vigorously resisted the trend, arguing that air power had an important role to play in the struggle within South Vietnam and an even more significant one in the future broader operations that were then coming under consid-

CHART 2—U.S. MILITARY ASSISTANCE COMMAND, VIETNAM, 31 DECEMBER 1964

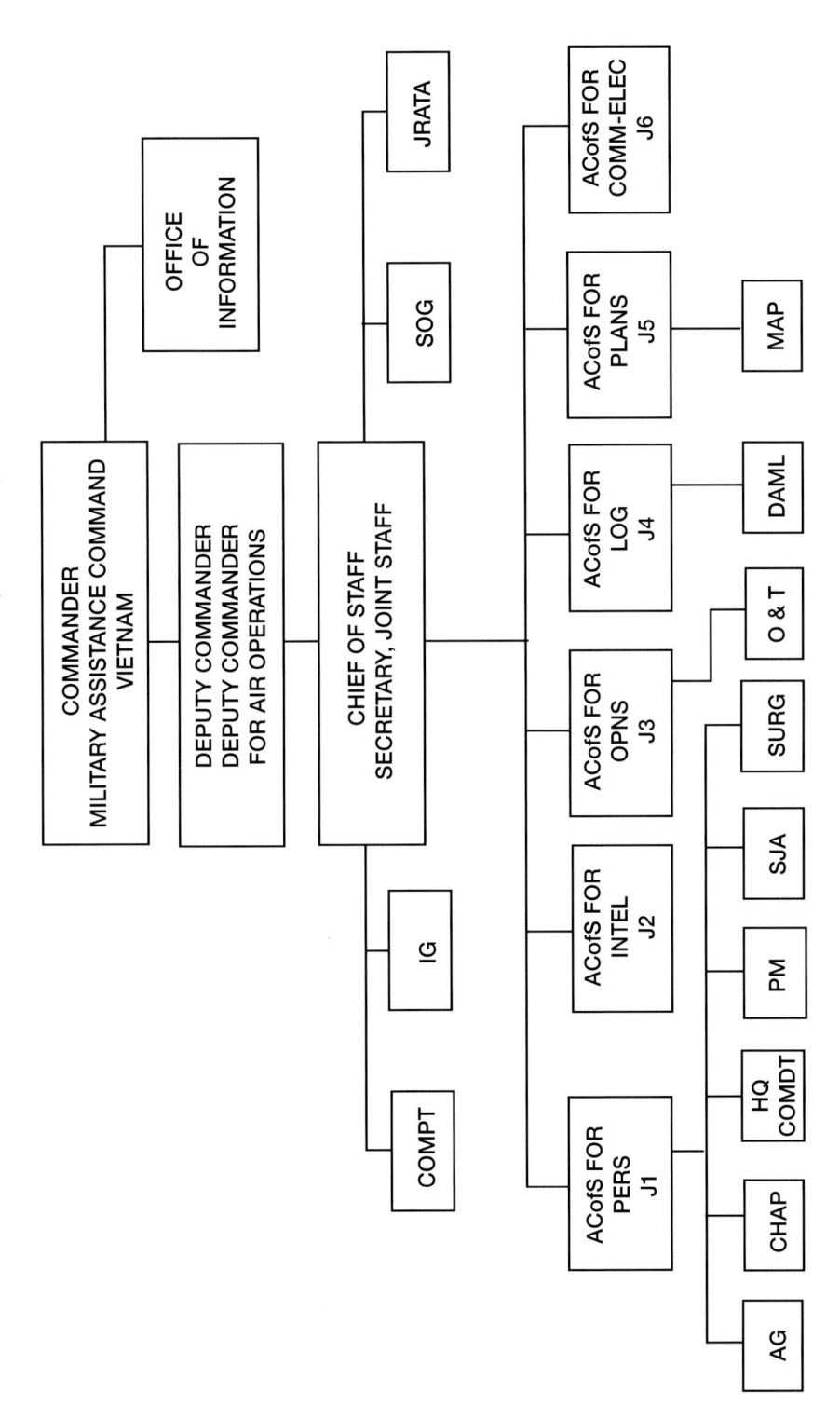

```
                    COMMANDER
          MILITARY ASSISTANCE COMMAND
                     VIETNAM
                        │───────────── OFFICE OF INFORMATION
              DEPUTY COMMANDER
          DEPUTY COMMANDER FOR AIR OPERATIONS
                        │
              CHIEF OF STAFF
          SECRETARY, JOINT STAFF
      ┌────────┬────────┬────────┬────────┬────────┬────────┬────────┬────────┐
    COMPT     IG     ACofS    ACofS    ACofS    ACofS    ACofS    SOG    JRATA
                     FOR      FOR      FOR      FOR      FOR
                     PERS     INTEL    OPNS     LOG      PLANS
                      J1       J2       J3       J4       J5
                                                                   ACofS FOR
                                                                   COMM-ELEC
                                                                       J6
      ┌────┬────┬────┐         ┌────┬────┐      │        │
     AG  CHAP  HQ   PM  SJA   SURG  O&T        DAML     MAP
              COMDT
```

Admiral Sharp
(Time Life Pictures/Getty Images)

eration. In an effort to strengthen its influence, the Air Force assigned Maj. Gen. Joseph H. Moore in January 1964 to replace General Anthis as 2d Air Division commander. A World War II combat veteran and former operations director of the Tactical Air Command, Moore was a boyhood friend of General Westmoreland—a fact that Air Force officials did not ignore in sending him to Vietnam. Westmoreland and Moore at once established a warm personal and professional relationship, and the 2d Air Division commander functioned in many respects as Westmoreland's air deputy. The two men cooperated to make the divided air control system in South Vietnam work as smoothly as possible.[39]

Nevertheless, Army–Air Force arguments persisted, both in South Vietnam and in Washington. The Air Force bitterly fought Westmoreland's and the Army's efforts to expand the missions of armed helicopters and to obtain more powerful such craft, complaining that the Army was taking advantage of strict operating restrictions on the FARMGATE unit to usurp the role of fixed-wing tactical aircraft. Discontent among FARMGATE pilots with those same restrictions and with their obsolescent, at times unsafe, equipment surfaced in the press early in 1964. Picking up on the issue, the influential Senator John Stennis of Mississippi and his Preparedness Investigating Subcommittee held hearings during June that provided a forum for Air Force allegations of neglect and misuse of air power in Vietnam. These were merely surface manifestations of a continuing interservice doctrinal battle that erupted periodically in deliberations of the Joint Chiefs of Staff and regularly threatened to spill over into the Congress. Persistent discontent among Air Force officers in Vietnam, General Wheeler warned Westmoreland, helped "stoke the fires" of conflict in the Pentagon; "conversely attitudes and beliefs in the Pentagon and elsewhere in the Air Force continue to supply fuel (or fire brands!) to the Air Force contingent in Vietnam." Indicating the intensity of service partisanship, General LeMay at one point personally scolded General Moore for allegedly undermining Air Force interests by too close cooperation with the Army.[40]

In an effort to mollify the Air Force, General Earle G. Wheeler, who had succeeded Taylor as chairman of the Joint Chiefs of Staff on 31 July 1964, pressed Westmoreland formally during the autumn to establish a deputy COMUSMACV for air operations, a position General Moore would hold in conjunction with his command of the 2d Air Division. Wheeler argued that giving Moore the additional title, along with a small staff section within MACV headquarters, would satisfy at least partially Air Force demands for continuous high-level participation in joint planning and operations.[41]

Westmoreland initially demurred. He insisted that General Moore already was functioning as his deputy for air matters, regularly attending daily MACV staff meetings, and that Air Force officers, as well as Navy and Marine aviators, occupied appropriate positions throughout the joint staff. Hence, redesignating Moore and adding a new headquarters element under him would only "create confusion and perhaps further cultivate seeds of dissension that we are trying to destroy." Admiral Ulysses S. Grant Sharp, who succeeded Admiral Felt as CINCPAC on 30 June 1964, also objected. He pointed out that "double-hatting" Moore would violate a JCS regulation against service component commanders performing additional staff duties and warned that the plan might merely provoke more controversy among the Joint Chiefs. Both men withdrew their objections after Wheeler reassured Sharp that the Joint Chiefs were prepared to waive the regulation and reiterated the political necessity for the action in staving off further interservice, congressional, and public controversy over the status of air power in Vietnam. In late October, Westmoreland submitted an amendment to MACV's Joint Table of Distribution, creating the position of deputy commander for air operations. The Joint Chiefs, however, did not get around to approving the change and confirming General Moore's new title until the following May. In the interim, General LeMay's retirement as Air Force chief of staff reduced, at least for a time, the stridency of the interservice controversy.[42]

MACV's forces in the field expanded moderately during 1964. Early in the year, the administration decided to increase the number of advisers with the South Vietnamese Army and in the provinces, on the largely unexamined assumption that an enhanced American presence throughout the chain of command would improve government performance. The Joint Chiefs of Staff during April and May developed ambitious plans for assigning American advisers to the South Vietnamese Army down to company level and for creating mobile training teams for the Civil Guard and Self-Defense Corps (now being redesignated the Regional and Popular Forces). General Westmoreland and Admiral Felt, however, objected that the Joint Chiefs' proposal would cause higher American casualties, offend Vietnamese nationalist sensitivities, and overburden MACV's logistical system. They favored a more modest augmentation of battalion advisory teams in the infantry, armor, and artillery, and the assignment of district advisers to work with the territorial forces. MACV during the spring deployed two-man experimental advisory teams in thirteen districts, with encouraging results in both military and civil affairs.[43]

At a conference in Honolulu early in June, Secretaries McNamara and Rusk, Ambassador Lodge, General Westmoreland, and Admiral Felt adopted Westmoreland's plan for additional battalion advisers and agreed to deploy five-man advisory teams to a total of 113 districts in the critical provinces. Westmoreland then submitted a formal request for about 900 additional advisers—the district and battalion teams and modest increases in the Navy and Air Force advisory groups. Doubling helicopter squadrons and support personnel required by the advisory buildup, brought his total reinforcement request to about 4,600 officers and men. McNamara approved immediately. These troops deployed incrementally to Vietnam during the last half of the year. Their arrival brought Military Assistance Command strength to a total of over 23,300 by the end of 1964.[44]

As part of this buildup, MACV expanded and reinforced the Special Forces while altering their command arrangements and mission assignment. The command wanted to integrate the Special Forces–advised Civilian Irregular Defense Groups (CIDGs), which it had inherited from the CIA, more fully into the general military campaign. As part of the reinforcement, the command enlarged its Special Forces contingent from about 500 officers and enlisted men on six-month temporary assignments to a full group of more than 1,200 on regular twelve-month tours. It also replaced the provisional Headquarters, U.S. Special Forces, Vietnam, with a regular command element, the 5th Special Forces Group (Airborne). At the same time, as the result of a study by General Westmoreland, MACV placed the Special Forces detachments in the field under the operational control of the corps senior advisers. Westmoreland intended this change to give these often free-wheeling elite troops the "focus, firm direction, and adequate supervision" he believed they had lacked up to that point. The 5th Special Forces Group retained command, less operational control, of the teams. Its commander advised Westmoreland on Special Forces matters, and the group advised and assisted the South Vietnamese Special Forces command. Besides altering command arrangements, MACV significantly changed the primary mission of the Green Berets and the irregulars they advised, from area pacification to the provision of strike forces to patrol and interdict Viet Cong infiltration routes across the border. It thereby largely diverted the Civilian Irregular Defense Group program from its original focus on paramilitary counterinsurgency to more conventional reconnaissance and combat.[45]

As the Military Assistance Command expanded, President Johnson and Secretary McNamara tried to improve the quality of its personnel, in both headquarters and the field. The president in December 1963 directed all government agencies to send only their best people to Vietnam. McNamara, in a private talk with the newly assigned MACV chief of intelligence, General Youngdale, expressed dissatisfaction with the qualifications and performance of the MACV staff, calling it "a second rate team" and expressing his determination to replace many of its members. Under pressure from McNamara and at General Harkins' recommendation, the Army, in particular, established strict standards for assignment to key MACV positions. Lieutenant colonels, for example, had to have graduated from the Command and General Staff College and not to have been passed over for promotion to colonel. At the outset, imposition of these criteria caused discontent and confusion in MACV. Incumbent officers who did not meet the criteria but were performing well resented an implied slur on themselves. Other personnel, on orders to Vietnam, were abruptly reassigned. While the effect of the new standards on the overall quality of the MACV staff was difficult to measure, their imposition reflected the administration's increasing concern over Vietnam as its only active war and principal foreign crisis, as well as a determination to commit the resources needed to secure victory.[46]

General Westmoreland, upon becoming acting commander in June, lost no time in imposing his own leadership philosophy and working methods on MACV headquarters. From the outset, he emphasized "professional and businesslike" advisory relations with the South Vietnamese; "open-minded and complete" cooperation with other U.S. agencies; and improved troop discipline, indoctrination, and welfare. He called for realistic, objective reporting, declaring that "we all seek the facts and the truth" and must aim at "the righting of the bad—not applauding success." He insisted that all personnel of the command follow his own example of correct military appearance and hard work, requiring a "minimum" sixty-hour week in both headquarters and the field. In contrast to Harkins, Westmoreland made himself accessible to American newsmen at command press briefings and in informal background sessions. He regularly took correspondents along on his trips outside Saigon and made special visits to places where his presence might draw reporters' attention to stories favorable to the allied war effort.[47]

Westmoreland employed the MACV staff intensively for consultation and anticipatory planning. He strengthened the Secretariate of the Joint Staff and transformed the commander's daily staff conferences into lengthy discussions of issues and policy, as well as using them to call the section chiefs' attention to complaints and deficiencies he had noted on his field trips. He established ad hoc groups to deal with special problems and often consulted directly with junior staff officers on matters of interest to him. The secretary of the Joint Staff declared that Westmoreland was "a great one for calling people directly, the section chiefs or even action officers if he knows them, telling them to come over and talk things over." Westmoreland employed his deputy, General Throckmorton, to make field investigations and follow through on special projects. Within headquarters, the chief of staff, General Stilwell, and the Assistant Chief of Staff for Operations, Brig. Gen. William E. DePuy, both men of strong intellect and dominant personality, were Westmoreland's most influential counselors and assistants. Westmoreland attempted to draw his component commanders and corps senior advisers into the development of strategy through monthly meetings of a MACV Executive Council. However, the council, established in October 1964, convened with increasing irregularity as the war, and the pressure on the members' time, expanded.[48]

Westmoreland and his staff worked in less than ideal surroundings. After combining with the MAAG, MACV headquarters occupied two principal facilities. MACV Compound 1, a converted hotel on Pasteur Street in downtown Saigon, housed the commander, his deputy, the chief of staff, the combat operations center, the communications center, and the directorates of intelligence, operations, and communications/electronics. Compound 2, a former MAAG facility some distance away in Cholon, Saigon's Chinese suburb, accommodated the personnel and logistics directorates and most of the special staff. Other elements, including the J5 section, the information office, and the Joint Research and Testing Agency, occupied separate quarters elsewhere. This dispersal of the headquarters forced personnel to do much time-consuming and potentially dangerous commuting across the crowded city. It divided some key agencies such as the communications center, which was split between Compounds 1 and 2 until October. Staff sections not located in the Pasteur Street complex complained of a lack of timely information and of inability to gain consideration of their views on major plans and policies. All the facilities, which depended for security on the South Vietnamese Army, were vulnerable to Viet Cong attack. Compound 1, for instance, was separated from a busy avenue only by a fence and a line of South Vietnamese army sentries.[49]

Even with these inconveniences and with the sixty-hour work week decreed by General Westmoreland, MACV headquarters personnel, until the end of 1964, enjoyed a relatively comfortable existence. Billeted in hotels and villas, most had leisure to sample the many excellent restaurants and other pleasures of Saigon. Higher ranking officers participated in a busy round of diplomatic receptions and dinners and found time for golf and tennis. The presence of American families created a semblance of peacetime post and garrison life. As the Viet Cong increased their terrorist attacks on Americans in Saigon, however, the wives and children had to cease their shopping and exploring trips. MACV during the year gradually reduced the number of accompanied positions on its roster. At the end of 1964, only 120 such slots remained. Nevertheless, although guerrilla bombings in the city and the deaths of friends or academy classmates in the fighting in the countryside brought home the actuality of war, there persisted, in the words of the MACV command historian, a "psychological gap between the Headquarters and the field, . . . [which] added to the remoteness and unreality of the war for Saigon staff officers."[50]

MACV: Executive Agent for Pacification?

Throughout 1964 the U.S. Mission struggled to revive the South Vietnamese campaign to recapture the countryside from the Viet Cong. The mission's pacification plans, and those of the Minh and Khanh governments, followed familiar principles. They called for regular forces, working out of relatively secure areas, to drive organized enemy units from steadily widening zones ("spreading oil spots"). Within those zones, territorial troops and police were to root out the Viet Cong guerrillas and political underground while civilian agencies of the government organized strategic hamlets, now called New Life Hamlets, and sought to win over the people through economic and social improvements. The allies, aware of the limitations on their resources and the difficulty of the task, planned to concentrate their efforts in the most heavily populated and strategically important provinces, primarily those of the upper Mekong Delta, those surrounding Saigon, and the populous coastal provinces of I and II Corps. At the urging of MACV and the mission, the Minh regime embodied these principles in its DIEN HUONG pacification plan, which General Khanh reissued, with minor modifications, under the title CHIEN THANG ("Struggle for Victory"). Khanh's plan constituted the framework for the allied campaign throughout 1964.[51]

In November 1963, at Secretary McNamara's behest and to guide its own deployment of personnel and allocation of resources, the U.S. Mission established a list of thirteen critical provinces, which were selected on the basis of size, strategic importance, and degree of Viet Cong domination. MACV and other mission agencies were to press the government to reinforce these provinces with troops and civilian personnel and were to concentrate additional American advisers, money, and materiel there. The White House and the State and Defense Departments continually demanded exhaustive reports on conditions in these provinces and on government progress (or lack of it) in pacifying them. The critical list, which had been reduced to nine by midyear, included Quang Tin in I Corps, Quang Ngai and Binh Dinh in II Corps, the provinces in III Corps surrounding Saigon, and several in the northern Mekong Delta in IV Corps.[52]

All the pacification plans called for the closest possible integration of military and civilian activities. Hence, they raised anew the issue, for both South Vietnamese and Americans, of how to combine the actions of numerous separate agencies, each jealous of its own prerogatives and advocating its own particular variant of the general pacification theory. On the American side, the Military Assistance Command throughout the year campaigned for its solution to this problem: placing all American pacification support under COMUSMACV as the ambassador's executive agent.

From the time of his arrival in Saigon, General Westmoreland pressed this cause with conviction and vigor. As XVIII Airborne Corps commander at Fort Bragg, he had worked closely with the Army Special Warfare Center and had absorbed much of the counterinsurgency doctrine under development there. He came to Vietnam well imbued with the idea that the struggle was essentially a political one for the allegiance of the people, with military force a subordinate element in a larger effort. Upon his assumption of command, a State Department official rejoiced that "we can shift from trying to kill every Viet Cong, to protecting the Vietnamese population."[53]

Westmoreland took every occasion to emphasize to his staff and to American advisers that "the real battle here is for the people." His recommendations for strengthening the allied effort dealt with land reform and political democratization, as well as improvement of the South Vietnamese Army. He early displayed concern for the effects of heavy weaponry in populated areas, questioning "the need for the 500 pound bomb in consideration of the targets available and the essentiality of winning the allegiance of the population." Even so, like many other Americans, civilians as well as military, Westmoreland tended toward a managerial, apolitical approach to counterinsurgency. He saw no incongruity in suggesting that the "young Saigon elite" be enlisted as government political cadres in the countryside (the enemy employed peasant youths for such activities—a major ingredient in his success). His headquarters spent much of the year trying to induce the Vietnamese to adopt an American-style system for programming pacification in the provinces on the basis of "time phased requirements of manpower, money, and materiel." The effort failed because, the MACV command historian concluded, "the already overburdened Vietnamese officialdom . . . was neither responsive nor sophisticated enough to absorb it."[54]

Westmoreland began campaigning to oversee pacification support while still MACV deputy commander. He was confronted at once with the disarray in the U.S. Mission caused by Lodge's alienation from Harkins and soon joined in the general consensus that the ambassador was a poor administrator who confined his coordination efforts to dealings with a few intimates. In an effort to overcome the country team's fragmentation, Westmoreland and the Deputy Chief of Mission, David G. Nes, in February organized an ad hoc Pacification Committee made up of the deputy heads of the interested agencies. After a promising start, Ambassador Lodge in April disbanded the committee, apparently because he feared that through it Nes and Westmoreland were effectively running the mission.[55]

Meanwhile, General Stilwell, the MACV chief of staff, proposed that the MACV commander be made the ambassador's executive agent for counterinsurgency, with representatives of the civilian agencies added to the MACV staff and with composite interagency teams, headed by military senior advisers, at corps and province levels. Such an arrangement, Stilwell argued, would unify American dealings with the South Vietnamese. It would also create an American parallel to General Khanh's organization for carrying out CHIEN THANG, which consisted of a largely civilian Central Pacification Committee chaired by Khanh, with the armed forces commanders in chief in charge of implementing decisions through the corps commanders and province chiefs. Westmoreland in June urged Lodge, then nearing the end of his tenure as ambassador, to designate him as his executive agent for coordination of all American pacification support. "Some designated individual," he declared, "must be appointed to exercise initiative in getting all interested parties together so as to effect an integrated program." Westmoreland recommended, as well, employment of a variation on Stilwell's military-civilian teams to expedite pacification in the most critical provinces. Attempting to assuage civilian fears that his proposals would lead to military domination of the counterinsurgency effort, he promised that, if assigned as executive agent, he would "work through committee arrangements designed to provide a consensus in approach." Lodge received Westmoreland's proposals with interest but took no action on them before leaving his Saigon post.[56]

Ambassador Taylor likewise declined to appoint the MACV commander his executive agent for pacification. Instead, he attempted to unify the American effort by establishing a Mission Council. This body, which Taylor instituted the day he arrived in Saigon, consisted of himself, Westmoreland, Deputy Ambassador U. Alexis Johnson, the local heads of the U.S. Operations Mission and the U.S. Information Agency, and the chief of the Central Intelligence Agency's Saigon station. The group, which Taylor used as a "miniature National Security Council," met weekly to make recommendations to the ambassador on all aspects of the mission's work. Supporting the council, a coordinating committee prepared the agenda and followed up on the carrying out of decisions. It also served as a vehicle through which the member agencies could resolve problems at the working level. The Mission Council did much to bring system and order to interagency deliberations, and it also contributed to more regular concert of action with the South Vietnamese, who established a National Security Council to work with it. It did not, however, bring about complete civil-military harmony among the Americans. Contact and cooperation between the MACV staff and those of USOM and the CIA, especially, remained occasional at best. The civilian agencies resented and resisted what they considered military interference with their counterinsurgency programs. The Operations Mission, for example, objected to MACV's giving civil affairs training to its newly established district military advisory teams, even though the teams were the only Americans then working regularly at that level of Vietnamese administration.[57]

General Westmoreland came close to achieving the executive agent role he desired in the mission's most ambitious pacification campaign

Ambassador Taylor, left, *with Secretary McNamara* (© Bettman/CORBIS)

of the year: Operation HOP TAC. In early June, the embassy and MACV, concerned at increasing Viet Cong inroads in the provinces adjoining the capital, developed a proposal for bringing the pacification activities of the entire region under a unified plan, administered by a single headquarters with a parallel American advisory and support organization. At the June Honolulu conference, Lodge and Westmoreland obtained approval of this concept from Rusk and McNamara. Lodge, in his final act as Ambassador, persuaded General Khanh to adopt it. General Westmoreland, meanwhile, put a special staff headed by the III Corps Senior Adviser, Col. Jasper Wilson, to work on a detailed plan. Khanh placed his III Corps commander, General Tran Ngoc Tam, in charge of the project on the Vietnamese side; a small Vietnamese element joined Wilson's planning task force.[58]

Completed late in August, the resulting plan, named Operation HOP TAC (the Vietnamese phrase for "cooperation"), called for a unified campaign in the six contiguous provinces—Gia Dinh, Bien Hoa, Binh Duong, Hau Nghia, Long An, and Phuoc Tuy—that together encircled Saigon. Regular and territorial troops, National Police, and

Reorganizing and Reviving Pacification

civilian ministries, working in close cooperation, were to pacify this area by moving outward from the capital, the center of the "oil spot," in a series of concentric rings. Hop Tac prescribed the familiar pacification sequence of military clearing and civil reconstruction for each ring. What was distinctive about it was the concentration in the area of sizable South Vietnamese military and police reinforcements, including the entire 25th ARVN Division, transferred from II Corps, and a strengthening of the American advisory presence, both civilian and military. Advisory teams, for instance, went into every district in the target provinces. Distinctive, too, was the commitment of all South Vietnamese and American agencies to a single plan and the establishment of a special organization to direct their operations. That organization, the Hop Tac Council, chaired by General Tam, included representatives of all the involved Vietnamese commands and civilian ministries accompanied by their MACV and mission advisers. Westmoreland, as Ambassador Taylor's representative to coordinate American Hop Tac support, played the role he desired as primary executive agent for the program. He established a special unit under Maj. Robert Montague, an experienced province adviser, within MACV headquarters to watch over the effort. The general himself, and other members of his staff, intervened frequently to keep the combined offensive moving.[59]

Initiated formally in September, Hop Tac in the end produced little cooperation and less progress. Hampered by divided command, repeated political upheavals in Saigon, frequent changes of commanders and province officials, and an insufficient number of trained people, the South Vietnamese were slow to deploy their troops, police, and civilian personnel. The Vietnamese Hop Tac Council, when finally established in October, lacked effective authority over the civilian elements and had no supporting staff of its own. On the American side, the civilian agencies objected to the plan as overcentralized and claimed that its concentric phase lines bore no relationship either to available South Vietnamese resources or to the actual centers of government and insurgent strength. Viet Cong main and guerrilla forces, steadily increasing in size, effectively obstructed government operations throughout the area and in some provinces forced the South Vietnamese Army onto the defensive. Perhaps most important, the South Vietnamese essentially regarded Hop Tac as a plan their American overseers had imposed upon them. Military and civilian officials alike accorded the effort less than top priority as a result, and their local subordinates, according to Westmoreland, displayed "a noticeable lack of . . . initiative and aggressiveness." Westmoreland nevertheless regularly found evidence of slow progress in Hop Tac. He considered the Hop Tac organization, both American and Vietnamese, to be the prototype for an effective unified approach to pacification.[60]

Struggling for Stability

The U.S. Mission attributed Hop Tac's disappointing results primarily to the persistent instability of the Saigon government. General Khanh proved unable to manage the cross-currents of military and political factionalism unleashed by the removal of Diem. Instead, the mercurial would-be strongman's penchant for often self-defeating intrigue plunged him into a complex series of power struggles with Saigon politicians, the organized Buddhists, and a faction-ridden officer corps.[61]

During the late summer, fall, and winter, political conspiracies; attempted military coups; and Buddhist, Catholic, student, and labor demonstrations and riots kept Saigon in turmoil, all but paralyzing orderly administration. In August, Khanh attempted to impose a new constitution making him president with near-dictatorial powers, but he backed down in the face of Buddhist street crowds and military opposition. In late October, under an uneasy multifactional compromise, a High National Council of civilian notables installed a more or less constitutional regime with Phan Khac Suu, an elderly politician, as chief of state and Tran Van Huong, a former mayor of Saigon, as premier. Khanh retained power as chairman of the Military Revolutionary Council and armed forces commander in chief. This regime satisfied neither Khanh nor the militant Buddhists, with whom Khanh increasingly allied himself. Also discontented was a group of young generals, originally promoted by Khanh after his takeover in January. In mid-September, these generals, nicknamed the Young Turks, suppressed a coup attempt by anti-Khanh officers and from then on were the dominant element in Saigon's armed forces.

In late December the Young Turks made their bid for power. They created a new political body, the Armed Forces Council, nominally headed by Khanh; tried to abolish the High National Council; and sought to purge the officer corps of what they considered deadwood. Their actions brought them, and Khanh, into open conflict with Ambassador Taylor, who supported the Suu-Huong government in the interests of political stability. Taylor publicly scolded Khanh and the generals for their disruptive meddling in politics. The military men in turn denounced Taylor for interfering in Saigon's internal affairs. Aware he no longer was America's man in South Vietnam, Khanh aligned himself more firmly with the Buddhists, who began open rioting against the United States. After weeks of confused wrangling, the crisis ended in February 1965 with the civilian government in place but with several Young Turks in the cabinet and Dr. Phan Huy Quat, a politician acceptable to the Buddhists, serving as premier instead of Huong. At the same time, after indications from Taylor that the United States no longer supported Khanh, the Armed Forces Council dispensed with the ambitious general. They took the occasion of another failed coup attempt (which they may have stage-managed for the purpose) to remove Khanh as armed forces commander and dispatch him to exile as an ambassador-at-large. South Vietnam thus staggered into 1965 with a weak civilian regime in office but with a generals' junta holding the balance of power behind the constitutional facade. In fact, at all levels of government, military officers exercised extensive civil authority; the corps commanders, especially those remote from Saigon, were evolving into semiautonomous regional warlords.[62]

Throughout this period of turmoil, Taylor and Westmoreland struggled to maintain South Vietnamese political stability, prevent coups, and keep the Vietnamese armed forces unified and protected from partisan disruption. At Taylor's direction, Westmoreland periodically reassured the often despondent Khanh of American support and that of the South Vietnamese armed forces. On occasion, he acted as an intermediary between Khanh and other generals. During actual and rumored coups, Westmoreland, frequently after advance warning from advisers with the involved units, convened his staff at the MACV combat operations center and dispatched what he called "coup-qualified" officers to the various Vietnamese headquarters to counsel moderation and prevent military actions in conflict with American desires. On one occasion in November, Westmoreland himself talked a leading Young Turk, the Air Force chief, Marshal Nguyen Cao Ky, out of moving against the government.[63]

After the failure of Khanh's constitution in August, and again after the attempted coup of mid-September, Westmoreland and his deputy, General Throckmorton, at Taylor's behest, visited every major Vietnamese headquarters to assess troop morale and the commanders' political intentions. On these occasions, they reminded the Vietnamese generals that armed forces unity and concentration on defeating the Viet Cong were essential to South Vietnam's survival and that persistent political chaos in South Vietnam alienated American public opinion and jeopardized the continuation of U.S. military and economic aid. Westmoreland used his influence with Khanh, and later with the Young Turks, to prevent the firing of capable officers whose parties or patrons temporarily were in eclipse. He consistently urged the Vietnamese authorities to resist demands, especially from the Buddhists, for purges of senior commanders. By late 1964 Westmoreland could report success in holding the armed forces together and protecting some "highly competent" officers whose factions were out of power; but he acknowledged that "we have . . . no assurance that these gains are more than superficial or more than a lull in the storm."[64]

In the midst of the government crisis in Saigon, the Military Assistance Command had to cope with a Montagnard revolt in the Central Highlands. There, Civilian Irregular Defense Groups recruited from among the aboriginal tribesmen, whom the Vietnamese referred to as *moi* ("savages") and treated as such, but who worked well with their U.S.

Special Forces advisers, had become a mainstay of the counterinsurgency effort. On the night of 19–20 September, irregulars of the Rhade Montagnard tribe, in a carefully planned uprising, seized four camps in Darlac Province. They arrested their American advisers, killed or locked up their Vietnamese Special Forces officers, and took hostage a couple of hundred other Vietnamese soldiers and civilians. However, their planned march on the province capital, Ban Me Thuot, failed due to rapid action by the South Vietnamese 23d Division. A military standoff then developed, with the government massing forces to retake the camps.[65]

The Military Assistance Command intervened, both to rescue its imprisoned personnel and to prevent a bloody battle that would have destroyed much of the pacification program in the Central Highlands. General Westmoreland dispatched his director of operations, General DePuy, to Ban Me Thuot as his representative. To quiet perennial Vietnamese suspicions that the United States was encouraging Montagnard separatism, Westmoreland provided DePuy with a letter to the rebel leaders expressing the "strong displeasure" of the American government at their actions and threatening to cut off pay and support to CIDG units that persisted in rebellion. DePuy apparently did not actually convey this message to the Montagnards. However, with some difficulty, and at one point only after a pre-dawn dash to 23d Division headquarters, he did prevent an ARVN assault on the camps. After a tense week, the American advisers, assisted at the end by a military show of force, secured the peaceable release of the hostages and surrender of the mutineers. In subsequent negotiations, the Saigon government at least promised to alleviate some Montagnard grievances, thus ending the crisis though not removing its underlying causes.[66]

The revolt revived General Westmoreland's concern about the irregular methods and command relationships of the American Special Forces, whom both Montagnards and South Vietnamese had viewed during the troubles variously as commanders, spokesmen, and advocates of the aborigines. On 6 October, he instructed his Special Forces commander, Col. John H. Spears, to remind his troops that they were to "advise and assist" but "not to command" the CIDGs and to take every possible measure to uphold the authority of the Vietnamese military commander of each camp. In the event of any future "dissidence, disagreement, or insurrection," the Green Berets, like all other U.S. representatives, were to speak and act "in support of the Government of Vietnam."[67]

In spite of the efforts of MACV and the rest of the American country team, a year of political upheaval undermined the effectiveness of the South Vietnamese government and brought pacification to a standstill. Military commanders and civilian officials, in the capital and the provinces, were changed too frequently to master their jobs; those who did last any length of time concentrated on remaining in office rather than waging the war. Not surprisingly, all elements of the American mission agreed that the pacification campaign had stood still during

Special Forces adviser briefs Montagnard strike force. (Stars and Stripes photo)

1964, except possibly in the HOP TAC area; and even there the extent of progress was debatable. The Americans overlooked the possibility that their programs might have been too complex, and too alien to indigenous ways, for even a stable Saigon regime to implement. Instead, they blamed South Vietnamese lack of political virtue for the absence of results. Typically, General Westmoreland declared: "the conduct of the government is characterized by inefficiency, corruption, disinterest and lack of motivation"; and he ruminated upon ways to attach more stringent conditions to American aid and to place Americans more directly in charge of the execution of the counterinsurgency program. Understandably, given their frustration with their Saigon ally, the Americans by the end of 1964 were planning for, and tentatively beginning to implement, an alternative strategy: direct military pressure on North Vietnam to end its support of the southern insurgency.[68]

Notes

¹ Quote is from Memo, McNamara for the President, 21 Dec 63, sub: Vietnam Situation, box 1, NSC CF, Vietnam, LBJL. For other assessments, see *U.S.–Vietnam Relations*, sec. 4.B.4, pp. 24–25; sec. 4.C.1, pp. 8–9, 19–20, 24–25, 30–32; Rpt, Col F. P. Serong to Gen Harkins, sub: Situation in South Vietnam Following Change of Government, Nov 63, tab 37, Westmoreland Hist File 1 (30 Mar 62–Nov 63), CMH. CIA Special Rpt, "Trends of Communist Insurgency in South Vietnam," 17 Jan 64; NSF, CF Vietnam, LBJL.

² *U.S.–Vietnam Relations*, sec. 4.C.1, pp. 49–50; sec. 4.C.9(a), pp. 5, 7–8; Rpt, Serong, Situation in SVN, Nov 63, pp. 4–5, 7–8. For a summary of early military improvements, see Talking Paper, 1 Dec 63, sub: Current Operations to Achieve US Objectives in RVN, tab 1–E, Westmoreland Hist File 2 (Jan–4 Feb 64), CMH. For the Minh regime's interest in dividing the NLF, see George McT. Kahin, *Intervention: How America Became Involved in Vietnam* (New York: Knopf, 1986), pp. 182–95.

³ For events of the coup, see ODCSOPS Summary–30 January Coup–Republic of Vietnam, 30 Jan 64, Historians files, CMH. See also Taylor, *Swords and Plowshares*, p. 308. Khanh criticism of Minh government is in CIA Info Rpt, 2 Dec 63, Historians files, CMH.

⁴ Kahin, *Intervention*, pp. 194–202. Msg, CIA to SecState, JCS, and ACSI, 28 Jan 64, ACSI–Army–64, box 138, 66A3106, RG 319, NARA. Msg, Harkins MAC 0325 to Taylor, 30 Jan 64, Historians files, CMH. Msgs, Lodge Saigon 1431 to SecState, 29 Jan 64, 8 PM; Ball State Flash 1149 to Lodge, 29 Jan 64; Harkins MAC 0321 to Taylor, 30 Jan 64. All in NSF VN, LBJL. Harkins Interv, Apr 74, p. 63. For what the Americans knew of Khanh's background, see Current Intel Memo, CIA, Ofc of Current Intel, 20 Mar 64, sub: Appraisal of Gen Nguyen Khanh, Historians files, CMH.

⁵ For analysis of the early 1964 decisions, see *U.S.–Vietnam Relations*, sec. 4.B.4, pp. 33–35; sec. 4.C.1, pp. i–iv; sec. 4.C.2(a), pp. xiii–xiv. NSAM 288 was based on recommendations of Secretary McNamara. Basic documents are Memo, McNamara for the President, 16 Mar 64, sub: South Vietnam; and NSAM 288, 17 Mar 64. Both in NSC History, Presidential Decisions, Gulf of Tonkin Attacks, box 38, LBJL.

⁶ McNamara's directive is quoted from *U.S.–Vietnam Relations*, sec. 4.B.4, p. 37; see also p. 35. MACV Fact Sheet, 3 Mar 64, sub: Phaseout of U.S. Forces, Historians files, CMH. "Essentially the same" phrase is from Memo, Adams for Ch, MAAGV; Cmdr, 2d AD; CG, USASCV; and CO, HSAS, 8 Apr 64, sub: Short Range Plan for RVN, File 204–58 (201–45) Organizational Planning Files (RVNAF 1964), box 2, 69A702, RG 334, NARA.

⁷ For typical allied assessments of Viet Cong progress, see Memo, Brig Gen C. A. Youngdale, USMC, MACV J2, for Distribution, 14 Feb 64, sub: Analysis of Viet Cong Posture during Period 1 July 1963 through 31 December 1963, File 204–58 (501–03) Intel Rpt Files (64), box 3, 69A702, RG 334, NARA. Serong, Situation in South Vietnam, Nov 63, pp. 5–6. CIA Special Rpt, 17 Jan 64; Memo, Colby for Distribution, n.d., no sub. Both in LBJL.

⁸ On Viet Cong assessments, see COSVN Standing Committee Directive Discussing the Tasks for the Last Six Months of 1963, Sep 63 (doc captured in Phuoc Long Prov, 29 Apr 69), pp. 4–16, 21–22, 24; and A Party Account of the Revolutionary Movement in South Vietnam from 1954 to 1963, and A Summary of the Situation in the South from 1962 to mid-1963 (doc captured by allied forces in Opn CRIMP, early 1966), pp. 36–38, 41–55, 57–59. Both in Historians files, CMH.

⁹ The Central Committee's Ninth Plenum Resolution Discussing the Situation in South Vietnam, December 1963 (trans. version of copy captured by U.S. forces in Cam-

bodia, 13 May 70), Historians files, CMH; quotes are from pp. 16–17. For interpretations of this momentous meeting and the arguments in Hanoi preceding and following it, see Duiker, *Road to Power*, pp. 221–27; and Wallace J.Thies, *When Governments Collide: Coercion and Diplomacy in the Vietnam Conflict* (Berkeley: University of California Press, 1980), pp. 242–53.

[10] Duiker, *Road to Power*, pp. 230–32. Thies, *When Governments Collide*, pp. 253–61. War Experiences Committee, Resistance War, pp. 62–63. Douglas Pike, *Vietnam and the Soviet Union: Anatomy of an Alliance* (Boulder, Colo.: Westview Press, 1987), pp. 45–49, attaches great importance to the removal of Khruschev as opening the way for more intensive military action by North Vietnam. Capture of North Vietnamese is reported in Msg, COMUSMACV MAC 6408 to JCS and CINCPAC, 21 Jul 64, NSF VN vol. 14 Cables 7/64, Box 6; Memo, CIA, 1 Sep 64, sub: The Situation in South Vietnam, NSF VN, vol. 18, Memos 9/1–15/64, box 8. Both in LBJL.

[11] For examples of American forecasts of enemy strategy, see Memo, Colby for Distribution, 11 Feb 64, LBJL; and Special National Intelligence Estimate (SNIE), 4 Mar 64, Historians files, CMH.

[12] McNamara quote is from Memo for the President, 21 Dec 63, sub: Vietnam Situation, NSC Country File, Vietnam, box 1, LBJL. Bundy quote is from Memo, McGeorge Bundy for William Bundy, 1 May 64, NSF/Intel File, box 9, LBJL. For Harkins' dealings with Khanh, see Msg, COMUSMACV MAC 2198 to CINCPAC and JCS, 23 Mar 64, NSC Country File, Vietnam, boxes 1 and 3, LBJL. On the authority conflict, see Ltr, Lodge to Rusk, 23 Apr 64, with encls, NSC Country File, Vietnam, box 3; and Ltrs, Lodge to Rusk, 30 Apr 64, Rusk to Lodge, 7 May 64, William P. Bundy to Lodge, 8 May 64, NSF Intel File, box 9. All in LBJL.

[13] Quote is from Memo, Forrestal for Bundy, 4 Feb 64, sub: South Vietnam, NSC Country File, Vietnam, LBJL; in same file, see Memo, Forrestal for Bundy, 30 Mar 64, sub: South Vietnam. Memo, McGeorge Bundy for the President, 4 Feb 64, sub: Your Luncheon with Secs Rusk and McNamara, NSF Aides Files/M Bundy/Luncheons w Pres, vol. 1(2), LBJL; Greene Interv, 6 Jun 65, p. 4. Weede Interv, 23 Jul 73, pp. 6–7; USMACV Command History, 1964, p. 9; Msg, Taylor JCS 6023 to CINCPAC and COMUSMACV, 27 Apr 64, Historians files, CMH.

[14] Msg, President Johnson to Harkins, 27 May 64; Msg, Harkins MAC 2647 to Johnson, 28 May 64; White House Press Release: Remarks of the President and Gen Paul D. Harkins upon Presentation of the Distinguished Service Medal to Gen Harkins . . . , 24 Jun 64. All in NSC Country File, Vietnam, box 5, LBJL. For Harkins' reaction, see Greene Interv, 6 Jun 65, pp. 4–7; and Interv, MACV Historian's Office with Lt Col Richard A. Naldrett, 22 Jun 65, Historians files, CMH. On Westmoreland as acting COMUSMACV, see Ernest B. Furgurson, *Westmoreland: The Inevitable General* (Boston: Little, Brown, 1968), pp. 297–99.

[15] The standard biography is Furgurson, *Westmoreland*. For a less flattering sketch, see Halberstam, *Best and Brightest*, pp. 663–82. Westmoreland, *A Soldier Reports*, pp. 9, 27–28, 39–43, 65–67, 102, and 240, describes his introduction to Vietnam and previous involvement with counterinsurgency. Other views of Westmoreland: Palmer, *25-Year War*, p. 40; Weede Interv, 23 Jul 73, pp. 11–12. Interv, Senior Officers Debriefing Program with Gen Harold K. Johnson, 27 Jan 72–30 Oct 74, sec. 15, pp. 20–21 and sec. 16, pp. 11–12, MHI.

[16] First quote is from Ltr, Palmer to Vann, 14 Jan 64, John P. Vann Papers, MHI. Second is from Memo, Forrestal for McGeorge Bundy, 26 May 64, Historians files, CMH.

[17] *U.S.–Vietnam Relations*, sec. 4.C.1, p. 85. Taylor, *Swords and Plowshares*, pp. 313–16. For Taylor's authority, see Msg, State 20 to AmEmb Saigon, 2 Jul 64, NSC Country File, Vietnam, box 6, LBJL. Westmoreland quote is from *A Soldier Reports*, p. 68; see also p. 70.

149

[18] Rosson, "Involvement in Vietnam," pp. 193–94. On embassy personnel, see Msgs, Taylor JCS 3118–64 to Westmoreland, 24 Jun 64; and Westmoreland MAC 3173 to Taylor, 24 Jun 64. Both in Westmoreland Msg Files, 1 Jan–31 Dec 64; CMH. Taylor and MACV staff: Greene Interv, 6 Jun 65, p. 8; Sternberg Interv, p. 1. Adams Interv, p. 2. Interv, MACV Historian's Office with Maj Gen Gen Sternberg, Historians files, CMH.

[19] MFR, Col J. E. Arthur, sub: Proposed Revision of MACV Structure, with att.; Memo, ACofS, J5 for Harkins, sub: Revision of MACV Command Structure, 1 Sep 62, Taylor Papers, NDU. "Consolidation of MAAG and MACV," pp. 1–2, in MACV Historical Records, File 206–02, Historians' Background Material (1965) Files, J1 Monthly Historical Summaries, Historians files, CMH. USMACV Command History, 1964, p. 10. Stilwell Interv, 11 Jul 65, p. 2, emphasizes Harkins' continuing belief that MACV was a "short term venture," as well as his reluctance to eliminate the job of his friend, General Timmes, the MAAG chief.

[20] "Consolidation of MAAG and MACV," pp. 2–3; USMACV Command History, 1964, pp. 10–11; Ltr, Harkins to CINCPAC, Mar 64, sub: Study on Reorganization of Hq MACV and MAAG, IS 322 (11 Jul 65), Historians files, CMH. For an example of Army support, see Memo, Mock for Distribution, 12 Mar 64 sub: CINCUSARPAC Observations, with encl, Ltr, Gen J. F. Collins to CofS, 29 Feb 64, CS 320 (12 Mar 64). On Westmoreland's role, see Ltr, Stilwell to Gen Johnson, 12 Mar 64. Both in Historians files, CMH.

[21] Harkins, MACV Reorganization Study, Mar 64. "Consolidation of MAAG and MACV," pp. 3–6; USMACV Command History, 1964, pp. 11–12.

[22] Msg, CINCPAC to JCS, 22 Mar 64; 1st end., CINCPAC, to Ltr, COMUSMACV MAC J1 Ser 0415, 23 Apr 64, 1 May 64. Both in Historians files, CMH. CINCPAC Command History, 1964, p. 307. "Consolidation MAAG and MACV," pp. 6–8.

[23] "Consolidation of MAAG and MACV," p. 10; Talking Paper for the JCS for the SecDef/JCS Meeting, 6 Apr 64, sub: JCS 2343/335–5—Vietnam and Southeast Asia, J5 T–49–64, Historians files, CMH; Note by the Secretaries to the JCS on Vietnam and Southeast Asia, 8 Apr 64; Memo, Gen Taylor for SecDef, 8 Apr 64, sub: Vietnam and Southeast Asia (JCSM–288–64), Memo, McNamara for JCS, sub: MACV/MAAG Reorganization. All in IS 322 (11 Jul 65), box 1, 68A3305, RG 330, NARA.

[24] MACV Command History, 1964, pp. 12–14, 17. "Consolidation MAAG and MACV," pp. 8–14; CINCPAC Command History, 1964, pp. 307–08. Msg, COMUSMACV MAC 3067 to CINCPAC, 20 Apr 64; HQ MACV Dirs 10–2, 25 Apr 64; 35–4, 21 May 64; 35–7, 14 Jul 64. All in Historians files, CMH. Msg, COMUSMACV MAC 3700 to DA, CNO, CSAF, CMC, JCS, 6 May 64, File 204–58 (201–45) Organizational Planning Files (RVNAF) (1964), box 2, 69A702, RG 334, NARA; Stilwell Interv, 11 Jul 65, pp. 3–4.

[25] In this period, the Joint Table of Distribution of the combined MACV and MAAG headquarters included the Army, Navy, and Air Force advisory teams as well as the command and staff. Hence, before the 15 May reorganization, MACV headquarters had a strength of 387 and the MAAG—headquarters and advisers combined—included 2,892 personnel. Under the 15 May JTD, total strength, consolidated headquarters and advisers, was 3,677 and by the end of 1964 had risen to 4,889 as a result of increases in the advisory force as well as the headquarters staff. These numbers did not include the American personnel in aviation and other support units.

[26] MACV Command History, 1964, pp. 14–15, 32; ibid., 1965, pp. 74–75; CINCPAC Command History, 1964, p. 308 and Chart IV–A. JTD, HQ, MACV, 15 May 64, in Ltr, HQ, MACV, to CINCPAC, 23 Apr 64, sub: MACV 15 May 64 JTD, with 1st end., CINCPAC to JCS, 1 May 64; Msgs, JCS 7765 and 8053 to CSA, CNO, CSAF, CMC, CINCPAC, 6 and 24 Aug 64. All in Historians files, CMH.

[27] Msg, JCS 9743 to CINCPAC, 3 May 63, File 204–58 (201–45) Org Planning Files—

Reorganizing and Reviving Pacification

Functions, Missions, and Command Relationships (1963), box 1, 69A702, RG 334, NARA. Fact Sheet, MACV, 4 Mar 64, sub: Test and Evaluation Activities, in SecDef Conf MACV Notebook, Mar 64, Historians files, CMH. MACV Command History, 1965, p. 439. CINCPAC Command History, 1965, pp. 344–46; MACV Dir 70–1, 21 Apr 64, no sub, Historians files, CMH.

[28] MACV Command History, 1964, pp. 22, 52–53, 63–64, 135, 157–59; ibid., 1965, pp. 94–95. MACV Fact Sheet, 3 Mar 64, sub: Review of COMUSMACV OPLAN 34A–64/ CAS Saigon OPLAN Tiger, in SecDef Conf MACV Notebook, Mar 64, Historians files, CMH.

[29] For an example of administration concern with intelligence and reporting, see Memo, Forrestal for Bundy, 8 Jan 64, sub: Reporting on the Situation in South Vietnam, NSC Country File, Vietnam, LBJL. Memo, ACSI for CofS, 3 Feb 64, sub: Intelligence Deficiencies in SVN; Memo, Ops Br/Collection Div, 19 Mar 64, sub: Vietnam; Memo, Brig Gen D. V. Bennett for DCSOPS, 29 Apr 64, sub: USAF Representation on the MACV Staff. All in Historians files, CMH. Intervs, Marine Corps Oral History Program with Maj Gen Carl A. Youngdale, USMC (Ret.), 3 Jun 75 and 5 Mar 81, pp. 362–63, 367–69, MCHC, Washington, D.C.

[30] MACV Command History, 1964, p. 40. Youngdale had been assistant chief of staff, G–2, at Headquarters, Marine Corps, during 1961–62; he came to MACV from command of the 1st Marine Brigade in Hawaii. See biographical sketch filed with Youngdale Intervs, 3 Jun 75 and 5 Mar 81.

[31] MACV Command History, 1964, pp. 41–42, 47–48. Youngdale Interv, 5 Jun 65, pp. 7–8, 17. U.S. Military Assistance Command, Vietnam, *Intelligence Guide and Operating Procedures*, 19 Nov 64; MFR, n.d., sub: Day-to-Day Reconnaissance Plan in the RVN, Historians files, CMH.

[32] The Army attaché in Saigon had become embroiled in institutional and personality clashes with Ambassador Lodge, and with Lodge's special military assistant, Lt Col John M. Dunn. These political considerations, and McNamara's preference for a single, unified source of military reporting, sealed the fate of the attachés. See: Memo, Maj Gen E. C. Doleman, ACSI, for Dir, DIA, 7 Jan 64, sub: Operational Control of the Service Attachés in Vietnam by COMUSMACV; ACSI Talking Paper, 16 Jan 64, same sub; and Memo, Col R. C. Roth for ACSI, 16 Mar 64, sub: Transfer of USARMA Attaché Saigon Personnel to COMUSMACV. All in ACSI VN Gen File, 66A3138 3/33:36–1, Washington National Records Center (WNRC).

[33] MACV Command History, 1964, pp. 42–45; ibid., 1965, p. 465. Youngdale Interv, 5 Jun 65, pp. 5–6, 8–9, 14. Paper, "The Validity of Intelligence on the Viet Cong," ca. 1963–64, att to Memo, Ops Br/Coll Div, 19 Mar 64, sub: Vietnam, Historians files, CMH. CIA Memo, 6 Apr 64, LBJL. Youngdale discusses MACV methods of developing Viet Cong order of battle in Msg, COMUSMACV MAC 7097 to CINCPAC, 29 Jul 64, NSF VN, vol. 14 Cables 7/64, box 6, LBJL.

[34] Msg, Westmoreland to Taylor and Sec Arthur Sylvester, 8 Jun 64, tab 3, Westmoreland Hist File 6 (1 June–3 Aug 64), CMH. Hammond, *Military and Media, 1962–1968*, pp. 80–82.

[35] Memo, CINCPAC for JCS, 13 Sep 63, sub: Reports of Counterinsurgency Progress, Vietnam, box 2, 71A226, RG 334, NARA. Msg, AmEmb Saigon to State, 21 Oct 63; NSF 201 VN, vol. 20, 10/18–28/63, Memos and Misc, JFKL. Msg, State 552 to AmEmb Saigon, 9 Oct 63; MACV Dir 69, 6 Nov 63, sub: MACV Province Studies Working Group, Historians files, CMH. Msg, JCS 3689 to CINCPAC, 26 Nov 63; Msg, Nes to State, 3 Feb 64. Both in NSC Country File, Vietnam, LBJL. CINCPAC Command History, 1964, p. 355. MACV Command History, 1964, pp. 53–54.

[36] Memo, William Bundy for Nes, 16 Jan 64, tab 4, Westmoreland Hist File 2 (Jan–4 Feb 64). Memo, Chester L. Cooper for McNamara, 12 Mar 64, sub: Recommendations

151

on Intelligence Reporting, tab 14, Westmoreland Hist file 3 (17 Feb–30 Apr 64). Memo, Cooper for Sullivan, 24 Feb 64, sub: Washington Requirements for Reporting on the War . . . Historians files, CMH; SecDef Conf, MACV Notebook, Mar 64; Memo, Westmoreland for Mission Council, n.d., sub: Summary of MACV Reports to Higher Headquarters. All in Historians files, CMH. Msg, Saigon 1925 to SecState, 7 Apr 64. Both in NSC Country File, Vietnam, Boxes 1 and 3, LBJL. MACV Command History, 1964, pp. 53–56. COC quote is from Interv, author with Paul E. Suplizio, 17 and 24 Jul 86, tape 1, side 2, CMH.

[37] Quote is from Ltr, Stilwell to Gen Johnson, 12 Mar 64, Historians files, CMH. MACV Command History, 1964, pp. 54–56; *U.S.–Vietnam Relations*, sec. 4.C.1, p. 86. For an example of Westmoreland's reports to Taylor, see his Memo for Taylor, 8 Oct 64, sub: Monthly Assessment of Military Activity, September 1964, tab 65, Westmoreland Hist File 8 (1 Sep–8 Oct 64), CMH. Fact Sheet, Requirement for Reporting on Effectiveness of RVNAF Units and Leaders, in File 204–58(1001–09), Trng Op Files (65), box 3, 69A702, RG 334, NARA.

[38] First quote is from Westmoreland MAC 2217 to Taylor, 6 May 64, Westmoreland Msg Files, 1 Jan–31 Dec 64, CMH. Second is from Greene Interv, 6 Jun 65, p. 24; see also pp. 26–27. MACV Command History, 1964, pp. 16–17; ibid.,1965, p. 92. MFR, Taylor, 15 May 64, sub: Discussion in Joint Chiefs of Staff of a Deputy COMUSMACV; Fact Sheet, n.d., sub: MACV 15 May 64 JTD; Taylor Papers, NDU. Msgs, Felt to Taylor, 7 May 64; and Wheeler WDC 4138 to Westmoreland, 20 Jun 64; Westmoreland Msg Files, 1 Jan–31 Dec 64, CMH. Hammond, *Military and Media, 1968–1973*, pp. 83–85. Memo, Brig Gen D. V. Bennett for DSCOPS, 29 Apr 64, sub: USAF Representation on the MACV Staff, Historians files, CMH.

[39] Futrell, *Advisory Years*, pp. 207–25; Adams Interv, p. 8. MACV Command History, 1964, pp. 85, 88. Msg, JCS 4661 to CINCPAC, 1 Feb 64; Ltr, CINCUSAF to JCS, 8 Apr 64, with encl. "Comments on Topics Discussed at Keehi Beach Meeting, 12 Mar 64," p. 3. Both in Historians files, CMH; Ltr, Adm Sharp to Westmoreland, 10 Oct 64, tab 53, Westmoreland Hist File 8 (1 Sep–8 Oct 64), CMH. Suplizio Intverv, 17 and 24 Jul 86, tape. 1, side 1, comments on the limited USAF representation in the MACV combat operations center.

[40] Quote is from Ltr, Wheeler to Westmoreland, 17 Sep 64, tab 23, Westmoreland Hist File 8 (1 Sep–8 Oct 64), CMH. Westmoreland, *A Soldier Reports*, pp. 86–87. Ltr, Moore to Westmoreland, 30 May 64, in Book of Misc Facts, box 1, 67A4064, RG 334, NARA; Ltr, Sharp to Westmoreland, 10 Sep 64, tab 15, Westmoreland Hist File 8 (1 Sep–8 Oct 64), CMH. Msgs, Wheeler JCS 3687–64, 3784–64 to Westmoreland, 28, 31 Jul 64, Westmoreland Msg Files, 1 Jan–31 Dec 64, CMH. Media and Congress: Hammond, *Military and Media 1962–1968*, pp. 76–78; Ltr, Sen John Stennis to McNamara, 9 Jul 64, with atts., tab 25, Westmoreland Hist File 6 (1 June–3 Aug 64), CMH. Msg, Westmoreland MAC 6373 to Wheeler, 9 Dec 64, Westmoreland Msg Files, 1 Jan–31 Dec 64, CMH.

[41] Msgs, Wheeler JCS 4371, 4409 to Westmoreland, 3 and 5 Sep 64; Gen Johnson WDC 5880 to Westmoreland, 3 Sep 64. Both in Westmoreland Msg Files, 1 Jan–31 Dec 64, CMH.

[42] Quote is from Msg, Westmoreland MAC 4790 to Wheeler, 4 Sep 64, Westmoreland Msg Files, 1 Jan–31 Dec 64, CMH. In same file, see Msgs, Westmoreland MAC 5335, 5549 to Wheeler, 3, 19 Oct 64; Sharp to Westmoreland, 6 Sep 64, 9 Oct 64; Wheeler JCS 4522, 4795 to Westmoreland, 14 Sep 64, 15 Oct 64; Wheeler DIASO–4 4726–64 to Sharp, 6 Oct 64. Ltr, Wheeler to Westmoreland, 17 Sep 64, tab 23, Westmoreland Hist File 8 (1 Sep–8 Oct 64), CMH. MACV Command History, 1965, p. 93.

[43] *U.S.–Vietnam Relations*, sec. 4.B.3, pp. 43–49, 54. Msgs, JCS 6473 and 6468 to

Reorganizing and Reviving Pacification

CINCPAC, 25 May 64; CINCPAC to JCS, 23 and 27 May, 64; COMUSMACV MAC 4259 to CINCPAC, 27 May 64. All in NSC Country File, Vietnam, Box 5, LBJL. Msg, State 2095 to AmEmb Saigon, 27 May 64, in COMUSMACV Book of Misc Facts, box 1, 67A4604, RG 334, NARA; MACV Command History, 1964, p. 76.

[44] MACV Command History, 1964, pp. 15–16, 56–61; ibid., 1965, pp. 75–76. *U.S.–Vietnam Relations*, sec. 4.B.3, pp. 50–55; sec. 4.B.4, pp. 37–39. Msgs COMUSMACV MAC 4460 to CINCPAC, 1 Jun 64; Rusk State 205 to AmEmb Saigon, 21 Jul 64. Both in NSC Country File, Vietnam, Boxes 5 and 6, LBJL. Msgs, COMUSMACV MAC 16180 to CINCPAC, 16 Jul 64; Taylor Saigon 125 to SecState, 17 Jul 64; CINCPAC to JCS, 20 Jul 64. All in Historians files, CMH. MFRs, Westmoreland, 22 and 23 Jul 64, sub: Meeting with Gen Khiem, tab 20, Westmoreland Hist File 6 (1 Jun–3 Aug 64), CMH.

[45] South Vietnamese Special Forces command arrangements paralleled the American, with the corps commander exercising operational control. *U.S.–Vietnam Relations*, sec. 4.C.1, p. 73. Fact Sheet for Sec Army, sub: Command and Operational Control of U.S. Army Special Forces in the RVN, File OSA 000.76 Vietnam, 6/23/64, Historians files, CMH. Westmoreland's concern about Special Forces command arrangements is expressed in the following, from which the quotes are taken: Memo for Spec Fcs Cmd, Apr 64, sub: Basis for Discussion of Special Forces Employment, tab 25, Westmoreland Hist File 3 (17 Feb–30 Apr 64), CMH; MACV Command History, 1964, pp. 56–57, 90; Kelly, *Special Forces*, pp. 46–49, 64–74.

[46] McNamara quotes are from Youngdale Interv, 3 Jun 75 and 5 Mar 75, pp. 361–63. Memo, President Johnson for Taylor, 2 Dec 63; Memo, Taylor for President, 6 Dec 63, sub: Assignment of Personnel to South Vietnam; Msg, COMUSMACV MAC 9407 to JCS, 8 Dec 63. All in NSC Country File, Vietnam, LBJL. MACV Command History, 1964, pp. 17–18. Talking Paper, sub: Quality of Military Personnel in Vietnam, tab 1, Westmoreland Hist File 6 (1 Jun–3 Aug 64), CMH. Greene Interv, 6 Jun 65, pp. 28–29, recalls confusion caused by the new criteria.

[47] Quotes are from Westmoreland, "Notes upon Taking Command," tab 29, Westmoreland Hist File 6 (1 Jun–3 Aug 64), CMH. In same historical file, see "Notes on Talk to Officers (Senior Advisers from Field) on Taking Command," Jun 64, tab 29; Ltrs, Westmoreland to All Officers and Men of USMACV, 20 Jun 64, tab 8; to Component Commanders and Senior Advisers, Jul 64, tab 14; and to various correspondents, 22 Jun 64, tab 10; HQ, MACV Dir 360–3, 2 Jul 64, tab 14. Hammond, *Military and Media, 1962–1968*, p. 82. Stilwell Interv, 11 Jul 65, p. 3.

[48] MACV Command History, 1964, p. 9. MACV Dir 10–8, 22 Oct 64, tab 15, Westmoreland Hist File 6 (1 Jun–3 Aug 64), CMH. Quote is from Greene Interv, 6 Jun 65, p. 25; see also pp. 10–11, 14, 17, 22–26. Stilwell Interv, 11 Jul 65, pp. 3–4; Naldrett Interv, 22 Jun 65, pp. 2–4; Youngdale Interv, 5 Jun 65, pp. 25–26; Suplizio Interv, 17 and 24 Jul 86, tape 1, sides 1 and 2; tape 4, side 1; Adams Interv, pp. 5–6, 17. Sternberg Interv, Historians files, CMH, pp. 4–5. Interv, Senior Officers Debriefing Program with Gen William B. Rosson, 1981, p. 328, MHI, notes Westmoreland's emphasis on anticipatory planning.

[49] Office locations are specified in MACV Dir 10–2, 25 Apr 64, Historians files, CMH. MACV Command History, 1964, pp. 140–41, 175; CINCPAC Command History, 1965, p. 537. Westmoreland, *A Soldier Reports* pp. 247–48; Suplizio Interv, 17 and 24 Jul 86, tape 1, side 1; tape 3, side 2; Adams Interv, pp. 5–6.

[50] Quote is from MACV Command History, 1964, p. 19; see also p. 18. Adams Interv, pp. 6, 15; 17 and 24 Jul 86, tape 3, sides 1 and 2; Col Francis F. Parry, "The War Generation," pt. 4, p. 7, in Parry Family Papers, MHI; Youngdale Interv, 3 Jun 75 and 5 Mar 81, pp. 13, 15, 22. Msg, COMUSMACV MAC 1120 to OSD, 13 Feb 64, Historians files, CMH.

[51] Msg, COMUSMACV MAC 0196 to CINCPAC, 9 Jan 64; Talking Paper, 30 Nov 63, sub: Additional Actions Which Could Be Taken to Facilitate Attainment of US Objectives in SVN, tabs 1–C and 1–E, Westmoreland Hist File 2 (Jan 64–4 Feb 64), CMH. Msgs, CINCPAC to JCS, 25 Jan 64; COMUSMACV MAC 1266 to CINCPAC, 19 Feb 64; Lodge Saigon 2331 to SecState, 28 May 64. All in NSC Country File, Vietnam, Boxes 1, 2, and 5, LBJL. CHIEN THANG Plan, 22 Feb 64, Historians files, CMH; MACV Command History, 1964, pp. 64–65.

[52] The original thirteen were Quang Ngai, Quang Tin, Binh Dinh, Dinh Tuong, Phuoc Thanh, Binh Duong, Tay Ninh, Hau Nghia, Long An, Kien Hoa, Kien Tuong, Chuong Thien, and An Xuyen. Evolution of the list is reviewed in Msg, Taylor Saigon 338 to SecState, 7 Aug 64, Historians files, CMH. Msg, SecDef to Lodge,12 Dec 63; Msg, Defense 934322 to CINCPAC, 21 Dec 63; Msg, AmEmb Saigon 1925 to SecState, 7 Apr 64; Msg, State/DOD/CIA/AID State 1674 to Lodge, 11 Apr 64. All in NSC Country File, Vietnam, LBJL. *U.S.–Vietnam Relations*, sec. 4.C.1, pp. 17–19, 81–82.

[53] Summary Record of the Meeting on Southeast Asia, Cabinet Room, June 10, 1964, 5:30 PM. . . . , NSC File—Files of McGeorge Bundy, LBJL.

[54] First Westmoreland quote is from Notes to Advisers on Day of Takeover, Historians files, CMH. Quote on bombs is from Memo, Westmoreland for Ch, JRATA, 1 May 64, sub: Type of Ordnance Being Used in South Vietnam, tab 5, Westmoreland Hist File 5 (6–30 May 64), CMH. Directive to All Officers and Men, USMACV, 1 Oct 64, sub: Civic Action in Vietnam, tab 49, Westmoreland Hist File 8 (1 Sep–8 Oct 64); Memo, Westmoreland for Taylor, 8 Dec 64, sub: Comments on Talking Paper re Strengthening the GVN, tab 6, Westmoreland Hist File 11 (7–31 Dec 64). All in CMH. The programming effort is recounted in MACV Command History, 1964, pp. 66–67.

[55] Westmoreland, *A Soldier Reports*, pp. 68–70. The rise and fall of the Nes Committee are traced in tab 9, Westmoreland Hist File 2 (Jan–4 Feb 64), CMH; and in tabs 4, 6, 10, 11, and 22, Westmoreland Hist File 3 (17 Feb–30 Apr 64). All in CMH.

[56] Paper, Stilwell, 10 Mar 64, sub: Counterinsurgency Vitalization, tab 13, Westmoreland Hist File 3 (17 Feb–30 Apr 64), CMH. Msg, COMUSMACV MAC 1370 to CINCPAC, 23 Feb 64, NSC Country File Vietnam, Box 2, LBJL, describes Khanh's organization. Msg, Westmoreland MAC 2815 to Taylor, 6 Jun 64, Westmoreland Msg Files, 1 Jan–31 Dec 64, CMH. Quote is from Memo, Westmoreland for Mr. Hurt, Dep Dir, USOM, 29 Jun 64, tab 9; see also MACV Draft Working Paper, 2 Jun 64, sub: United States–Vietnamese Province Task Force Executive and Administrative Mission . . . , tab 2. Both in Westmoreland Hist File 6 (1 Jun–3 Aug 64), CMH.

[57] *U.S.–Vietnam Relations*, sec. 4.C.1, pp. 86–87; sec. 4.C.8, pp. 8, 21–22. Taylor, *Swords and Plowshares*, pp. 317–18. Eckhardt, *Command and Control*, p. 48. Msg, Taylor Saigon 41 to SecState, 7 Jul 64, NSC Country File, Vietnam, Box 6, LBJL. Mission Council Action Memo 1, tab 16, Westmoreland Hist File 6 (1 June–3 Aug 64), CMH. Suplizio Interv, 17 and 24 Jul 86, tape 4, side 1; Sternberg Interv, pp. 1–3. On district advisers, see Memos, James S. Killen for Westmoreland, 27 Aug 64; Westmoreland for Killen, 2 Sep 64, sub: Terms of Reference; tab 8, Westmoreland Hist File 8 (1 Sep–8 Oct 64), CMH.

[58] MACV Command History, 1964, p. 68; *U.S.–Vietnam Relations*, sec. 4.B.3, pp. 66–67; sec. 4.C.8, p. 1. Talking Paper for Gen Westmoreland with Gen Khanh, sub: Task Force for Coordination of Pacification in the Area of Saigon, tab 7, Westmoreland Hist File 6 (1 Jun–3 Aug 64); Memo, Westmoreland for Taylor, 14 Nov 64, sub: Assumption by the US of Operational Control of the Pacification Program . . . , tab 3, Westmoreland Hist File 10 (14 Nov–7 Dec 64). Both in CMH. Msg, COMUSMACV MAC 5423 to CJCS, 25 Jun 64, NSC Country File, Vietnam, LBJL. MACV Fact Sheet, 19 Jun 64, sub: Combined GVN–US Effort to Intensify Pacification Efforts in Critical Provinces. Historians files, CMH.

Reorganizing and Reviving Pacification

⁵⁹ MACV Command History, 1964, p. 68; ibid., 1965, pp. 231–32; *U.S.–Vietnam Relations*, sec. 4.C.8, pp. 1–2. MFR, Col M. J. L. Greene, 9 Sep 64, sub: Hop Tac Briefing, tab 14; Msg, Taylor to SecState, 18 Sep 64, tab 28. Both in Westmoreland Hist File 8 (1 Sep–8 Oct 64), CMH. Memo, Westmoreland for Taylor, 19 Oct 64, sub: Weekly Assessment of Military Activity . . . , tab 14, Westmoreland Hist File 9 (9 Oct–13 Nov 64); Memo, Westmoreland for Taylor, 14 Nov 64, sub: Assumption by US of Operational Control of the Pacification Program . . . , tab 3, Westmoreland Hist File 10 (14 Nov–7 Dec 64). All in CMH. Suplizio Interv, 17 and 24 Jul 86, tape 4, side 1.

⁶⁰ For varying assessments of Hop Tac, see *U.S.–Vietnam Relations*, sec. 4.B.3, pp. 67–69; sec. 4.C.8, pp. 2–5; MACV Command History, 1964, p. 68; Westmoreland, *A Soldier Reports*, pp. 84–86. Westmoreland quote is from Memo for Taylor, 18 Jan 65, sub: Weekly Assessment of Military Activity . . . , tab 26, Westmoreland Hist File 12 (1–22 Jan 65), CMH; in same file, see tab 7. Westmoreland sees progress in Msgs MAC 4830 and 6191 to Wheeler and Sharp, 6 Sep 64 and 28 Nov 64, Westmoreland Msg Files, 1 Jan–31 Dec 64, CMH.

⁶¹ Typical American views of the effect of government instability on the counterinsurgency effort, and of the sources of that instability, can be found in Msg, Taylor Saigon 377 to President and SecState, 10 Aug 64; and U.S. Intelligence Board, Special National Intelligence Estimate (SNIE), 8 Sep 64. Both in Historians files, CMH.

⁶² *U.S.–Vietnam Relations*, sec. 4.C.1, pp. 88–98, 102; sec. 4.C.2(c), pp. 69–72, 79–80; sec. 4.C.3, p. 53; sec. 4.C.9(a), pp. i–ii, 54–66; Taylor, *Swords and Plowshares*, pp. 317–37. Memo, Brig Gen William E. DePuy for Westmoreland, 26 Feb 65, sub: The Armed Forces Council, William E. DePuy Papers, MHI, evaluates that political body from the MACV perspective. MACV Command History, 1964, pp. 2–5, describes the civil functions of South Vietnamese military commanders.

⁶³ *U.S.–Vietnam Relations*, sec. 4.C.1, pp. 56–58, 60, 63–64, 95; sec. 4.C.9(a), pp. vi, 50; Taylor, *Swords and Plowshares*, pp. 318, 355–56. MACV Command History, 1964, p. 42; Youngdale Interv, 5 Jun 65, p. 2; Suplizio Interv, 17 and 24 Jul 86, tape 1, sides 1 and 2; and Greene Interv, 6 Jun 65, p. 23, recount MACV's efforts to keep track of coup activity. Westmoreland, *A Soldier Reports*, pp. 62–74, 90–98, gives his version of coup events. Westmoreland's contacts with the Vietnamese generals on a variety of matters can be sampled in his Historical Files, Jun 64–Feb 65, CMH. Memo, Maj W. E. LeGro, 27 Aug 64, sub: Changes in Government, Vietnam, with att. Resume of Questions and Answers, Telecon with Gen Westmoreland, 25 Aug 64, Historians files, CMH.

⁶⁴ Quote is from Msg, Westmoreland MAC 6191 to Wheeler, 28 Nov 64, Westmoreland Msg Files, 1 Jan–31 Dec 64, CMH; in same file, Msg, Westmoreland MAC 4830 to Wheeler, 6 Sep 64. Msgs, Westmoreland MAC 0961 and 0985 to Wheeler, 24 Feb 65, Westmoreland Msg Files, 1 Jan–31 Mar 65, CMH. Memo, Westmoreland for Taylor, 14 Sep 64, sub: Military Personnel to be Contacted, tab 18; "Discussion with Senior Officers of the RVNAF," Sep 64, tab 34; Memo, Westmoreland for Taylor, 1 Oct 64, sub: Your Memorandum of September 16th . . . ; tab 52, Westmoreland Hist File 8 (1 Sep–8 Oct 64), CMH.

⁶⁵ MACV Command History, 1964, pp. 122–24. Kelly, *Special Forces*, pp. 63–64. Westmoreland, *A Soldier Reports*, pp. 77–80.

⁶⁶ Ltr, Westmoreland to Gen Khanh, 25 Sep 64, tab 39, Westmoreland Hist File 8 (1 Sep–8 Oct 64), CMH. DePuy's account of his mission is in Romie L. Brownlee and William J. Mullen III, *Changing an Army: An Oral History of General William E. DePuy, USA Retired* (Washington, D.C.: Military History Institute and Center of Military History, 1988), pp. 126–28;. Negotiations are recounted in Kelly, *Special Forces*, p. 64.

⁶⁷ Memo, Westmoreland for Col John H. Spears, 6 Oct 64, sub: Mission and Command Relationships, tab 62, Westmoreland Hist File 8 (1 Sep–8 Oct 64), CMH.

155

[68] Quote is from Memo, Westmoreland for Taylor, 31 Oct 64, sub: U.S. Posture toward the Emerging GVN, tab 24, Westmoreland Hist File 9 (9 Oct–13 Nov 64), CMH. See also, Memo, Westmoreland for Taylor, 14 Nov 64, sub: Assumption by U.S. of Operational Control of the Pacification Program in SVN, tab 3, Westmoreland Hist File 10 (14 Nov–7 Dec 64), CMH. For examples of U.S. pessimism, see *U.S.–Vietnam Relations*, sec. 4.C.1, p. 98; sec. 4.C.3, pp. 9–11; sec. 4.C.9(a), pp. i–ii. For views that American programs were unrealistic at best, see MACV Command History, 1964, p. 125; also pp. 68–69 and Paper, Earl J. Young, 31 Jul 64 sub: Strategic Hamlet Program in Long An Prov, Historians files, CMH.

5

The Beginning of Escalation

During 1964 the Johnson administration slowly moved toward a decision to implement the second track of NSAM 288: carrying the war to North Vietnam. From the beginning of the enlarged American role in the conflict, the Joint Chiefs of Staff had favored direct use of U.S. forces against the insurgency's support base. The president and his civilian advisers gradually came around to their point of view, as did Ambassadors Lodge and Taylor. Different advisers at different times held varying views on the reasons for going north, on the manner of doing so, and on the results to be expected. The Joint Chiefs consistently advocated heavy air strikes aimed at destroying Hanoi's will and ability to support the southern insurgency; Lodge, Taylor, and many State and Defense Department civilians believed that a more limited campaign would bring the war's costs home to the North Vietnamese leaders and result in negotiations on acceptable terms. Officials also argued that bombing the north would strengthen South Vietnamese confidence in America's commitment to the struggle and that the prospect of such operations would constitute an additional inducement to the Saigon leaders to stabilize and reform their government. Finally, as the pacification effort floundered and seemed headed for defeat, attacks on the north came to be seen as the only additional expedient available for halting, and perhaps reversing, the adverse course of events. Ambassador Taylor declared early in January 1965: "We are presently on a losing track and must risk a change. . . . The game needs to be opened up and new opportunities offered for new breaks which hopefully may be in our favor."[1]

Widening the War

President Johnson edged into escalation a step at a time, his apparent doubts about its effectiveness reinforced by election campaign politics and by a desire to have something resembling a stable government in place in Saigon before attacking North Vietnam in force.[2] During the first half of 1964, the president combined diplomatic warnings to Hanoi with the launching of a not very successful campaign of small-scale South Vietnamese maritime and airborne commando raids into the north. In May he authorized limited American air operations in Laos, both to counter a new Pathet Lao offensive and to reconnoiter and harass the Ho Chi Minh Trail. At the same time, the Joint Chiefs, the Pacific Command, and MACV began contingency planning for American and South Vietnamese air attacks on North Vietnam.

Those plans received their initial implementation in August, with Navy air raids in retaliation for North Vietnamese attacks on U.S. destroyers in the Gulf of Tonkin. President Johnson took this occasion to secure from Congress, on 7 August, a resolution authorizing him to "take all necessary steps, including the use of armed force," to assist any Southeast Asian nation threatened by Communist aggression. Yet the cautious Johnson delayed decisive action until well after his reelection. Following a climactic civilian-military policy review in late November, the president early in December committed himself to a two-phase program. The first phase was to consist of continued commando raids, intensified air operations in Laos, and bombing of North Vietnam in reprisal for major Viet Cong depredations in the south. At the same time, the United States and South Vietnam were to plan together for the second phase—a campaign of gradually intensifying air strikes against the north, to be launched once the Saigon government met certain minimum requirements for stability and effectiveness.

The Military Assistance Command played a major part in the planning and execution of each escalatory step. However, throughout 1964, Generals Harkins and Westmoreland took a conservative attitude toward expansion of the conflict, and especially toward attacking North Vietnam. Both commanders assessed South Vietnam's short-term prospects for survival more optimistically than did other American officials; they believed that with a stable, reasonably efficient government, the South Vietnamese could beat the Viet Cong on their own ground. Conversely, they feared that premature assaults on the north would provoke strong Communist retaliation in the south before Saigon was prepared to counter it. Both commanders also insisted that even if Hanoi could be forced to reduce or halt its support of the insurgency, the struggle in the south for control of the people still would decide the issue.

In May, during early discussions of going north, General Harkins commented: "Declarations of war, bombing of North Vietnam and the other peripheral actions proposed or discussed can only be helpful after the GVN has demonstrated by concrete results its . . . capability to win the pacification campaign on the home grounds." General Westmoreland strongly supported commando raids on North Vietnam and air and ground operations in Laos against the Ho Chi Minh Trail. He also favored air reprisals against the north for major Viet Cong attacks on American installations. Nevertheless, until early 1965 he urged that the United States delay any sustained campaign against the north until the South Vietnamese had achieved a measure of governmental stability

The Beginning of Escalation

Aerial view of Bien Hoa Air Base after a Communist mortar attack (AP photo)

and were militarily better prepared to defeat any Communist counterescalation. "We must assure ourselves that [the] GVN is established on [a] reasonably firm political, military and psychological base," he declared on 27 November, "before we risk the great strains that may be incurred by vigorous external operations." Consistent with his view on reprisals, Westmoreland supported Ambassador Taylor's unsuccessful calls for a forceful U.S. response to the Viet Cong's destructive mortaring of Bien Hoa Air Base in November and the blowing up of the Brink Hotel (which was serving as a bachelor officers quarters) in Saigon the following month. At the end of the year, in the light of continuing political upheaval in Saigon, the MACV commander finally joined the ambassador in recommending an immediate bombing campaign. He recalled later that, "like Ambassador Taylor, . . . I could see no viable alternative within current policy restrictions and a reasonable time frame."[3]

OPLAN 34A

The Military Assistance Command planned and conducted a program of covert South Vietnamese airborne and amphibious raids into North Vietnam. Pacific Command had developed the concept for these operations in mid-1963, expanding on a Central Intelligence Agency effort carried on, without much effect, during the previous two years. At a Honolulu conference shortly after Diem's overthrow, Secretary Mc-

Namara reviewed CINCPAC's concept and directed MACV and the CIA jointly to prepare a detailed twelve-month plan for implementing it.[4]

The two agencies completed their Operation Plan (OPLAN) 34A in mid-December. They proposed a total of over 2,000 activities, in three ascending categories of scale and severity, to include reconnaissance, psychological warfare, and sabotage operations as well as small-scale military attacks. All were to be conducted by South Vietnamese air, ground, and naval units supplemented by Asian, mostly Chinese Nationalist, mercenaries. MACV and the CIA would furnish equipment, advisers, and base facilities within South Vietnam; but no Americans were to enter North Vietnam. After an interdepartmental committee in Washington reviewed the plan and refined the proposed list of actions, President Johnson on 16 January 1964 authorized commencement of the first, most limited, phase of OPLAN 34A on 1 February. Ambassador Lodge and General Harkins then secured South Vietnamese approval of the plan—an essential step since the Saigon government would furnish most of the forces involved.[5]

Aside from a jurisdictional dispute over responsibility for certain agency-run activities along the North Vietnam–Laos border, the Military Assistance Command and the Central Intelligence Agency cooperated with little difficulty in carrying out OPLAN 34A. To conduct the commando operations, General Harkins in March established the Special Operations Group, later retitled Studies and Observations Group, within MACV headquarters. Headed by an Army colonel with a CIA deputy and with an initial strength of 99 military people and 31 civilians, the group commanded the American personnel engaged in 34A and other special operations and advised, assisted, and supported the South Vietnamese armed forces in planning and carrying out the missions. Although the MACV commander had operational control of SOG, final implementing authority for its activities rested elsewhere. On the basis of monthly lists of activities recommended by MACV, the Defense Department, in consultation with the White House and State Department, made the final selections of operations to be conducted and retained a veto over the launching of every raid.[6]

Operations under OPLAN 34A began slowly and initially produced only meager results, due to shortages of equipment and inadequately trained, undermotivated personnel. However, they gradually expanded in number and destructiveness. By mid-1964, besides a variety of propaganda and psychological warfare activities, they included small amphibious raids and bombardments of shore targets by fast armed motorboats. In August, the Tonkin Gulf incident, which grew out of the 34A raids, caused the United States to suspend the operations and temporarily to shift the maritime forces involved from their base at Da Nang farther south to Cam Ranh Bay. The allies resumed the attacks early in October, but the stormy weather of the northeast monsoon limited their number and effectiveness. As 1964 ended, nevertheless, the headquarters in Honolulu and Saigon were planning for continuation of the program, to include additional shore attacks and capture of North Vietnamese naval and civilian vessels. The Johnson administration at the same time granted Westmoreland more flexibility in scheduling activities on the monthly approved list. The MACV commander favored keeping up the incursions, without publicly acknowledging them, less for their military effect than for the display they made of American determination and their potential as a "real boost" to South Vietnamese morale.[7]

Air and Ground Operations in Laos

Simultaneously with its preparations for 34A operations, the Military Assistance Command in cooperation with South Vietnamese forces developed a series of plans for ground reconnaissance, harassment, and blockage of the enemy's supply routes through the panhandle of southern Laos. MACV badly needed information about Viet Cong infiltration and base construction in the area, but most sources for intelligence of that sort had dried up after the Geneva Accords of mid-1962. Early in 1964 the command reoriented the Special Forces' CIDG program toward border surveillance, and it sought the opportunity to use these and other forces to penetrate Laos. That became possible in March 1964 when Laotian Premier Souvanna Phouma, as part of a reestablishment of diplomatic relations with South Vietnam, granted Saigon's forces the right to conduct limited air and ground operations in the panhandle against the common enemy. About the same time, the Defense Department and the CIA agreed to transfer the agency's remaining paramilitary activities in southern Laos to MACV's control.[8]

To take advantage of the emerging opportunity, the MACV J5 section developed plans during March for employing patrols and aerial surveillance to locate enemy forces in the panhandle and then larger ground attacks and air strikes to disrupt their activities. At Secretary McNamara's recommendation, President Johnson in mid-March incorporated incursions into Laos into NSAM 288, his first major Vietnam policy directive. However, Ambassador Leonard Unger in Vientiane objected to operations on any but the smallest scale to avoid upsetting the fragile Laotian balance of power. Eventually, he agreed to the launching of covert six-man reconnaissance patrols, inserted and withdrawn by air. Early in May, at the direction of the Joint Chiefs, the Military Assistance Command and the South Vietnamese high command began combined preparation for these operations, code-named Leaping Lena. The American and South Vietnamese Special Forces headquarters, coordinated by MACV's Intelligence Directorate, did the detail work. The allies set up training facilities at Nha Trang for the personnel, selected from the South Vietnamese Special Forces, and dispatched their first five teams across the border on 24–25 June. At the same time, they began planning for more ambitious overt company- and battalion-size cross-border incursions, to involve regular infantry elements from I and II Corps as well as the Special Forces.[9]

These plans and preparations came to naught. The Vietnamese Special Forces (VNSF), which had suffered severe disruption in the aftermath of Diem's overthrow, lacked the leadership, training, and motivation for the airborne operations originally contemplated. Most members of the first teams inserted were lost or straggled back to South Vietnam on foot after obtaining no significant information. VNSF leadership deficiencies meanwhile gave rise to riots among the troops at the Nha Trang base that set back preparations for the entire program. MACV and the Joint General Staff then shifted to planning for limited incursions on foot by CIDG elements, with possible larger ground offensives to follow. However, continued disagreements with the Vientiane embassy, the South Vietnamese political upheavals, and the Montagnard revolt prevented any significant action. In late October, General Westmoreland had to report to the Joint Chiefs that the South Vietnamese could not undertake cross-border operations before 1 January 1965. For the rest of the year, the allies' harassment of the Ho Chi Minh Trail was limited to occasional strikes by T–28s from the Royal Laotian Air Force with U.S. Air Force combat air patrols flying cover.[10]

In contrast to the stumbling pace of ground operations, American air activity over Laos expanded rapidly during 1964. Early in May the administration, with Souvanna Phouma's acquiescence, directed MACV to conduct low-level reconnaissance flights with Air Force and Navy jets over the panhandle and over the Plain of Jars in northern Laos, the major battlefield of the Royal Laotian and Pathet Lao forces. Besides providing MACV with information on enemy infiltration into South Vietnam, these missions, code-named YANKEE TEAM, were to furnish intelligence to friendly Laotians and demonstrate to both allies and enemies U.S. resolve in Southeast Asia. General Westmoreland, through the 2d Air Division, coordinated YANKEE TEAM operations, which involved Thailand-based Air Force RF–101s and Navy RF–8As from carriers in the South China Sea. He allocated sorties in response to his own intelligence requirements, and to those of the Joint Chiefs, the Pacific Command, and the American embassy in Vientiane.[11]

Begun as a reconnaissance program, YANKEE TEAM soon took on a more lethal aspect. In June, after Pathet Lao gunners shot down a Navy jet over the Plain of Jars, fighter escorts began accompanying YANKEE TEAM missions. They conducted suppressive strikes against Communist positions and, after the Tonkin Gulf incident, were authorized to engage any enemy planes that interfered with the operations. In August, General Westmoreland recommended expansion of YANKEE TEAM to include outright attacks in the panhandle by Vietnamese Air Force and FARM GATE planes. The State Department vetoed this proposal, on the familiar grounds that the raids would excessively compromise Souvanna's increasingly pro forma neutrality, but later in the fall agreed to operations by Laotian aircraft with YANKEE TEAM escorts. Finally, on 12 December, as part of President Johnson's program of increased pressure on North Vietnam, the United States inaugurated Operation BARREL ROLL, a campaign of deliberate air attacks against enemy troops, infiltration routes, and installations throughout the panhandle and Plain of Jars. As with YANKEE TEAM, General Westmoreland acted as CINCPAC's coordinator for these missions, but CINCPAC and the Joint Chiefs occasionally intervened in matters of operational detail. By the end of the year, American aircraft had flown more than 1,500 sorties over Laos, all but a handful under YANKEE TEAM.[12]

Ambassador Sullivan
(© Bettmann/CORBIS photo)

As coordinator of YANKEE TEAM and BARREL ROLL, and as planner and potential executor of cross-border ground incursions, Westmoreland had to work closely with the U.S. ambassador to Vientiane. Both Ambassador Unger and William L. Sullivan, who replaced Unger in December, through the defense attaché office in the Vientiane embassy, were conducting an unacknowledged but expanding ground and air war against the Pathet Lao and North Vietnamese centered around the Plain of Jars, with the ground fighting done by the Royal Laotian Army and by CIA-assisted Meo tribal irregulars. For practical purposes Unger and Sullivan could veto any Military Assistance Command proposal for operations in Laos. The ambassadors, understandably, evaluated such proposals from the perspective of their own war in Laos rather than the one MACV was waging in South Vietnam. In an effort to improve coordination of American activities in South Vietnam, Laos, and Thailand (the base for some YANKEE TEAM aircraft and an occasional clandestine participant in the ground fighting in Laos), Ambassador Taylor during the autumn secured State Department permission to form a Coordinating Committee for U.S. Missions in Southeast Asia (SEACOORD). This body consisted of the ambassadors to Saigon, Vientiane, and Bangkok and their military assistants, as well as representatives of Pacific Command. Westmoreland participated in both his own capacity and as commander of U.S. forces in Thailand. The committee met monthly to review and harmonize the activities of the three country teams, concentrating at its initial sessions on the details of air operations in Laos.[13]

In deference to JCS and CINCPAC concern that SEACOORD would duplicate or disrupt existing military chains of command, Taylor abandoned plans for a formal parallel military committee. Instead, General Westmoreland consulted informally with the other military country team members during SEACOORD meetings. Westmoreland reassured General Wheeler that he would keep CINCPAC and the JCS informed of what went on in SEACOORD meetings and that "the interest of the military will be protected during the course of committee deliberations." Further reassuring the military leaders, Secretary McNamara declared on 9 December that, as far as he was concerned, the establishment of SEACOORD did not change existing command relationships. The question of command relations aside, Westmoreland expected SEACOORD to be "helpful to us locally through the forum that it provides to exchange ideas and points of view and to effect operations."[14]

The Military Assistance Command's interest in air and ground operations in Laos was only one aspect of its larger effort to determine the dimensions of, and to interfere with, the movement of enemy troops, equipment, and supplies across South Vietnam's borders. Besides Laos, the command devoted much attention to formally neutral Cambodia, which it believed was the source of the increasing number of Communist–bloc weapons appearing in the Mekong Delta. During 1964 the MACV J3 developed plans for a physical barrier along stretches of the Cambodian border; and the country team pressed the Saigon government to tighten its controls on vessels passing up the Mekong to Phnom Penh. In connection with border control, Westmoreland welcomed a JCS proposal late in the year for stationing an international so-called KANZUS (Korea, Australia, New Zealand, United States) force along the Demilitarized Zone. Built around a U.S. division, this force would deploy in conjunction with renewed bombing of the north to deter or repel any retaliatory North Vietnamese ground attack. Westmoreland put his own staff and that of the U.S. Military Assistance Command, Thailand, to work on proposals for using the force to restrict enemy infiltration into South Vietnam, as well as to block a direct assault. The MACV commander argued throughout 1964 that "border control operations *into* Laos and positive control actions *at* the border of Cambodia" would benefit the counterinsurgency campaign more than would attacks on North Vietnam.[15]

Early Planning for the Air War

MACV's planning for the 34A raids and for operations in Laos took place within the framework of more general escalation planning by CINCPAC. On 18 March the Joint Chiefs of Staff directed Admiral

Felt to prepare plans for three levels of action: antiinfiltration operations on and across South Vietnam's borders, retaliatory air raids to be launched on 72 hours' notice against North Vietnam, and sustained air operations against the north to be undertaken on 30 days' notice. These actions were to be executed primarily with South Vietnamese forces reinforced as necessary by the FARM GATE unit and by other U.S. air elements. Pacific Command in response prepared its Operation Plan 37–64, completing the basic draft by 30 April. Thereafter, it gradually altered and expanded the plan, adding, for example, a list of ninety-four targets in North Vietnam with detailed air strike plans for each. Late in the year, the command incorporated all its plans and those of its subordinate commands for action outside South Vietnam into a single document titled Plan 37.[16]

The Military Assistance Command, with the J5 section doing most of the work and the 2d Air Division contributing detailed target selections and strike plans, prepared its own supporting Operation Plan 37–64 as well as the separate 34A–series plans. The command also recommended air strike targets for the list of ninety-four, both for one-time reprisals and for the sustained bombing campaign; but the Joint Chiefs and CINCPAC determined the final roster. In Washington, a MACV representative participated in a JCS escalation war game, SIGMA I–64, in which officials attempted to assess the effects of increased U.S. military pressure on the North Vietnamese. The results of the game indicated that the proposed strategy would lead only to a larger war. Especially after the Tonkin Gulf reprisal in August, MACV's strike planning concentrated on the requirements for attacking particular North Vietnamese targets with Vietnamese Air Force, FARM GATE, and U.S. Air Force planes. General Westmoreland reported in late November that planning for strikes against the north was "well underway" and provided "smooth phasing" from initial Vietnamese raids through rising levels of intensity which would engage FARM GATE, U.S. Air Force, and U.S. Navy aircraft "as required to accomplish assigned missions." Ancillary to the air war planning, MACV intelligence initiated studies of what effect an order from Hanoi to suspend hostilities, accompanied by reduction or termination of logistic support from the north, might actually have on the southern insurgency. All this activity was in addition to the command's continuous review and updating of its entire range of U.S. and SEATO contingency plans.[17]

Besides taking part in unilateral American planning for attacks on the north, the Military Assistance Command, as directed by the ambassador, engaged in combined planning for such operations with the South Vietnamese. This activity went forward with frequent interruptions, as the Johnson administration tried to use suspension of the planning as a bargaining chip in pressuring the South Vietnamese to stabilize their government. In the aftermath of the Tonkin Gulf incident, the MACV J3 set up a Combined Planning Section to cooperate

President Johnson confers with Secretary of Defense McNamara and Ambassador Taylor. (© Bettmann/CORBIS photo)

with personnel of the RVNAF high command on short-range escalation and defense preparations. By late August, MACV and the Joint General Staff were working together on 34A operations and projected incursions into Laos, as well as "targeting aspects" of air strikes against North Vietnam. In late November, General Westmoreland informed Ambassador Taylor that his command could offer the South Vietnamese a chance to participate in combined planning for actions ranging from small covert air strikes as part of OPLAN 34A to a full-scale overt campaign involving all the allied air forces.[18]

In connection with this air strike planning, in the immediate aftermath of the Tonkin Gulf incident Westmoreland sought for his headquarters to have command of both future reprisal strikes and of the prospective sustained campaign. On 7 August, he proposed to Admiral Sharp, Felt's successor, that General Moore be made the allied combined air commander in South Vietnam, with operational control of U.S. aircraft in the country and also of the South Vietnamese Air Force. Under Westmoreland, Moore then would assign missions to all those forces, including strikes into North Vietnam and Laos. Admiral Sharp, however, had other ideas. On the 8th, the admiral informed Westmoreland that he intended to conduct operations directly through his Air Force and Navy component commanders. MACV, at Sharp's direction, would control the operations only of the FARM GATE unit and the VNAF. General Moore would receive orders from Pacific Air Forces for U.S. Air Force missions and from Westmoreland for those by FARM GATE and the Vietnamese. This arrangement, Sharp believed, would "best utilize the command and control facilities available to me"; and it would allow the MACV commander to concentrate on the war within South Vietnam while monitoring air operations through General Moore. Westmoreland raised no immediate objection to Sharp's dictum, in large measure because he was preoccupied during the next several months with the consequences of the Tonkin Gulf incident in South Vietnam.[19]

After Tonkin Gulf: Reinforcing the South

The Military Assistance Command had little influence upon and only secondary involvement in the Tonkin Gulf naval engagements of 2–4 August and the ensuing American air strikes on North Vietnamese boat bases and oil storage sites. MACV received intelligence on North Vietnamese coast defenses from the DE SOTO patrols which the destroyers were conducting when they came under fire, but the patrols themselves were directed by CINCPAC through Pacific Fleet.[20] The president, the Joint Chiefs, and CINCPAC decided upon the 5 August reprisal without reference to MACV and employed Navy carrier planes for the mission. General Westmoreland participated only by accompanying Ambassador Taylor when he notified General Khanh of the raids.[21]

The Tonkin Gulf engagements and retaliatory raids, nevertheless, had significant effects on Military Assistance Command's plans and activities. In response to the incidents and reprisals, the command had to prepare for the potential consequences within South Vietnam of further escalation. It also had to absorb a rapid buildup of American forces within its theater and deal with an increasing tempo of Viet Cong attacks on U.S. installations.

On the day of the air strikes, 5 August, General Westmoreland met with General Khanh and his senior RVNAF commanders to warn them that the Viet Cong would probably strike back within South Vietnam. He urged the Vietnamese to strengthen the defense of ports, airfields, and other vital installations and to launch offensive operations to throw the enemy off balance and disrupt his activities. Besides taking the security measures, Khanh placed his ground forces in I and II Corps, his air force, and his navy on maximum alert. In line with earlier statements of his advocating that the allies "Go North," he grandiloquently threatened air reprisals of his own if the North Vietnamese or Chinese attacked his country. On a more practical level, Khanh established an emergency command post at Vung Tau, for which MACV provided communications and a small staff liaison element. MACV and the Joint General Staff rapidly sketched out a combined plan for countering a North Vietnamese or Chinese ground invasion of South

MACV: The Years of Escalation, 1962–1967

Vietnam. In response, however, to the end of the crisis and to unexpectedly intense Vietnamese objection to foreign command of their forces, the headquarters soon suspended this planning, and the 2d Air Division prepared for unilateral American retaliation for any new attacks on DE SOTO patrols. Those plans also proved academic, for the administration suspended the operations after another Tonkin Gulf incident on 18 September.[22]

Simultaneously with the Tonkin Gulf reprisal, the United States began building up its air and naval forces in Southeast Asia. On 5 August the Joint Chiefs of Staff directed the immediate deployment of certain units earmarked for the third phase of OPLAN 37–64, a sustained air campaign, with the dual purpose of deterring enemy attacks and preparing for further offensive action. During the next several weeks, in consequence, an additional carrier air group and an amphibious task group with a Marine brigade embarked took station in the South China Sea. Meanwhile, two squadrons of Air Force B–57 Canberra jet bombers deployed to Bien Hoa Air Base north of Saigon; the equivalent of two more squadrons of interceptors and fighter-bombers flew into Tan Son Nhut and Da Nang; detachments of reconnaissance and aerial refueling craft took station at Tan Son Nhut; and other squadrons, already in the Western Pacific or transferred from the United States, moved to airfields in Thailand, Okinawa, and the Philippines. On Okinawa, a Marine aircraft wing and an Army brigade both received alerts for possible movement to South Vietnam. In Hawaii, another Army brigade increased its readiness for possible deployment to Thailand.[23]

To accommodate the influx of aircraft and personnel into South Vietnam, the Military Assistance Command adjusted its air control facilities and hurriedly resumed planning—suspended under the 1963 withdrawal program—for enlarging its air bases and other installations. On 6 August, General Moore established a new 2d Air Division command post at Tan Son Nhut, separate from the combined USAF/VNAF control system, through which to discharge his expanding command responsibilities throughout Southeast Asia. General Westmoreland had begun air base expansion planning in June, when he realized that deployments under CINCPAC's contingency plans would overload South Vietnam's three jet fields at Tan Son Nhut, Bien Hoa, and Da Nang. He accelerated this effort in August, appointing master planning boards at the major bases and conducting engineering surveys of sites for an additional field. At the end of the year, he and Admiral Sharp joined in proposing construction of a new jet base at Chu Lai in southern I Corps, and they had under discussion the building of a second runway at Da Nang.[24]

As the air bases filled up with American aircraft and their supporting personnel and equipment, they presented tempting targets for Viet Cong and North Vietnamese retaliation for any future allied strikes against North Vietnam. General Westmoreland, in the aftermath of Tonkin Gulf, saw a twofold threat. Return air strikes by the rapidly expanding North Vietnamese jet force, possibly reinforced by the Communist Chinese, were unlikely but not out of the question, especially against Da Nang in far northern South Vietnam. More probable, in Westmoreland's view, were infantry and mortar attacks on the airfields by Viet Cong, possibly reinforced with North Vietnamese regular units. In Westmoreland's assessment, the South Vietnamese Army, which was responsible for protecting the American bases, could do so only by diverting already thinly spread units from pacification and territorial security missions at the risk of "serious loss of government control over sizeable areas and their populations."[25]

On 15 August, accordingly, Westmoreland recommended to Admiral Sharp and General Wheeler that a Marine expeditionary brigade (MEB) and an Army brigade, either the 173d Airborne on Okinawa or one from the 25th Infantry Division in Hawaii, be prepared for deployment to the Da Nang and Tan Son Nhut–Bien Hoa areas. Already alerted as part of the post–Tonkin Gulf buildup, these units should be sent to South Vietnam as quickly as possible "in the event of an attack on Da Nang judged by COMUSMACV to be beyond the capability of the RVNAF to handle or a decision to execute operation plans . . . likely to cause retaliatory actions against SVN." Westmoreland also asked for other forces. To counter the air threat, he requested the immediate deployment of one Marine and two Army HAWK (Homing All the Way Killer) antiaircraft missile battalions, to Da Nang, Saigon, and Nha Trang.[26] He also asked for augmentation of his U.S. Army component command, which had been renamed in February U.S. Army Support Command, Vietnam (USASCV), by a small Army logistical command, an engineer group, and a signal battalion, all of which would be needed to support the additional American forces actually deploying and those projected for the future.[27] Admiral Sharp endorsed Westmoreland's proposals, with the reservation that deployment of the air defense battalions for Saigon and Nha Trang could be deferred until the enemy threat became more immediate. Ambassador Taylor withheld specific concurrence with the recommendations but accepted them in principle as precautions that should be taken before the United States launched any further attacks on North Vietnam.[28]

Westmoreland's recommendations received a mixed response from the Joint Chiefs of Staff. With the immediate crisis at an end, the chiefs saw no need for action on the Marine and Army brigades beyond continuation of existing plans and preparations, which were designed for rapid reaction in emergencies. They promised to give "full consideration," however, to Westmoreland's proposals for "prudent deployment of additional forces" upon the launching of any major new escalation. The forces that Westmoreland wanted for Da Nang, at any event, already were prepared for deployment. On 6 August, Pacific Command had activated the 9th Marine Expeditionary Brigade as an amphibious force in readiness. It was composed of a reinforced regiment from the Okinawa-based 3d Marine Division and aircraft units from Japan and the Philippines. Units of this brigade cruised off South Vietnam regularly during the remainder of 1964, drawing closer to Saigon and Da Nang during each government crisis and coup attempt. The entire brigade could move rapidly to Da Nang by sea and air on short notice, and if necessary it could fight its way ashore.[29]

The Joint Chiefs also responded negatively to Westmoreland's request for support and engineer troops. They declared on 1 September that, because of an armed forces-wide shortage of logistical units, it was "inadvisable" to assign any to Vietnam solely in anticipation of the "possibility" of future combat force deployments. Westmoreland, however, continued to press this issue, in an effort to resolve existing MACV logistical problems as well as to prepare for contingencies. Since early in the year, his chief of logistics, Brig. Gen. Frank A. Osmanski, had been urging reform of the existing supply system, under which each service provided for its own forces and furnished Military Assistance Program materiel to its South Vietnamese counterpart while an increasingly overburdened Headquarters Support Activity, Saigon, sustained MACV headquarters and attempted to maintain a joint supply operation throughout the country. Barely sufficient for existing demands, this system could not accommodate the force buildup envisioned in escalation plans.[30]

Seeking to remedy this situation, Westmoreland, with Admiral Sharp's support, asked in December and again in early 1965 for an Army logistic command of 3,500 officers and men and for an engineer group of 2,400. While not completely replacing the multiple support systems, the logistic command, he argued, could at least serve as a single source for items used by all services. In addition, it could unify some facilities maintenance and other functions, and it could operate a more efficient transportation and distribution system throughout South Vietnam. The engineer group would reduce MACV's dependence on civilian contractors in meeting its growing construction needs. In December, as the United States stepped up planning for air attacks on North Vietnam, the Joint Chiefs, reversing their earlier stand, endorsed Westmoreland's proposal. Secretary McNamara, however, responded more cautiously. After a review of MACV's logistical situation by a team from his own office, in February 1965 he approved the deployment only of a tiny nucleus of the logistic command—thirty-eight planners and thirty-seven other personnel.[31]

Although the other two parts of his proposal met with a tepid response, Westmoreland's request for air defense missile battalions received immediate approval. During September, preparation for the movement of the Marine HAWK battalion to Da Nang and preliminary steps toward establishment of the Army missile units farther south got under way. Marine and Army teams surveyed sites for the batteries and drew up detailed deployment plans. The marines initially proposed to

The Beginning of Escalation

send to Da Nang an entire HAWK battalion of over 500 men, with a security force of 1,500 more. Believing this complement excessive for the air defense mission he had in mind and seeking to minimize the American presence at Da Nang, Westmoreland secured a reduction of the force to two batteries with 422 personnel, accompanied by a 153-man rifle company for ground defense.[32]

In mid-November, at JCS direction, the Marine 1st Light Antiaircraft Missile (LAAM) Battalion left California by ship for South Vietnam. The deployment, however, hit a series of snags early in December. Because the Vietnamese authorities at Da Nang were slow in turning over land for the battery positions, Taylor and Westmoreland on 3 December had to divert the battalion to Okinawa. Disagreements then developed among the Joint Chiefs, Admiral Sharp, and Westmoreland over the exact sites for the batteries and over whether civilian contractors or Navy Seabees should build their permanent positions. At the same time, over Westmoreland's protests, Ambassador Taylor decided to hold the battalion on Okinawa so that he could use its deployment as a bargaining counter in his confrontation with Khanh and the Young Turks. Only the Marine infantry company intended to protect the batteries reached Da Nang during December. The rest of the deployment stood in abeyance as the new year began.[33]

As if to justify General Westmoreland's requests for American base defense forces, the Viet Cong during late 1964 intensified their campaign of terrorism and sabotage against American personnel and installations. Since late 1962, the Communist underground in Saigon and elsewhere had carried out, in the words of a North Vietnamese official history, "many surprise attacks on U.S. lairs." Agents threw grenades and planted bombs in bars, restaurants, movie theaters, and stadiums frequented by Americans. They sabotaged aircraft and fuel dumps. In one of their most dramatic coups, Viet Cong frogmen in April 1964 mined and sank the aircraft ferry USS *Card* in the port of Saigon.[34]

The Military Assistance Command responded by developing internal defense plans for its headquarters, airfields, depots, housing, and communications centers. The command obtained a reduced strength Military Police company from the United States in April to protect its facilities in Saigon, but, in accord with longstanding U.S. policy, it left perimeter defense of air bases and other major installations to the Vietnamese armed forces. Their performance of the task left much to be desired, in spite of the efforts of American advisers at every level from Westmoreland on down. Over and above inefficiency and lack of resources, Vietnamese politics hindered effective use of the available forces. On the air bases, for example, hard feelings between the South Vietnamese Army and Air Force stemming from one of the many coup attempts prevented full interservice cooperation.[35]

Taking advantage of the allies' lapses, the Viet Cong hit hard during the last two months of 1964. On the night of 1 November, they slipped past the outer defenses of Bien Hoa Air Base and launched a destructive mortar bombardment. In half an hour, their gunners killed four Americans, wounded seventy-two, and put the equivalent of a squadron of B–57s out of action. On Christmas Eve, the Viet Cong bombed the Brink Hotel officers quarters in Saigon, inflicting heavy casualties upon both Americans and Vietnamese. Besides vainly recommending retaliation against North Vietnam, MACV responded to these attacks by surveying the security of its installations, pinpointing defects, and pressing the South Vietnamese to correct them.[36]

In reaction to the Brink Hotel bombing, for example, a MACV committee chaired by General DePuy and with representation from all mission agencies reviewed defense arrangements for the 60-odd American installations in Saigon. After analyzing the manpower requirements for their proper protection, the MACV provost marshal recommended that the mission obtain a full battalion of American Military Police to reinforce the available South Vietnamese troops and police. Agency for International Development (AID) officials, however, refused to concur, preferring to leave the task entirely to the Vietnamese. This deadlock over means continued into the new year.[37]

In the light of intensifying Viet Cong terrorism, and also of the threat of South Vietnamese factional mob violence, MACV and the U.S. Mission, under anxious prodding from Washington, examined the question of evacuating the over 1,700 American dependents still in Saigon. As had General Harkins before him, Westmoreland, preferred to let the number of wives and children shrink by attrition as tours ended. He pointed out that an abrupt evacuation, especially in the midst of the continuing political crisis, might indicate to the Vietnamese that the United States was abandoning the struggle. By the end of the year, nevertheless, it was clear that the dependents' presence in Saigon had become an obstacle to action against North Vietnam. President Johnson, for example, cited concern for the dependents' safety as a consideration in declining to retaliate against North Vietnam for the Brink bombing.[38]

Air War in the North: Planning and Command

Early in the new year, driven by fear that a South Vietnamese collapse might be imminent, the administration decided to launch its air offensive against North Vietnam without waiting for a stable Saigon government. On 7 February 1965, after a Viet Cong raid on an American advisers' barracks and helicopter base near Pleiku in the Central Highlands, the United States sent its aircraft northward in a long-planned reprisal code-named FLAMING DART. A second FLAMING DART raid followed on the 11th, responding to a Viet Cong attack on Americans at Qui Nhon. Two days later, President Johnson expanded FLAMING DART into a sustained air campaign against North Vietnam that

McGeorge Bundy, center, with General Westmoreland (NARA)

was subsequently named Rolling Thunder. Political turmoil in Saigon during late February along with bad weather over the north delayed the start of the program until 2 March, but the United States had nonetheless taken its final step toward what would become a prolonged, though limited, air war against North Vietnam.[39]

Westmoreland and his staff were much involved in the final preliminaries to the bombing campaign. Early in December, after President Johnson decided to intensify pressure on the north, Westmoreland helped Ambassador Taylor explain the decision to South Vietnamese military leaders and then oversaw the resumption of combined planning, both for one-time reprisals and for the prospective sustained bombing. The 2d Air Division and VNAF headquarters selected targets in the southern part of North Vietnam for combined U.S. and Vietnamese Air Force reprisal strikes, to be launched within twenty-four hours of a Viet Cong provocation. General Westmoreland considered it "important that we get the VNAF in the act" in such operations. He had his air commander, General Moore, working to "get them cranked up on short notice, provided . . . that their participation is cleared with appropriate authorities."[40]

MACV: The Years of Escalation, 1962–1967

On 7 February, after the spectacular Viet Cong mortar and sapper attack on the American advisers' compound at Pleiku, Westmoreland joined Ambassador Taylor and visiting presidential National Security Adviser McGeorge Bundy in recommending what became the first FLAMING DART reprisal. Westmoreland notified General Khanh, then in his last days of power, of the American decision for the raid. Later in the day, accompanied by Bundy, he met with Khanh at Pleiku to confirm which reprisal targets the Vietnamese Air Force was to hit. Westmoreland subsequently briefed Khanh on the results of the initial strikes and on U.S. plans for a sustained bombing campaign. Meanwhile, the MACV J5, Air Force Brig. Gen. Milton B. Adams, began work with his Joint General Staff counterpart on a final list of reprisal targets for the Vietnamese Air Force. In all these consultations, the Vietnamese, although welcoming the start of attacks on the north, made clear their wish to participate in both planning and execution of each new step in escalation. They also urged that the reprisals be justified in terms of general Communist aggression against their country rather than simply the killing of Americans.[41]

These Vietnamese sensitivities figured prominently in General Westmoreland's determined challenge to Admiral Sharp's 8 August command directive, under which the FLAMING DART raids were conducted. Westmoreland's drive to overturn this arrangement began after the second FLAMING DART operation on 11 February. In the aftermath of the strikes, in which the Vietnamese Air Force participated, Westmoreland complained to Sharp that the South Vietnamese, who Westmoreland believed must appear to play the "central role" in this new stage of the conflict, had been denied any voice in initiating and planning the reprisal. To avoid such a political error in the future, Westmoreland suggested that, after assignment of targets by Sharp, MACV coordinate the rest of the mission, at least those portions flown by South Vietnamese and U.S. Air Force units based on the Southeast Asian mainland. He declared: "My vantage point would seem to make me a logical candidate for target selection (recommendation) and for operational coordination to be exercised through my Air Force component commander. I take this position because of the essentiality of adaptation and coordination with the U.S. Ambassador, the GVN and the RVNAF."[42]

Admiral Sharp emphatically disagreed. The administration, Sharp declared, desired rapid action on reprisals, which Westmoreland's proposed procedure would not provide. The admiral stated that he intended to keep in force his August directive on command arrangements. Westmoreland, in response, disclaimed any intention to challenge Sharp's procedures. However, he went over the Admiral's head to plead his case to the Joint Chiefs, arguing that the political necessity of keeping the South Vietnamese in the forefront should take precedence over the administration's desire for the most rapid possible reprisals.[43]

Receiving no satisfaction from the JCS, Westmoreland returned to the attack early in March, after the first four ROLLING THUNDER missions had been ordered and then cancelled due either to bad weather or diplomatic considerations. Westmoreland again emphasized the importance of giving the South Vietnamese a significant part in decisions on target selection, attack timing, and force levels. He also asked for authority to brief the Vietnamese on strikes at least twenty-four hours in advance so as to give their air force the needed time for planning and preparation; and he requested more freedom of action in diverting squadrons to operations within South Vietnam when weather delayed scheduled raids on the north. Summing up, he suggested with the concurrence of Ambassador Taylor and General Moore that the MACV commander have responsibility for all ROLLING THUNDER operations south of the 19th Parallel. In that case, MACV would use a list of preauthorized targets but would determine the timing and details of strikes on its own. Admiral Sharp and the Seventh Fleet would have responsibility for air attacks north of the parallel.[44]

Westmoreland's proposal received a definitive rejection from both General Wheeler and Admiral Sharp. While he sympathized with Westmoreland's desire for more operational flexibility, Wheeler declared that the Washington authorities, because of political and diplomatic considerations, would have to continue to dictate most details of ROLLING THUNDER. Admiral Sharp was blunter: "In this one phase of the war," he said, the United States was "a major participant with an overwhelming share of the forces involved" and hence would make the decisions. Since Vietnamese security precautions were questionable and one of their pilots sooner or later inevitably would be captured and interrogated by the enemy, Westmoreland should give them only the minimal information they required for their own missions and "not before we have to." Finally, Sharp "most emphatically" rejected Westmoreland's proposal for dividing strike control. He reiterated the principles of his August directive and declared, "I intend to use this method in the future and would appreciate it if you would accept that fact."[45]

Westmoreland did so. From then on, as each subsequent ROLLING THUNDER operation occurred, he and Ambassador Taylor briefed South Vietnamese authorities on it in general terms. General Moore informed his Vietnamese counterpart, Air Vice Marshal Ky, of the details of the strikes only insofar as they affected VNAF operations and only just before the Vietnamese planes took off. As for unilateral American attacks on the north, they took place under the command of Pacific Air Forces, which passed tasking orders to the 2d Air Division and Pacific Fleet. "My headquarters," Westmoreland reported in mid-April, "is bypassed on these."[46]

The Marines Land at Da Nang

Responding to anxious questions from the Joint Chiefs about the adequacy of his base security following the Pleiku and Qui Nhon incidents, General Westmoreland modified MACV's long-standing policy of relying for protection on the South Vietnamese. He detailed increased numbers of Americans to close-in defense of their own quarters and facilities, even though such diversion of personnel from their regular duties would "adversely affect our operational efficiency." Well before the February attacks, Westmoreland, with Ambassador Taylor's support, had requested a full Military Police battalion for installation security. The Joint Chiefs approved the deployment on 18 February, after additional urging from Taylor; but the unit did not reach Saigon until 19 March. In the meantime, MACV brought in almost 300 Air Police and other U.S. military personnel on temporary assignment to protect its principal air bases. On 9 and 11 February, General Westmoreland warned the Joint Chiefs of Staff that the attacks on Pleiku and Qui Nhon marked the start of a new phase of the war and that he might need the equivalent of a division of American troops to guard his vital installations against retaliation.[47]

As the administration approached a decision to start bombing North Vietnam, the question became not whether but when to extricate the American dependents and how to present the measure to the South Vietnamese. Westmoreland on 6 February suggested immediate removal of the families with small children, leaving the others, including his own wife, to be sent out as a group in response to a major emergency or, preferably, on a gradual basis as their husbands' tours of duty ended. "With this plan," he argued, "the disappearance of U.S. dependents from the scene would be so gradual as to pass almost undetected by the Vietnamese."

The first FLAMING DART raid cut short the discussion. President Johnson on 8 February ordered removal of all dependents. Ambassador Taylor justified the action to the Saigon government as an effort to clear the way for an expanded U.S. commitment. Under a previously prepared MACV evacuation plan, the civilians departed on commercial flights during the next ten days. Keenly aware of reported Viet Cong threats to American facilities, including the children's school, General Youngdale declared later, "I was never so glad to see dependents leave in all my life."[48]

With the bombers going north and the Viet Cong assaulting American installations apparently at will, U.S. troop deployments planned earlier came with a rush. On 23 January, the same day he called for the MP battalion, Ambassador Taylor concurred in Westmoreland's recommendation that the Joint Chiefs dispatch the HAWK battalion from Okinawa. President Johnson approved the move on 8 February, when he ordered the evacuation of American dependents. One battery arrived at Da Nang by air the following day. The main body of the 1st

The Beginning of Escalation

Military dependents at Tan Son Nhut Air Base, waiting to depart to the United States (NARA)

LAAM Battalion and a supporting Marine engineer company arrived by ship a week later.[49]

Even as the final elements of the HAWK battalion disembarked, the dispatch of the full 9th Marine Expeditionary Brigade to Da Nang also came under active consideration. On 12 February, as part of a general program of force deployments for the first eight weeks of ROLLING THUNDER, the Joint Chiefs of Staff recommended movement of a Marine expeditionary brigade from Okinawa and Japan to Da Nang, to deter and if necessary to repel attacks on the base. Asked to provide his views on this proposal, General Westmoreland sent his deputy, General Throckmorton, to make a quick security survey of Da Nang. On the 16th, on the basis of Throckmorton's report and proposed deployment plan, Westmoreland endorsed immediate landing of the Marine brigade. In doing so, he pointed out that Da Nang was a key base for air operations in Laos and North Vietnam, that it was more exposed than any other American airfield to attack by both infiltrators from the north and the Viet Cong, and that it was defended by South Vietnamese troops of doubtful political and military reliability. Westmoreland saw no immediate need for American ground forces elsewhere than at Da Nang but warned that troops might soon be required as well for base defense in the Saigon area and at Nha Trang and Cam Ranh Bay.[50]

Admiral Sharp promptly supported the proposal to land the Marine brigade, emphasizing the deterrent value of its presence on the ground. Ambassador Taylor, however, expressed reluctance. In a lengthy message to the Joint Chiefs on 22 February, he questioned the ability of even a full MEB to prevent stand-off mortar barrages of the sort that had devastated Bien Hoa. He also warned against drifting into a series of troop requests and commitments that would end with Americans trying to wage the entire antiguerrilla war by themselves amid a sea of hostile Vietnamese. Nevertheless, respecting Westmoreland's "understandable concern" for the security of Da Nang, Taylor supported immediate placement of one battalion landing team (BLT) there. That size force, he believed, would eliminate any "substantial" danger of a Viet Cong infantry assault on the airfield. In conjunction with the South Vietnamese, it also would provide an "acceptable level" of protection against mortar bombardment.[51]

In deference to Taylor's views, Westmoreland scaled down his request for marines. On 22–23 February, after a visit to Da Nang, he recommended landing only those elements of the 9th MEB required for the security mission—two BLTs, a helicopter squadron, and "minimum" command and support contingents. The remaining battalion and other units would stand offshore for commitment later if required.[52] The marines were to come in partly by airlift and partly by amphibious landing, with the mission of occupying "defensive positions on critical terrain features in order to secure the airfield and as directed communications facilities, supporting installations, port facilities and landing beaches at Da Nang against attack."[53]

Admiral Sharp endorsed this reduced program, although he expressed himself in favor of early deployment of the third battalion landing team and an F–4 squadron; and the ambassador also accepted it. On 26 February, President Johnson ordered the landing of the Marine elements Westmoreland had recommended. Secretary of State Rusk instructed Taylor to obtain approval of the landing from Premier Phan Huy Quat and other top South Vietnamese civilian and military leaders. Rusk emphasized to the ambassador that in all discussions with the Vietnamese he should define the marines' role as "general security" and avoid giving the impression that they would be involved in any way in pacification.[54]

Ambassador Taylor and General Westmoreland lost no time in preparing the ground, politically and militarily, for the landing. Taylor on 1 March secured the consent of Premier Quat to the introduction of the brigade—which, it should be noted, the South Vietnamese government had not requested. General Westmoreland then opened negotiations on the details with General Minh, once more RVNAF commander in chief, and General Nguyen Van Thieu, Quat's Minister of Defense. Both Vietnamese urged caution in introducing this substantial American force into the Da Nang area, where Buddhist antigovernment dem-

The Beginning of Escalation

onstrators were active and well-organized and apparently enjoyed the tacit support of the I Corps commander, Maj. Gen. Nguyen Chanh Thi. A member of the Young Turks' group, Thi governed his region as a virtually autonomous warlord and was rumored to be contemplating secession from South Vietnam and a separate peace with the north. Whatever the case, after a personal visit from Westmoreland, Thi and his staff cooperated smoothly with representatives of MACV and the 9th MEB in planning for the marines' reception.[55]

The greater threat of disruption came from Washington, where policy makers, having made their decision, began to have second thoughts. On 2 March, with diplomatic and military preparations under way for deploying the MEB, Assistant Secretary of Defense for International Security Affairs John McNaughton cabled Ambassador Taylor with a proposal to substitute the U.S. Army's Okinawa-based 173d Airborne Brigade for the marines. Sharp, Taylor, and Westmoreland all dissented vigorously from McNaughton's proposal. They pointed out that the South Vietnamese government had approved bringing in the marines, that both United States and South Vietnamese preparations for the marines' landing were far advanced, and that the marine brigade, which could supply itself over the beach, was more easily supportable through the limited Da Nang port facilities than would be an Army brigade. Admiral Sharp meanwhile objected to having the 173d, which constituted the Pacific Command's air-transportable reserve, tied down in a static security mission. He and Westmoreland also noted that all Pacific Command contingency plans called for placement of the 173d Airborne Brigade at Saigon and the MEB at Da Nang, where substantial Marine elements, including a helicopter squadron engaged in supporting the South Vietnamese, were already established. Under this barrage of adverse facts, the substitution plan died quietly. On 7 March, the Joint Chiefs of Staff ordered CINCPAC to land the 9th MEB (–) at Da Nang. The landings, which began the next day, were hampered by heavy seas but not by the Viet Cong. Smiling Vietnamese girls carrying flower leis met the battalion that landed across the beach.[56]

During their first month on shore, the marines operated under highly restrictive instructions from General Westmoreland. Issued on 8 March, the instructions specified that the 9th MEB would not "engage in combat operations against enemy forces except for its own protection or the protection of installations, facilities or other units it is charged with defending or assisting in defending." The marines were not to perform any counterinsurgency functions. Under the operational control of MACV, the brigade was to work with the ARVN corps on a basis of "coordination and cooperation in the mutual self-interest of both commands." Following these instructions, the Marine battalions took positions on the airfield perimeter and on hills immediately west of the base, in a largely unpopulated tactical area of responsibility (TAOR) assigned by General Thi. The rifle companies manned de-

Marines take up defensive positions after landing at Da Nang. (AP photo)

fensive positions and conducted short-range patrols within their area. They made no contact with the enemy, and most of their casualties came from heat prostration.[57]

The landing of the 9th MEB at Da Nang marked the culmination of efforts to reinforce American positions in South Vietnam in counterpoint to the bombing of the north. Concern for security of the vital air bases had been present throughout discussion of the bombing offensive in both Washington and Saigon, and plans for related force deployments in the western Pacific had always included sending Marines to Da Nang. The terms under which President Johnson approved the Marine deployment and Westmoreland's initial operational directive to the 9th Marine Expeditionary Brigade reflected a continuing desire to keep American fighting men out of the counterguerrilla war. Truthfully, Westmoreland recalled: "I saw my call for Marines at Da Nang not as a first step in a growing American commitment but as . . . a way to secure a vital airfield and the air units using it, . . . an airfield essential to pursuing the adopted strategy."[58]

Because of the context in which it occurred, nevertheless, the landing at Da Nang on 8 March was to acquire in retrospect precisely the significance which Westmoreland claimed it did not have. Even as the marines settled into their bunkers and ran their first patrols, General Westmoreland and his superiors, on the basis of a growing volume of disturbing information about the military situation in South Vietnam, were beginning to consider seriously the most drastic intensification yet of the U.S. commitment: the direct engagement of large American ground forces in the battle against the Viet Cong.

The Beginning of Escalation

Notes

[1] Quote is from Msg, Taylor Saigon 2052 to the President, 6 Jan 65, tab 14, Westmoreland Hist File 12 (1–22 Jan 65), CMH. For earlier, similar views, see William H. Sullivan, Memorandum on Situation in South Vietnam, 13 Jul 64; and Memo, Palmer for CSA, 1 Sep 64, sub: Analysis of Situation in Vietnam. Both in Historians files, CMH.

[2] Unless otherwise noted, this discussion of the sequence of administration decisions is based on: *U.S.–Vietnam Relations*, sec. 4.C.1 through sec. 4.C.3; Berman, *Planning a Tragedy*, pp. 33–37; Palmer, *25-Year War*, pp. 34–35; Taylor, *Swords and Plowshares*, pp. 309–13, 320–21, 325–27; Gelb and Betts, *Irony of Vietnam*, pp. 96–120; and Thies, *When Governments Collide*, pp. 19–94.

[3] Harkins quote is from Msg, Harkins MAC 2247 to Taylor, 7 May 64, in Conference for Gen Taylor, 11 May 64, Book 1/3, box 1, 67A4604, RG 334, NARA. First Westmoreland quote is from Msg, MAC 6164 to Wheeler, 27 Nov 64, Westmoreland Msg Files, 1 Jan–31 Dec 64, CMH. Second Westmoreland quote is from *A Soldier Reports*, p. 114; see also pp. 89, 105–06, 109–14 for his retrospective views on escalation. Memos for Taylor, 28 Aug 64, sub: Feasibility of OPLAN 37, tab 51, Westmoreland Hist File 7 (27 Jul–31 Aug 64); and 9 Nov 64, tab 33, Westmoreland Hist File 9 (9 Oct–13 Nov 64), CMH.

[4] *U.S.–Vietnam Relations*, sec. 4.C.2(a), p. 2. Westmoreland, *A Soldier Reports*, pp. 106–07. An example of early planning for clandestine operations is Memo for the Special Group, 29 Dec 62, sub: North Vietnam Operational Plan, NSF 197/VN Jan 63, JFKL.

[5] MACV Command History, 1964, pp. 158–59. COMUSMACV/CAS Saigon OPLAN 34A–64/Tiger, 15 Dec 63, I–35034/64, OPLAN 34A File, box 2, 73A1350; Ltr, CINCPAC 3010, Ser 465, to JCS, 19 Dec 63, sub: Combined MACV–CAS Saigon Plan for Actions against North Vietnam, I–35033/64, ISA 092 NVN, box 8, 67A4660; both in RG 330, NARA. Msg, SecDef to Lodge, 12 Dec 63; Memo, McGeorge Bundy for the President, 7 Jan 64; Msg, Lodge Saigon 3943, to SecState, 21 Jan 64. All in NSC Country File, Vietnam, LBJL.

[6] Westmoreland, *A Soldier Reports*, pp. 106–07. *U.S.–Vietnam Relations*, sec. 4.C.2(a), pp. 1–2. Memo, Bennett for DCSOPS, 29 Apr 64, sub: USAF Representation on the MACV Staff; Msg, JCS 7391 to CSA, CNO, CSAF, CMC, CINCPAC, 14 Jul 64. All in Historians files, CMH. MACV–CIA jurisdiction issue: Msg, COMUSMACV MAC 5521 to JCS, 28 Jun 64, NSC Country File, Vietnam, LBJL. For a typical monthly operations proposal, see Msg, COMUSMACV MAC 15084 to White House, 27 Nov 64, NSC Country File, Vietnam, LBJL.

[7] Marolda and Fitzgerald, *Assistance to Combat*, pp. 339–43, 406–10, 466–72, summarize the course of 34A operations. For the operation's difficulties, see MACV Fact Sheet, 3 Mar 64, sub: Review of COMUSMACV OPLAN 34A–64/CAS Saigon OPLAN Tiger; and Remarks by COMUSMACV Preceding Review of OPLAN 34A. Both in SecDef Conf MACV Notebook, Mar 64; Historians files, CMH. Example of Westmoreland view of 34A operations: Memo, Westmoreland for Taylor, 17 Aug 64, tab 22, Westmoreland Hist File 7 (27 Jul–31 Aug 64), CMH.

[8] MACV Command History, 1965, p. 208. *U.S.–Vietnam Relations*, sec. 4.C.2(a), p. xv. Paper, "Validity of Intelligence on the Viet Cong," att to Memo, Ops Br, Collection Div, 19 Mar 64, sub: Vietnam, encl. 1; CIA Info Rpt, 1 Aug 63, sub: Assessment of the Progress of the War against the Viet Cong . . . during the First Half of 1963, Fact Sheet, 9 Jan 63. All in Historians files, CMH. Memo for the President, sub: Actions Taken Pursuant to Specified Paragraphs of NSAM 273, NSC Country File, Vietnam, LBJL.

[9] MACV Command History, 1964, pp. 163–64. *U.S.–Vietnam Relations*, sec. 4.C.1, p. 73; sec. 4.C.2(b), p. 4; Msgs, State 1630 and 836 to AmEmbs Saigon and Vientiane, 7 Apr 64; Msgs, Vientiane 1116 and 1119 to SecState, 10 and 11 Apr 64; Memo, M.

MACV: The Years of Escalation, 1962–1967

V. Forrestal for Bundy, sub: Laos, 5 May 64. All in NSC Country File, Vietnam, LBJL. Msgs, JCS 6163 to CINCPAC, 5 May 64; COMUSMACV MAC 3232 to JCS, 27 Jun 64; COMUSMACV MAC 5646 to CINCPAC, 1 Jul 64. All in Historians files, CMH. MACV Fact Sheet, 20 May 64, sub: Operation Delta, in Book of Misc Facts, box 1, 67A4064, RG 334, NARA.

[10] MACV Command History, 1964, p. 164; *U.S.–Vietnam Relations*, sec. 4.C.2(b), pp. 5, 7, 8–10, 22–23; Msg, COMUSMACV MAC 6068 and 6935 to CINCPAC, 14 and 25 Jul 64, Historians files, CMH; Msg, COMUSMACV to CINCPAC, 16 Aug 64, tab 20, Westmoreland Hist File 7 (27 July–31 Aug 64), CMH. Ltr, Westmoreland to Maj Gen Tran Thien Khiem, 25 Jul 64, File 204–58 (1007–03) Foreign Trng Prog Files (64), box 3, 69A702, RG 334, NARA.

[11] Westmoreland, *A Soldier Reports*, p. 110. Marolda and Fitzgerald, *Assistance to Combat*, pp. 380–81. MACV Command History 1964, pp. 107–08; ibid., 1965, pp. 208–09. CINCPAC Command History, 1964, pp. 269–70. Msg, State 1976 to Saigon, 18 May 64, NSC Country File, Vietnam, LBJL.

[12] Evolution of Yankee Team rules of engagement is traced in Marolda and Fitzgerald, *Assistance to Combat*, pp. 381–92. MACV Command History, 1964, pp. 46–48, 107–08, 113–14; ibid., 1965, p. 209. Memo, Westmoreland for Taylor, 28 Aug 64, sub: Concept for Attack of Panhandle Targets, tab 50, Westmoreland Hist File 7 (27 July–31 Aug 64), CMH. Msg, Rusk to AmEmb Saigon, 14 Oct 64, tab 6, Westmoreland Hist File 9 (9 Oct–13 Nov 64), CMH. Msg, Sharp to Westmoreland, 21 Oct 64, Westmoreland Msg Files, 1 Jan–31 Dec 64, CMH.

[13] How the U.S. ambassadors to Vientiane ran the war in Laos is discussed in Charles A. Stevenson, *The End of Nowhere: American Policy Toward Laos since 1954* (Boston: Beacon Press, 1972), pp. 206–17. Westmoreland, *A Soldier Reports*, pp. 76–77. CINCPAC Command History, 1964, p. 21. MACV Command History, 1964, pp. 166–67.

[14] CINCPAC Command History, 1964, pp. 21–22. Quotes are from Msg, Westmoreland MAC 5908 to Wheeler, 11 Nov 64; see also Msg, Westmoreland MAC 5849 to Sharp, 6 Nov 64; both in Westmoreland Msg Files, 1 Jan–31 Dec 64, CMH.

[15] Memo, Senior Member, Vietnam Delta Infiltration Study Group, for COMUSMACV, 15 Feb 64, sub: Report of Recommendations Pertaining to Infiltration into South Vietnam of Viet Cong Personnel, Supporting Materials, Weapons and Ammunition, Westmoreland Hist File 4 (15 Feb 64). MACV Command History, 1964, pp. 88–92. Talking Paper for the JCS for Their Meeting with General Westmoreland on 21 December 1964, 18 Dec 64, tab 23, Westmoreland Hist File 11 (7–31 Dec 64), CMH; Msg, Gen Easterbrook BNK 054 to Westmoreland, 18 Jan 65, Westmoreland Msg Files, 1 Jan–31 Mar 65, CMH. Quote is from Memo, Westmoreland for Taylor, sub: Feasibility of OPLAN 37, 28 Aug 64, tab 51, Westmoreland Hist File 7 (27 July–31 Aug 64), CMH.

[16] *U.S.–Vietnam Relations*, sec. 4.C.2(a), pp. xv, 11; sec. 4.C.3, pp. 2–3. CINCPAC Command History, 1964, pp. 49–54.

[17] Quote is from Msg, Westmoreland MAC 6191 to Wheeler, 28 Nov 64, Westmoreland Msg Files, 1 Jan–31 Dec 64, CMH; in same file, see Msg, Westmoreland MAC 4830 to Wheeler and Sharp, 6 Sep 64. MACV Command History 1964, pp. 160–65. Msg, Lodge Saigon 1937 to President; Msg, State 1677 to Saigon, 12 Apr 64; Memo, Rear Adm J. W. Davis, for Asst SecDef (ISA), 25 Jun 64, sub: Military Planning in Support of NSAM 288. All in NSC Country File, Vietnam, LBJL. JCS Final Rpt, Sigma I–64, 15 Apr 64, Historians files, CMH. Memo, Westmoreland for Taylor, sub: SNIE 10–3–64, 9 Oct 64, 13 Nov 64, tab 43, Westmoreland Hist File 9 (9 Oct–13 Nov 64), CMH.

[18] Memo, Asst CofS, J3, for CofS, MACV, 9 Aug 64, sub: Summary of Accomplishments, 3–9 Aug 64, Historians files, CMH. Memo, Westmoreland for Taylor, 17 Aug 64, tab 22, Westmoreland Hist File 7 (27 July–31 Aug 64), CMH. Memo, Westmoreland for

The Beginning of Escalation

Taylor, 23 Nov 64, sub: Items We Can Offer to the GVN Now, tab 16, Westmoreland Hist File 10 (14 Nov–7 Dec 64). For an example of use of planning as a bargaining chip, see Msg, Taylor to Amb Johnson et al., 3 Nov 64, Westmoreland Msg Files, 1 Jan–31 Dec 64, CMH.

[19] Westmoreland's proposal is summarized in Futrell, *Advisory Years*, p. 232. Sharp's directive is in Msg, CINCPAC to COMUSMACV, 8 Aug 64, Historians files, CMH.

[20] The North Vietnamese, in attacking the USS *Maddox,* apparently associated the destroyer with concurrent OPLAN 34A coastal raids, in spite of MACV's efforts to keep its operations separate from the DE SOTO activities. Marolda and Fitzgerald, *Assistance to Combat*, pp. 393–444, recounts the relationship between MACV, 34A operations, and the destroyer incidents.

[21] MACV Command History, 1964, ann. A, p. IV–3. Msg, COMUSMACV MAC 7358 to SecState, OSD, JCS, White House, 4 Aug 64, NSC Country File, Vietnam, LBJL. Msg, Taylor Saigon 303 FLASH to SecState, 5 Aug 64, NSC History, Presidential Decisions, Gulf of Tonkin Attacks, Box 38, LBJL.

[22] Msg, COMUSMACV MAC 7425 and AmEmb to CINCPAC, 5 Aug 64, NSC History Tonkin Gulf. Msg, COMUSMACV MAC 7429 to CINCPAC, 5 Aug 64, Historians files, CMH. MACV Command History, 1964, pp. 161–62, 174. Msgs, Westmoreland MAC 5147 and 6191 to Wheeler, 21 Sep 64 and 28 Nov 64, Westmoreland Msg Files, 1 Jan–31 Dec 64, CMH. Marolda and Fitzgerald, *Assistance to Combat*, pp. 453–62, recount the September incident and subsequent suspension of DE SOTO operations.

[23] Msg, JCS 7729 to CINCPAC, 5 Aug 64, NSC History Tonkin Gulf. For air unit deployments, see Futrell, *Advisory Years*, pp. 229–30.

[24] Futrell, *Advisory Years*, p. 230. MACV Command History, 1964, pp. 140–41, 158. Msg, Westmoreland MAC 6260 to Sharp, 2 Dec 64, Westmoreland Msg Files, 1 Jan–31 Dec 64, CMH.

[25] Msg, COMUSMACV MAC 8149 to CINCPAC, 15 Aug 64, NSC History Tonkin Gulf. MACV Command History, 1964, p. 162. For the appearance of jets at North Vietnamese fields in August, see Futrell, *Advisory Years*, p. 230.

[26] The HAWKs, mobile surface-to-air missiles effective against low-flying aircraft, would complement the medium- and high-altitude coverage of the already deployed Air Force F–102 interceptors. See MACV Command History, 1964, pp. 110–11.

[27] In February 1964, at COMUSMACV's recommendation, U.S. Army, Ryukyus, redesignated the U.S. Army Support Group, Vietnam, as U.S. Army Support Command, a title more appropriate to its missions, roles, and responsibilities, which were "an amalgam of combat support and logistics command functions." Msgs, CINCUSARPAC to CINCPAC, 14 Jan 64; CINCPAC to CINCUSARPAC, 28 Jan 64; CINCUSARPAC to CINCUSARYIS, 10 Feb 64; General Orders (GO) 14, HQ, US Army, Ryukyu Islands, 18 Feb 64. All in Historians files, CMH.

[28] Msg, COMUSMACV MAC 8149 to CINCPAC, 15 Aug 64, NSC History Tonkin Gulf. Westmoreland had requested the HAWKs by themselves earlier, on 9 August; see Msg, COMUSMACV MAC 7604 to CINCPACAF, 9 Aug 64, Historians files, CMH. Msg, CINCPAC to JCS, 18 Aug 64, NSC Country File, Vietnam, LBJL. Msg, Taylor Saigon 465 to SecState, 18 Aug 64, Historians files, CMH.

[29] *U.S.–Vietnam Relations*, sec. 4.C.2(b), p. 38. Quotes are from Msg, JCS 8230 to CINCPAC, 1 Sep 64, NSC Country File, Vietnam, LBJL. For organization and activities of the 9th MEB, see Jack Shulimson and Maj Charles M. Johnson, USMC, *U.S. Marines in Vietnam: The Landing and the Buildup, 1965* (Washington, D.C.: History and Museums Division, Headquarters, U.S. Marine Corps, 1978), pp. xiii, 3. Msg, Taylor to SecState, 20 Aug 64, tab 27, Westmoreland Hist File 7 (27 July–31 Aug 64); and Msg, MACV MAC 4966 to JCS, 13 Sep 64, Westmoreland Msg Files, 1 Jan–31 Dec 64, both in CMH, reflect contemplated and actual uses of the MEB as a force afloat.

183

[30] Quotes are from Msg, JCS 8230 to CINCPAC, 1 Sep 64, NSC Country File, Vietnam, LBJL. Background on logistic problem: MACV Command History, 1964, pp. 135–36; ibid., 1965, p. 104. Memo, Brig Gen Frank A. Osmanski for DEPCOMUSMACV, 11 Feb 64, sub: Logistics of the Counterinsurgency in RVN, tab 7, Westmoreland Hist File 2 (Jan 64–4 Feb 64). Marolda and Fitzgerald, *Assistance to Combat*, pp. 358–61.

[31] MACV Command History, 1964, p. 136; ibid.,1965, pp. 104–05. Westmoreland, *A Soldier Reports*, p. 127. CINCPAC's part in the logistical debate is described in Marolda and Fitzgerald, *Assistance to Combat*, pp. 361–65.

[32] MACV Command History, 1964, pp. 110–11. Msgs, CINCUSARPAC ARP 12523 to CINCPAC, Aug 64; CINCPAC to JCS, 12 Aug 64; COMUSMACV MAC 8387 to CINCPAC and CINCUSARPAC, 19 Aug 64; CINCPAC to CINCPACFLT, CINCUSARPAC, and COMUSMACV, 2 Sep 64. All in Historians files, CMH. Msgs, Westmoreland MAC 5849 and 6138 to Sharp, 6 and 25 Nov 64, Westmoreland Msg Files, 1 Jan–31 Dec 64, CMH.

[33] MACV Command History, 1964, p. 111. Msgs, Westmoreland MAC 6373 to Wheeler, 9 Dec 64 and Wheeler PRS 3198 to Westmoreland, 10 Dec 64. In Westmoreland Msg files, 1 Jan–31 Dec 64. Memo, Westmoreland for Taylor, 9 Dec 64, sub: LAAM Battalion Programmed for Da Nang, tab 8; tab A, app. B, Talking Paper for the JCS for Their Meeting with Gen Westmoreland on 21 December 1964, 18 Dec 64, sub: Items for Discussion with General Westmoreland, tab 23; both in Westmoreland Hist File 11 (7–31 Dec 64), CMH.

[34] Quote is from *Resistance War*, pp. 66–67. MFR, Maj Peter T. Barrett (ACSI), 13 Apr 64, sub: Viet Cong Terrorist and Sabotage Activities against US Personnel and Installations in the Republic of Vietnam, Historians files, CMH. *Card* sinking, and subsequent refloating and salvage, are described in Marolda and Fitzgerald, *Assistance to Combat*, pp. 355–56.

[35] MACV Command History, 1964, pp. 20, 101–02, 107, 156–57. MP company: Msgs, COMUSMACV MAC 2952 to JCS, 16 Apr 64; JCS 5921 to CINCSTRIKE/USCINCMEAFSA, CSA, CINCPAC, 17 Apr 64; NSC Country File, Vietnam, LBJL. ARVN–VNAF friction: Memo, Westmoreland for Taylor, 24 Nov 64, sub: Fact Sheet on Bien Hoa Incident, tab 18, Westmoreland Hist File 10 (14 Nov–17 Dec 64), CMH.

[36] For results of the Bien Hoa attack, see Futrell, *Advisory Years*, pp. 253–54; and Memo, Westmoreland for Taylor, 24 Nov 64, sub: Fact Sheet on Bien Hoa Incident, tab 18, Westmoreland Hist File 10 (14 Nov–7 Dec 64). Ltr, Westmoreland to Khanh, 4 Nov 64, tab 29, Westmoreland Hist File 9 (9 Oct–13 Nov 64) is typical of efforts to pressure the South Vietnamese to improve security. Taylor, *Swords and Plowshares*, pp. 323–24, 332–33, summarizes mission requests for reprisals.

[37] MACV Command History, 1964, pp. 101–07; ibid., 1965, pp. 424–25.

[38] Harkins' views on removing U.S. dependents are in Msg, MAC 2247 to Taylor, 7 May 64, in Conference for Gen Taylor, 11 May 64, Book 1/3, box 1, 67A4604, RG 334, NARA. Msg, Pres Johnson State 1281 to Lodge, 21 Feb 64, NSC Country File, Vietnam, LBJL. Msg, Pres Johnson to Taylor, 31 Dec 64, tab 46, Westmoreland Hist File 11 (7–31 Dec 64), CMH. Msg, Sharp to Wheeler, 6 Jan 65; Msg, Sharp to Westmoreland and Wheeler, 27 Jan 65, Westmoreland Msg Files, 1 Jan–31 Mar 65, CMH. MACV Command History, 1965, p. 425. Westmoreland, *A Soldier Reports*, pp. 87–88.

[39] *U.S.–Vietnam Relations*, sec. 4.C.1, pp. v–vii; sec. 4.C.2(c), pp. vii, 76–80; sec. 4.C.3, pp. i–vi, 31–44, 48–50, 69, 71–72. MACV Command History, 1965, pp. 199–201.

[40] Quote is from Msg, Westmoreland MAC 110 to Sharp, 9 Jan 65, Westmoreland Msg Files, 1 Jan–31 Mar 65, CMH. *U.S.–Vietnam Relations*, sec. 4.C.2(c), pp. 68–69, 71. Taylor, *Swords and Plowshares*, pp. 329, 334. Msg, Rusk State 1419 to Taylor, 7 Jan 65, tab 15; and Memo, Westmoreland for Taylor, 10 Jan 65, tab 1. Both in Westmoreland

The Beginning of Escalation

Hist File 12 (1–22 Jan 65), CMH. Msgs, Taylor to SecState, 23 and 25 Jan 65, tabs 2 and 7, Westmoreland Hist File 13 (21 Jan–28 Feb 65), CMH.

[41] Westmoreland, *A Soldier Reports*, pp. 115–18, and Taylor, *Swords and Plowshares*, p. 335, describe activities on 7 February. Msgs, Westmoreland MAC 0582 and 0619 to Sharp, 6 and 8 Feb 65, Westmoreland Msg Files, 1 Jan–31 Mar 65, CMH; MFRs, Westmoreland, 7 Feb 65, sub: Meetings with Gen Khanh, tab 25; Westmoreland, 8 Feb 65, sub: Visit with Gen Khanh, tab 26; Adams, 10 Feb 65, sub: Combined Planning for Operations against DRV, tab 34; Westmoreland, 18 Feb 65, sub: Meeting with Gen Khanh, 18 February 1965, tab 47. All in Westmoreland Hist File 13 (21 Jan–28 Feb 65), CMH.

[42] Msg, Westmoreland MAC 0732 to Sharp, 12 Feb 65, Westmoreland Msg Files, 1 Jan–31 Mar 65. See also MACV Command History, 1965, p. 200; and Westmoreland, *A Soldier Reports*, p. 117.

[43] Msgs, Sharp to Westmoreland, 13 Feb 65; Westmoreland MAC 0781 to Gen Goodpaster, OCJCS, 15 Feb 65; Goodpaster JCS 05720–65 to Westmoreland, 16 Feb 65; Wheeler JCS 0587–65 to Westmoreland, 17 Feb 65; Westmoreland MAC 0848 to Wheeler, 18 Feb 65. All in Westmoreland Msg Files, 1 Jan–31 Mar 65, CMH. Msg, Westmoreland to Sharp, 14 Feb 65, tab 37, Westmoreland Hist File 13 (21 Jan–28 Feb 65), CMH.

[44] Msgs, Westmoreland MAC 1061 to Wheeler, 1 Mar 65; Westmoreland MAC 1387 to Sharp, 14 Mar 65. Both in Westmoreland Msg Files, 1 Jan–31 Mar 65, CMH; MACV Command History, 1965, pp. 200–201.

[45] Msgs, Wheeler JCS 0739–65 to Westmoreland and Sharp, 1 Mar 65; Sharp to Westmoreland, 2 and 16 Mar 65. All in Westmoreland Msg Files, 1 Jan–31 Mar 65, CMH. Sharp quotes are from the latter two messages.

[46] Msg, Westmoreland MAC 2027 to Wheeler, 12 Apr 65, Westmoreland Msg Files, 1 Apr–30 Jun 65, CMH. MACV Command History, 1965, p. 202.

[47] MACV Command History, 1965, pp. 38, 424–25. Quote is from Msg, Westmoreland MAC 0712 to Wheeler, 11 Feb 65, Westmoreland Msg Files, 1 Jan–31 Mar 65, CMH. In same file, see Msgs, Wheeler JCS 0498–65, 0512–65, and 0602–65 to Westmoreland, 10 Feb 65 and 18 Feb 65; Westmoreland MAC 0675 to Gen Andrew J. Goodpaster, 10 Feb 65. Msg, Taylor to SecState, 23 Jan 65, tab 3, Westmoreland Hist File 13 (21 Jan–28 Feb 65), CMH. Msg, Taylor Saigon 2552 to SecState, 13 Feb 65, in NSC History, Deployment of Major US Forces to Vietnam, July 1965, box 40, LBJL. MACV J3 Historical Summary, Mar 65, in MACV History Backup Files, 1965, Historians Files, CMH.

[48] First quote is from Memo, Westmoreland for McNaughton, 6 Feb 65, sub: Evacuation of Dependents, tab 24, Westmoreland Hist File 13 (21 Jan–28 Feb 65), CMH; in same file, see Msg, Taylor to McGeorge Bundy, 1 Feb 65, tab 15; and MFR, Westmoreland, 10 Feb 65, sub: Visit with Gen Khanh, 8 Feb 65, tab 26. Msg, Westmoreland MAC 0666 to Gen Waters, Westmoreland Msg Files, 1 Jan–31 Mar 65, CMH. MACV Command History, 1965, p. 425. Westmoreland, *A Soldier Reports*, p. 118. Youngdale quote is from Interv.

[49] Msg, Taylor to SecState, 23 Jan 65, tab 4, Westmoreland Hist File 13 (21 Jan–28 Feb 65), CMH. Shulimson and Johnson, *Marines in Vietnam, 1965*, pp. 4–6.

[50] Msgs, JCS 005147 to CINCPAC, 12 Feb 65; COMUSMACV MAC 4614 to CINCPAC, 16 Feb 65; COMUSMACV MAC 4999 to JCS, 17 Feb 65. All in NSC History, Major Forces, box 40. Memo, Throckmorton for Westmoreland, 15 Feb 65, sub: Deployment of MEB (RLT/MAG) to Da Nang; Memo, Moore for COMUSMACV, 18 Feb 65. Both in MACV History Backup Files, 1965, 68A1395, RG 334, NARA. MACV Command History, 1965, p. 30.

[51] Msg, CINCPAC to JCS, 18 Feb 65; Msg, Taylor to JCS, 22 Feb 65; NSC History, Major Forces, box 40. For retrospective comments on this issue, see Westmoreland, *A Soldier Reports*, p. 123; and Taylor, *Swords and Plowshares*, p. 338.

[52] A Marine expeditionary brigade normally consisted of a regimental headquarters, three infantry battalions, an artillery battalion, combat and service support units, and a composite Marine aircraft group (MAG) including fixed-wing and helicopter squadrons. Gen Moore objected to bringing in the Marine air squadrons on the grounds that the marines were not going to conduct offensive combat operations that would require air support and that Da Nang Air Base already was overcrowded with U.S. and South Vietnamese aircraft. See Memo, Maj Gen J. H. Moore for Westmoreland, 17 Mar 65, sub: Marine Fighter Squadrons at Da Nang Air Base, Historians files, CMH.

[53] Msgs, Westmoreland MAC 5515 and 5604 to CINCPAC, 22 and 23 Feb 65, NSC History, Major Forces, box 40.

[54] Msgs, CINCPAC to JCS, 24 Feb 65; State 1840 to Saigon, 26 Feb 65. Both in NSC History, Major Forces, box 40. Msg, Wheeler to Sharp and Westmoreland, 27 Feb 65, tab 75, Westmoreland Hist File 13 (21 Jan–28 Feb 65), CMH.

[55] Msg, Taylor Saigon 2789 to SecState, 28 Feb 65, NSC History, Major Forces, box 40. Msg, Westmoreland to CINCPAC, 2 Mar 65, tab 7; Memo, Westmoreland MAC 1107 for Taylor, sub: MEB, to Wheeler, tab 22 Both in Westmoreland Hist File 14 (1–26 Mar 65). Msg, Westmoreland to Wheeler and Sharp, 3 Mar 65, Westmoreland Msg Files, 1 Jan–31 Mar 65, CMH. Concern over Thi's possible separatist aspirations is expressed in Memo, DePuy for Westmoreland, 12 Jan 65, sub: Separatism in I Corps, William E. DePuy Papers, MHI.

[56] Certain DOD officials evidently thought use of the airborne brigade would be less politically conspicuous and provocative than landing the more heavily equipped marines; see *U.S.–Vietnam Relations*, sec. 4.C.4, pp. 6–8. Shulimson and Johnson, *Marines in Vietnam, 1965*, p. 9. Westmoreland, *A Soldier Reports*, pp. 123–24. Msg, Taylor Saigon 2820 to SecState, 3 Mar 65, NSC History, Major Forces, box 40. Msg, Westmoreland MAC 1107 to Wheeler and Sharp, 3 Mar 65, Westmoreland Msg Files, 1 Jan–31 Mar 65. Memo, Westmoreland for Taylor, 7 Mar 65, sub: MEB, tab 22, Westmoreland Hist File 14 (1–26 Mar 65), CMH.

[57] Memo, Westmoreland for CG, 9th MEB, 8 Mar 65, sub: Regulations Governing Operations of the US Marine Expeditionary Brigade in the Republic of Vietnam, tab 26, Westmoreland Hist File 14 (1–26 Mar 65), CMH. For details of the landings and initial Marine operations, see Shulimson and Johnson, *Marines in Vietnam, 1965*, pp. 7–20.

[58] Westmoreland, *A Soldier Reports*, pp. 122–23. See also *U.S.–Vietnam Relations*, sec. 4.C.4, pp. 21–22.

6

Beginnings of the Ground Troop Commitment, January–June 1965

Early in 1964, soon after General Westmoreland arrived in Saigon, he received a "one classmate to another" letter of advice from Maj. Gen. William P. Yarborough, commanding general of the Army Special Warfare Center. On one point, General Yarborough was especially adamant:

Under no circumstances that I can foresee should US strategy ever be twisted into a "requirement" for placing US combat divisions into the Vietnamese conflict as long as it retains its present format. I can almost guarantee you that US divisions . . .could lie almost unattacked for months or years, would reap nothing but propaganda reverses as alleged "representatives of a new colonialism," and could find no targets of a size or configuration which would warrant division–sized attack in a military sense. The key to the beginning of the solution to Vietnam's travail now lies in a rising scale of population and resources control.[1]

At the time he wrote them, Yarborough's views constituted the conventional wisdom about Vietnam among American officials in both Saigon and Washington. However, as South Vietnam's military situation deteriorated early in 1965, General Westmoreland and other American civilian and military leaders gradually discarded their former assumptions and committed their country's ground forces to the struggle. Reports and recommendations from MACV did much to bring about the American intervention in the ground war and to determine the pattern of U.S. deployments and operations.

Plans and Proposals, 1954–1964

Civilian and military leaders discussed committing U.S. troops at several crisis points during the American involvement in Indochina. The Eisenhower administration considered such action in 1954 but decided against it because opposition from Congress and America's allies reinforced the president's own reluctance to make the commitment. In the fall of 1961, as President Kennedy examined measures for strengthening the Saigon regime, several of his key advisers along with Ambassador Nolting, the Joint Chiefs of Staff, and the military members of the Taylor mission urged deployment of U.S. and SEATO ground forces to protect South Vietnam's borders, block infiltration routes in Laos, and demonstrate American resolve. Kennedy rejected these suggestions in favor of an expanded advisory and combat support effort.[2]

Over the years, The PACOM and MACV commanders made and periodically revised contingency plans for employing U.S. troops in Southeast Asia, either unilaterally or under SEATO, to counter various possible levels of North Vietnamese and Chinese Communist aggression. By the mid-60s, the principal plan covering ground operations in Indochina was Pacific Command's OPLAN 32, with its supporting plans from MACV and other subordinate commands. This scenario identified four degrees, or phases, of Communist threat: Phase I—alert; Phase II—counterinsurgency; Phase III—direct North Vietnamese attack; and Phase IV—direct Chinese attack. In Phases III and IV, the United States was to deploy a Marine Expeditionary Force to Da Nang, an Army division and a corps headquarters to Qui Nhon and the Central Highlands, and an Army airborne brigade to Saigon. These forces would help the South Vietnamese halt Communist drives down the coast and through the Mekong Valley. The Phase II (counterinsurgency) plan for Vietnam entailed simply a scaled-down version of the Phase III deployment, with a portion of the Marine force going to Da Nang and two Army brigades to the Saigon area. Their principal mission would be to defend vital areas for the South Vietnamese, thereby freeing ARVN units for offensive operations; but the plan left open the possibility that the American troops might engage in unspecified counterguerrilla activities. The 32-series plans were intended primarily for Korea-style conventional warfare and did not apply directly to the situation as it actually developed in early 1965. Even so, the Marine deployments to Da Nang were in conformity with them. Further, the planning process had acquainted commanders and staffs with the practical aspects of placing large forces in Vietnam, and the contingency plans influenced the identities and locations of the first units to go in.[3]

Troop deployments to South Vietnam came under consideration repeatedly during the Johnson administration's escalation debates of 1964. State Department officials suggested insertion of sizable ground forces in northern South Vietnam as a substitute for a bombing offensive against the north. The Joint Chiefs of Staff gave consideration to an anti-infiltration cordon of U.S. troops across both South Vietnam and Laos. Late in the year, the chiefs also undertook intensive study of a more modest plan for an international force, built around an American division, to guard the Demilitarized Zone within South Vietnam. This force would deploy in conjunction with the bombing offensive to deter retaliatory North Vietnamese ground assaults. All these proposals envisioned a static, defensive mission for the American forces. However National Security Adviser McGeorge Bundy contemplated more aggressive action. In late August, he declared: "A still more drastic possibility which no one is discussing is the use of substantial U.S. armed forces in operations against the Viet Cong. I myself believe that before we let this country go we should have a hard look at this grim alternative. . . . It seems to me at least possible that a couple of brigade-size units put in to do specific jobs about six weeks from now might be good medicine everywhere."[4]

In spite of this interest in the issue in Washington, Ambassador Taylor and General Westmoreland opposed any direct commitment of American soldiers to counterinsurgency combat, although both men saw a need for troops to defend air bases in South Vietnam if the United States began bombing the north. They held to this position even when President Johnson expressed interest in enlarging the role of American ground forces in the fighting. On 30 December, the president rejected Taylor's and Westmoreland's call for reprisal air strikes in response to the Brink BOQ bombing but urged upon them greater attention to new initiatives within South Vietnam. "I have never felt that this war will be won from the air," Johnson told Taylor:

and it seems to me that what is much more needed and would be more effective is a larger and stronger use of rangers and special forces and marines, or other appropriate military strength on the ground and on the scene. I am ready to look with great favor on that kind of increased American effort, directed at the guerrillas and aimed to stiffen the aggressiveness of Vietnamese military units up and down the line. Any recommendation that you or General Westmoreland make in this sense will have immediate attention from me, although I know that it may involve the acceptance of larger American sacrifices. We have been building our strength to fight this kind of war ever since 1961, and I myself am ready to substantially increase the number of Americans in Vietnam if it is necessary to provide this kind of fighting force against the Viet Cong.[5]

In saying this, the president opened a door, but Taylor and Westmoreland declined to walk through it. On 6 January, Taylor, with Westmoreland's concurrence, renewed his call for retaliatory bombing. He also transmitted a MACV staff analysis endorsed by Westmoreland of the question of using more American ground troops. The MACV staff, Taylor reported, believed that the number of American advisers and support personnel with the South Vietnamese forces had nearly reached the maximum that the Vietnamese could absorb. Beyond the advisory and combat support role, the staff had analyzed three possible uses of American troops: employment of Army and Marine infantry battalions as mobile reserves to counter major Viet Cong offensives and attack enemy units and base areas; integration of a U.S. infantry battalion into each ARVN regiment "to lead the way and set the standards"; and use of division-size forces of American, Vietnamese, and allied troops to hold coastal enclaves protecting vital ports and airfields. The staff had recommended none of these courses of action, arguing in each case that the political disadvantages outweighed the military benefits. Taylor passed on to the president the MACV conclusion:

> The Vietnamese have the manpower and basic skills to win this war. What they lack is motivation. The entire advisory effort has been devoted to giving them both skill and motivation. If that effort has not succeeded there is less reason to think that U.S. combat forces would have the desired effect. In fact, there is good reason to believe that they would have the opposite effect by causing some Vietnamese to let the U.S. carry the burden while others, probably the majority, would turn actively against us. . . . Intervention with ground combat forces would at best buy time and would lead to ever increasing commitments until, like the French, we would be occupying an essentially hostile foreign country.[6]

South Vietnamese officials at this time saw no need for U.S. troops. Late in January, for example, General DePuy, on his own initiative, sounded out his Vietnamese counterpart, Colonel Nguyen Duc Thang, on "whether or not he thought we should make a larger military effort in Vietnam and if so, in what manner." Thang, an officer highly regarded by both DePuy and Westmoreland, replied that "additional air power might well be applied against the VC secret war zones." However, he declared that introducing American ground combat troops would be "a great psychological error" unless the United States planned "to escalate into a limited war throughout Southeast Asia."[7]

Taylor's, Westmoreland's, and Thang's statements reflected a longstanding consensus that South Vietnam should fight and win its own ground war and that it possessed the resources, if properly employed, to do so. Within two months, however, that consensus would change.

Collapse of the CHIEN THANG Plan

Throughout 1964 the Military Assistance Command had worked to enlarge and improve the South Vietnamese armed forces and to deploy them for effective support of the CHIEN THANG pacification plan. In March, after Secretary McNamara scrapped the Model Plan, with its projections of U.S. and South Vietnamese force reductions, the American mission and the Khanh government hurriedly made plans to increase the ARVN and territorial forces by about 50,000 men. In April, General Khanh decreed nationwide mobilization for military or civilian public service of all able-bodied males between 20 and 45 years of age. He established a Mobilization Directorate to enforce the decree and to strengthen the government's existing conscription system. The Americans provided additional MAP funds and advisory support for the increase. Although nothing resembling Khanh's proclaimed total call-up occurred, and although government inefficiency and Viet Cong obstruction hampered conscription, the government secured enough new recruits during the year to meet its expansion goal and to reinforce its many understrength units. At the same time, the government, at MACV's urging, increased the pay, dependent housing, and benefits of regular and territorial troops; and it promised more equitable, rapid promotion for both officers and NCOs. These reforms, officials hoped, would improve unit leadership and reduce the continuing drain that desertions imposed upon the armed forces.[8]

Encouraged by these developments, General Westmoreland planned further expansion of Saigon's military establishment during 1965. On the basis of a combined MACV–High Command force structure survey, he presented Admiral Sharp and the Joint Chiefs with two alternative plans for increasing the regular and territorial forces. Under alternative one, the ARVN would expand by another 31,000 men and the Regional and Popular Forces by over 110,000, providing strength sufficient, in Westmoreland's estimation, to accelerate progress in Hop Tac and to forestall Viet Cong gains in other high-priority areas. Alternative two called for the same territorial force expansion as the first but would add an extra 17,000 men to the ARVN. This alternative would permit larger gains in pacification, according to Westmoreland, but would place greater strain on the government's manpower resources and training facilities and take more time to complete. He therefore recommended Alternative one, and the U.S. government agreed to provide Military Assistance Program support for it. Under the plan adopted, South Vietnam was to have over 590,000 men under arms by the end of 1965, about 275,000 of them in the regular army, navy, and air force.[9]

Qualitative improvements accompanied the expansion. Pressed continuously by MACV, the South Vietnamese reorganized their high command along lines favored by the Americans. After lengthy negotiations, Westmoreland also secured the merger of several competing, ineffective hamlet-level militias into a single paid, full-time component, the Popular Forces. South Vietnamese military intelligence, under the influence of some 250 American intelligence advisers and with the support of specialized American units and personnel, provided a growing amount of reliable information about the Viet Cong. Intensified training and new equipment—A–1H Skyraiders and H–34 helicopters for the Air Force; 105-mm. and 155-mm. howitzers, M41 tanks, and additional armored personnel carriers for the South Vietnamese Army—enhanced their firepower, mobility, and combat performance. In spite of the persistence of high desertion rates and inadequate or insufficiently aggressive leadership at all levels, General Westmoreland felt justified in declaring at the end of the year that the RVNAF now possessed the "greatest, most flexible and responsive combat power in its history."[10]

The Military Assistance Command worked throughout the year to translate the Chien Thang plan from the broad concept promulgated by General Khanh into practical military plans that would lead to what Westmoreland called "thoroughgoing operations on the ground." To that end, Westmoreland during July defined the various military missions in aid of pacification for the guidance of American advisers. The most important were "search and destroy"—attacks on enemy units and base areas; "clearing"—prolonged operations to expel organized Viet Cong forces from areas to be pacified; and "securing"—elimination of the Viet Cong shadow government and protection of the restored civil administration. At MACV's inducement, the High Command specified on 25 December two principal military phases of pacification—clearing and securing. In the clearing phase, ARVN forces were to drive organized Viet Cong forces out of areas targeted for pacification while simultaneously attacking enemy units and bases outside the pacification zones. In the securing phase, the Regional and Popular Forces and the National Police were to take over defensive tasks from the ARVN and to root out the Viet Cong infrastructure in order to provide the necessary underpinning for a restored civil administration. The ARVN at this point would move on to new areas and begin clearing them, leaving behind units to assist in securing operations if the territorials and police lacked sufficient strength.[11]

By the time this directive was issued, MACV had already made much progress in concentrating ARVN forces in the priority pacification areas—the "spreading oil spots"—established in the CHIEN THANG plan. There were several of these in each corps besides the large HOP TAC zone around Saigon. General Westmoreland and his senior advisers gradually persuaded corps and division commanders to commit a large proportion of their infantry battalions to these zones for long-term clearing and securing operations, conducted under province control and emphasizing day and night small-unit patrols and ambushes. By the end of 1964, about 70 percent of the ARVN infantry battalions in I and II Corps, and 78 percent of those in III Corps, were engaged in operations of this type. MACV also secured redeployments of troops within and between corps and division areas and some changes in corps boundaries to increase manpower in and around the principal oil spots. In the largest single redeployment, the South Vietnamese in October transferred their entire 25th Division from II Corps to Long An and Hau Nghia Provinces in III Corps to reinforce HOP TAC. At the end of 1964 the government's military dispositions and operations at last were coming into line with its national pacification plan.[12]

By then, the Viet Cong were countering the CHIEN THANG program with increasing effectiveness. Like the government, the insurgents expanded their forces during the year, and at a greater rate. MACV's estimates of Viet Cong main force strength, which generally lagged behind actual developments, increased from about 27,000 at the beginning of 1964 to 34,000 in July and to more than 48,000 in March 1965. These figures did not include the enemy's guerrillas and hamlet militia, whose strength MACV intelligence estimated to be between 80,000 and 100,000, an admittedly rough and arbitrary approximation that probably understated the total. In the same way, the number of main force

Beginnings of the Ground Troop Commitment, January–June 1965

formations grew from an estimated 5 regiments, 46 battalions, and 132 separate companies in mid-1964 to an estimated 10 regiments, 79 battalions, and 160 companies in early 1965. The enemy's armed forces, even with their rapid growth, remained much smaller than those of the government. Since government forces needed overwhelming superiority in manpower to carry out their clear-and-secure operations, however, any significant increase in Viet Cong numbers threatened to upset the balance of forces essential to success of the CHIEN THANG plan.[13]

The Viet Cong filled their expanding ranks mainly with southerners, often promoting men from the guerrilla ranks to form new main force units. However, they continued to rely heavily on infiltrators from the north for officers, NCOs, and specialists. In October 1964, working from an expanded base of captured documents and prisoner interrogation reports, MACV's J2 section tripled its estimate of infiltration between 1959 and August 1964 from 13,000 to 34,000 personnel. It also projected that total enemy infiltration into the south during 1964 would be on the order of 10,000 men. By the middle of the year, the Military Assistance Command had established the presence of native North Vietnamese, as well as regrouped southerners, among infiltrators in the northern corps areas; but until well into 1965 it failed to verify South Vietnamese reports that organized northern army units were moving into the south.[14]

An enemy soldier holds his AK–47 rifle.
(CMH collection)

Besides growing in size, the Viet Cong's main forces acquired heavier armaments and began to replace their old French, Japanese, and captured American weapons with newer ones of Communist-bloc manufacture. Beginning in late 1964, Chinese copies of the excellent Soviet automatic assault rifle, the AK–47, appeared among weapons captured by the South Vietnamese, as did other small arms and machine guns firing the same 7.62-mm. cartridge. Main-force units also were more abundantly equipped with mortars, antitank rocket launchers, and recoilless rifles. By introducing these Communist-bloc weapons, the Viet Cong standardized their infantry's armament and increased its firepower.[15]

Gradually implementing the directive of the Ninth Plenum to intensify their military effort, the Viet Cong used their growing forces to bloody the ARVN so as to erode the principal pillar of the unstable gov-

MACV: The Years of Escalation, 1962–1967

Covered by a U.S. Army helicopter, South Vietnamese marines advance into Binh Gia, 30 December 1964. (AP photo)

ernment and to roll back pacification. More frequently than in the past, Viet Cong units from platoon to battalion size sought opportunities to inflict casualties on government regulars. Typically, they would besiege a strategic hamlet or government outpost, then ambush the relieving unit, usually with a superior force fighting from carefully prepared positions. Less frequently, Viet Cong in battalion or greater strength would seize a hamlet or district town and then stand their ground for one or two days against counterattacking ARVN or Regional Force elements. Cumulatively, these actions cost the government heavily. Average casualties per month rose from about 1,900 at the beginning of 1964 to 3,000 at the end. Although the Viet Cong suffered severely in many engagements, the overall loss ratios shifted steadily against the Saigon forces.[16]

In late December, at Binh Gia in Phuoc Tuy Province about thirty miles southeast of Saigon, the Viet Cong used their assault and ambush tactics to deal the ARVN its most severe defeat of the year. Invading a hitherto relatively quiet portion of the HOP TAC area, two main force Viet Cong regiments, newly equipped with Communist-bloc weapons and supported by local units and guerrillas, seized a progovernment Catholic village and then stayed to fight the troops who came to retake it. In a series of engagements between 28 December and 3 January, they destroyed a battalion of marines and another of rangers, killed almost 200 government troops and 5 U.S. advisers, captured more than 300 individual and crew-served weapons, and shot down 2 helicopters. The III Corps mounted a multibattalion search-and-destroy operation in response but failed to engage the Communist regiments. This battle, in the view of many Americans at the time, presaged a Viet

Cong advance from guerrilla warfare to large-unit operations.[17]

To break up the pacification oil spots, the Viet Cong employed main force elements, guerrillas, and political cadres in combination. They developed their counter-pacification campaign most fully in the piedmont and coastal plain of I and II Corps, where the government previously had seemed to be gaining ground through effective application of the "spreading oil spot" technique, but where the South Vietnamese Army was weakened late in 1964 by the transfer southward of the 25th Division. Working from mountain base areas, main-force and regional elements, in conjunction with local guerrillas, terrorized government village and hamlet officials, harassed small posts and defended hamlets, destroyed hamlet fortifications, and blocked road traffic. To immobilize the South Vietnamese Army, main-force and regional units made occasional large attacks on outposts and district capitals. Behind the military units came Viet Cong political cadres who gradually gained access to and control over the villagers of the piedmont and coast.[18]

By the first anniversary of its inception, the CHIEN THANG pacification plan, with its associated dispersal of the South Vietnamese Army to clear and hold selected areas, was failing. The plan's American and Vietnamese authors had assumed that the Viet Cong would continue operations on about the same scale and with the same combination of guerrilla and main force activity as in 1963. When the Viet Cong, employing main forces as well as guerrillas, began systematically to attack all elements of the pacification program simultaneously, from ARVN units on clearing and securing missions to strategic hamlets in supposedly secure zones, the government lacked the forces, whether regular or territorial, to protect the pacification oil spots effectively, let alone expand them or seek out and destroy the Viet Cong battalions. Its dispersed forces risked defeat in detail by well-armed Viet Cong regulars, who could concentrate seemingly at will against undermanned or isolated objectives. Especially in I and II Corps, Saigon's troops, to avoid piecemeal annihilation, had to abandon outlying and hard-to-defend pacified areas, which then promptly reverted to Viet Cong control. According to a later MACV estimate, the government, between mid-1964 and mid-1965, lost an additional 6 percent of South Vietnam's population to the Viet Cong. Only continued Viet Cong inability to manipulate the urban political factions and the persistent loyalty of the armed forces to the government stood in the way of an insurgent victory at the end of 1964. By then North Vietnamese regular units were moving into South Vietnam to provide what Communist planners hoped would be the final impetus for Saigon's military and political collapse.[19]

A Limited Response

The Military Assistance Command was slow to acknowledge any major change in the relative balance of power. Throughout 1964 General Westmoreland and his intelligence section interpreted Viet Cong strategy as essentially a continuation, somewhat intensified, of the previous pattern of terrorism, guerrilla warfare, and occasional opportunistic larger attacks. While expressing concern at the frequency and deadliness of Viet Cong ambushes, Westmoreland noted on several occasions that the overall number of enemy large-unit operations was actually declining. He suggested that, in the face of stronger government forces, the Viet Cong were shifting their resources to terrorism and small-unit action, expedients that were less costly and more effective in extending their control in the countryside. At the end of the year, a MACV study of Viet Cong strategy and tactics, while it took note of the increases in enemy main force strength and the appearance of new Communist-bloc weapons, concluded that "the VC still have not reached the . . . 'mobile warfare phase' of their 'people's war'" and that they had not yet "faced up to the full risk of prolonged pitched battles of the conventional type." [20]

As Westmoreland and Taylor indicated in their January response to President Johnson's suggestion that the United States introduce ground troops into the war, MACV and the mission still attributed the lack of pacification progress primarily to South Vietnamese political instability and administrative inefficiency rather than to Viet Cong strength. Westmoreland initially even played down the military significance of the debacle at Binh Gia, claiming that the South Vietnamese Army's defeat had resulted from the preoccupation of senior III Corps commanders with Saigon politics. "We must not," he told Taylor, "be overwhelmed by the loss of one battle. There will be more wins and more losses. If the GVN will turn its attention back to the war, there will be more wins than losses." [21]

During the first two months of 1965, the tone of Westmoreland's and MACV's assessments changed rapidly. The change came in response to continued Viet Cong battlefield successes, especially in I and II Corps, and to accumulating evidence from prisoners and captured weapons and documents of the enemy's rearmament and expansion. By March, MACV was not only revising upward its estimates of Viet Cong strength but also making alarming projections of future growth. Based on the Viet Cong's apparent rate of expansion during 1964, the command estimated that the enemy could have as many as 100 battalions in the field by the end of 1965, and that estimate did not include North Vietnamese regular units, whose presence in the south now seemed increasingly probable. The command also acknowledged a possible enemy movement toward large-unit warfare. Late in January, General Westmoreland called Ambassador Taylor's attention to "increasing appearances of VC main forces which either sought open engagement or occupied friendly villages with determination to stay until the RVNAF produced enough combat power to force them to withdraw." A month later he informed the Joint Chiefs that the government's military position was deteriorating everywhere but in IV Corps. "These trends indicate," he warned, "that the situation visualized in OPLAN 32 Phase II (RVN) [a requirement for U.S. troops to reinforce the South Vietnamese Army in the counterguerrilla war] may be approaching."[22]

Enemy pressure slackened throughout the country during March, but the situation remained ominous. In II Corps, South Vietnamese forces, supported by American air strikes and reinforced by a large part of Saigon's general reserve, checked a Viet Cong offensive in populous Binh Dinh Province and reopened a number of key highways. The enemy, however, continued to build up his strength in the region, so much so that the hard-pressed corps commander was considering withdrawal of some of his exposed garrisons. In the cities the Viet Cong continued terrorist attacks on American facilities, severely damaging the U.S. embassy in Saigon with a car bomb on 30 March. Most disturbing of all, allied intelligence confirmed during the first days of April the presence of a battalion of the *PAVN 325th Division* northwest of Kontum in the Central Highlands and strongly suspected that other elements of the division were there as well. The infiltration of North Vietnamese combat units to reinforce the still-expanding Viet Cong main forces, long considered possible by MACV, appeared to be under way.[23]

General Westmoreland issued a comprehensive, pessimistic review of the situation on 6 March, even before much of this bad news reached him. Surveying the corps tactical zones, he declared that enemy forces in I Corps were extending their influence from the piedmont into the lowlands and erasing what pacification gains the government had made. In II Corps, where some ARVN units were already "in a pessimistic frame of mind and . . . reluctant to engage in offensive operations," Westmoreland expected the enemy to reinforce his troops in the region's northern provinces and try to cause a "psychological collapse" of the government side. In III Corps, the Hop Tac campaign had come to a stop for lack of additional forces. The general reserve, on which the program relied to counter enemy attacks and to conduct peripheral search and destroy operations, had been committed elsewhere, opening the way for the Viet Cong to wipe out government gains by throwing in their own available reserves. Only in IV Corps did the government appear to be holding its ground and perhaps gaining a bit in pacification; but even there the Viet Cong were reportedly forming main force regiments and seemed capable of raising the intensity of military action at any time.

Looking ahead over the next six months, Westmoreland expected more of the same, only worse. He predicted that the Viet Cong, "holding the initiative," would increase the tempo and intensity of their political-military offensive, especially in the northern and central parts of South Vietnam. They would add to their military manpower through conscription and recruiting in the south and infiltration from the north, organize new units, and consolidate their main force elements into large formations with standardized weapons. By means of large- and small-unit actions, they would try to compress the South Vietnamese Army and territorials into strongholds isolated from the people while cutting roads and communications and wearing down the marine and airborne battalions of the South Vietnamese general reserve. As its military campaign went forward, the enemy would consolidate political control of the territory it already dominated while striving to expand its influence over the people of militarily contested areas. In addition, it would intensify all forms of propaganda and subversion in government-held districts to create "a massive popular peace movement" among religious, ethnic, and political groups. Westmoreland concluded:

> With the continuance of present trends, and provided that no new power elements are brought into play, six months from now the configuration of the RVNAF will essentially be a series of islands of strength clustered around district and province capitals clogged with large numbers of refugees in a generally subverted countryside; and the GVN itself will be beset by "end the war" groups openly advocating a negotiated settlement. . . . We are headed toward a VC takeover of the country, sooner or later, if we continue down the present road at the present level of effort.[24]

In the context of this rather cataclysmic projection, Westmoreland's immediate proposals for additional American action were modest and did not include any major request for ground forces. He sought only to "postpone indefinitely the day of collapse" until "other pressures" on North Vietnam—presumably the bombing campaign—could take effect. To this end, he repeated a request he had made in January for freedom of action in using U.S. tactical aircraft against the Viet Cong and put forward a number of proposals for enhancing MACV's reconnaissance and targeting capabilities. To increase ARVN mobility and counter enemy road-cutting, he requested three more UH–1B helicopter companies and a half squadron of C–130 transport planes. Noting that the enemy, conducting larger operations and using standardized Communist-bloc weapons, would have to depend on supplies infiltrated by sea as well as land, Westmoreland urged more extensive use of Pacific Fleet vessels to interdict Vietnamese coastal waters. In his only reference to ground troops, he declared that the deployment of marines to Da Nang would enhance base security there and that "it may be necessary to bring in ground forces elsewhere, for identical purposes or indeed to prevent a collapse in some particular area at a critical time." Ending on a note of incongruous optimism, Westmoreland suggested that the Viet Cong were "not 10 feet tall" and that they suffered from tactical and logistical problems of their own. The South Vietnamese people meanwhile showed "remarkable resiliency" and little enthusiasm for the Communists. In that light, he held out hope that the United States, by an "increased show of strength and determination," might not only buy itself and the Saigon government more time but also "start the pendulum in the opposite direction."[25]

Beginnings of the Ground Troop Commitment, January–June 1965

F–4B Phantom II over South Vietnam (NARA)

Westmoreland's optimism may have stemmed in part from the fact that his campaign to bring the full weight of American air power to bear on the Viet Cong was nearing success in early March. At the beginning of 1965, Westmoreland could not employ U.S. jets in South Vietnam, and the FARM GATE piston engine aircraft still had to carry a Vietnamese pilot or observer on all their missions, which were supposedly for training rather than combat. On 26 January, "as a matter of prudence," Westmoreland asked the Pacific Commander and the Joint Chiefs for authority to launch jet strikes when important enemy targets were unreachable by the Vietnamese Air Force and when a combat situation was "of such criticality that the VC could obtain a major victory or numbers of American lives would be lost." The administration granted his request, with the proviso that Westmoreland himself, with the ambassador's concurrence, approve each mission. Westmoreland used this authority twice during February, once for a raid on a Viet Cong concentration in Phuoc Tuy Province, site of the Binh Gia battle, and the second time to relieve an ambushed Ranger and CIDG force near Pleiku.[26]

Although enemy pressure on the South Vietnamese Army mounted, the initial jet strikes had favorable military results with no visible adverse Vietnamese governmental or popular reaction. Thus, during late February and early March, Westmoreland pressed for complete discretionary authority to employ air power. He wanted to eliminate the cumbersome mission-by-mission approval requirement and to locate strike request and control in the established MACV/VNAF tactical air control system. The administration was at first reluctant to give Westmoreland the broad mandate he requested, but it relented after increasingly urgent representations from the MACV commander, seconded by Admiral Sharp. On 9 March 1965, the Joint Chiefs granted Sharp full discretion to employ U.S. aircraft in South Vietnam as he and his subordinate commanders deemed prudent. On the same day, also at Westmoreland's and Sharp's recommendation, the Joint Chiefs removed the restrictions on FARM GATE combat operations and authorized the air commando unit to replace with U.S. Air Force markings the Vietnamese insignia their planes had borne hitherto. From that point onward, American jet and propeller-driven aircraft were fully committed to the fight in South Vietnam, and heavy American air strikes could be expected to accompany every sizable engagement.[27]

Westmoreland had campaigned vigorously to bring American air power into the battle, but until well into March he was much less aggressive in advocating the use of ground troops. This was true even though MACV was rapidly realizing the extent of the enemy's force buildup and the degree to which it was tipping the balance against the government in the countryside. Westmoreland mentioned troops only in general terms and largely in connection with base defense in his 6 March situation estimate. This was at the time when the 9th Marine Expeditionary Brigade was preparing to land at Da Nang. In endorsing Westmoreland's estimate, Admiral Sharp was equally conservative. He emphasized only the need for troops "in security missions within Vietnam" and the desirability of expanding the U.S. logistical base there.[28] Only after receiving a strong signal from Washington that more expansive proposals were desired and expected did Westmoreland submit his first major recommendation for introducing American soldiers into the ground war.

Three Proposals for Sending Troops

The signal came during a visit to Vietnam by the Army Chief of Staff, General Harold K. Johnson. As he had indicated in suggesting the deployment of U.S. troops to Taylor and Westmoreland in December, President Johnson was intent on taking every possible measure to infuse energy into the campaign against the Viet Cong. In addition, during the first months of 1965, the president and his principal advisers had come to share General Westmoreland's concern that South Vietnam might be in danger of collapse. Driven by both considerations, the president on 2 March dispatched General Johnson to Saigon to review with the mission the existing American effort and decide what more could and should be done. In particular, General Johnson told Ambassador Taylor, his task was to evaluate "present use of all DOD assets and . . . determine what additional forces and techniques, if any, can be of value." President Johnson himself phrased his instructions more colorfully. After a breakfast meeting on the day of General Johnson's departure for Saigon, the Army chief of staff later recalled, the president "bored his finger into my chest and . . . said 'get things bubbling'" in Vietnam.[29]

The president's dispatch of the chief of staff of the Army to investigate and report on what additional military measures should be taken in Vietnam in itself pointed toward an interest in more activity on the ground. In fact, General Johnson's trip resulted in three separate but related proposals to that end, one from the Army chief of staff himself, one from Westmoreland, and one from the Joint Chiefs. During the months that followed, officials outlined the shape of the American commitment on the basis of those proposals.

General Johnson (NARA)

General Johnson arrived in Saigon on 5 March 1965, with a party composed of fourteen military and civilian members. During a week's stay, he and his group conferred with Ambassador Taylor, General Westmoreland, and the mission council and received extensive briefings from the MACV staff. The Army chief of staff also met with South Vietnamese officials, including Premier Quat, Minister of Defense Thieu, and Air Vice Marshal Ky. The briefings and conversations generally sounded the same note as Westmoreland's assessment of 6 March, with emphasis on indications that the enemy might be preparing for a large takeover of territory in the Central Highlands, possibly as the base for an alternative National Liberation Front government.[30]

General Johnson brought with him for discussion a list of proposals for additional actions. The embassy and MACV furnished him with their own lists, prepared, at Secretary McNamara's direction, on the assumption of "no limitation on funds, equipment or personnel." The ensuing talks and briefings included much mention of American troops. At their first meeting, Johnson and the mission council agreed to explore a number of subjects, among them "use of U.S. manpower to offset present shortage in Armed Forces of GVN." Westmoreland submitted to the chief of staff an extensive array of possible new military actions. These included employment of U.S. troops to act as corps and general reserve reaction forces, to defend enclaves, and to provide "ground security for critical areas." During March his staff was making an intensive study of the enclave plan and also of the feasibility of an antiinfiltration cordon across northern South Vietnam and the Laos panhandle. At some point during the visit, Westmoreland broached to Johnson the idea of deploying a U.S. Army division around Pleiku to help relieve pressure on II Corps. The chief of staff indicated that the new airmobile division might be available for that assignment.[31]

The Army chief of staff left Vietnam a convinced proponent of putting in American ground troops in substantial numbers and with a combat mission. On his way back to Washington, Johnson told the staff of U.S. Army, Pacific: "I am the first Chief of Staff, I think, since World War II who believes that if it is in the interest of the United States to hold South Vietnam . . . , then it is in the interest of the United States to commit ground troops to Asia." He dismissed as "fictional" the post-Korea doctrine that the United States should stay out of Asian land wars and declared: "Where the U.S. interest requires it, that is where the Army belongs, and so far as I am concerned, that's where I am going to recommend that it go. That's our job."[32]

In his trip report, delivered on 14 March 1965, Johnson was as good as his word. The chief of staff repeated much of General Westmoreland's 6 March assessment, declaring that the Vietnam situation had "deteriorated rapidly and extensively in the past several months and that major new remedial actions must be quickly undertaken." He reported that the South Vietnamese armed forces, even with the planned increase, lacked the resources to deal by themselves with the "magnitude and scope" of Viet Cong aggression.

To reinforce the South Vietnamese, Johnson proposed three categories of American action. The first consisted of twenty-one specific measures for reinforcing the existing advisory and support effort, intensifying the air war against North Vietnam, and bringing U.S. air and sea power to bear more effectively in South Vietnam. General Johnson's second category was a proposal to send a "tailored division force" of American troops to South Vietnam, either to defend certain key towns and installations or (as Johnson preferred) to operate offensively against the Viet Cong in the Central Highlands in order to allow the ARVN in II Corps to concentrate more of its troops in the coastal provinces. Implementation of his twenty-one points and deployment of the division, Johnson declared, would "alleviate but may not remedy" the military situation and probably would not provide "the power increase needed to support an acceptable political solution to the war." Hence, Johnson suggested a third and final step: emplacement of a U.S. or SEATO anti-infiltration cordon of at least four divisions below the Demilitarized Zone and across the Laotian panhandle. Besides stopping infiltration, Johnson argued, the cordon force would supplement

Beginnings of the Ground Troop Commitment, January–June 1965

the bombing as a threat to North Vietnam and provide leverage in any negotiations that might develop in the future.[33]

General Westmoreland expressed satisfaction with the chief of staff's proposals, which, he later declared, "reflected much of my thinking." Johnson's visit evidently convinced the MACV commander that a major troop request would receive favorable consideration in Washington and indeed now was expected, and he lost no time in submitting one. Immediately after General Johnson's departure, Westmoreland put his staff to work on a plan incorporating many ideas they had discussed. He outlined the results in a 17 March message to General Wheeler, and at the end of the month he sent the full plan to Washington in the form of a voluminous "Commander's Estimate of the Military Situation in South Vietnam."[34]

In both documents, Westmoreland defined the immediate problem as a need to gain time by preventing a South Vietnamese collapse under intensifying Viet Cong pressure until Saigon's armed forces could complete their projected 1965 expansion and/or ROLLING THUNDER could cause North Vietnam to stop supporting the insurgency. To accomplish this, U.S. ground forces were required to "offset security deficiencies and stabilize the situation pending the buildup of the RVNAF."

Westmoreland began his argument with an extended analysis of the enemy threat. He reviewed the latest, most alarming estimates of Viet Cong main force and guerrilla strength and pointed out that by recruiting and conscription within South Vietnam supplemented by infiltration from the north the enemy could raise at least twenty new battalions a year and an indeterminate number of irregulars. Reviewing a number of possible Viet Cong courses of action, Westmoreland believed the insurgents would most likely pursue a campaign of small-scale attacks, subversion, assassination, sabotage, and propaganda designed to expand the Viet Cong's political, administrative, and security infrastructure in the south. They would couple this effort with "maximum feasible buildup of forces in preparation for a higher level of military operations" and "occasional large scale attacks where there is a high assurance of success." As a supplement, they might also introduce regular North Vietnamese combat units of up to division size into I and II Corps "to attack and overrun a major installation or city. . . in an attempt to break the will to resist in the northern corps [and] establish a pseudo government." The South Vietnamese Army, Westmoreland declared, even with its projected 1965 increase, could barely contain an intensified guerrilla offensive with occasional large-unit attacks. If North Vietnamese units joined the battle as well, the government might suffer in I and II Corps major defeats and territorial losses severe enough to lead to the sort of military and political disintegration the Viet Cong sought.[35]

To ensure against such a disaster, the United States must commit ground forces at once. Like General Johnson, Westmoreland advocated deploying a U.S. Army division (if possible the new airmobile unit) to conduct offensive operations against the Viet Cong on the axis between Qui Nhon and Pleiku in the Central Highlands. As an alternative, the division could secure coastal enclaves around the ports of Qui Nhon, Nha Trang, and Tuy Hoa. Westmoreland preferred the first course of action because it seemed more immediately beneficial to the military balance in the critical highlands. It also gave American soldiers an offensive mission away from the densely populated lowlands where their presence might provoke political hostility. In addition to the division, Westmoreland asked for a separate Army brigade for use in III Corps to protect bases at Bien Hoa and Vung Tau and to conduct mobile operations in defense of the HOP TAC area. Finally, he proposed rounding out the Marine force at Da Nang with a third battalion landing team and the placement of a fourth Marine infantry battalion at Phu Bai, north of Da Nang, to protect the airfield and Army communications intelligence unit there. Counting the 2 Marine battalions already at Da Nang, the units requested would constitute a force of 13 Army and 4 Marine infantry battalions plus supporting elements. Westmoreland estimated that their presence would release at least 10 ARVN battalions for redeployment or for reconstitution of Saigon's general reserve. He asked that the deployment of the units and the logistic elements required for their support begin as soon as possible and that it be completed not later than early June. He warned in addition that if ROLLING THUNDER had not succeeded by the middle of the year, "additional deployments of U.S. and third country forces should be considered, including introduction of the full [Marine expeditionary force] into I Corps."[36]

In what was to become a recurring rationale when the Military Assistance Command made troop requests, Westmoreland emphasized the contribution his proposed reinforcement would make to improving the overall ratio of allied to enemy strength as measured in comparative numbers of maneuver battalions. Abandoning the 10-to-1 ratio of government to enemy forces usually deemed essential to success in counterinsurgency but obviously unattainable in South Vietnam, Westmoreland set 3-to-1 as the desirable margin instead. However, even with its projected 1965 increase, the South Vietnamese Army would end the year with a ratio to the Viet Cong of only 1.6 battalions to 1, assuming a comparatively modest Viet Cong buildup and no large injection of North Vietnamese units. The insertion of American units, Westmoreland contended, would improve the ratio considerably, especially since each U.S. Army battalion could be considered as equal in combat power to two ARVN or Viet Cong battalions and each Marine battalion as equal to three. With the 13 Army and 4 Marine battalions, the ARVN thus would gain the equivalent of 38 of its own battalions, bringing the nationwide troop ratio to 1.9 to 1 by the end of 1965 and the ratio in critical II Corps close to the desired 3 to 1. Further, if the American units arrived by the middle of the year, they would shift the balance

Beginnings of the Ground Troop Commitment, January–June 1965

toward the government much sooner than would the ARVN buildup alone, giving the U.S. force still greater military and political impact.[37]

Westmoreland gave extended consideration to an antiinfiltration cordon across northern South Vietnam and the Laotian panhandle. However, he saw it as no immediate solution to the military problem he faced. He acknowledged that perhaps five divisions of American, South Vietnamese, Thai, and Laotian troops, once deployed from the South China Sea to the Mekong, effectively would prevent North Vietnam from supporting the Viet Cong buildup. The disadvantage, he pointed out, was that it would take at least the remaining months of 1965, and perhaps longer, to put the ports and roads in I Corps into condition to supply such a force, not to mention opening the necessary line of communications through Thailand. In addition, extension of the conflict into nominally neutral Laos would undoubtedly provoke heated political opposition in the United States and lead to a multitude of diplomatic difficulties, further delaying establishment of the cordon. Westmoreland suggested that if ROLLING THUNDER performed as hoped, the cordon would be superfluous by the time it was in place. In any event, he concluded, the blocking force could not be in position soon enough to help reduce the immediate threat to the Saigon government.[38]

General Westmoreland sent his commander's estimate to Washington at the end of March, carried by General DePuy, who accompanied Ambassador Taylor to the capital for a policy reassessment. High Defense Department officials and the Joint Chiefs of Staff received a briefing on the estimate. By the time it reached Washington, however, the chiefs already had developed a more ambitious proposal of their own based on General Johnson's report and earlier communications from Westmoreland.[39]

General Johnson's report, indeed, had set off a flurry of top-level discussion. At a 15 March 1965 meeting with McNamara and the Joint Chiefs, the president approved in principle most of the Army chief of staff's twenty-one recommendations for strengthening the existing American effort. He also made apparent his interest in more far-reaching military proposals, urging the chiefs to devise measures to "kill more VC." The Joint Chiefs reviewed General Johnson's suggested ground force deployments. They also considered the possibility of introducing a South Korean division into South Vietnam to give the troop commitment an international flavor, something much desired by the administration, and heard a proposal from the commandant of the Marine Corps to establish six coastal "beachheads" defended by American forces.[40]

On 20 March, after a study by the Joint Staff and considerable negotiation among themselves, the chiefs delivered their own proposal to the secretary of defense. Declaring that "the requirement is not simply to withstand the Viet Cong, . . . but to gain effective operational superiority and assume the offensive," the Joint Chiefs called for dispatch of a Marine expeditionary force to Da Nang, a U.S. Army division to Pleiku, and a Republic of Korea division (assuming one could be obtained) to a location to be determined later. The mission of the marines and Army troops would be "counterinsurgency combat operations," while that of the Koreans would be "counterinsurgency and base security operations." On the day they submitted their proposal to Secretary McNamara, the chiefs directed Admiral Sharp and General Westmoreland to comment on the logistical requirements for deploying and supporting the three-division force and on command arrangements to permit the MACV commander effectively to coordinate allied and South Vietnamese ground operations. From that point on, the JCS proposal became the basis for planning at all echelons and also eventually for presidential deployment decisions.[41]

Edging into the Ground War

By the end of March, Westmoreland, the chief of staff of the Army, and the Joint Chiefs of Staff all had recommended commitment of large numbers of U.S. troops to ground combat. President Johnson and his closest advisers strongly favored in principle reinforcement of the South Vietnamese Army with American soldiers. Nevertheless, during the next two months, the president moved only slowly and cautiously, albeit steadily, toward implementing the military leaders' recommendations. He and his advisers were concerned with keeping all Executive Branch participants in the policy debate on board at each step and hence sought to keep the steps small. They also wanted to avoid overly abrupt or conspicuous acts of escalation so as to placate domestic public opinion and neutralize opponents of the war. Finally, they had to deal with Vietnam in relation to other military and diplomatic problems, including a major crisis in the Dominican Republic that had led to U.S. military intervention.[42]

Even had the administration wanted to move faster, a number of circumstances worked against any immediate large infusion of U.S. troops into South Vietnam. For one thing, as of late March, no American logistical base existed in the country capable of supporting a multidivision force. Insertion of major units, General Westmoreland and Admiral Sharp told the Joint Chiefs, would have to await formation of an Army logistic command; deployment of thousands of support troops; and extensive port, airfield, and road improvements. Those preparations had yet to begin or even to be authorized.[43]

During April and May 1965, the military situation in South Vietnam, as reported by MACV and the U.S. Mission, appeared less desperate than it had at the beginning of the year. The civilian government of Premier Quat proved unexpectedly effective, restoring a semblance of cohesive administration and moderating Saigon's endemic faction-

Beginnings of the Ground Troop Commitment, January–June 1965

The Joint Chiefs of Staff: left to right, *General McConnell, Admiral McDonald, Generals Wheeler, Johnson, and Greene* (© Bettmann/CORBIS photo)

al strife. On the battlefield, Viet Cong offensive activity diminished, while the South Vietnamese Army regained the initiative and won victories in some areas. Westmoreland felt optimistic enough to suggest in his monthly evaluation for April that the government "may have actually turned the tide at long last." To be sure, there were less favorable indications. The Viet Cong main forces continued to increase in size and appeared to be concentrating for probable new attacks in the I, II, and III Corps areas. Evidence continued to mount, moreover, of the presence of North Vietnamese regular units in the Central Highlands. General DePuy believed, as a result, that South Vietnam was in "the lull before a storm" and that the outcome of the war "seems to be hanging in the balance." These ill omens notwithstanding, the sense of crisis that had given rise to the March troop proposals abated during April and early May, enough to encourage second thoughts about major commitments.[44]

For his own part, Ambassador Taylor had long advised a slow, cautious approach to the commitment of American combat units. An early and consistent advocate of bombing the north, he acknowledged that the force ratio in the south was changing in favor of the enemy and that at some point American soldiers might be needed to redress the balance. Even so, until late May, he repeatedly counseled against any immediate large-scale use of Americans to fight the Viet Cong. He doubted that the "white-faced soldier" could engage the guerrillas effectively on their own ground. Major troop involvement, he contended, would expose the United States to charges of colonialism and give the Chinese Communists an excuse to send their own forces into North Vietnam. In the south, American fighting men would have difficulty distinguishing Vietnamese friends from foes and would come into politically abrasive contact with the civilian population. The war-weary Saigon government and army would turn the more difficult missions over to the Americans, thereby generating still further demands for U.S. troops. Given these disadvantages, Taylor argued, only the gravest threat to South Vietnam's survival could justify commitment of major U.S. combat units, and no such threat yet existed. Therefore, to avoid tying down mobile Army and Marine forces unnecessarily and counterproductively, he urged the White House to minimize combat unit deployments and instead to bring in support troops to build a logistic base capable of sustaining large forces in case it became necessary to commit them later.[45]

The administration's first major decision on troop commitments strongly reflected Taylor's advice. On 1 April, after conferences with his advisers and with the ambassador, President Johnson directed the deployment to Vietnam of two additional Marine battalions, a Marine aircraft squadron, and the 9th MEB headquarters and support elements. One battalion was to round out the brigade at Da Nang; the other, in accord with General Westmoreland's recommendation in his commander's estimate, was to defend the Army radio unit and airfield at Phu Bai. Johnson also authorized the dispatch of 18,000–20,000 U.S. support troops to Vietnam "to fill out existing units and supply needed logistic personnel." Subsequent directives and messages made clear that these troops were to establish a series of coastal bases capable of supporting the three-division force proposed by the Joint Chiefs. Seeking allied troops to balance the new American commitment, President Johnson ordered "urgent exploration" of force contributions with the South Korean, Australian, and New Zealand governments.

Finally, in perhaps his most portentous decision, the president altered the mission of all Marine battalions in Vietnam "to permit their more active use under conditions to be established and approved by the Secretary of Defense in consultation with the Secretary of State." Secretaries Rusk and McNamara and Ambassador Taylor construed this language as authorizing a shift from static positional defense to at least limited offensive operations against the Viet Cong, including, in Taylor's view, a "strike role" in support of the South Vietnamese Army anywhere within fifty miles of American bases. The President and his advisers postponed a final decision on the Joint Chiefs' three-division plan. They recognized, however, that deployment of the additional marines and logistic troops was the first step in implementing the larger program and expected to review further steps within about sixty days.[46]

Beginnings of the Ground Troop Commitment, January–June 1965

In the meantime, the Joint Chiefs, at Secretary McNamara's direction, began detailed planning for introduction of the entire three-division allied force into Vietnam "at the earliest practicable date." At the chiefs' direction, Admiral Sharp convened representatives of all the major Pacific commands, MACV among them, as well as delegations from the Defense Department, the JCS, and interested commands in the United States, for a deployment conference that ran between 9 and 11 April at his Honolulu headquarters. The conference developed specific logistic requirements and movement schedules for the forces contemplated for deployment. In the course of their discussions, the conferees fleshed out many portions of the chiefs' plan. They suggested Qui Nhon and Nha Trang as coastal bases for the Army division and reiterated that the division's mission should be counterinsurgency operations in the Central Highlands. Adopting MACV recommendations, the conference proposed Quang Ngai, in southern I Corps, as the most worthwhile location for the Korean division and added to the original plan a separate Army brigade for Bien Hoa/Vung Tau. For all these units, as well as the marines at Da Nang and Phu Bai, the conferees proposed a concept of operations calling for movement by stages from initial securing of coastal bases to wide-ranging offensive maneuvers, and they made proposals for command and control of the force in unilateral and combined operations.[47]

According to the U.S. Army, Pacific, historian, this conference, for the Pacific Command and its components, signaled imminent U.S. movement from a limited advisory role to preparation for full combat participation in the war. The Joint Chiefs incorporated the conference version of troop locations, concepts of operations, and command relations into an expanded version of their three-division proposal, which they presented to McNamara on 17 April. Subsequent discussions of all aspects of committing troops to Vietnam among the Joint Chiefs, Sharp, and Westmoreland revolved around the three-division plan as modified by the April CINCPAC conference.[48]

General Westmoreland, whose commander's estimate had been overshadowed in Washington by the Joint Chiefs' three-division proposal, sought to incorporate MACV ideas into the chiefs' plan. For example, he argued successfully for Quang Ngai as the location for the Korean division, in preference to the Saigon area initially favored by the Joint Chiefs. Recognizing that a full division for the Central Highlands was more than the administration could accept at once, he concentrated on separate requests for the smaller forces mentioned in his commander's estimate. Hence, late in March, he pressed for an additional Marine battalion for Phu Bai, emphasizing the need to protect the Army radio unit and the desirability of securing an additional airstrip for Marine helicopters to relieve congestion at Da Nang. Ambassador Taylor supported Westmoreland in this recommendation, which became part of the president's 1 April troop decision.[49]

Westmoreland then shifted to a campaign for deployment of an Army brigade to Bien Hoa and Vung Tau, also part of his commander's estimate. The CINCPAC conference of 9–11 April, which General Stilwell, the MACV chief of staff, reported was "heavily influenced" by Westmoreland's ideas, incorporated this deployment into its recommendations. Westmoreland then repeated it as a separate proposal on 11 April l965. Declaring that the brigade would enhance the security of vital American installations while reinforcing the Hop Tac area against growing Viet Cong main forces, he added that it would also serve as an air-transportable reserve for the Central Highlands. While Westmoreland did not specify a unit in his request, the most likely candidate was the Okinawa-based 173d Airborne Brigade, long earmarked for Vietnam in contingency plans and briefly considered as a substitute for the 9th Marine Expeditionary Brigade at Da Nang. On the basis of a MACV staff study of the possibility of bringing the 173d into Vietnam periodically for short-duration offensive operations, Westmoreland early in April asked Admiral Sharp's permission to begin planning for deployment of the brigade. After Sharp, the Joint Chiefs, and Secretary McNamara approved Westmoreland's 11 April proposal, the chiefs on the 14th directed CINCPAC to deploy the 173d to Bien Hoa. U.S. Army, Pacific; U.S. Army, Ryukyu Islands; and MACV began making the preliminary arrangements for the movement.[50]

A protest from Ambassador Taylor brought these preparations to an abrupt halt. Taylor complained to the secretary of state that the order came as a "complete surprise" to him, conflicted with his understanding of administration policy at that point, and had not been accompanied by State Department instructions to obtain agreement from Premier Quat. Always concerned with keeping all his advisers on board, President Johnson suspended the order pending another full-dress conference on troop deployments.[51]

A new conference was necessary, as well, because the Johnson administration, even more than General Westmoreland, was pressing the question of introducing American troops. On 15 April, McGeorge Bundy informed Ambassador Taylor that the president believed that the United States must use "all practicable means" to strengthen its position in South Vietnam and that "additional United States troops are [an] important if not decisive reinforcement." That same day, the State and Defense Departments, in a joint message to Taylor and Westmoreland, directed MACV to plan for insertion of a brigade at Bien Hoa and additional multibattalion forces at several coastal points. All were to conduct counterinsurgency operations. The same message called on the country team to undertake a number of other "experimental steps" suggested by the president himself, aimed at adding "something new" to American programs in South Vietnam in order to "achieve victory." These included encadrement of Americans into ARVN battalions, brigading of ARVN battalions with American ones, use of American experts

Beginnings of the Ground Troop Commitment, January–June 1965

and techniques to improve South Vietnamese recruiting, employment of American mobile dispensaries to bring medical care to the peasantry, reinforcement of province administration with American civil affairs teams, and U.S. distribution of food directly to South Vietnamese soldiers and their families. Eager for immediate action, the administration proposed to send a large military-civilian party to Saigon within the week to begin implementing the new programs.[52]

If Westmoreland and Taylor had been out of step on the question of deploying the 173d Airborne Brigade, they responded in concert to these new proposals, which the ambassador later characterized as "the product of Washington initiative flogged to a new level of creativity by a President determined to get prompt results." Taylor protested vehemently against rushing American deployments without sufficient planning, justification, and diplomatic clearance. He also complained that the administration was piling more programs on a Saigon government already floundering in its efforts to execute the existing ones. Supporting Taylor's position, Westmoreland argued against all the encadrement plans as duplicating much of the advisory effort. He added that they would create morale and logistical problems for both the Americans and South Vietnamese out of all proportion to any military benefits. In the face of these objections, President Johnson suspended introduction of any new troops or programs until after a policy conference called for Honolulu on 20 April.[53]

When that conference convened, Secretary McNamara, accompanied by General Wheeler and other officials, met with Ambassador Taylor, Admiral Sharp, and General Westmoreland. Besides quietly burying most of the president's cadre proposals, the conferees agreed to speed up the insertion of American combat units into South Vietnam, a move they rationalized as helping to break the will of the Viet Cong by denying them victory. Adopting a scaled-down version of the JCS plan, the group recommended the deployment to Vietnam during May and June of 3 additional American brigades, 2 Army and 1 Marine, along with substantial logistic elements, an Australian battalion (already promised by that country), and a Korean regimental combat team yet to be obtained. These deployments would bring American troop strength in Vietnam to about 82,000 men and 13 maneuver battalions before even counting the 7,200 Australians and South Koreans. One U.S. Army brigade was to go to Bien Hoa–Vung Tau and the other to Qui Nhon and Nha Trang. The Marine brigade and aviation units were to take position at Chu Lai in southern I Corps, the site of a planned new American airfield. The Australians were to reinforce the Army brigade at Bien Hoa and the Koreans to operate in southern Quang Ngai. As possible later deployments "not recommended now," the conferees designated the U.S. Army airmobile division for use in the Central Highlands, a U.S. corps headquarters for Nha Trang, a full Korean infantry division for Quang Ngai, and three more Marine battalions for Da Nang.[54]

Left to right, *Secretary McNamara, Air Vice Marshal Ky, President Johnson, and General Thieu* (NARA)

President Johnson accepted these proposals, but he implemented them gradually. The Marine brigade targeted for Chu Lai and the 173d Airborne Brigade for Bien Hoa deployed early in May. The Australians and large numbers of American support troops followed shortly thereafter. The Koreans and the final Army brigade for Qui Nhon and Nha Trang did not begin to move until after events made the deployment plan for them obsolete. In the end, nonetheless, the 20 April decisions committed the United States to large-scale ground combat in Vietnam. Under them, indeed, Westmoreland obtained as many battalions as he had requested in his March commander's estimate, though not the division for the Central Highlands.[55]

Questions of Command and the Concept of Operations

As each of the U.S. units deployed, the Military Assistance Command helped prepare the way diplomatically and militarily. While Ambassador Taylor secured Premier Quat's approval of each new American commitment, General Westmoreland informed the commander in chief of the South Vietnamese armed forces and the chief of the Joint General Staff and reached an understanding with them on the military arrangements. He also helped prepare for the introduction of third-country allied forces. For example, he worked out with the Australian ambassador in Saigon the location and missions of that country's battalion. For the American forces, Westmoreland and his principal staff officers arranged cooperation with the ARVN commands in their areas of operation and tried to ensure the orderly arrival of the troops. On one occasion, he dissuaded the 9th Marine Expeditionary Brigade from conducting a full-scale amphibious assault at Chu Lai, complete with preparatory air strikes and naval gunfire, on a beach which contained friendly civilians and was to be secured beforehand by the 2d ARVN Division.[56]

While the first deployments were being debated, decided upon, and carried out, MACV, the Pacific Command, and the JCS engaged in continuing discussions aimed at refining aspects of the three-division plan. They concentrated their attention on three issues: tactical command and control of American forces; command relations between American and South Vietnamese forces; and the question of exactly what combat missions American troops should perform and by what stages they should enter upon them. Through a constant exchange of messages, and through the Honolulu conferences, the senior commanders reached a general consensus on these clusters of issues. Thus they made a number of decisions that would shape the future course of American ground operations in South Vietnam.

Marines wade across a neck-deep river. (© The Mariners' Museum/CORBIS)

The simplest, most straightforward problem was that of tactical command of U.S. and allied field forces once they entered the country in significant numbers. Since most of the units would be in the northern corps areas remote from Saigon, MACV obviously would require a subordinate headquarters of some sort to direct day-to-day operations of the Army and Korean divisions and to coordinate their activities with those of the marines, who already had their own command structure in the form of the III Marine Expeditionary Force (MEF) and its subordinate division and aircraft wing. Accordingly, during March, Westmoreland began considering formation of a Northern Area Command to direct operations of all non–South Vietnamese combat units. Spurred by General Wheeler and following OPLAN 32, he and Admiral Sharp decided during April that a U.S. Army corps headquarters should probably deploy to Nha Trang soon after the Army division did. This headquarters was to assume operational control of the III MEF, the

Army troops, and the Koreans. Westmoreland proposed to assign his deputy, General Throckmorton, to command the headquarters since Throckmorton was familiar with MACV plans and policies and possessed the rank and prestige to deal with the Vietnamese corps commanders. After the Marine landings at Chu Lai in early May, the III Marine Expeditionary Force, the 3d Marine Division, and the 1st Marine Aircraft Wing headquarters moved into Da Nang and went into operation. The force headquarters was retitled, at Westmoreland's request, the III Marine Amphibious Force (MAF) to avoid evoking unpleasant Vietnamese memories of the French Expeditionary Corps. Deployment of the Army corps headquarters and formation of the northern field force remained in abeyance along with deployment of the Army and Korean divisions.[57]

The question of American–South Vietnamese command relations was more complicated. With a large U.S. troop buildup and major American combat involvement in prospect, General Westmoreland in March launched a low-keyed but insistent campaign for establishment of a combined allied command that, in effect, would place the ARVN under operational control of MACV. He believed that, beyond any military benefits, such a command would enhance the Saigon government's stability by bringing politically active South Vietnamese generals under American supervision and restraint. Prime Minister Quat and at least a few senior RVNAF officers shared Westmoreland's views on this point. They agreed that only some form of combined command and staff could restore the government forces' military effectiveness.[58]

Seeking to exploit this opportunity, Westmoreland during March and April 1965 developed plans for a small American–South Vietnamese staff to assist him and the RVNAF High Command in planning and directing combined operations. Westmoreland believed that creation of such a staff, serving otherwise independent national forces, would not offend Vietnamese nationalist sensitivities; at the same time it would be a first step toward a full-fledged combined command. During General Johnson's visit early in March, Premier Quat expressed support for a combined staff. At Westmoreland's direction the MACV J3 and J5 sections drew up terms of reference and a table of distribution for it. In April, Westmoreland secured a tour extension for his candidate for chief of the combined staff, Col. James L. Collins, Jr., then senior adviser to the Regional and Popular Forces. Soon to be promoted to brigadier general, Collins spoke fluent French and had a good relationship with senior Vietnamese officials. Westmoreland also intended to establish similar combined staffs at corps and lower level headquarters when U.S. troops arrived. In addition, General Throckmorton developed plans for creating an international field force headquarters in the northern corps areas, initially to be built around the 9th MEB and later around the U.S. corps, which would exercise tactical control over American, South Korean, and some South Vietnamese combat units.[59]

Beginnings of the Ground Troop Commitment, January–June 1965

This planning came to an abrupt halt early in May. The senior Vietnamese generals, increasingly the dominant force in the Saigon government, expressed strong opposition to any form of combined command. Complicating matters, the Saigon newspapers picked up rumors, probably planted by the generals, that a combined command was under consideration. They issued passionate editorial denunciations of any such surrender of Vietnamese sovereignty. Faced with this opposition, Westmoreland and Taylor abandoned the campaign for even a combined staff. On 8 May, in his first comprehensive concept of operations for U.S. forces in Vietnam, Westmoreland declared that the command relationship between the Americans and the South Vietnamese armed forces would be one of "combat support through coordination and cooperation in the mutual self-interest of both commands." Later in the month, when Secretary McNamara formally endorsed creation of a combined high-level staff and field force headquarters, Taylor and Westmoreland both responded that such action was no longer politically feasible or desirable. From then on, the MACV commander concentrated on making the existing advisory and cooperative relationship work as well as possible. He did manage to install General Collins in the Joint General Staff compound as his personal representative. General DePuy continued informally to promote combined contingency planning at the JGS and corps levels.[60]

Even before significant American ground combat forces arrived, MACV had thus decided, by default, against a Korea-style unified allied command. General Westmoreland later justified this decision as essential to appease South Vietnamese nationalist sensibilities and as desirable in enhancing their forces' capacity to operate on their own when American troops eventually departed. He believed that, with advisers at every level of the Vietnamese armed forces, with his network of personal relationships with senior RVNAF commanders, and with the leverage he could exert through his control of American resources, he could influence South Vietnamese operations sufficiently for his purpose without "puppetry or proconsulship." Incoming MACV Chief of Staff, Maj. Gen. William B. Rosson, who arrived just after the effort for a combined staff collapsed, fully endorsed Westmoreland's reasoning. Rosson, who had been in Indochina during the French war, declared that "anyone possessing even a cursory knowledge of the French colonial period in Vietnamese history could and should have dismissed out of hand . . . a scheme calling for foreign—particularly Occidental—encadrement and command of GVN forces." He "frankly was irritated to find that the staff recently had been required to devote substantial time and effort to that subject."[61]

Closely related to the question of command was that of a concept of operations for the U.S. forces. When American troops entered South Vietnam in substantial numbers, where were they to go and what, beyond static base defense, were they to do? Every troop commitment proposal addressed this question, directly or indirectly. By the end of May, at least the military participants in the policy debate were approaching a consensus on the subject.

From the start, General Westmoreland thought in terms of using U.S. units aggressively, especially against the Viet Cong's main forces. He told General Wheeler on 17 March that American troops, besides protecting the principal ports and air bases, "must be available and committed when necessary as quick-reaction forces against the VC once he comes out into the open and chooses to engage." In his commander's estimate, Westmoreland envisioned employment of a division deep in the Central Highlands for mobile offensive operations; and he wanted the Army brigade at Bien Hoa and Vung Tau as a reaction force for III Corps. Aware of widespread official interest in concentrating U.S. forces for the defense of coastal enclaves, the MACV commander acknowledged that this concept, which his staff had studied, possessed "attractive features" from a logistical standpoint, and "to some degree" was "integral to all other plans." Even so, he declared, this approach represented "an inglorious, static use of U.S. forces in an overpopulated area with little chance of direct or immediate impact on the outcome of events."[62]

To varying degrees, Admiral Sharp, the Joint Chiefs, and Ambassador Taylor shared Westmoreland's preference for the offensive. Sharp opposed sending the Army division inland until its coastal bases were secured, but he emphasized that any American units committed should "phase into the counterinsurgency role," which would involve "active, mobile search and destroy operations." The Joint Chiefs, in their three-division proposal, favored placing the Army division in the Central Highlands for mobile operations and emphasized the need to "gain operational superiority and assume the offensive." Although skeptical of the necessity and desirability of introducing a division-size American force, Ambassador Taylor considered an offensive mission in the highlands the most militarily useful role for such a force if it did go in. Late in March he expressed preference for an "offensive enclave" strategy, under which U.S. troops would establish secure coastal bases and then operate up to fifty miles inland from them in support of the South Vietnamese. This idea seems to have been the basis of President Johnson's 1 April expansion of the mission of the 9th Marine Expeditionary Brigade.[63]

Commenting on 27 March on the Joint Chiefs' three-division plan, Admiral Sharp outlined a concept of operations that all the military participants were able to accept. Sharp proposed that American forces move into South Vietnam and onto the offensive in four phases. In the first, they were to protect vital U.S. installations and establish secure coastal enclaves from which they could support South Vietnamese operations. In the second, they were to conduct offensive operations from those enclaves. In the third and fourth phases, they would move inland and repeat the process, first establishing bases and then attack-

Beginnings of the Ground Troop Commitment, January–June 1965

ing outward from them. The 9–11 April CINCPAC conference adopted this four-phase concept, adding the proviso that the phases were "not necessarily sacrosanct" and could overlap or be conducted simultaneously in different areas, depending on the situation. Discussing specific operations of the three divisions, the conference members, partially endorsing Westmoreland's views, recommended that the Army division first establish coastal bases at Qui Nhon and Nha Trang and then, "when logistically feasible," conduct mobile operations in the highlands. The Joint Chiefs, with Secretary McNamara's approval, incorporated the PACOM conference concept into their own further revisions and expansions of their plan.[64]

General Westmoreland included the phase concept in his instructions to the 9th MEB implementing President Johnson's 1 April expansion of the marines' mission, but his initial effort was not aggressive enough for Admiral Sharp. On 11 April, after obtaining consent from South Vietnamese authorities, Westmoreland directed the Marine brigade commander to move onto the offensive by stages, beginning with extended patrolling, then undertaking small heliborne attacks within a fifty-mile radius of Da Nang, and finally launching battalion-size offensives throughout I Corps in cooperation with the Vietnamese. He told Sharp that he did not expect the marines to reach the third stage for "several weeks." Westmoreland's directive drew strong criticism from Sharp. The admiral informed Westmoreland that the Joint Chiefs of Staff desired the "earliest feasible" involvement of the 9th MEB in offensive counterinsurgency combat, and he insisted that the MACV commander strengthen the wording of his instructions to that effect. Westmoreland complied. On 14 April, he sent the 9th MEB an amended directive that included a sentence, drafted by Sharp, calling for "an intensifying program of offensive operations to fix and destroy the VC in the general Da Nang area."[65]

Admiral Sharp's phases were even more evident in Westmoreland's first general concept of operations for American troops, which he issued on 8 May after discussions with the South Vietnamese High Command. Westmoreland defined four missions for American and other non–South Vietnamese units, to be assumed successively and cumulatively as the units arrived in the country and gained experience in operating there: base area security; "deep patrolling and offensive operations"; "reaction operations in coordination with RVNAF"; and implementation of U.S. contingency plans. He discussed only the first three, which coincided roughly with phases one and two of Sharp's concept. The first mission, base security, could entail close-in perimeter defense of an installation; but it also could mean protection of a wider area around the base, extending out to the limits of light artillery range. In the deep patrolling and offensive stage, the troops were to move farther out into the countryside and attack Viet Cong units and bases, normally in areas of operation assigned by local South Vietnamese commanders. These operations could take place at some distance from a base but should contribute to its security by disrupting enemy offensive preparations. In the third stage, the troops were to be prepared to reinforce the South Vietnamese Army anywhere within a corps area, and they were to engage in wide-ranging search and destroy operations, either unilaterally or in cooperation with the South Vietnamese.[66]

Even before he issued this general concept, Westmoreland, on 5 May, embodied its principles in letters of instruction to the commanders of the III Marine Amphibious Force and the 173d Airborne Brigade. He directed each force to protect designated installations and prepare to conduct deep patrolling, offensive, and reserve/reaction operations in cooperation with the ARVN corps. Both were to move progressively from base defense onto the offensive through the stages outlined in the 8 May MACV concept. In Stage III, the marines were to operate in cooperation with and support of I Corps. Besides similarly working with III Corps, the 173d Airborne Brigade was to be available at Westmoreland's order for search-and-destroy and reserve/reaction operations in other corps areas, meaning primarily the Central Highlands.[67]

The Marine amphibious force and the Army brigade moved only gradually into the second and third stages of operations. During April and May, the marines concentrated on close-in defense of their three enclaves and on experiments in population security and pacification in the few villages in their tactical areas of responsibility (TAORs). At Da Nang in late May, they entered the deep patrolling and offensive stage, but their operations were restricted by General Thi's refusal to allow the marines into densely populated, Viet Cong–infested areas such as one that lay immediately south of the airfield. In all three of their TAORs, the marines encountered Viet Cong units of only platoon and smaller size. They suffered about 200 casualties, including 18 killed in action, during their first two months of combat operations. The story was substantially the same for the 173d Airborne. Initially divided between Bien Hoa and Vung Tau, the brigade would not begin preparing for major offensive action until mid-June, when its two infantry battalions were reunited at Bien Hoa and reinforced by the newly arrived Australian battalion.[68]

Where the Question Stood, June 1965

At the beginning of June, after three months of argument and decision-making within the U.S. government, American ground combat forces in South Vietnam were still few in numbers and limited in activity. The larger part of a Marine division and aircraft wing were on shore at Da Nang, Phu Bai, and Chu Lai. Elsewhere, the 173d Airborne Brigade (on temporary duty status and scheduled to be replaced by another brigade from the United States) and the Australian battalion were the only non–South Vietnamese combat elements. Another Army

Beginnings of the Ground Troop Commitment, January–June 1965

brigade, from the 1st Infantry Division, had been authorized for deployment to Qui Nhon, and a South Korean regimental combat team also was on the way. The forces in South Vietnam, Marine and Army alike, had yet to mount a major offensive operation and yet to engage battalion-size or larger enemy formations.

Nevertheless, President Johnson and his advisers had crossed a critical threshold by deciding to commit American soldiers to fight the Viet Cong and, however deliberately and cautiously, committing them to combat. The president and his men also set in motion a military planning and preparation process predicated on the deployment of a much larger force than had yet been authorized and on engagement of that force in an offensive aimed at defeating the enemy militarily within South Vietnam. In the course of that planning, MACV, CINCPAC, and the Joint Chiefs of Staff had sketched the outlines of tactical command and control for the force, had decided against creating a combined command with their South Vietnamese ally, and had developed a concept of operations for feeding American units into the fight.

As of early June, Westmoreland and his superiors had nonetheless avoided discussing one vital question: how American troops would contribute to the achievement of the overall U.S. military and political objectives in South Vietnam. They had examined at length the commitment of particular units; but except for generalities about improving force ratios, preventing a South Vietnamese collapse, and regaining the initiative, they had not addressed the larger strategic issue. Westmoreland's 8 May concept of operations laid out how individual units were to go about entering the fight, but it hardly constituted a plan of conduct for the war. Instead, it treated the introduction of ground combat units as simply an extension of American advice and assistance to the South Vietnamese armed forces. The troops would function, Westmoreland said, "in . . . a logical extension and expansion of [the] role already performed by a wide range of US units and forces throughout RVN."[69] This formula, adequate for the limited forces thus far committed, would wear thin as American numbers and firepower overwhelmed those of the army they were supposedly supporting. Yet until the beginning of June, it seemed as if the Johnson administration would have time to work out these problems in the course of a continued gradual introduction of American forces. Time, however, was about to run out.

Notes

[1] Ltr, Maj Gen William P. Yarborough to Westmoreland, 26 Feb 64, tab 5, Westmoreland Hist File 3 (17 Feb–30 Apr 64), CMH.

[2] For the 1954 proposals, see Spector, *Early Years*, pp. 194–214. The 1961 proposals are in Porter, *Vietnam Documentation* 2:128–34. Msg, Nolting to SecState, 31 Oct 61; Memo, McGeorge Bundy for the President, 21 Nov 61; Msg, CHMAAG, Vietnam, to CINCPAC, 21 Nov 61; Historians files, CMH. Taylor Rpt, tab D.

[3] Spector, *Early Years*, pp. 268–72, 300–301, 358–60, covers the early planning. MACV Command History, 1965, pp. 29, 157; COMUSSEASIA OPLAN 32–64–Ph III, IV, 15 May 64, p. 1 and ann. B; COMUSMACV OPLAN 32–64–Ph II (RVN), ann. B, 1 Jul 63, with changes, 1 May 64; Historians files, CMH; Memo, Westmoreland for Taylor, 5 Mar 65, sub: Ground Force Deployments into South Vietnam Under US/SEATO Contingency Plans, Folder: Buildup Problems, Fact Sheets, Misc Studies, MACV History Backup Files 65, box 68A1395, RG 334, NARA.

[4] Quote is from Memo, McGeorge Bundy for the President, 31 Aug 64, NSF Aides Files, Memos for Pres 6/64–2/65, McGeorge Bundy Memos, box 2, LBJL. *U.S.–Vietnam Relations*, sec. 4.C.2 (c), pp. 24–25, 66–67. Memo, Robert. H. Johnson and P. M. Kattenburg, sub: Alternative to Air Attacks on North Vietnam: Proposals for Use of U.S. Ground Forces in Support of Diplomacy in Vietnam, Paul Warnke Papers, John McNaughton Files, box 8, LBJL. Msg, JCS to CINCPAC and COMUSMACV, 2 Dec 64, tab 31, Westmoreland Hist File 10 (14 Nov–7 Dec 64); see also tab 23, Westmoreland Hist File 11 (7–31 Dec 64). Westmoreland, *A Soldier Reports*, pp. 114–15.

[5] Msg, Johnson to Taylor, 30 Dec 64, in NSC History, Major Forces, box 40, LBJL. For comment and interpretation, see Berman, *Planning a Tragedy*, pp. 34–35.

[6] Msg, Taylor to the President, 6 Jan 65, NSC History, Major Forces, box 40, LBJL. Compare with draft embassy telegram, tab 9, Westmoreland Hist File 12 (1–22 Jan 65), CMH. For a similar, earlier MACV staff conclusion, see Paper, Maj Gen Richard G. Stilwell, 10 Mar 64, sub: Counterinsurgency Vitalization, tab 13, Westmoreland Hist File 3 (17 Feb–30 Apr 64), CMH.

[7] Memo, DePuy for Westmoreland, 29 Jan 65, sub: Conversation with General Thang . . . , DePuy Papers, MHI. Westmoreland transmitted this report to Ambassador Taylor; see Memo, Westmoreland for Ambs Taylor and Johnson, 30 Jan 65, DePuy Papers, MHI.

[8] *U.S.–Vietnam Relations*, sec. 4.C.1, pp. 59–60, 64, 72. CINCPAC Command History, 1964, pp. 315–18. MACV Command History, 1964, pp. 23–24, 61, 136–37, 155–56; Ltr, Harkins to Khanh, 5 Apr 64, file 204–58 (1418–03) MAP Files (64), box 3, 69A702; Memo, Stilwell for Distribution, 20 May 64, sub: Transmittal of FY 65–66 Force Structure Plan, file 204–55 (201–45) Organizational Planning Files (RVNAF) (1964), box 2, 69A702; RG 334, NARA. Msg, Westmoreland MAC 1840 to Wheeler, 3 Apr 65, Westmoreland Msg Files, 1 Jan–31 Dec 64 and 1 Apr–30 Jun 65, CMH

[9] MACV Command History, 1964, pp. 61–62; ibid., 1965, pp. 57–58. CINCPAC Command History, 1964, pp. 323–24; Westmoreland emphasizes his desire to avoid overstraining the South Vietnamese manpower system in Memo for Taylor, 16 Nov 64, sub: Measures of National Mobilization to Put SVN on a War Footing, tab 5, Westmoreland Hist File 10 (14 Nov–7 Dec 64), CMH.

[10] Quote is from Msg, Westmoreland MAC 6468 to Brig Gen E. C. Dunn, 15 Dec 64, Westmoreland Msg Files, 1 Jan–31 Dec 64, CMH. In same file, see Msgs, Westmoreland MAC 4830, 6164, 6191 to Wheeler, 6 Sep, 27 and 28 Nov 64. MACV Command History, 1964, pp. 116–22, 159–60. CINCPAC Command History, 1964, p. 306. Msgs, COMUSMACV MAC 3299 to JCS, 27 Apr 64, and Saigon 774 to State, 8 Sep 64. Both in NSC File

Beginnings of the Ground Troop Commitment, January–June 1965

Vietnam, LBJL. Memo, Col Walter Greenwood, Jr., 6 Aug 64, Historians files, CMH.

[11] Quotes are from Msg, COMUSMACV MAC 4568 to CINCPAC, 4 Jun 64, Historians files, CMH. MACV Command History, 1964, pp. 65–66; Westmoreland Paper, "Military and Security Situation and Trends," tab 2; Msg, Westmoreland MAC 5423 to Taylor and Adm Harry D. Felt, 25 Jun 64; tab 11, Westmoreland Hist File 6 (1 Jun–3 Aug 64), CMH. MACV Directive 320–1, 15 Jul 64, Historians files, CMH. RVNAF High Command Directive AB 139, 25 Dec 64, ann. E, Historians files, CMH. MACV Memo, sub: RVNAF Counterinsurgency Roles and Missions, 4 Feb 65, tab 23, Westmoreland Hist File 13 (21 Jan–28 Feb 65), CMH.

[12] MFR, Westmoreland, 23 Jul 64, sub: Meeting with Gen Khiem, 22 Jul 64, tab 20, Westmoreland Hist File 6, (1 Jun–3 Aug 64); Fact Sheet, sub: Background Material— Hop Tac, tab 33, Westmoreland Hist File 7 (27 Jul–31 Aug 64); MFR, Westmoreland, 4 Dec 64, sub: Meeting with Gen Khanh, tab 33, Westmoreland Hist File 10 (14 Nov–7 Dec 64). All in CMH. Msg, Lodge Saigon 2479 to SecState,13 Jun 64, box 5, NSC File, Vietnam, LBJL. Execution of the redeployments is surveyed in Maj Paul E. Suplizio, "Military Support of Pacification in South Vietnam, April 1964–April 1965" (Thesis, U.S. Army Command and General Staff College, 1966), pp. 176–79, 223–28, 234–36, 256–61. Historians Files, CMH.

[13] Msg, Saigon 107 to State, 15 Jul 64, box 6, NSC Country File, Vietnam, LBJL. Suplizio, "Military Support of Pacification," pp. 158–62, 165–66. Youngdale Interv, 3 Jun 65, p 9. MACV Command History, 1964, p. 121. The March strength estimate is in U.S. Military Assistance Command, Vietnam, Commander's Estimate of the Situation in South Vietnam, 26 Mar 65, pp. 12–13, in tab 38, Westmoreland Hist File 14 (1–26 Mar 65), CMH.

[14] The higher infiltration figure is discussed in tab A, app. A, of Talking Paper for the JCS for Their Meeting with Gen Westmoreland on 21 December 1964, 18 Dec 64, sub: Items for Discussion with Gen Westmoreland, tab 23, Westmoreland Hist File 11 (7–31 Dec 64), CMH. See also *U.S.–Vietnam Relations*, sec. 4.C.2(c), pp. 1–2. The earlier estimate is in Memo, Youngdale for Distribution, 20 Apr 64, sub: Viet Cong Infiltration, file 204–58(501–03) Intel Rept Files (64), box 3, 69A702, RG 334, NARA. Memo, CIA, 1 Sep 64, sub: The Situation in South Vietnam, box 8, NSC Country File, Vietnam, LBJL.

[15] Memo, Youngdale for Distribution, 15 Mar 65, sub: Viet Cong Strategy and Tactics during 1964 (Historical Monograph), pp. 24–25, MACV Command History, 1965, pp. 10–11. Historians files, CMH; MACV Command History, 1965, pp. 10–11. Intel Memo, CIA Ofc of Current Intel, Intel Memo, 20 Apr 65, sub: Modernization of Viet Cong Armament, Warnke Papers, McNaughton Files, LBJL.

[16] For an overview of military events in 1964, see Admiral U. S. G. Sharp and General W. C. Westmoreland, *Report on the War in Vietnam (as of 30 June 1968)* (hereafter cited as *Report on the War*) (Washington, D.C.: Government Printing Office, 1968), pp. 92–95. The North Vietnamese in War Experiences Committee, *Resistance War*, pp. 64–65, emphasizes the need to increase large-unit operations and smash the ARVN in order to complete the overthrow of the Saigon government. For an analysis of Viet Cong strategy and operations in 1964, see Suplizio, "Military Support of Pacification," pp. 95–96, 105–29, 143–47, 262–66.

[17] A North Vietnamese account of the campaign can be found in *Resistance War*, pp. 65–66. American accounts and analysis can be found in Memo, Westmoreland for Taylor, 4 Jan 65, sub: Weekly Assessment of Military Activity for Period 27 December 1964 to 2 January 1965, and the same document for the period 3–9 January 1965; tabs 7 and 19, Westmoreland Hist File 12 (1–22 Jan 65), CMH. Suplizio, "Military Support of Pacification," pp. 282–83; Westmoreland, *A Soldier Reports*, p. 104.

[18] Paper, 15 Oct 64, sub: I Corps Trends, tab 8, Westmoreland Hist File 9 (9 Oct–13 Nov 64), CMH.

[19] Suplizio, "Military Support of Pacification," pp. 12–13, 147, 179–82, 233n, 238–44, 285, 303–312, analyzes the effect of the changing balance of military forces on the oil-spot plan. See also Suplizio Intervs, 17 and 24 Jul 86, tape 4, side 1. From May 1964–May 1965, Suplizio served as a J3 operations briefing officer and hence was deeply involved in the continuous monitoring of military operations during the period. The 6 percent population loss estimate is from MACV Command History, 1965, pp. 235–36. Duiker, *Road to Power*, pp. 232–33, notes the paradox of continued Viet Cong success in the countryside but inability to bring down the Saigon government.

[20] Quote is from Memo, Youngdale for Distribution, 15 Mar 65, sub: Viet Cong Strategy and Tactics During 1964 (Historical Monograph), p. 25; see also pp. 24, 26, Historians files, CMH. MACV Fact Sheet, 24 May 64, sub: Synopsis of VC Strategy and Tactics Study, in Book of Misc Facts, box 1, 67A4064, RG 334, NARA. Msg, COM-USMACV MAC 7627 to CJCS, 9 Aug 64, Historians files, CMH. For typical views on the reduction in large-scale Viet Cong attacks, see Msg, COMUSMACV MAC 7124 to CINCPAC, 30 Jul 64, Historians files, CMH; and remarks by General Westmoreland to *Life* magazine symposium with Mission Council members, 14 Nov 64, pp. 10–11, in tab 1, Westmoreland Hist File 10 (14 Nov–7 Dec 64), CMH.

[21] Quote is from Memo, Westmoreland for Taylor, 10 Jan 65, tab 17, Westmoreland Hist File 12 (1–22 Jan 65), CMH. See also Msgs, Westmoreland MAC 5147 and 0081 to Wheeler, 21 Sep 64 and 7 Jan 65, Westmoreland Msg Files, 1 Jan–31 Dec 64 and 1 Jan–31 Mar 65, CMH. A MACV J2 study characterized Binh Gia as simply "a large size ambush operation." Memo, Youngdale for Distribution, 15 Mar 65, sub: Viet Cong Strategy and Tactics During 1964 (Historical Monograph), p. 26, Historians files, CMH.

[22] First quote is from Memo, Westmoreland for Taylor, 25 Jan 65, sub: Weekly Assessment of Military Activity for Period 17–23 Jan 65, tab 8, Westmoreland Hist File 13 (21 Jan–28 Feb 65), CMH. Second is from Msg, COMUSMACV MAC 4999 to JCS, 17 Feb 65, NSC History, Major Forces, box 40, LBJL. The 100-battalion estimate is in USMACV, Commander's Estimate of the Military Situation in South Vietnam, 26 Mar 65, p. 13, tab 38, Westmoreland Hist File 14 (1–26 Mar 65), CMH; in same file, see Memo, Westmoreland for Taylor, 1 Mar 65, sub: Weekly Assessment of Military Activity for Period 21–27 February 1965, tab 5.

[23] MACV Command History, 1965, pp. 5–6. Msgs, Westmoreland MAC 1221 to Wheeler and Sharp, 7 Mar 65; Westmoreland MAC 1842 to Taylor, 3 Apr 65; Westmoreland Msg Files, LBJL. CMH. Memo, CIA, 6 Apr 65, sub: Communist Intentions in South Vietnam, NSC History, Major Forces, box 41 LBJL. Taylor, *Swords and Ploughshares*, pp. 340–41.

[24] COMUSMACV, "Military Estimate of the Situation in Vietnam," cabled to JCS 6 Mar 65, in Gen Harold K. Johnson, "Report on Survey of the Military Situation in South Vietnam,"14 Mar 65, tab B, box 5A, Harold K. Johnson Papers, MHI. The message form of this document is Msg, Westmoreland MAC 1190 to Wheeler and Sharp, 6 Mar 65, Westmoreland Msg Files, 1 Jan–31 Mar 65, CMH.

[25] Msg, Westmoreland MAC 1190 to Wheeler and Sharp, 6 Mar 65, Westmoreland Msg Files, 1 Jan–31 Mar 65. These proposals closely paralleled ideas that General Wheeler had informed Westmoreland and Sharp were already under consideration by the Washington "principals." See Msg, Wheeler to Sharp and Westmoreland, 27 Feb 65, tab 75, Westmoreland Hist File 13 (21 Jan–28 Feb 65), CMH.

[26] Chronology: COMUSMACV Recommendations and Observations on Use of U.S. Airpower in Vietnam War, 1965–1968, pp. 1–4, file TS–0192–80, Westmoreland Papers, CMH. MFR, Westmoreland, 8 Feb 65, sub: Visit with Gen Khanh, tab 26, Westmoreland Hist File 13 (21 Jan–28 Feb 65), CMH. Sharp and Westmoreland, *Report on the War*, pp. 107–08, recounts the first U.S. jet strikes.

Beginnings of the Ground Troop Commitment, January–June 1965

[27] COMUSMACV, "Chronology of Recommendations," pp. 1–4. Quote is from Msg, Westmoreland MAC 6127 to Wheeler and Sharp, 27 Feb 65, tab 81, Westmoreland Hist File 13 (21 Jan–28 Feb 65), CMH; in same file, see also tabs 54 and 55. Msg, Westmoreland to Wheeler and Sharp, 6 Mar 65, tab 20, Westmoreland Hist File 14 (1–26 Mar 65), CMH. Memo, Wheeler JCSM–161–65 for Sec of Defense, 6 Mar 65, NSC History, Major Forces, box 40. Historical Division, Joint Secretariat, JCS, *The History of the Joint Chiefs of Staff: The Joint Chiefs of Staff and the War in Vietnam, 1960–1968* (hereafter cited as *JCS and Vietnam, 1960–1968*) (Washington, D.C.: Historical Division, Joint Chiefs of Staff, 1 Jul 70), ch. 24, pp. 12–14.

[28] Msg, Sharp to Wheeler, 6 Mar 65, Westmoreland Msg Files, 1 Jan–31 Mar 65, CMH.

[29] First quote is from Msg, Gen Johnson to Taylor, 2 Mar 65, Close Hold File no. 6, Johnson Papers, MHI. In same collection, box 2, see Msg, McNamara to Taylor, 2 Mar 65. Interv, Senior Officer Debriefing Program with Gen Harold K. Johnson, 27 Jan 72–30 Oct 74, sec. 11, pp. 12–13, and sec. 12, pp. 14–15, MHI. Quote from the president is from Interv, Charles B. MacDonald and Charles von Luttichau with Gen Harold K. Johnson, 20 Nov 70, p. 8, Historians files, CMH.

[30] Gen Johnson Trip Report, 14 Mar 65. Gen Johnson Interv, 27 Jan 72–30 Oct 74, sec. 12, pp. 16–18. Memo, Col M. J. Berenzweig for the Secretary of the General Staff, 26 Mar 65, sub: Memoranda of Discussions in Vietnam, March 1965, box 5B, H. K. Johnson Papers, MHI. Berman, *Planning*, p. 54. Westmoreland, *A Soldier Reports*, pp. 125–27. Johnson already had received a gloomy assessment of the situation in late February, including a warning from his deputy chief of staff for operations that only commitment of U.S. troops could save the country. See Palmer, *25-Year War*, pp. 38–40.

[31] MACV Command History, 1965, pp. 106, 421–22. Msgs, Westmoreland MAC 1228 to Waters, 8 Mar 6; Westmoreland MAC 1463 to Wheeler, 17 Mar 65. Both in Westmoreland Msg Files, 1 Jan–31 Mar 65, CMH. Memo, Westmoreland for Gen Johnson, 5 Mar 65, sub: Items for Discussion, Close Hold file 4, Johnson Papers, MHI; Johnson Trip Rpt, 14 Mar 65, tab A.

[32] Transcript of briefing for USARPAC staff, 12 Mar 65, folder 5, tab 47, box 9, Johnson Papers, MHI.

[33] Johnson Trip Report, 14 Mar 65.

[34] Quote is from Westmoreland, *A Soldier Reports*, pp. 127–30. Msg, Westmoreland MAC 1463 to Wheeler, 17 Mar 65, Westmoreland Msg Files, 1 Jan–31 Mar 65, CMH. USMACV, "Commander's Estimate of the Military Situation in South Vietnam," 26 Mar 65, tab 38, Westmoreland Hist File 14 (1–26 Mar 65), CMH.

[35] USMACV Commander's Estimate, 26 Mar 65, pp. 2–3, 12–16, 19–20, and ann. A.

[36] Msg, Westmoreland MAC 1463 to Wheeler, 17 Mar 65; USMACV "Commander's Estimate," 26 Mar 65, pp. 2–11.

[37] Westmoreland justified his abandonment of the 10-to-1 rule of thumb on grounds that, with the Communist shift toward larger actions in which air power and artillery could be brought to bear, the conventional attack superiority ratio of 3-to-1 could be considered sufficient. MACV Commander's Estimate, 26 Mar 65, pp. 7–10.

[38] MACV Commander's Estimate, 26 Mar 65, pp. 5, 25–26, ann. E. See also Msg, Westmoreland MAC 1463 to Wheeler, 17 Mar 65, Westmoreland Msg Files, 1 Jan–31 Mar 65, CMH.

[39] *U.S.–Vietnam Relations*, sec. 4.C.5, pp. 84–85. The briefing is mentioned in Memo, William P. Bundy for Secretaries Rusk and McNamara and McGeorge Bundy, 28 Mar 65, sub: Major Issues During Ambassador Taylor's Visit, Warnke Papers, McNaughton Files, box 8, LBJL.

[40] *U.S.–Vietnam Relations*, sec. 4.C.5, p. 13; Historical Division, JCS, *JCS and Vietnam, 1960–1968*, ch. 24. Johnson Interv, 27 Jan 72–30 Oct 74, sec. 12, pp. 19–20.

[41] *U.S.–Vietnam Relations*, sec. 4.C.5, pp. 92–93. Historical Division, JCS, *JCS and Vietnam, 1960–1968*, ch. 19, pp. 13–14. Msg, Wheeler to Sharp and Westmoreland, 20 Mar 65, Westmoreland Msg Files, 1 Jan–31 Mar 65, CMH.

[42] For examples of the administration approach, see Memo, 1 Apr 65, sub: Key Elements for Discussion, Thursday, April 1; Msg, SecState to AmEmb Saigon, 3 Apr 65; and Memo, McGeorge Bundy for the President, 14 Apr 65. All in NSC History, Major Forces, boxes 40 and 41, LBJL. See also MFR of Meeting, 10:30 A.M., 3 Apr 65, in Secretary Rusk's Office, 6 Apr 65; and Msg, McGeorge Bundy to Taylor, 15 Apr 65; tabs 5 and 24, Westmoreland Hist File 15 (27 Mar–7 May 65), CMH. For a general account of the president's manipulation of his advisers, see Berman, *Planning a Tragedy*.

[43] Msgs, Westmoreland MAC 1463 to Wheeler, 17 Mar 65, and MAC 1566 to Sharp, 22 Mar 65; Sharp to Wheeler, 27 Mar 65; Westmoreland Msg Files, 1 Jan–31 Mar 65, CMH.

[44] Quotes are from Memo, DePuy for Throckmorton, 28 May 65, sub: How Goes the War, DePuy Papers, MHI. MACV Command History, 1965, pp. 5–6. *U.S.–Vietnam Relations*, sec. 4.C.5, pp. 41–47. Msgs, Westmoreland MAC 1463 to Wheeler, 17 Mar 65, and to Sharp, 12 Apr 65; Msg, Taylor Saigon 701 to Wheeler, 15 Apr 65. All in Westmoreland Msg Files, 1 Jan–31 Mar 65 and 1 Apr–30 Jun 65, CMH. Msgs, Taylor to SecState, 13 Apr 64 and 4 May 65; CIA Office of National Estimates, Special Memo 12–65, 30 Apr 65, sub: Current Trends in Vietnam. All in NSC History, Major Forces, box 41, LBJL.

[45] Historical Division, JCS, *JCS and Vietnam, 1960–1968*, ch. 21, pp. 10–13. Msgs, Taylor to JCS, 22 Feb 65, and to SecState, 18 Mar 65, box 40; and Msgs, Taylor to SecState, 12 and 14 Apr 65, and 19 May 65, box 41; NSC History, Major Forces, LBJL. Taylor, *Swords and Ploughshares*, p. 338.

[46] Msg, JCS to CINCPAC, 3 Apr 65, National Security Council (NSC) Action Memo 328, 6 Apr 65. Both in NSC History, Major Forces, boxes 40 and 41. *U.S.–Vietnam Relations*, sec. 4.C.5, pp. 59–61; MFR, 6 Apr 65, sub: Meeting 10:30 A.M., 3 Apr 65, in Secretary Rusk's Office, tabs 3 and 5, Westmoreland Hist File 15 (27 Mar–7 May 65), CMH; Taylor quote is from Msg, Taylor to SecState, 4 Apr 65, Taylor Papers, NDU. Taylor, *Swords and Ploughshares*, p. 341; Westmoreland, *A Soldier Reports*, p. 131. Memo, 1 Apr 65, sub: Key Elements for Discussion, Thursday, April 1, at 5:30 P.M., NSC History, Major Forces, box 40, LBJL.

[47] Msgs, Gen Burchinal JCS 008507 to Adm Sharp, 6 Apr 65; and CINCPAC to JCS, 6 Apr 65. Both in Taylor Papers, NDU. Memo, JCS for CINCPAC, 8 Apr 65, sub: Terms of Reference for the Honolulu Conference, (SM–333–65). In folder: Buildup Problems, Fact Sheets, Misc, MACV History Backup files 65, 68A1395, RG 334, NARA. *U.S.–Vietnam Relations*, sec. 4.C.5, pp. 16–17. Historical Division, JCS, *JCS and Vietnam, 1960–1968*, ch. 21, pp. 2–7; CINCPAC Command History, 1965, 2:280–88; MACV Command History, 1965, pp. 39, 48–49.

[48] USARPAC Historical Summary, *1964–65*, p. 66. CINCPAC Command History, 1965, pp. 288–89. Historical Division, JCS, *JCS and Vietnam, 1960–1968*, ch. 21, pp. 7–10. *U.S.–Vietnam Relations*, sec. 4.C.5, pp. 20–21.

[49] Msgs, Sharp to Westmoreland, 7 Apr 65; Westmoreland MAC 1968 to Sharp, 9 Apr 65; Stilwell HWA 0869 to Westmoreland, 10 Apr 65. In Westmoreland Msg Files, 1 Apr–30 Jun 65, CMH. Memo, Throckmorton for Westmoreland, 24 May 65, sub: Deployment and Command Arrangements for ROK Brigade, tab 9, Westmoreland Hist File 16 (10 May–30 Jun 65), CMH. Marines for Phu Bai: *U.S.–Vietnam Relations*, sec. 4.C.5, pp. 14–15, 56–59; Msg, Taylor to SecState, 18 Mar 65, NSC History, Major Forces, Box 40, LBJL.

[50] Msg, COMUSMACV MAC 11682 to CINCPAC, 11 Apr 65, tab 15, Westmoreland Hist File 15 (27 Mar–7 May 65), CMH; Msg, Stilwell HWA 0887 to Westmoreland, 13

Beginnings of the Ground Troop Commitment, January–June 1965

Apr 65, Westmoreland Msg Files, 1 Apr–30 Jun 65, CMH; Msg, CINCPAC to JCS, 13 Apr 65; Msg, JCS to CINCPAC and CINCSTRIKE/USCINCMEAFSA,14 Apr 65; NSC History, Major Forces, Box 41. Memo, Adams for CofS, MACV, 19 Mar 65, sub: Proposal for Employing 173d Abn Bde in RVN, Folder: COMUSMACV's 1965 Files, MACV History Backup Files, 65, 68A1395, RG 334, NARA.

[51] The confusion evidently arose from a 12 April message from Taylor to the State Department favoring accelerated logistic preparations for a U.S. brigade-size force at Bien Hoa/Vung Tau. Msg, Taylor to SecState,12 Apr 65, in NSC History, Major Forces, Box 41, LBJL. In same collection and box, see Msg, Taylor to SecState,14 Apr 65. *U.S.–Vietnam Relations*, sec. 4.C.5, pp. 19, 62–64. Historical Division, JCS, *JCS and Vietnam, 1960–1968,* ch. 21, pp. 8, 13–15.

[52] Msg, State and Defense to AmEmb Saigon, CINCPAC, and COMUSMACV, 15 Apr 65, NSC History, Major Forces, box 41. Quote is from Msg, Bundy to Taylor, 15 Apr 65, tab 24, Westmoreland Hist File 15 (27 Mar–7 May 65), CMH.

[53] Taylor's comment is in *Swords and Ploughshares*, pp. 341–42; see also pp. 339–40. Westmoreland, *A Soldier Reports*, pp. 131–32. On cadreing, see MACV Command History, 1965, pp. 81–82; and Rosson, "Involvement in Vietnam," p. 197. Msgs, Taylor to SecState,17 Apr 65; White House to AmEmb Saigon, 17 Apr 65; NSC History, Major Forces, box 41, LBJL.

[54] Memo, McNamara for the President, 21 Apr 65; Msg, Rusk to Taylor, 22 Apr 65; NSC History, Major Forces, box 43. Historical Division, JCS, *JCS and Vietnam, 1960–1968,* ch. 21, pp. 15–16; Taylor, *Swords and Ploughshares*, pp. 342–43.

[55] Historical Division, JCS, *JCS and Vietnam, 1960–1968,* ch. 21, pp. 18–20. Memo, Bundy for President Johnson, 27 Apr 65, sub: Cable from Max Taylor; Msg, JCS to CINCPAC and CINCSTRIKE/USMEAFSA, 30 Apr 65; Msg, Rusk to Taylor, 19 May 65. All in NSC History, Major Forces, box 41. Msg, Taylor to SecState, 1 May 65, tab 52, Westmoreland Hist File 15 (27 Mar–7 May 65), CMH; *U.S.–Vietnam Relations*, sec. 4.C.5, pp. 22–23, 64, 78–79, 93–94.

[56] MFRs, Westmoreland, 28 Apr 65, sub: Conference with Gens Thieu and Minh, tab 45; and Westmoreland, 29 Apr 65, sub: Conference with Australian Ambassador, tab 47; Westmoreland Hist File 15 (27 Mar–7 May 65), CMH; Msgs, Sharp to Westmoreland, 14 Apr 65; Westmoreland MAC 2115 to Sharp,16 Apr 65; Westmoreland MAC 2270 to Gen V. H. Krulak, USMC, 26 Apr 65; Krulak to Westmoreland, 29 Apr 65. All in Westmoreland Msg Files, 1 Apr–30 Jun 65, CMH. Shulimson and Johnson, *Marines in Vietnam 1965*, pp. 30–32.

[57] Memo, Gen Throckmorton for Westmoreland, 4 Apr 65, sub: Organization of Northern Area, tab 7; Msg, Westmoreland to CINCPAC, 11 Apr 65, tab 15. Both in Westmoreland Hist File 15 (27 Mar–7 May 65), CMH; Msgs, Westmoreland MAC 2029 and 2135 to Sharp,12 and 17 Apr 65, Westmoreland Msg Files, 1 Apr–30 Jun 65, CMH; Historical Division, JCS, *JCS and Vietnam, 1960–1968,* ch. 22, pp. 15–16; CINCPAC Command History, 1965, 2:283–84. For activation of the III MAF, see Shulimson and Johnson, *Marines in Vietnam, 1965,* p. 36.

[58] USMACV Commander's Estimate, 26 Mar 65, p. 7. MFRs, DePuy, 26 Feb 65 and 9 Mar 65, sub: Conversation with Gen Thang; Memo, DePuy for Westmoreland, 13 Apr 65, sub: Moratorium on Further Changes in the Command Structure of RVNAF. All in DePuy Papers, MHI. Msg, Taylor to SecState, 23 Jan 65, tab 5, Westmoreland Hist File 13 (21 Jan–28 Feb 65), CMH. MFR, Johnson, 8 Mar 65, sub: Meeting with Prime Minister Quat, box 5B; Transcript of Briefing for USARPAC Staff,12 Mar 65, box 9, Johnson Papers, MHI; Rosson, "Involvement in Vietnam," pp. 195–99.

[59] MACV Command History, 1965, pp. 100–101; Msgs, Westmoreland MAC 1463 to Wheeler, 17 Mar 65; Westmoreland MAC 1566, 1968, and 2029 to Sharp, 22 Mar

225

65, 9 and 12 Apr 65; Sharp to Wheeler, 27 Mar 65; Westmoreland MAC 1776 to Gen Johnson,1 Apr 65. All in Westmoreland Msg Files, 1 Jan–31 Mar 65, 1 Apr–30 Jun 65. Papers Concerning Advisers in the Support Role, Mar 65, tab 28, Westmoreland Hist File 14 (1–26 Mar 65). Memo, Col J. L. Collins, Jr., for CofS, MACV, 14 Apr 65, sub: Development of Combined Staff Organization, tab 20, Westmoreland Hist File 15 (27 Mar–7 May 65), CMH.

[60] MACV Command History, 1965, pp. 101–02. Memo, Westmoreland for Taylor, 21 May 65, sub: Combined Command, tab 8, Westmoreland Hist File 16 (10 May–30 Jun 65). Both in CMH. Msgs, Taylor to SecState, 29 Apr and 24 May 65; COMUSMACV to CINCPAC, 8 May 65. All in NSC History, Major Forces, box 41. Rosson, "Involvement in Vietnam," pp. 195–200; MFR, DePuy, 24 Jul 65, sub: Conversation with Gens Thang and Phong. Memo, DePuy for Thang, 24 Jul 65, sub: Combined Planning. Both in DePuy Papers, MHI.

[61] For Westmoreland's rationale, see Westmoreland, *A Soldier Reports*, pp. 133–34; and Sharp and Westmoreland, *Report on the War*, p. 104. Rosson's comments are in "Involvement in Vietnam," pp. 195, 200. See also Taylor, *Swords and Ploughshares*, pp. 349–50.

[62] First two quotes are from Msg, Westmoreland MAC 1463 to Wheeler, 17 Mar 65, Westmoreland Msg Files, 1 Jan–31 Mar 65; USMACV "Commander's Estimate," 26 Mar 65, ann. G; Draft Memo, Westmoreland for Taylor, in Folder: COMUSMACV's 1965 Files, MACV History Backup Files 65, 68A1395, RG 334, NARA. Final quote is from Westmoreland, *A Soldier Reports*, pp. 128–30.

[63] *U.S.–Vietnam Relations*, sec. 4.C.5, pp. 15, 67, 92–93; Historical Division, JCS, *JCS and Vietnam, 1960–1968*, ch. 19, pp. 12–14. Msgs, Wheeler JCS 1008 to Sharp and Westmoreland, 20 Mar 65; Sharp to Westmoreland, 21 Mar 65; Sharp to Wheeler, 27 Mar 65. All in Westmoreland Msg Files, 1 Jan–31 Mar 65, CMH. For the 1 April decision, see *U.S.–Vietnam Relations*, sec. 4.C.5, p. 59; and MFR, 3 Apr 65, tab 5, Westmoreland Hist File 15 (27 Mar–7 May 65), CMH.

[64] CINCPAC Command History, 1965, 2:280–83. Msgs, Sharp to Wheeler, 27 Mar 65; Stilwell HWA 0869 to Westmoreland, 10 Apr 65. Both in Westmoreland Msg Files, 1 Apr–30 Jun 65, CMH. USARPAC Historical Summary, 1964–65, pp. 67–68; Historical Division, JCS, *JCS and Vietnam, 1960–1968*, ch. 21, pp. 6–10. *U.S.–Vietnam Relations*, sec. 4.C.5, p. 18.

[65] Msgs, Westmoreland MAC 1985 to Wheeler, 11 Apr 65; Sharp to Westmoreland, 14 Apr 65. Both in Westmoreland Msg Files, 1 Apr–30 Jun 65, CMH. Msg, CINCPAC to COMUSMACV, 14 Apr 65, NSC History, Major Forces, box 41. MACV J3 Historical Summary, Apr 65, in Folder: Buildup Problems, Fact Sheets, Misc Studies, MACV History Backup Files 65, 68A1395, RG 334, NARA; Shulimson and Johnson, *Marines in Vietnam, 1965*, p. 27.

[66] Msg, COMUSMACV to CINCPAC, 8 May 65, NSC History, Major Forces, box 41; Westmoreland, *A Soldier Reports*, p. 135. Westmoreland issued this concept in response to decisions of the 20 April Honolulu meeting; see Historical Division, JCS, *JCS and Vietnam, 1960–1968*, ch. 22, p. 18.

[67] These instructions are summarized in Msg, Taylor to SecState, 9 May 65, NSC History, Major Forces, box 41. See also Shulimson and Johnson, *Marines in Vietnam, 1965*, p. 36.

[68] Memo, Westmoreland for Taylor, 3 Jun 65, sub: Authority for the Commitment of US Ground Combat Forces, tab 21, Westmoreland Hist File 16 (16 May–30 Jun 65), CMH; Shulimson and Johnson, *Marines in Vietnam, 1965*, pp. 27–30, 36–42; MACV Command History, 1965, pp. 40, 166; *U.S.–Vietnam Relations*, sec. 4.C.5, pp. 79–82.

[69] Msg, COMUSMACV to CINCPAC, 8 May 65, NSC History, Major Forces, box 41, LBSL.

7

The Fateful Decisions, June 1965–February 1966

During the first six months of 1965, the Johnson administration moved slowly and cautiously, almost experimentally, toward committing American soldiers to fight the Viet Cong. Its actions in the last half of the year, however, contrasted starkly. In that period, responding to the absence of results from the bombing of the north and to the apparently accelerating political and military deterioration of South Vietnam, President Johnson made a rapid succession of decisions that plunged U.S. ground forces into battle without reservation and in great numbers before their effectiveness in the conflict had been fully tested. At the same time, he altered the objective of the commitment, from the limited goal of preventing South Vietnamese collapse to the more ambitious one of defeating the Viet Cong insurgency by a predominantly American effort.

South Vietnam in Peril

On 3 June, in reply to a State Department request for his views on future ROLLING THUNDER targets, Ambassador Taylor warned that the air campaign by itself never would compel the Hanoi government to stop supporting the Viet Cong. While he advocated continued, heavier bombing of North Vietnam, the ambassador declared that only "a conviction on their part that the tide has turned or soon will turn against them in the South" would break the enemy's will.[1]

By the time Taylor sent this message, the tide in South Vietnam seemed instead to be turning in favor of the enemy. Military events were taking much the course that Westmoreland had forecast back in March. Viet Cong main forces and guerrillas—steadily increasing in numbers and effectiveness—bled Saigon's regulars and territorials in large and small engagements, opening the way for further subversion of the countryside and posing a threat of physical and moral collapse of the government forces. At the same time, the enemy conducted a systematic road-cutting campaign to isolate the towns and cities, paralyze the economy, and break up the remaining government territory into separate, vulnerable islands of resistance.[2]

While most Viet Cong actions continued to be small hit-and-run attacks, their campaign also included main force engagements with ominous implications. Between mid-May and mid-June, Viet Cong troops in at least regimental strength fought three sustained battles with government regulars—at Song Be and Dong Xoai north of Saigon in III Corps and at Ba Gia in southern I Corps. In each, the enemy attacked district towns or small ARVN units to draw out relief forces and then slaughtered the reinforcements piecemeal as they arrived. In the engagement at Dong Xoai, the worst government defeat of the three, several Viet Cong battalions stormed a South Vietnamese Special Forces camp and district town, then remained in the vicinity for five days to maul a succession of South Vietnamese battalions, including one from the supposedly elite airborne. Over 400 government soldiers died before the enemy broke contact and withdrew, and the toll of missing men and lost equipment was high. In all these fights, the Viet Cong demonstrated continued improvement in tactical proficiency and weaponry, as well as determination to destroy government forces in prolonged combat, even at the cost of heavy casualties to themselves. South Vietnamese commanders, by contrast, became ever more defensive minded. In some regions, notably II Corps, they became hesitant to reinforce posts under attack or simply gave up exposed positions, including half a dozen district headquarters.[3]

The South Vietnamese commanders' caution reflected in part an increasingly unfavorable balance of regular forces. The Viet Cong, while replacing severe battlefield losses, continued to expand their regular contingent, drawing on a seemingly inexhaustible reservoir of southern recruits and northern infiltrators. Their troops seemed well trained and led, and their new array of Soviet- and Chinese-made infantry weapons gave them formidable firepower which the artillery and air support available to the ARVN could not always overmatch. Behind the Viet Cong stood a growing force of North Vietnamese regulars in their own combat formations. By early June the Military Assistance Command had confirmed the presence in northern II Corps of elements of the North Vietnamese *325th Division*. Another division, the *304th*, was suspected to be in the Laos panhandle within easy reinforcing distance. According to General Westmoreland, the Viet Cong had built up their strength to a point where they could mount regimental-size operations in all four corps areas and at least battalion-size attacks in "virtually all" provinces. Still worse, as of early June, only a small fraction of the Viet Cong main force and none of the North Vietnamese units had been committed to major attacks. The enemy's heaviest blows had yet to fall.[4]

By contrast, the South Vietnamese Army was forced to suspend its expansion and suffered a gradual decline in combat strength. Early in June, at Westmoreland's suggestion, the government indefinitely post-

Chief of State Thieu, left, *and Air Vice Marshal Ky*
(© Bettmann/CORBIS)

poned the activation of eleven new infantry battalions that had been scheduled under the 1964 RVNAF mobilization plan. Instead, it used new soldiers coming out of the training centers to bring its existing battalions, which casualties and desertion had reduced to an average of less than 380 men, up to something resembling effective combat strength. To produce still more replacements quickly, the government shortened basic recruit training from 12 weeks to 9 and battalion training from 21 weeks to 18. Yet the hemorrhage of ARVN manpower continued. By mid-June, MACV estimated that four South Vietnamese Army regiments and nine battalions were unfit for combat due to personnel losses. With no new battalions scheduled for activation until November, the projected government-to-Viet Cong strength ratio appeared worse than it had been in March, when General Westmoreland made his first request for substantial American reinforcements. Ambassador Taylor declared early in July that the South Vietnamese forces needed "an injection of new vitality which can only come from U.S. sources."[5]

As enemy military pressure increased, civilian government in Saigon once again collapsed. Premier Quat stumbled into a political and constitutional standoff with Chief of State Suu, who challenged the premier's authority to dismiss three members of his cabinet. Mediation efforts by Ambassador Taylor failed, due, Taylor reported, to tactical mistakes by Quat and to the ambiguous language of South Vietnam's provisional constitution, which provided no legal way out of the impasse. Finally, on 9 June, Quat asked the senior military commanders to mediate the dispute. The generals, who had held aloof from the controversy while growing increasingly impatient at the paralysis of the government, responded by forcing out both Suu and Quat. On the 14th, they set up a ten-man military governing council, chaired by General Nguyen Van Thieu, who became de facto chief of state. The Vietnamese Air Force commander, Air Vice Marshal Nguyen Cao Ky, assumed the premiership under the cumbersome title of Commissioner in Charge of the Executive Branch. Ky formed an all-military cabinet composed of relatively young, supposedly reform-minded officers and promulgated an ambitious 26-point national mobilization program. In the midst of a battlefield crisis, Saigon's military leaders thus once more immersed themselves in the cauldron of politics.[6]

The new regime did not inspire great confidence among members of the U.S. Mission. General Thieu, Quat's former defense minister, had impressed many Americans favorably as a division and corps commander. However, the reserved, cautious native of central Vietnam, who had been involved in Saigon politics since the anti-Diem coup of 1963, had a reputation for self-seeking and intrigue. As chief of state, he was an unknown quantity. Air Vice Marshal Ky, a northerner by birth and a Buddhist, was Thieu's opposite in personality—impulsively outspoken, a high-liver who affected purple jump suits and twin pearl-handled revolvers. A member of the young generals' group that first backed and then got rid of Khanh, Ky had made a creditable record as head of the air force. As premier, he again showed great energy, zeal for good government, and a desire for aggressive action against the Viet Cong. But Ambassador Taylor regarded him as "completely without the background and experience for an assignment as difficult as this one." The Catholics, Buddhists, and other political factions took a noncommittal attitude toward the new regime, responding tepidly at best to its calls for austerity, unity, and sacrifice. The American embassy prepared to give all possible moral and practical support to this, the fifth Saigon government in eighteen months, but its members expressed little hope of immediate improvements. "With governments coming and going as if Saigon was a revolving door," General Westmoreland later stated, "I could see little possibility of the South Vietnamese themselves overcoming the military crisis."[7]

Air Power Holds Back the Enemy

To check the enemy offensive, General Westmoreland resorted first to the American forces on hand. Since his ground units still were few, that meant primarily air power. Westmoreland took full advantage of the authority granted him and Admiral Sharp early in March to employ jet fighter-bombers in South Vietnam. He also made the most of a decision by Sharp, soon after the Honolulu conference in April, to give the war in South Vietnam priority in allocating air resources, even at

The Fateful Decisions, June 1965–February 1966

the cost of occasionally canceling strikes in North Vietnam and Laos.[8]

U.S. Air Force, Navy, and Marine fighter-bombers played perhaps the decisive role in blunting major Viet Cong attacks. These aircraft, although hampered until mid-summer by limited reconnaissance and forward air control support, flew an ever-increasing number of combat sorties. In engagements such as Song Be, Ba Gia, and Dong Xoai, the American and South Vietnamese air forces at a minimum prevented even worse government losses. They also substantially increased enemy casualties and made it prohibitively costly for the Viet Cong to hold their positions for any length of time. General Westmoreland declared on 11 June that maintenance of the government presence in a number of important areas of South Vietnam "is becoming more and more dependent upon air" and that "air capabilities . . . constitute the current difference between keeping the V. C. buildup under reasonable control and letting the enemy get away from us throughout most of the countryside."[9]

To supplement his tactical air power, Westmoreland acquired a major new resource: B–52 heavy bombers of the Strategic Air Command (SAC). In February the Air Force had moved thirty of these aircraft, refitted to carry large conventional bomb loads, to Andersen Air Force Base on Guam for possible use against North Vietnam. However, for a variety of political and military reasons, the Defense Department kept the Stratofortresses out of ROLLING THUNDER. Early in March, the Joint Chiefs of Staff, partly to "assist in opening the door" for eventual use of the planes over the north, suggested their employment against selected Viet Cong targets in South Vietnam. Although General John D. Ryan, USAF, the SAC commander, and Admiral Sharp (who later changed his mind) initially resisted the proposal, General Westmoreland took a more favorable view. In messages to Sharp and the Joint Chiefs and in person at the 20 April Honolulu conference, the MACV commander emphasized the value of the big bombers for attacking major Viet Cong base areas, such as War Zones C and D north of Saigon, where enemy facilities were too widely dispersed, deeply dug in, and well concealed to be seriously damaged by tactical aircraft.[10] With the B–52s, which flew at altitudes beyond enemy sight and hearing and could carpet a wide area with bombs within a very short time, Westmoreland could disrupt Viet Cong bases while using his fighter-bombers for other more suitable missions.[11]

Early in May, the Defense Department approved in principle use of the B–52s in South Vietnam and directed Admiral Sharp and General Ryan to work out procedures for strikes on targets proposed by General Westmoreland. At the outset, either President Johnson or Secretary McNamara had to approve each individual mission. The first B–52 raid, code-named ARC LIGHT I, took place on 18 June, against a suspected Viet Cong troop concentration in War Zone D, forty miles north of Saigon. At the cost of two Stratofortresses lost with most of their crews in a mid-

A B–52 Arc Light bombing mission (U.S. Air Force photo)

air collision, the aircraft from Guam churned up a portion of Vietnamese landscape with 1,300 bombs, all dropped within thirty minutes. Results of this initial attack were unimpressive. South Vietnamese troops searching part of the target area after the strike found little evidence of enemy casualties or damage to installations. Nevertheless, General Westmoreland was convinced that, with improved preattack security and more rapid planning and strike authorization, the B–52s would be effective against otherwise unreachable enemy forces and facilities. Admiral Sharp concurred in the MACV commander's assessment and urged him to propose additional missions as soon as possible so as to "establish a pattern for the employment of this capability." In spite of many references in the news media to swatting flies with sledgehammers, and in spite of objections by members of the Air staff in Washington to diversion of the strategic nuclear bombers to conventional tactical missions, by the end of June the B–52s were well on the way to becoming a permanent part of the Military Assistance Command's arsenal of weapons.[12]

Decisions for an American Ground War

By the time the B–52s went into action, a new round of debate and decision-making on commitment of U.S. ground troops was well under way. On 5 June, two days after his declaration that bombing the north alone would not end Hanoi's aggression, Ambassador Taylor submitted to Washington a general political-military assessment of the situation in South Vietnam. Drafted by the Mission Intelligence Committee and concurred in by himself, Deputy Ambassador U. Alexis Johnson, and General Westmoreland, the assessment summed up how dangerously the tide was running against the allies. The ambassador reviewed the difficulties of the Quat regime, then still clinging to office; the developing enemy offensive; and the manpower and morale problems of the South Vietnamese armed forces.

General Wheeler
(© Bettmann/CORBIS)

He warned that during the next several months the South Vietnamese, their inadequate military reserves spread increasingly thin, would likely suffer additional defeats comparable to those of late May and early June. Such reverses, combined with economic hardship caused by Viet Cong blocking of communication arteries, "will have a serious adverse impact on popular confidence and morale, exacerbating political instability in Saigon." Even worse, the "cumulative psychological impact" of a series of lost battles "could lead to a collapse in ARVN's will to continue the fight." To prevent such a collapse, Taylor concluded, "it will probably be necessary to commit U.S. ground forces to action."[13]

General Westmoreland followed up Taylor's political assessment with a military one of his own and with a proposal for reversing the adverse trend in the south by a major infusion of American troops. As in his previous reinforcement requests, he acted in response to a cue from his superiors in Washington. The administration, disturbed by Taylor's situation assessments, summoned the ambassador home for another policy review. In preparation for Taylor's visit, the Joint Chiefs of Staff decided to reopen the question of committing some of the forces discussed in the 20 April Honolulu conference, particularly additional marines and the Army division for the Central Highlands. On 4 June, General Wheeler asked Westmoreland and Sharp for their opinions on the desirability of early introduction of the division and for an estimate of when the American logistic base in South Vietnam would be built up enough to support it.[14]

On 7 June, Westmoreland furnished answers to Wheeler's questions and much more besides. Assessing the military situation in the same terms and language as the Mission Intelligence Committee, he emphasized the presence of North Vietnamese regulars, the growing but as yet largely uncommitted Viet Cong main force, and the likelihood of heavy new attacks north of Saigon, in the Quang Ngai and Quang Tin provinces of I Corps, and in the Central Highlands and Binh Dinh province of II Corps. After recapitulating the decline in ARVN strength and aggressiveness, Westmoreland concluded: "In order to cope with the situation . . . , I see no course of action open to us except to reinforce our efforts . . . with additional U.S. or third country forces as rapidly as is practical during the critical weeks ahead." He also advocated planning for commitment of "even greater forces, if and when required, to attain our objectives or counter enemy initiatives."

Westmoreland built his troop request on the recommendations of the 20 April Honolulu conference. Besides the two Army brigades and the Korean regimental combat team agreed upon at that conference, the MACV commander asked for early dispatch of the units designated at that time for later decision: the airmobile division, a South Korean infantry division, an Army corps headquarters, and two Marine battalion landing teams, all to be accompanied by large contingents of Army logistical troops. Going beyond the units previously considered, he expressed a need for another U.S. Army division, either the 1st Infantry or 101st Airborne; another Marine amphibious brigade; additional tactical air, helicopter, and combat and logistic support units; and three antiaircraft missile battalions. Later in June, he asked to keep the 173d Airborne indefinitely, rather than return it to Okinawa when the other Army brigades arrived. After some initial confusion, especially over the 173d, Westmoreland and the Joint Chiefs settled upon a request for 44 maneuver battalions—34 American, 9 Korean, and 1 Australian—all to be in South Vietnam by the end of the year. Ten of those battalions—7 U.S. Marine, 2 U.S. Army, and 1 Australian—already were deployed. Six more Army battalions (a brigade each from the 1st Infantry and 101st Airborne Divisions) and a South Korean regimental combat team were to enter South Vietnam during July. Westmoreland asked that the rest of the troops be sent during August, September, and October, on a schedule that matched closely one worked out by the Army staff late in April as part of its contingency planning.[15] When these deployments were completed, U.S. forces in South Vietnam would number about 175,000 men, with the allies providing additional troops.[16] *(Map 3)*

In his 7 June message and in more detail a week later, Westmoreland elaborated upon his plans for employing these forces. The additional marines all would go to build up the 3d Marine Division so that it could provide "adequate reserve reaction forces" for I Corps, which then had "virtually no reserve" and was "barely able to hold the major population centers, province and district towns." The airmobile division, the brigade from the 1st Infantry Division, and the Korean units all were to reinforce II Corps, where two ARVN divisions had "a hopelessly large area to cover with the meager forces available." The Koreans would secure coastal logistic bases at Qui Nhon and Cam Ranh Bay

MAJOR U.S. AND ALLIED FORCES
SOUTH VIETNAM
1966

MAP 3

while the American units swept the plateau around Kontum and Pleiku and kept open the main supply route into those towns, Highway 19. To reinforce III Corps against the enemy main forces that had demonstrated their power at Song Be and Dong Xoai, Westmoreland intended to use the 173d Airborne, the brigade from the 101st Airborne, and the rest of the additional Army division in the provinces north of Saigon. Westmoreland believed that IV Corps was "standing on its own two feet," because of the nature of the region's delta terrain and the effectiveness of the South Vietnamese divisions stationed there. "Whether or not US forces will be required in this area cannot now be forecast."

The MACV commander expected that the majority of maneuver battalions he had requested would be tied down defending American bases and holding lines of communication. Nevertheless, in his dispatches he emphasized the importance of the troops' offensive role. He acknowledged that defeat of the Viet Cong guerrillas and political underground in the heavily populated Mekong Delta and nearby coastal regions was essential to final allied victory, but he insisted that only the South Vietnamese could "make real progress and succeed" in that part of the war. Since South Vietnamese troops, however, were being diverted from pacification to counter the growing enemy main forces in the Central Highlands and elsewhere, he declared, "my concept is basically to employ US forces, together with Vietnamese airborne and marine battalions of the general reserve, against the hardcore North Vietnam/Viet Cong forces in reaction and search and destroy operations, and thus permit the concentration of Vietnamese troops in the heavily populated areas." He added: "We will be conducting mobile warfare from fixed and defended bases. Some of these bases will be major logistics centers at ports and airfields, such as Chu Lai and Cam Ranh. Others will be tactical bases such as An Khe or Pleiku. The tactical bases will move as necessary and that may be with some frequency as the battle develops."[17]

Westmoreland's proposals received prompt endorsement from his military superiors, at least as far as the size of the reinforcement was concerned. Admiral Sharp concurred on 7 June. Four days later, the Joint Chiefs of Staff formally recommended to Secretary McNamara the deployment on Westmoreland's schedule of all the requested reinforcements except the additional Army division and a Marine amphibious brigade. On the question of troop dispositions, both Sharp and Air Force Chief of Staff General John P. McConnell expressed strong reservations about immediate movement inland of the airmobile division, which still was in the process of formation and had yet to be tested in combat. Both men argued that the division should operate initially around Qui Nhon, where it would not have to rely so completely on air transport for supply. Sharp also suggested that a coastal deployment would contribute more to controlling the populated lowlands, which he considered strategically and politically more important than the plateau. From a broader perspective, General McConnell warned against committing American ground forces to a potentially endless battle of attrition in the south without a strong accompanying air campaign to knock North Vietnam out of the war.[18]

Ambassador Taylor and the new leaders of South Vietnam supported the MACV commander's bid for reinforcements. On 28 June, Generals Thieu and Ky, "sober-faced and depressed" according to the ambassador, informed Taylor that they could not raise forces rapidly enough during the next few months to match the Viet Cong and North Vietnamese buildup. They must have American or other allied troops to hold off the enemy while they put their own political and military affairs in order. In contrast to his earlier hesitancy on the subject, Taylor now attested to the need for more American troops to contain the Viet Cong offensive, to compensate for declining ARVN strength and morale, and to prevent major defeats that could cause collapse of the still-fragile Thieu-Ky regime. He warned on 11 July, in his most urgent statement:

ARVN is alone clearly incapable of coping with growing Viet Cong capabilities as already reinforced by PAVN and we are faced with prospect of successive tactical reverses, piecemeal destruction of ARVN units, and gradual loss of key communication and population centers, particularly in the highlands. Unless this trend is reversed, there will be a growing danger of attrition of RVNAF will to fight in months ahead, accompanied by a similar loss of civilian confidence. Only early commitment of U.S., third country forces . . . in strength greater than that now available in SVN can blunt and bloody the . . . offensive to the point of convincing Hanoi's leaders that they cannot win in the South.[19]

President Johnson and his senior advisers, most of whom were determined at least to avoid losing in Vietnam, inexorably moved toward acceptance of the 44-battalion reinforcement, although at different rates and with varying degrees of misgiving. Secretary McNamara, after a lengthy review of Westmoreland's plan, formally recommended it to the president on 26 June. To support the troop deployment and to rebuild the U.S. strategic reserve, he also urged a call-up of 100,000 reservists and National Guardsmen and extension of enlistment terms in all services. Secretary of State Rusk, National Security Adviser McGeorge Bundy, and CIA Director William Raborn, after some skeptical questioning, fell into line with McNamara's request.

Yet dissent remained. What Bundy called "second level men" in the State and Defense Departments and the CIA raised questions. Some, including at one point Deputy Ambassador Johnson, expressed doubt that South Vietnam was as near collapse as Westmoreland and the mission were indicating or questioned whether the enemy really was shifting to large-unit warfare to an extent that would justify the commitment of so many American combat troops. Under Secretary of State George Ball, the most outspoken, articulate dissenter, considered South Vietnam already a lost cause and warned that the United States was heading for an interminable, costly, and ultimately futile struggle in which Americans would repeat the French failure in a "white man's war" against Asian nationalists. He urged the president to minimize additional force commitments and to begin preparing to disengage, which he said could be done at less diplomatic cost before, rather than after, deeper American involvement in the fighting. President Johnson himself seemed to favor another intensification of the American military effort. Yet he delayed his decision, to allow a consensus to form among his advisers, to explore alternatives, and to buy time to prepare the domestic political ground.[20]

Throughout the lengthy administration consideration of his proposal, General Westmoreland was in constant communication with General Wheeler and Admiral Sharp. He refined and defended his reinforcement request and concept of operations. He also furnished arguments against alternatives that Wheeler proposed, possibly as straw men in many instances, on behalf of Secretary McNamara. Westmoreland rejected as inadequate several variant deployment schemes that called either for a smaller total force or for substitutions for the airmobile division. He commented negatively on a new series of proposals for encadrement of small American units in South Vietnamese regiments and battalions. Westmoreland also pronounced as politically undesirable or militarily impractical a number of suggested employments for American combat units, such as taking over protection of Saigon to release the South Vietnamese general reserve airborne and marine battalions for field operations—a mission, Westmoreland pointed out, that would detract from the appearance of Vietnamese sovereignty and might involve Americans in politically embarrassing riot control duty. Responding to frequently expressed fears in Washington, Westmoreland, strongly seconded by Admiral Sharp, insisted that with proper troop leadership and indoctrination, American forces could maintain good relations with the Vietnamese people, thereby minimizing the danger of a mass xenophobic reaction.[21]

Yet Westmoreland, as he pressed his campaign for reinforcements with increasing urgency, envisioned no short or easy struggle. Instead, on 24 June, he told General Wheeler that "we are in for the long pull. The struggle has become a war of attrition. Short of [a] decision to introduce nuclear weapons against sources and channels of enemy power, I see no likelihood of achieving a quick, favorable end to the war." Two days later, he declared: "We are deluding ourselves if we feel some novel arrangement is going to get quick results. We must think in terms of an extended conflict; be prepared to support a greatly increased effort; give the commander on the scene the troops that he requires and the authority to deploy these troops in accordance with his best judgment. . . . We need more troops, and we need them quickly."[22]

Even while the Johnson administration debated Westmoreland's reinforcement request, it took significant steps toward unrestricted U.S.

The Fateful Decisions, June 1965–February 1966

participation in the ground war. To begin with, the administration reaffirmed and strengthened the MACV commander's authority to commit his troops to offensive action. Westmoreland had possessed such authority since early April, and his May concept of operations had as its final stage entry of American units into active combat alongside the South Vietnamese. However, a public relations mishap resulted in confusion about the extent of the MACV commander's tactical discretion. On 8 June 1965, a State Department briefing officer, more or less offhandedly, informed a press conference that U.S. troops in Vietnam were available to support their allies in combat beyond the boundaries of American-protected bases and had been for some time. A predictable furor erupted. The media and members of Congress denounced the executive branch for trying to maneuver the country into a full-fledged land war without open public debate. Attempting to appease the critics, White House Press Secretary George F. Reedy and Secretary of State Rusk issued statements to the effect that the troops' primary mission remained base defense. They denied that the president had ordered any change in that mission. Rusk especially appeared to tie any combat activity quite strictly to installation security.[23]

These pronouncements, issued just as the battle at Dong Xoai was approaching a crisis, left Westmoreland in a quandary. By mid-June, his available American units—the marines in I Corps and the 173d Airborne Brigade at Bien Hoa—were ready to move into offensive operations. Indeed, after the commander of I Corps came close to asking for Marine assistance at Ba Gia, Ambassador Taylor on 3 June had requested and promptly received State Department confirmation that the MACV commander could "authorize commitment [of] U.S. ground forces to action in combat support on the basis of operational coordination and cooperation with RVNAF." The new policy declarations, taken literally, seemed to nullify the previous authorizations. Specifically, they raised doubts as to whether Westmoreland could commit forces at Dong Xoai, which was far from any major American-protected base.[24]

On 12 June, in an effort to clarify his position, Westmoreland sent a message to Admiral Sharp, with copies to the Joint Chiefs of Staff and the State Department, asking for a redefinition of his authority and suggesting new wording which he thought would conform to the most recent administration statements. This message drew a strong rebuke from Sharp. The Pacific commander told Westmoreland that, as far as he and the Joint Chiefs were concerned, the MACV commander already possessed ample discretion to "conduct operations necessary to achieve our objectives." Emphasizing that the chiefs had carefully constructed the phrase "counterinsurgency combat operations" to provide that discretion, Sharp warned Westmoreland that more precise directives, if issued in the current Washington climate, likely would be more restrictive. At Sharp's urging, Westmoreland withdrew his message of the 12th. However, when he simultaneously informed Sharp that he might be required to exercise his discretion by committing the 173d Airborne to rescue the South Vietnamese at Dong Xoai within the next 12 hours, it was the admiral's turn to be cautious. By telephone call and teletype message, Sharp acknowledged that Westmoreland, as "the man on the ground," had the responsibility and power to act; but he left little doubt that he preferred to avoid a troop commitment at that time. He urged Westmoreland to take a "hard look" at the possibility of driving off the enemy with intensive air strikes, and he directed the MACV commander to consult with him before ordering the brigade into action.[25]

The crisis at Dong Xoai passed without involvement of American ground forces, but the scope of Westmoreland's tactical discretion remained in doubt. Finally, on 26 June, in response to a query from Taylor, Secretary Rusk settled the question. He informed Taylor that Westmoreland could commit U.S. troops "independently of or in conjunction with" the South Vietnamese "in any situation in which the use of such troops is requested by an appropriate GVN commander and when, in COMUSMACV's judgment, their use is necessary to strengthen the relative position of GVN forces." This statement for practical purposes gave Westmoreland a tactical free hand with the soldiers and marines at his disposal.[26]

Besides giving Westmoreland freedom to use what troops he had, the administration took preliminary steps toward deploying the reinforcements he had requested. On 19 June, Secretary McNamara authorized the Army to establish the airmobile division, under the name and colors of the 1st Cavalry Division, as part of its permanent force structure. A week later, he directed the division to prepare for movement overseas. At the same time, President Johnson authorized deployment of two Marine battalion landing teams that were part of the 7 June reinforcement request. On 9 July, McNamara directed the secretary of the Army to plan for commitment of the entire 44-battalion force as well as for expansion of the Army by 1 additional division, 6 separate brigades, 19 airmobile companies, and large support and service forces, to be provided by adding 250,000 men to the active Army through the draft and calling up 100,000 National Guardsmen and reserves. The following day, McNamara informed the Joint Chiefs that President Johnson on 8 July had approved the deployment of all the troops Westmoreland had requested. Also on 10 July, the president ordered to Vietnam 10,400 additional quartermaster, engineer, ordnance, transportation, medical, and signal troops, needed to support U.S. forces already in South Vietnam and to receive the 1st Cavalry Division "if deployed."[27]

A final initiative had even more significant implications. On 29 June, McNamara, through General Wheeler, asked Sharp and Westmoreland what forces beyond the forty-four battalions then under consideration would be needed during 1966 to "prove to the VC/DRV that they cannot win in South Vietnam." Shortly thereafter, in a face-to-face confer-

The Fateful Decisions, June 1965–February 1966

ence, McNamara told the Pacific commander that he "did not want to depend upon further ARVN buildup since thus far it had not been sufficient to offset losses plus VC gains and further it was too unreliable a factor." The defense secretary wanted Sharp to make estimates without regard to the restrictions of "what up to now has been limited use of our assets"; and he indicated that at least "partial mobilization" remained a real possibility. Sharp and Westmoreland both replied that they would almost certainly need more forces, although they could not yet specify how many. Westmoreland declared on 30 June that the 44-battalion reinforcement, which was about the maximum that could be brought into South Vietnam during the rest of 1965, "should re-establish the military balance" by the end of the year but "will not . . . cause the enemy to back off." Beyond that, he added, he tended "instinctively" to believe that he would need "substantial" additional forces. By these questions, and the answers they evoked, McNamara subtly but profoundly altered the terms of reinforcement planning, from what was needed to prevent the South Vietnamese from losing to what the Americans on their own required for winning.[28]

Immediately after receiving Wheeler's 29 June query, Westmoreland set his staff to work on an estimate of additional troop requirements for 1966. In the absence of firm information on American unit combat performance and the future rate of the enemy buildup, the planners perforce based their initial estimate on a combination of mathematical rules of thumb, professional judgment, and what the MACV chief of staff called "a degree of wizardry." Starting from their best guess of how many battalions the enemy would add during 1966 and a forecast of South Vietnamese strength, and assuming that each U.S. Army infantry battalion equaled in combat power two ARVN or Viet Cong battalions and each U.S. Marine battalion equaled three friendly or enemy Vietnamese ones, the planners calculated how many more American battalions the allies would require to maintain the three-to-one ratio deemed essential to seizing the tactical initiative. As a check, they also added up the number of battalions necessary for essential defensive and offensive missions; and they played a series of war games that pitted various combinations of American and South Vietnamese forces against projected enemy strength in different regions of the country. By these methods, the staff arrived at a recommended 1966 reinforcement of twenty-four U.S. maneuver battalions plus proportional combat and logistic support units and tactical air squadrons, a total of about 100,000 additional men.[29]

General Westmoreland presented this estimate to Secretary McNamara in mid-July, when McNamara visited Saigon for a comprehensive review of the progress, or lack of it, of the war, the final preliminary to a presidential decision on reinforcements. McNamara arrived in the South Vietnamese capital on the 16th, with an entourage that included General Wheeler and Ambassador Taylor's designated successor, Henry

Ambassador-designate Lodge and Secretary McNamara meet with Head of State Thieu and Premier Ky in Saigon. (© Bettmann/CORBIS photo)

Cabot Lodge.[30] His group spent five busy days with the mission. They also heard extensive briefings from Chief of State Thieu, Premier Ky, and officials of their regime on South Vietnamese political, economic, and military plans. Discussions ranged over most aspects of the war, including a review of proposed allied field command arrangements, consideration and rejection of press censorship, and an evaluation of ROLLING THUNDER.

Throughout, U.S. troop reinforcements were the issue of most concern. Preparatory to his visit, McNamara had asked the country team for estimates of troop needs for the rest of 1965 and "the probable requirements for additional forces next year." The MACV briefing to McNamara, presented by General DePuy, addressed both points. DePuy laid out MACV's force requirements in two phases, each of which denoted a stage in the progress of the military campaign as well as a reinforcement increment. In Phase I, the 44-battalion reinforcement

The Fateful Decisions, June 1965–February 1966

would enable the allies to "stem the tide" that until then had been running against them. This meant containing the Viet Cong offensive during the rest of the year and preventing a South Vietnamese political or military collapse. In Phase II, which should begin early in 1966, the second contingent of American reinforcements would give the allies the strength to "turn the tide" by attacking enemy main forces and base areas while simultaneously resuming the pacification of economically and politically important regions. This phase would require an estimated 24 additional American maneuver and 17 combat support battalions with helicopter and logistic units and 9 Air Force squadrons.

Both troop requests met a favorable response. Indeed, discussion of Phase I ended almost at once. During the second day of the meetings, Deputy Secretary of Defense Cyrus Vance telephoned from Washington to inform McNamara that President Johnson had decided to deploy the entire forty-four battalions and was "favorably disposed" toward mobilizing reserves and extending the tours of active duty personnel. The conferees then turned to the reinforcement for 1966. McNamara accepted the Phase II proposal as a basis for further planning and appeared to support it. He also left his field commander in little doubt that the war from then on would be primarily an American effort. Discussion throughout the conference, according to the MACV Chief of Staff, Maj. Gen. William B. Rosson, "revolved almost exclusively around the need for a major US effort—one calling for greater assets, greater vigor, greater effectiveness. . . . McNamara himself was dynamic and convincing—one who had a tremendous grasp for detail and who exuded confidence and a positive approach." Rosson found himself "not only surprised by the numbers of forces that Washington was prepared to send . . . , but somewhat awed by the realization that General Westmoreland was to play a key role in determining the numbers and types of forces that would be considered."[31]

The long–awaited presidential decision quickly followed McNamara's return to Washington. On 20 July, the defense secretary reiterated his endorsement of the 44-battalion reinforcement, a reserve call-up, and extension of active-duty tours. He also called for gradual intensification of ROLLING THUNDER, renewed pacification efforts in South Vietnam, and a diplomatic peace offensive, possibly to include a temporary cessation of bombing in the north. This proposal constituted the agenda for a final round of administration policy deliberations. During them, most participants gave evidence that they realized the troops under consideration were a first installment rather than a final payment and that they were contemplating what amounted to an American takeover of the war. McNamara himself declared that deployment of another 100,000 men early in 1966 likely would be necessary and that acceptance of his proposal implied a "commitment to see a fighting war clear through at considerable cost in casualties and materiel." No one was optimistic about the new Saigon regime. Ambassador-designate Lodge observed that "we shouldn't take the Government too seriously" and must "do what is necessary" to hold South Vietnam "regardless of the Government." Only George Ball continued to argue for withdrawal rather than deeper involvement; the other advisers, and President Johnson himself, rejected that alternative.[32]

At the end of a final National Security Council session on 27 July, Johnson, as expected, went ahead with the 44-battalion program. However, he ruled out an immediate reserve call-up, a request to Congress for large supplemental military appropriations, and a declaration of a national emergency, claiming that such actions would divide the country politically and might provoke more direct Russian and Chinese intervention on North Vietnam's side. In fact, Johnson wanted to avoid a potentially divisive congressional and public debate on the war; his overriding consideration was implementing his domestic Great Society legislation. He planned to meet Westmoreland's requirements for 1965 out of the resources of the active military establishment, but he indicated that more drastic mobilization measures might come at the beginning of the next year if renewed diplomatic initiatives proved fruitless. Further to minimize the domestic and foreign political impact of his decision, on the 28th, Johnson announced the deployment of only a portion of the 44-battalion reinforcement, including the airmobile division. Privately, General Wheeler informed Sharp and Westmoreland that "COMUSMACV's requests for units, personnel and materiel . . . will be met in full according to the desired schedule" and that preparations were under way to "ensure that we can meet follow-on requirements" in 1966.[33]

Johnson's decision for an open-ended commitment of U.S. forces to the war without mobilization dismayed the Joint Chiefs. They recognized that a reserve call-up was needed to carry out the Vietnam buildup efficiently while maintaining American military readiness elsewhere in the world. In addition, they believed that the president was understating the number of American troops that would be needed for victory, which some thought could go as high as a million men. General Johnson, whose service was most affected by the failure to mobilize, seriously considered resigning in protest. In the end, he stayed on—a decision he later characterized as "the worst, the most immoral" he had ever made. General Wheeler, the chairman, did not convey his colleagues' doubts to other policymakers. When asked for his views in White House councils and meetings with congressional leaders, he raised no objection to Johnson's course of action.[34]

The president's decision against mobilization of the reserves had the immediate result of slowing the deployment of the troops that Westmoreland had requested. Over the longer term, the effects on the armed services and the country were much more severe. As the Military Assistance Command requested additional U.S. reinforcements, the point at which reserves would have to be mobilized would set the limit on force deployments. To make commitments short of that point, the administration gradually would hollow out its forces in the United States and elsewhere in the world, undermining their discipline, cohesion, and combat readiness. Even worse, by deliberately understating the scale and costs of the U.S. commitment in July 1965, President Johnson made inevitable an erosion of congressional and public trust in his administration as the conflict went on. During the years to come, the "credibility gap" would only grow wider, until it engulfed both the president and South Vietnam.

Implementing Phase I

Once President Johnson had made his fateful decision, General Westmoreland and his staff turned their attention to carrying out the 44-battalion deployment and to fleshing out their proposals for Phase II. The deployment was largely a matter of putting into effect decisions reached and policies established during the lengthy discussion of the Joint Chiefs' three-division plan. In addition, the command in Saigon solved practical problems as they arose, modified the buildup schedule and troop list in response to unfolding events, and attempted to articulate an overall plan for the conduct of the war.

The major ground combat elements involved entered South Vietnam at the places and more or less at the times Westmoreland had specified. During July two Army infantry brigades deployed, the 2d of the 1st Infantry Division to the Saigon area and the 1st of the 101st Airborne to Cam Ranh Bay in II Corps. The following month, the 7th Marines disembarked at Chu Lai to augment the III Marine Amphibious Force (MAF). In September the 1st Cavalry Division (Airmobile) occupied its base at An Khe, midway between Qui Nhon and Pleiku. This location was Westmoreland's concession to Admiral Sharp, who was still unwilling to place the division too far inland and thought it should concentrate initially on controlling the coastal regions. During October the remainder of the 1st Infantry Division joined its 2d Brigade north of Saigon. In the same month, the Korean Capital Division—two infantry regiments with a marine brigade attached—took position at Qui Nhon and Cam Ranh Bay. Combat and service support troops and fixed- and rotary-wing air units arrived in a steady stream, although delays in construction of additional airfields capable of handling jets held up deployment of several Air Force tactical squadrons.[35]

General Westmoreland conducted this buildup on a very limited logistical base. Engineers and support troops had begun deploying to South Vietnam in April in response to repeated MACV requests; during the same month U.S. Army, Pacific, activated a logistic command in the country. In June engineers started building an extensive port and airfield complex at Cam Ranh Bay. Nevertheless, American base facilities still were rudimentary when the movement of major reinforce-

Soldiers of the 1st Cavalry Division disembarking at Qui Nhon
(© Bettmann/CORBIS)

ments commenced. Taking a calculated risk, Westmoreland accepted combat troops simultaneously with their supporting elements, rather than bringing in the supporting forces first. His logisticians, in several frantic months of improvisation, kept their part of the buildup barely abreast of that of the fighting forces, with no adverse consequences worse than occasional local supply shortages and administrative mix-ups and a growing backlog of vessels awaiting discharge off the ports. By the end of the year, a support structure was taking shape, with major supply facilities at Da Nang, Cam Ranh, Qui Nhon, Nha Trang, Saigon, and Vung Tau. Under a policy established by Admiral Sharp, the Navy provided common item support to all U.S. forces in I Corps; the Army 1st Logistical Command covered the other three corps areas.[36]

As his combat forces expanded, Westmoreland put into effect the plan that he, Admiral Sharp, and General Wheeler had adopted in April for a field command built around an Army corps headquarters. Details of the new command were still unsettled, however, when an argument broke out over its service composition. During June and July, Sharp and Wheeler pressed Westmoreland to organize a joint, rather than an Army, field force headquarters. They contended that it would likely have to control tactical air support and might have III MAF attached to it; hence, it should include officers of all concerned services. Westmoreland held out for the scaled-down Army corps headquarters originally contemplated, promising to add liaison officers from other

Aerial view of the Cam Ranh Bay complex (NARA)

services as required. That arrangement, he said, would give him more flexibility in restructuring the headquarters as the situation changed and would keep the details of its organization and personnel out of Washington interservice politics. The Joint Chiefs in late June ruled in favor of a joint headquarters but subsequently reversed themselves when they realized that Westmoreland, in line with long-standing contingency plans, intended to retain the III Marine Amphibious Force as a separate corps-level command.[37]

On 1 August, Westmoreland activated the tactical headquarters at Nha Trang under the designation Task Force Alpha. He assigned it the mission of exercising operational control over U.S. and South Korean units in II and III Corps and providing combat support to the South Vietnamese Army on the basis of "coordination and cooperation." Initially modest in size and number of attached troops, the task force expanded to corps level when the 1st Cavalry Division came under its control. On 25 September, MACV redesignated it Field Force Vietnam, a title chosen to avoid confusion with the numbered South Vietnamese corps and to denote the American command's supporting relationship to them. He enlarged the field force's responsibilities to include conduct of the MACV advisory effort in its area of operations. The force commander then became senior adviser to his counterpart Vietnamese corps commander, an arrangement that took careful explaining to General Vinh Loc of II Corps, who at first considered it a reduction in his own status. Westmoreland since April had intended to assign his deputy, General Throckmorton, to command the tactical headquarters. However, he discovered that he needed Throckmorton for other more urgent tasks. Hence, he placed Maj. Gen. Stanley R. Larsen, Throckmorton's designated deputy, in command of the field force, a job Larsen had held in an acting capacity since early August. In part because Larsen was junior in rank to the major general commanding the 1st Infantry Division, and partly because he expected to form a second field force in III Corps early in 1966, Westmoreland restricted Field Force Vietnam's area of control to II Corps. He placed the 1st Division, when it arrived, directly under MACV.[38]

General Larsen (NARA)

Besides organizing an American field headquarters, Westmoreland negotiated command arrangements with his Australian and Korean allies as their forces reached South Vietnam. The Australians readily agreed to place their battalion and its supporting elements, which were attached to the 173d Airborne Brigade at Bien Hoa, under the general's operational control. They were slow in permitting its use, however, in offensives at any distance from the base. Only in October, after Westmoreland's low-key persuasion, did the Australian government authorize free employment of the unit throughout III Corps. The Koreans' much larger forces were more difficult to deal with. Their division entered South Vietnam under a "Military Working Arrangement" with the United States, which vested control of Korean forces in a commander, Republic of Korea Forces, Vietnam. They refused to place their units under formal operational control of MACV, claiming that to do so would make them seem like mercenaries and puppets of the United States. After prolonged negotiations, General Westmoreland and the Korean commander, General Chae Myung Shin, reached a gentlemen's agreement (with nothing in writing) under which Chae placed his division under General Larsen's de facto control. As a formal device for defining the missions, command relations, and operational areas of the Koreans, and for looking after their military interests, the allies, as provided in the Working Arrangement, set up a tripartite committee consisting of General Chae, the chief of the RVNAF Joint General Staff, and the chief of staff of MACV.[39]

Following Westmoreland's May concept of operations, the newly arrived American ground forces first established and secured their bases and then launched progressively more ambitious offensives. In late June the 173d Airborne Brigade drove into War Zone D north of Saigon, killing some enemy and uncovering base facilities. The marines, however, had the distinction of first bringing a Viet Cong main force element to battle. On 17–18 August, in Operation STARLITE, the newly arrived 7th Marines encircled two battalions of an enemy regiment south of Chu Lai and inflicted a claimed 700 casualties while losing 45 marines killed and 203 wounded.[40]

During the autumn U.S. Army troops also engaged the enemy main force. Pushing into the war zones north of Saigon, the 1st Infantry Division and the 173d Airborne Brigade fought elements of the *5th and 9th PLAF Divisions* in a series of battles. In the Central Highlands of II Corps, the 1st Cavalry Division, making extensive use of helicopters for mobility, during November waged the largest American campaign of the war thus far. Battling a North Vietnamese division, the cavalrymen suffered casualties of 305 dead and 524 wounded while claiming to have killed at least 1,500 enemy. Although enemy losses were undoubtedly substantial, in these engagements as in subsequent ones, American units posted "body counts" that were based on questionable estimates and at times deliberately inflated. For lack of a better measurement of success, however, MACV and other U.S. agencies used these statistics as indicators of trends in the war and when the numbers looked favorable exploited them for public relations purposes.[41]

As Americans entered battle, officials in Saigon, Honolulu, and Washington grappled with the problem of designing a long-range plan of campaign and of determining what role U.S. forces should play in carrying it out. General Westmoreland issued his own first comprehensive campaign plan on 1 September, entitled "Concept of Operations in the Republic of Vietnam." He intended it partly as a guide for the activities of subordinate commands and partly as a framework for his requests for more forces in 1966.

Essentially an expansion upon the ideas he had presented to McNamara in July, his concept envisioned war in three phases, each associated with an American troop commitment. In Phase I, which would run through the rest of 1965, the allies were to hold their existing positions; continue pacification in a few areas, principally around Saigon; and launch limited forays against Viet Cong combat units and bases to forestall enemy attacks. In Phase II, which Westmoreland at first estimated would take up the first half of 1966, the allies, strengthened by a second wave of American troops, would mount sustained large-scale offensives against the enemy's main forces, occupy or neutralize the most important Viet Cong base areas, and restore government control to high-priority sections of the countryside, specifically the heavily populated coastal portions of I and II Corps, the Hop Tac provinces around Saigon, and a belt of provinces across the middle of the Mekong Delta. By the end of this phase, Westmoreland envisioned that the allies would have reduced considerably Viet Cong and North Vietnamese fighting power and reestablished Saigon's authority over much of the rural population. If the enemy still fought on after these setbacks, Phase III would run for a year to a year and a half after the end of Phase II. In that period, U.S. forces, augmented by as many as sixty-three more maneuver battalions and by a much enlarged South Vietnamese Army, would conduct offensive and pacification operations "designed to destroy the remaining organized VC/DRV units in S[outh] V[iet] N[am], and to clear and secure all populated areas . . . with concurrent and follow-on pacification" of the entire country. They also might move into Laos to sever the Ho Chi Minh Trail and take unspecified actions to stop Cambodian support of the Viet Cong.[42]

Westmoreland's general concept of the development of the campaign within South Vietnam had the concurrence of Admiral Sharp and the Joint Chiefs and incorporated much of their thinking. There was, however, lengthy discussion during the autumn among both military and civilian leaders of two intertwined issues: the extent to which U.S. troops should engage directly in pacification; and the geographical and military division of responsibility between American and South Vietnamese forces.

Westmoreland initially expected American units to concentrate on defending their own bases and attacking large organized enemy formations while the South Vietnamese went after the guerrillas and political infrastructure. However, other presidential advisers, including Secretaries McNamara and Rusk, expressed interest in American participation in territorial security and population control, especially during September and October when a lull in main force activity raised the possibility that the Viet Cong, in response to the American buildup, were reverting to purely guerrilla warfare. Such a change in enemy tactics, Rusk and McNamara suggested in mid-September, might even allow a slowdown in U.S. troop deployments. If only to forestall such a decision, Westmoreland and Sharp were quick to affirm that American troops could undertake pacification, something the marines already had begun on a limited scale. They and the Joint Chiefs argued that if the enemy persisted in the big-unit war, U.S. troops should be used primarily in that aspect of the struggle. If the enemy did go back to small-unit activity, American forces should work with the South Vietnamese to clear and secure the countryside. At any event, they always would try to root out the Viet Cong in

The Fateful Decisions, June 1965–February 1966

the immediate vicinity of their own bases. The reemergence of enemy main forces during November, highlighted by the bloody engagements in the Ia Drang Valley, rendered this question largely moot.[43]

The issue of division of responsibility was closely related to that of pacification. Westmoreland, from the time of his March commander's estimate, envisioned that American troops would take on much of the burden of maintaining pressure on enemy main forces and base areas. Indeed, South Vietnam's urgent need for men, mobility, and firepower for that mission was at the heart of the rationale for committing American troops. The South Vietnamese themselves favored such an allocation of tasks. General Thieu and other officials of his government told McNamara during his July visit to Saigon that, for both military and political reasons, American forces should operate in thinly populated regions, notably the Central Highlands, while the South Vietnamese Army regrouped for another try at controlling the settled lowlands. Westmoreland and Sharp preferred a less rigid demarcation of duties, based on the CHIEN THANG pacification support plan. Under it, both nations would share responsibility for each military mission. The Americans and the South Vietnamese general reserve would primarily but not exclusively conduct search and destroy and clearing operations on the fringes of the pacification "oil spots." The ARVN and the territorials, with American help as needed and available, would perform the securing mission among the hamlets and villages. This allocation of functions found widespread acceptance, although General Taylor, among others, expressed concern that it would result in American forces taking upon themselves too much of the burden of the war.[44]

The Phase I reinforcement increased in size during the summer and early autumn. As the buildup continued and American combat activity intensified, General Westmoreland and his staff discovered that in preparing their initial troop list they had underestimated the number of support units needed to sustain the forty-four maneuver battalions at full effectiveness. During August and September, in response to a series of MACV requests for additional air transport, air defense, artillery, engineer, medical, and tactical air units, as well as miscellaneous elements needed to fill out other organizations, the administration enlarged Phase I from 175,000 American troops to more than 220,000. President Johnson, at Secretary McNamara's insistence, readily approved these supplemental requests, known as the Phase I Add-ons. So enlarged, Phase I would take until April 1966 to complete, overlapping the troop movements of the prospective Phase II. It also would compete with Phase II for ready units, especially Army combat and service support organizations. Thus, enlargement of Phase I complicated the planning of Phase II, which went forward even as the troops of the first reinforcement contingent were deploying.[45]

Planning Phase II

At Secretary McNamara's behest, development of the 1966 reinforcement proposal followed a more orderly procedure than that of the 44-battalion plan. Westmoreland told Admiral Sharp the number of troops he required and the schedule on which he wished to receive them. Sharp then assembled a planning conference at his headquarters, attended by representatives of the Joint Chiefs of Staff, the service staffs, and all concerned commands, both in the Pacific and in the continental United States. At this conference, the providers and movers of the forces reviewed the MACV proposal and revised it to bring it into line with their capabilities and resources. As a final step the Pacific commander placed the conference's decisions before McNamara and the Joint Chiefs as a formal recommendation. Phase II went through two of these cycles. In the process, it changed in both time schedule and number of troops involved.

General Westmoreland opened the first round of planning on 18 September. He dispatched to Admiral Sharp a reiteration of his three-phase concept of operations, along with a list of major combat units for the 1966 reinforcement increment. These included two-thirds of another Marine division for III MAF; two more Army infantry divisions, one for the Saigon area and one for coastal II Corps; an armored cavalry regiment, also for coastal II Corps; and an additional battalion for the two-battalion 173d Airborne Brigade—in all, twenty-eight maneuver battalions. He also asked for another Army corps headquarters as the nucleus of a second field force; about 30,000 additional support troops; and seven Air Force fighter-bomber and two transport squadrons, bringing the total reinforcement to about 117,000 men. He wanted most of these troops to arrive in South Vietnam during the first half of 1966, with the Army and Marine divisions and the armored cavalry regiment deploying before the end of April.[46]

Westmoreland expected to encounter "tough sledding" in obtaining administration approval for a second major troop deployment hard on the heels of the first. Accordingly, he and General DePuy, his principal spokesman on Phase II planning, developed a carefully crafted presentation of the MACV proposal. In the form of a briefing, the presentation outlined the campaign phases of Westmoreland's concept of operations and then related the two reinforcement increments to the military tasks they were designed to address. Using the briefing and its extensive charts and graphs, General DePuy made the point that the first forty-four battalions would prevent the military situation from getting any worse, but that significant progress in pacification and the destruction of enemy forces and base areas would come when the Military Assistance Command received the Phase II reinforcements. As delivered by the forceful, articulate DePuy before various audiences in Honolulu, Washington, and Saigon, the MACV briefing impressed, among others, Secretary McNamara, who characterized it as the "best professional performance" that he had seen in five years in the Pentagon.[47]

Well-prepared briefings, however, could not save Westmoreland's preferred deployment schedule from a collision with the reality of limited service resources and the effects of President Johnson's decision against mobilizing the reserves. That collision occurred almost immediately, at the Pacific Command Phase II planning conference, held at Admiral Sharp's headquarters from 27 September through 1 October. After hearing General DePuy present MACV's program, the delegation from the Army staff, headed by Maj. Gen. Frank J. Sackton, Assistant Deputy Chief of Staff for Operations and Plans, declared that the plan was unworkable. The Army representatives demonstrated conclusively that in the absence of a reserve call-up their service would be unable to provide the additional troops Westmoreland wanted for Phase I and at the same time meet his proposed Phase II deadlines.[48]

With little choice in the matter, Westmoreland, who headed the MACV delegation, reluctantly agreed to a revised timetable hastily worked out by the staffs from Washington and Saigon. Under it, most Army deployments were to be held back until the second half of 1966. Of the two infantry divisions, one, the 25th, would enter South Vietnam in September, as would the armored cavalry regiment. The other division, the 4th, was to be delayed until December. Aviation and logistic unit deployments were to stretch well into 1967. In partial compensation for these delays, Westmoreland was to receive a brigade of the 25th Division at Saigon late in January and one from the 4th Division in II Corps in June. Marine, Navy, and Air Force deployments remained about as on Westmoreland's original schedule.

Westmoreland insisted that "for the record" his preferred earlier deployment dates be included in the final conference report, which would constitute Admiral Sharp's recommendation to the Joint Chiefs. Nevertheless, he acquiesced in the stretch-out, even though it nullified his projection that Phase II of the campaign might end by mid-1966. He and Admiral Sharp had been backing away from that projection even before the conference. At Honolulu they agreed upon phraseology, previously formulated by the admiral, to the effect that, while second-phase deployment plans should include a fixed time schedule, no dates should be set for the start and finish of the military operations. Westmoreland reported to Ambassador Lodge that the conference had been "highly successful." Privately, he expressed concern about the growing tension between himself and the Army staff over his expanding force requirements, which he acknowledged were "cutting into the meat and vitals of the Army."[49]

To General Westmoreland's surprise, Phase II met with an immediately favorable reception in Washington. On 15 and 18 October, General DePuy presented the conference recommendations to the Joint

Chiefs and Secretary McNamara in the form of a revised version of the MACV briefing. On the 18th, McNamara directed the services to prepare plans to complete both deployment phases, with and without a reserve call-up. On 3 November he recommended to the president full implementation of the Phase II plan, noting that the services could furnish the proposed forces by the end of 1966 without using the reserves. In justification of the new reinforcement, the defense secretary repeated DePuy's quantitative analysis of how the troop commitment would hasten military and pacification progress. He warned, however, that if the enemy also continued his buildup, the United States could face by early 1967 "stagnation at a higher level and . . . a need to decide whether to deploy Phase III forces, probably in Laos as well as in South Vietnam." In hopes of avoiding this grim prospect through diplomacy, and at a minimum of establishing the administration's good faith in the search for peace, McNamara recommended that Johnson try another bombing pause before he committed the Phase II forces. This formula received general endorsement from the president and his senior advisers. They appeared resigned to the inevitability of another large troop deployment and devoted most of their attention to arguments about the tactics and timing of the bombing pause. Although he postponed a decision on Phase II, Johnson in mid-November authorized McNamara to prepare his budget requests for the next fiscal year on the assumption that the deployments would take place.[50]

Meanwhile, the second cycle of Phase II planning got under way, largely in response to enemy actions. During October and November, the Military Assistance Command's intelligence section and other U.S. intelligence agencies reported a continuing, rapid increase in all catagories of the opposing forces. The Viet Cong continued to form new local and main-force battalions even as they suffered and replaced heavy battle losses. At the same time, North Vietnamese regulars moved south in ever-increasing numbers. This buildup, and the persistent enemy willingness to make main force attacks during the autumn when the situation favored them, had ominous implications for Phase II. According to MACV staff projections based on these strength increases, even with the Phase II reinforcements and with small augmentations of the South Vietnamese forces, the allies would fall short of the 3-to-1 ratio in maneuver battalions. The only solution, it seemed to the MACV commander, was to ask for still more American or other allied troops.[51]

Westmoreland did so on 23 November, after receiving a combined study by his intelligence and operations directorates of the enemy buildup and the force needed to counter it and after securing assent from Ambassador Lodge and the Mission Council. He asked for nearly a doubling of the Phase II reinforcement of maneuver battalions from 28 to 53, with a corresponding increase in Army aviation and support units and Air Force tactical squadrons. To reduce the burden on American resources, Westmoreland suggested that part of this reinforcement

The Fateful Decisions, June 1965–February 1966

could be South Korean: a regimental combat team to round out the Capital Division and another full infantry division to protect coastal areas in II Corps and release the U.S. 4th Infantry Division for mobile operations in the highlands. He also asked for more American combat units: another infantry division to reinforce III Corps and operate in the northern part of the Mekong Delta, a separate infantry brigade for II Corps, an additional airmobile infantry battalion to augment the 1st Cavalry Division, and an air cavalry squadron each for the 1st Cavalry and 4th Infantry Divisions. Westmoreland requested deployment of the Koreans during the second quarter of 1966 and of the American units during the third and fourth quarters. He emphasized that before these deployments could take place he must have prior shipment of a much expanded list of logistical support forces. Otherwise, he argued, by further straining his already barely adequate support base, the new arrivals would reduce rather than increase his command's capacity for sustained combat.[52]

The expanded Phase II proposal, like the original, received rapid, unquestioning administration acceptance. On 30 November and again on 6 December, McNamara endorsed the enlarged reinforcement, restating his October rationale and again urging a preparatory bombing pause. The proposal met with mild dissent from General Taylor and from the Air Force Chief of Staff, General McConnell. Both advocated a much intensified air campaign against North Vietnam, and both questioned the wisdom of trying to match the projected enemy buildup, whose dimensions Taylor thought might be overestimated, man for man with American troops. Most senior administration officials, however, accepted the enlargement of Phase II with little argument. Late in December, in connection with a Christmas holiday truce, President Johnson took the first step in McNamara's recommended scenario. He halted the bombing of North Vietnam and then kept the pause in effect through the end of January as background to a global flurry of American diplomatic activity. Fully expecting the diplomatic effort to fail, the president intended the pause primarily to prepare American opinion for the larger war toward which his course was set.[53]

Accordingly, military preparations for Phase II continued parallel to the diplomatic effort. On 1 December, McNamara instructed his principal civilian and uniformed subordinates to make detailed plans for carrying out the doubled Phase II, working toward a late-January Honolulu conference that would establish final troop lists and movement schedules. Also during December, Sharp and Westmoreland prepared their own comprehensive deployment plan, by quarters, for all the remaining Phase I forces and for Phase II. Their program, which incorporated the units already deployed during 1965, called for 102 allied maneuver battalions, 79 of them American, and over 440,000 men to be in South Vietnam by the end of 1966. Reflecting Sharp's theater-wide concerns, it also included substantial American reinforcements for Thailand and another Army division for Hawaii to replace the 25th as Pacific Command reserve. Westmoreland meanwhile made additional plans of his own. Aware that the military services were suffering from manpower and unit shortages, he instructed his staff to draw up a list of the minimum additional forces he would need to stay even and to prepare "alternative and lesser force packages" as fallback positions for the conference.[54]

Movement of some Phase II units occurred before the definitive planning conference and before the end of the bombing pause. On 9 December, citing the steady enlargement of North Vietnamese and Viet Cong main forces in II and III Corps and the threat they posed to Pleiku and Saigon, Westmoreland asked for and received early deployment of two brigades of the 25th Infantry Division. The 3d Brigade went by air to Pleiku late in December, leapfrogging the congested South Vietnamese ports. It strengthened the defenses of Pleiku and released more of the 1st Cavalry for offensive operations. A month later the division's 2d Brigade deployed by ship to Saigon and established itself at Cu Chi, located about fifteen miles northwest of the capital, to reinforce the none-too-steady ARVN 25th Division in that vital area.[55]

Decisions at Honolulu

The final Phase II planning conference opened in Honolulu on 17 January, as the bombing pause was nearing its diplomatically unproductive end. Running through 9 February, it began with two weeks of meetings at which over 450 staff officers and civilians from the involved commands thrashed out the details of the air and ground deployments and campaign plans for the coming year. It ended as a political summit meeting between President Johnson and the South Vietnamese leaders, Thieu and Ky. U.S. troop commitments had an important place in both sets of deliberations.

The staff discussions revolved around three alternative plans, called cases, which the Joint Chiefs of Staff, at McNamara's direction, had drawn up for carrying out Sharp and Westmoreland's 102-battalion program. Case I called for a reserve mobilization and extension of enlistments. Cases II and III did not, and Case III also included withdrawal of fewer men from forces outside the United States. The first two cases would provide all 102 maneuver battalions, but in Case II the deployment of 9 would be postponed until early 1967. Case III required outright deletion of 18 American battalions, including a complete division, 2 brigades, and some smaller combat elements. As a result of prospective shortages of Army aviation and logistic units and personnel, none of the cases would provide full helicopter, artillery, and service support to the fighting units, although Case I came close to doing so. Not surprisingly, General DePuy, who again headed the MACV delegation, expressed preference for Case I as most fully contributing to

Secretary Rusk and President Johnson at the Honolulu conference, 1966 (NARA)

the achievement of the Military Assistance Command's campaign objectives for 1966. He pronounced Case II acceptable but less desirable because of its reduction in support forces and its stretch-out of combat unit deployments. While "adequate for the safety of the command," he said, Case III would leave MACV without sufficient power to take the offensive. Admiral Sharp, in his final conference report to the Joint Chiefs, substantially adopted the Military Assistance Command's position, in effect recommending implementation of Case I while expressing a willingness to settle for Case II.[56]

President Johnson and the South Vietnamese leaders, in their formal sessions and conference communique, concentrated on the promotion of pacification and political and social reform. In private, they made important decisions on strategy and troop commitments. The allies adopted a set of quantitative campaign objectives for 1966, based primarily on Westmoreland's concept of operations, which the general took as his "marching orders." The objectives included defending key military and civilian centers and food-producing areas, opening roads and railroads, clearing and securing the four national priority pacification zones, and bringing 60 percent of South Vietnam's people within secure territory by the end of 1966. Along with these security-related goals, the leaders promised to intensify their offensive against Viet Cong and North Vietnamese units, bases, and lines of communication within South Vietnam and infiltration routes in Laos and North Vietnam, with the objective of destroying 40–50 percent of the enemy's base areas during the coming year and of inflicting casualties on their forces "at a rate as high as their capability to put men into the field."[57]

Westmoreland was present for these final meetings, which were the occasion of his first face-to-face conference with President Johnson since taking command of MACV. The general held lengthy talks with Johnson and with McNamara, who had accompanied the president. Both men assured the MACV commander that he would receive all of his Phase II forces. McNamara told Westmoreland to expect deployments under the planning conference's Case I schedule but without a reserve call-up. This meant that the general would have to prepare to compensate for the resulting shortages in logistic support by arranging interservice exchanges of resources, employing civilian contractors, and, if possible, reducing requirements.[58]

Even as the Phase II reinforcements began moving into Vietnam during the first months of 1966, McNamara and the Joint Chiefs engaged in a lengthy tug-of-war over implementation of the Honolulu decisions. At issue was the persistent question of a reserve call-up. On 9 February the secretary of defense instructed all Defense Department agencies as planned to prepare to meet the troop requirements and movement dates of Case I, but without mobilization and extension of enlistments. The Joint Chiefs objected that this could be done only at the cost of unacceptably large withdrawals from U.S. forces in Europe and elsewhere. They argued for a stretchout of deployments through the first half of 1967 to allow time for new units to be formed from men raised by enlarged draft calls. McNamara on 11 April reluctantly approved a lengthened Case I schedule prepared by the Joint Chiefs that in fact much resembled the original Case II, although he delayed fewer units than the chiefs had proposed. Minor adjustments of the schedule continued until 30 June, when McNamara issued a final version, which the Defense Department dubbed Program Three.[59]

From General Westmoreland's standpoint, this debate was not of immediate concern, as the various changes had no effect on troop movements during the first part of 1966. The forces he most urgently needed, the 1st Marine Division and the remainder of the 25th Infantry Division, entered Vietnam during the first quarter. Under the plan adopted at Honolulu and later confirmed in Program Three, other major combat formations were to arrive somewhat earlier than previously contemplated. The 4th Infantry Division, for example, was scheduled for July rather than December and in fact completed its deployment in mid-October.[60]

Westmoreland knew by the end of February that he could count on greatly expanded American forces with which to pursue victory in

The Fateful Decisions, June 1965–February 1966

South Vietnam. Yet the Phase II he finally received was very different from the one he had proposed half a year before. Instead of a rapid infusion of a comparatively modest additional force during the first half of 1966 to accelerate the momentum of allied operations, Phase II had turned into a much larger but also much slower reinforcement that would not have its full effect on the balance of forces in South Vietnam until late in the year. By that time, the enemy's buildup also would have had its effect.

Notes

[1] Msg, Taylor 4035 to SecState, 3 Jun 65; see also Msg, Under SecState Ball 2769 to Ambs Taylor and Johnson, 1 Jun 65. Both in NSC History, Major Forces, box 41, LBJL.

[2] MACV Command History, 1965, pp. 5–6, 235–36. *U.S.–Vietnam Relations*, sec. 4.C.5, pp. 49–55. Memo, Westmoreland for Taylor, 30 May 65 sub: Comparison of the Rural Reconstruction Situation, 25 Jan and 25 Apr 65, tab 15, Westmoreland Hist File 16 (10 May–30 Jun 65), CMH. Memo, Westmoreland for Political Section, U.S. Embassy Saigon, 18 Jan 66, sub: Comparison of 1964 and 1965 Statistics, tab E–3, Westmoreland Hist File 3 (20 Dec 65–29 Jan 66), CMH. Msg, Taylor to SecState, 6 Jul 65, Historians files, CMH.

[3] MACV Command History, 1965, pp. 6, 220–23, 227–28. *U.S.–Vietnam Relations*, sec. 4.C.5, pp. 47, 49–50. For growing ARVN defensiveness, see Msg, Taylor 4220 to SecState for the President, 17 Jun 65, NSC History, Major Forces, box 42, LBJL.

[4] *U.S.–Vietnam Relations*, sec. 4.C.5, pp. 50–51, summarizes intelligence estimates. For Westmoreland's assessment, see Msg, COMUSMACV MAC 19118 to CINCPAC, 7 Jun 65; see also Msg, Taylor 4074 to SecState, 5 Jun 65. Both in NSC History, Major Forces, box 41, LBJL.

[5] Quote is from Msg, Taylor to SecState, 6 Jul 65, copy in Historians files, CMH. RVNAF buildup plans are summarized in *U.S.–Vietnam Relations*, sec. 4.C.5, p. 89; see also pp. 49–50 and in this volume ch. 6, pp. 192–93. Msg, Taylor 4074 to SecState, 5 Jun 65; Msg, COMUSMACV MAC 19118 to CINCPAC, 7 Jun 65. Both in NSC History, Major Forces, box 41, LBJL. Msg, Taylor 4220 to SecState, 17 Jun 65, NSC History, Major Forces, box 42, LBJL. Memo, Maj Gen Ben Sternberg for COMUSMACV, 7 Jul 65, sub: RVNAF Strength Summary, tab 11, Westmoreland Hist File 17 (1 Jul–28 Aug 65), CMH.

[6] Taylor analyzes the causes of the crisis in Msg 4074 to SecState, 5 Jun 65, NSC History, Major Forces, box 41, LBJL. MFR, Westmoreland, 31 May 65, sub: Call on Gen Thieu, tab 17, Westmoreland Hist File 16 (10 May–30 Jun 65), reflects initially aloof attitude of the generals. For narrative of events, see MACV Command History, 1965, pp. 18–19; *U.S.–Vietnam Relations*, sec. 4.C.5, pp. 41–42; and Taylor, *Swords and Ploughshares*, pp. 343–45.

[7] Biographical data is from CMH files. Taylor quote is from Msg, EmbTel 4220 to SecState, 17 Jun 65, NSC History, Major Forces, box 42, LBJL; see also his *Swords and Ploughshares*, pp. 345–46. Westmoreland quote is from *A Soldier Reports*, p. 138; see also pp. 90–91. MACV Command History, 1965, pp. 19–20.

[8] John Schlight, *The War in South Vietnam: The Years of the Offensive, 1965–1968*, The United States Air Force in Southeast Asia (Washington, D.C.: Office of Air Force History, 1988), pp. 31–33, 39–42; Msgs, Sharp to Westmoreland, 4 Apr 65; Westmoreland MAC 2027 to Wheeler, 12 Apr 65; Stilwell HWA 0887 to Westmoreland, 13 Apr 65; Westmoreland Msg Files, 1 Apr–30 Jun 65, CMH.

[9] Quote is from Msg, Westmoreland MAC 3052 to Sharp, 11 Jun 65, Westmoreland Msg Files, 1 Apr–30 Jun 65, CMH. For air operations, see Schlight, *Years of the Offensive*, pp. 41–49, 81–82, 99–111 and app. 5. MACV Command History, 1965, pp. 33–35, 46–48. Shulimson and Johnson, *Marines in Vietnam, 1965*, pp. 152–54.

[10] On 15 April, Westmoreland used his tactical aircraft in a saturation strike, Operation BLACK VIRGIN, against part of War Zone C. The operation took twelve hours to carry out, tied up most of MACV's combat aircraft, and achieved no significant results. See Schlight, "USAF South Vietnam," pp. 44–47; and Briefing Notes, in Westmoreland Hist Notes, 29 Aug–4 Sep 65, Westmoreland Hist File 1 (29 Aug–24 Oct 65), CMH.

[11] Schlight, *Years of the Offensive*, pp. 49–51. Msgs, Burchinal JCS 0789–65 to West-

The Fateful Decisions, June 1965–February 1966

moreland, Sharp, and Gen Ryan, 4 Mar 65; Ryan CINC 03072 to Burchinal, 4 Mar 65; Sharp to Burchinal, 5 Mar 65; Westmoreland MAC 1187 to Burchinal, 6 Mar 65. All in Westmoreland Msg Files, 1 Jan–31 Mar 65, CMH. COMUSMACV, "Chronology of Recommendations," p. 2. Sharp and Westmoreland, *Report on War*, p. 98.

[12] Historical Division, JCS, *JCS and Vietnam, 1960–1968,* ch. 24, pp. 2–6; COMUSMACV, "Chronology of Recommendations," pp. 4–7. Schlight, *Years of the Offensive*, pp. 51–55, 82–83. Quote is from Msg, Sharp to Westmoreland, 19 Jun 65; see also Msg, Westmoreland MAC 3172 to Sharp, 20 Jun 65. Both in Westmoreland Msg Files, 1 Apr–30 Jun 65, CMH. Westmoreland's views on the value of B–52s are summarized in Briefing Notes, in Westmoreland Historical Notes, 29 Aug–4 Sep 65, Westmoreland Hist File 1 (29 Aug–24 Oct 65), CMH.

[13] Msg, Taylor 4074 to SecState, 5 Jun 65; see also Taylor 4035 to SecState, 3 Jun 65. Both in NSC History, Major Forces, box 41, LBJL.

[14] For administration reaction to Taylor's reports, see Berman, *Planning a Tragedy*, p. 67. Msgs, Wheeler JCS 2080 to Sharp and Westmoreland, 4 Jun 65; Westmoreland MAC 2932 to Wheeler, 5 Jun 65. Both in Westmoreland Msg Files, 1 Apr–30 Jun 65, CMH.

[15] The 1st Infantry and 82d Airborne Divisions long had been designated for Vietnam in Army contingency plans. The 101st Airborne replaced the 82d when the latter was committed in the Dominican Republic during the spring and summer. For the Army planning, see MS, Walter G. Hermes, "The Department of the Army: The Buildup," ch. 3, pp. 11–14, 56; ch. 4, pp. 7–8; ch. 5, pp. 16–19. CMH files.

[16] Msg, COMUSMACV MAC 19118 to CINCPAC and JCS, 7 Jun 65, NSC History, Major Forces, box 41, LBJL; Westmoreland, *A Soldier Reports*, pp. 140–41; *U.S.–Vietnam Relations*, sec. 4.C.5, p. 91. Msgs, Westmoreland MAC 3240 to Wheeler and Sharp, 24 Jun 65; Westmoreland MAC 3283 to Wheeler, 27 Jun 65; Wheeler JCS 2400–65 to Sharp and Westmoreland, 29 Jun 65; and Westmoreland MAC 3320 to Wheeler and Sharp, 30 Jun 65. All in Westmoreland Msg Files, 1 Apr–30 Jun 65, CMH. See also Memo, DePuy for Westmoreland, 3 Jul 65, sub: Deployment of Units, tab 4, Westmoreland Hist File 17 (1 Jul–28 Aug 65), CMH.

[17] Msg, COMUSMACV MAC 19118 to CINCPAC and JCS, 7 Jun 65; text of telegram from Gen Westmoreland COMUSMACV 20055, 14 Jun 65; NSC History, Major Forces, boxes 41 and 42, LBJL. Of the 34 U.S. and 1 Australian battalions called for, Westmoreland expected to use 19 for defensive tasks, leaving 16, plus the 11 of the RVNAF general reserve, for offensive maneuver. All the Koreans would have essentially defensive missions. See Msg, Westmoreland MAC 3275 to Wheeler, 26 Jun 65, Westmoreland Msg Files, 1 Apr–30 Jun 65, CMH.

[18] Msgs, CINCPAC to JCS, 7 and 11 Jun 65; Memo, Wheeler JCSM–457–65 for SecDef, 11 Jun 65, sub: US/Allied Troop Deployments to South Vietnam. All in NSC History, Major Forces, boxes 41 and 42, LBJL. General McConnell's arguments are summarized in Schlight, *Years of the Offensive*, pp. 69–70.

[19] Quote is from Msg, Taylor 108 to SecState, 11 Jul 65, NSC History, Major Forces, box 43, LBJL. In same collection, see Msgs, Taylor 4220 to SecState, 17 Jun 65; Taylor 4265 to SecState, 18 Jun 65; and Taylor 4434 to SecState, 30 Jun 65. All in NSC History, Major Forces, boxes 42 and 43, LBJL. For South Vietnamese views and attitudes, see Msgs, Taylor 4422 to SecState, 29 Jun 65; and Taylor 009 to SecState, 1 Jul 65; Historians files, CMH. See also MFR, Westmoreland, 29 Jun 65, sub: Meeting with Gen Co, Minister of Defense, GVN, tab 42, Westmoreland Hist File 16 (10 May–30 Jun 65), CMH. Taylor recounts his change of mind in *Swords and Ploughshares*, p. 347.

[20] This discussion of the administration's decision-making process is based on Berman, *Planning a Tragedy*, pp. 67–129, 135–38, 146–48, 167; and Gelb and Betts, *Irony of*

261

Vietnam, pp. 120–23. For Ambassador Johnson's views, see Memo, John T. McNaughton, sub: McNaughton–Alexis Johnson Conversation, 25 Jun 65, in box 1, Warnke Papers, McNaughton Files, LBJL; for other comments on the debate, see *U.S.–Vietnam Relations*, sec. 4.C.6, p. 1.

[21] Msg, JCS 003800 to CINCPAC, 11 Jun 65, NSC History, Major Forces, box 42, LBJL. Msgs, Wheeler JCS 2323–65, JCS 2331–65, JCS 2360–65 to Sharp and Westmoreland, 22 Jun 65; 23 Jun 65; 24 Jun 65; Msgs, Westmoreland MAC 3237 to Sharp, 24 Jun 65; MAC 3275 to Wheeler, 26 Jun 65; and MAC 3320 to Wheeler and Sharp, 30 Jun 65; Sharp to Wheeler, 23 Jun 65, 25 Jun 65, and 27 Jun 65. All in Westmoreland Msg Files, 1 Apr–30 Jun 65, CMH.

[22] Quotes are from Msgs, Westmoreland MAC 3240 to Wheeler and Sharp, 24 Jun 65; and Westmoreland MAC 3275 to Wheeler, 26 Jun 65. Both in Westmoreland Msg Files, 1 Apr–30 Jun 65, CMH.

[23] For development of the "credibility gap" on this issue, see Hammond, *Military and the Media, 1962–1968*, pp. 161–68, and *U.S.–Vietnam Relations*, sec. 4.C.5, pp. 81–82. White House statement is quoted in Msg, OSD to CINCPAC, 1 Jun 65, tab 23, Westmoreland Hist File 16 (10 May–30 Jun 65), CMH. Taylor, *Swords and Ploughshares*, pp. 344–45. Westmoreland, *A Soldier Reports*, pp. 134–36.

[24] Msg, Taylor to SecState, 3 Jun 65; Msg, State/Defense to AmEmb Saigon, 5 Jun 65. NSC History, Major Forces, box 41, LBJL.

[25] Msg, COMUSMACV MAC 19912 to CINCPAC, 12 Jun 65, NSC History, Major Forces, box 42, LBJL; Msgs, Sharp to Westmoreland, 13 Jun 65; Westmoreland MAC 3074 to Sharp, 13 Jun 65; Westmoreland Msg Files, 1 Apr–30 Jun 65, CMH. See also Westmoreland, *A Soldier Reports*, pp. 138–39. On the 173d Airborne Bde, see Msgs, COMUSMACV MAC 3072 to CINCPAC info JCS, 13 Jun 65; Sharp to Westmoreland, 13 Jun 65; Westmoreland MAC 3077, to Sharp, 13 Jun 65. All in Westmoreland Msg Files, 1 Apr–30 Jun 65, CMH. Memo, Maj Lloyd J. Matthews for Westmoreland, 13 Jun 65, sub: Telephone Call from Adm Sharp at 1555, tab 26, Westmoreland Hist File 16 (10 May–30 Jun 65), CMH.

[26] Msg, Taylor EmbTel 4370 to State, 25 Jun 65; Msg, State 3057 to Saigon, 26 Jun 65; copies in Historians files, CMH. *U.S.–Vietnam Relations*, sec. 4.C.5, p. 104.

[27] Lt Gen John J. Tolson, *Airmobility, 1961–1971*, Vietnam Studies (Washington, D.C.: Department of the Army, 1973), pp. 61–62. *U.S.–Vietnam Relations*, sec. 4.C.5, p. 110. Msg, State and Defense to AmEmb Saigon, 10 Jul 65, NSC History, Major Forces, box 43, LBJL. Hermes, "Buildup," ch. 4, pp. 31–36. Johnson's 8 July decision is described in H. R. McMaster, *Dereliction of Duty: Lyndon Johnson, Robert McNamara, the Joint Chiefs of Staff, and the Lies That Led to Vietnam* (New York: Harper Collins, 1997), pp. 304–05.

[28] Quotes are from Msgs, Wheeler JCS 2400–65 to Sharp and Westmoreland, 29 Jun 65; Sharp to Westmoreland and Lt Gen Paul S. Emrick, 30 Jun 65; and Westmoreland MAC 3320 to Wheeler and Sharp, 30 Jun 65; see also Msg, Sharp to Wheeler, 4 Jul 65. All in Westmoreland Msg Files, 1 Apr–30 Jun 65, CMH.

[29] Rosson, "Involvement in Vietnam," pp. 201–07; Quote is from p. 205. For another description of calculation methods, see USMACV, Concept of Operations in the Republic of Vietnam, 1 Sep 65, ann. B, app. 12. *U.S.–Vietnam Relations*, sec. 4.C.6, pp. 10, 40–41, suggests the requirements were based more on what was available in the United States than on any other consideration.

[30] The year Taylor had promised the president he would serve ended in July. For Lodge, the visit was an opportunity to participate in decisions he would be implementing, and it would help him prepare for his Senate confirmation hearing. See Taylor, *Swords and Ploughshares*, p. 348; and Msg, McGeorge Bundy CAP 65391 to the Presi-

dent, 4 Jul 65, 1:10 p.m., copy in Historians files, CMH.

[31] Westmoreland quote is from *A Soldier Reports*, p. 142; see also pp. 141–43. Historical Division, JCS, *JCS and Vietnam*, ch. 22, p. 6. *U.S.–Vietnam Relations*, sec. 4.C.5, pp. 108–10, and sec. 4.C.6, p. 8. Taylor, *Swords and Ploughshares*, pp. 348–51. Msg, SecDef 5319 to AmEmb Saigon, 7 Jul 65, NSC History, Major Forces, box 43, LBJL; in same collection, see Chronology of Presidential Decisions, and Msg AmEmb Saigon to State, 27 Jul 65. Msg, Taylor Saigon 136 to SecState,13 Jul 65, copy in Historians files, CMH. Rosson quotes are from Rosson Interv, 1981, pp. 328–30; see also his "Involvement in Vietnam," p. 208.

[32] First McNamara quote is from his Memo for the President, 20 Jul 65, sub: Recommendations of Additional Deployments to Vietnam. Other quotes are from MFR, 22 Jul 65, sub: Meetings on Vietnam July 21, 1965. Both in NSC History, Major Forces, box 43, LBJL.

[33] Johnson's decision is recorded in Summary Notes of 553d NSC Meeting, July 27, 1965, 5:40 pm–6:20 pm, sub: Deployment of Additional U.S. Troops to Vietnam, NSC History, Major Forces, box 43, LBJL. Quote is from Msg, Wheeler JCS 2800–65 to Sharp and Westmoreland, 28 Jul 65, Westmoreland Msg Files, 1 Jul–30 Sep 65, CMH.

[34] The Joint Chiefs' acquiescence is detailed in McMaster, *Dereliction of Duty*, pp. 312–20, and U.S. Senate, Committee on Foreign Relations, *The U.S. Government and the Vietnam War: Executive and Legislative Roles and Relationships, Part IV: July 1965–January 1968* (Washington, D.C.: Government Printing Office, 1994), pp. 21–22; the quote from General Johnson is on p. 22.

[35] MACV Command History, 1965, pp. 42–44, 365. CINCPAC Command History, 1965, 2:292–94. Sharp and Westmoreland, *Report on War*, pp. 107–11. For air buildup, see Schlight, *Years of the Offensive*, pp. 85–88, 93–94, 113. 1st Cavalry location: Westmoreland, *A Soldier Reports*, pp. 144–45, 156; Interv, Senior Officer Debriefing Program with Gen William E. DePuy, Mar–Apr 79, p. V–23, MHI.

[36] MACV Command History, 1965, pp. 106–08. Msgs, Westmoreland MAC 4128 to Wheeler, 14 Aug 65; Westmoreland MAC 5419 to Gen Johnson, 30 Oct 65. Both in Westmoreland Msg Files, 1 Jul–30 Sep 65 and 1 Oct–31 Dec 65, CMH. Westmoreland Hist Notes, 23 Nov 65, Westmoreland Hist File 2 (25 Oct–20 Dec 65), CMH. Sharp and Westmoreland, *Report on War*, pp. 99, 254.

[37] Msgs, Westmoreland MAC 3277 to Lt Gen James L. Richardson, Jr, 26 Jun 65; Westmoreland MAC 3307 to Gen Johnson, 29 Jun 65; Wheeler JCS 2413 to Westmoreland, 29 Jun 65; Westmoreland MAC 3322 to Wheeler, 30 Jun 65; Sharp to Westmoreland, 6 Jul 65. All in Westmoreland Msg Files, 1 Apr–30 Jun 65 and 1 Jul–30 Sep 65, CMH. Historical Division, JCS, *JCS and Vietnam, 1960–1968*, ch. 22, pp. 21–22. Eckhardt, *Command and Control*, pp. 52–53.

[38] Maj Gen Jonathan O. Seaman, the 1st Division commander, was the senior Army major general in MACV. Msgs, Richardson WDC 05151 to Westmoreland, 16 Jun 65; Westmoreland MAC 4052 to Gen Johnson, 9 Aug 65; Westmoreland MAC 4217 to Gen Johnson, 20 Jun 65; Westmoreland MAC 4749 to Sharp, 23 Sep 65. All in Westmoreland Msg Files, 1 Apr–30 Jun 65 and 1 Jul–30 Sep 65, CMH. Westmoreland Hist Notes, 20 Sep 65, 18 Oct 65, and 17 Nov 65, in Westmoreland Hist Files 1 (29 Aug–24 Oct 65) and 2 (25 Oct–20 Dec 65), CMH. Eckhardt, *Command and Control*, pp. 53–55, summarizes headquarters activations.

[39] Eckhardt, *Command and Control*, p. 60. Msgs, Westmoreland MAC 3876 to Goodpaster, 30 Jul 65; Westmoreland MAC 4097 to Sharp, 12 Aug 65; Westmoreland MAC 4114 to Wheeler, 13 Aug 65; Westmoreland Msg Files, 1 Jul–30 Sep 65, CMH. MFR, Westmoreland, sub: Meeting with Lt Gen Sir John Wilton, 25 Jun 65, tab 37, Westmoreland Hist File 16 (10 May–30 Jun 65), CMH. Military Working Arrangement between

COMROKFORV and COMUSMACV, 6 Sep 65, copy in Historians files, CMH. Westmoreland Hist Notes, 5 Sep 65 and 6 Dec 65, Westmoreland Hist Files 1 (29 Aug–24 Oct 65) and 2 (25 Oct–20 Dec 65), CMH.

[40] Sharp and Westmoreland, *Report on War*, pp. 107–11. Shulimson and Johnson, *Marines in Vietnam 1965*, pp. 69–83.

[41] John M. Carland, *Stemming the Tide: Combat Operations, May 1965 to October 1966*, United States Army in Vietnam (Washington, D.C.: U.S. Army Center of Military History, 2000), chs. 4–6; the body count problem is discussed on p. 150.

[42] USMACV, Concept of Operations, 1 Sep 65, pp. 1–3, ann. B; Quote is from ann. B, app. 5. MACV Command History, 1965, pp. 137–48, 152–53. Westmoreland, *A Soldier Reports*, pp. 145–46.

[43] CINCPAC Command History, 1965, 2:298–303; Msg, Rusk DepTel 753 to AmEmb Saigon, 14 Sep 65; Msg, Lodge EmbTel 953 to SecState, 18 Sep 65; copies in Historians files, CMH. MFR, Gen Creighton W. Abrams, 27 Sep 65 sub: JCS Executive Session with Secy of Defense and Dep Secy of Defense, 20 Sep 65, 1400 hrs, Close Hold File 3, H. K. Johnson Papers, MHI; Msgs, Wheeler JCS 3428–65 to Sharp and Westmoreland, 16 Sep 65; Westmoreland MAC 4642 and 4675 to Wheeler and Sharp, 17 and 18 Sep 65; Sharp to Wheeler, 22 Sep 65; Westmoreland Msg Files, 1 Jul–30 Sep 65, CMH.

[44] Msg, Taylor Saigon 182 to State, 18 Jul 65, Historians Files, CMH. Historical Division, JCS, *JCS and Vietnam*, ch. 23, pp. 2–11. Taylor, *Swords and Ploughshares*, pp. 363–65. Msgs, Sharp to Westmoreland, 2 Nov 65; Wheeler JCS 4500–65 to Sharp and Westmoreland, 20 Nov 65; Sharp to Wheeler, 23 Nov 65; Westmoreland MAC 5875 to Wheeler and Sharp, 21 Nov 65; Westmoreland Msg Files, 1 Oct–31 Dec 65, CMH.

[45] CINCPAC Command History, 1965, 2:292–95. MACV Command History, 1965, pp. 42–43, 117; Historical Division, JCS, *JCS and Vietnam, 1960–1968*, ch. 22, pp. 8–9; Hermes, "Buildup," ch. 7, p. 26; Memo, McNamara for the President, 22 Sep 65, NSC History, Major Forces, box 40, LBJL. MFR, 29 Sep 65, sub: Luncheon Meeting with the President, Ball, McNamara, McGeorge Bundy, Raborn, Moyers, and Califano, NSC Country File, Vietnam, LBJL.

[46] MACV Command History, 1965, pp. 43–44; see also p. 36. CINCPAC, Command History, 1965, 2:295–97; Westmoreland Hist Notes, 15 Sep 65, Westmoreland Hist File 1 (29 Aug–24 Oct 65); MFR, Maj Gen F. R. Sackton, 4 Oct 65, sub: CINCPAC Phase II Planning Conference, 27 September–1 October 1965, Blue Tab D, Hermes Backup Files. Both in CMH.

[47] First quote is from Msg, Westmoreland MAC 4701 to Sharp, 20 Sep 65; second is from Msg, Gen Johnson WDC 10453 to Westmoreland, 1 Dec 65. Both in Westmoreland Msg Files, 1 Jul–30 Sep 65 and 1 Oct–31 Dec 65, CMH. Westmoreland Hist Notes, 15 Sep 65, Westmoreland Hist File 1 (29 Aug–24 Oct 65), CMH. MACV J3 Briefing, 18 Oct 65, in National Military Command Center, Pentagon, copy in Historians files, CMH. Summary of the DePuy Briefing for Secretary of Defense, 18 Oct 65; and MFR, Acting Secy of the Army Willis M. Hawkins, 18 Oct 65, sub: Presentation by General DePuy to the JCS and Service Secretaries, 18 Oct 65. Both in file TS–0175–80, Westmoreland Papers, CMH.

[48] Without a reserve call-up, the Army would have to carry out its planned expansion and furnish units for Vietnam by forming new organizations with draftees, using cadres and trainers drawn from the active forces. It could do this, at the cost of reduced unit readiness everywhere but in Southeast Asia, but not as rapidly as with a reserve mobilization. See Hermes, "Buildup," ch. 4, pp. 41–46; ch. 6, p. 54; and ch. 7, pp. 26–29. Also Ltr, Paul D. Phillips to DePuy, 2 Sep 65, DePuy Papers, MHI. The other services had similar difficulties; see for example Schlight, *Years of the Offensive*, pp. 85–86.

[49] MFR, Sackton, 4 Oct 65, sub: CINCPAC Phase II Planning Conference, 27 Sep–

The Fateful Decisions, June 1965–February 1966

tember–1 October 1965, Hermes Backup Files, CMH; Hermes, "Buildup," ch. 7, pp. 29–33; CINCPAC Command History, 1965, 2:297–98, 306–07; MACV Command History, 1965, pp. 44, 51, 117. First Westmoreland quote is from Msg, HWA 2667 to Amb Lodge, 2 Oct 65, Westmoreland Msg Files, 1 Oct–31 Dec 65, CMH. Second is from Westmoreland Hist Notes, 25 Sep–3 Oct 65, in Westmoreland Hist File 1 (29 Aug–24 Oct 65), CMH. CINCPAC Command History, 1965, 2:295–97. Msg, Sharp to Wheeler, 22 Sep 65, Westmoreland Msg Files, 1 Jul–30 Sep 65.

[50] Wheeler JCS 3912–65, JCS 3931–65, and JCS 4431–65 to Sharp and Westmoreland, 18 and 19 Oct 65 and 17 Nov 65, Westmoreland Msg Files, 1 Oct–31 Dec 65, CMH; MFR, Acting Secy of the Army Willis M. Hawkins, 18 Oct 65, sub: Presentation by Gen DePuy to the JCS and Service Secretaries, 18 October 1965; file TS–0175–80, Westmoreland Papers, CMH. McNamara quote is from Memo for the President, 3 Nov 65, sub: Courses of Action in Vietnam, 1st Rough Draft, copy in Historians files, CMH. Memo, William P. Bundy, 23 Oct 65, sub: Policy Choices and Decision-Making Procedures on Vietnam, Memos, McGeorge Bundy for Jacobsen for the President, 8 Nov 65; and McGeorge Bundy for the President, 27 Nov 65, sub: Once More on the Pause. Copies in Historians files, CMH.

[51] Enemy buildup: Briefing by Brig Gen Joseph A. McChristian, J–2 MACV, HQ MACV, 28 Nov 65, box 43; HQ MACV, Office of the AC/S J–2, Order of Battle Study no. 66–1: Enemy Force Buildup, July 1964–December 1965, 18 Feb 66; box 31, Joseph A. McChristian Papers, MHI. Msg, Westmoreland MAC 5358 to Sharp, 27 Oct 65, Westmoreland Msg Files, 1 Oct–31 Dec 65, CMH. Historical Division, JCS, *JCS and Vietnam*, ch. 23, pp. 14–16. MACV Command History, 1965, pp. 7–9, 14–15, 58.

[52] Westmoreland Hist Notes, 20 and 22 Nov 65, Westmoreland Hist File 2 (25 Oct–20 Dec 65), CMH; *U.S.–Vietnam Relations*, sec. 4.C.6, pp. 21–23; Msg, Westmoreland MAC 6053 to Gens Johnson and Waters, 30 Nov 65, Westmoreland Msg Files, 1 Oct–31 Dec 65, CMH; MACV Command History, 1965, pp. 44–45, 117–18.

[53] *U.S.–Vietnam Relations*, sec. 4.C.6, pp. 24–25. Memos, McNamara for President, 30 Nov 65; and sub: Military and Political Actions Recommended for South Vietnam, 6 Dec 65; Memos, McGeorge Bundy for President, 3 and 9 Dec 65; Memo, Taylor for McNamara, 6 Dec 65, sub: Comments on Reference Documents; Msg, Bundy CAP 65828 to President, 7 Dec 65. All in Historians files, CMH. McConnell's views are in Schlight, *Years of the Offensive*, pp. 114–15. For the bombing pause, see Thies, *When Governments Collide*, pp. 115–22; and Hammond, *Military and the Media, 1962–1968*, pp. 218–26.

[54] Msgs, Wheeler JCS 4658–65 to Sharp, 1 Dec 65; Gen Johnson WDC 10453 to Westmoreland, 1 Dec 65; DePuy MAC 6456 to Westmoreland, 15 Dec 65; Westmoreland Msg Files, 1 Oct–31 Dec 65, CMH. *U.S.–Vietnam Relations*, sec. 4.C.6, pp. 25–26, 28; Historical Division, JCS, *JCS and Vietnam, 1960–1968*, ch. 32, pp. 1–2; CINCPAC Command History, 1965, 2:308. Westmoreland Hist Notes, 9 Dec 65 and 11 and 16 Jan 66, Westmoreland Hist Files 2 (25 Oct–20 Dec 65) and 3 (20 Dec 65–29 Jan 66), CMH.

[55] MACV Command History, 1965, p. 45; and ibid., 1966, pp. 69–70. Msg, Westmoreland MAC 0006 to Sharp, 1 Jan 66, Westmoreland Msg Files, 1 Jan–31 Mar 66; CMH. Westmoreland Hist Notes, 9 and 11 Dec 65; MFR, Maj C. M. Putnam, 30 Dec 65, sub: COMUSMACV Conference with FFORCEV Commanders and II Corps Advisers. Both in Westmoreland Hist Files 2 (25 Oct–20 Dec 65) and 3 (20 Dec 65–29 Jan 66), CMH.

[56] *U.S.–Vietnam Relations*, sec. 4.C.6, pp. 26–27, 35–37; Historical Division, JCS, *JCS and Vietnam, 1960–1968*, ch. 32, p. 2. MACV Command History, 1966, pp. 66–67; Hermes, "Buildup," ch. 8, pp. 29–32. Work and positions of the MACV delegation can be followed in detail in a series of Msgs from DePuy to Westmoreland, 19 to 30, Jan 66, Westmoreland Msg Files, 1 Jan–31 Mar 66, CMH.

[57] Goals are summarized in "1966 Program to Increase the Effectiveness of Military Operations and Anticipated Results Thereof," 8 Feb 66, tab A–6, Westmoreland Hist File 4 (30 Jan–1 Mar 66), CMH. "Marching orders" quote is from Col Paul L. Miles, USA (Ret.), Specific Comments on "MACV: The Joint Command," 11 Mar 2002, p. 1, CMH.

[58] Msgs Sharp to Westmoreland and Stilwell, 1 Feb 66; Sharp to Wheeler, 1 Feb 66; Westmoreland Msg Files, 1 Jan–31 Mar 66, CMH. "NSC History, Honolulu Conference," box 44, NSC Files, LBJL. Westmoreland Hist Briefing, 16 Feb 66, tab A; Declaration of Honolulu, 9 Feb 66, tab A–10; Text of Joint Communique, tab A–11; MFR, Brig Gen W. K. Jones, USMC, 20 Feb 66, sub: MACV Commander's Conference, 10 Mar 66, tab C–1. All in Westmoreland Hist File 4 (30 Jan–13 Mar 66), CMH. *U.S.–Vietnam Relations*, sec. 4.C.6, pp. 21–22; Westmoreland, *A Soldier Reports*, pp. 159–60.

[59] *U.S.–Vietnam Relations*, sec. 4.C.6, pp. 29–33, 37–40, 48–50; Historical Division, JCS, *JCS and Vietnam*, ch. 32, pp. 2–5. Hermes, "Buildup," ch. 8, pp. 36–37.

[60] MFR, W. K. Jones, 10 Mar 66, sub: MACV Commanders' Conference, 20 Feb 66, tab C–1, Westmoreland Hist File 4 (30 Jan–13 Mar 66), CMH, contains Westmoreland's report to his commanders on reinforcements to be expected. For actual arrivals, see Westmoreland and Sharp, *Report on War*, pp. 123–29; and Jack Shulimson, *U.S. Marines in Vietnam: An Expanding War, 1966* (Washington, D.C.: History and Museums Division, Headquarters, U.S. Marine Corps, 1982), pp. 128, 130–31.

8

MACV Headquarters: The Years of Expansion, 1965–1967

During the period between President Johnson's troop commitment decisions of July 1965 and the end of 1967, the United States attempted to win the war in Vietnam by an escalating application of its military power on the ground in South Vietnam and in the skies over North Vietnam and Laos. The Military Assistance Command, Vietnam, directed much but not all of this effort. In the process, the command grew from an advisory and support organization into what amounted to the headquarters of a field army of American and allied troops actively battling a growing enemy main force. Yet at the same time, MACV continued to be responsible for equipping, training, and advising the armed forces of the Republic of Vietnam. It also took a major part in the American mission's effort to promote a stable, constitutional, democratic Saigon government; and it became the central directing agency for an ambitious new American-sponsored try at pacifying the South Vietnamese countryside. Beyond the boundaries of South Vietnam, MACV, in not always harmonious collaboration with American authorities in Vietiane and Bangkok, conducted a covert air and ground war in Laos. It also cooperated, and at times quarreled, with CINCPAC over the bombing campaign against North Vietnam.

As MACV's missions proliferated, its organization grew in size and complexity. The expansion was largely ad hoc and unplanned, with new agencies springing up or hiving off of old ones and command relationships being improvised under pressure of circumstances and service interests. Each new mission, and each policy or institutional conflict, brought an organizational response, as did each fresh initiative from an administration in Washington increasingly desperate to achieve some measurable amount of progress in the war.

Enlarging the Headquarters

As allied strength in Vietnam mushroomed to over half a million American, Australian, South Korean, New Zealand, Filipino, and Thai military personnel and nearly 80,000 civilian employees of various nationalities, the Military Assistance Command headquarters grew in proportion. Between December 1964 and December 1967, the MACV headquarters complement tripled in size, from about 1,100 officers and enlisted men to almost 3,300. The addition of personnel to the headquarters ran ahead of formal Joint Table of Distribution changes. Because Westmoreland since August 1964 had possessed authority to requisition personnel for staff increases at the same time as he submitted the enlarged organization tables for JCS approval, the new people were usually at work long before the formal organizational revisions went into effect.[1]

The central structure of the headquarters—the six joint general staff ("J") sections and the special staff offices—remained largely unchanged during this period of rapid growth. However, within the major staff sections, branches and divisions multiplied, merged, and divided at a bewildering pace to deal with new functions and responsibilities, and additional staff elements grew up in response to a variety of new tasks. Early in 1967, a contract team studying MACV's requirements for automatic data processing declared itself unable to develop formal flowcharts for the headquarters because it was "too large, too dispersed, and too dynamic in structure." Not surprisingly, much of the expansion in manpower and organizational complexity came in the intelligence, operations, and logistics sections, which provided much of the command, control, and management impetus for the American force buildup. By early 1967, MACV's intelligence staff alone numbered more than 600, well over twice the size of the entire headquarters in 1962.[2]

With expansion, the MACV staff dispersed into a proliferating number of buildings throughout downtown Saigon, adding to the command's existing security vulnerabilities and communications difficulties. In March 1965, even before the American buildup got under way, General Westmoreland began a search for a new location large enough to accommodate the entire headquarters. He initially tried to obtain a site near the Joint General Staff compound at Tan Son Nhut Airport, desirable from the standpoint of removing Americans from central Saigon and placing MACV conveniently close to its Vietnamese counterpart. The Vietnamese government, however, refused to turn over the most suitable location, a soccer field near the civilian air terminal, allegedly because Premier Ky wanted to keep the property for a postwar tourist hotel. MACV in October 1965 settled for a triangular 31-acre site along Petrus Ky Street in western Saigon, which afforded adequate space. Ironically, it bordered upon the residence area of the International Control Commission which was still supposedly overseeing the 1954 Geneva cease-fire in Indochina.[3]

The big American construction contractor, Raymond, Morrison-Knudsen, Brown and Root, and J. A. Jones (RMK-BRJ) barely had ordered prefabricated buildings from the United States and begun

MACV Headquarters: The Years of Expansion, 1965–1967

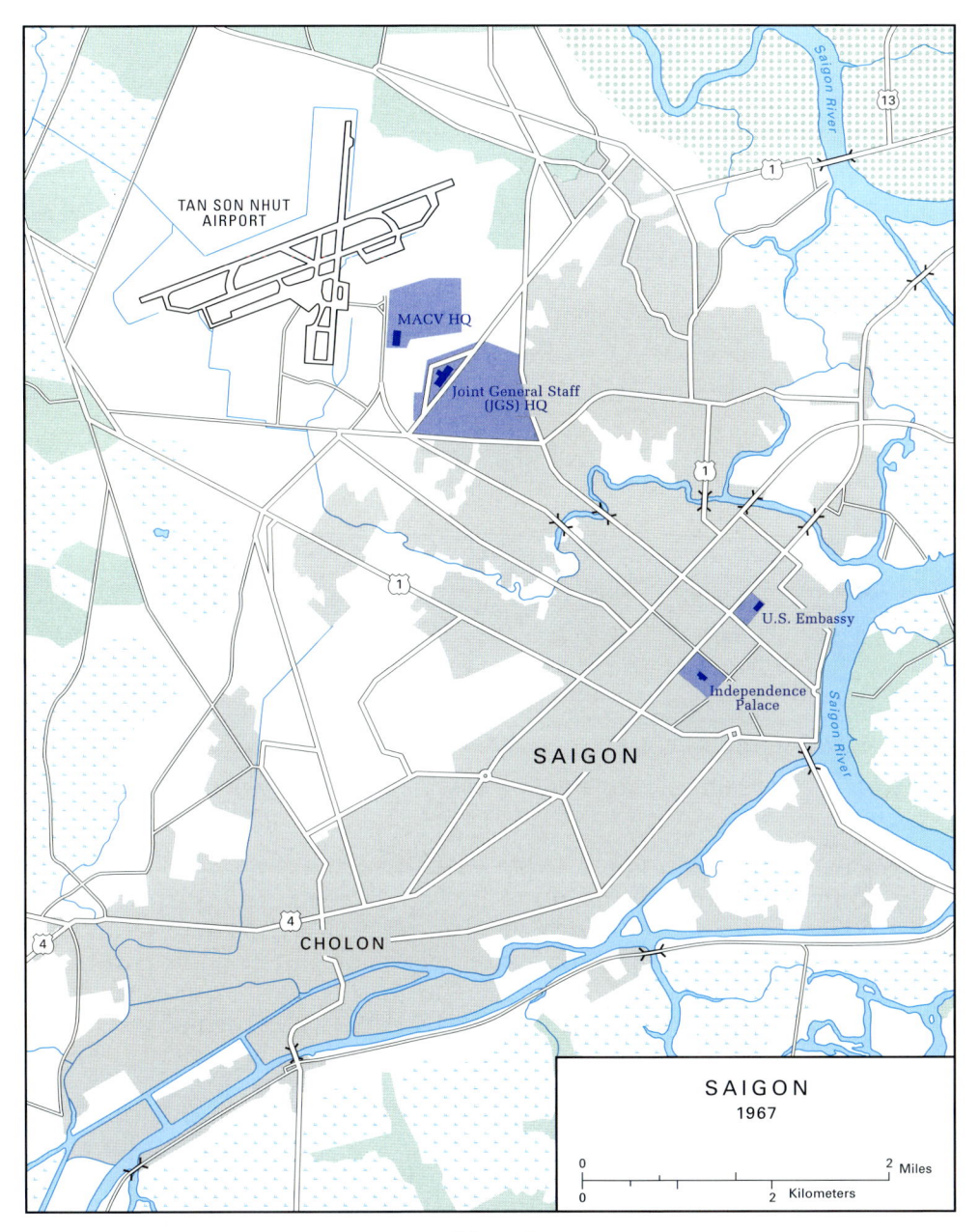

MAP 4

clearing land and pouring concrete foundations when MACV and the U.S. Mission decided on a change of site. MACV always had regarded the Petrus Ky plot as a second choice; residents of the area had protested location of the American headquarters there; and, most serious, the site was close to a Buddhist institute militantly opposed to the Thieu-

MACV: The Years of Escalation, 1962–1967

MACV headquarters, with Tan Son Nhut in the background (DOD files)

Ky government. In late April 1966, with the Saigon regime locked in a tense confrontation with Buddhist and ARVN rebels in I Corps, Ambassador Lodge and General Westmoreland reopened the effort to acquire the Tan Son Nhut soccer field. Under their combined remonstrations, Ky gave way. At the cost of about six months' delay in completing the project and an additional $3 million, the Americans turned the Petrus Ky site over to the U.S. Agency for International Development (USAID) for a trade school and began construction at Tan Son Nhut.[4] *(Map 4)*

MACV occupied its new headquarters early in August the following year. Completed at a total cost of $25 million, the new complex soon earned the nickname "Pentagon East." The air-conditioned structure of two-story prefabricated buildings, a little more than a third the size of its Washington namesake, included some twelve acres of enclosed office space. In addition to the headquarters offices, the complex included a barracks, a mess hall, a refrigerated storage building, and its own power plant and telephone exchange. Inside, according to one staff officer, "the well-waxed corridors had the fluorescent feel of an airport terminal." A cyclone fence, topped with barbed wire and with watch towers at intervals, provided close-in protection. While long in coming, the move to Tan Son Nhut unified all elements of the headquarters in one place, conveniently near the Joint General Staff and the headquarters of MACV's Air Force component command.[5]

At MACV headquarters, as throughout the command, most officers and enlisted men served unaccompanied one-year tours of duty under a Defense Department policy that dated back to the advisory years before the American buildup. Generals and a small number of key field grade officers remained longer for the sake of continuity in important posts; their tours ranged in length from eighteen months to two years, depending on the requirements of the command, individual circumstances, and the needs of their parent services. Under a program established by General Westmoreland, officers in important positions who volunteered, at COMUSMACV's invitation, to spend additional time in Vietnam received special incentives, including the privilege of moving their families to government quarters in the Philippines. While he supported longer service in Vietnam for selected individuals, Westmoreland favored the one-year tour as a general policy, on the grounds men could not keep up the pace of work he expected of them for more than a year in Vietnam's tropical climate and that frequent personnel changes infused fresh ideas and viewpoints into the command. Frequent rotation also allowed the services to give their best commanders Vietnam experience while at the same time distributing their leadership talent among Southeast Asia and other important theaters. According to Lt. Gen. Frederick Weyand, his deputy chief of staff for personnel, Army Chief of Staff Johnson "feels quite strongly that with the talent we have on the bench, it would be a mistake to play the whole ball game, or even a major portion thereof, with only one G[eneral] O[fficer] team. . . . The long range needs of the Army and the nation require maximum utilization of this opportunity to give as many of our GO's as possible the actual counter-insurgency combat experience they can acquire only in RVN."[6]

Selection and assignment of general officers to key command and staff positions was a matter of continuous negotiation between General Westmoreland, Admiral Sharp, General Wheeler, and the service chiefs. The MACV commander left Navy, Air Force, and Marine selections largely to the respective services. If he intervened at all, he did so only occasionally, very circumspectly, and when possible in concert with his component commanders. He exercised much greater influence over the assignment of Army general officers, on which he dealt directly, as Army component commander, with General Johnson. As commanders and key staff officers became due for rotation, Westmoreland, his deputy Army component commander, and the chief of staff would work out a "slate" of replacements. Westmoreland's wishes carried great weight in this process, and he usually could block assignment of officers he definitely did not want; but he had to yield on occasion to other Army requirements enunciated by General Johnson, including the aforementioned career management considerations. Nevertheless, the MACV commander's personal preferences normally prevailed when he expressed them strongly. As a result, the Military Assistance Command appears to have received the best talent the Army and the other services could provide.[7]

For members of the MACV staff, derisively referred to by combat troops as "Saigon Commandos" or by the unprintable acronym REMFs, a tour at headquarters combined long working hours and a lingering threat of terrorism with access to the amenities, wholesome and otherwise, of a booming wartime capital. Veterans of the pre-1965 MACV saw a decline in the quality of Saigon life as the influx of Americans and war refugees brought price inflation, overcrowding, pollution, traffic jams, and a growing air of squalor and brutalization. Nevertheless, there were still tennis and swimming available at the exclusive *Cercle Sportif* (officers only), golf at the Saigon Golf Club, and horseback riding at the *Cercle Hippique*. Well-stocked post exchanges offered merchandise, snacks, and a variety of concessions. Special Services operated a library, bowling center, swimming pool, and craft shop, as well as the out-of-country rest and recuperation (R & R) program; and by mid-1966 two USO clubs were open. Armed Forces Radio and Television stations carried American music, news, and other programs. The 17th Field Hospital provided American military and civilian personnel with a full range of inpatient and outpatient medical services. Senior officers continued to live in rented villas and lower ranking personnel in hotels converted into officer and enlisted quarters. Residents of the hotels could take their drinks up to the roofs at sundown and watch the flares and gunflashes of the distant war on the horizon while awaiting the start of the evening's motion picture. Leisure time for most MACV headquarters personnel, however, was increasingly limited. General Westmoreland considered a seven-day, sixty-hour work week "par for the course"; he himself averaged close to eighty hours.[8]

As time went on, an increasing number of American personnel from MACV and the many other headquarters in the Saigon area moved out of the city. As South Vietnam's capital and only major seaport, Saigon naturally attracted more than its share of the American buildup. As a result, by April 1966 the city and its environs contained nearly 36,000 U.S. personnel. The American influx overburdened the city's real estate, drove up prices, and created an embarrassingly conspicuous foreign presence at the political heart of South Vietnam. At the urging of Admiral Sharp and the Joint Chiefs, and under personal instructions from President Johnson to accelerate the exodus from downtown Saigon, General Westmoreland directed his staff and his component commanders to halt further deployment of American units to the capital and to plan for the dispersal of those already there.[9]

The resulting program, known as Operation MOOSE (Move out of Saigon Expeditiously), and to some harassed planners as GOOSE (Get

MACV Headquarters: The Years of Expansion, 1965–1967

out of Saigon Eventually), took until early 1968 to complete and cost at least $40 million for the required construction and relocations. In the process, besides MACV's move to Tan Son Nhut, U.S. Army, Vietnam (USARV), and the 1st Logistical Command relocated to Long Binh about fifteen miles north of the capital. Numerous facilities went to Bien Hoa, Cam Ranh Bay, and other locations in the provinces. By the end of 1967, the number of American personnel working in Saigon and its Chinese suburb, Cholon, had fallen to about 7,900, while nearly 20,000 were located at Tan Son Nhut. MACV and its subordinate commands at the same time turned back to the South Vietnamese some seventy office and residential properties.[10]

The threat of Viet Cong terrorism was present wherever Americans lived and worked in the Saigon area. The capital city constituted a separate Viet Cong special zone, with its own main and local forces, guerrillas, and political cadres. Many Viet Cong native to the area lived and moved about legally as ostensibly loyal citizens. They kept up a campaign of assassination, sabotage, and harassment against United States and South Vietnamese personnel and installations. On 1 April 1966, after a short, violent gunfight with U.S. MPs, the enemy set off a large truck bomb at the Victoria Bachelor Officers Quarters, causing over 120 American, Vietnamese, and Australian casualties. A little less than a year later, Communist gunners managed to fire five 81-mm. mortar rounds at the old main MACV building, using a house with the roof removed as a firing position. The shells missed their target but one hit an ARVN truck killing twelve soldiers. A time bomb left behind at the Viet Cong mortar site caused several more casualties.[11]

To protect its installations, MACV, for political reasons, continued to rely primarily on South Vietnamese Army regulars, territorial forces, and police of the South Vietnamese Capital Military District. In cooperation with these forces, the U.S. 716th Military Police Battalion under Headquarters Support Activity, Saigon, and its successor the U.S. Army Headquarters Area Command manned reinforced concrete guard posts at American military installations, the U.S. embassy, and the major billets and conducted nightly roving patrols with machine gun-equipped jeeps. In addition, the residents of each billet were organized for security and self-defense. At Tan Son Nhut, the American and South Vietnamese Air Forces protected their own installations. The command imposed curfews on Americans and warned individual personnel to exercise caution in using public transportation, to vary their routes to and from work, to inspect their vehicles frequently for hidden bombs and booby traps, and to travel in groups when in the city. These precautions kept terrorism at a relatively low level until the Tet offensive in early 1968 for the first time brought full-scale warfare to Saigon's streets.[12]

As American forces in Vietnam expanded, so did the stream of official and semi-official visitors to the Military Assistance Command. Official visitors included President Johnson himself, who made two hastily

General Westmoreland (second from left) *receives the Boy Scout Silver Buffalo Award for distinguished service in Washington, D.C.* (© Bettman/CORBIS)

arranged stopovers at Cam Ranh Bay in October 1966 and December 1967. Vice President Hubert Humphrey, Secretary McNamara, General Wheeler, the service chiefs and secretaries, and a host of people from the Defense Department and its civilian contractors passed through Saigon on a more or less regular basis, as did officials of other government departments and senators, congressmen, and their staffs. Numerous private citizens, ranging from clergymen through advice columnist Ann Landers, also toured Vietnam. These persons either traveled on their own or were sponsored by the government for various purposes, usually related to enhancing American public support for the war. The number of visitors to MACV swelled to an average of 552 per month during 1966 and 740 per month the following year.[13]

General Westmoreland welcomed these visitations as an opportunity to educate Americans in and out of government in the realities of the war as MACV understood them. Even so, he also recognized the burden they placed on his command. Visits by senior officials called for extensive preparatory staff work, followed by lengthy schedules of conferences, briefings, and trips to the field, usually requiring the presence of Westmoreland and his principal subordinates. Lesser figures were the responsibility of lower-ranking members of the staff, but these officers also had duties that suffered from their absence. Senators and congressmen could be especially demanding and, depending on their importance to the administration, usually had to be accommodated.[14]

MACV and the Defense Department attempted repeatedly to curtail the flood of visitors to Saigon. In early 1967, for example, the Defense Department directed all its agencies to hold trips to Vietnam and Thailand to an "absolute minimum" and required each visit to meet one or more of three criteria: helping field commanders and staffs acquire needed resources; aiding future operations; and providing field commanders or higher echelons with significant information not otherwise available. Similarly, the ambassador asked the State Department to help keep down the number of non-Defense delegations. Nevertheless, the flow continued and reached an all-time high of 1,429 people in December 1967.[15]

With practice, the MACV system for entertaining and instructing visitors achieved considerable polish, with social occasions as well as briefings delivering the command's message. Westmoreland, for example, often invited junior officers from combat units to his dinners for congressmen, journalists, and other prominent civilians, to give the officers "a pleasant occasion" and the guests "some feel for the fighting." He also used his visitors as sources of information for himself on policy trends in the administration and public sentiment in the country.[16]

Planning and Control of Operations

As the American role in the war changed from advice and support of the South Vietnamese to direct combat participation, General Westmoreland endeavored to keep all aspects of the effort under his close personal control. He claimed later that "although the line of authority ran to me in several different ways, I was able to provide unity of command for the entire American military effort in South Vietnam, and . . . to give my personal attention to the entire range of advisory, combat, and support activities."[17] To accomplish this, he relied both on his individual efforts and on an expanding network of staff agencies for command and control, planning, logistical management, communications, and intelligence.

Sometimes characterized as a "workaholic," Westmoreland filled his sixteen-hour days in Saigon with staff conferences, meetings with the ambassador and country team, discussions with Vietnamese counterparts, and an endless round of welcoming, informing, persuading, and entertaining his command's many visitors. The general devoted several days each week to field trips, during which he orchestrated plans with his tactical commanders, saw and talked with the troops,

CHART 3—ORGANIZATION OF MACV HEADQUARTERS, MAY 1967

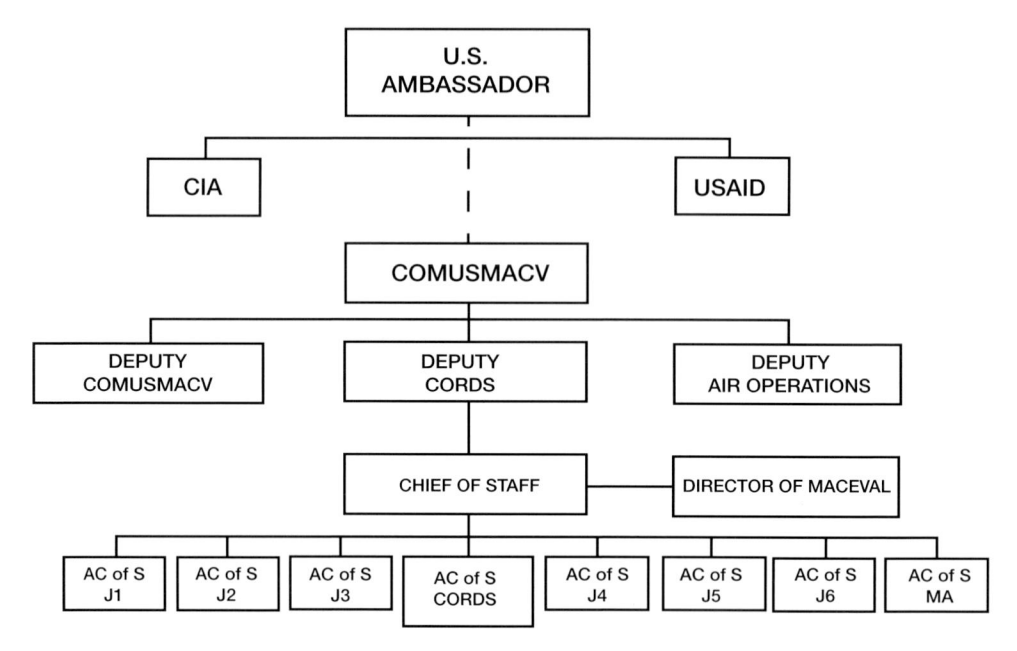

```
                    ┌──────────────────┐
                    │  U.S. AMBASSADOR │
                    └──────────────────┘
         ┌─────────────────┼─────────────────┐
     ┌───────┐             │             ┌───────┐
     │  CIA  │             │             │ USAID │
     └───────┘             │             └───────┘
                    ┌──────────────┐
                    │   COMUSMACV  │
                    └──────────────┘
         ┌─────────────────┼─────────────────┐
   ┌──────────┐      ┌──────────┐      ┌──────────────┐
   │  DEPUTY  │      │  DEPUTY  │      │   DEPUTY     │
   │ COMUSMACV│      │  CORDS   │      │ AIR OPERATIONS│
   └──────────┘      └──────────┘      └──────────────┘
                           │
                  ┌────────────────┐      ┌────────────────────┐
                  │ CHIEF OF STAFF │──────│ DIRECTOR OF MACEVAL│
                  └────────────────┘      └────────────────────┘
  ┌──────┬──────┬──────┬──────┬──────┬──────┬──────┐
┌─────┐┌─────┐┌─────┐┌─────┐┌─────┐┌─────┐┌─────┐┌─────┐
│AC of││AC of││AC of││AC of││AC of││AC of││AC of││AC of│
│ S J1││ S J2││ S J3││  S  ││ S J4││ S J5││ S J6││ S MA│
│     ││     ││     ││CORDS││     ││     ││     ││     │
└─────┘└─────┘└─────┘└─────┘└─────┘└─────┘└─────┘└─────┘
```

and attempted to gain a firsthand impression of conditions in the four corps areas. Paperwork occupied most of the long hours he spent on airplanes, whether traveling within South Vietnam or to periodic high-level conferences at Honolulu; Bangkok and Udorn, Thailand; and other points. To break the work routine, he played an occasional game of tennis or took brief holiday trips to visit his wife and children, who had left Saigon in the 1965 dependent exodus and were quartered in the Philippines.[18]

A self-confessed believer in conferences as "a useful, even essential, tool of command," Westmoreland held regular Saturday morning meetings with his principal staff officers in the headquarters combat intelligence center. During these sessions, which evolved from simple intelligence briefings, he reviewed events, issued oral guidance on planning and operations, announced major tactical decisions, and directed staff agencies to produce studies and recommendations on particular issues.[19]

Outside of these formal staff meetings, Westmoreland depended heavily on certain members of his staff for advice and information. Brig. Gen. William E. DePuy, highly intelligent, articulate, and forceful, was perhaps Westmoreland's most influential counselor on a wide range of matters until he left the MACV Operations Directorate to command the 1st Infantry Division in March 1966. Until then, "there was much truth to the assertion that the chain of command was Westmoreland to DePuy to the field." After his wife and children

MACV Headquarters: The Years of Expansion, 1965–1967

left Saigon, Westmoreland had certain key staff officers, including at various times his surgeon, his science adviser, and officers involved in intelligence and relations with the South Vietnamese, live with him in his villa. At breakfast and dinner, which the men usually ate together, Westmoreland drew out members of this "kitchen cabinet" on matters of interest and sometimes made decisions on the basis of their discussions.[20]

The position of the deputy MACV commander expanded in importance and increased in rank as the Military Assistance Command's operations and responsibilities multiplied. Although the other services periodically angled for the slot, Westmoreland insisted on an Army second-in-command.

General Abrams (NARA)

The deputy COMUSMACV, Westmoreland repeatedly declared, had to be qualified to direct ground operations and to deal with the Army-dominated Vietnamese Joint General Staff in order to be able to fill in for him during absences or to replace him in the event of his death or incapacitation. Only an Army general could fulfill those requirements.[21]

Westmoreland's first two deputies, John L. Throckmorton and John A. Heintges, were lieutenant generals.[22] In March 1967, Secretary McNamara, Admiral Sharp, and General Westmoreland decided the job should go to a four-star general who would also be Westmoreland's designated successor. The increase in rank would strengthen the deputy's authority over the Army lieutenant generals who headed the Army component command and the two field forces, as well as the three-star Marine general commanding the III Marine Amphibious Force (MAF). At McNamara's, Sharp's, and Westmoreland's recommendation, President Johnson on 6 April appointed General Creighton W. Abrams, Jr., to the position. *(Chart 3)* Abrams, then serving as vice chief of staff of the Army, was one of that service's ablest, most respected leaders. The new deputy's arrival in Saigon in June sparked rumors at MACV headquarters of Westmoreland's imminent departure, an expectation apparently shared by Abrams and by Maj. Gen. Walter T. Kerwin, the new MACV chief of staff, who had served with Abrams in the Pentagon and accompanied him to Vietnam. In fact, Abrams would spend nearly a year and a half as Westmoreland's deputy before succeeding him. Although Abrams and Westmoreland differed greatly in personality and command style, the two generals worked harmoniously together. Increasingly preoccupied with tactical operations and pacification, Westmoreland put Abrams in charge of advice and assistance to the South Vietnamese armed forces. Previous deputy MACV commanders had also been involved in this task, but Abrams brought to it additional rank, prestige, and force of character, qualities needed both to unify the diffuse American advisory effort and to pressure and persuade the South Vietnamese into improving their military performance.[23]

To monitor operations, furnish information to higher headquarters, and make short-term plans, General Westmoreland drastically enlarged his headquarters' hitherto rudimentary combat operations center. Planning for the new center, part of the J3 section, began late in October 1965, with the assistance of a team of officers sent out by the Joint Chiefs of Staff and the National Military Command Center. To improve service balance in MACV headquarters and to strengthen his ties to the III Marine Amphibious Force—which then constituted close to half his U.S. ground combat power—Westmoreland proposed that the command center be headed by a Marine brigadier general. Pending final JCS approval of the new organization, Westmoreland and General DePuy activated the Combat Operations Center (COC) under direction of Marine Col. Francis F. Parry, a member of DePuy's section. The designated director, Brig. Gen. William K. Jones, USMC, reached Saigon early in January 1966, whereupon Colonel Parry became his deputy. Later in the year, Parry was joined by a second, Army, deputy director, assigned at the instigation of DePuy, who did not want to leave this powerful staff agency under exclusively Marine control.[24]

From a modest start—when Jones arrived, "they had the office space, they had a few desks and chairs and so forth," as well as some officers assigned—the Combat Operations Center grew within a year into virtually a staff within a staff. With its more than 200 personnel, the center took over most of the old MACV command compound until it moved to specially designed secure facilities in the new headquarters at Tan Son Nhut. By early 1967, the center had six divisions. Surface Plans and Operations did most of MACV's short-term ground operational planning, as well as overseeing the politically sensitive employment of herbicides and other chemicals. Air Plans and Operations maintained current information on U.S. and South Vietnamese fixed-wing air activity throughout Southeast Asia and planned and monitored B–52 strikes. According to Colonel Parry, the office provided the forum in which Westmoreland himself chose the B–52 targets. Army Aviation kept track of the allocation of Army helicopters among tactical commands. Joint Operations followed the activities of the South Vietnamese forces. It provided advisers and liaison officers to the J3 and Joint Operations Center of the Joint General Staff. A Tactical Air Support Element processed field command requests for air missions.[25]

MACV Headquarters: The Years of Expansion, 1965–1967

The Command Center Division, heart of the new staff element, manned and operated the MACV Command Center. This facility, according to Colonel Parry, "became the center of day-to-day activity, the show place of headquarters, and the sine qua non for all visiting firemen of consequence." Manned around the clock, with secure communications links to MACV's subordinate headquarters in South Vietnam and to Pacific Command and the Joint Chiefs of Staff, the Command Center was MACV's focal point for the assembly of information on current operations and the dispatch of orders to the field and reports to higher authority. Each duty watch included desk officers for each corps area and for air and naval operations, as well as representatives of the Intelligence, Logistics, and Communications/Electronics Directorates. Also part of the Command Center Division, a Briefing and Reports Branch conducted major portions of the headquarters' regular command and staff briefings, prepared the MACV daily and weekly Situation Reports (SITREPs), and contributed to Westmoreland's weekly military reports to the embassy.[26]

General Chaisson (as a lieutenant general in 1970) (U.S. Marine Corps photo)

The Combat Operations Center did more than transmit information. General DePuy, who oversaw the COC's creation, assigned it responsibility for all operational planning within the current year. The COC issued six-month operational guidance to the senior U.S. tactical commanders. It also managed the details of allocating to the corps areas MACV airlift, sealift, air support, and helicopter resources and of conducting major force redeployments. The COC directors, key members of General Westmoreland's inner official family, arranged for the general's monthly commanders' conferences, frequently accompanied him on field trips, and regularly made inspection tours of their own for the commander. The Marine Corps appreciated the importance of the COC directorship and provided some of its best officers for it. General Jones, the first director, went on to command Fleet Marine Force, Pacific. His replacement, Brig. Gen. John R. Chaisson, formerly G3 of III MAF, where Westmoreland met him and was impressed by him, was one of the Marine Corps' most popular and promising officers, a likely future candidate for commandant. Chaisson developed a close working relationship with Westmoreland, who personally had requested his

279

assignment to MACV and who retained him as COC director beyond the end of his regular tour.[27]

General Westmoreland placed great emphasis on contingency planning by his headquarters so as to have a plan on file for every foreseeable eventuality. Long-range plans and studies were the province of the J5 office, headed throughout the conflict by an Air Force major general—an appropriate allocation of service responsibility since the directorate dealt with many contingencies in which air operations would predominate. The office produced an endless stream of studies, many personally called for by Westmoreland, on subjects that ranged from blocking enemy infiltration routes through Laos and Cambodia to posthostilities nation-building by the South Vietnamese armed forces. One subdivision within the directorate maintained and revised MACV's portions of Pacific Command and SEATO contingency plans; another developed plans for special operations by American and allied forces. Most of these projects, for example those dealing with Laos and Cambodia, never went beyond the paper stage but were available for prompt implementation had the administration decided to broaden the war. In addition to formulating plans, the J5 section at Westmoreland's direction also reviewed current tactics and strategy and occasionally proposed alternatives. "Since J5 was not involved in actual operations," the MACV commander declared, "this provided me with an outside view."[28]

Occasionally, at General Westmoreland's direction, several staff sections combined their efforts to examine contingencies. In May 1967, for example, with enemy forces building up in northern I Corps, the intelligence, operations, and planning directorates conducted a "wargaming exercise" to analyze North Vietnamese and Viet Cong "capability and possible courses of action" and to recommend countermeasures. Later in the year, after the North Vietnamese siege of Con Thien, Westmoreland instructed the intelligence directorate to form a DMZ Front Command, which was to review, from the enemy's viewpoint, the tactics of the engagement and try to forecast possible new Communist courses of action. Special problems produced special arrangements. When Westmoreland decided to establish a division-size Army force in southern I Corps, for instance, he assigned Kerwin's predecessor as chief of staff, Maj. Gen. William B. Rosson, who also was commander-designate of the unit, to plan the deployment. Rosson did so, using office space furnished by the Army component headquarters and a skeleton division staff pulled from a variety of Army units.[29]

The Military Assistance Command headquarters had to make adjustments to manage the logistics of the American buildup. Early in 1966 General Westmoreland decided to employ his J4 office primarily to plan and coordinate logistical support while the service components handled the details of execution. The directorate, hitherto mainly concerned with advising its RVNAF counterpart, reorganized to become "in effect a joint logistical staff for a theater of operations." It established a system for keeping track of the month-by-month balance between MACV's requirements and capabilities in key areas such as port operations, supply, maintenance, and transportation. It also absorbed the Directorate of Army MAP Logistics, previously a separate staff agency, and pulled together a number of small engineer organizations into a single MACV Engineer's Office. Westmoreland, in selecting his assistant chiefs of staff, J4, took account of the changing problems of the buildup. In spring 1966, when base development and construction constituted MACV's principal joint logistical concern, he selected Maj. Gen. Carroll H. Dunn, an Army engineer, as his J4. When Dunn finished his tour in September of the following year, Westmoreland replaced him with Maj. Gen. Henry A. Rasmussen, an officer skilled in supply management, since that function had assumed first priority.[30]

General Dunn's selection as MACV J4 came after a prolonged debate between General Westmoreland on one side and the Office of the Secretary of Defense and the Joint Chiefs on the other over how best to direct the huge construction effort in support of the American buildup. The newly established MACV engineer, a colonel, lacked the rank and staff to bring unity to the actions of the various services; the planning, funding, and execution initially fell to the service component commanders and to a flag-rank Navy officer in charge of construction who directed the work of the private contractor combine, RMK-BRJ. As the total programmed cost of military construction rose toward the billion dollar mark, these agencies were unable to develop a joint construction plan or agree on priorities. They competed with each other for scarce real estate, building materials, engineer units, port access, and transportation.[31]

Anticipating this situation, the staff of the secretary of defense, in mid-1965, began promoting creation of a "Construction Czar" within Military Assistance Command, separate from the Logistics Directorate. This official, preferably an Army engineer major general with a sizable staff, would have authority to make unified construction plans for the entire command and to allocate tasks, manpower, and resources among the services. Pressed by Secretary McNamara, the Joint Chiefs and the chief engineers of the Army, Navy, and Air Force all endorsed the concept. In December, General Wheeler proposed it to Westmoreland and Admiral Sharp. At the same time, Wheeler recommended then-Brigadier General Dunn, a major general designee, for construction chief, noting that Dunn possessed the necessary technical qualifications and had the confidence of Secretary McNamara and his civilian subordinates.[32]

General Westmoreland resisted this proposal, fearing that the "czar" would function as an independent agent of the Defense Department rather than a subordinate of his own. He declared that construction was too intertwined with other aspects of logistics, port clearance for example, to be separated from the jurisdiction of his J4. All he needed to manage the development effort, he contended, was a strengthened J4 engineer office and authority to allocate military construction funds among the services. McNamara and Wheeler, however, insisted that the construction program needed "strong, centralized operating direction on a big scale" with its own independent chief. Acknowledging that Westmoreland should have maximum authority and flexibility in fund allocation, Wheeler emphasized that the Defense Department would grant that authority only if it were exercised through a separate MACV chief of construction. Gaining the support of Admiral Sharp, who initially had taken Westmoreland's side, they overrode Westmoreland's protests against dictation by Washington of the structure of his staff.[33]

The MACV Construction Directorate, headed by General Dunn as assistant chief of staff for construction, went into operation on 15 February 1966. Dunn had authority over all military construction in South Vietnam, except the activities of engineers assigned to tactical units. He also served as adviser to the South Vietnamese Army engineer. Although Dunn and his 144-man office were quickly integrated into MACV headquarters and served Westmoreland well in bringing order to the construction effort, the MACV commander had the last organizational word. Still preferring to have the construction effort under his J4, he finally won over Undersecretary of Defense Cyrus Vance, hitherto a strong advocate of the construction czar concept, to his position. In July, with the concurrence of CINCPAC and the JCS, he appointed General Dunn his J4 and placed the Construction Directorate, headed by a brigadier general, under supervision of the Logistics Directorate, where it remained thereafter.[34]

Similar questions of organization and control arose concerning the increasingly complex communications system through which MACV directed its forces' expanding operations and maintained contact with higher headquarters in Hawaii and Washington. When the American buildup began, MACV relied for communications with the field on the South Vietnamese civilian and military radio, telephone, and teletype systems, which had been modernized with American equipment and advice, and on a U.S.-built and -operated long-distance or "backbone" system, called BACK PORCH, which transmitted messages between Saigon and other major centers in Vietnam, as well as Bangkok and Udorn in Thailand. High frequency radio and undersea cable systems, supplemented by a satellite ground terminal near Saigon, connected MACV with the Philippines, Okinawa, Hawaii, and the continental United States. The message traffic generated by the 1965 troop buildup quickly overwhelmed these facilities. MACV and the services responded with ad hoc expansions using tactical signal equipment, most of it provided by the Army. The command, in conjunction with the Defense Department, also hastily developed plans for a new Integrated Wideband Communications System to replace BACK PORCH, as well as for automated telephone and data transmission networks—the latter essential to managing the supply buildup.[35]

Before these plans could be implemented, MACV, the Department of the Army, and the Defense Department had to resolve a jurisdictional dispute over control of Army signal troops in Southeast Asia. The dispute involved the Defense Communications Agency (DCA), an organization established in the late 1950s to build and manage a worldwide Defense Communications System, and the Army's Strategic Communications Command, which operated BACK PORCH and MACV's other communications links in Vietnam and also built, maintained, and manned the Southeast Asia portions of the Defense Communications System. After much discussion, all sides accepted a compromise originated by Brig. Gen. Walter E. Lotz, Jr., the MACV director of communications/electronics, which unified Army signalmen under General Westmoreland by a roundabout route. Under it, the Army on 1 April 1966 consolidated its signal units in Vietnam, except those attached to tactical formations, into a signal brigade nominally attached to the Strategic Communications Command but under the operational control of MACV's Army component command. Under the brigade, a Regional Communications Group operated the Defense Communications System network in South Vietnam, and other Army signal groups directly supported the field forces and divisions. The brigade shared responsibility for communications at theater level and above with the Defense Communications Agency office in Saigon and both organizations were under the oversight of the MACV J6.[36]

The communications system the two agencies jointly managed took until mid-1968 to complete, due to delays in construction and procurement of equipment. Even before all its elements were in place, it provided MACV headquarters with comprehensive telephone, radio, and teletype network links to most places of significance in Vietnam and Southeast Asia, as well as to Hawaii and the continental United States. The system routinely handled a huge volume of messages and raw data and was indispensable to coordinating military operations, especially air support. However, it also deluged higher authorities with undigested information and facilitated constant intervention in the details of MACV's activities by CINCPAC, the Joint Chiefs, the Defense Department, and the White House.[37]

Throughout the elaboration of MACV's command, control, and communications structure, one key element, the commander's instrument for detecting deficiencies and abuses and responding to soldiers' complaints, the Office of the Inspector General, developed only slowly. MACV, until well into the buildup, left the conduct of inspections and investigations for U.S. forces to the component commands, all of which included substantial inspector general offices. The MACV Inspector General's Office, which consisted until 1965 of one officer and one enlisted man, did little more than keep the commander informed about the work of the components and make occasional visits to field advisory teams.

The MACV inspector general's functions and staff slowly grew during the years of the buildup, as inspection and investigation requirements developed that the individual services could not meet. General Westmoreland formally made his inspector general responsible for monitoring the entire inspection effort within MACV in 1965, but he rejected suggestions that the position be upgraded from colonel to general officer. During the next two years, the office acquired responsibility for advising the Joint General Staff Inspector General's Office, for making regular inspections of the MACV advisory teams, and for investigation of matters that cut across service jurisdictions or involved both American and South Vietnamese forces. In the latter cases, the MACV inspector general began conducting combined investigations with his Joint General Staff counterpart. General Abrams, as deputy COMUSMACV responsible for improving the South Vietnamese forces, initiated combined inspections as well, both of RVNAF units and their American advisers. Col. Robert M. Cook, who became MACV inspector general in August 1967, aggressively pressed the expansion of his office in all these areas, with strong support from General Abrams, under whom Cook had commanded a tank platoon in the Battle of the Bulge. Nevertheless, the MACV Inspector General's Office remained small through the first part of 1968, its eleven officers and five enlisted men struggling to meet its increasing inspectional, investigative, and advisory responsibilities.[38]

Combined Intelligence

The expansion of the Military Assistance Command's operational and planning elements, and also of its combat forces, created an all but insatiable demand for timely, accurate intelligence. As of mid-1965, the Intelligence Directorate, in spite of considerable enlargement during 1964, was far from able to meet that demand. Still engaged primarily in advising South Vietnamese military intelligence agencies and transmitting to MACV and higher headquarters information obtained from them, the office possessed little independent capacity for collection, analysis, and production and was ill-prepared to furnish combat intelligence to units in the field.[39]

The task of expanding MACV's intelligence capabilities fell to Maj. Gen. Joseph A. McChristian, who replaced Maj. Gen. Youngdale as assistant chief of staff, J2, at the beginning of July 1965, just as the large-scale commitment of U.S. troops was getting under way. A veteran Army intelligence officer whose counterinsurgency experience dated back to the Greek civil war in 1949–1950, McChristian was familiar with conditions in South Vietnam from his previous assignment as G2 of U.S. Army, Pacific. He arrived in Saigon just in time for

MACV Headquarters: The Years of Expansion, 1965–1967

the crucial mid-July visit of Secretary of Defense McNamara. As part of discussions of the American troop commitment, McNamara directed Westmoreland to specify the requirements for a full-fledged American combat intelligence system in Vietnam and promised to provide whatever resources the MACV commander and his new intelligence chief requested. McChristian, an officer of formidable energy, took full advantage of the secretary's support and also that of Westmoreland, with whom he occasionally played tennis. Within two weeks of his arrival in Vietnam, McChristian and his staff had put together a proposed MACV intelligence organization, which Westmoreland promptly approved.[40]

General McChristian (DOD files)

McChristian enlarged and reorganized the MACV J2 office. In mid-1967, after several interim reorganizations, the intelligence staff included over 600 personnel. Three deputy J2s, for combat intelligence, production, and support, supervised the work of the office's divisions, which included Intelligence Operations, Exploitation, Estimates, Plans and Training, Production, Management, and Counterintelligence. Other elements maintained contact with foreign military attachés and provided representatives for the Combat Operations Center. To keep track of his office's proliferating activities, McChristian instituted a management system that made periodic checks of the status of major functions and projects. In an effort to pull together the intelligence activities of all services, McChristian issued annual MACV collection programs that specified particular command requirements and areas of interest. McChristian drew the Special Forces and Studies and Observations Group deeper into the intelligence collection program and reestablished ties with the foreign military attachés in Saigon, many of whom possessed access to people and governments not directly approachable by the Americans. To enhance dissemination of his product, McChristian in August 1966 instituted a widely distributed monthly Periodic Intelligence Report (PERINTREP). He also revised the weekly MACV headquarters intelligence briefing to include recommended courses of action based on his estimate of the enemy situation. General Westmoreland soon made this enhanced briefing the basis of his weekly strategy conference.[41]

In the field, McChristian built up the Army G2 advisory elements with Vietnamese corps and divisions into full-scale intelligence detachments. He also secured Army military intelligence units to enhance MACV's capabilities in imagery interpretation, counterintelligence, and other technical functions. All these units were subordinate to the 525th Military Intelligence Group, over which McChristian, in a departure from normal joint staff practice, exercised operational control. In late 1967 MACV organized all the American field intelligence and advisory elements under the 525th into five integrated battalions, one for each corps area and one for the Capital Military District. Each battalion performed counterintelligence, collection, and advisory functions within its area of responsibility. It also provided direct support for the American divisions and separate brigades and coordinated U.S. and ARVN intelligence efforts. Under MACV, a special operations intelligence battalion worked against *COSVN* and other high-priority targets. Further to support the combat troops, McChristian and his staff sped up the dissemination to field commands of intelligence from the most highly classified American sources.[42]

While building up purely American intelligence resources, General McChristian also sought to capitalize on those of the South Vietnamese. He knew that his allies possessed a familiarity with their own language and culture and an intimate, detailed understanding of the enemy that the Americans, for all their organizational and technical sophistication, lacked. To combine the strengths of both allies while making more effective the MACV J2 Directorate's advice and assistance to its Vietnamese counterpart, McChristian undertook to create a full-fledged combined American and South Vietnamese intelligence organization soon after assuming his duties. He had the support of General Westmoreland, who generally resisted creation of combined staff agencies because he wanted to promote RVNAF self-sufficiency but made an exception in the case of intelligence. Westmoreland negotiated the necessary agreements with the Vietnamese high command. McChristian's counterpart, Col. Ho Van Loi, Joint General Staff chief of intelligence, accepted the combined concept at once and committed his resources to it.[43]

When it reached its full development late in 1966, the system in Saigon consisted of four combined centers. Each had American and Vietnamese codirectors and a staff of intelligence specialists, technicians, translators, and clerical personnel of both nationalities. The American contingent came from MACV's Intelligence Directorate, which supervised the centers and reviewed, revised, or rejected their product. Three of the centers performed specialized functions. The Combined Military Interrogation Center questioned selected enemy prisoners and defectors; coordinated interrogation throughout South Vietnam; helped to develop standard operating procedures for handling POWs and Viet Cong who came over to the government; and sent teams to field commands for immediate exploitation of captives during operations. The Combined Document Exploitation Center, with an American-Vietnamese staff of over 300, evaluated and translated the growing volume of enemy unit and headquarters files uncovered by allied offensives. Distilling the results into spot reports for immediate exploitation by combat units, it also stored these findings in an automated data base from which it could produce longer studies on demand. The document exploitation center also maintained "go teams," for quick on-the-scene evaluation of captured material during operations. The third specialized element, the Combined Materiel Exploitation Center, examined and evaluated items of captured enemy equipment and issued technical intelligence reports, summaries, and analyses.[44]

The fourth agency, the Combined Intelligence Center, Vietnam (CICV), brought together the product of all the other centers into "an all-source intelligence data base" for use by MACV and the Joint General Staff. Housed initially in a converted warehouse at Tan Son Nhut and later in a specially constructed building close to the new MACV headquarters at the air base, CICV eventually reached a strength of more than 600 Americans and Vietnamese. In operation twenty-four hours a day, its branches prepared detailed terrain studies and correlated the products of photographic, infrared, and radar reconnaissance. The center's largest element, its Order of Battle Branch, maintained complete, up-to-date listings by corps area of *PAVN* and *PLAF* units, with histories and estimates of their strengths. It also assembled information on enemy infiltration from North Vietnam and on the Viet Cong's political underground and issued specialized studies on enemy organization and operations. Another key unit, the center's Targets Acquisition Branch, compiled information that MACV used to direct air strikes and ground operations. This branch made extensive use of "pattern analysis," a technique for assembling and analyzing data from multiple sources on all forms of enemy activity in a given area in order to determine the most profitable objectives.[45]

The combined centers, with their heavily automated data bases, produced a steadily growing volume of intelligence with increasing responsiveness to the needs of commanders and staffs. The document exploitation center alone during 1967 printed some 1,400 pounds of reports per day. Yet the system had its limitations. Because of the security risk created by the presence of its Vietnamese personnel, the Combined Intelligence Center lacked access to data from the most sensitive U.S. technical sources, which was reserved to the purely American elements of MACV intelligence. As a result, its estimates—for example on enemy strength and infiltration—were often altered or disregarded farther up the chain of command. For lack of technical talent, the Vietnamese were underrepresented in many elements of the system. As a result, Americans in the Combined Intelligence Center outnumbered Vietnamese by about five to one. American members within the combined agencies, moreover, distrusted their South Vietnamese associates, whose competence the Americans doubted and whose language they did not speak. In consequence, a de facto separation of the two nationalities prevailed within offices and branches. The Vietnamese, for their part, were reluctant to share the output of their unique sources with other American and Vietnamese agencies that they viewed as potential rivals for power and influence. The worst drawback of the system, from the standpoint of its effect on the conduct of the war, was the timing of its creation. Set up after, rather than before, American troops were committed to battle, it took the better part of two years to become fully operational and to assemble a really comprehensive body of data on the enemy. Until then, MACV and its subordinate commands had to fight, in the words of a Marine officer, "half-blind and nearly deaf."[46]

The Advisory Mission

MACV's responsibility for advice and support to the South Vietnamese armed forces continued after the arrival of American troops, and its organization for discharging this duty became the subject of periodic review. Command and administration of the advisers was divided between MACV and its service components. Navy and Air Force advisers were under the operational control of their respective component headquarters. Army advisory teams in the field worked under the III MAF and I and II Field Force commanders, who functioned as senior advisers to their counterpart Vietnamese corps commanders. The advisory groups in IV Corps, where no major U.S. combat units operated, and those with the Airborne Division and other specialized Vietnamese commands, remained directly under MACV.[47]

After the abolition of the Military Assistance Advisory Group in mid-1964, MACV was without a single staff focal point for the advisory program. Each headquarters directorate advised its Joint General Staff counterpart on matters within its regular cognizance. Under J3 supervision, the MACV Training Directorate controlled the U.S. Army advisers with the South Vietnamese Central Training Command, the ARVN schools and training centers, and the ranger, artillery, and armor commands. Also under J3, the Political Warfare Advisory Directorate worked with the RVNAF General Political Warfare Department—the armed forces' propaganda, troop indoctrination, and social welfare agency—as well as discharging a variety of staff responsibilities for American psychological warfare and civic action. The Military Assistance Program (MAP) Directorate, which reported directly to the MACV chief of staff, oversaw the management of financial and materiel aid to the South Vietnamese. The MACV comptroller, through his Vietnamese Advisory Division, for practical purposes made up the South Vietnamese defense budget and monitored Saigon's spending and fiscal management. By late 1967, the Military Assistance Command's headquarters contained about 1,000 American advisers—not counting those with tactical units, provinces, and districts—distributed among or reporting to more than a score of different staff agencies.[48]

At the top, the advisory effort possessed a degree of unity. General Westmoreland, as senior American adviser to the South Vietnamese armed forces, conferred regularly with General Cao Van Vien, chief of the Joint General Staff. Westmoreland used his deputies to oversee the South Vietnamese forces, and in mid-1967 he placed General Abrams in charge of the entire RVNAF improvement program. He also employed a special assistant for liaison with the South Vietnamese Ministry of Defense and Joint General Staff. The holders of this position, Brig. Gen. James L. Collins and his successor, Brig. Gen. John F. Freund, represented Westmoreland at conferences with the Vietnamese and on combined inspections. They also cultivated informal contacts with key Vietnamese officers, both to obtain information and to exercise behind-the-scenes influence on Saigon's political and military affairs. Below Westmoreland, his deputy, and his special assistant, however, no element existed in the MACV staff to pull together the effort to strengthen the South Vietnamese forces. In consequence, as General Bruce Palmer put it, there was "a lack of cohesiveness, a lack of overall direction and control, a lack of . . . supervision, and a lack of coordination" in the command's dealings with the South Vietnamese.[49]

During 1966 an initiative by Secretary McNamara forced MACV to review its advisory organization and procedures. McNamara directed the transfer of the foreign aid-funded Military Assistance Program to the individual armed services, each of which from then on was to support its Vietnamese counterpart out of its own appropriations. This change involved the service component commands in planning and funding military assistance, necessitating a reconsideration of the MACV advisory structure. The review, however, was inconclusive. Arguing that only one American headquarters should deal with Saigon's army high command, General Westmoreland rejected a recommendation from his Army component command—which had been retitled U.S. Army, Vietnam (USARV), in July 1965—that it should assume responsibility for the entire Army advisory program in much the same way as the other service components had taken charge of their own advisers. In July, Westmoreland approved the shift of the logistical advisory mission from the MACV Logistics Directorate to USARV, which established a general staff section to conduct it; but he kept the rest of the Army advisers under MACV. Further, to pull together the advisory effort, the MACV commander in December established a deputy J3 for RVNAF matters. The first incumbent of this position, Brig. Gen. Albert R. Brownfield, later succeeded General Freund as Westmoreland's liaison officer with the Joint General Staff.[50]

The issue arose again the following year, in the context of a reorganization of American support for pacification and of a new emphasis by the Johnson administration on improving the South Vietnamese forces. In June 1967, the J5 directorate undertook a full-dress study, called Project 640, of a number of alternatives for unifying the command's advisory function. These included reestablishing the Military Assistance Advisory Group, enlarging or reducing the advisory role of USARV, and creating some new advisory focal point in the MACV staff. The J5 planners rejected the idea of a revived MAAG as proliferating headquarters and re-creating an arrangement earlier found unsatisfactory. In September, they recommended that MACV establish an assistant chief of staff for military assistance to handle both Military Assistance Program and advisory matters and that it take back from USARV the Army advisory functions so as to avoid division of authority and duplication of effort.[51]

Westmoreland approved these recommendations. The Office of Assistant Chief of Staff for Military Assistance went into operation in November 1967, headed by an Army brigadier general. Its mission was "to supervise, coordinate, monitor, and evaluate, in conjunction with appropriate agencies," the joint advisory effort and the Military Assistance Program. The section's 29-man staff came largely from the MAP Directorate, which the new agency absorbed, and was broken into two divisions: one for military assistance and the other for plans, policy, and advisory support. Early the following year MACV transferred the ARVN logistics advisory program, and the personnel who administered it, from USARV headquarters back to itself. While some improvement, these changes still left the actual conduct of advice to the South Vietnamese scattered throughout the headquarters, with the new military assistance office limited to oversight and coordination. MACV, for example, dispersed the logistical functions it reclaimed from U.S. Army, Vietnam, among four separate staff divisions. As a result, at the beginning of 1968, four years after abolition of the MAAG, Westmoreland's headquarters still lacked a single advisory organization capable of bringing to bear unified, effective American influence for reform and modernization of the South Vietnamese armed forces.[52]

Reporting, Research, and Analysis

The Military Assistance Command confronted steadily expanding requirements for the collection, reporting, and analysis of data about its multifarious activities. In response, the number of reports generated by MACV and its subordinate headquarters grew to impressive proportions. The Intelligence Directorate produced, among others, a monthly enemy order of battle summary; daily, weekly, and monthly intelligence summaries; the weekly estimates updates that were the basis of General Westmoreland's Saturday staff conferences; and the PERINTREPs. The Operations Directorate issued a daily SITREP, a weekly operations summary, weekly and monthly U.S./RVNAF/Free World Forces orders of battle, and a monthly herbicide use summary. Still other reports, many requiring extensive data-gathering in the field, dealt with subjects of special concern to MACV and higher authorities. Thus, in February 1966, MACV instituted a monthly measurements-of-progress briefing, summarized quarterly for CINCPAC, on achievement of the military and pacification goals set at the Honolulu conference. Another series of reports dealt with RVNAF improvement. The Hamlet Evaluation System (HES), introduced early in 1967, attempted to measure the degree of government and Viet Cong control in each of Vietnam's thousands of hamlets. By early 1967 MACV and its component commands were producing nearly 400 different reports on a regular basis. In addition, MACV received constant demands for special reports from the National Military Command Center and the White House, especially when controversial or unfavorable Vietnam stories broke in the news media.[53]

Authorities in Washington and Saigon tinkered continually with the reporting system. They attempted to resolve discrepancies between the various sets of statistics and to arrive at common terminology and criteria for measuring such significant indicators as the number of enemy attacks, the rate of infiltration from North Vietnam, and the percentage of peasants under government control. Above all, they sought a simple set of reliable indexes of progress, or lack of it, in the many-faceted campaign. In late 1967 a presidentially appointed interagency working group reviewed the data then used to measure trends in the war in South Vietnam. The group concluded that "data most frequently used [are] not adequate for [the] task" and recommended creation of still another interagency task force, chaired by the director of central intelligence, to develop "new ways of measuring progress." Admiral Sharp and General Abrams, who responded for Westmoreland, both endorsed the goals of the interagency group. Abrams pointed out that MACV already had efforts of its own under way to improve its evaluation of RVNAF development and pacification. The command's aim, he reported to General Wheeler in a masterpiece of management jargon, was to be able to conduct "extensive analysis using all systems . . . to develop management utility devices, concentrating on correlating program progress/effectiveness indicators against burden parameters to assist in program planning, control, and feedback for re-planning."[54]

With ever-growing amounts of data to process, the Military Assistance Command headquarters inevitably turned to automation. The various staff agencies made early and extensive use of punch-card and tape machines, and the Intelligence Directorate secured a computer to manage its growing data bases. However, the headquarters as a whole was slow to acquire its own computer and instead sent most of its operational data to Pacific Command for processing in its machine—an arrangement that seemed satisfactory until the extent of MACV's information requirements became apparent. During 1965 and 1966 study teams from Pacific Command, the Joint Chiefs of Staff, and the Advanced Research Projects Agency all reviewed MACV's information management practices and problems. While their conclusions varied in specifics, they all indicated the desirability of establishing a central computerized data processing agency for the headquarters.[55]

During 1967, at the ARPA team's recommendation, MACV installed in its new building an IBM 360 model computer, then the most advanced available, as the centerpiece of a Data Management Agency serving the entire staff. Within a year, the Data Management Agency automated most of the command's operational, intelligence, and logistics files, as well as the Hamlet Evaluation System and the reports on military assistance and RVNAF performance. To simplify the transfer of data to other headquarters, MACV whenever possible used computer programs and information formats compatible with those elsewhere in the Defense Department. The Combat Operations Center, for example, managed its computerized daily journal with the same system used by the National Military Command Center.[56]

With increasing amounts of readily retrievable, easily manipulated data, MACV expanded its capacity to analyze its operations, both to improve efficiency and effectiveness and to support its positions in discussions with the Department of Defense. In September 1967 General Westmoreland decided to establish a MACV Systems Analysis Division under his deputy chief of staff. The new division was to perform primarily short-range operational studies of immediate benefit to the command and also to coordinate analysis by the service components. Seeking to place the eighteen-man office in operation as rapidly as possible, Westmoreland secured agreement from the Joint Chiefs to expedite approval of the necessary change to the MACV organization table and assistance from the Office of the Secretary of Defense in recruiting qualified civilian analysts and computer programmers. As a nucleus for the division, he obtained three officer-analysts and three enlisted men from within Vietnam. With this skeleton staff, the MACV Operations Research/Systems Analysis Office (MACEVAL) began work in mid-November. It had the missions of conducting studies employing "the disciplines of operations research" as directed by the MACV commander, advising him on systems analysis matters, and overseeing the overall analysis effort within the command. As its first major assignment, the office undertook an examination of methods for measuring the comparative combat capabilities of American and South Vietnamese forces.[57]

The systems analysis agency was a latecomer to the Military Assistance Command's effort to apply science and technology to the Vietnam conflict. Throughout the buildup, the service testing and development units—the Army Concept Team in Vietnam, the Air Force Test Unit, and the more recently created U.S. Navy Research and Development Team, Vietnam—continued in operation, as did the Advanced Research Projects Agency's field unit which assisted South Vietnamese military research and development. In addition, MACV drew upon the resources of the Office of the Director, Defense Research and Engineering, and outside contractors such as the RAND Corporation for studies of problems ranging from hamlet security to assessment of the effects of allied propaganda on the Viet Cong and North Vietnamese.

During 1966 General Westmoreland once again reorganized MACV's research, development, and testing elements. With the concurrence of Admiral Sharp and the Joint Chiefs, the MACV commander abolished the Joint Research and Testing Agency. He transferred the service test units, and the responsibility for service-peculiar development and testing, to the respective component commanders. In Westmoreland's view, this function properly belonged to the components, which with the buildup of American forces possessed the resources to discharge it. The MACV commander, through his assistant chief of staff, J3, continued to supervise the services' research and testing. He retained the right to veto projects unrelated to immediate operational needs and to assign projects of joint significance to particular service test agencies.[58]

The ARPA Field Unit remained in MACV headquarters and came under the supervision of the newly established scientific adviser to the commander. In March 1966, the Joint Chiefs of Staff suggested that General Westmoreland add to his staff a prominent civilian scientist who could serve as his technical adviser and maintain contact with the scientific and engineering communities in the United States. Westmoreland, who had been thinking along the same lines, at once accepted the proposal. The Office of MACV Scientific Adviser went into operation in December, headed by Dr. William G. McMillan. A chemistry professor from the University of California at Los Angeles, McMillan possessed an extensive background as a Defense Department scientific consultant; he had been nominated for the MACV position by Assistant Secretary of Defense for Research and Engineering Dr. John W. Foster. As MACV scientific adviser, Dr. McMillan counseled General Westmoreland on scientific and technical matters, exercised staff supervision over the ARPA field unit, and continually reviewed development, testing, and evaluation within the command. He also kept in touch with the director of defense research and engineering and alerted Westmoreland to new technologies potentially worth trying out in Vietnam.[59]

During his office's first year in operation, Dr. McMillan's responsibilities rapidly expanded. At General Westmoreland's invitation, the scientific adviser lived with the MACV commander in his villa and participated in the weekly MACV staff conferences. Westmoreland assigned McMillan specific projects of command interest, for example, assessment of all available advanced technologies that might help locate and destroy the North Vietnamese artillery bombarding American positions from north of the Demilitarized Zone. To help unify the decentralized research efforts of the services, the science adviser during 1967 instituted biweekly seminars attended by representatives of all commands even peripherally involved in development and testing, including the Special Forces and the Studies and Observations Group, and also the scientific office of the U.S. embassy.[60]

Inevitably, the scientific adviser sought to enlarge his empire. Early in December 1967, McMillan presented Westmoreland with a plan to attach science advisers to field commanders down to independent brigade level and to bring the "fragmented" service research and development agencies back under MACV's direct control. To manage all this, the Office of the Scientific Adviser would add to its existing strength of 1 civilian, 4 officers, and 2 enlisted men a brigadier general deputy scientific adviser, 5 other officers, a warrant officer, and 4 enlisted men. Still not satisfied with his command's ability to bring scientific expertise quickly to bear on operational problems, General Westmoreland proved receptive to McMillan's proposals. Elsewhere, however, the MACV historian dryly recorded, they "did not experience smooth sailing." The combat commanders saw no need for scientific advisers, and Admiral Sharp and the Joint Chiefs rejected the proposal out of hand. In the end, it produced only one tangible result. General Westmoreland early in 1968 "double-hatted" Dr. McMillan as science adviser to the deputy commanding general of USARV and placed a civilian deputy to McMillan at the Army component headquarters. According to the USARV deputy commander, this arrangement strengthened the tie between the combat forces and the research and development community. Field commanders, however, continued to complain that it took too long for new devices, once the need for them had been established, to be produced and delivered to troops.[61]

While MACEVAL and the Office of the Scientific Adviser generated an increasing volume of studies, the extent of their influence on command decisions is open to question. Significantly, the chief of the Systems Analysis Office did not regularly attend General Westmoreland's weekly strategy meetings, though "requirements for him emerged from those meetings." Westmoreland later insisted that he based his major decisions on "the feel of the battlefield, the situation, and knowledge of the fundamentals of tactics and history" and that systems analysis "usually verified the tactical judgment." The terms in which he discussed such issues in private "back channel" messages to Admiral Sharp and General Wheeler tend to bear out this statement.[62]

Most of the reports and analyses emanating from MACV and the echelons below and above it were based on quantitative measurements of various aspects of the war—friendly and enemy casualties, weapons captured, miles of road and waterway opened, percentage of population under government control, number of battalion-size North Vietnamese and Viet Cong attacks, and so on and on. From General Westmoreland down, American commanders in Vietnam realized that many of the numbers upon which they relied so heavily were of questionable origin and accuracy. They also appreciated that many aspects of the unconventional, diffuse conflict in which they were engaged did not lend themselves to quantification. Admiral Sharp declared in August 1967: "In my opinion, we have trapped ourselves because of our obsession to quantify everything. . . . I suggest that we attempt to move away from the great dependence on demonstrating our results with numbers and concentrate on the less tangible but more important results of our operations." Nevertheless, in a war without front lines and decisive battles, statistics remained the only available measurement of progress; and Secretary McNamara continually demanded more of them. Moreover, even flawed data, when properly analyzed, could yield valid insights and contribute to a more effective strategy.[63]

Unfortunately, statistics also were used for public relations. As the war became more controversial in the United States, MACV felt increasingly heavy pressure from higher authorities to produce data demonstrating progress. Inconsistencies in the figures or changes in them that appeared unfavorable—even if they resulted from alterations in terminology or counting methods—regularly led to questions in Congress and the news media and consternation in the White House, Pentagon, and State Department. Major substantive controversies within MACV and between MACV and other agencies, such as that over what forces should be included in the enemy order of battle, became inextricably intertwined with administration efforts to shape public perceptions of the war. In these and other instances, statistics and their analysis became not management tools, but weapons in public relations campaigns and policy battles. Operational analysis in the Vietnam conflict too often served, to paraphrase Clausewitz, as a continuation of politics by other means.[64]

How Joint the Command?

As the Military Assistance Command headquarters expanded, the services continued their tug-of-war over the distribution of key staff positions. Underlying the disputes over control of particular slots remained the question whether the MACV headquarters should have genuinely balanced service representation or whether it should continue—as the absorption of the MAAG in 1964 had left it—as essentially an Army organization with limited participation by the other services. General Westmoreland, backed by the Army chief of staff and to a lesser degree by the Chairman of the Joint Chiefs, General Wheeler, adhered to the latter position. He maintained that, since ground operations predominated in the Vietnam conflict; since MACV performed a number of purely U.S. Army functions, such as administering the Army advisory program; and since the South Vietnamese Army was the largest and most important of the Vietnamese armed forces that received MACV's assistance and advice, U.S. Army members had to occupy the majority of command and staff positions in the joint headquarters.[65]

The other services disagreed, particularly the Air Force. Air Force leaders persisted in their claim that the Joint Chiefs and the secretary of defense intended MACV to be "a single unified headquarters with a well-balanced Joint Staff," not a thinly disguised single service command. They also contended that MACV was not making use of the full range of American military expertise, particularly that of airmen, in conducting an increasingly complex war. Lt. Gen. Joseph H. Moore, the 2d Air Division commander, told Westmoreland late in 1965, "The size of the forces assigned to your command and the complexity of the policy, planning, and management problems generated by these combined forces surely favors the requirement for a strong, well-balanced unified joint staff."[66]

The Army's grip on MACV tightened during 1965. Lacking a replacement for General Youngdale, the Marine Corps surrendered by default the post of assistant chief of staff, J2, to the Army, which had long coveted it and which possessed a qualified candidate in General McChristian. When General Throckmorton had to step down as deputy COMUSMACV due to a back ailment, the Marine Corps and the Air Force both nominated general officers to succeed him. General Westmoreland, however, preferred an Army deputy, and the Joint Chiefs reluctantly appointed General Heintges, only because he was the MACV commander's first choice for the position. The Air Force won a partial victory in May, with the assignment of General Moore to additional duty as MACV deputy commander for air, but complained that Moore's terms of reference, issued by Westmoreland, gave him only nominal authority. Army predominance extended to the lower ranks as well. At the end of 1965, more than 1,600 of the 2,400 MACV headquarters personnel were from the Army.[67]

Early in 1965, under pressure from the Joint Chiefs, General Westmoreland incorporated increased Navy, Air Force, and Marine Corps representation in a new MACV headquarters Joint Table of Distribution (JTD) then being prepared. The changes, he declared, were "in consideration of the greater emphasis now being placed on air and naval activities." Early in April, Westmoreland also recommended creation of a new MACV deputy chief of staff position, to be filled by an Air Force brigadier general, and the advancement of the chief of the Naval Advisory Group, the senior naval officer at MACV, to flag rank. He also expanded Air Force and Navy representation in the intelligence, operations, logistics, and planning directorates by transferring to those services various branch chief or deputy chief positions or by adding Navy and Air Force deputies to Army-headed branches. Out of a proposed total increase of 100 officers in the general staff directorates, Westmoreland reserved about one-third for the Navy, Air Force, and Marine Corps.[68]

This JTD, submitted in May, was overtaken by the accelerated American troop buildup of the last half of the year. Accordingly, in late August, with another headquarters distribution table in preparation,

MACV Headquarters: The Years of Expansion, 1965–1967

Westmoreland assigned four senior officers, one from each service, to make an "objective" analysis of each position and to determine which service was "best able to provide the expertise" to fulfill its "functional requirements." He perhaps slanted the outcome, however, by requiring that the officers take into account the service composition of forces under the Military Assistance Command; the fact that COMUSMACV was not responsible for out-of-country air operations; and MACV's three principal missions: as a subordinate unified headquarters, as adviser to the South Vietnamese armed forces, and, "most pertinent," as a senior ground force tactical headquarters.[69]

The board reported to Westmoreland in October. Besides endorsing the earlier changes in favor of the other services, it recommended the addition of an Air Force deputy director of personnel and more Navy and Air Force division and branch chiefs in the other general staff sections. General Moore, the board's Air Force member, refused to endorse the recommendations on grounds that they still left his service underrepresented. He argued that the positions of MACV directors of intelligence and communications/electronics should go to the Air Force, along with those of deputy assistant chiefs of staff for operations and logistics and deputy chief, Engineering Division, J4. Partially meeting Moore's requests, Westmoreland, in order "to mollify . . . the Air Force zealots who are interested in greater representation on the MACV staff," agreed to shift the J6 position from the Army to the Air Force after the departure of the incumbent, General Lotz, who was then engaged in establishing MACV's communications organization. At the same time, as a gesture to the marines, he awarded them the post of chief of the Combat Operations Center. When he submitted the new JTD to General Wheeler and Admiral Sharp early in November, he declared that the resulting staff was "reasonably balanced with regard to the composition of the forces and the character of the operations" and "provides the professional expertise we need to do the job, considering the unique conditions under which we operate here as opposed to the classic organization of a joint staff."[70]

In spite of Westmoreland's concessions to the Air Force and Marine Corps, among the Joint Chiefs, only Army Chief of Staff Johnson, fully supported the new headquarters organization. The Navy, Air Force, and Marine chiefs all believed their services deserved more representation. Each service had its list of desired MACV staff positions, most then held by the Army. Air Force Chief of Staff McConnell, insisted his service should have the personnel, intelligence, or operations directorates in addition to communications/electronics and also made a bid, quickly quashed, to take the Combat Operations Center away from the marines. General Wheeler loyally upheld his joint commander but privately told Westmoreland that he thought the proposed JTD short-changed the other services. The Joint Chiefs did not act on the November JTD proposal until mid-May of 1966 and then they submitted a split paper. The Air Force and Marine Corps formally dissented while the Navy endorsed the MACV proposal but with reservations. Deputy Secretary of Defense Vance, acting for McNamara, approved the majority recommendation.[71]

Westmoreland had won the battle, but by the narrowest of margins, as General Wheeler made clear in transmitting the final Defense Department decision. The chairman warned Westmoreland that Navy, Air Force, and Marine discontent with their representation at MACV was "deep-seated and will persist"; hence, Westmoreland in the future must "go further in bringing officers of other Services into important positions. . . . Within the confines of efficiency," Wheeler concluded, "the staffing of the joint effort should move in the direction of wider participation." In response, Westmoreland promised that service representation in his headquarters would "continue to be the object of timely, objective analysis," although in the future he planned to review specific functions rather than, as in the August 1965 effort, attempting to study the entire headquarters. To be sure, as new staff organizations proliferated, the general did attempt to promote service balance. In the MACV Construction Directorate, for instance, one-fourth of the 144 personnel were Navy and Marine and another fourth Air Force. General Dunn had a Navy Civil Engineering Corps captain as deputy and an Air Force lieutenant colonel as executive officer. Air Force officers headed two of the directorate's seven divisions.[72]

After mid-1966, the interservice battle over MACV's composition declined in intensity. The headquarters remained predominately Army in personnel and procedures, but the other services, while still less than satisfied with their representation, appear to have accepted Army domination of MACV as a fact of life. General Westmoreland emphasized interservice teamwork and fair play, seemingly to good effect. The first marine to head the Combat Operations Center, General Jones, recalled that his Army colleagues were "quite interested in knowing the viewpoints of the other services and in trying to develop a teamwork that was necessary to run the command." From his viewpoint, Admiral Sharp preferred an Army-heavy MACV headquarters. So constituted, the Military Assistance Command was sure to remain oriented on its main task, carrying on the ground war in South Vietnam. In addition, MACV's lack of a truly joint staff reduced the likelihood of its being removed from under Sharp and made a separate unified command—an eventuality that the Navy had been determined to prevent since the first discussions of MACV's establishment.[73]

During the years of the American buildup, the internal structure of Military Assistance Command headquarters became steadily more complex. New or expanded functions produced new organizations. Individual efforts at staff empire-building further accelerated this process. The insatiable information demands of the American policy establishment brought proliferation of reports and the elaboration of the

MACV Headquarters: The Years of Expansion, 1965–1967

headquarters' data management and communications systems. As new offices were created and old ones expanded, the services maneuvered for staff positions and command influence, the better to promote their interests and advance their views on the conduct of the war. The complexity of MACV's internal structure was matched by that of its external relationships as it attempted to carry out its combat, advisory, and pacification missions in South Vietnam and to influence operations in the wider Southeast Asian theater.

MACV: The Years of Escalation, 1962–1967

Notes

[1] *U.S.–Vietnam Relations*, sec. 4.B.3, p. 125. MACV Command History, 1965, pp. 74–75, 91.

[2] MACV Command History, 1965, pp. 91–92. Quote is from Rpt, ARPA, Project AGILE, "Information Handling in Headquarters MACV: An Analysis and Recommendation for ADP Support (hereafter cited as "MACV Information Handling")," 1 Feb 67, p. iii, Historians files, CMH. For an overview of MACV's structure early in 1967, see pp. 34–117 of this report. For the structure later in the year, see HQ MACV Interim Telephone Directory, copy in NAVFORV Ops Files (7), box 431, COMNAVFORV Records, Naval Historical Center.

[3] Westmoreland, *A Soldier Reports*, pp. 247–48; MACV Command History, 1965, pp. 135–36. Msgs, Westmoreland MAC 1811 to Wheeler, 2 Apr 65; and Westmoreland MAC 5017 to Wheeler and Sharp, 8 Oct 65. Both in Westmoreland Msg Files, 1 Apr–30 Jun 65 and 1 Oct–31 Dec 65, CMH. MS, Lt Col Adrian G. Traas, "Builders and Fighters: Military Engineering in Southeast Asia," ch. 11, pp. 26–27, CMH.

[4] MACV Command History, 1966, p. 145. Westmoreland Hist Briefings, 26 Apr 66 and 3 May 66, tab F, Westmoreland Hist File 5 (13 Mar–23 Apr 66) and tab A, Westmoreland Hist File 6 (24 Apr–28 May 66). Both in CMH. MFR, Westmoreland, 6 May 66, sub: Meeting with Prime Minister Ky, 1100–1130 hrs, 6 May 66, tab B–3, Westmoreland Hist File 6 (24 Apr–28 May 66), CMH. Msgs, Westmoreland MAC 3332 and 3628 to Sharp, 28 Apr 66 and 6 May 66, Westmoreland Msg Files, 1 Apr–30 Jun 66, CMH. Traas, "Builders and Fighters," ch. 11, pp. 27–28.

[5] Sharp and Westmoreland, *Report on War*, p. 154; Westmoreland Hist Notes, 6–18 Aug 67, tab A, Westmoreland Hist File 20 (4–20 Aug 67), CMH. For description of the complex, see Traas, "Builders and Fighters," ch. 11, p. 28. Quote is from Bruce E. Jones, *War Without Windows: A True Account by a Young Army Officer Trapped in an Intelligence Cover-Up in Vietnam* (New York: Vanguard, 1987), p. 142.

[6] Quote is from Msg, Woolnough WDC 8360 to Westmoreland, 29 Sep 65, Westmoreland Msg Files, 1 Jul–30 Sep 65, CMH. Msgs, Westmoreland MAC 1587 to Wheeler and Sharp, 24 Mar 65; Westmoreland MAC 8578 to Sharp, 1 Oct 66; Westmoreland MAC 1888 to Johnson, 25 Feb 67; Westmoreland MAC 7684 to Lt Gen Frederick Weyand, 16 Aug 67. All in Westmoreland Msg Files, 1 Jan–31 Mar 65; 1 Oct–31 Dec 66; 1 Jan–31 Mar 67; and 1 Jul–30 Sep 67, CMH. MACV Command History, 1966, pp. 160–63. Westmoreland's rationale for the one-year tour can be found in *A Soldier Reports*, pp. 294–97.

[7] On selections in other services, see Msg, Westmoreland MAC 0293 to Krulak, 13 Jan 66; Wheeler JCS 3299–67 to Westmoreland, 4 May 67; Sharp to Westmoreland, 9 May 67; Westmoreland MAC 7454, to Sharp and Lt Gen Horace M. Wade, USAF, 9 Aug 67; Westmoreland Msg Files, CMH. Westmoreland Hist Notes, 25 Feb 67, tab B, Westmoreland Hist File 13 (27 Jan–25 Mar 67). Westmoreland's dealings with Gen Johnson on Army rotations can be followed through his Msg Files and History Files. See also Interv, Senior Officers Debriefing Program with Gen Bruce Palmer, Jr., 1975, pp. 202, 205–06, 210–12, 214–15, 246–47, MHI.

[8] Detail on life in Saigon can be found in USMACV, *General Information Brochure*, 1 Jun 66, copy in CMH files; Suplizio Interv, 17 and 24, Jul 86, passim; Col Francis Fox Parry, USMC, *Three-War Marine* (New York: Jove Books, 1989), pp. 260–62, 272–74; and Jones, *War Without Windows*, passim. MACV Command History, 1966, pp. 145–46. Westmoreland's views on working hours can be found in address to Joint US Senior Officers' Conference, 13 Oct 67, summarized in Westmoreland Hist Notes, 1–13 Oct 67, tab A, Westmoreland Hist File 23 (1–15 Oct 67), CMH.

[9] MACV Command History, 1966, pp. 144–47. Ibid., 1967, p. 901. Msgs, Westmore-

land MAC 3332 to Sharp, 28 Apr 66; Wheeler JCS 5039–66 to Sharp and Westmoreland, 24 Aug 66; Westmoreland MAC 7441 to Lodge, Sharp, and Wheeler, 27 Aug 66; Westmoreland Msg Files, 1 Apr–30 Jun 66 and 1 Jul–30 Sep 66, CMH.

[10] Sharp and Westmoreland, *Report on War*, pp. 146–47. MACV Command History, 1966, pp. 147–48; ibid., 1967, 901–05; ibid., 1968, 2:803–06.

[11] MACV Command History, 1966, pp. 192–93, 196–97; Westmoreland Hist Briefing, 25 Feb 67, tab B, Westmoreland Hist File 13 (27 Jan–25 Mar 67), CMH.

[12] MACV Command History, 1966, pp. 191–93. MACV, *General Information Brochure*, 1 Jun 66, pp. 19–20, CMH files. Interv, Charles B. MacDonald with Brig Gen Robert Ashworth, Columbia, S.C., 21 Jun 73, Notes in CMH files. For a personal view, see Jones, *War Without Windows*, pp. 41–43, 46–48.

[13] Statistics on visitors: MACV Command History, 1967, p. 1199; see also ibid., 1965, pp. 260–61. A sense of the dimensions of the visitor influx, and of MACV's methods for handling them, can be gained from the Westmoreland Msg Files for 1965–67 and the Westmoreland Historical Briefings in his Hist Files for the same period.

[14] For Westmoreland's views on visitors, see Ltr, Westmoreland to Wheeler, 11 Nov 64, tab 39, Westmoreland Hist File 9 (9 Oct–13 Nov 64); Westmoreland Hist Notes, 5–11 Sep 65 and 1–20 May 67, Westmoreland Hist File 1 (29 Aug–24 Oct 65), and tab A, Westmoreland Hist File 17 (1–31 May 67); All in CMH. MACV Command History, 1967, pp. 1201–03. Msg, Westmoreland MAC 6077 to Sharp et al., 1 Dec 65, Westmoreland Msg Files, Dec 65, CMH. Memo, Westmoreland for CINCPAC, 18 Aug 67, sub: Assignment of C–140B Aircraft, SVN, COMUSMACV Signature (Sig) File, Aug 67.

[15] DOD rules are summarized in MACV Command History, 1967, pp. 1199–2000; see also pp. 1202–04 and MACV Command History, 1965, p. 261. Msgs, Johnson WDC 10558 to Westmoreland, 3 Dec 65; Sharp to Wheeler, 30 Dec 66; Westmoreland MAC 12668 to Sharp, 26 Dec 67. All in Westmoreland Msg Files, CMH.

[16] Quote is from Westmoreland, *A Soldier Reports*, p. 277. Msgs, Wheeler JCS 7227–66 to Sharp and Westmoreland, 25 Nov 66; Westmoreland MAC 5693 to Momyer, et al., 16 Jun 67; Westmoreland Msg Files, CMH. Westmoreland Hist Notes, 11 Oct 65, Westmoreland Hist File 1 (29 Aug–24 Oct 65) and 16 Feb 66, tab A, Westmoreland Hist File 4 (30 Jan–13 Feb 66), CMH. For a sardonic view of MACV's system for handling visitors, and of the visitors themselves, see William R. Corson, *The Betrayal* (New York: Ace Books, 1968), ch. 11.

[17] Sharp and Westmoreland, *Report on War*, p. 101.

[18] "Workaholic" characterization is from Palmer, *25-Year War*, p. 40; see also pp. 134–35. Westmoreland describes his routine and methods in *A Soldier Reports*, pp. 265–68, 277–78, 284; but the best sense of his activities can be gained through his Historical Notes and Briefings in the Westmoreland Hist Files, 1965–68, CMH. Msg, Westmoreland MAC 11106 to Sharp, 21 Dec 66; Westmoreland Msg Files, CMH.

[19] Quote is from Westmoreland, *A Soldier Reports*, p. 268. Palmer Interv, 1975, p. 227, MHI. Parry, *Three-War Marine*, p. 284. Westmoreland Hist Briefing, 20 Mar 66, tab A, Westmoreland Hist File 5 (13 Mar–23 Apr 66), CMH. MFRs of some of these meetings are reproduced in the Westmoreland Historical Files, CMH. For an example, see tab D–3, Westmoreland Hist File 8 (17 Jul–17 Sep 66).

[20] Quote is from Parry, *Three-War Marine*, pp. 262–63. Interv, Marine Corps Oral History Program with Lt Gen William K. Jones, USMC, 13 Apr–5 Jun 73, p. 26, MCHC. For an account of Westmoreland's housemates, see Interv, Senior Officers Oral History Program with Maj Gen Spurgeon H. Neel, Jr., 1985, pp. 168–71, MHI.

[21] Westmoreland explains his insistence on an Army deputy in Msgs MAC 5286 and 5387 to Wheeler, 23 and 29 Oct 65, Westmoreland Msg Files, 1 Oct–31 Dec 65, CMH.

[22] General Heintges replaced General Throckmorton in November 1965 after Throckmorton was disabled by a back ailment. Westmoreland Hist Notes, 21 Oct 65, Westmoreland Hist File 1 (29 Aug–24 Oct 65), CMH. Msgs, Westmoreland MAC 5261 to Wheeler, 21 Oct 65; Wheeler JCS 4001–65 to Westmoreland, 22 Oct 65; Woolnough WDC09469 to Westmoreland et al., 2 Nov 65. All in Westmoreland Msg Files, 1 Oc–31 Dec 65, CMH.

[23] Westmoreland, *A Soldier Reports*, pp. 214, 222; Westmoreland Hist Notes, 27 Mar–8 Apr 67, tab A, Westmoreland Hist File 15 (27 Mar–30 Apr 67), CMH. Msgs, Wheeler JCS 2166–67 to Westmoreland, 22 Mar 67; Westmoreland MAC 2816 to Wheeler and Sharp, 24 Mar 67; Abrams to Westmoreland, WDC 4617, 10 Apr 67. All in Westmoreland Msg Files, CMH. Headquarters speculation is recounted in Lt Gen John R. Chaisson, USMC, Oral History Transcript, 1975, pp. 56–58, History and Museums Div, HQMC, and Kerwin Interv, 1980, pp. 347–48, 350–53; Palmer Interv, 7 and 10 Jun 68, p. 470.

[24] MACV Command History, 1965, p. 95; ARPA, Project AGILE, "MACV Information Handling," pp. 11–12; Westmoreland Hist Notes, 22 and 29 Oct 65, Westmoreland Hist Files 1 (29 Aug–24 Oct 65) and 2 (25 Oct–20 Dec 65), CMH; Msg, Westmoreland MAC 5416 to Sharp, 30 Oct 65, Westmoreland Msg Files, 1 Oct–31 Dec 65, CMH. Parry, *Three-War Marine*, pp. 264–65, 286; Ltr, Col F. F. Parry, USMC, to E. O. Parry, 30 May 66, Parry Family Papers, MHI; Ltr, Westmoreland to Wheeler, 2 Dec [65], 1966 R–Z Folder, William E. DePuy Papers, MHI.

[25] Quote is from Jones Interv, MCHC, pp. 3–4. Parry, *Three-War Marine*, pp. 264–266. ARPA, Project AGILE, "MACV Information Handling," pp. 93–102.

[26] ARPA, Project AGILE, "MACV Information Handling," pp. 96–100. Quote is from Parry, *Three-War Marine*, p. 265.

[27] Jones Interv, 13 Apr and 5 Jun 73, pp. 23–25, p. 88; Parry, *Three-War Marine*, pp. 266, 270; Ltr, Brig Gen John R. Chaisson to Mrs Chaisson, 22 Jan 67, box 6, John R. Chaisson Papers, Hoover Institution, Stanford, Calif. For Chaisson's background, see sketch in Chaisson Oral History. Westmoreland comments on his respect for Chaisson in Notes of General Westmoreland's Conference with CMH Historians, 6 Dec 89, author's files. CMH. Msg, Westmoreland MAC 8055 to Gen Greene, CMC, 25 Aug 67, Westmoreland Msg Files, 1 Jul–30 Sep 67, CMH.

[28] Typical Westmoreland demands for contingency planning are in Westmoreland Hist Briefings, 24 Jul 66, tab A, Westmoreland Hist File 8 (17 Jul–17 Sep 66), and 4 Jan 67, tab C, Westmoreland Hist File 12 (13 Dec 66–26 Jan 67), CMH. MACV Command History, 1965, pp. 421–23; ibid., 1966, pp. 745–54; ibid., 1967, pp. 1024–31. Quote is from Interv, MacDonald with Westmoreland, 28 Jan 73, in MacDonald Notes, CMH files; in same file, see Westmoreland Interv, 12 Mar 73.

[29] Westmoreland Hist Notes, 1–20 May 67; MFR, Brig Gen A. M. Hendry, Jr., USAF, 12 May 67, sub: CIIC Meeting, 12 May 1967, tabs A and A–11, Westmoreland Hist File 17 (1–31 May 67), MFR, Col R. S. Breen, USMC, 22 Oct 67, sub: CIIB Meeting, 21 October 1967, tab A–1, Westmoreland Hist File 24 (15 Oct–12 Nov 67). Both in CMH. For the I Corps reinforcement planning, see Rosson Interv, 1981, pp. 358–61.

[30] Quote is from MACV Command History, 1965, p. 134; see also ibid., 1966, pp. 232–35. Sharp and Westmoreland, *Report on War*, p. 253. Traas, "Builders and Fighters," ch. 9, pp. 37–38. Westmoreland, *A Soldier Reports*, p. 418.

[31] MACV Command History, 1967, pp. 839–40. Traas, "Builders and Fighters," ch. 9, pp. 1–10.

[32] MACV Command History, 1965, pp. 134–35. Traas, "Builders and Fighters," ch. 9, pp. 10–11. Msgs, Throckmorton HWA 2069 to Westmoreland, 5 Aug 65; Wheeler JCS 4658–65 to Sharp, 1 Dec 65; JCS to CINCPAC, 4 Dec 65. All in Westmoreland Msg Files, CMH.

MACV Headquarters: The Years of Expansion, 1965–1967

[33] Traas, "Builders and Fighters," ch. 9, pp. 11–16; MACV Command History, 1965, p. 135; Msgs, Westmoreland MAC 6176, 6257, 0179, 0215 to Sharp and Wheeler, 5 and 6 Dec 65 and 9 and 10 Jan 66; Westmoreland MAC 0459 to Wheeler, 18 Jan 66; Msgs, Wheeler JCS 4761–65, 4934–65, 0205–66, 0227–66 to Westmoreland and Sharp, 7 and 18 Dec 65 and 13 and 15 Jan 66; Wheeler JCS 0103–66 to Westmoreland, 6 Jan 66; Sharp to Wheeler, 22 Dec 65. All in Westmoreland Msg Files, CMH.

[34] Traas, "Builders and Fighters," ch. 9, pp. 19–38. Dunn came to South Vietnam from South Korea by way of Washington, where he met with senior DOD officials; Msgs, Woolnough WDC 00369 and 00411 to Beach, 11 and 12 Jan 66; Westmoreland MAC 2751 to Sharp, Wheeler, and Johnson, 7 Apr 66. All in Westmoreland Msg Files, 1 Jan–31 Mar 66, and 1 Apr–30 Jun 66, CMH.

[35] This discussion is based on Maj Gen T. M. Rienzi, *Communications-Electronics, 1962–1970,* Vietnam Studies (Washington, D.C.: Department of the Army, 1972), chs. 1 and 2. See also MACV Command History, 1965, pp. 392–94.

[36] John D. Bergen, *Military Communications: A Test for Technology*, United States Army in Vietnam (Washington, D.C.: Center of Military History, 1986), pp. 167, 170–71, 175–85; Rienzi, *Communications-Electronics*, pp. 22–27, 40– 41, 47–48, 57–59; Westmoreland Hist Notes, 16 Nov 65, tab D, Westmoreland Hist File 2 (25 Oct–20 Dec 65); and 23 Jan 66, tab F, Westmoreland Hist File 3 (20 Dec 65–29 Jan 66), CMH.

[37] Bergen, *Military Communications*, pp. 291, 310–11. Rienzi, *Communications-Electronics*, ch. 7. For comment on the effect of rapid communications, see Parry, *Three-War Marine*, p. 266.

[38] MS, Col Robert Sholly, "The Role of the Inspector General, Military Assistance Command, Vietnam, 1964–1971," n.d., pp. i–iii, 1–43, CMH files. Manuscript provided the author by Colonel Sholly. Westmoreland's views on IG: Westmoreland Hist Notes, 5 Nov 65, tab B, Westmoreland Hist File 2 (25 Oct–20 Dec 65). Msgs, Westmoreland to Wheeler, MAC 2837, 10 Apr 66; Wheeler to Westmoreland and Sharp, JCS 2256–66. Both in Westmoreland Msg Files, 1 Apr–30 Jun 66, CMH.

[39] The deficiencies of the MACV J2 as of early 1965 are described in Interv, Senior Officers Oral History Program with Brig Gen Glenn Muggleberg, 1985, pp. 6–7, 18–19, 20–22, MHI. For additional comment on U.S. intelligence deficiencies, see Palmer, *25-Year War*, pp. 39–40.

[40] Maj Gen Joseph A. McChristian, *The Role of Military Intelligence,* Vietnam Studies (Washington, D.C.: Department of the Army, 1974), pp. 3–5. Msgs, Westmoreland MAC 2621 to Johnson, 17 May 65; Richardson WDC 04380 to Westmoreland and Walters, 20 May 65. Both in Westmoreland Msg Files, 1 Apr–30 Jun 65, CMH. McChristian's work habits and relationship with Westmoreland are described in Muggleberg Interv, 1985, pp. 23–24; see also pp. 8–9.

[41] McChristian, *Military Intelligence*, pp. 6–20, 148–49. ARPA, Project AGILE, "MACV Information Handling," pp. 45–89, describes the MACV intelligence establishment as of early 1967. Ltr, McChristian to Maj Gen J. E. Thomas, ACSI, USAF, 1 Nov 66, CMH files. Rosson Interv, 1981, pp. 326–327; MACV Command History, 1965, pp. 465–67; ibid., 1968, 2:582–88. MACV J2 PERINTREP, vol. 1, 1 Jan–30 Jun 66, pp. i–ii, copy in MHI, is the first issue of the series. Muggleberg Interv, 1985, pp. 13–16, describes J2's contacts with the Studies and Observations Group and the attachés.

[42] MACV Command History, 1968, 2:569–70. Muggleberg Interv, 1985, pp. 9–10.

[43] McChristian, *Military Intelligence*, pp. 11, 21–24. The Vietnamese intelligence establishment and its relation to MACV J2 are discussed in Col Hoang Ngoc Lung, *Intelligence*, Indochina Monographs. (Washington, D.C.: Center of Military History, 1982), pp. 11–17, 37–78, 82–83. MACV Command History, 1968, 2:569. Westmoreland Hist Notes, 1 Sep 65, Westmoreland Hist File 1 (29 Aug–24 Oct 65), CMH. *A Soldier Reports*, p. 254.

MACV: The Years of Escalation, 1962–1967

[44] MACV Command History, 1968, 2: 571, 574–80. McChristian, *Military Intelligence*, pp. 26–44.

[45] Quote is from MACV Command History, 1968, 2:571–72. McChristian, *Military Intelligence*, pp. 45–64. Jones, *War Without Windows*, chs. 5 and 6, describes CICV from the perspective of a junior intelligence officer.

[46] Quote is from Brig Gen Edwin H. Simmons, USMC, in Graham A. Cosmas and Lt Col Terrence P. Murray, USMC, *U.S. Marines in Vietnam: Vietnamization and Redeployment, 1970–1971* (Washington, D.C.: History and Museums Division, HQMC, 1986), p. 255. McChristian, *Military Intelligence*, pp. 38, 127, 149–54. Muggleberg Interv, 1985, pp. 16–17. Jones, *War Without Windows*, pp. 61–62, 92–94; Memo, CO, U.S. Naval Amphibious School, for CNO, 17 Aug 66, sub: Debrief of Kidd, James L. . ., and Sutherland, Ronald "V". . ., pp. 3–4, 6, Vietnam Command Files, Naval Hist Ctr. Interv, Charles B. MacDonald with Lt Gen Phillip Davidson, 7 Sep 73, in MacDonald Notes, CMH files. Lung, *Intelligence*, p. 11.

[47] MACV advisory organization is surveyed in Jeffrey J. Clarke, *Advice and Support: The Final Years, 1965–1973,* United States Army in Vietnam (Washington, D.C.: Center of Military History, 1988), pp. 53–57. See also MACV Command History, 1967, pp. 129–32.

[48] Clarke, *Final Years*, pp. 54–55, 76–77; Gen Cao Van Vien, et al., *The U.S. Advisor*, Indochina Monographs (Washington, D.C.: Center of Military History, 1980), pp. 34–38; MACV Command History, 1965, pp. 94–96, 253–54, 448–50; ibid., 1967, pp. 221–31; Msg, Westmoreland MAC 8807 to Sharp, 17 Sep 67, Westmoreland Msg Files, 1 Jul–30 Sep 67, CMH; Memo, Col J. L. Clancy for COMUSMACV, et al., 17 Sep 67, sub: Briefing on the Overall Status of the CY 1967 and CY 1968 GVN Defense Budgets, tab A–7, Westmoreland Hist File 22 (10–30 Sep 67), CMH.

[49] Quote is from Exit Interv, Historical Section, USARV, with Lt Gen Bruce Palmer, Jr., 7 and 10 Jun 68, p. 253; See also Palmer Interv, 1975, pp. 217–18, MHI. Vien, et al., *The U.S. Advisor*, pp. 38–40. MACV Command History, 1966, pp. 453, 748. Westmoreland Hist Notes, 5 Jun 66; and Chronology, 1 Jan–30 Jun 66; tabs A and D–5, Westmoreland Hist File 7 (29 May–16 Jul 66), CMH. Msgs, Westmoreland MAC 4074 and MAC 5197 to Gen Johnson, 22 May 66 and 1 Jun 67. Both in Westmoreland Msg Files, 1 Apr–30 Jun 66 and 1 Apr–30 Jun 67, CMH. Neel Interv, 1985, p. 171.

[50] Sharp and Westmoreland, *Report on War*, p. 67. MACV Command History, 1966, pp. 244–245, 284–288, 453–454. Palmer Interv, 7 and 10 Jun 68, p. 252. Westmoreland Hist Notes, 13 Dec 66, tab D, Westmoreland Hist File 11 (30 Oct–12 Dec 66), CMH. Clarke, *Final Years*, p. 210.

[51] Clarke, *Final Years*, pp. 209–10. MACV Command History, 1967, pp. 226–27, 231–32.

[52] Sharp and Westmoreland, *Report on War*, p. 142. MACV Command History, 1967, pp. 233–35; ibid., 1968, 2:621–22. Clarke, *Final Years*, p. 210.

[53] ARPA, Project AGILE, "MACV Information Handling," apps. A and B, lists and summarizes the major MACV reports. Msgs, Westmoreland to Sharp, 25 Sep 65; Westmoreland MAC 1362 to Sharp, 17 Feb 66, Westmoreland Msg Files; Westmoreland Hist Briefings, 8 Mar 66, tab D, Westmoreland Hist File 4 (30 Jan–13 Mar 66); CMH. Westmoreland Hist Notes, 1–20 May 67, tab A, Westmoreland Hist File 17 (1–31 May 67), CMH. MACV Command History, 1967, pp. 191–93, 622–25. Ltr, Col F. F. Parry, USMC, to E. O. Parry, 30 May 66, Parry Family Papers, MHI.

[54] First quote is from Msg, Wheeler JCS 9573–67 to Sharp and Westmoreland, 8 Nov 67; second is from Msg, Abrams MAC 11159 to Wheeler and Sharp, 21 Nov 67. Both in Westmoreland Msg Files, 1–30 Nov 67, CMH. See also Msgs, Wheeler CJCS 0547–67 to Westmoreland and Sharp, 20 Jan 67; Westmoreland MAC 0753 to Wheeler, 23 Jan 67;

Sharp to Wheeler, 12 Feb 67; Sharp to Wheeler, 29 Nov 67. All in Westmoreland Msg Files. Ltr, Abrams to Gen Johnson, 23 Dec 67, Westmoreland Sig File, Dec 67.

[55] Youngdale Interv, 5 Jun 75, p. 4. J2 automation is covered in McChristian, *Military Intelligence*, pp. 152–54. ARPA, Project AGILE, " MACV Information Handling," pp. 9–20, 143–70, summarizes earlier studies and gives its own recommendation.

[56] Msgs, Sharp to Wheeler, 12 Feb 67; Westmoreland MAC 1550 to Sharp, 14 Feb 67. Both in Westmoreland Msg Files, 1 Jan–31 Mar 67, CMH. Westmoreland Hist Notes, 1–13 Oct 67, tab A, Westmoreland Hist File 23 (1–15 Oct 67); and 29 Nov–16 Dec 67, tab A, Westmoreland Hist File 26 (29 Nov–16 Dec 67). Both in CMH. MACV Command History, 1968, 2:711–12, 803–804. MACV Data Management Agency, *Command Manual for Journal Data System*, 6 Aug 68, copy in CMH files. In same collection, see manuals for other automated data bases.

[57] Msgs, Westmoreland MAC 8829 to Gen McConnell, 18 Sep 67; Westmoreland MAC 9558 to Gen Johnson, 12 Oct 67; Gen Johnson JCS 8692–67 to Westmoreland, 14 Oct 67; Westmoreland MAC 10169 to Wheeler, 27 Oct 67; Wheeler JCS 9242–67 to Westmoreland, 30 Oct 67. All in Westmoreland Msg Files, CMH. MACV Command History, 1967, pp. 1251–52; ibid., 1968, 1:332–33.

[58] MACV Command History, 1965, p. 457; ibid., 1966, pp. 763–64; ibid., 1967, pp. 863–65; ibid., 1968, 2:743–46. Ltr, Westmoreland to Dr John S. Foster, Jr., 30 Jul 67, Westmoreland Sig File, July 67, CMH.

[59] MACV Command History, 1966, pp. 763–64; ibid., 1967, pp. 862–63; ibid., 1968, 2:744–46. Westmoreland Hist Briefings, 15 Mar 66, tab E, Westmoreland Hist File 4 (30 Jan–13 Mar 66) and 8 Oct 66, tab C, Westmoreland Hist File 9 (18 Sep–17 Oct 66), CMH. Westmoreland, *A Soldier Reports*, pp. 267–68. Msg, Wheeler JCS 5516–66 to Westmoreland and Sharp, 14 Sep 66, Westmoreland Msg Files, 1 Jul–30 Sep 66.

[60] Msg, COMUSMACV MAC 33247 to CINCPAC, 10 Oct 67, Westmoreland Sig File, 1967, CMH. Westmoreland, *A Soldier Reports*, pp. 265–68. MACV Command History, 1967, p. 866.

[61] Quote is from MACV Command History, 1968, 2:746–47; ibid., 1967, pp. 865–66. Msgs, Westmoreland MAC 11794 to Sharp, 6 Dec 67; Dr. Foster, OSD (DDR&E) 11234 to Westmoreland, 30 Dec 67. Both in Westmoreland Msg Files, 1–31 Dec 67, CMH. Westmoreland Hist Notes, 29 Nov–16 Dec 67, tab A, Westmoreland Hist File 26 (29 Nov–16 Dec 67), 28 Dec 67–31 Jan 68, tab A–1, Westmoreland Hist File 28 (27 Dec 67–31 Jan 68), CMH. Palmer Interv, 7 and 10 Jun 68, p. 257. R & D delays are commented on in Interv, Senior Officer, Debriefing Program with Lt Gen William R. Peers, 26 Jan and 12–15 Apr 77, sec. 3, pp. 18–19, MHI. Copy in CMH.

[62] Westmoreland quotes are from Interv with MacDonald, 20 Feb 73, MacDonald Notes, CMH Files.

[63] Quote is from Msg, Sharp to Wheeler, 3 Aug 67; Westmoreland Msg Files, 1 Jul–30 Sep 67, CMH; for similar caution by Westmoreland, see his Msg MAC 3102 to McNamara, 20 Apr 66, Westmoreland Msg Files, 1 Apr–30 Jun 66, CMH. Westmoreland, *A Soldier Reports*, p. 273 presents a standard defense of use of statistical measurement. Thomas C. Thayer, "How to Analyze a War without Fronts: Vietnam 1965–1972," *Journal of Defense Research, Series B, Tactical Warfare*, vol. 7B (Fall 1975), ch. 1, provides an OSD systems analyst's view of the usefulness of Vietnam statistics in understanding the course of the conflict.

[64] The public relations implications of statistics are illustrated in Msgs, Wheeler CJCS 0624–67 to Westmoreland, 23 Jan 67; and Westmoreland MAC 0869 to Wheeler and Sharp, 26 Jan 67. Westmoreland Msg Files, 1 Jan–31 Mar 67, CMH. In same source, see Msgs, Westmoreland MAC 9127 to Wheeler, 19 Oct 66; Wheeler JCS 4476–67 to Sharp and Westmoreland, 15 Jun 67; and Wheeler JCS 9468–67 to Westmoreland, 5

MACV: The Years of Escalation, 1962–1967

Nov 67. Hammond, *Military and the Media 1962–1968*, pp. 279–84, 315–20, 325–27. Parry, *Three-War Marine*, p. 279, recalls the pressure to report progress.

[65] Westmoreland defends the Army-heavy MACV staff in Ltr, no. 01562, 30 Nov 65 sub: JTD, HQ Staff, USMACV, 15 Nov 65, quoted in MACV Command History, 1965, p. 94; and Msg MAC 5601 to Wheeler and Sharp, 9 Nov 65, Westmoreland Msg Files, 1 Oct–31 Dec 65, CMH.

[66] Quote is from Ltr, Moore to Westmoreland, 8 Oct 65, sub: Air Force Representation on MACV Staff, tab F–7, Westmoreland Hist File 1 (29 Aug–24 Oct 65), CMH. Air Force complaints are summarized in Schlight, *Years of the Offensive*, pp. 10–11.

[67] MACV Command History, 1965, pp. 92–93, 274. Msgs, Denholm WDC 1576 to Westmoreland, 27 Feb 65; Westmoreland MAC 2602 to Gen Johnson, 15 May 65; Wheeler JCS 4098–65 to Sharp and Westmoreland, 28 Oct 65; Throckmorton WDC 9824 to Westmoreland, 13 Nov 65. All in Westmoreland Msg Files, CMH. Westmoreland Hist Notes, 5–11 Sep 65, 16 and 21 Oct 65, Westmoreland Hist File 1 (29 Aug–24 Oct 65), CMH.

[68] MACV Command History, 1965, p. 93. Msgs, Westmoreland MAC 1787 to Gen Johnson, 1 Apr 65; Westmoreland MAC 1850 to Sharp, 3 Apr 65; Westmoreland MAC 5601 to Wheeler and Sharp, 9 Nov 65. All in Westmoreland Msg Files, CMH.

[69] Msg, Westmoreland MAC 5601 to Wheeler and Sharp, 9 Nov 65, Westmoreland Msg Files, 1 Oct–31 Dec 65, CMH.

[70] First quote is from Westmoreland Hist Notes, 8 Nov 65, tab C, Westmoreland Hist File 2 (25 Oct–20 Dec 65); see also Westmoreland Hist Notes, 12 Oct 65, Westmoreland Hist File 1 (29 Aug–24 Oct 65). Both in CMH. Second quote is from Msg, Westmoreland MAC 5601 to Wheeler and Sharp, 9 Nov 65, Westmoreland Msg Files, 1 Oct–31 Dec 65, CMH. Ltr, Moore to Westmoreland, 8 Oct 65, sub: Air Force Representation on MACV Staff, tab F–7, Westmoreland Hist File 1 (29 Aug–24 Oct 65), CMH. Ltr, Wheeler to Westmoreland, 18 May 66, Att. 2, tab D–26, Westmoreland Hist File 6 (24 Apr–28 May 66), CMH.

[71] Msgs, Wheeler JCS 4220–65 to Westmoreland and Sharp, 3 Nov 65; Westmoreland MAC 5674 to Throckmorton, 12 Nov 65; Throckmorton WDC 9824 to Westmoreland, 13 Nov 65. All in Westmoreland Msg Files, 1 Oct–31 Dec 65, CMH. Ltr, Wheeler to Westmoreland, 18 May 66, tab D–26, Westmoreland Hist File 6 (24 Apr–28 May 66), CMH; Att. 1 to this letter summarizes the services' demands for additional MACV staff slots.

[72] Quotes are from Ltrs, Wheeler to Westmoreland, 18 May 65; and Westmoreland to Wheeler, 27 May 66. Both in tab D–26, Westmoreland Hist File 6 (24 Apr–28 May 66), CMH. Makeup of the MACV Construction Directorate is summarized in Traas, "Builders and Fighters," p. 24.

[73] Quote is from Jones Interv, 13 Apr–5 Jun 73, pp. 1–2. Adm U. S. Grant Sharp, "Reminiscences of Adm U. S. Grant Sharp, USN (Ret.)," 2 vols., Transcript of Intervs by Cdr Etta Belle Kitchen, USN (Ret.), for Oral History Program, U.S. Naval Institute, 20 Sep 69–7 Jun 70, pp. 246–47.

9

Controlling U.S. Forces

During the buildup, the command and control structure for U.S. forces evolved along established lines. General Westmoreland remained a subtheater commander under CINCPAC. Within South Vietnam, he exercised command of his American units through the service component headquarters and through the field forces and the III Marine Amphibious Force. All these organizations expanded and evolved to meet growing operational and administrative requirements. Their relationships with MACV often became the subject of controversies within and between the services. As such issues arose, General Westmoreland, in conjunction with Admiral Sharp and General Wheeler, sought resolutions which both accommodated service interests and doctrines and preserved his ability to give central direction to the campaign in South Vietnam.

Military Assistance Command, Pacific Command, and the JCS

Even as the Military Assistance Command, Vietnam's forces and activities expanded far beyond what had been contemplated at its establishment, it remained a subordinate unified command under Admiral Ulysses S. Grant Sharp, the Commander in Chief, Pacific. Under Sharp, General Westmoreland conducted all American operations within South Vietnam as well as those portions of the air war in Laos and North Vietnam that Sharp delegated to him. From his Honolulu headquarters Sharp directed the bombing campaign against North Vietnam through his Air Force and Navy component commanders. He also retained control of the American forces stationed in Thailand and the Seventh Fleet carriers and other vessels that supported operations in South Vietnam.

Admiral Sharp closely supervised MACV's activities. He periodically issued an overall concept of operations for Southeast Asia, in which he emphasized the interdependence of the campaigns in North and South Vietnam and Laos and of American support activities in Thailand. He transmitted Defense Department and JCS directives on matters such as rules of engagement for South Vietnam's border areas. As the officer in charge of military construction throughout the Pacific, Sharp reviewed the Military Assistance Command's proposals on, including the location of new jet airfields in South Vietnam, to ensure their compatibility with theater strategy. In spite of the distance between his headquarters and Saigon, Sharp kept himself informed of the details of the counterinsurgency campaign through frequent exchanges of messages with General Westmoreland, periodic visits to South Vietnam, and regular conferences with Westmoreland in Saigon and Honolulu. Sharp rarely interfered in Westmoreland's day-to-day running of the war, but the admiral did not hesitate to express his views on tactics and other matters, and Westmoreland often incorporated Sharp's ideas into his own policies and recommendations. Sharp also intervened directly in the allocation and use of certain scarce air munitions and in the cross-border activities of MACV's Studies and Observations Group. Finally, as MACV's principal source of logistical support, Sharp and his component commanders played a central role in planning and carrying out troop deployments to South Vietnam.[1]

Sharp's Army, Navy, Air Force, and Marine component commanders maintained constant contact with their service subordinates in Vietnam, who were under their direction in all but operational matters. This linkage provided MACV's component commanders, notably those of the III Marine Amphibious Force, with a channel of communication to Westmoreland's immediate superior and a potential means of reversing the MACV commander's decisions. A Marine Corps observer praised Admiral Sharp for "his conscientious actions in seeking Marine Corps counsel . . . on purely Marine Corps affairs affecting forces under MACV authority." Marines welcomed Sharp's oversight as protecting their interests in the "strongly Army-oriented" Military Assistance Command. On more than one occasion, they took advantage of this channel to challenge MACV decisions that they deemed adverse to Corps interests.[2]

As the conflict in South Vietnam expanded, so did direct communication between the authorities in Washington and Westmoreland. General Wheeler found it convenient to deal with Westmoreland directly instead of through Sharp, especially when he needed a quick MACV response to an urgent policy question. Such exchanges became frequent and informal. The Army Chief of Staff, General Johnson, recalled that, when serving as acting chairman of the Joint Chiefs while Wheeler was incapacitated by a heart attack, "there were periods when I would call . . . Westmoreland once or twice a day and talk to him direct on a private line." President Johnson increasingly regarded Westmoreland, rather than Sharp, as his principal military commander in Southeast Asia and sought to develop a personal relationship with him. Thus, in August 1966 Johnson summoned the general and his wife to the LBJ Ranch for what was largely an informal get-acquainted visit. Later in the year, when he met at Manila with the heads of state of America's Far Eastern allies, the president saw to it that Westmoreland rather than Sharp attended as the senior American military representative. Eventually, Johnson drew a reluctant Westmoreland into his administration's political defense of the war.[3]

The enlargement of Westmoreland's forces, responsibilities, and public visibility created the potential for conflict between the MACV commander and Admiral Sharp, a strong-willed officer who was determined to maintain his own prerogatives and to promote his views on strategy. Through tact and diplomacy, and with cooperation from General Wheeler, the two commanders avoided a rupture. When communicating directly with Westmoreland, Wheeler customarily sent Sharp information copies of his messages. Westmoreland did the same with his replies to Wheeler, an arrangement that allowed Sharp to add his own comments when he chose to do so. Frequently, Wheeler simultaneously sought the views of both commanders.

Admiral Sharp
(Naval Historical Center photo)

Westmoreland went out of his way to keep Sharp informed on the details of ground operations and troop deployments. He consulted his superior on plans and recommendations and often deferred to his preferences, for example on locating the 1st Cavalry Division base at An Khe instead of Pleiku. For his part, Sharp respected Westmoreland's substantial autonomy, including the MACV commander's right to deal directly with the ambassadors to Thailand and Laos. However, Sharp was quick to rebuke his subordinate for any failure to keep him informed of such dealings and took steps to block any direct communication between MACV staff sections and agencies in Washington. He also kept himself at the center of operations evaluation and policy-making for the ROLLING THUNDER campaign.[4]

Wheeler, Sharp, and Westmoreland for the most part maintained a united front in discussing Vietnam policy and strategy with Secretary of Defense McNamara and other high administration officials. Preparing for McNamara's periodic trips to Honolulu and Saigon, Westmoreland and Sharp carefully coordinated their briefings for the secretary, especially on ROLLING THUNDER issues. Wheeler regularly coached Sharp and Westmoreland as to what issues to raise with McNamara, as well as soliciting suggestions from them on matters he should bring up with the secretary and the Joint Chiefs in Washington. The result of this continuous consultation was a seamlessness in military advice and reporting from the field, with the rough edges of disagreement smoothed away. Wheeler operated similarly with the Joint Chiefs. He went to great lengths to prevent the issuance of "split papers" which might give McNamara and his civilian analysts an opportunity to intervene in technical military questions. While these methods achieved the chairman's immediate tactical purposes, they also prevented a full airing at the administration's highest levels of important disagreements among the armed services, for example over the efficacy of bombing North Vietnam.[5]

Naval Forces, Vietnam

At the beginning of 1965 the principal naval element of MACV, the 600-man Naval Advisory Group, although nominally a service component command headquartered in Saigon, in practice carried out only advisory and support functions for the South Vietnamese Navy. During the year, it acquired operational responsibilities. In July, to facilitate coordination with the South Vietnamese, the Seventh Fleet transferred to the advisory group operational control of the U.S. Navy vessels and aircraft participating in Operation MARKET TIME, a combined U.S.–South Vietnamese coastal patrol aimed at preventing seaborne supply and reinforcement of the Viet Cong. In addition to these units, designated Task Force (TF) 115, the advisory group also commanded the U.S. Navy and Coast Guard boats patrolling South Vietnam's rivers (TF 116). Even with these additions, the advisory group was overwhelmingly outnumbered by the III Marine Amphibious Force, which quickly grew into the largest naval organization in South Vietnam. In May 1965 the III MAF commander, Maj. Gen. William R. Collins, as the senior naval officer on shore, assumed the naval component command. The advisory group and its subordinate task forces, however, remained outside Collins' jurisdiction, reporting directly to MACV.[6]

The resulting situation was anomalous and unsatisfactory to all concerned. General Collins' successor, Maj. Gen. Lewis W. Walt, as senior U.S. commander in I Corps, directed the operations of more than 40,000 marines in a reinforced division and air wing, acted as senior adviser to the ARVN corps commander, and provided common-item logistical support to all American forces in his area through a large Naval Support Activity at Da Nang. Understandably, he had little time to spare for his duties as naval component commander, although he maintained a small III MAF staff element for that purpose. With his headquarters located at Da Nang, over 300 miles from Saigon, Walt was hardly in a position to provide timely advice to General Westmoreland on naval matters. The Naval Advisory Group, for its part, was considered a MACV staff element rather than a Navy command, even though it had task forces under it. It lacked a formal channel to General Walt, and its small Saigon staff had all it could do to cope with its new operational responsibilities.[7]

Admiral Ward (Naval Historical Center photo)

For practical purposes, as of the end of 1965 MACV included two naval component headquarters, neither of which was fully effective. The Navy at the same time had no single coordinator or authoritative spokesman within MACV. In the light of these facts, Westmoreland, with the support of Admiral Sharp, in September 1965 directed the Chief, Naval Advisory Group, Rear Adm. Norvell G. Ward, to initiate a study of alternative command arrangements.[8]

In January 1966, after nearly three months of work and consultation with the Pacific Fleet, the advisory group staff presented a rather convoluted proposal. They recommended that the III Marine Amphibious Force commander, with a strengthened staff, retain his naval component "hat" and that a new headquarters in Saigon, Naval Forces, MACV, under a flag-rank deputy naval component commander, control the two task forces and perform naval component functions outside I Corps. Although nominally under III MAF, the commander of Naval Forces, MACV, would be considered directly subordinate to Westmoreland in his advisory and operational capacities. This plan, its authors argued, would keep all Navy and Marine forces in Vietnam under a single component commander, avoid placing a naval officer between the MACV Commander and one of his principal ground force headquarters, and yet ensure effective control of naval forces while providing MACV with authoritative Navy representation.[9]

MACV: The Years of Escalation, 1962–1967

Presented with this proposal on 9 January, General Westmoreland rejected it as too complicated. Instead, he recommended that Admiral Sharp establish a "straightforward" naval component command in Saigon that would exercise operational control of all naval forces in South Vietnam except those of III MAF, which should become a "separate uniservice command" under MACV. To protect the "prestige and political view" of the South Vietnamese Navy and Marine Corps, the naval component commander would also serve as chief of the Naval Advisory Group. Westmoreland's proposal received the endorsement of Sharp, of General Walt (who was more than willing to be relieved of his component responsibilities), and of General Wallace M. Greene, Jr., Commandant of the Marine Corps, whom Westmoreland made sure to consult during one of the commandant's periodic trips to Vietnam. With such support behind it, the plan received quick approval from the Joint Chiefs of Staff.[10]

On 1 April 1966, the Pacific Fleet activated the new component headquarters, U.S. Naval Forces, Vietnam (NAVFORV), under Admiral Ward's command. NAVFORV, under operational control of COMUSMACV and administrative control of Pacific Fleet, took command of the Naval Advisory Group, of Task Forces 115 and 116, and of Naval Support Activity Da Nang. It conducted all naval combat and logistical operations in MACV's purview, provided common-item supply and other services to U.S. forces in I Corps, advised and assisted the South Vietnamese Navy and Marine Corps, and assumed certain United States and SEATO contingency planning tasks. At the same time, the III Marine Amphibious Force became a separate single-service command, under the operational control of the MACV Commander and the administrative control of the commanding general, Fleet Marine Force Pacific (FMFPAC), at Honolulu. Charged with the conduct of land and air combat in I Corps, and responsible for the logistics and administration of its attached Marine units, III MAF for practical purposes constituted a fourth service component command.[11]

As part of these rearrangements, Headquarters Support Activity Saigon, which since 1962 had provided logistical support to MACV headquarters and to American forces elsewhere in South Vietnam, went out of existence. The Army, through its 1st Logistical Command, assumed common support functions in II, III, and IV Corps. Another Army organization, the newly established Headquarters Area Command, took over housekeeping and security chores for MACV headquarters and the other installations in and around Saigon.[12]

The establishment of Naval Forces Vietnam did not resolve all naval command problems within MACV. Command of the joint Army-Navy Mobile Riverine Force, established early in 1967 to seek out and destroy the Viet Cong along the innumerable waterways of the Mekong Delta, was one such problem. Eventually designated Task Force 117, the force comprised an Army infantry brigade and a supporting

A vessel of the riverine force patrols waters of the Mekong Delta. (U.S. Navy photo)

Navy element of gunboats, landing craft, and other shallow-draft vessels. Both NAVFORV and Pacific Fleet rejected a bid by MACV and U.S. Army, Pacific, to place the joint force under a single Army-dominated headquarters. As a compromise, MACV established separate headquarters for the Army and Navy elements of the force, with the latter under operational control of Admiral Ward but assigned to "close support" of the Army brigade. The Army and Navy commanders of the force conducted operations by mutual coordination, much as had their counterparts in nineteenth century joint expeditions. The commander of the Pacific Fleet, who had been concerned over the "long range impact" of precedents set by the riverine force on future amphibious command relationships, accepted this arrangement as a unique solution of a special problem which yet prevented Army dictation of the movement of Navy ships. The compromise remained in effect until the joint riverine force ceased operations in August 1969, in spite of repeated attempts by MACV commanders and IV Corps senior advisers to establish a greater degree of Army control over the Navy elements.[13]

Amphibious command relationships lay at the heart of another persistent issue: control of the operations of the Seventh Fleet's Special Landing Force (SLF). This unit, which consisted of a reinforced Marine infantry battalion and a helicopter squadron embarked in amphibious shipping, constituted Pacific Command's mobile landing force reserve for contingencies throughout the Far East. Admiral Sharp made the landing force available to MACV and the III Marine Amphibious Force to attack Viet Cong targets along the coasts and to reinforce ground operations in I Corps and throughout South Vietnam. Under well-established joint doctrine, strongly supported by the Navy and marines, command during any landing operation, including control of the airspace over the beachhead, was to be exercised by the Navy officer commanding the amphibious task force until the ground troops were firmly established on shore. This system, designed for assaults upon hostile coastlines, created problems when applied in Vietnam, where the Special Landing Force normally disembarked into the operating areas of friendly units. It effectively excluded the overall commander, who was ultimately accountable for success or failure, from the planning and execution of the amphibious portion of the operation. It also infringed upon Seventh Air Force's coordination of tactical air support.[14]

General Westmoreland first encountered this problem in March 1966, during the planning of Operation JACKSTAY, a combined assault near Saigon by the SLF and elements of the Vietnamese Marine Corps. Westmoreland and Vice Admiral John J. Hyland, the Seventh Fleet commander, improvised liaison between MACV and the amphibious task force for JACKSTAY. At a formal conference on Okinawa in late May, representatives of MACV and of the Pacific Fleet worked out a permanent agreement that provided for more systematic joint scheduling and planning of SLF operations by the two headquarters. However, joint doctrine on the separation of amphibious and onshore commands remained in effect, to General Westmoreland's dismay. To no avail, he recommended to Admiral Sharp that all SLF operations in South Vietnam be "planned and executed under operational control of CG, III MAF, or other field commander designated by me." After early 1967, the Special Landing Force rarely was employed outside I Corps, thereby limiting conflicts of authority between MACV and the fleet. Nevertheless, the question of command of the landing force remained an irritant in MACV-Navy relations until the end of its operations in Vietnam in late 1969.[15]

U.S. Army, Vietnam: A Question of Roles

When major troop commitments came under serious consideration in March 1965, control over the Army elements in Vietnam was divided. Since abolition of the MAAG the year before, Westmoreland had directly commanded the Army advisers with the South Vietnamese forces. The Army combat support and combat service support units in the country were attached to the U.S. Army Support Command, Vietnam (USASCV), which performed primarily logistical functions. Under an arrangement established in 1963, General Westmoreland, as an additional duty, acted as MACV's Army component commander, with the USASCV commander as his deputy for Army matters. These arrangements were adequate for the size and missions of the Army contingent through 1964. With the deployment of major combat units, however, Army leaders had to reconsider their command structure in Vietnam.[16]

Army Chief of Staff Harold K. Johnson; the commander of U.S. Army, Pacific, General John K. Waters; and General Westmoreland agreed early that MACV would direct Army combat operations through one or more corps-level headquarters, which were to deploy when the divisions did. They differed, however, over the role of MACV's Army component command. Johnson and Waters wanted to upgrade U.S. Army Support Command, Vietnam, into a full-fledged Army component headquarters under its own commander. That headquarters, they argued, should relieve Westmoreland of as many as possible of his nontactical, noncombat Army functions, including the entire Army advisory effort as well as all service-related logistics and administration. Westmoreland objected to this proposal. Removal of the Army advisers from MACV, he argued, would re-create the division of responsibility that had existed under the MAAG. In addition, creation of a full-fledged Army component command would result in the presence of "two large headquarters in the Saigon area [with] the same span of control I now have, and complicate the relationship between my headquarters and the [South Vietnamese Joint General Staff] which is also the senior Army headquarters."[17]

These considerations notwithstanding, MACV headquarters by itself could not conduct all the affairs of an Army force that was expanding rapidly toward a projected total strength of at least 300,000. In late March 1965 the Defense Department, after repeated urging from Westmoreland, established in Vietnam the 1st Logistical Command to support Army and other U.S. and allied forces. The logistical command, along with Army aviation, engineer, signal, and medical organizations, the Special Forces, and the combat divisions and brigades, required at least a minimal component headquarters to handle its administration and coordinate its activities.[18]

The solution was another compromise. On 20 July 1965, U.S. Army, Pacific, redesignated the U.S. Army Support Command as United States Army, Vietnam (USARV), with Westmoreland as its commander and the former USASCV commander, Brig. Gen. John Norton, as his deputy. The deputy, whose position was upgraded to three stars when Lt. Gen. Jean E. Engler replaced Norton early in 1966, commanded USARV for all practical purposes under Westmoreland's general direction. By retaining the Army component command, however, Westmoreland remained the sole point of contact between USARV and the Joint General Staff. Reflecting Westmoreland's preferences, USARV exercised command in all but tactical matters over Army forces attached to MACV

315

MACV: The Years of Escalation, 1962–1967

General Norton, center (NARA)

and furnished them with supply and combat service support. It also provided common-item supply to all U.S. forces in South Vietnam outside I Corps, as well as much logistical and combat assistance to the Free World allies and the South Vietnamese. U.S. Army, Vietnam, nominally was under the administrative control of USARPAC. However, as the Vietnam command expanded in size and functions, it increasingly communicated on many issues directly with the Department of the Army in Washington rather than the Pacific component headquarters in Honolulu.[19]

As a theater commander, Westmoreland was following well-established practice in retaining for himself the direct command of his Army forces. During World War II, General Dwight D. Eisenhower served simultaneously as Supreme Commander, Allied Expeditionary Force, and as Commanding General, European Theater of Operations, U.S. Army. General Douglas MacArthur made similar arrangements, both as commander of the Southwest Pacific Area during World War II and as commander in chief of United Nations Forces in Korea.[20]

Westmoreland intended U.S. Army, Vietnam, to function primarily as a logistic support command, roughly analogous to the Services of Supply and Communications Zone theater headquarters of World Wars I and II. In spite of his intentions, however, as American ground forces expanded and began active campaigning, USARV took on many of the tasks of a field army headquarters. To provide the tactical field force commands with sufficient, timely supplies and replacements, as well

USARV headquarters at Long Binh (NARA)

as essential aviation, engineer, artillery, and medical support, the component headquarters had to enter into the planning and execution of operations. Its staff and those of the field forces established a network of contacts for this purpose. In addition, USARV controlled and allocated the theater reserve of helicopters and other combat support units, a function for which the MACV staff lacked the time and technical expertise. USARV, through its aviation, supply, and medical support channels, usually possessed earlier and more complete combat information than did MACV. According to Lt. Gen. Bruce Palmer, Engler's successor, "the people who know there is a fight going on somewhere are the medics who handle the dustoffs. By the same token, the aviators know right away where the action is. When we hit a hot LZ, our Aviation Brigade people know about it very quickly. When somebody runs low of ammunition, we know it right away. . . . Thus, First Log . . . and our other commands have a very close and rapid feel for the basic situation."[21]

General Westmoreland himself steadily expanded USARV's responsibilities. The component command's headquarters at Long Binh constituted MACV's alternate combat operations center, for use if the Tan Son Nhut facility was put out of action. Westmoreland delegated to the component headquarters much of the administration and logistical support of Army field advisers and assigned to it as well as an ever-expanding role in assistance to Free World and South Vietnamese forces. At his direction, the USARV staff helped prepare MACV's operational contingency plans and did much work on force structure, base development, and the reception of newly arrived combat units. USARV also became involved in operations because of its responsibility for training Army troops, for instance in detecting and destroying Viet Cong booby traps.[22]

General Waters, the U.S. Army, Pacific, commander, as well as Generals Engler and Palmer, pressed for a formal expansion of USARV's charter, but with only limited success. After one of Waters' periodic visits to Saigon, Westmoreland complained: "He apparently feels that the Army component should become operational like the Air Force and Navy components." During 1966 Engler made his abortive bid to take over the Army advisory program. When he succeeded Engler in June of the following year, General Palmer strongly advocated that his headquarters be given full operational control over Army forces, including tactical command, thereby freeing Westmoreland to concentrate on joint matters and assistance to the South Vietnamese. Palmer's proposal may have reflected his experience in command of U.S. forces in the Dominican Republic in 1965, where he employed a separate Army tactical commander. MACV's existing command relationships, Palmer declared, were "not sound from either a joint or service point of view" and made it "extremely difficult to develop operational and support plans in any logical fashion." Palmer's views reflected those of General Johnson, who pressed unsuccessfully during early 1967 for transfer of Westmoreland's component responsibilities to a separate four-star field army commander. *(Chart 4)*[23]

Westmoreland refused to attempt any fundamental redistribution of responsibilities, claiming that such proposals reflected "a lack of understanding of the situation and the nature of the operations." At Palmer's request, he did grant the deputy commanding general, USARV, the right to prepare efficiency ratings for field force commanders and to review those for commanders at division level and below, tasks hitherto reserved respectively to the MACV and field force commanders. He also permitted Palmer to assign officers to brigade commands without veto by the divisions. These authorities, Palmer recalled, gave him "a little teeth" in dealing with the tactical headquarters. Nevertheless, the formal division between tactical and logistical commands in MACV's Army component remained, allowing the field forces and divisions, in Palmer's words, to "play both sides against the middle. Where they cannot get their way in the command channel, they simply go to the OPCON channel."[24]

General Westmoreland's retention of extensive Army command responsibilities involved him continually in Army service matters. He and Army Chief of Staff Johnson together managed the rotation of general officers in and out of MACV and its subordinate commands. Sometimes directly and sometimes through his deputies at USARV, the MACV commander negotiated continually with Johnson and the Army staff about a myriad of other details of Army administration, ranging

CHART 4—PACIFIC COMMAND RELATIONSHIPS, 1967

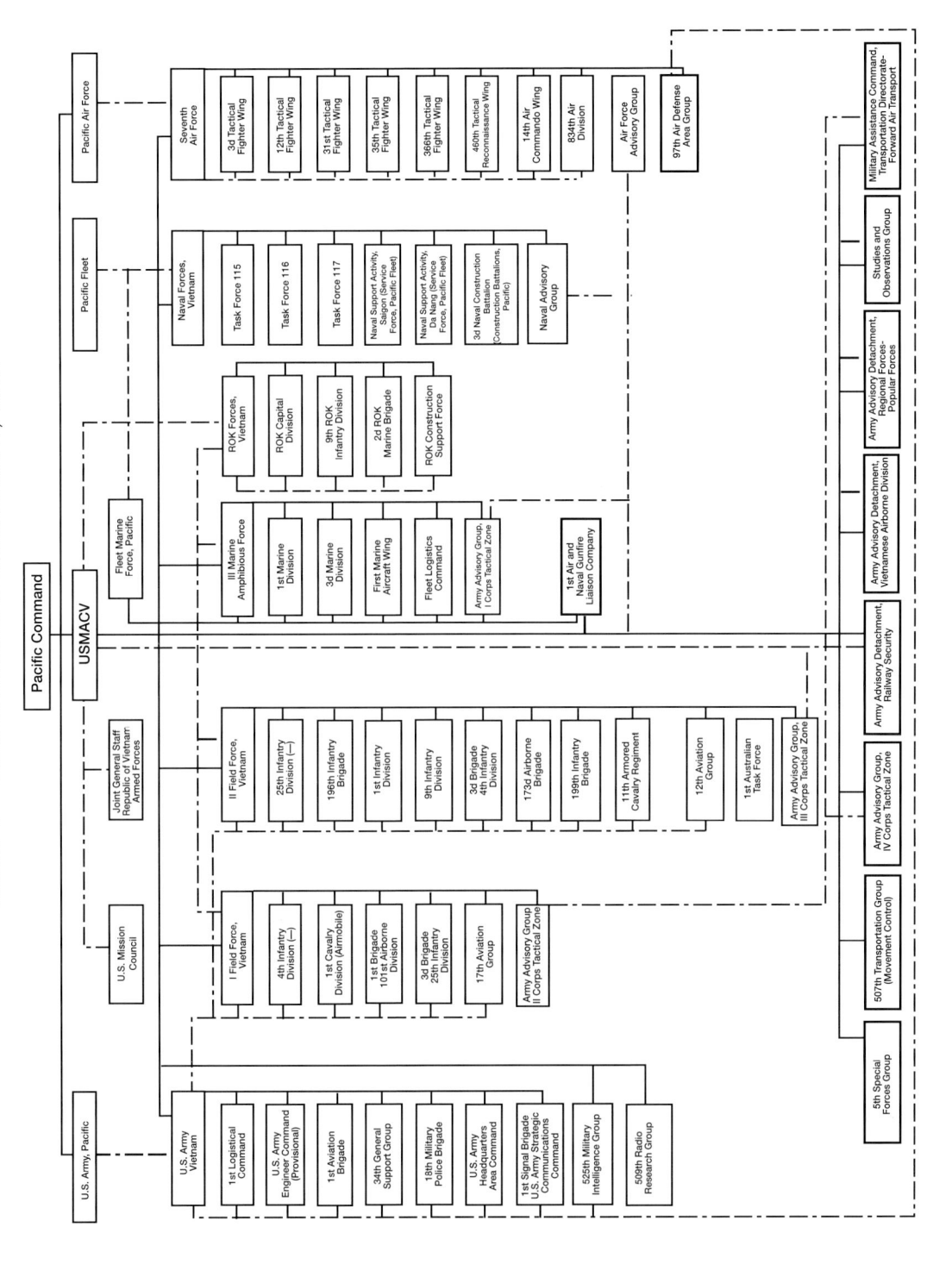

from the flow of replacements to reorganization and standardization of infantry battalions. General Johnson attempted to keep informed about affairs in Vietnam through regular visits and daily reading of the cable traffic, but his relations with Westmoreland, if amicable in tone, were strained by personality differences and by an underlying mutual distrust. More fundamentally, the interests of the two clashed since Westmoreland sought all possible reinforcements for his theater while Johnson tried to protect the Army's worldwide capabilities against the voracious demands of the war in Vietnam.[25]

Although less involved in the internal affairs of the other services, Westmoreland paid constant attention to their interests and sensitivities. He could hardly avoid doing so since the other service chiefs, like General Johnson, kept close watch over their forces in Vietnam. The Air Force and Marine chiefs were especially vigilant in protecting their prerogatives, at times to the point where they themselves seemed to be trying to command their components from Washington. In Vietnam, the component headquarters developed their own informal contacts with MACV to help defend their interests. Especially when major issues of command relations or roles and missions were involved, the components were quick to appeal MACV decisions to Honolulu and Washington through their service chains of command. To avoid such complications, MACV staff officers as a result frequently cleared even routine directives with the components. As the MACV Surgeon, Maj. Gen. Spurgeon H. Neel, recalled: "you had a unified commander there . . . but . . . he had to be sure that he didn't ruffle the feathers of the Army component, the Navy component, and the others." [26]

The Seventh Air Force: A Multiplicity of Masters

No interservice issues were more contentious than those related to command and control of air power. Air power, both fixed and rotary wing, profoundly affected the way in which the United States fought the war. The availability of airborne fire support, of air transport for troops and cargo, and of aerial reconnaissance permitted the Military Assistance Command to carry out otherwise impossible ground operations and to occupy and hold positions otherwise untenable. In addition, through most of the conflict, the United States relied almost exclusively on air power for offensive action against North Vietnam and for attacks on enemy bases and lines of communication in nominally neutral Laos and Cambodia.[27]

For his part, General Westmoreland viewed air power as a key element in his effort to defeat the Viet Cong and North Vietnamese. "Air capabilities . . . constitute the current difference between keeping the V. C. buildup under reasonable control," he avowed in June 1965, "and letting the enemy get away from us throughout most of the countryside."[28] In that light, his objectives with regard to air power were simple:

to obtain as much of it as possible for his operations in South Vietnam and to influence the air wars in Laos and North Vietnam so that they would have the maximum effect in reducing enemy reinforcement and supply of the Viet Cong.

The Military Assistance Command's position as a subtheater within CINCPAC's domain greatly complicated its efforts to evolve proper command and control arrangements for its air assets. The American armed forces during World War II and the Korean conflict had evolved the practice of centralizing control of air power at the theater level, normally under an Air Force general who served as both air component commander and deputy theater commander for air operations. In the Air Force view, which amounted to an article of faith within that service, theater air power could function at full efficiency and effectiveness only under such unified direction. Hence, any parceling-out of air elements to subordinate commands had to be avoided. Adhering to this principle, the commanders of Pacific Command's Air Force component, Pacific Air Forces (PACAF), successively Generals Jacob E. Smart and Hunter Harris, were concerned throughout the early years of the Vietnam War with keeping their forces unified and able to respond rapidly and flexibly to any contingency, including a theater-level conflict with the Soviet Union and Communist China. To that end, they worked to restrict the number of air units assigned to the Military Assistance Command and the size and status of MACV's subordinate Air Force headquarters. So effective were they that MACV's air component at the outset consisted only of the small advance echelon of the 2d Air Division (2d ADVON), which in turn was subordinate to the Philippines-based Thirteenth Air Force, the command through which PACAF directed its operations in Southeast Asia.[29]

As the war in Vietnam intensified and the role of American combat forces grew, Pacific Air Forces had to enlarge its command structure in South Vietnam and Thailand. In October 1962 the Air Force expanded the 2d ADVON into the 2d Air Division. At that point, the division's commander served two masters. As air component commander under COMUSMACV, he exercised operational control of Air Force units based in South Vietnam. Simultaneously, under direction of Thirteenth Air Force, he commanded the Air Force elements in Thailand and was to conduct operations in Laos and elsewhere in Southeast Asia, should the need arise.[30]

Further evolution occurred during 1964 and 1965, as the number of American aircraft in Southeast Asia increased and they began striking targets in Laos as well as the two Vietnams. Late in 1965 Air Force Chief of Staff John P. McConnell formally separated the 2d Air Division from the Thirteenth Air Force and placed the command directly under Pacific Air Forces for its functions in both South Vietnam and Thailand. The Air Force at the same time settled for half a loaf on the long-debated issue of whether Westmoreland's deputy should be an Air Force

MACV: The Years of Escalation, 1962–1967

General McConnell, portrayed as a lieutenant general
(Defense Visual Information Center photo)

officer by agreeing to designation of Maj. Gen. Joseph H. Moore, the 2d Air Division commander, as deputy to Westmoreland—but for air operations only. Air Force units in Thailand, in deference to diplomatic considerations, came under a deputy commander, Thirteenth Air Force who served simultaneously as deputy commander of the 2d Air Division. This arrangement maintained the formality of a separate American Air Force commander in Thailand; yet in practice General Moore, who delegated only logistical functions to his deputy, still could assign missions to all U.S. aircraft based in Southeast Asia. The arrangement also had the advantage, from PACAF's point of view, of keeping the Thai-based squadrons out from under the Military Assistance Command, Vietnam's control.[31]

The final stage in the evolution of MACV's Air Force component command quickly followed. As a tactical headquarters, the 2d Air Division lacked the staff to manage the large Air Force base development program in South Vietnam. By early 1966, its strength—nearly 1,000 aircraft and 30,000 men—had grown to that of a higher organizational unit, a numbered air force. Accordingly, with JCS approval, on 1 April

Controlling U.S. Forces

1966, General McConnell redesignated the division as the Seventh Air Force. Besides solving immediate organizational problems, the change, in McConnell's view, increased Air Force influence in the joint headquarters by elevating MACV's air component commander from a major general to a lieutenant general. The new air force's command relationships to MACV and PACAF were identical to those of the 2d Air Division, with the deputy commander of the Seventh Air Force retaining his dual position as Thirteenth Air Force deputy in Thailand. In that capacity, he kept Ambassador Graham Martin in Bangkok informed about Air Force operations from Thai bases and also served as principal Seventh Air Force liaison officer with the embassy in Vientiane, Laos.[32]

By the time the Seventh Air Force went into operation, Admiral Sharp had confirmed his intention to direct ROLLING THUNDER from Honolulu through his Air Force and Navy component commanders. His decision required the Seventh Air Force commander to serve several masters. In South Vietnam, General Moore and his successor, Lt. Gen. William W. Momyer, directed air operations as deputies and component commanders to General Westmoreland, although their authority over Navy, Marine, and Army aircraft, as well as the Strategic Air Command's B–52s, was limited. For the offensive against North Vietnam, the Seventh Air Force received its missions from Admiral Sharp through Pacific Air Forces and employed aircraft based in Thailand as well as South Vietnam in executing them. (Thailand-based aircraft, in deference to Thai political concerns, did not fly missions in South Vietnam but could be used in the North and in Laos.) The Seventh Air Force also provided aircraft for missions in Laos, some flown under Westmoreland's orders and others under direction of the American ambassador in Vientiane. Perhaps understating the case, a Seventh Air Force staff officer declared that "it became . . . fragmented and awkward for the Commander at Seventh Air Force to meet the requirements of these . . . different people who could tell him to do different things with a single set of forces."[33]

The Air War in the South: A Single Manager?

At the 20 April 1965 Honolulu conference, Secretary McNamara put the war in South Vietnam ahead of ROLLING THUNDER and strikes in Laos, where the allocation of American air power in Southeast Asia was concerned. General Westmoreland took maximum advantage of this decision to ensure lavish air support of his ground operations. His ever-escalating demands for sorties, which included periodic bids to control the squadrons based in Thailand and on the offshore carriers, irritated Admiral Sharp. The admiral believed that the air war against North Vietnam was of equal importance with that in the south and that Westmoreland's requirements for support of his command often exceeded the number of profitable targets. Sharp declared that Westmoreland always wanted to "get the absolute maximum of ordnance dropped on every objective he could find," including some targets "that could just barely be justified." Nevertheless, Westmoreland had the support of Secretary McNamara, who repeatedly reiterated his South Vietnam–first ruling—as much, Sharp suspected, to limit bombing of the north, about which the defense secretary had increasing doubts, as to ensure sufficient air power in the south. Sharp, however, did succeed in limiting Westmoreland's access to the aircraft in Thailand. He also kept the Seventh Fleet's carriers firmly under his own control, forcing Westmoreland to request Navy sorties through Sharp's headquarters.[34]

Although, in the Air Force view, the theater air component commander, under general guidance from the joint commander, needed the broadest possible authority and autonomy in conducting the air war, conditions in Vietnam never approached that ideal. Viewing air power as an implement in the ground campaign, General Westmoreland retained many important air command-and-control functions in his Army-dominated MACV staff. By so doing, he limited the purview and authority of his deputy for air operations. In September 1965, for example, he established a board under MACV to review air strike control procedures and rules of engagement, rejecting protests from General Moore that such a task properly belonged to the 2d Air Division. In the same way, Westmoreland entrusted the allocation of air sorties[35] among missions and corps areas to the Tactical Air Support Element (TASE) of the MACV Combat Operations Center, and he kept most target evaluation and selection for both fighter-bombers and B–52s a function of the MACV staff. The Seventh Air Force, which possessed extensive reconnaissance and intelligence capabilities, could nominate targets; but its suggestions had to compete for approval with those of the field forces, the Combined Intelligence Center, and other agencies. Air Force officers objected that these arrangements denied MACV the full benefit of their own technical and tactical expertise and shackled air power too closely to the requirements of ground commanders—conditions exacerbated by the continuing underrepresentation of their service in the MACV intelligence and operations directorates.[36]

Despite the tensions that arose because of Westmoreland's approach to air power, the general's relations with his air deputies were characterized more by cooperation than conflict, if only because MACV and the Seventh Air Force shared an interest in unified control of all air operations in Southeast Asia. Enhancing the effect was Westmoreland's high regard for Moore, an old friend, and for Momyer, Moore's successor. Commanders and staff officers of Pacific Air Forces and Seventh Air Force almost unanimously praised Westmoreland for his understanding and fairness. The Seventh Air Force commander regularly participated in the MACV commander's weekly headquarters strategy meetings. His staff and that of MACV gradually developed close cooperation, to the point where the air component headquarters eventually came to draft most MACV messages and position papers on air power questions.[37]

Unified control of air operations, however, proved to be an elusive goal. The Strategic Air Command, for example, kept its B–52s outside MACV's and Seventh Air Force's authority. General Westmoreland placed great value on the heavy bombers as a weapon for disrupting enemy base areas and troop concentrations and increasingly for providing close-in fire support to American and South Vietnamese ground forces in combat. Although SAC and the Air staff continued to question the effectiveness of the strikes, code-named Arc Light, and to object to diversion of a growing number of B–52s from their primary strategic mission, Westmoreland secured Defense Department approval of repeated increases in his monthly allocation of bomber sorties. By late 1967, the authorized B–52 sortie rate for Southeast Asia had reached 1,200 per month, flown by planes operating out of U Tapao in Thailand as well as from their main base on Guam. Along with more sorties, Westmoreland obtained greater freedom of action in their use. Whereas in 1965 each individual Arc Light mission required JCS, State and Defense Department, and White House approval, within a year the administration, at Westmoreland's urging, had delegated the responsibility to Admiral Sharp. Sharp in turn permitted Westmoreland, in consultation with the embassy in Saigon and the South Vietnamese government, to select all targets in South Vietnam.[38]

To the persistent displeasure of the Seventh Air Force, Westmoreland concentrated Arc Light targeting in his own headquarters. On recommendations from the field forces, the Seventh Air Force, and the targeting section of the Combined Intelligence Center, the MACV commander personally established the target list and set priorities. At the outset, target selection was largely a process of guesswork on the basis of very limited information. With the expansion of MACV's intelligence establishment, the process became more sophisticated. The multiservice staff of the Combined Intelligence Center assembled a weekly list of preplanned targets, using information from the entire range of sources available to MACV. CICV's list then underwent review and amendment by the J2 and other staff sections and final evaluation and approval by General Westmoreland. Combat units could also submit immediate Arc Light requests to MACV through the field forces for rapid review, clearance with the South Vietnamese, and transmission to the Strategic Air Command, which then either diverted missions in flight or launched planes kept on alert at Guam or U Tapao.[39]

While the B–52s were highly responsive to MACV's requirements, they remained under the operational control of the Strategic Air Command, exercised through the Guam-based Eighth Air Force. The Air Force refused to assign any of the bomber units to either Pacific Command or MACV on grounds that SAC, a specified command directly under the secretary of defense, must keep its planes under unified control, ready for instant reversion to their strategic nuclear mission.

General Momyer, center, receives his fourth star from Generals Westmoreland and Abrams. (Defense Visual Information Center photo)

Instead, SAC directed the Eighth Air Force to provide a fixed monthly number of sorties in support of MACV and maintained a small liaison group, the SAC Advance Echelon (ADVON), at MACV headquarters to expedite the processing of strike requests.

This arrangement was acceptable to General Westmoreland since it permitted the Military Assistance Command to select targets for the Arc Light strikes. However, when General Momyer took command of the Seventh Air Force in July 1966, he was less satisfied and launched a campaign to bring Arc Lght operations under the more direct control of his own headquarters. One of his sevice's leading exponents of tactical air power, Momyer believed that the B–52s, when used in a tactical role as they were in Vietnam, should be under the theater air component commander, who then could employ them as part of a unified pool of aircraft. He also was convinced that MACV, dominated as it was by ground officers, was using the strategic bombers uneconomically for strikes on targets of dubious validity and for missions that could be performed as effectively and more efficiently by fighter-bombers. Under the existing system, the Seventh Air Force, which possessed the expertise on proper B–52 use, was all but excluded from mission plan-

Controlling U.S. Forces

ning, relegated to escorting the Stratofortresses over Vietnam and coordinating their bombing runs with other tactical air activities.[40]

While he acknowledged MACV's final authority in B–52 targeting, General Momyer urged Westmoreland to transfer the details of mission planning and execution, along with the SAC Advance Echelon, from MACV to Seventh Air Force headquarters. However, he remained unable to overcome Westmoreland's determination to control B–52 targeting and Air Force opposition to any parceling out of SAC's airplanes. Momyer obtained only the formal attachment of the advance echelon to himself as deputy MACV commander for air operations, although in practice the echelon's members worked as part of the Seventh Air Force staff. General Westmoreland withheld from the advance echelon any role in planning strike requests. As a result, General Momyer acquired in the end simply a more effective liaison body for air traffic control of the Arc Light missions. Arc Light planning remained concentrated in the MACV staff for the rest of the joint command's existence.[41]

The debate within the Air Force over control of the B–52s paralleled a much more vehement interservice dispute about the air component commander's authority over Army, Navy, and Marine aircraft. On this question, which involved doctrinal convictions of near-religious intensity on all sides, the Air Force differed sharply with the other services. General Momyer, a dedicated and effective advocate of the Air Force position, summarized the controversy:

The flexibility of airpower and its capacity to concentrate large quantities of firepower in a short time make it a most desirable addition to an army or navy. As a consequence, these two forces have sought the division of airpower, placing it under their control when needed for their own mission.

Airmen, on the other hand, have argued that airpower is a decisive element of war in its own right and that the full effects of airpower can only be achieved when it is centrally controlled and directed against the most vital part of the enemy, whether that part be the industrial base or the military forces deployed to a theater of war. . . . Thus, for airpower to be employed for the greatest good of the combined forces in a theater of war, there must be a command structure to control the assigned airpower coherently and consistently and to ensure that the airpower is not frittered away by dividing it among army and navy commands.[42]

This issue, along with disputes over the airmobility concept, had embittered Army–Air Force relations during the early years of MACV's existence. However, by mid-1966, the two services had resolved their major differences, largely as the result of an unusual top-level agreement between their respective chiefs of staff, Generals Johnson and McConnell. Under this agreement, signed in April 1966, the Air Force in effect acknowledged the Army's complete control over its helicopters; the Army in return transferred its fixed-wing Caribous and other transports to the Air Force and promised not to procure or develop such aircraft in the future. In Vietnam, Army helicopters continued to operate under the control of field force and division commanders; reserves were parceled out by USARV under MACV's direction, exercised through the Army Aviation Division of the Combat Operations Center. To enhance coordination of airmobile maneuvers with artillery and air support, the Army and Air Force linked their separate aircraft control networks through a MACV Joint Air–Ground Operations System. These arrangements ended Army–Air Force feuding over air power in Vietnam. As a result, Army commanders, ultimately including Westmoreland, increasingly sided with Seventh Air Force in its efforts to secure control over the other services' fixed-wing aircraft.[43]

With the Army air issue settled and with the Navy carriers firmly under Admiral Sharp's control, the Marine Corps became the principal target of Westmoreland's air deputies. Marine Corps doctrine called for employment of aircraft as part of a unified air-ground team, under control of the amphibious force commander, with the primary mission of supporting marines in ground combat. During the Korean conflict, marines had seen their air-ground team broken up, with their air wing placed under operational control of the Fifth Air Force and employed wherever needed along the front. Recalling that arrangement, which marines believed had resulted in less responsive support to frontline troops, the leaders of the Corps were determined to maintain the integrity of their air-ground team in Vietnam.[44]

The marines had the backing of CINCPAC, who reserved to himself the right to establish policies and procedures for the conduct of tactical air support in South Vietnam, as elsewhere in his theater. In late 1963 Admiral Felt, Sharp's predecessor, had appointed a board of officers, representing all the services, to develop general principles for tactical air support in joint operations. The board was headed by Marine Brig. Gen. Keith B. McCutcheon, the PACOM assistant chief of staff for operations, who had been a leader since World War II in the development of the Corps' air support doctrine. It produced a document reflecting strong Marine Corps influence, laying down as a central principle that each service component of a joint force should retain command and control of its air element "in order to take maximum advantage of its organization, equipment, training, and uni-service doctrine." The joint force commander should exercise operational control of the different air elements through the component commanders, one of whom he was to designate as "coordinating authority"for tactical air support.[45] The designated coordinator, in consultation with the other component commanders, was to draw up joint operational procedures but was not to exercise anything resembling genuine command of the different air forces. Further reinforcing the Marine Corps position, the board stated that Marine forces in joint operations "normally will be employed as air-ground teams."[46]

In developing tactical support procedures for the growing American forces in Vietnam, Admiral Sharp followed the principles of the McCutcheon board. He did so in part because he shared the Marine view on the merits of the issue and also out of a desire to avoid interservice wrangling over air power doctrine. "My goal," he told General Westmoreland, "has been to establish procedures which satisfy operational requirements, while minimizing the interservice debate which has much newspaper appeal but little in the way of constructive suggestion." In accord with this approach, in March 1965 Sharp vetoed a proposal by Westmoreland to place the first Marine fighter-bomber squadron to arrive at Da Nang under operational control of General Moore as Air Force component commander. The following month, in a directive establishing policies and procedures for control of tactical air support throughout Pacific Command, Sharp declared that in South Vietnam close support of ground forces in contact with the enemy should have first priority in the allocation of air power and that authority to control strikes should be exercised at the level of command as close as possible to the action. He reiterated that MACV's air component commander should function as no more than a "coordinating authority" for tactical air support and air traffic control.[47]

After Admiral Sharp blocked his initial move to place the 1st Marine Aircraft Wing's fighter-bombers under the 2d Air Division, General Westmoreland in effect let the marines keep their own planes. The Military Assistance Command's basic air command and control directive, published in July 1965 and reissued with minor amendments the following year, provided that the commanding general of III MAF, in his role as what amounted to a component commander under MACV, would exercise operational control over the 1st Marine Aircraft Wing through the marines' tactical air control system. The wing's aircraft flew missions in support of the III MAF, which had first call upon them except in the direst emergencies. Under an agreement with 2d Air Division/Seventh Air Force, III MAF daily placed fixed-wing sorties in excess of those needed for its own operations at the disposal of MACV's air component commander for employment throughout the theater. In addition, III MAF committed itself to transfer certain of its fighter-bombers, HAWK missiles, and control facilities at Da Nang to the command of the Seventh Air Force, as MACV air defense coordinator, in the event of a North Vietnamese air attack. Westmoreland defined the functions of his air component commander in terms of "coordinating authority," with responsibility for air traffic control and for promoting cooperation among the different services' air forces, but no command over them.[48]

General Moore considered these arrangements wrong in both principle and practical effect. Under them, air power in South Vietnam was geographically divided between two separate control systems: a Marine one in I Corps and an Air Force one, which included the South Vietnamese Air Force, encompassing the rest of the country. In addition, the Seventh Air Force retained responsibility for supporting South Vietnamese and non-Marine U.S. ground units in I Corps, a circumstance that occasionally created confusion in requesting and directing tactical air power. Late in 1965, in connection with plans for deployment of additional Marine squadrons to South Vietnam, Moore reopened the issue with Westmoreland, who expressed unhappiness at having "three air forces in I Corps" and "alluded to the possibility" of putting the Marine squadrons under the operational control of the 2d Air Division.

Westmoreland commissioned his J3, General DePuy, to review the question of control of Marine air power. DePuy recommended against breaking up the Marine air-ground team and favored continuing the practice of having III MAF turn over its excess sorties to the 2d Air Division. The alternative, DePuy declared, "would be certain to arouse a violent and emotional opposition on the part of the Marines which would be registered at every echelon from here to the White House and I can not see that it would be worth the trouble." Accepting DePuy's reasoning, Westmoreland left the existing arrangement in place.[49]

General Moore and his successor, General Momyer, attempted repeatedly to obtain at least more Marine sorties for employment under their control, but to no avail. They did secure a proviso in MACV's air support directive allowing COMUSMACV, "in the event of a major emergency or disaster," to place all U.S. tactical air resources under the commander, Seventh Air Force; but until 1968 General Westmoreland did not see fit to exercise that authority. The marines, at both III MAF and FMFPAC headquarters, vigorously and in the main successfully resisted every Air Force encroachment on their air-ground team. Late in 1967, Lt. Gen. Victor H. Krulak, the FMFPAC commander, told his fellow Marine generals: "Today we have what we longed for in Korea. It is no accident. We have CINCPAC to thank for putting his foot down and saying, 'No, the Marines fight as a team. I will not see them broken up.' We have him to thank, plus the stubborn persuasion on him by a few Marines. Today we have our [air-ground] team in its classic sense and for the first time really in combat history."[50]

Through 1967, Westmoreland and Sharp took a pragmatic approach to the interservice conflicts over tactical air power. They tried, with considerable success, to accommodate differing service doctrines while still maintaining a unified air effort. In spite of rivalry and divisions of authority, the services in Vietnam managed to mesh their air control systems sufficiently to provide the Military Assistance Command with a powerful, flexible tactical air weapon. In I Corps, the Seventh Air Force and III MAF worked out techniques for effective cooperation, for example in so-called SLAM operations, concentrated strikes by B–52s and fighter-bombers against enemy troops and infiltration routes. Nevertheless, by the end of 1967, the issue of air command and control in III MAF's area of operations was coming up for reconsideration. Changing tactical circumstances in I Corps, combined with General Westmoreland's growing dissatisfaction with III MAF's overall conduct of the campaign in the north, were eventually to permit General Momyer to reopen the air command question.[51]

The Field Forces and the III Marine Amphibious Force

The tactical commands under MACV developed parallel to the service components. Westmoreland, Sharp, and the Joint Chiefs had settled upon the general features of the Army field force headquarters by mid-1965. The first such command, Field Force, Vietnam, essentially built around an Army corps headquarters, went into operation at Nha Trang on 25 September, after several months' existence as Task Force Alpha, initially controlling all U.S. ground forces in II Corps. In III Corps, the commander of the 1st Infantry Division, who reported directly to Westmoreland, directed American combat operations. On 15 March 1966, Westmoreland activated II Field Force, Vietnam, with headquarters at Bien Hoa and jurisdiction over American forces in III Corps. At the same time, the MACV commander redesignated Field Force, Vietnam, as I Field Force, Vietnam. As had been the case since the initial Marine landing at Da Nang, American ground operations in I Corps remained under the control of the III Marine Amphibious Force. In IV Corps, where no major American ground units were deployed, the corps senior adviser directed U.S. military activities.[52]

The lieutenant generals commanding the two field forces and III MAF all reported directly to General Westmoreland on operational matters and were under their service components, respectively USARV and FMFPAC, for administrative and logistical purposes. They exercised operational control over combat and support units attached to them and also over Army Special Forces detachments in their areas. They planned and executed American combat operations and coordinated activities with the South Vietnamese and Free World allied forces. As senior advisers to their counterpart ARVN corps commanders, they were Westmoreland's agents for directing Army advisory activities. When MACV took over pacification during 1967, they assumed extensive responsibilities in that field as well. The III MAF commander, due to the marines' air-ground organization, controlled as well his own fixed- and rotary-wing air force, with which he executed operations in I Corps and elsewhere at COMUSMACV's direction. In order to oversee varied, complex activities over extended territory, the field force staffs expanded to nearly 500 officers and enlisted men in I Field Force, over 1,000 in II Field Force, and more than 700 in III Marine Amphibious Force. Even with these resources, and with deputy commanders, which they acquired in 1967, the field force commanders found themselves stretched to the limit by their many responsibilities. One declared flatly that at his level "the span of control was unmanageable," requiring him to "operate by exception and . . . only . . . on crises."[53]

Acting in effect as his own field army commander, General Westmoreland closely supervised and guided his corps-area subordinates. Besides issuing yearly and six-month campaign plans and formal letters of instruction on particular subjects, Westmoreland assembled his field commanders, along with those of the service components and often representatives of other American agencies and the allied forces, for periodic conferences. Invariably held outside Saigon, most frequently at Nha Trang or Cam Ranh Bay, these meetings provided a forum for policy guidance by Westmoreland and for briefings by the field commanders on their operations, successes, and problems. They also included occasional presentations by the ambassador and other mission officials on non-military aspects of the conflict. Westmoreland valued these meetings as opportunities for widely separated commanders to exchange information and ideas and for himself to emphasize problems or issues of current importance. At least in bringing the commanders together, the meetings seem to have served their purpose. A commander of I Field Force commented: "Hell, I never left II Corps. If we didn't have those meetings, I would never have seen anybody."[54]

Formal plans and conferences, however, were not the primary means by which Westmoreland guided the day-to-day course of operations. The few combat units available, especially during 1965 and 1966, required careful allocation to keep maximum pressure on the enemy and to counter his initiatives. The field force headquarters were slow to acquire essential staff personnel and to develop their full operational capabilities. Even when they did, they lacked MACV's access to the most reliable and sensitive sources of intelligence. Hence, Westmoreland sometimes had no alternative but to exercise close personal direction over operational planning and over deployment of units as small as battalions.[55]

He did so largely through regular visits, at least once a month and more often during crisis periods, to field force, division, and brigade headquarters. Westmoreland went to the commanders rather than summoning them to Saigon, he later explained, to keep the field generals alert and because tactical decisions were best made on the spot where he could get the "feel" of the situation and obtain the most complete, up-to-date information. Normally traveling with his combat operations center chief and a few aides, Westmoreland typically received briefings from the host commander and his staff on the military situation and on current and projected operations. He then commented and issued instructions. To confirm the decisions reached, Westmoreland, using a practice he claimed that he copied from General J. Lawton Collins in World War II, had the field force or division commander send him a message summarizing the results of the meeting, to be checked against a similar record prepared by his own staff officers.[56]

With the Army field forces, which were subordinate to him in both his MACV and component capacities, Westmoreland maintained a generally harmonious working relationship; but he had continual difficulty imposing his will upon his third, and in some respects most important, regional command, the III Marine Amphibious Force. The III MAF functioned under the close supervision of FMFPAC and Marine Corps headquarters, to which it reported in detail on operational matters as well as on the administrative and logistical concerns proper to a component command. The FMFPAC commander, General Krulak, who had been involved in counterinsurgency in various capacities since the Kennedy administration, had strong views on ground strategy in Vietnam that he vigorously promoted to his immediate superior, Admiral Sharp. According to General Johnson, Marine Corps Commandant Greene "made a call once or twice a day from his own headquarters in Washington to Da Nang . . . , and always had up-to-date information on what was going on by phone at any meeting of the JCS that we both attended." Westmoreland confided to his diary late in 1965: "I detect a tendency for the Marine chain of command to try to unduly influence the tactical conduct of III MAF which is under my operational control."[57]

General Walt
(Time Life Pictures/Getty Images)

The III MAF was at odds with MACV and the other services on a number of matters. The marines' retention of their own air arm kept them perpetually in contention with the Seventh Air Force. The I Field Force and III MAF during 1966 had repeated difficulty coordinating operations along their mutual boundary, in part due to poor personal relations between Generals Larsen and Walt. Both in their military operations and in their pacification efforts, the marines at times infringed on the prerogatives of South Vietnamese authorities in I Corps, resulting in Vietnamese complaints to the U.S. Mission and MACV. More substantively, MACV and III MAF disagreed, at least in emphasis and priorities, on how best to conduct the ground war. Strongly convinced of the importance of winning the struggle for the allegiance of the rural population, the marines were more inclined than Westmoreland and his Army commanders to commit their American battalions to territorial defense and security as opposed to mobile operations against the North Vietnamese and Viet Cong main forces. The marines developed their approach almost entirely through their own chain of command, without review of its potential costs and policy implications by the embassy, MACV, or the State and Defense Departments. In Westmoreland's view, they were unresponsive to his efforts to modify their tactics. Westmoreland criticized the marines' overcentralization of control of their helicopters; he pressed Walt, Krulak, and Greene in vain to reorganize Marine units so as to make what he considered would be more efficient use of their available manpower; and he became increasingly dissatisfied with the quality of III MAF's operational planning.[58]

Public relations were another source of irritation. The marines aggressively publicized their own activities in contravention of MACV's policy of maintaining a unified military information program—an offense of which the other services also were guilty to one degree or another. In part to restrain such Marine activities, Westmoreland in October 1965 established a jointly staffed MACV information center in Da Nang. The marines, however, quickly transformed the center into what amounted to their own public affairs office. Word of Army-Marine disagreements reached the press, provoking strongly worded directives from General Wheeler that Sharp, Westmoreland, and their component commanders stop their subordinates' public airing of interservice disputes. The commanders in Vietnam promised stern action against violators while insisting on the innocence of their own people, but the leaks and news stories kept coming.[59]

In the belief that "it is in the best interest of this command to avoid any inter-service conflicts," Westmoreland relied on diplomacy more than command authority to move III MAF in the directions he desired. He tactfully tried to dissuade General Greene from intervening in the affairs of his command and succeeded in maintaining cordial relations with the strong-willed commandant. He also lost no time in courting Greene's successor, General Leonard D. Chapman. At the end of General Walt's tour as commander of III MAF in May 1967, Westmoreland made a point of flying to Da Nang for the change of command ceremony, at which he presented Walt with a decoration and publicly praised his service in Vietnam.[60]

Westmoreland attempted to guide III MAF's operations through the same mixture of formal directives and personal visits that he used with the two field forces. To improve Marine planning, he directed III MAF to conduct numerous studies and war games and reviewed and at times criticized the results. He also required the marines to plan for specific operations against enemy main force units and base areas in an effort to reduce what he thought was their excessive defensive-mindedness. Marine commanders, however, never fully accepted Westmoreland's concept of how to fight the war and continued as much as possible to adhere to their own. Even after Lt. Gen. Robert E. Cushman replaced Walt at the head of III MAF, Westmoreland in turn remained dissatisfied with the methods and policies of the amphibious force headquarters and increasingly doubted its competence to direct the expanding and increasingly violent battle for I Corps. By late 1967, the development of large-scale fighting along the Demilitarized Zone, and the need to reinforce III MAF with growing numbers of Army troops were rapidly bringing to a head issues of both ground and air command in the northernmost military region.[61]

Notes

[1] For examples of Sharp's intervention in South Vietnam, see Sharp, "Reminiscences," pp. 203–04, 261–62, 308–10, 326–27. MACV Command History, 1967, 1: 310–16, 350–51. Msgs, Sharp to Westmoreland, 9 Apr 66, 26 Aug 67, 29 Oct 67, 4 Nov 67, and 19 Dec 67; Westmoreland MAC 12505 to Sharp, 22 Dec 67; Sharp to Amb Sullivan, 17 Feb 67. All in Westmoreland Msg Files, 1966–1967, CMH. Westmoreland Hist Briefings, 17 Aug 66 and 4 Jan 67, tab C, Westmoreland Hist File 8 (17 Jul–17 Sep 66) and tab C, Westmoreland Hist File 12 (13 Dec 66–26 Jan 67). Both in CMH.

[2] Aide Memoir for Use by the CMC in Discussion with CINCPAC . . . , box 2, Victor H. Krulak Papers, MCHC.

[3] Quote is from Gen Johnson Interv, 20 Nov 70, pp. 15–17. Westmoreland, *A Soldier Reports*, pp. 189–92. Msgs, Wheeler JCS 6313–66 to Westmoreland and Sharp, 15 Oct 66; Lt Gen George S. Brown, USAF, JCS 7472–67 to Sharp and Westmoreland, 9 Sep 67. Both in Westmoreland Msg Files, 1 Oct–31 Dec 66, 1 Jul–30 Sep 67, CMH. Westmoreland describes his acquaintanceship with President Johnson in Interv, Lyndon B. Johnson Library with William C. Westmoreland, 8 Feb 69, LBJL.

[4] Westmoreland, *A Soldier Reports*, pp. 76, 261–62; Westmoreland Interv, 8 Feb 69, sec. 1, p. 14; Rosson Interv, 1981, pp. 334–35; Peers Interv, 26 Jan and 12–15 Apr 77, sec. 3, p. 36. Ltr, Westmoreland to Lt Gen Leonard D. Heaton, 28 Jan 67, Westmoreland Sig File, Jan 67, CMH; in same file, see Ltr, Heaton to Westmoreland, 10 Jan 67. Msg, Sharp to Wheeler, 26 May 67, Westmoreland Msg Files, Apr–Jun 67. The relationship between Sharp, Westmoreland, and Wheeler can be followed through the Westmoreland Msg Files, 1966–1967.

[5] For examples of coordination, see Msgs, Westmoreland MAC 5690, MAC 8757, MAC 6052 to Sharp, 7 Jul 66, 7 Oct 66, 27 Jun 67; Sharp to Westmoreland, 7 Oct 66, 20 Jan 67, 12 Oct 67; Wheeler JCS 6428–66, JCS 1691–67 to Westmoreland, 20 Oct 66, 6 Mar 67; Wheeler JCS 6200–67 to Sharp and Westmoreland, 3 Aug 67. All in Westmoreland Msg Files, 1966–1967, CMH. Westmoreland Hist Notes, 13–28 Nov 67, tab A, Westmoreland Hist File 25 (13–28 Nov 67), CMH. Wheeler's avoidance of split JCS recommendations is commented on in Palmer, *25-Year War*, pp. 34–35.

[6] MACV Command History, 1965, pp. 54–56, 99–100; Shulimson and Johnson, *Marines in Vietnam, 1965*, p. 36; Staff Study, Ch, NAVADVGRP, MACV, sub: An Examination of the Naval Component Commander Requirement for the Military Assistance Command, Vietnam, (hereafter cited as Naval Component Commander Requirement) 5 Jan 66, pp. 9–13, COMNAVFORV Plans Files, 1966 Da Nang Conference Folder, box 471, COMNAVFORV Records, Naval Historical Center (NHC), Washington, D.C.

[7] Ch, NAVADVGRP, MACV, Naval Component Commander Requirement, 5 Jan 66, pp. 11, 14, 17–18; Memo, 51 for 05, 12 Feb 66, sub: Report of Field Trip to NCC Staff, Da Nang. Both in COMNAVFORV Plans Files, 1966 Da Nang Conference Folder, box 471, COMNAVFORV Records, NHC. Msg, Rear Adm N. G. Ward to Rear Adm Thomas F. Connolly, 11 Aug 65, Rear Adm N. G. Ward's Personal Msg Files, 1965, box 108, COMNAVFORV Records, NHC.

[8] MACV Command History, 1965, p. 100. Westmoreland Hist Notes, 25 Sep–3 Oct 65, in Westmoreland Hist File 1 (29 Aug–24 Oct 65), CMH. Msg, Westmoreland MAC 32718 to Adm McDonald, 17 Sep 65, Rear Adm Ward's Personal Msg File, 1965, box 108, COMNAVFORV Records, NHC.

[9] Ch, NAVADVGRP, MACV, Naval Component Commander Requirement, 5 Jan 66, pp. 18–21, COMNAVFORV Plans Files, 1966 Da Nang Conf Folder, box 471, COMNAVFORV Records, NHC. Staff Study, NAVADVGRP Dec 65, sub: Requirements for a Naval

MACV: The Years of Escalation, 1962–1967

Component Commander under COMUSMACV; Ch, NAVADVGRP, MACV, Naval Component Commander Requirement, 8 Jan 66. Both in Vietnam Command Files, NHC.

[10] Msg, Westmoreland MAC 0185 to Sharp, 9 Jan 66, Westmoreland Msg Files, 1 Jan–31 Mar 66, CMH. Westmoreland Hist Notes, 9 Jan 66, tab D, Westmoreland Hist File 3 (20 Dec 65–29 Jan 66), CMH. Memo, 51 for 05, sub: Report of Field Trip to NCC Staff, Da Nang, 12 Feb 66; Memo, Ch, NAVADVGRP, sub: Assignment of Tasks to COMNAVFORV and CG III MAF, 28 Mar 66. Both in 1966 Da Nang Conference (Conf) Folder, box 471, COMNAVFORV Records, NHC. Msg, CNO to CINCPACFLT, 072103Z Mar 66, Buildup of Forces Folder, NAVFORV Ops Files (7), box 432, COMNAVFORV Records, NHC.

[11] Westmoreland Hist Notes, 3 Apr 66, tab C, Westmoreland Hist File 5 (13 Mar–23 Apr 66), CMH. Memo, Ch, NAVADVGRP, sub: Assignment of Tasks to COMNAVFORV and CG III MAF, 28 Mar 66, 1966 Da Nang Conf Folder, box 471; Memo, Ch, NAVADVGRP for MACJ02, sub: Assignment of Tasks to COMNAVFORV, 7 Apr 66, box 558; Memo, Cdr J. P. Iredale for N–5, N–3, 0–2, 15 Mar 68, box 471. All in COMNAVFORV Records, NHC. MACV Command History, 1967, pp. 126–28.

[12] MACV Command History, 1966, pp. 240–42; Chronology, 1 Jan–30 Jun 66, tab D–5, Westmoreland Hist File 7 (29 May–16 Jul 66), CMH.

[13] Eckhardt, *Command and Control*, pp. 78–80. Msg, CINCPACFLT to COMNAVFORV, 22 Oct 66, Command Relations Folder; Memo, Brig Gen A. R. Brownfield for CofS, sub: U.S. Command Relationships, IV CTZ; Memo, Capt J. D. Eaton for COMNAVFORV et al., 24 Mar 68, sub: U.S. Command Relations, IV CTZ; Memo, COMNAVFORV for ACofS J3 MACV, sub: U.S. Command Relations, IV CTZ, 31 Mar 68. All in box 471, COMNAVFORV Records, NHC. Msg, COMNAVFORV to CINCPACFLT, 21 Aug 68, box 477, COMNAVFORV Records, NHC.

[14] For doctrinal issues of command of the SLF, which arose between III MAF and Pacific Fleet as well as between the fleet and MACV, see Shulimson, *Marines in Vietnam, 1966*, pp. 297–99.

[15] MACV Command History, 1966, pp. 415–20; Shulimson, *Marines in Vietnam, 1966*, pp. 300–304; Jones Interv, pp. 8–12, MCHC; Westmoreland Hist Notes, 27 Mar 66, tab B, Westmoreland Hist File (13 Mar–23 Apr 66), CMH. Quote is from Msg, Westmoreland MAC 00196 to Sharp, 5 Jan 68, tab A–13, Westmoreland Hist File 28 (27 Dec 67–31 Jan 68), CMH.

[16] MACV Command History, 1965, p. 96.

[17] Eckhardt, *Command and Control*, pp. 49–50; MACV Command History, 1965, pp. 96–97. Quote is from Msg, Westmoreland MAC 3307 to Gen Johnson, 29 Jun 65; see also Msgs, Westmoreland MAC 1724 to Johnson, 30 Mar 65; and Westmoreland MAC 5387 to Wheeler, 29 Oct 65. All in Westmoreland Msg Files, 1 Jan–31 Mar 65, 1 Apr–30 Jun 65, and 1 Oct–31 Dec 65. See also Rosson Interv, 1981, pp. 346–47.

[18] Interv, Senior Officers Oral History Program with Lt Gen Jean E. Engler, 1981, pp. 244–45, MHI. MACV Command History, 1965, pp. 105–06. MS, Joel Meyerson, "Logistics in the Buildup," 1989, pp. 2–3, CMH. Eckhardt, *Command and Control*, pp. 44–45.

[19] MACV Command History, 1965, p. 97; ibid., 1967, pp. 125–26, 128–29; Engler Interv, 1981, pp. 218, 242, MHI; Westmoreland Hist Notes, 7 Nov 65, tab C, Westmoreland Hist File 2 (25 Oct–20 Dec 65), CMH. Interv, Senior Officers Debriefing Program with Lt Gen Stanley R. Larsen, 1977, sec. 8, pp. 1–2, MHI.

[20] These precedents are cited in Eckhardt, *Command and Control*, pp. 51–52. Army doctrine as of 1965 is summarized in MS, Maj Steve E. Dietrich, "Corps-Level Command-and-Control in an Unconventional Conflict: U.S. Army Field Forces in Vietnam," Military Studies Branch, CMH, 1989, ch. 2, p. 3, CMH files.

[21] Ltr, Lt Gen Bruce Palmer, Jr., to Gen Johnson, 14 Nov 67, Close Hold Misc File,

H. K. Johnson Papers, MHI. Quote is from Exit Interv, Historical Section, USARV, with Lt Gen Bruce Palmer, Jr., 7 and 10 Jun 68, in Interv, Senior Officers Debriefing Program with Gen Bruce Palmer, Jr., 1975, p. 258, MHI; see also pp. 261–63, 240, 280. Interv, Senior Officers Debriefing Program with Lt Gen Jonathan O. Seaman, 1971–1972, sec. 5, pp. 27–28, MHI.

[22] Ltr, Palmer to Gen Johnson, 14 Nov 67, Close Hold Misc File, H. K. Johnson Papers, MHI. Msg, COMUSMACV MAC 27658 to DCG USARV, 19 Aug 67, Command Relations Folder, box 471, COMNAVFORV Records, NHC. See also 9th Division's Move to the Delta Folder, box 477, COMNAVFORV Records, NHC. Palmer Interv, 7 and 10 Jun 68, pp. 250, 252; Palmer Interv, 1975, pp. 225–26. Memo, Westmoreland for DCG USARV, 24 Jun 67, sub: Establishment of Mine and Booby Trap Confidence Courses, Westmoreland Sig File, Jun 67, CMH.

[23] First quote is from Westmoreland Hist Notes, 20 Mar 66, tab A, Westmoreland Hist File 5 (13 Mar–23 Apr 66), CMH. Second is from Ltr, Palmer to Gen Johnson, 14 Nov 67, Close Hold Misc File, H. K. Johnson Papers, MHI. Palmer, *25-Year War*, pp. 31–32, 49; Palmer Interv, 7 and 10 Jun 68, pp. 258–59. General Bruce Palmer, Jr., *Intervention in the Caribbean: The Dominican Crisis of 1965* (Lexington: University Press of Kentucky, 1989), p. 155. Other Army generals had varying views on this subject; see for example Seaman Interv, 1971–72, sec. 5, p. 33; and Rosson Interv, 1981, pp. 346–47.

[24] First quote is from Westmoreland Hist Notes, 20 Mar 66, tab A, Westmoreland Hist File 5 (13 Mar–23 Apr 66), CMH. Second is from Palmer Interv, 1975, p. 511; see also pp. 221–22. Third is from Palmer Interv, 7 and 10 Jun 68, pp. 258–59; see also pp. 257–58, 260. Ltr, Palmer to Gen Johnson, 14 Nov 67, Close Hold Misc File, H. K. Johnson Papers, MHI. Memos, Palmer for Westmoreland, 25 Jun 67, sub: Role of USARV, and sub: Efficiency Report Chain, 25 Jun 67; Memo, Westmoreland for Palmer, sub: Role of USARV, 30 Jun 67. All in Westmoreland Sig File, Jun 67, CMH.

[25] Westmoreland's dealings with General Johnson can be followed in the Westmoreland Message Files and Historical Files for the 1965–1968 period. Johnson describes his efforts to keep abreast of Vietnam developments in his Interv, 27 Jan 72–30 Oct 74, sec. 13, pp. 31–32, and sec. 14, pp. 6–7. For the relationship between Johnson and Westmoreland, see Interv, Charles B. MacDonald and Charles von Luttichau with Gen Harold K. Johnson, McLean, Va., 20 Nov 70, p. 21, CMH; MacDonald-Westmoreland Interv, 12 Mar 73; and Palmer Interv, 1975, p. 204. Both in CMH.

[26] Quote is from Interv, Senior Officers Oral History Program with Maj Gen Spurgeon H. Neel, Jr., 1985, p. 172, MHI. H. K. Johnson Interv, 20 Nov 70, pp. 42–45. Memo, Cdr J. P. Iredale for Force Plans Officer, sub: U.S. Command Relations, IV CTZ, 31 Mar 68, box 471, COMNAVFORV Records, NHC, indicates the complex informal relationships that developed between service component and MACV staffs.

[27] The overall impact of air power on the Vietnam conflict is surveyed in Donald J. Mrozek, *Airpower and the Ground War in Vietnam* (Washington, D.C.: Pergamon–Brassey's, 1989).

[28] Msg, Westmoreland MAC 3052 to Sharp, 11 Jun 65, Westmoreland Msg Files, 1 Apr–30 Jun 65, CMH.

[29] Momyer, *Airpower in Three Wars*, pp. 70–71; see ch. 2 in this volume for an overview of the evolution of U.S. command and control of tactical air power. Schlight, *Years of the Offensive*, pp. 31–32.

[30] Momyer, *Airpower in Three Wars*, pp. 71–73. See also ch. 2, pp. 42–44 in this volume for the command rearrangements of October 1962.

[31] Momyer, *Airpower in Three Wars*, pp. 80–83. Interv, Project Corona Harvest with Maj Gen Gilbert L. Meyers, USAF, 27 May 70, pp. 51–54. AFCHO.

[32] Momyer, *Airpower in Three Wars*, pp. 80, 83–84. Schlight, *Years of the Offensive*,

pp. 129–30. Interv, Project Corona Harvest with Gen John P. McConnell, USAF, 4 Nov 70, pp. 6–7. AFCHO.

[33] Air command is summarized in Sharp and Westmoreland, *Report on War*, pp. 101–03. Quote is from Interv, Project Corona Harvest with Maj Gen Gordon F. Blood, USAF, 6 Apr 70, p. 25, AFCHO.

[34] Schlight, *Years of the Offensive*, pp. 32–33, 54. Quote is from Sharp, "Reminiscences," pp. 369–70; see also pp. 310–32, 360–62, 636–37. Msgs, Sharp to Westmoreland, 24, 27 Jul 66; Sharp to Wheeler, 13 Apr 66; Wheeler JCS 9682–67 to Westmoreland, 10 Nov 67. All in Westmoreland Msg Files, 1965–1967, CMH. Msgs, Wheeler JCS 8297 to Sharp and Westmoreland, 12 Apr 66, tab E–2; Westmoreland MAC 12815 to Wheeler and Sharp, 13 Apr 66, tab E–5; Wheeler JCS 8463 to Westmoreland and Sharp, 14 Apr 66, tab E–7; Westmoreland Hist File 5 (13 Mar–23 Apr 66), CMH. MACV Command History, 1966, pp. 394, 398–99.

[35] A sortie consists of one mission by one aircraft.

[36] Schlight, *Years of the Offensive*, pp. 126–27. MACV Command History, 1965, pp. 188–90. Westmoreland Hist Notes, 5–11 Sep 65, 15 Sep 65, and 5 Oct 65; Memo, MACV for Distribution, 10 Sep 65, sub: Joint Board to Study Tactical Air Firepower. Both in Westmoreland Hist File 1 (29 Aug–24 Oct 65), CMH; in same file, see tabs C–2 and H–4. Muggleberg Interv, 1985, pp. 25–26, 28; Memo, Joint Coordinator, Ofc, Dep CofS (Plans and Programs) for CofS [HQMC], sub: Trip Report to WestPac, tab A, in HQMC Staff Visit WestPac, Nov–Dec 65, MCHC Archives; Meyers Interv, 27 May 70, pp. 49–51; Blood Interv, 6 Apr 70, pp. 22–24.

[37] Momyer, *Airpower in Three Wars*, p. 293. Westmoreland's views of his air commanders are in: Westmoreland Hist Briefing, 3 Jul 66, tab D, Westmoreland Hist File 7 (29 May–16 Jul 66), CMH. Msg, Westmoreland MAC 6073 to Gen McConnell, 18 Jul 66, Westmoreland Msg Files, 1 Jul–30 Sep 66, CMH; and MacDonald-Westmoreland Interv, 18 Jun 73. For typical Air Force praise of Westmoreland, see McConnell Interv, 4 Nov 70, p. 7. Interv, Project Corona Harvest with Gen George S. Brown, USAF, 19–20 Oct 70, pp. 10–11, AFCHO, and Interv, Project Corona Harvest with Lt Gen David C. Jones, USAF, 4–6 May 69, pp. 6–8, AFCHO.

[38] Schlight, *Years of the Offensive*, pp. 82–83, 148, 150–54, 256–58; MACV Command History, 1965, pp. 192–99; ibid., 1966, pp. 400–401; Msg, COMUSMACV MAC 35970 to CINCPAC, 1 Nov 67, Westmoreland Sig File, 1967, CMH. MacDonald-Westmoreland Interv, 28 Jan 73, CMH.

[39] Momyer, *Airpower in Three Wars*, p. 283; Ltr, Westmoreland to Lt Gen J. C. Meyer, USAF, 15 Aug 67, COMUSMACV Sig File, 1967, CMH. Parry, *Three-War Marine*, pp. 266–67. Sharp and Westmoreland, *Report on War*, p. 126. Intervs, Project Corona Harvest with Gen Hunter Harris, USAF, 22 Apr 71, pp. 33–34; with Maj Altha M. Stewart, USAF, and with Adm Ulysses S. Grant Sharp, 19 Feb 71, pp. 4–6. All in AFCHO.

[40] Schlight, *Years of the Offensive*, pp. 148–49. Momyer, *Airpower in Three Wars*, pp. 99–101. MACV Command History, 1965, p. 193.

[41] Schlight, *Years of the Offensive*, pp. 149–50. Momyer, *Airpower in Three Wars*, pp. 101–04. Westmoreland Hist Briefing, 13 Dec 66, tab D, Westmoreland Hist File 11 (30 Oct–12 Dec 66); Msg, Westmoreland MAC 11160 to Sharp, 23 Dec 66, Westmoreland Msg Files, 1 Oct–31 Dec 66. Both in CMH.

[42] Momyer, *Airpower in Three Wars*, p. 39. General Momyer had participated in the early development of Air Force tactical air support doctrine as a fighter group commander in North Africa in World War II. Thereafter, against the tide of Air Force emphasis on strategic nuclear warfare, Momyer, in various command and senior staff positions, continued as a proponent of tactical air power within his service. His career is outlined in Schlight, *Years of the Offensive*, p. 139.

[43] The Johnson-McConnell agreement is recounted in Schlight, *Years of the Offensive*, pp. 122–25; and in Tolson, *Airmobility*, pp. 104–08. Text of the agreement is in Msg, Johnson WDC 4210 to Westmoreland and Waters, 6 Apr 66, Westmoreland Msg Files, 1 Apr–30 Jun 66, CMH. For control of Army helicopters, see HQ MACV Directive (Dir) 95-4, 28 Jun 66, ann. C, copy in III MAF Command Relations Files, MCHC.

[44] Air command relations in Korea are summarized in Momyer, *Airpower in Three Wars*, pp. 59–62. The marines' determination not to repeat the Korean experience is noted in Shulimson and Johnson, *Marines in Vietnam, 1965*, p. 151. Schlight, *Years of the Offensive*, pp. 110–11, succinctly summarizes the Marine Corps–Air Force argument over control of air power.

[45] The Joint Chiefs of Staff defined "coordinating authority" as "a commander or individual assigned responsibility for coordinating specific functions or activities involving forces of two or more services, or two or more forces of the same service. He has the authority to require consultation between the agencies involved but does not have the authority to compel agreement. In the event he is unable to obtain essential agreement he shall refer the matter to the appointing authority." JCS Pub. 1, *Dictionary of US Military Terms for Joint Usage*, July 1962, p. 57.

[46] HQ CINCPAC, Report of the CINCPAC Tactical Air Support Procedures Board, 18 Dec 63, box 14, Keith B. McCutcheon Papers, pp. 1–2 and app. H, p. 7, MCHC. In same collection, box 13, see Ltrs, McCutcheon to Col E. E. Anderson, USMC, 18 Dec 63, and to Brig Gen G. S. Bowman, USMC, 23 Jan 64. Neither Felt nor Sharp adopted this report in its entirety, but they incorporated its recommendations in other directives. Brig Gen Keith B. McCutcheon, "Marine Aviation in Vietnam," in *The Marines in Vietnam, 1954–1973: An Anthology and Annotated Bibliography* (Washington, D.C.: History and Museums Div, HQMC, 1974), p. 175.

[47] Quote is from Msg, Sharp to Westmoreland, info Wheeler, McConnell, Chapman, and Krulak, 18 Jan 68, Westmoreland Msg Files, 1–31 Jan 68, CMH. Msgs, COMUSMACV MAC 9775 to CINCPAC, 28 Mar 65; CINCPAC to COMUSMACV, 29 Mar 65 and 24 Apr 65. Both in CINCPAC Msg Files, NHC. Sharp Interv, 19 Feb 71, p. 19; Sharp, "Reminiscences," pp. 638–40.

[48] MACV Dir 95-4, 28 Jun 66, copy in III MAF Command Relations File, MCHC Archives; Memo, Westmoreland for Moore, 25 Aug 65 sub: TOR, Deputy for Air Operations, HQ U.S. MACV, copy in box 14, McCutcheon Papers, MCHC; 1st MAW Operations Order (OpOrd) 303-65, 15 Jul 65, in app. 3, 1st MAW Command Chronology, MCHC Archives; in same document, see pt. 3, sec. 11. Shulimson and Johnson, *Marines in Vietnam, 1965*, p. 152.

[49] Westmoreland quotes are from his Historical Notes, 28 Dec 65, tab B, Westmoreland Hist File 3 (20 Dec 65–29 Jan 66), CMH; see also tab C in same file. MacDonald-Westmoreland Interv, 7 May 73. Memo, DePuy for Westmoreland, 3 Mar 66, sub: Tactical Air Control, 1966 R–Z Folder, DePuy Papers, MHI. For the Air Force view, see Momyer, *Airpower in Three Wars*, pp. 81–82; and Schlight, *Years of the Offensive*, pp. 108–10.

[50] Msg, Westmoreland to Sharp, 9 Apr 66, Westmoreland Msg File, 1 Apr–30 Jun 66; Westmoreland Historical Briefing, 13 Dec 66, tab D. Westmoreland Hist File 11 (30 Oct–12 Dec 66), CMH. Emergency provision is in MACV Dir 95-4, 28 Jun 66, par. 3.e., in III MAF Command Relations File, MCHC Archives. Interv, USMC Oral History Program with Lt Gen Victor H. Krulak, 1970, sess. 5, p. 2, MCHC. Quote is from Krulak, Speech to 1967 HQMC General Officers' Symposium, p. 21, box 2, Krulak Papers, MCHC.

[51] Momyer, *Airpower in Three Wars*, pp. 277–78, outlines the scope and effectiveness of tactical air support in Vietnam. For favorable assessments of air support, see Sharp

MACV: The Years of Escalation, 1962–1967

Interv, 19 Feb 71, p. 15; and Peers Interv, 26 Jan and 12–15 Jan 77, sec. 3, pp. 60–61. Both the successes and growing difficulties of Air Force–Marine cooperation in I Corps are outlined in MACV Command History, 1967, 1: 325, 450–52; and ibid., 1968, 1: 423–24, 434–36.

[52] For establishment of the field force headquarters, see Dietrich, "Field Forces," ch. 1, pp. 9–21; ch. 2, p. 1; ch. 3, passim.

[53] MACV Command History, 1967, p. 128. Strengths of the headquarters are in Dietrich, "Field Forces," ch. 3, pp. 58, 69; and Maj. Gary L. Telfer, USMC; Lt. Col. Lane Rogers, USMC; and V. Keith Fleming, Jr., *U.S. Marines in Vietnam: Fighting the North Vietnamese, 1967* (Washington: History and Museums Division, HQMC, 1984), p. 319. Lt Gen Fred C. Weyand, Senior Officer Debriefing Report, 15 Jul 68, pp. 6–7, CMH; Peers Interv, sec. 4, pp. 6–7, MHI. Msg, Johnson WDC 0195 to Westmoreland, 6 Jan 67, Westmoreland Msg Files, 1 Jan–31 Mar 67, CMH. Quote is from Douglas Kinnard, *The War Managers* (Hanover: University Press of New England, 1977), p. 58.

[54] HQ MACV Dir 525-4, 17 Sep 65, sub: Tactics and Techniques for Employment of U.S. Forces in the Republic of Vietnam, Westmoreland Hist File 1 (29 Aug–24 Oct 65), CMH. Msgs, Westmoreland MAC 02916 to Component and Field Force Commanders, 24 Jan 67; COMUSMACV MAC 35945 to CGs, III MAF, I and II FFORCEV, and DCG, USARV, 1 Nov 67. All in Westmoreland Sig File, 1967, CMH. Westmoreland, *A Soldier Reports*, pp. 268–69. MFR, Chaisson, 9 Feb 67, sub: MACV Commanders' Conference, 22 January 1967, tab D–11, Westmoreland Hist File 12 (13 Dec 66–26 Jan 67), CMH. Quote is from Peers Interv, sec. 3, pp. 75–76, MHI.

[55] MacDonald-Westmoreland Interv, 18 Jun 73, CMH; Westmoreland, *A Soldier Reports*, p. 271. Early field force headquarters difficulties are recounted in Dietrich, "Field Forces," ch. 3, pp. 18–19.

[56] Westmoreland, *A Soldier Reports*, pp. 269–70; MacDonald-Westmoreland Interv, 28 Jan 73 and n.d., CMH; Westmoreland Conference with CMH Historians, 6 Dec 89, Notes in CMH; Interv, Charles B. MacDonald and Charles von Luttichau with Lt Gen Stanley R. Larsen, 6 Dec 68, pp. 1–2, copy in CMH; Seaman Interv, sec. 3, pp. 42–43, MHI; Palmer, *25-Year War*, p. 63. Records of Westmoreland's conferences are scattered throughout his History Files for 1965–1968, CMH.

[57] First quote is from H. K. Johnson Interv, sec. 12, p. 16, MHI. Second is from Westmoreland Hist Notes, 4 Oct 65, Westmoreland Hist File 1 (29 Aug–24 Oct 65), CMH; in same file, see Notes for 17 Oct 65. Larsen Interv, 1977, sec. 5, pp. 13–14, CMH. Peers Interv, sec. 3, pp. 35–36, MHI. MacDonald-Westmoreland Interv, 25 Apr 73, CMH. Msg, Westmoreland MAC 5038 to Gen W. M. Greene, CMC, 9 Oct 65, Westmoreland Msg Files, 1 Oct–31 Dec 65, CMH. General Krulak's views and influence on strategy are summarized in Shulimson, *Marines in Vietnam, 1966*, pp. 11–14.

[58] Larsen Interv, 1977, sec. 5, pp. 9–13, CMH. MacDonald-Westmoreland Interv, 17 and 19 Jun 73, CMH. Westmoreland Hist Notes, 17 Oct 66, tab D, Westmoreland Hist File 9 (18 Sep–17 Oct 66); 29 Jan 67, tab D, Westmoreland Hist File 12 (13 Dec 66–26 Jan 67); 6–18 Aug 67, tab A, Westmoreland Hist File 20 (4–20 Aug 67). All in CMH. Chaisson Oral History, pp. 223–25, MCHC. Msg, Westmoreland MAC 7598 to Sharp, 13 Aug 67; Msg, Krulak to Westmoreland, 19 Aug 67; tabs A–11 and A–26. Both in Westmoreland Hist File 20 (4–20 Aug 67), CMH. *U.S.–Vietnam Relations*, sec. 4.C.11, pp. 17–19.

[59] Service rivalry, media leaks, and the Da Nang press center are covered in Hammond, *Military and Media, 1962–1968*, pp. 243–44. Msgs, Wheeler JCS 5419–66 to Sharp and Westmoreland, 12 Sep 66; Engler MAC 7999 to Gen Johnson, 14 Sep 66; Larsen NHT 0648 to Johnson, 14 Sep 66; Westmoreland MAC 8020 to Wheeler and Sharp, 14 Sep 66. All in Westmoreland Msg Files, 1 Aug–30 Sep 66, CMH.

[60] Quote is from Msg, Westmoreland MAC 9128 to Johnson, 29 Sep 67; Westmoreland Msg Files, 1 Jul–30 Sep 67, CMH. Westmoreland, *A Soldier Reports*, p. 166. Westmoreland Hist Notes, 16 Jan 67, tab D, Westmoreland Hist File 12 (13 Dec 66–26 Jan 67), and 23–31 May 67, tab B, Westmoreland Hist File 17 (1–31 May 67). Both in CMH. MFR, Westmoreland, 20 Jan 68, sub: Meeting with General Chapman, Newly Appointed Commandant of the Marine Corps . . . , Westmoreland Hist File 28 (27 Dec 67–31 Jan 68), CMH.

[61] Ltr, Westmoreland to CG III MAF, 21 Nov 65, sub: Letter of Instruction (LOI–4), tab E–1, Westmoreland Hist File 2 (25 Oct–20 Dec 65); MFR, Jones, 16 Sep 66, sub: COMUSMACV's Visit to III MAF . . . , tab A–5, Westmoreland Hist File 9 (18 Sep–17 Oct 66); Msg, III MAF COC to COMUSMACV COC, 20 Jan 67, tab D–5; Westmoreland Hist File 12 (13 Dec 66–26 Jan 67), CMH, are examples of Westmoreland's guidance to III MAF. Other examples can be found throughout Westmoreland's History and Message Files. For Marine response to MACV guidance, see Shulimson, *Marines in Vietnam, 1966*, pp. 14–15.

10

The Allies and Pacification

Besides controlling its U.S. units, the Military Assistance Command had to coordinate the operations of allied forces that varied greatly in capabilities and in willingness to accept American tactical direction. In addition, after much interagency squabbling within the U.S. government, MACV became responsible for managing the pacification campaign. To meet these challenges, General Westmoreland, his subordinates, and his military and civilian superiors resorted to piecemeal adjustments and modifications of existing arrangements and institutions. The expedients they adopted were shaped in part by operational realities, in part by American interservice and intergovernmental politics, and in part by the requirements of interallied diplomacy.

The Allies

MACV's forces included sizable contingents from America's Asian and Pacific allies. Beginning in mid-1964, the Johnson administration pressed anti-Communist nations around the world to join in the struggle in Vietnam. The administration valued such assistance not only for the additional resources it provided but also because it lent multilateral respectability to a domestically and internationally controversial venture.

This "more flags" appeal elicited only token humanitarian contributions from America's principal European, Middle Eastern, and Western Hemisphere allies; but a number of countries closer to Vietnam dispatched significant forces as an accompaniment to the U.S. troop buildup. The Republic of Korea, which in late 1964 had contributed a 1,900-man paramilitary civic action ("DOVE") unit, during the next two years sent a marine brigade and two full infantry divisions. Australia and New Zealand early furnished advisers, then added the equivalent of a brigade of combat troops. Thailand first sent a regiment and later enlarged it to an undersize division. The Philippines provided a 2,000-man paramilitary force. At peak strength, Free World allied forces in South Vietnam amounted to more than 68,000 men and included 31 maneuver battalions—more allied troops, though of mixed qual-

MACV: The Years of Escalation, 1962–1967

ity, than had served alongside Americans during the United Nations-sponsored Korean War. Each contributing country sent forces under a separate agreement with the United States and South Vietnam, and each—except for Australia and New Zealand, which largely paid their own way—received in return substantial American support in money and new arms and equipment for its Vietnam contingent and in some instances for its forces at home. In Vietnam each allied unit drew combat and logistical support from MACV, normally through its counterpart American service component.[1]

In December 1964 the Military Assistance Command set up a special staff element, the International Military Assistance Office, under supervision of the J5 section, to oversee the affairs of the third country forces. Renamed the Free World Military Assistance Office in October 1965, this agency acquired its own building in downtown Saigon, which it shared with representatives of the troop-contributing countries. Codifying earlier ad hoc arrangements, the Free World Military Assistance Office outlined command relationships between MACV, the allied forces, and the South Vietnamese. Each allied force was under the command of a general officer of its own nationality who maintained his headquarters in Saigon. The national commander, cooperating with representatives of MACV and the South Vietnamese Joint General Staff (JGS) (in practice Generals Westmoreland and Cao Van Vien for major contingents, such as the Koreans), formed a policy council that implemented the terms of the military agreements between the United States, South Vietnam, and the contributing country. The council's most important task was the establishment of an exact command relationship between the allied force, MACV, and the JGS. In practice, this meant that the allies dealt directly with MACV, since the third countries ruled out any subordination of their forces to those of Saigon.[2]

The Australians, New Zealanders, Thais, and to a degree the Filipinos placed their troops under General Westmoreland's operational control and that of his subordinate American tactical commanders. These arrangements, however, were less militarily absolute and straightforward than their formal terms might have suggested. Each country kept close watch over its contingent and negotiated with MACV the exact extent of its forces' participation in combat. Concerned about the domestic political effects of heavy casualties, for example, the Australian government was reluctant to engage its soldiers in risky offensive operations and also wanted to keep them out of internationally sensitive areas such as the Vietnam-Cambodia border region. After lengthy negotiations with Lt. Gen. John Wilton, chief of the Royal Australian Army General Staff, and other Australian officials, as well as with the South Vietnamese, Westmoreland early in 1966 assigned the Australian–New Zealand task force its own area of operations in Phuoc Tuy Province east of Saigon. There, in a province well away from Cambodia that large enemy main-force units rarely

The Allies and Pacification

entered, the task force could protect an important highway and fight Viet Cong guerrillas.[3]

The South Koreans, whose troops eventually took over defense of most of the populated coastal region of II Corps, rejected any semblance of formal American operational control. Viewing their presence in Vietnam as a bargaining lever in their relations with the United States and as an occasion to assert themselves as an Asian anti-Communist power in their own right, the Koreans from the outset insisted that their expeditionary force be treated as independent of, and coequal with, the U.S. and South Vietnamese armies. Since the United States needed Korean soldiers in Vietnam much more than the Koreans needed to be there, the Seoul government was able to extract large financial and diplomatic concessions in return for the two army divisions and the marine brigade it contributed to the war. It also obtained generally what it wanted in terms of command relationships in Vietnam.[4]

The Koreans' attitude compelled Westmoreland to engage in some delicate diplomacy. Early in 1965 the Koreans agreed to place their DOVE unit under Westmoreland's operational control. When planning began for deployment of their divisions and brigade, however, the Commander, Republic of Korea Forces, Vietnam, Maj. Gen. Chae Myung Shin, withdrew the concession. A new military working arrangement signed on 6 September 1965, after lengthy conferences between Chae, Westmoreland, and Cao Van Vien, provided for MACV logistical and intelligence support for the Korean force, but Chae, on grounds of national sovereignty and prestige, refused to sign any document formally placing his troops under Westmoreland's operational control. On the question of command, the document simply declared that the Korean units would "execute necessary operational missions in support of the National Pacification Program" under their own commander. Privately, Chae and other Korean officials assured Westmoreland that their forces would act as though they were under his orders and those of the I Field Force commander, General Larsen, as long as nothing was put in writing and the orders were couched as requests. Westmoreland accepted this gentlemen's agreement as "probably more durable and certainly more politically palatable than a formal arrangement that would create unnecessary controversy . . . , be politically awkward to the Koreans, and in the final analysis not be binding."[5]

At the field force level, considerable jockeying for position ensued over the exact terms of the informal command arrangement. General Larsen initially assumed that he could exercise operational control of the Korean divisions, transmitting instructions to them directly through Korean liaison elements at I Field Force headquarters. General Chae, however, denied that Larsen had operational control and insisted that the field force commander deal with the divisions through Chae's headquarters, Republic of Korea Forces, Vietnam (ROKFORV), on the basis of requests rather than orders. After the second Korean infantry division arrived during 1966, Chae tried to channel all of Larsen's communications with the Korean forces through a small ROKFORV field headquarters that he set up at Nha Trang at Westmoreland's suggestion. Chae also sought to establish his own contacts with the ARVN II Corps commander and considered attaching Korean advisers to South Vietnamese Army units within his area of responsibility. During 1966, the Korean government promoted Chae to lieutenant general, compelling Westmoreland hastily to obtain a third star for General Larsen, who otherwise would have labored under a disadvantage in rank. Westmoreland responded to the Koreans' stubbornness with more personal diplomacy by both himself and Larsen. He told the Mission Council in October 1966 that he was "simply letting water find its own level and not raising difficult questions which would require formalized answers at this time." He continued to rely as far as possible on "informal accommodations" in defining MACV-ROKFORV command relations.[6]

Brig. Gen. Edward H. de Saussure, 196th Brigade commander, with General Chae (NARA)

Under these arrangements, the Koreans obtained the independence they wanted. Westmoreland and his I Field Force commanders took care to maintain cordial personal and working relationships with General Chae and to respect Korean nationalist sensitivities. In practice, engaging in only minimal cooperation with the South Vietnamese, the Korean divisions largely conducted their campaign in their own area of responsibility and under only the most general American direction. Continuing to assert his status as an independent third force, General Chae in late 1967 demanded that he be made a cosigner with Generals Westmoreland and Vien of the annual American-Vietnamese combined campaign plan, even though Chae's forces operated in only two of the four corps areas. Westmoreland sidestepped this bid by suggesting that the Koreans and Vietnamese adopt supplemental combined plans for the regions where the Koreans were deployed.[7]

Apparently under instructions from Seoul to minimize casualties, the Koreans concentrated on defense and pacification of the coastal strip they controlled. While seemingly effective in suppressing the

Viet Cong, their pacification methods provoked repeated complaints from the South Vietnamese and from American advisers that the Koreans were killing and torturing civilians. The Koreans attacked enemy main forces and base areas only occasionally, after much persuasion by I Field Force and after being assured of lavish American tactical air, helicopter, and artillery support. Korean offensives, in the view of American commanders, were usually inefficient in proportion to the resources tied up in supporting them. General Larsen and his successors respected the discipline and professionalism of their Korean allies but, because of their defensive-mindedness, considered them, in Larsen's words, "on balance . . . about one half as effective in combat as our best US units."[8]

South Korean troops inspect a dead Viet Cong guerrilla. (© Bettmann/CORBIS)

Besides working out command relationships and operational missions for the allied contingents, General Westmoreland participated in continuing U.S. diplomatic efforts to obtain still more third-country soldiers. He cooperated with U.S. ambassadors as well as military commanders and advisers in negotiating with contributing countries about the size, composition, equipment, and missions of their units. During 1967, for example, he and his staff worked with Ambassador Graham Martin in Bangkok and with the commander of the U.S. Military Assistance Command, Thailand, Maj. Gen. Richard G. Stilwell (and his successor, Maj. Gen. Hal D. McGown) on plans for expanding the Thai contingent from a regimental combat team to a small division. Throughout these discussions, Westmoreland took the position that allied units must come to Vietnam fully trained and ready for combat because MACV lacked resources to complete their preparation and to protect them until they could defend themselves. He also tried to minimize drafts on MACV for men and equipment to aid in activating allied units in their own countries. Such assistance, he contended, should come from outside his theater so as not to hinder either the American buildup or efforts to expand and improve the South Vietnamese military. In accord with this policy, he persuaded U.S. Army, Pacific, and the Department of the Army to reduce by 50 percent the number of personnel taken from USARV and the MACV advisers to help organize and train the Thai division.[9]

The allied contingents kept the MACV commander and staff busy with a host of minor military and political problems, most requiring international diplomacy to solve. The distribution of M16 rifles, for example, became a question of face for the Koreans, who insisted that, in recognition of the size and importance of their forces, they should receive them ahead of the other allies and the South Vietnamese. Provision of national food and entertainment for the foreign contingents generated message traffic and consumed command and staff time, as did occasional scandals, such as the Koreans' clandestine shipments home of spent brass artillery shell casings and allegations of brutality in their pacification campaigns. In coping with such problems, MACV often enlisted the aid of U.S. commanders stationed in the contributing countries, who used their military and government contacts to secure information and smooth over irritations. Those commanders, in turn, often transmitted concerns of their host governments to MACV. Westmoreland, for example, maintained constant communication with General Charles Bonesteel, commander of U.S. forces in Korea, on matters concerning that country's contingent.[10]

Overall, the allied forces were a mixed blessing for the Military Assistance Command. On the one hand, they made a significant, if limited, contribution to the war effort. The Koreans, for example, protected a large, heavily populated area containing several major ports and allied bases, freeing American and South Vietnamese troops for other tasks. The Australians and New Zealanders, though few in numbers, were competent professional soldiers experienced in antiguerrilla operations. The Thais and Filipinos, much less effective, nevertheless enhanced security in the areas where they were stationed. On the other hand, the allied forces, and most notably the Koreans, required disproportionate amounts of American logistical and combat support and of MACV command and staff attention. Their presence further complicated the persistent question of establishing an American–South Vietnamese combined command.

The South Vietnamese: Cooperation and Coordination

As American and allied participation in the war expanded, General Westmoreland continued to reject proposals that surfaced periodically in Washington and Saigon for a combined command. He commissioned several MACV staff studies of the subject, but all concluded that the political and military difficulties and disadvantages of attempting to establish an international headquarters would outweigh any possible benefits. Westmoreland argued that he already exercised de facto control of South Vietnamese operations through the advisory system and through the provision of logistical and combat support, and that imposition of an American supreme commander on the Vietnamese would add substance to Communist charges of U.S. imperialism. He asserted that a combined staff would be divided by language barriers and could not be given access to the most sensitive intelligence for fear of security breaches by its South Vietnamese members. Westmoreland pointed out that the other allies would have to be given "various prestige command positions" in any such headquarters. Finally, a combined military command would require an international political authority of some kind to direct its activities, adding still more diplomatic complications. Westmoreland preferred to stick with the existing system, imperfect as it was, and his superiors accepted his judgment.[11]

Accordingly, the Military Assistance Command continued to work with the South Vietnamese forces on the basis of "mutual coordination and cooperation." Each nation retained control of its own forces, and field commanders were to collaborate as equals in planning and executing operations. The South Vietnamese were considered to be ultimately responsible for the defense of all their national territory, with the Americans and other allies assisting in particular assigned areas.[12]

By late 1965, the command structure of Saigon's armed forces had assumed the form it would retain throughout the rest of the war. At the top, the Joint General Staff, which served as a counterpart to MACV, functioned as both an army and a joint headquarters, planning and directing all aspects of the Vietnamese military effort. Its general staff sections corresponded closely to those of MACV and were grouped into three directorates, for operations, personnel, and logistics. Two other specialized directorates oversaw training and political warfare. Directly subordinate to the JGS were separate commands for the air force, navy, marine corps, and airborne forces, as well as administrative headquarters for branches of the army, the territorials, and the Special Forces. In the field, four corps commanders under the JGS controlled the South Vietnamese Army's infantry divisions and other regular formations. Almost invariably military officers, the province chiefs exercised command over the Regional and Popular Forces under the operational control of the divisions and the political authority of the corps commanders, who did additional duty as civil governors of their regions.[13]

As a matter of policy, General Westmoreland enjoined his subordinates to work closely and continually with the Vietnamese. He told his commanders early in 1966: "We are not taking over. Our objective is to keep them in the war. We must use diplomacy, tact, and finesse to get them more and more into the act, to use their forces in joint op-

General Vien, center, *confers with Lt. Gen. Le Nghen Khan and Lt. Col. Ted Gordiner.*
(U.S. Army photo)

erations. They must share in any battlefield victory. It pays to defer to some senior commanders, to make them feel that they have responsibility. We must not let them lose face, lose interest, and lessen their interest."[14]

The MACV commander himself was as good as his word. He conferred several times a week with his counterpart, General Vien, on all aspects of the war effort, and he communicated with Vien by formal letter on important matters. Westmoreland continued to urge Vien, Thieu, and Ky to correct their forces' many persistent deficiencies, especially the crippling inadequacy of leadership. Recognizing the political character of RVNAF command assignments and the desirability of avoiding any appearance of a direct American role in making them, Westmoreland approached such issues with circumspection, the more so because changes in senior military command amounted to changes in the government that the armed forces dominated. He told General Wheeler that he preferred to give advice on personnel "in connection with proposals made by the Vietnamese as opposed to exercising positive . . . initiative in proposing personalities, although I do this discreetly from time to time." An officer with a good combat record whom Westmoreland and other Americans considered nonpolitical and reasonably free of corruption, General Vien also was a friend and supporter of President Thieu, who retained the general in his post throughout the life of the Saigon government. Vien was usually responsive to Westmoreland's suggestions insofar as Vietnamese military politics allowed. According to General Chaisson, Westmoreland "could get . . . Vien to do mostly what he would suggest to him—if it was within his capability; if it wasn't getting into a big power struggle or something like that."[15]

In form at least, Americans and South Vietnamese at all levels of command engaged in close and continuing cooperation. MACV and JGS staff sections and committees, guided by parallel directives from Westmoreland and Vien, regularly collaborated in combined studies and plans. The most important of these, the annual Combined Campaign Plans, were prepared by representatives of the general staffs of both headquarters and signed by Westmoreland and the chief of the JGS with great ceremony. Supplemented by subordinate plans for each corps area, the plans constituted the authoritative statements of allied strategy. Growing more detailed and elaborate with each passing year, they specified military and pacification objectives and assigned roles and missions to American, South Vietnamese, and third-country forces.[16]

Yet cooperation and coordination between MACV and the JGS often consisted more of form than substance. Combined planning was frequently little more than a facade for unilateral American staff work. The MACV staff, for instance, did most of the drafting of the first three Combined Campaign Plans, for 1966, 1967, and 1968, with only comments and suggestions from the South Vietnamese. Except for the combined intelligence centers, genuine combined headquarters agencies did not develop, for lack of Vietnamese technical competence and American fear of Viet Cong penetration of the South Vietnamese armed forces. Each headquarters maintained its own combat operations center, with MACV liaison officers stationed at that of the JGS. For security reasons, MACV staff sections often withheld information from their JGS counterparts. The command, for example, notified the Joint General Staff of American annual plans for military assistance to South Vietnam only after Washington had approved them. At times, MACV left the JGS entirely out of the planning for major operations until the moment of execution.[17]

Much the same pattern prevailed at the field force level. Generals Westmoreland and Vien attempted to encourage combined efforts by American field forces and ARVN corps, through such devices as joint visits to their subordinate commanders and the holding of combined tactical conferences and quarterly reviews of progress under the campaign plans. Nevertheless, although they maintained overtly cordial relationships with their ARVN counterparts, American field force commanders were preoccupied with direction of their own forces. Their visits to Vietnamese units and headquarters tended to be infrequent and mostly ceremonial. In their turn, Vietnamese corps commanders devoted much of their time to their political responsibilities, often at the expense of their military functions. The Vietnamese commanders, untrained in systematic planning and staff work on the American model, short of qualified officers, and in some instances convinced their headquarters were Viet Cong-infiltrated, did little long- or middle-range operational planning. They found it easier to leave the initiative to the Americans, who in any event controlled most of the logistical and combat support. American commanders, in turn, found it simpler to operate without the less efficient South Vietnamese units. Coordination and cooperation usually meant in practice that each army operated separately, the Americans attacking enemy main forces and base areas with at best token Vietnamese participation, and the ARVN trying to protect the populated regions.[18]

Occasionally, the allies attempted closer cooperation. For example, between December 1966 and November 1967 MACV and the JGS conducted Operation Fairfax/Rang Dong in the Capital Military District surrounding Saigon. In this operation, the U.S. 199th Light Infantry Brigade, commanded by Westmoreland's RVNAF-relations troubleshooter, General Freund, and the Vietnamese 5th Ranger Group cooperated in an effort to improve security in the environs of the capital. Results of Fairfax/Rang Dong were ambiguous. The allied troops inflicted significant enemy casualties and reduced Viet Cong activity to the point that Westmoreland in November 1967 felt justified in removing the 199th Brigade from the operation and returning responsibility for the capital's outskirts entirely to the Vietnamese. However, the combined command and intelligence arrangements worked imperfectly at best, due mostly to rivalry and distrust among the Vietnamese agencies involved; and the South Vietnamese rangers were less effective than the American troops, both in antiguerrilla combat and in winning the confidence of the villagers. Above all, as so often occurred in this period of the war, American resources, initiative, and energy were the driving force behind the operation. When the American brigade left, security and pacification in the region declined.[19]

During the years of the American buildup, the U.S. and South Vietnamese forces, with only occasional exceptions, failed to commit the effort and resources that would have been required to make combined operations a day-to-day reality. They conducted more or less parallel, rather than truly combined, campaigns. Overwhelmed by the resources and power of their ally, South Vietnamese commanders fell into a habit of operational dependence on the Americans. "Gradually," one of them admitted, "they lost interest in the combat situation outside of the pacification areas. It was as if the war was being fought in a distant and alien world." Whether formation of a genuine combined command with Vietnamese units under direct control of American generals would have produced better ARVN performance and closer interallied cooperation will remain forever a matter of conjecture and controversy. A combined command had worked in the Korean War, but South Korea in the 1950s had possessed a strong civilian national leadership independent of the armed forces. In South Vietnam by contrast, the armed forces in essence constituted the national government, so that an American assumption of military control would have amounted to an assumption of political control as well, lending an unacceptable colonialist aura to the entire arrangement. Besides this political obstacle, considering the limited results of Operation Fairfax and similar experiments, it seems likely that the fundamental deficiencies of Saigon's forces, rooted in South Vietnamese society and culture, would have prevented the full integration of operations under any command relationship.[20]

Pacification and Saigon Politics

Although often overshadowed by the escalating armed conflict, pacification—Revolutionary Development in the terminology of the Thieu-Ky regime—continued to command the attention of influential men and organizations in both Washington and Saigon. Henry Cabot Lodge, who began his second term as ambassador to South Vietnam in August 1965, regarded pacification as "the heart of the matter." He sided with those members of the U.S. Mission who questioned the increasing weight of the military in the American effort and considered securing the countryside more important than destroying enemy units. In Washington, a number of conferences and studies of varying agency sponsorship called anew for an integrated American military and nonmilitary strategy in Vietnam. Though preoccupied with staying in power, the Thieu-Ky government showed stirrings of new attention to the problem, for example by establishing a Ministry of Revolutionary Development to pull together Saigon's pacification programs.

At the Honolulu conference in February 1966, President Johnson, Chief of State Thieu, and Premier Ky formally accorded pacification equal importance with the military offensive. They publicly committed themselves to ambitious social and economic programs and to the promotion of democracy and justice for the Vietnamese people. Johnson, in private sessions, told American officials that he expected in the ensuing months not promises but tangible progress toward those objectives. He used the oft-quoted phrase, "Nail those coonskins on the wall."[21]

The reemphasis on pacification reopened the long-standing issue of how best to unify American military and civilian support of a campaign that had to be carried out primarily by the South Vietnamese. In Saigon, the U.S. Mission was still essentially a congery of separate bureaucratic baronies, each of which pursued its own version of the common strategy under the loose coordination of the Mission Council and which maintained its own lines of communication to its parent agency in Washington. Ambassador Lodge, for all his interest in pacification, proved no better an administrator in his second tour than he had been in his first. Viewing himself as a presidential representative and policy advocate rather than as director of the mission, he refused to involve himself in the internal workings of the agencies under him, thereby rendering himself ineffective at ensuring unity of purpose and action. In Washington, a State Department-chaired Vietnam Coordinating Committee coordinated in name only; in practice, no one below President Johnson and Secretaries Rusk and McNamara was pulling the effort together.[22]

In contrast to his predecessor, General Harkins, Westmoreland maintained cordial and cooperative relations with Ambassador Lodge and with Lodge's successor, Ellsworth Bunker. Westmoreland and Lodge worked together effectively in trying to stabilize the Saigon government. The ambassador generally avoided interference in military operations. On most occasions, Lodge asked Westmoreland to review military portions of his messages or sought the MACV commander's suggestions on the drafts. This harmonious relationship became somewhat frayed as Lodge came under increasing White House pressure for pacification progress. The ambassador then began blaming military preoccupation with large-unit operations and failure to orient the ARVN toward counterinsurgency for the deteriorating security in the countryside. Westmoreland responded with extensive defenses of MACV's operational and advisory performance. Privately, he complained that Lodge lacked "a deep feel of military tactics and strategy" and was "inclined to over-simplify the military situation and to deal with it on a . . . formula basis." This disagreement notwithstanding, the two men maintained a friendly working relationship until Lodge's departure in April 1967.[23]

If anything, the cooperative relationship between the MACV commander and the ambassador improved under Ellsworth Bunker. A veteran diplomat who replaced Lodge in May 1967, Bunker had worked closely with soldiers during the 1965 Dominican intervention and in Westmoreland's view was a strong friend of the military. He could be counted on to take the soldiers' side on such issues as recommendations for expanded operations in Laos and Cambodia. Early in his ambassadorship, Bunker included Westmoreland in a small executive committee that gathered over lunch after each weekly Mission Council meeting to resolve major policy questions outside the cumbersome formality of the larger body.[24]

As the largest single component of the U.S. Mission, in manpower, resources, and presence in the countryside, MACV inevitably played a major part in nonmilitary activities. Representatives of the command sat on mission committees dealing with economic warfare and psychological operations. They participated in and often initiated periodic mission attempts to persuade the Vietnamese to undertake general mobilization. At Ambassador Lodge's request, the Military Assistance Command assumed responsibility for the debriefing, transportation, and medical care of American civilians recovered from Viet Cong captivity. In mid-1966, when the embassy established a committee on strategy and priorities, the MACV representative, according to Westmoreland, "had a major influence over the committee and the end product was therefore fully acceptable to me."[25]

Since the armed forces constituted the political framework of South Vietnam, MACV's advisory function kept the command embroiled in

General Thi, center (© Bettmann/CORBIS)

South Vietnamese politics. By late 1965 the armed forces and the government had achieved a precarious stability dependent upon a balance of power between the officer factions headed by Chief of State Thieu and Premier Ky. In close coordination with the ambassador, Westmoreland employed his advisers with the senior commanders to help keep this factional balance stable and to guide the military leaders toward reestablishment of constitutional, democratic government. The MACV commander himself devoted many hours to counseling various generals, advising on removals and replacements of commanders, and encouraging the officers to maintain their precarious unity. He also kept a wary watch on Vietnamese relations with the Montagnards and on the activities of his own Special Forces teams among the tribespeople, seeking to prevent a repetition of the 1964 revolt.[26]

The Military Assistance Command played a crucial part in resolving the most severe crisis of the Thieu-Ky regime. Early in March 1966, in the midst of political maneuvering over the first steps toward drafting a new constitution, the military directorate in Saigon dismissed the commander of I Corps, Lt. Gen. Nguyen Chanh Thi, whom the Saigon generals viewed as a threat to their power. Thi's ouster set off a rebellion in his corps area, where he enjoyed wide popularity and ruled as an independent satrap. Mutinous ARVN soldiers, allied with Buddhists and other non-Communist dissidents, took control of Hue, Da Nang, and other towns in the military region. Thieu and Ky sent troops from Saigon to quell the uprising. The resulting armed confrontation raised the imminent possibility of an intra-South Vietnamese civil war, to the consternation of American authorities in Saigon and Washington.

In this crisis General Westmoreland became the major American agent working to restore stability. Through his advisory network, he communicated on a soldier-to-soldier basis with leaders of all factions and secured up-to-date information on the unfolding events for the embassy, CINCPAC, and the Joint Chiefs of Staff. He influenced Saigon's actions by providing or withholding air transport and other forms of military assistance. At the outset, Westmoreland directed General Walt at Da Nang to maintain strict neutrality between the contending forces, whose actions periodically threatened Walt's own troops and installations. The marines, through an astute combination of diplomacy and shows of force, kept an uneasy peace.

After pro-Saigon troops forcibly suppressed the rebels at Da Nang in mid-May, Westmoreland, at the direction of General Wheeler and with the concurrence of Ambassador Lodge, undertook to divide the insurgent military leaders and to separate them from the Buddhists and other civilian elements. To develop strategy, he established an ad hoc "Think Group" at MACV headquarters. There followed a period of tortuous negotiations, arranged by MACV, between generals of the two sides, as well as a rapid series of appointments and reliefs of new I Corps commanders. While the MACV effort did not bring about the rebels' surrender, it appears to have weakened and divided them. A final government military drive into Hue early in June effectively ended the revolt without full-scale fighting and without a mass defection of the dissidents to the Viet Cong, who, to the Americans' surprise, had remained passive throughout the troubles.[27]

MACV's political involvements did not end with the defeat of the I Corps rebels. During 1967, as South Vietnam drafted a new constitution and then held village, hamlet, presidential, and national assembly elections, General Westmoreland and Ambassadors Lodge and Bunker worked to keep the generals united and committed to the political program. Westmoreland reported to General Wheeler on 25 June: "The Ambassador and I are discussing the matter almost daily, keeping our ears to the ground and exercising discreet influence without suggesting any preference for candidates. We are by all means encouraging unity within the armed forces, and stressing the importance of free and fair elections." As Thieu and Ky maneuvered for the presidency, Westmoreland maintained impartiality between the two aspirants while urging them not to let their rivalry split the nation's armed forces. The MACV commander and Ambassador Bunker greeted with relief Ky's eventual decision, after lengthy negotiations among the Vietnamese generals, to settle for the vice presidency on a Thieu-Ky ticket. During the campaign and election that followed, the Military Assistance Command cooperated closely with the South Vietnamese armed forces in protecting the polling places from Viet Cong attack and harassment. In addition, the command helped transport ballots and conducted nonpartisan get-out-the-vote psychological operations. As the Americans had hoped, Thieu and Ky won a contest that, despite some controversy, U.S. observers and the American news media rated as largely fair and honest.[28]

CORDS: A Single Manager at Last

By the time the Vietnamese held their presidential election in September 1967, the Military Assistance Command had taken control of the American side of the pacification campaign. It did so as the result of a prolonged struggle within the U.S. government over pacification management that began in earnest in the period immediately preceding the Honolulu conference and accelerated during the months following it. The central issue in the debate was the establishment of an American single manager for pacification in Saigon who could pull together the personnel and activities of all the U.S. agencies working in the Vietnamese countryside.

The champions of single management included Secretary McNamara and Robert W. Komer, whom President Johnson in March 1966 appointed his special assistant to coordinate pacification efforts in Washington. Within six months of the Honolulu conference, McNamara and Komer concluded that the single manager should be the MACV commander, since the provision of military security was central to effective pacification and since MACV controlled more manpower and resources in the countryside than any other agency. In addition, Komer believed that the military would pay adequate attention to pacification only if they received responsibility for it. Led by the State Department, the civilian agencies vigorously opposed a MACV takeover of pacification. They were unwilling to sacrifice their own independence, doubted the military's competence to perform the task, and objected to further militarization of what they considered essentially a political struggle. Rather than have the military take over, the civilian agencies, along with Ambassador Lodge who championed their views, preferred to continue coordinating their efforts through the Mission Council.[29]

In his principal gesture at unified management of pacification, Lodge brought into the mission Brig. Gen. Edward G. Lansdale, USAF, a veteran practitioner of anti-Communist political warfare in Asia who was credited with defeating the Hukbalahap insurgency in the Philippines. Lodge gave Lansdale, who arrived with a ten-man staff, the title Special Liaison Officer and a vague mandate to coordinate civilian and military pacification activities. Lansdale, whose management approach was as unsytematic as Lodge's, engaged in jurisdictional quarrels with MACV and other mission agencies. He spent most of his time making contacts among South Vietnamese civilian and military figures in an effort to find dynamic new popular leaders and to promote an anti-Communist people's revolution. Lacking support from the other elements of the mission, Lansdale and his assistants accomplished nothing tangible and were gradually isolated from the rest of the U.S. establishment in Saigon.[30]

President Johnson early made clear his own desire for tighter management, but he hesitated to impose military control and instead directed a series of reorganizations of the civilian side of the mission. Soon after the Honolulu conference Ambassador Lodge, at White House insistence, formally named Deputy Ambassador William Porter as coordinator of civilian pacification programs. Porter, however, lacked the staff, the ambassadorial support, and the administrative skill to unify the effort. Lodge and the mission civilians resisted further reorganization and seemed to the increasingly impatient president to lack a sense of urgency about the problem.

During October, under the influence of McNamara and Komer, Johnson appears to have decided to turn over pacification to MACV. Nevertheless, he gave the civilians one last chance. Early in November, he ordered Lodge to unify the pacification programs of all civilian agencies except the CIA under one embassy official with his own staff and with single managers under him in the field at corps, province, and district levels. The Office of Civil Operations (OCO), which Lodge established on 21 November under Deputy Ambassador Porter, constituted a unified chain of command for civilian pacification operations; but it started life on borrowed time. President Johnson warned Lodge in his November message that OCO would be "on trial" for 90–120 days, "at the end of which we would take stock of progress and reconsider whether to assign all responsibility for [pacification] to COMUSMACV."[31]

Throughout these maneuvers, General Westmoreland kept to the sidelines. He had been convinced since 1964 of the need for a unified military-civilian approach to pacification and had volunteered himself as the ambassador's agent for managing it. Even as the U.S. troop buildup and military operations absorbed much of his attention, Westmoreland continued to emphasize publicly and privately that victory rested ultimately on restoring the connection between the Saigon government and the rural population. He remained a supporter of Operation Hop Tac, which he considered a model for an integrated American-Vietnamese, civilian-military campaign, and persisted in promoting it until July 1966, when a Vietnamese command reorganization in III Corps provided an opportunity to give the faltering operation a decent burial. Westmoreland cooperated in U.S. Mission experiments with province team chiefs and informally tried to coordinate MACV pacification activities with those of other agencies. He was quick to offer MACV staff support to Deputy Ambassador Porter as pacification coordinator and provided the deputy ambassador, at his request, with a brigadier general as a military assistant.[32]

When invited to comment on questions of American organization for pacification, Westmoreland advocated single management. He declared that military and nonmilitary efforts must be completely in-

The Allies and Pacification

tegrated; he called attention to the large existing involvement of his command, especially the 1,100 MACV district advisers, in civilian as well as military aspects of the effort; and he proposed various plans for unified management under the ambassador. However, to avoid a confrontation with the civilian agencies, he allowed other officials, such as McNamara and Komer, to argue for designating him as single manager, telling visitors only that he was not volunteering for the job but would accept it if directed to do so.[33]

During the summer and autumn of 1966, Westmoreland received regular reports from Generals Wheeler and Johnson on the president's growing inclination to give the pacification effort to MACV. During a mid-October visit to Saigon, McNamara informed Westmoreland of administration plans for the last-chance civilian reorganization and expressed his belief that a military takeover was inevitable. The MACV commander in response put his J5 section to work on a contingency plan for transformation of his headquarters into a directorate of field operations for the U.S. embassy, controlling both civilian and military activities. At the urging of Wheeler and Johnson, Westmoreland strengthened the pacification element of the MACV staff. On 7 November 1966, he established a Revolutionary Development Support Directorate under the staff supervision of his J3. Headed by Brig. Gen. William A. Knowlton, former secretary of the MACV Joint Staff, the new directorate assumed inspection and liaison functions with the South Vietnamese Revolutionary Development Ministry, duties that were formerly performed by a division of J3. It also assumed oversight of MACV's general support for pacification. Its ulterior purpose, as Wheeler told Westmoreland, was "first, to plug in a pacification channel between the Embassy and your headquarters; and, second, to permit a transfer of authority and direction of the whole operation to you at some future time."[34]

MACV cooperated with and assisted the Office of Civil Operations during that agency's brief existence. "I sure as hell knew OCO wouldn't work," General Westmoreland later recalled, "but I gave it the best I had." He furnished Ambassador Porter with a military deputy, Brig. Gen. Paul Smith, former commander of the 173d Airborne Brigade, whom Westmoreland considered a "superlative staff officer." Members of MACV's Revolutionary Development Support Division worked with the OCO staff on analyses of hamlet self-defense requirements and development and evaluation of pacification plans. When Porter appointed the four OCO regional directors, the key men of the new civilian chain of command, Westmoreland instructed the commanders of I and II Field Forces and III MAF and the IV Corps senior adviser to provide them with support and assistance. Tensions developed, however, both in Saigon and in the field, when Porter and his regional directors tried to intervene in what Westmoreland considered strictly military decisions such as the deployment of U.S. infantry battalions and the train-

359

Ambassador Bunker, right, with Generals Westmoreland and Wheeler (U.S. Air Force photo)

ing of South Vietnamese Regional Force troops. Westmoreland told Wheeler in February that "the civilian side of the house is tending to exercise authoritative prerogatives in military matters. If this trend continues, a clash is inevitable although we are doing our utmost to avoid such a collision." A visit to Saigon by Robert Komer, the president's overseer of pacification, prevented a full-scale MACV-OCO confrontation; but OCO's days were numbered in any event.[35]

In spite of OCO's success in unifying civilian pacification activities at every level from Saigon to the districts, the new organization, in the short time allowed it, could not produce significant change in the actual balance between government and Viet Cong control in the countryside. This apparent lack of results, as well as Lodge's persistent foot-dragging on reorganization and the civilian agencies' lack of enthusiasm in supporting OCO, opened the way for McNamara, Komer, and other advocates of a military takeover to resume their campaign. During the first two months of 1967, they explored the possibility of appointing Westmoreland ambassador to South Vietnam to succeed Lodge, who had expressed his intention to step down. As ambassador, with deputies for military operations and pacification, Westmoreland could then direct the entire American war effort in what Wheeler called a "MacArthur-type operation." Early in March, however, President Johnson, at Secretary Rusk's urging, rejected this proposal on grounds that the United States should not have a military man as ambassador in Saigon when the Vietnamese appeared likely to elect a general as president.[36]

The final decision came in late March 1967, during a conference on Guam between President Johnson and the South Vietnamese leaders. With all the American principals from Washington and Saigon, including newly appointed Ambassador Bunker, on hand, Johnson placed pacification support under Westmoreland and assigned Komer to head the program as a deputy MACV commander with the personal rank

The Allies and Pacification

of ambassador. Under a plan outlined by Westmoreland, Komer's organization was to be formed by merging OCO and the MACV Revolutionary Development Support Directorate into a new MACV joint staff section, the Office of Civil Operations and Revolutionary Development Support (OCORDS). Komer and a small staff then flew back to Saigon with Westmoreland to work out the details of the new organization. On 11 May, soon after arriving in Saigon, Ambassador Bunker formally announced the establishment of CORDS and the assignment of pacification responsibility to General Westmoreland with Komer as his civilian deputy. Two days later, at a commanders' conference at Cam Ranh Bay, Westmoreland, Bunker, and Komer explained the new organization to the senior American military leaders.[37]

In its final form, worked out in prolonged negotiations between Komer, Westmoreland, and their staffs, CORDS represented a unique infusion of civilians into a military organization. The CORDS office in MACV had a civilian chief, L. Wade Lathram, the former OCO staff director, who was designated assistant chief of staff for CORDS. General Knowlton, who had headed MACV's Revolutionary Development Directorate, served as Lathram's deputy. Besides engaging in planning and analysis, CORDS exercised operational control over pacification in the field. Under it, the four OCO regional directors became deputies to the field force and III MAF commanders for CORDS, on an equal footing with the deputy senior military advisers. The CORDS deputies in turn controlled single managers, some military and some civilian, for each province, who had charge of the MACV provincial and district advisory teams as well as personnel of the civilian agencies. In a fully integrated chain of command, soldiers came under the authority of civilians who wrote their efficiency reports; civilians similarly came under the command of soldiers.[38]

Komer, who well deserved the nickname "Blowtorch," made the most of his ambassadorial rank and his at times abrasive personality in establishing his position within the Military Assistance Command. He secured, for example, the right of direct access to both Westmoreland and Ambassador Bunker. Although in theory he was to communicate with the CORDS organization only through the MACV chief of staff, in practice he regularly bypassed the chief of staff and operated what amounted to a separate chain of command for pacification that stretched from MACV headquarters down to the districts. He secured comparable authority for his deputies for CORDS at corps level. "Basically," Komer recalled, "the corps commanders left us alone. The pacification business was run autonomously."[39]

Komer owed much of his success in building up his agency to his own aggressiveness and skill as a bureaucratic infighter and to his White House connections and backing. He also benefited from the strong support of General Westmoreland. Throughout the crucial formative period of Komer's agency, the MACV commander repeatedly overrode his military staff and his field commanders on questions of CORDS authority and autonomy. For example, when Komer clashed with General McChristian over whether CORDS or the MACV Intelligence Directorate should conduct a new campaign against the Viet Cong infrastructure, Westmoreland ruled in favor of Komer. He also upheld Komer on the question of the regional deputies' authority over province and district military advisers. At the same time Westmoreland protected his own prerogatives as MACV commander by quickly suppressing Komer's attempts to communicate directly with Washington. Nonetheless, the two men developed a working relationship of mutual trust and confidence. Westmoreland permitted Komer wide latitude within the pacification sphere, and Komer deferred to Westmoreland on military operational matters.[40]

Komer's relations with the rest of the MACV hierarchy were far from placid. General Abrams—like Komer, a man of strong opinions and colorful language—became a rival of the CORDS deputy. MACV Chief of Staff Kerwin, an Abrams protégé, resented Komer's free-wheeling tendency to bypass his office on pacification matters, a habit that made coordination of the sprawling MACV staff even more difficult. Partly to ease relations between Komer and the military elements of MACV, Westmoreland provided the CORDS deputy with a personal military assistant, Maj. Gen. George Forsythe, an officer with much advisory experience, pacification expertise, and diplomatic skill. In agreeing to assign Forsythe to this position, the Army chief of staff noted that the new deputy was "an individual known by Komer who can work with him and yet is fully conscious of the complexities of military/civilian relationships."[41]

Within MACV headquarters, CORDS constituted one of the larger staff sections, both in manpower and demands on facilities. Its divisions for Plans and Programs, Operations and Analysis, and Regional and Popular Forces were located in the main MACV complex at Tan Son Nhut. A number of specialized divisions, many inherited from OCO, occupied an Agency for International Development building, known as USAID Number Two, in downtown Saigon. The CORDS Operations and Analysis Division, responsible for assembling and analyzing pacification data and managing the Hamlet Evaluation System, alone included about 100 personnel, half of them military people and civil servants and half contract computer technicians. The division, which worked closely with the MACV Data Management Agency, used more than 50 percent of the time and capacity of the headquarters' IBM computer in preparing its many reports. As seemed to be true of every reorganization, the establishment of CORDS created demands in MACV for still more military manpower, both in Saigon and in the field. Westmoreland shifted personnel within his organization wherever possible, to stay within increasingly tight strength ceilings, but he also had to request additional officers and men from outside the theater.[42]

The Allies and Pacification

As a merger of civilians and soldiers in one organization, CORDS achieved a high level of success. Civilian pacification operatives initially greeted its establishment with near despair, anticipating their complete submergence by the military. However, Komer's strong influence in MACV, the U.S. Mission, and Washington, coupled with the placement of civilians in high posts, as exemplified by the elevation of Lathram over Knowlton, did much to alleviate these fears. Cooperation between the MACV staff and the divisions of CORDS was informal and effective; the Operations and Analysis Division chief, for example, maintained a direct exchange of information with the Intelligence and Operations Directorates of the military staff. At the field force level also, the new organization proved to be workable, although commanders complained occasionally that their CORDS deputies bypassed them in dealing with MACV headquarters.[43]

The placement of pacification under the Military Assistance Command led to other organizational adjustments within the U.S. Mission. Representatives of the command began attending USAID regional planning conferences. Late in 1967 MACV, by agreement with USAID and with the Mission Council's approval, took over advice and support to the South Vietnamese civil highway construction and veterans' affairs administrations, hitherto USAID responsibilities but closely connected with the military and pacification programs.[44]

During the formation of CORDS, MACV and the Joint U.S. Public Affairs Office (JUSPAO) engaged in much discussion and many studies of the proper division of labor in psychological warfare. Since 1965, JUSPAO, an agency formed by combining elements of the U.S. Information Service (USIS), MACV, and USAID, had been responsible for both U.S. Mission relations with the press and propaganda directed at friends and enemies. MACV during the ensuing years had built up its own Psychological Operations Directorate to attack enemy military morale; OCO had formed a similar office of its own to support pacification. In July 1967 a MACV study group, formed at General Wheeler's request, recommended that the command replace JUSPAO as mission coordinator of psychological warfare, leaving it to concentrate on the increasingly difficult problem of press relations. However, after negotiations with Ambassador Barry Zorthian, Embassy Minister–Counselor for Public Affairs and Director of JUSPAO, Westmoreland agreed instead to retain roughly the existing division of labor. The Public Affairs Office continued to set overall psychological warfare policy and conducted certain nationwide propaganda campaigns; the Military Assistance Command carried out military psychological operations through its Psychological Operations Directorate and propaganda support of pacification through the CORDS Psychological Operations Division.[45]

With the establishment of CORDS, the entire direction of the interrelated military and political campaign against the Viet Cong was vested in the Military Assistance Command as the principal operating agent of the U.S. Mission. General Westmoreland occupied the center of a complex web of relationships with American, allied, and South Vietnamese military forces; with the South Vietnamese government; and with American civilian agencies. Yet the structure of his command was a ramshackle one created by a long series of piecemeal accretions, most of them heavily influenced by internal U.S. bureaucratic politics and by the imperatives of international diplomacy. He directed it more by negotiation among semi-independent fiefdoms than by the authority of rank.

With the American services, Westmoreland had to tread carefully through a minefield of doctrinal issues and to accommodate differing concepts of operations and tactics. His employment of his Free World allies was circumscribed both by their varying military capabilities and by the policies of their governments. As a matter of what he considered political necessity, Westmoreland denied himself real command authority over the South Vietnamese forces and relied instead on persuasion backed by indirect pressure to guide their operations. Finally, while the establishment of the Office of Civil Operations and Revolutionary Development Support brought the political and paramilitary campaigns under his purview, the new agency constituted a separate, semi-autonomous entity within MACV under a civilian chief who enjoyed direct access to the ambassador and possessed considerable influence with Westmoreland's superiors in Washington. General Westmoreland made this system work through diplomacy, patience, and a high degree of adaptability to the complicated requirements of an unconventional conflict. He confonted similar complexities, and responded with similar tactics, in attempting to influence the war in Southeast Asia outside South Vietnam.

The Allies and Pacification

Notes

[1] Allied contributions are conveniently summarized in Lt Gen Stanley R. Larsen and Brig Gen James L. Collins, Jr., *Allied Participation in Vietnam,* Vietnam Studies (Washington, D.C.: Department of the Army, 1975). A table of allied strengths is on p. 23. The political importance of securing more flags is illustrated in Msg, Wheeler JCS 2904–65 to Sharp and Westmoreland, 5 Aug 65, Westmoreland Msg Files, 1 Jul–30 Sep 65, CMH.

[2] MACV Command History, 1965, pp. 72, 94–95, 354–57; ibid., 1966, pp. 288–89.

[3] MACV Command History, 1965, pp. 71–72, 359–62. MFR, Westmoreland, 25 Jun 65, sub: Meeting with Gen Wilton . . . , tab 37, Westmoreland Hist File 16 (10 May–30 Jun 65). Westmoreland Hist Notes, 2 Sep 65 and 6 Oct 65, Westmoreland Hist File 1 (29 Aug–24 Oct 65); and 20 Mar 66, tab A, Westmoreland Hist File 5 (13 Mar–23 Apr 66); Msgs, Westmoreland MAC 3876 to Lt Gen Goodpaster, 30 Jul 65; MAC 4097 to Sharp, 12 Aug 65; MAC 2163 to Sharp, 17 Mar 66; Westmoreland Msg Files, 1 Jul–30 Sep 65 and 1 Jan–31 Mar 66. All in CMH.

[4] Negotiations for the Korean troops are described in Larsen and Collins, *Allied Participation*, pp. 120–31.

[5] First quote is from Military Working Arrangement between COMROKFORV and COMUSMACV, 6 Sep 65, copy in CMH files. Second is from Westmoreland Hist Notes, 6 Dec 65, Westmoreland Hist File 2 (25 Oct–20 Dec 65), CMH. MACV Command History, 1965, pp. 72–73, 363–67; Msg, Westmoreland MAC 3888 to Beach, 30 Jul 65, Westmoreland Msg Files, 1 Jul–30 Sep 65; Westmoreland Hist Notes, 5 Sep 65, Westmoreland Hist File 1 (29 Aug–24 Oct 65). Both in CMH. Interv, Charles B. MacDonald with Gen William C. Westmoreland, 11 Feb 73, CMH.

[6] Quote is from Mission Council Action Memo 129, 5 Oct 66, tab C–1, Westmoreland Hist File 9 (18 Sep–17 Oct 66); Westmoreland Hist Notes, 8 Mar 66, tab D, Westmoreland Hist File 4 (30 Jan–13 Mar 66); 17 Sep 66, tab E, Westmoreland Hist File 8 (17 Jul–17 Sep 66); 25 Nov 66, Westmoreland Hist File 11 (30 Oct–12 Dec 66). All in CMH. Msgs, Westmoreland MAC 5718 to Beach, 8 Jul 66; Gen Johnson WDC 8006 to Westmoreland, 8 Jul 66; Larsen NHT 0609 and NHT 0654 to Westmoreland, 2 Sep, 17 Sep 66. All in Westmoreland Msg Files, 1 Jul–30 Sep 66, CMH.

[7] Debriefing Rpt, Lt Gen Stanley R. Larsen, CG I FFV, 31 Jul 67 (DTIC Tech Rpt), p. 27, CMH files. Westmoreland Hist Notes, 5 Jun 66, tab A, Westmoreland Hist File 7 (29 May–16 Jul 66). MFRs, Westmoreland, 13 Nov 67, sub: Meeting with General Vien on 25 October 1967; and 13 Nov 67, sub: Signing of Combined Campaign Plan for CY 68 . . . ; tabs A–20 and A–22, Westmoreland Hist File 24 (15 Oct–12 Nov 67). All in CMH. Msgs, Westmoreland MAC 5978 to Sharp, 25 Jun 67; Rosson NHT 1249 to Westmoreland, 7 Oct 67; Westmoreland Msg Files, 1 Apr–30 Jun 67 and 1–31 Oct 67. All in CMH.

[8] Larsen is quoted in Msg, Westmoreland to Sharp, 28 Jan 66, Westmoreland Msg Files, 1 Jan–31 Mar 66, CMH. In same file, see Msg, Westmoreland MAC 0184 to Wheeler, 9 Jan 66. Msgs, Larsen NHT 0522 and 0747 to Westmoreland, 5 May 67 and 28 Jun 67; Westmoreland MAC 5978 to Sharp, 25 Jun 67. All in Westmoreland Msg Files, 1 Apr–30 Jun 67, CMH. MacDonald-Westmoreland, Interv, 17 Jun 73, CMH. Rosson Interv, 1981, pp. 384–86; Larsen and Collins, *Allied Participation*, pp. 147–59.

[9] MACV Command History, 1965, pp. 72, 361, 367–68, 371–72; ibid., 1967, pp. 248–76; ibid., 1968, 1: 346–48, 351–52. Westmoreland Hist Notes, 27 Mar–8 Apr 67, tab A, Westmoreland Hist File 15 (27 Mar–30 Apr 67); Memo, Westmoreland for Clifford and Taylor, 25 Jul 67, sub: Requirements for Free World Military Assistance Forces, tab A–15A, Westmoreland Hist File 19 (6 Jul–3 Aug 67); CMH. Msg, COMUSMACV MAC 41358 to CINCPAC, 12 Dec 67, Westmoreland Sig File, Dec 67, CMH. Details of

MACV: The Years of Escalation, 1962–1967

Westmoreland's negotiations with the Thais and other nationalities can be followed in Westmoreland Msg Files, 1965–1968, CMH.

[10] On M16 issue, see Msgs, Bonesteel KRA 101 to Westmoreland and Sharp, 19 Jan 67; Westmoreland MAC 0755 to Bonesteel, 23 Jan 67; Westmoreland Msg Files, 1–31 Jan 67, CMH. For rations and special services, see Msgs, MAC 9256 Westmoreland to Sharp, 22 Oct 66; Bonesteel KRA 1730 to Sharp, Beach, and Westmoreland, 1 Nov 66; Westmoreland MAC 9752 to Bonesteel, 7 Nov 66. Brass: Msgs, Bonesteel KRA 2075 and KRA 2021 to Westmoreland, 24 Dec 66 and 6 Sep 67; Westmoreland MAC 0182 to Bonesteel, 6 Jan 67. All in Westmoreland Msg Files, 1966–67.

[11] Westmoreland sums up his objections to a combined command in Msg to CINCPAC, 19 Feb 68, reproduced in MACV Command History, 1968, 1:221–22. See also Clarke, *Final Years*, p. 212; MacDonald-Westmoreland Interv, 11 Feb 73, CMH files; MACV Command History, 1966, p. 246; Westmoreland Hist Notes, 16 Feb 66, tab A, Westmoreland Hist File 4 (30 Jan–13 Mar 66), CMH.

[12] MACV Command History, 1967, p. 133, contains the official definition of U.S.–RVNAF relationships.

[13] Organization of the JGS and RVNAF is described in Clarke, *Final Years*, ch. 2. Useful information also can be found in Truong, *Cooperation and Coordination*, pp. 20–22, 42–43.

[14] MFR, Jones, 24 Apr 66, sub: MACV Commanders' Conference, tab A–2, Westmoreland Hist File 6 (24 Apr–28 May 66), CMH.

[15] First quote is from Msg, Westmoreland MAC 7988 to Wheeler and Sharp, 23 Aug 67, Westmoreland Msg Files, 1 Jul–30 Sep 67, CMH. In same file see Msg, Westmoreland MAC 8807 to Sharp, 17 Sep 67. Second quote is from Chaisson Oral History, pp. 252–53, MCHC. A typical expression of Westmoreland's approach to dealing with the Vietnamese is in Memo, Westmoreland for MACV Officer Advisers, 8 Jan 67, sub: U.S. Adviser/Counterpart Relationship, Westmoreland Sig File, Jan 67, CMH. Westmoreland sketches Cao Van Vien's character in *A Soldier Reports*, pp. 242–43. For Vien's relations with the military directorate, see Clarke, *Final Years*, pp. 109–10 and 266–68.

[16] Truong, *Cooperation and Coordination*, pp. 22–25, 53–56; Sharp and Westmoreland, *Report on War*, pp. 104, 142. Westmoreland Hist Notes, 1 Sep 65, Westmoreland Hist File 1 (29 Aug–24 Oct 65), CMH; 26 and 31 Dec 65, tabs A and B, Westmoreland Hist File 3 (20 Dec 65–29 Jan 66); MFR, Westmoreland,13 Nov 67, sub: Signing of Combined Campaign Plan for CY 68 (AB 143) at JGS, 0800 hrs, 13 November 1967, tab A–22, Westmoreland Hist File 24 (15 Oct–12 Nov 67); Msg, Westmoreland MAC 10574 to Sharp, 7 Nov 67, Westmoreland Msg Files, 1–30 Nov 67. All in CMH. See also texts of the combined plans in CMH files.

[17] MFR, Westmoreland, 13 Nov 67, sub: Meeting with Gen Vien on 25 October 1967, tab A–20, Westmoreland Hist File 24 (15 Oct–12 Nov 67), CMH, discusses desirability of the JGS's originating the next combined campaign plan. Truong, *Cooperation and Coordination*, pp. 26–27. Gen Cao Van Vien et al., *The U.S. Advisor,* Vietnam Monographs (Washington, D.C.: Center of Military History, 1980), pp. 44–45.

[18] Msg, Westmoreland MAC 6018 to Sharp, 16 Jul 66, Westmoreland Msg Files, 1 Jul–30 Sep 66, CMH; Westmoreland, *A Soldier Reports*, pp. 243–46; MFR, DePuy, 3 Sep 65, sub: Combined Tactical Conference . . . , Westmoreland Hist File 1 (29 Aug–24 Oct 65), CMH; MFR, Col John Hayes, 27 Oct 67, sub: Vietnamese–US Commanders' Conference, tab A–5, Westmoreland Hist File 24 (15 Oct–12 Nov 67), CMH; Vien et al., *U.S. Advisor*, p. 41. Truong, *Cooperation and Coordination*, pp. 59–61, 69–72, 177–80; Larsen Debrief, 31 Jul 67, pp. 17, 25–26, CMH; Seaman Interv, 1971–72, sec. 5, pp. 34–35; and Peers Interv, sec. 3, 1977, pp. 69–70. Both in MHI. Palmer, *25-Year War*, pp. 56–57.

[19] Clarke, *Final Years*, pp. 250–51. Truong, *Cooperation and Coordination*, pp. 128–

The Allies and Pacification

34. The importance of Freund's experience in dealing with the South Vietnamese to his command of this operation is emphasized in Westmoreland Hist Notes, 25 Feb 67, tab B, Westmoreland Hist File 13 (27 Jan–25 Mar 67), CMH.

[20] Quote is from Truong, *Coordination and Cooperation*, p. 165. Some U.S. commanders believed that a combined command would have been beneficial; see Throckmorton Interv, 14–15 Mar 78 and 14 Apr 78, sec. 3, pp. 4–5; Senior Officer Debriefing Rpt, Lt Gen Frederick C. Weyand, 15 Jul 68, p. 7, CMH; and Palmer, *25-Year War*, pp. 64, 194. Robert W. Komer also criticizes the absence of combined military control; see his *Bureaucracy Does Its Thing*, pp. 94–102. Clarke, *Final Years*, pp. 500–501, summarizes the political obstacles.

[21] The revival of interest in pacification is traced in *U.S.–Vietnam Relations*, sec. 4.C.11, pp. 1–45. "Coonskins" quote is on p. 41. Vietnamese efforts are recounted in MACV Command History, 1967, pp. 562–63; and Westmoreland Hist Notes, 10 Dec 65, Westmoreland Hist File 2 (25 Oct–20 Dec 65), CMH.

[22] The management problem is summarized in Thomas W. Scoville, *Reorganizing for Pacification Support* (Washington, D.C.: Center of Military History, 1982), p. vi and ch. 1; Komer, *Bureaucracy Does Its Thing*, ch. 6; Westmoreland, *A Soldier Reports*, p. 210; and MACV Command History, 1967, p. 565. *U.S.–Vietnam Relations*, sec. 4.C.11, p. 8; and MacDonald-Westmoreland Interv, 24 Apr 73, CMH, are typical comments on Lodge's lack of interest in administration.

[23] Quote is from Westmoreland Hist Notes, 13 Dec 66, tab D, Westmoreland Hist File 11 (30 Oct–12 Dec 66), CMH. His relations with the ambassador can be followed in Westmoreland's Historical and Message Files, 1965–67. MACV Command History, 1965, p. 402; and ibid., 1968, 1:222–23. Disagreements over pacification are reflected in Msgs, Westmoreland MAC 10822 to Wheeler and Sharp, 12 Dec 66, Westmoreland Msg Files, 1 Oct–31 Dec 66, CMH; and Msg, Lodge Saigon 10204 to SecState, 6 Nov 66, tab B–3, Westmoreland Hist File 11 (30 Oct–12 Dec 66), CMH. Also MacDonald-Westmoreland Interv, 17 Jun 73, CMH files.

[24] MACV Command History, 1967, pp. 584–85. Bunker's character is sketched in Westmoreland, *A Soldier Reports*, p. 217; and Palmer, *25-Year War*, pp. 47–48. Westmoreland Hist Notes, 1–20 May 67, tab A, Westmoreland Hist File 17 (1–31 May 67) and 1 June–5 Jul 67, tab A, Westmoreland Hist File 18 (1 Jun–5 Jul 67), CMH. MacDonald-Westmoreland Interv, 12 Mar 73, CMH files. Scoville, *Pacification Support*, pp. 60–61.

[25] Quote is from Westmoreland Hist Notes, 10 Jul 66, tab E, Westmoreland Hist File 7 (29 May–16 Jul 66); see also notes of 23–31 May 67, tab B, Westmoreland Hist File 17 (1–31 May 67); both in CMH. MACV Command History, 1965, pp. 249, 406–07; ibid., 1966, pp. 178–91, 557. Ltr, Lodge to Westmoreland, 13 Mar 67; Memo, Westmoreland for Lodge, 29 Mar 67, sub: Handling of Civilian Personnel Recovered from the Enemy; Westmoreland Sig File, Mar 67, CMH.

[26] Saigon's military politics are discussed in detail in Clarke, *Final Years*, chs. 2, 7, and 14. Westmoreland's relationships with the Vietnamese generals can be followed through his Msg Files and Historical Files for 1965–1968, CMH. Memo, Westmoreland for Taylor, 27 Jul 65, sub: The Montagnards and FULRO, tab 17, Westmoreland Hist File 17 (1 Jul–28 Aug 65); MFR, Maj Carl M. Putnam, 30 Dec 65, sub: COMUSMACV Conference with FFORCEV Commanders and II Corps Advisers, tab B–1, and Westmoreland Hist Notes, 27 Jan 66, tab F, Westmoreland Hist File 3 (20 Dec 65–29 Jan 66); and Ltr, Westmoreland to Col W. A. McKean, 2 Feb 66, tab A–2, Westmoreland Hist File 4 (30 Jan–13 Mar 66). All in CMH.

[27] Events of the crisis are covered in Clarke, *Final Years*, ch. 7; and Shulimson, *Marines in Vietnam, 1966*, pp. 73–74, 81–91. Westmoreland's part in events can be followed through his Msg Files, 1 Jan–31 Mar 66 and 1 Apr–30 Jun 66; and his Historical

MACV: The Years of Escalation, 1962–1967

Files 5 (13 Mar–23 Apr 66), 6 (24 Apr–28 May 66), and 7 (29 May–16 Jul 66). All in CMH. Jones Interv, p. 32, MCHC, comments on the extent to which the embassy allowed Westmoreland to manage the crisis.

[28] Quote is from Msg, Westmoreland MAC 5994 to Wheeler and Sharp, 25 Jun 67, Westmoreland Msg Files, 1 Apr–30 Jun 67, CMH. Political events are covered in Clarke, *Final Years*, ch. 14. Election results are summarized in Sharp and Westmoreland, *Report on War*, pp. 152–56. Westmoreland Hist Notes, 1–20 May 67, tab A, Westmoreland Hist File 17 (1–31 May 67); and 10–29 Sep 67, tab A, Westmoreland Hist File 22 (10–30 Sep 67); Msg, COMUSMACV MAC 32676 to CINCPAC, 5 Oct 67, Westmoreland Sig File, 1967. Both in CMH.

[29] The controversy over pacification management is recounted in Scoville, *Pacification Support*, chs. 2 and 3, and *U.S.–Vietnam Relations*, sec. 4.C.11, pp. 53–121. Msg, Lodge Saigon 10204 to SecState, 6 Nov 66, tab B–3, Westmoreland Hist File 11 (30 Oct–12 Dec 66), CMH, is an expression of Lodge's views. See also Westmoreland, *A Soldier Reports*, p. 211.

[30] Msgs, Rosson MAC 6481 to Westmoreland, 16 Dec 65; Westmoreland HWA 3420 to Lodge, 17 Dec 65; Westmoreland Msg Files, 1 Oct–31 Dec 65, CMH. Draft Talking Paper for Gen Westmoreland with Amb Lodge and Amb Porter, Dec 65, tab A–3, Westmoreland Hist File 3 (20 Dec 65–29 Jan 66), CMH. U.S. Congress, Senate, Committee on Foreign Relations, *The U.S. Government and the Vietnam War, Executive and Legislative Roles and Relationships, Pt. IV, July 1965–January 1968* (Washington, D.C.: Government Printing Office, 1994), pp. 58–61.

[31] Quote is from Msg, SecState 78865 to AmEmb Saigon, 4 Nov 66, tab A–1, Westmoreland Hist File 11 (30 Oct–12 Dec 66), CMH; in same file, see Msg, Lodge Saigon 10204 to SecState, 6 Nov 66, tab B–3.

[32] MACV Command History, 1965, pp. 403–05; ibid., 1966, pp. 739–41. Ltrs, Westmoreland to Gens Cao Van Vien and Nguyen Huu Co, 3 Sep 65, tabs A–5 and A–6, Westmoreland Hist File 1 (29 Aug–24 Oct 65); Westmoreland Hist Notes, 26 Feb 66, tab C, Westmoreland Hist File 4 (30 Jan–13 Mar 66); and 25 Nov 66, tab C, Westmoreland Hist File 11 (30 Oct–12 Dec 66). All in CMH. Msgs, Westmoreland MAC 4642 to Wheeler and Sharp, 17 Sep 65; Westmoreland MAC 5021 to Wheeler, 8 Oct 65; Westmoreland MAC 7242 to Gen Johnson, 20 Aug 67; Westmoreland Msg Files, Jul 65–Sep 66. All in CMH.

[33] Msg, Westmoreland MAC 0117 to Collins, 7 Jan 66, Westmoreland Msg Files, 1 Jan–31 Mar 66, CMH, is typical of Westmoreland's position. Westmoreland, *A Soldier Reports*, pp. 210–12. Westmoreland Hist Notes, 11 Dec 65, Westmoreland Hist File 2 (25 Oct–20 Dec 65), and 16 Sep 66, tab D, Westmoreland Hist File 8 (17 Jul–17 Sep 66), CMH.

[34] Quote is from Msg, Wheeler JCS 6339–66 to Sharp and Westmoreland, 17 Oct 66, Westmoreland Msg Files, 1 Oct–31 Dec 66; Msgs, Sharp to Westmoreland, 8 Oct 66; Gen Johnson WDC 13803 to Westmoreland, 23 Nov 66; Westmoreland Msg Files, 1 Oct–31 Dec 66; Draft Msg (not sent), Westmoreland to Wheeler and Sharp, Oct 66, tab D–8, Westmoreland Hist File 9 (18 Sep–17 Oct 66); Westmoreland Hist Notes, 17 Oct 66, tab A, Westmoreland Hist File 9 (18 Sep–17 Oct 66); All in CMH. MACV Command History, 1966, p. 532; ibid., 1967, pp. 566, 583–84.

[35] First quote is from MacDonald-Westmoreland Interv, 4 Feb 73, CMH files. Second is from Westmoreland MAC 1523 to Wheeler, 13 Feb 67, Westmoreland Msg Files, 1 Jan–31 Mar 67, CMH. In same file, see Msg, Westmoreland MAC 01629 to Wheeler, 16 Feb 67. Westmoreland and Sharp, *Report on War*, p. 119. Msg, Westmoreland MAC 10050 to Sharp, Wheeler, and Johnson, 17 Nov 66, Westmoreland Msg Files, 1 Oct–31 Dec 66. All in CMH. MACV Command History, 1967, p. 568. For examples of OCO entrance into military affairs, see Westmoreland Sig Files, Jan and Feb 67, CMH.

[36] Scoville, *Pacification Support*, pp. 43–48. *U.S.–Vietnam Relations*, sec. 4.C.11, pp. 122–26. Msgs, Wheeler JCS 0831-67, JCS 1190-67, JCS 1527-67, JCS 1528-67, JCS 1573-67, JCS 1637-67, JCS 1815-67 to Westmoreland, 30 Jan 67; 14, 28 Feb 67; 1, 3, 10 Mar 67; Msgs, Westmoreland MAC 1629 and MAC 1998 to Wheeler, 16, 28 Feb 67, Westmoreland Msg Files, 1 Jan–31 Mar 67. All in CMH.

[37] Scoville, *Pacification Support*, pp. 49–55. *U.S.–Vietnam Relations*, sec. 4.C.11, pp. 127–30. Westmoreland, *A Soldier Reports*, pp. 213–15. Westmoreland Hist Notes, 25 Mar 67, tab C, Westmoreland Hist File 13 (27 Jan–25 Mar 67); 1–20 May 67, tab A, Westmoreland Hist File 17 (1–31 May 67). Both in CMH. In latter file, AmEmb Saigon, Admin Ops Notice 473, 11 May 67, sub: Statement by Ambassador Ellsworth Bunker, tab A–10; and MFR, Chaisson, 21 May 67, sub: MACV Commanders' Conference, 13 May 1967, tab A–13. MACV Command History, 1967, pp. 585–87.

[38] Scoville, *Pacification Support*, pp. 62–69. MACV Command History, 1967, pp. 587–88. For a description of the mixed staff of one major CORDS office, see Interv, CMH with Col James R. Loome, USA (Ret.), 27 Feb 91, tape in CMH files.

[39] Quote is from Scoville, *Pacification Support*, p. 73. Komer's personality and operating methods are sketched in Westmoreland, *A Soldier Reports*, p. 215; Chaisson Oral History, pp. 54–55, MCHC; and Interv, Charles B. MacDonald with Lt Gen George Forsythe, 16 Jun 73, CMH files.

[40] The infrastructure dispute is recounted in Scoville, *Pacification Support*, pp. 78–79; see also pp. 71–78. McChristian, *Military Intelligence*, p. 78, gives his view of the issue. Forsythe Interv, 16 Jun 73. MacDonald-Westmoreland Interv, n.d., in Personalities Section of Notes, CMH files; Westmoreland Hist Notes, 1–20 May 67, tab A, Westmoreland Hist File 17 (1–31 May 67); 1 Jun–5 Jul 67, tab A, Westmoreland Hist File 18 (1 Jun–5 Jul 67); and 6 Jul–3 Aug 67, Westmoreland Hist File 19 (6 Jul–3 Aug 67). All in CMH.

[41] Kerwin Interv, 1980, pp. 351–56, 362–64. Westmoreland, *A Soldier Reports*, p. 215. Quote is from Msg, Gen Johnson WDC 5845 to Westmoreland, 4 May 67, Westmoreland Msg Files, 1 Apr–30 Jun 67; Forsythe Interv, 16 Jun 73. Both in CMH.

[42] Loome Interv, 27 Feb 91. Msgs, Westmoreland MAC 3126 to Johnson, 3 Apr 67; Gen Johnson WDC 4282 and WDC 4882 to Westmoreland, 4 Apr 67 and 14 Apr 67; Westmoreland MAC 8230 to Sharp, 31 Aug 67; Sharp to Westmoreland, 2 Sep 67. All in Westmoreland Msg Files, 1 Apr–30 Jun 67 and 1 Jul–30 Sep 67, CMH. Ltr, Weyand to Westmoreland, 21 Jul 67, Westmoreland Sig File, Jul 67, CMH.

[43] For civilian reaction, see *U.S.–Vietnam Relations*, sec. 4.C.11, pp. 130–31. Loome Interv, 27 Feb 91. Ltr, Weyand to Westmoreland, 21 Jul 67, Westmoreland Sig File, CMH. See also Larsen Interv, 6 Dec 68, p. 5; and Msg, Westmoreland MAC 11573 to Wheeler, 30 Nov 67, Westmoreland Msg Files, 1–30 Nov 67, CMH.

[44] Memo, D. G. MacDonald for Westmoreland, 31 Jul 67; Memo, Westmoreland for MacDonald, 7 Aug 67, sub: MACV Participation in USAID's Forthcoming Honolulu Conference. Both in Westmoreland Sig File, Aug 67, CMH. Westmoreland Hist Notes, 19–26 Dec 67, tab A, Westmoreland Hist File 27 (19–26 Dec 67); and 28 Dec 67–31 Jan 68, Westmoreland Hist File 28 (27 Dec 67–31 Jan 68), CMH. Sharp and Westmoreland, *Report on War*, pp. 261–62.

[45] MACV Command History, 1965, p. 253; ibid., 1966, pp. 555–57; ibid., 1967, pp. 7–8, 634–39. Westmoreland Hist Notes, 1 Jun–5 Jul 67, tab A, Westmoreland Hist File 18 (1 Jun–5 Jul 67), CMH. Msgs, Wheeler JCS 5742-67 to Sharp and Westmoreland, 22 Jul 67; Westmoreland MAC 6964 to Wheeler, 24 Jul 67; Westmoreland MAC 9882 to Sharp, 20 Oct 67. All in Westmoreland Msg Files, 1 Jul–30 Sep 67 and 1 Oct–31 Dec 67, CMH; Memo, Westmoreland for Bunker, 12 Oct 67, sub: Psychological Operations in the US Mission, Westmoreland Sig File, Oct 67, CMH.

11

The Wider Theater

Besides conducting the many-faceted campaign in South Vietnam, General Westmoreland's command was heavily engaged in the other three separate "wars" into which, for policy reasons, the Johnson administration felt compelled to divide the struggle for Indochina. The same pool of Seventh Air Force aircraft that bombed and strafed Viet Cong troops and base areas in South Vietnam also struck targets in North Vietnam in ROLLING THUNDER and flew missions against the Ho Chi Minh Trail and the Plain of Jars in Laos. Irregulars of the Military Assistance Command's Studies and Observations Group harassed and reconnoitered the trail and carried on the OPLAN 34A operations in North Vietnam.

Westmoreland shared the direction of these operations with other civilian and military officials whose interests and strategic priorities often differed from his. Admiral Sharp kept control of ROLLING THUNDER. The U.S. ambassador in Vientiane exercised ultimate authority over the semi-clandestine American campaigns in Laos. His counterpart in Bangkok closely supervised the actions of American forces based in Thailand. Westmoreland thus had to rely on negotiation in his effort to influence operations on what he considered an extension of the South Vietnam battlefield.

Fragmentation of Command

As the enemy understood and waged them, the Southeast Asian wars in fact constituted interdependent parts of a single politico-military struggle. Many American leaders also appreciated the unity of the conflict and submitted suggestions from time to time for the establishment of a single U.S. military commander for all Southeast Asia, either subordinate to CINCPAC or reporting directly to the secretary of defense. Secretary McNamara had initially proposed that MACV be separated from the rest of Pacific Command and in 1967 told Westmoreland that he had "made a mistake in not having set up a Southeastern Asia theater with [Westmoreland] in command." Westmoreland, at least in retrospect, held the same view. Among the services, the

Army and Air Force favored a unified American theater command for all Southeast Asia.[1]

Nevertheless, seemingly intractable bureaucratic and political obstacles stood in the way of creating such a command. Admiral Sharp insisted, as had his predecessor, Admiral Felt, that Southeast Asia was an integral part of the Pacific theater and could not practically be separated from it. He and his Navy superiors continued to resist any command rearrangement that would divide the Pacific Fleet and attach any major element of it to an Army-dominated headquarters on the Asian mainland. The State Department, echoed by officials of the Southeast Asian countries, pointed to the diplomatic difficulty of establishing a single American military commander for South Vietnam, an active belligerent, and for Thailand, Cambodia, and Laos, which were neutral at least in name. In a mid-1965 study of the problem, the MACV staff concluded that creation of a single U.S. commander under CINCPAC for South Vietnam, Thailand, and Laos would be desirable from a strictly military standpoint but that the political complications attending such a reorganization would outweigh the military benefits. In the end, all concerned accepted the existing system (or lack of it) as the lesser evil and attempted to make it work through coordination and cooperation.[2]

Indeed, the only change during the buildup was in the direction of further fragmentation. Since the Laotian crisis of 1962, the MACV commander had performed additional duty as commander, U.S. Military Assistance Command, Thailand (COMUSMACTHAI). In this capacity, he commanded the growing American forces in Thailand, which included a joint military assistance group working with the Thai armed forces, an Army logistics command laying the groundwork for U.S. troop deployments in the event of a broadening of the Southeast Asian war, and a rapidly expanding number of Air Force installations and units involved in operations over Laos and North Vietnam. Westmoreland delegated the day-to-day oversight of operations in Thailand to the commander of the assistance group, Maj. Gen. Ernest F. Easterbrook, who served also as deputy COMUSMACTHAI.[3]

As the Vietnam conflict intensified, Thai officials increasingly expressed discontent with this arrangement. They considered that having the American forces in their country commanded from Saigon, a foreign capital, was an affront to their national dignity. They also were concerned that the link between MACV and MACTHAI might entangle Thailand too deeply in the war in South Vietnam. The U.S. Ambassador to Bangkok, Graham Martin, respected Thai concerns. Seeking to increase his own influence over American military activity in Thailand, he campaigned for separation of the assistance command in that country from MACV. Accepting the need to mollify the Thais, General Westmoreland initially endorsed Martin's proposal, as did Admiral Felt during his final months as CINCPAC. However, in early 1965, the MACV commander changed his position. He called for continued unification of the two commands, on grounds that with the growing battlefield crisis in South Vietnam, "Thai sensitivities should take second place to practical military solutions."[4]

The Johnson administration, valuing at least the appearance of Thai neutrality, accepted Martin's, rather than Westmoreland's, arguments. In late May, Secretary McNamara directed the formation of a U.S. Military Assistance Command, Thailand (MACTHAI), separate from MACV and reporting to CINCPAC, with an Army major general in command. Formal activation of the new headquarters came on 10 July. General Westmoreland succeeded in having Maj. Gen. Richard G. Stilwell, his former chief of staff, appointed to head the neighboring command; but, Westmoreland recalled, "Martin ran a one-man show, operated out of his hip pocket. Stilwell [was] not always consulted."[5]

In spite of the formal separation of the two commands, General Westmoreland remained much involved in military affairs in Thailand. He retained his position as commander-designate of U.S. and SEATO ground forces in the event of a general Southeast Asian war; hence, the MACV J5 directorate carried on extensive regional contingency planning. In addition, Westmoreland continued to employ a small SEATO planning staff in Bangkok, and MACV and MACTHAI developed a facility at Korat as the site for a command post in case of a region-wide war. Working closely with Ambassador Martin and the MACTHAI commander, General Westmoreland coordinated the steady expansion of Thailand-based American air operations against North Vietnam and the Ho Chi Minh Trail and prepared plans for the deployment to South Vietnam of Thai troops and for possible operations from Thailand into the Laotian panhandle. His headquarters and the Bangkok embassy exchanged information on enemy activity in Cambodia, and he received briefings on the Communist insurgency in Thailand. Such practical cooperation notwithstanding, the separation of MACV and MACTHAI further complicated American command relations in Southeast Asia, creating another set of independent authorities with whom Westmoreland had to negotiate in order to shape operations outside South Vietnam.[6]

The Ho Chi Minh Trail and the Plain of Jars

Although they preserved a facade of neutrality, Laos and Cambodia contained major North Vietnamese and Viet Cong supply depots, headquarters, training facilities, and rest areas. Some of those in Cambodia were within fifty miles of Saigon. Both countries served in addition as conduits for the flow of troops and war material from North Vietnam and the Soviet bloc. The Ho Chi Minh Trail complex ran through the jungled mountains of the Laotian panhandle, the elongated extension of that country that bordered South Vietnam from the Demilitarized Zone to the Central Highlands. The trail continued southward through eastern Cambodia, a region studded with Communist bases and largely abandoned by Cambodians. Seeking to destroy the enemy base areas and stem the flow of supplies and troops into South Vietnam, General Westmoreland continually sought authority to use his air power against the enemy-controlled portions of Laos and Cambodia. He also tried to obtain permission for ground operations, ranging from clandestine reconnaissance to full-scale multidivision offensives. Political and command complications attended, and frequently frustrated, all these efforts.[7]

By the end of 1965, an active American air war was in progress in Laos. MACV had initiated these operations, code-named BARREL ROLL, late in 1964, as part of the Johnson administration's early intensification of pressure on the North Vietnamese. During 1965, as both the air campaign and the continuing Laotian civil war intensified, CINCPAC and MACV divided the BARREL ROLL area of operations. In the northernmost portion, which retained the BARREL ROLL designation, American aircraft flew in support of the Royal Laotian Army and CIA-organized Meo tribal irregulars fighting the Pathet Lao and North Vietnamese on and around the Plain of Jars. The two southern zones, STEEL TIGER and TIGER HOUND, covered the eastern portion of the panhandle, respectively north and south of the Demilitarized Zone in Vietnam, and were the scene of air attacks and limited ground incursions against the Ho Chi Minh Trail. These operations were most intensive in the TIGER HOUND zone, where MACV obtained wide freedom to attack both fixed facilities and moving vehicles located by aerial reconnaissance. Supporting TIGER HOUND, MACV's Studies and Observations Group late in 1965 began inserting ground reconnaissance teams into the panhandle, in an operation code-named SHINING BRASS. These teams, recruited from the ethnic groups of the region and led by American Special Forces personnel, had the mission of locating targets hidden in the rough terrain and of conducting raids on lightly defended command posts, way stations, and other facilities.[8]

From the beginning of the air war in Laos late in 1964, Admiral Sharp delegated all aspects of the actual conduct of operations to General Westmoreland, even though Laos was outside the MACV commander's territorial jurisdiction. Westmoreland in turn entrusted the day-to-day running of the campaign to the commanders of 2d Air Division/Seventh Air Force. The air component commander and his staff obtained target clearance from the American embassy in Vientiane and then planned, scheduled, and executed strikes. He was responsible, however, to two employers. In the STEEL TIGER and TIGER HOUND areas, he operated under General Westmoreland's direction; but in BARREL ROLL, he received mission assignments from the American embassy in Vientiane.[9]

The ground reconnaissance and raiding portion of the campaign was the province of MACV's Studies and Observations Group. Formed in February 1964 to conduct clandestine OPLAN 34A operations against North Vietnam, this agency enlarged its functions to encompass the entire array of MACV's irregular cross-border activities. It also incorporated Pacific Command's Joint Personnel Recovery Center, charged with efforts to rescue American servicemen missing anywhere in Southeast Asia. At the height of its activities, SOG had a strength of about 2,500 American personnel and 7,000 Southeast Asian irregulars organized in reconnaissance and other special operations teams as well as company- and battalion-size reinforcement and reaction forces. These personnel, besides continuing the original OPLAN 34A airborne and naval operations against North Vietnam, fought a covert and small-scale but dangerous and deadly ground war in Laos and eventually Cambodia.[10]

Directed by an Army colonel, SOG headquarters constituted a more or less autonomous entity within the Military Assistance Command. With a staff that eventually numbered more than 400 personnel representing all the armed services and the Central Intelligence Agency, the headquarters performed its own operational planning, intelligence, logistical, and communications functions but relied heavily on U.S. Army, Vietnam, for supply and helicopter lift. SOG "could do anything," one of its commanders recalled, "that a corps, division, or what have you [headquarters] could do." The organization received missions from Westmoreland, who had to secure authorization from Washington for certain operations. Its commander reported to Westmoreland through the MACV chief of staff and was under the "cognizance" of the J5 Directorate. Even so, whenever possible SOG avoided the regular MACV headquarters channels of coordination and supervision, in order to preserve the secrecy of its activities. Col. Donald D. Blackburn, who originated SHINING BRASS and presided over much of SOG's expansion, explained: "Considering the sensitivity of the . . . operations, I felt that there was too much of a risk for leaks if I had to coordinate everything with the MACV staff."[11]

In every aspect of operations in Laos, General Westmoreland and his Seventh Air Force and Studies and Observations Group commanders had to deal with the U.S. Ambassador to Vientiane, William L. Sullivan. A skillful bureaucratic warrior with strong connections within the Johnson administration and extensive experience in Southeast Asia policy-making, Sullivan directed the entire American military and paramilitary effort in Laos through his country team. With the technical assistance of his Air Force attaché, he selected targets for air strikes in the BARREL ROLL area, and he established rules of engagement and approved targets in STEEL TIGER and TIGER HOUND. He also set territorial limits and operating rules for SHINING BRASS.

Where in Westmoreland's view the war in South Vietnam took precedence and Laos was merely an extension of that battlefield, to Sullivan the preservation of Laos and of U.S. interests there came first. Sullivan was willing to accommodate Westmoreland's desire to sever the Ho Chi Minh Trail, but not at the cost of America's interest in preserving Souvanna Phouma's government and the forms of Laotian neutrality ratified under the 1962 Geneva Agreement. Because of that, Sullivan was usually in the position of resisting MACV efforts to intensify the campaign in the panhandle. At minimum, he sought to keep American activity clandestine and small in scale. He was also determined to prevent Westmoreland from encroaching upon his territory and his war. According to one associate, "The biggest job Bill Sullivan had was to keep Westmoreland's paws off Laos."[12]

General Blackburn (1968 photo) (NARA)

As was to be expected, the ambassador's insistence on retaining veto power over all military operations in Laos irritated and frustrated General Westmoreland and his Seventh Air Force commanders. Westmoreland confided repeated complaints to his diary about what he called Sullivan's "field marshal" complex. For their parts, Generals Moore and Momyer and their subordinates chafed under Vientiane's tight restrictions on targets and objected to Sullivan's attempts to dictate the types of aircraft and ordnance to be used in Barrel Roll missions. They also had constantly to resist attempts by the ambassador to secure guaranteed numbers of sorties for Laos at the expense of what air commanders considered more important operations in North and South Vietnam.[13]

To exchange information, resolve differences, and coordinate military and political activity, the ambassadors and military commanders in South Vietnam, Thailand, and Laos, together with Admiral Sharp, continued regular meetings of the Coordinating Committee for U.S. Missions in Southeast Asia (SEACOORD), established in 1964. For military coordination, however, SEACOORD, with its proliferating working committees and elaborate procedures for setting agendas and arranging meetings, proved too cumbersome. Westmoreland and Sullivan, usually joined by Ambassador Martin from Bangkok, did most of their negotiating in less formal and more frequent sessions, most often held at the American base at Udorn, Thailand. Westmoreland regularly brought his Seventh Air Force and SOG commanders, his intelligence director, and the chief of his Combat Operations Center to these conferences. Occasionally, the Political Counselor or other officials from the U.S. embassy in Saigon also attended. It was at Udorn, in an informal, at times jocular atmosphere, that the MACV commander and the "field marshal" from Vientiane hammered out the shape of the American war in Laos. They incorporated their understandings in parallel recommendations to the State and Defense Departments or sought formal ratification of them from SEACOORD.[14]

Over two years of negotiation, Westmoreland, often assisted by Admiral Sharp and General Wheeler on particularly difficult points, gradually obtained Sullivan's agreement to expanded MACV operations against the Ho Chi Minh Trail. As a result, by late 1967 American aircraft could strike very nearly at will throughout the TIGER HOUND area.

Prince Souvanna Phouma
(© Bettmann/CORBIS)

Even so, they could attack targets of opportunity such as moving supply convoys only within a fixed distance of roads and tracks and only after obtaining clearance through Laotian military representatives on board airborne command and control planes. With Vientiane's agreement, B–52s were also striking targets throughout the Laotian areas of operation, in some instances under the cover of missions near the border in South Vietnam. However, restrictions likewise remained on these operations. For example, although he allowed ARC LIGHTS in Laos, Souvanna Phouma, for political reasons of his own, refused to permit Thailand-based B–52s to fly over his country on the way to targets in South Vietnam. On the ground, the SHINING BRASS zone of operations, renamed PRAIRIE FIRE early in 1967, expanded into a twenty-kilometer deep strip extending from the Demilitarized Zone to the Cambodian border. Within it, the Studies and Observations Group could employ reconnaissance and raiding forces of up-to-company size. In addition, American artillery at positions in northwestern I Corps had begun firing in support of Laotian irregular units operating in the panhandle.[15]

Sullivan nevertheless continued to protect his prerogatives within Laos and to enforce limits on those of COMUSMACV. During August 1967 General Westmoreland made a determined effort, in the context of a further enlargement of the PRAIRIE FIRE zone and of planning for an electronic sensor barrier across the DMZ, to have the PRAIRIE FIRE boundary redefined as a "line of coordination" rather than a rigid barrier. This would enable SOG teams to pursue the enemy across it when permitted by Vientiane. While willing to adjust the PRAIRIE FIRE line to incorporate roads and terrain features of interest to MACV, Sullivan refused to weaken the boundary in any way. He stated that PRAIRIE FIRE was "not a piece of territory which has been detached from my responsibilities . . . and given over to your command. It is instead an area in Laos where MACSOG is permitted to conduct certain types of operations which have been agreed to by higher authority in Washington, subject to my concurrence." Sullivan reserved the right to send his own road-watch teams of Laotian irregulars into the PRAIRIE FIRE area when he deemed it desirable, and in spite of appeals by Westmoreland to Wheeler and Sharp, he won his point. Strict territorial limits on MACV's penetrations into the panhandle remained in effect. They would do so, Sullivan told Westmoreland acidly, until "the JCS turns . . . MACSOG . . . over to me or else the President names you Ambassador to Laos. The larger national interests would suggest that we avoid both these extremes."[16]

Besides seeking to expand air operations and ground reconnaissance, General Westmoreland kept his headquarters at work on contingency plans for full-scale American and South Vietnamese offensives into Laos aimed at blocking the Ho Chi Minh Trail with ground forces and destroying the enemy troops and supplies already in the panhandle. The military logic of creating a solid barrier to North Vietnamese reinforcement of the Viet Cong had been apparent to many American officials from the beginning of the war. General Johnson, for instance, had recommended such action in his pivotal report of March 1965. Westmoreland likewise recognized the importance of cutting the Ho Chi Minh Trail with significant forces, the more so as it became apparent that air strikes and ground harassment by themselves could not halt infiltration and as enemy reaction units began regularly driving PRAIRIE FIRE teams out of key base areas.[17]

During 1966 and 1967 the Military Assistance Command developed a series of plans for large-scale incursions into Laos. The most ambitious of these, Operation FULL CRY, completed late in 1966, called for several U.S. infantry divisions, after extensive logistical preparation, to drive into Laos along Route 9, which ran just south of the Demilitarized Zone and seemed the most practical line along which to establish a cordon. Simultaneously, the airmobile 1st Cavalry Division was to descend upon the Bolovens Plateau in the southern panhandle. The force moving along Route 9 was to block the infiltration routes while the division from the Bolovens pushed northward to meet it, destroying bases and supply depots as it advanced.[18]

The plan for FULL CRY assumed the availability of a "corps contingency force" to supplement the American troops already in South Vietnam. During 1967, as it became apparent that the Johnson administration had no intention of providing such a force, General Westmoreland scaled back his planning. Under his direction, the MACV staff developed proposals, dubbed SOUTHPAW and HIGH PORT, for employing respectively brigade- and division-size forces of elite South Vietnamese

The Wider Theater

troops in limited cross-border search and destroy operations. Closely coordinated with intensive B–52 and tactical air strikes, they essentially formed an expansion of the existing PRAIRIE FIRE campaign. At the end of the year, anticipating a possible change of administrations and hence of national policy during 1968, Westmoreland resumed more ambitious planning. He set his J5 section and the deputy commander of USARV to work on Operations EL PASO I and II, both of which envisioned a westward advance along Route 9 by American and ARVN divisions, to occur possibly during late fall or early winter of 1968.[19]

None of these plans came anywhere near adoption. The Johnson administration was determined to confine the ground war, at least, within South Vietnam. Ambassador Sullivan adamantly opposed any large-scale, overt allied invasion of Laos, even the predominately South Vietnamese SOUTHPAW and HIGH PORT operations. Such actions, he and his country team insisted, would compromise irretrievably Laotian neutrality, probably bring down Souvanna Phouma's government, and provoke dangerous counteraction by China and the Soviet Union. Equally important, both Admiral Sharp and General Westmoreland were less than urgent in advocating major operations in Laos. Sharp had no desire to commit American forces to a new land front in Southeast Asia. Instead, he preferred to strengthen the naval and air campaigns against North Vietnam. Westmoreland, while affirming the eventual necessity of a drive into Laos, initially declared it logistically and politically unfeasible. As his forces expanded, he treated the offensive as a supplement to his campaign in South Vietnam, a project to be undertaken sometime in the future after the enemy was already well on the way to defeat and when additional large American reinforcements were available. He never considered or advocated a movement into Laos as an alternative and potentially more worthwhile employment for the U.S. troops he already had in hand.[20]

Cambodia

In Cambodia, command relationships were much simpler. No active war was going on in that country and no American ambassador was present, Prince Norodom Sihanouk having broken off formal relations with the United States over earlier cross-border incursions by the South Vietnamese. Hence, Westmoreland had complete authority over all American military activity in Cambodia. There was, however, very little of it to direct. Following a policy of strict respect for Cambodian neutrality and sovereignty in hopes of regaining Sihanouk's cooperation against the Communists, the Johnson administration closely restricted allied military operations along the South Vietnamese–Cambodian border. Under the rules of engagement prescribed by the JCS and CINCPAC, MACV's air and ground forces could strike enemy positions in Cambodia only to protect themselves against North Vietnamese and Viet Cong attack; they could not fire on places inhabited by Cambodians under any circumstances.[21]

For the most part, General Westmoreland rigorously enforced these regulations on his field commanders, although he was willing to stretch them to some degree to gain a tactical advantage. In March 1966, for example, he turned down a suggestion by General Larsen that MACV simply move the Cambodian border with II Corps, which was disputed, several kilometers westward to facilitate a I Field Force search and destroy operation. Instead, with General Wheeler's concurrence, Westmoreland urged Larsen to interpret the self-defense aspect of the regulations liberally when maneuvering within South Vietnam against enemy troops near or at the border.[22]

By the time Westmoreland gave these instructions to Larsen, he was well aware that Cambodia's posture as a neutral haven of peace in Southeast Asia was a facade. Beginning as early as 1964, South Vietnamese and later U.S. military intelligence had gradually accumulated evidence that the North Vietnamese, with at least the passive support of Prince Sihanouk's government, were making extensive use of Cambodia not only as a location for camps and supply depots but also as a conduit and source of food, weapons, and munitions. By late 1966, the MACV Intelligence Directorate and other U.S. agencies were well on the way to establishing that the North Vietnamese were feeding their troops in the Central Highlands with Cambodian rice and that Communist arms were being delivered by ship to Sihanoukville, from whence they were flowing into the Mekong Delta. The extent of the enemy base network paralleling the South Vietnamese–Cambodian border also was well known.[23]

The Johnson administration nevertheless declined to take action against the enemy's facilities in Cambodia for fear of diplomatic opprobrium over a U.S. attack on a neutral, ostensibly peaceful state. President Johnson and his advisers believed that Prince Sihanouk might yet be drawn to the allied side, especially as he learned the extent of North

Prince Norodom Sihanouk with President Kennedy (CMH files)

The Wider Theater

Vietnamese and Viet Cong violation of his nation's jealously guarded sovereignty. Disagreements within the intelligence community also made for inaction. The Central Intelligence Agency persistently rejected military claims that major arms shipments were coming through Sihanoukville and insisted that the enemy's border bases were being stocked primarily from within South Vietnam or via the Ho Chi Minh Trail. Constrained by these considerations, President Johnson throughout his term relied primarily on quiet diplomacy in attempting to turn Sihanouk against his not altogether welcome Communist guests.[24]

The president and his advisers also gradually enlarged the scope of military action, especially in gathering additional information on enemy activities with which to influence Sihanouk. To that end, during 1966 and 1967, at the urging of the Joint Chiefs and General Westmoreland, they instituted step by step a highly secret program of air and ground reconnaissance of eastern Cambodia.

The effort began in mid-June 1966, when the administration authorized General Westmoreland to conduct a one-time series of aerial photographic missions over a twenty-kilometer-deep strip of Cambodia along the South Vietnamese border. Carried out by the Seventh Air Force and code-named DORSAL FIN, the missions were limited to a total of twelve, with no more than four aircraft over Cambodia at any one time. MACV confined information about the flights and distribution of the intelligence gained from them to a minimum number of key command and staff personnel. It made no public announcements of the missions and provided the crews with cover assignments on the South Vietnamese side of the border. When the initial incursions produced no international furor, the administration over the following year gradually enlarged the program. It allowed MACV to carry out continuous aerial reconnaissance within the twenty-kilometer zone, although at a rate of no more than twenty missions per month and with tight security restrictions remaining in effect.[25]

Supplementing the aerial surveillance, in May 1967 the president authorized General Westmoreland to send SOG teams into the twenty-kilometer border strip. Code-named DANIEL BOONE, these incursions were initially limited to only the northern part of the border zone, with a ceiling of ten missions a month and three teams in Cambodia at any one time. To avoid attracting attention, the teams were to enter and leave their operating areas on foot, avoid contact with Cambodian troops and civilians, and engage only in reconnaissance. As was the case with DORSAL FIN, the administration gradually relaxed the restrictions. By the end of 1967, MACV could conduct thirty missions a month along the entire length of the border and insert a limited number of teams by helicopter. Even so, the command had to inform Pacific Command of each mission forty-eight hours in advance, and it had to obtain JCS approval of each individual patrol in the southern part of the border strip. Despite these restrictions, the reconnaissance effort grew to substantial size, with ninety-nine teams inserted into Cambodia during the last half of 1967.[26]

Besides executing the limited operations permitted him, General Westmoreland sought to promote more extensive U.S. efforts, both diplomatic and military, to eliminate the enemy's Cambodian sanctuaries. As early as December 1965, he directed the chief of MACV's Naval Advisory Group to prepare plans for a naval blockade of Sihanoukville and the Mekong River, Cambodia's principal outlets to the sea. Late the following year, he organized a staff committee chaired by the MACV J5, code-named STEAM BATH, to recommend courses of both military and nonmilitary action in Cambodia. MACV headquarters worked closely with SEACOORD in promoting the establishment of interdepartmental Cambodia monitoring groups in Washington and Southeast Asia; Westmoreland kept Australian officials, whose embassy represented U.S. interests in Phnom Penh, informed about North Vietnamese and Viet Cong violations of Cambodia's neutrality; and early in 1968 MACV headquarters provided intelligence support for an effort by Ambassador Chester Bowles to reopen diplomatic contact with Sihanouk.[27]

On the military side, Westmoreland, with encouragement from SEACOORD and Ambassador Bunker, pressed forward with plans and proposals for seizing or blockading Sihanoukville, for blockading the Mekong, for limited ground operations against enemy base areas, and for air attacks, including B–52 strikes, into Cambodia. In December 1967, in his most ambitious proposal up to that time, he asked Admiral Sharp and the Joint Chiefs for permission to conduct artillery fire from within South Vietnam and tactical air and B–52 strikes against enemy forces in the so-called Tri-Border Area where Laos, Cambodia, and South Vietnam came together. This region, according to MACV intelligence, contained a North Vietnamese division headquarters, important supply depots and road junctions, and several enemy regiments recuperating from recent heavy fighting in South Vietnam. Westmoreland argued that a surprise bombardment of a base complex hitherto safe from attack would inflict heavy enemy losses. Since the area was remote and had few civilian inhabitants, the attack should produce little diplomatic reaction and might be conducted without publicity. Both Ambassador Bunker and Admiral Sharp endorsed the tri-border plan. Nevertheless, the administration withheld approval rather than risk disrupting the Bowles mission. At the end of 1967, MACV's military activity in Cambodia remained confined to reconnaissance.[28]

MACV and ROLLING THUNDER

From its beginning in February 1965, the bombing campaign against North Vietnam gradually expanded in the number of raids and in the importance of the industrial, transportation, and military targets struck. American public and official debate over the campaign—its jus-

The Wider Theater

tification, objectives, and effectiveness—intensified even as the bombing did. Within the government, the Joint Chiefs of Staff and Admiral Sharp continuously pressed for heavier bombing of more significant targets. Civilian officials from the State Department and Central Intelligence Agency, and increasingly from the Department of Defense, challenged the political wisdom and military value of ROLLING THUNDER and urged that Johnson reduce the program or even halt it entirely. By late 1966 Secretary McNamara had joined their ranks. Pressed from all sides and concerned as well with congressional and public opinion, President Johnson held back. He authorized incremental expansion of the campaign, but never to the levels desired by the military. While not directly responsible for ROLLING THUNDER, Westmoreland of necessity became involved in both the campaign and the debate. He sought to influence the conduct of operations in order to assist his efforts in South Vietnam, and he added his voice to the military's advocacy of the air offensive.[29]

Westmoreland followed closely the activities of his 2d Air Division/Seventh Air Force commander, to whom Pacific Air Forces, Admiral Sharp's agent for directing the northern air war, delegated much of the responsibility for coordinating Air Force and Navy raids against North Vietnam. At Sharp's request, Westmoreland offered recommendations for improving ROLLING THUNDER's effectiveness in interdicting the flow of enemy troops and supplies into the south. In addition, at the insistence of the American embassy in Saigon, late in 1965 he took on the task of investigating periodic mistaken bombings in the Demilitarized Zone by jets, usually from the carriers, trying to hit targets in the southernmost part of North Vietnam and instituted more rigorous control procedures for strikes close to the buffer zone between the two Vietnams.[30]

From the beginning of major air attacks on the north, General Westmoreland had argued with Admiral Sharp, to no avail, that he should be CINCPAC's agent for direction of the campaign. In mid-March 1966 he made a more modest bid for jurisdiction over operations in Route Packages One and Two, the segments of North Vietnam just above the Demilitarized Zone.[31] Concerned about an enemy force buildup in the area that appeared to threaten the two northernmost provinces of I Corps, he proposed that MACV take over direction of air strikes in the zone, which had become, in effect, an extension of the southern battlefield. The operations he envisioned, patterned on the TIGER HOUND concept used in Laos, would feature strikes directed by forward air controllers on the basis of continuous air reconnaissance and intensive intelligence gathering. *(Map 5)*

The MACV commander argued that with these route packages under his jurisdiction, he could readily shift air power between infiltration targets in Laos and North Vietnam in response to changing weather and tactical conditions. He also contended that a more clear-cut division

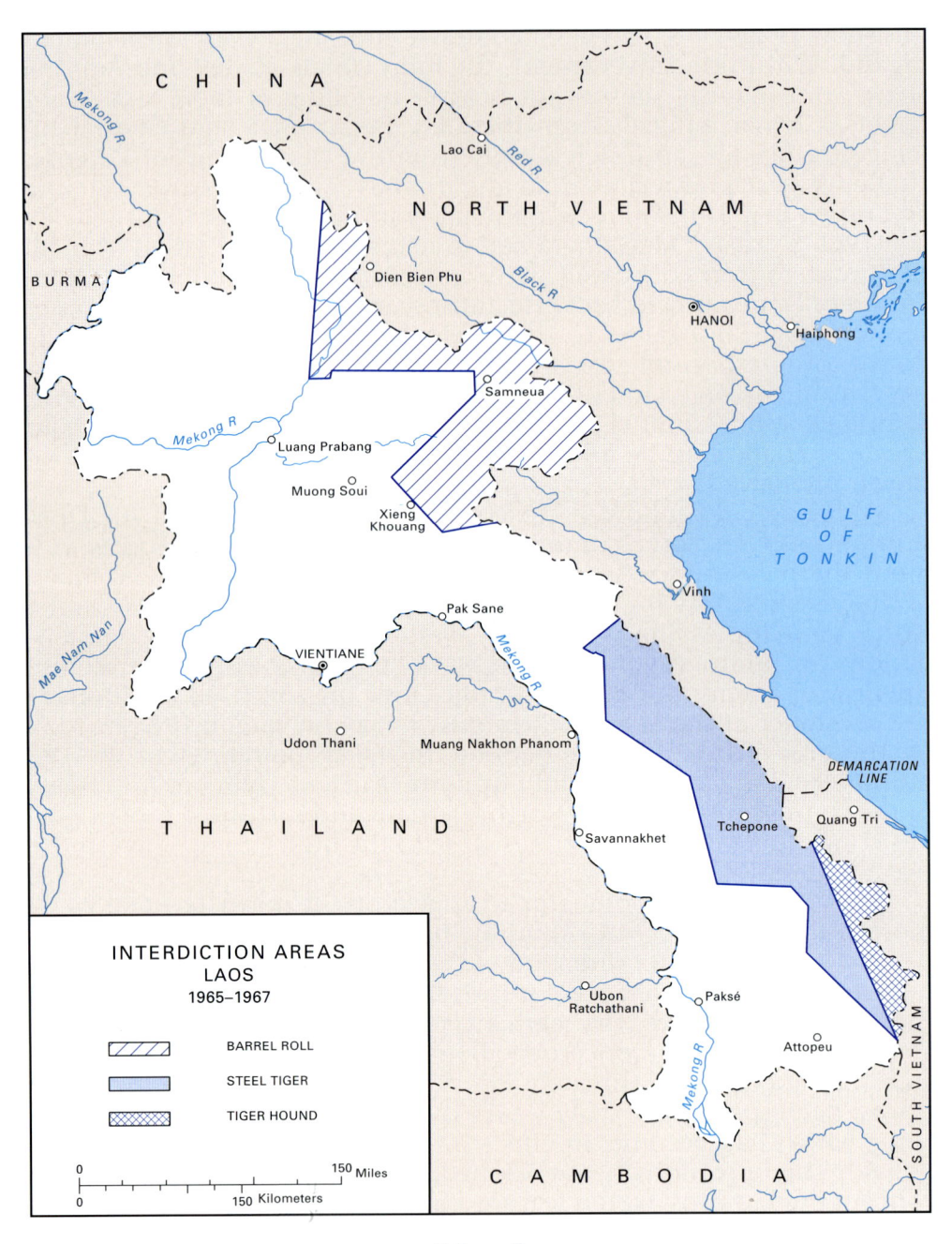

MAP 5

The Wider Theater

of labor would result, with Sharp directing the "strategic" bombing of the upper portions of North Vietnam and Laos while MACV conducted what was essentially a "tactical" air war in the lower regions. To avoid any appearance of an appeal over his superior's head, Westmoreland addressed this recommendation only to Sharp, with no information copy to General Wheeler. He explained, "It is Admiral Sharp's prerogative to organize this command as he sees fit and I did not want my recommendation with respect to internal command relations to be known outside of this headquarters."[32]

Initially reluctant, Sharp on 26 March granted the MACV commander authority over Route Package One, whose boundaries were expanded slightly northward. Route Package Two, however, he kept out of Westmoreland's jurisdiction because strong North Vietnamese air defenses there prevented the use of TIGER HOUND tactics. Sharp provided Westmoreland an allowance of sorties from Thailand and from the carriers for use in both the Laotian panhandle and Route Package One, and he permitted the MACV commander to use aircraft based in South Vietnam in those same areas when Westmoreland considered such employment "advantageous to the overall battle." From that time on, the Seventh Air Force flew missions in Route Package One under Westmoreland's direction.[33] *(Map 6)*

With Route Package One in hand, Westmoreland reached out for control of more of the northern air war. During one of Admiral Sharp's visits to Saigon early in July 1966, the MACV commander suggested that he also receive responsibility for Route Package Two, again on grounds that the area was an extension of the battlefield in South Vietnam. Sharp refused. He declared that South Vietnam, Laos, and Route Package One were plenty for Westmoreland to handle and that carriers of Task Force 77 were providing adequate coverage of Route Package Two. Subsequently, Sharp turned down a proposal by Westmoreland that the air effort against the northern route packages be reduced in favor of an all-out interdiction campaign in southern North Vietnam. Insisting that "pressure on the northern area may be what is needed to convince Hanoi that they are embarked on an unprofitable course of action," Sharp instructed Westmoreland to reallocate his own already ample air resources for interdiction if he considered the mission that important. The admiral reminded Westmoreland that "the responsibility for ROLLING THUNDER remains with me, including the allocation of sorties." Following this exchange, Westmoreland made no further efforts to encroach on Sharp's ROLLING THUNDER preserve.[34]

Even as he tried to extend his jurisdiction over ROLLING THUNDER, Westmoreland joined Admiral Sharp and General Wheeler in defending the bombing offensive and advocating its expansion. Westmoreland was a relatively late convert to this position. During the policy deliberations of 1964 and early 1965, he repeatedly expressed doubt that air attacks would bring Hanoi to terms while its forces were winning in the south. He also warned against provoking the North Vietnamese until the Saigon government and army were strong enough to withstand enemy retaliation. The arrival of American troops relieved Westmoreland's anxieties on the latter point. Nevertheless, he continued to regard ROLLING THUNDER as having at best peripheral effects on the war in the south, his primary concern. He informed General Wheeler as late as February 1967 that air interdiction in North Vietnam and Laos, while it had inflicted "appreciable damage" on the enemy's logistical system, had not affected "in drastic degree" the movement of troops on foot into South Vietnam. In allocating air power, Westmoreland favored giving priority to tactical support in South Vietnam, if necessary at the expense of ROLLING THUNDER. "We continually were faced with trying to make Westy realize that the air campaign in the north was an essential part of the whole operation," Admiral Sharp declared. "It was probably late 1966 or early 1967 before he fully understood how important the air campaign against North Vietnam was."[35]

Whatever his initial reservations, Westmoreland did join Admiral Sharp and General Wheeler in their advocacy of the northern air campaign. He had no objection to putting direct pressure on Hanoi, provided that such action did not jeopardize South Vietnam or divert resources from the campaign there; and he appears to have wanted to maintain a united front with Sharp and Wheeler in favor of strong military action, especially in the face of rising challenges from "dovish" civilians. Accordingly in June 1966, at Sharp's and Wheeler's suggestion, Westmoreland recommended attacks on North Vietnam's petroleum storage and distribution facilities. He argued that such an escalation, by demonstrating American resolve, would improve the morale of the South Vietnamese government, then recovering from near-civil war in I Corps. In October, Westmoreland repeated his endorsement of ROLLING THUNDER directly to McNamara when the defense secretary visited Saigon. He told McNamara that South Vietnam was secure enough that "we are now in a position to apply whatever pressure is necessary to influence the leadership in the North."[36]

As the sole senior military representative at the Manila conference later that month, Westmoreland, coached in advance by Wheeler, delivered a still stronger endorsement of ROLLING THUNDER to President Johnson and other Washington officials. He claimed at that time that the bombing was reducing the flow of enemy troops and munitions into South Vietnam and undermining Hanoi's general ability to carry on the war. He declared that any halt to air attacks in the north would have an "adverse psychological effect" on South Vietnamese and allied fighting forces. Echoing a persistent theme of Admiral Sharp's, he deplored the slow and cautious expansion of the air offensive to that point and urged heavier bombing of a wider range of targets.[37]

During 1967, as the military-civilian debate over ROLLING THUNDER approached a critical stage, Westmoreland closely coordinated his com-

The Wider Theater

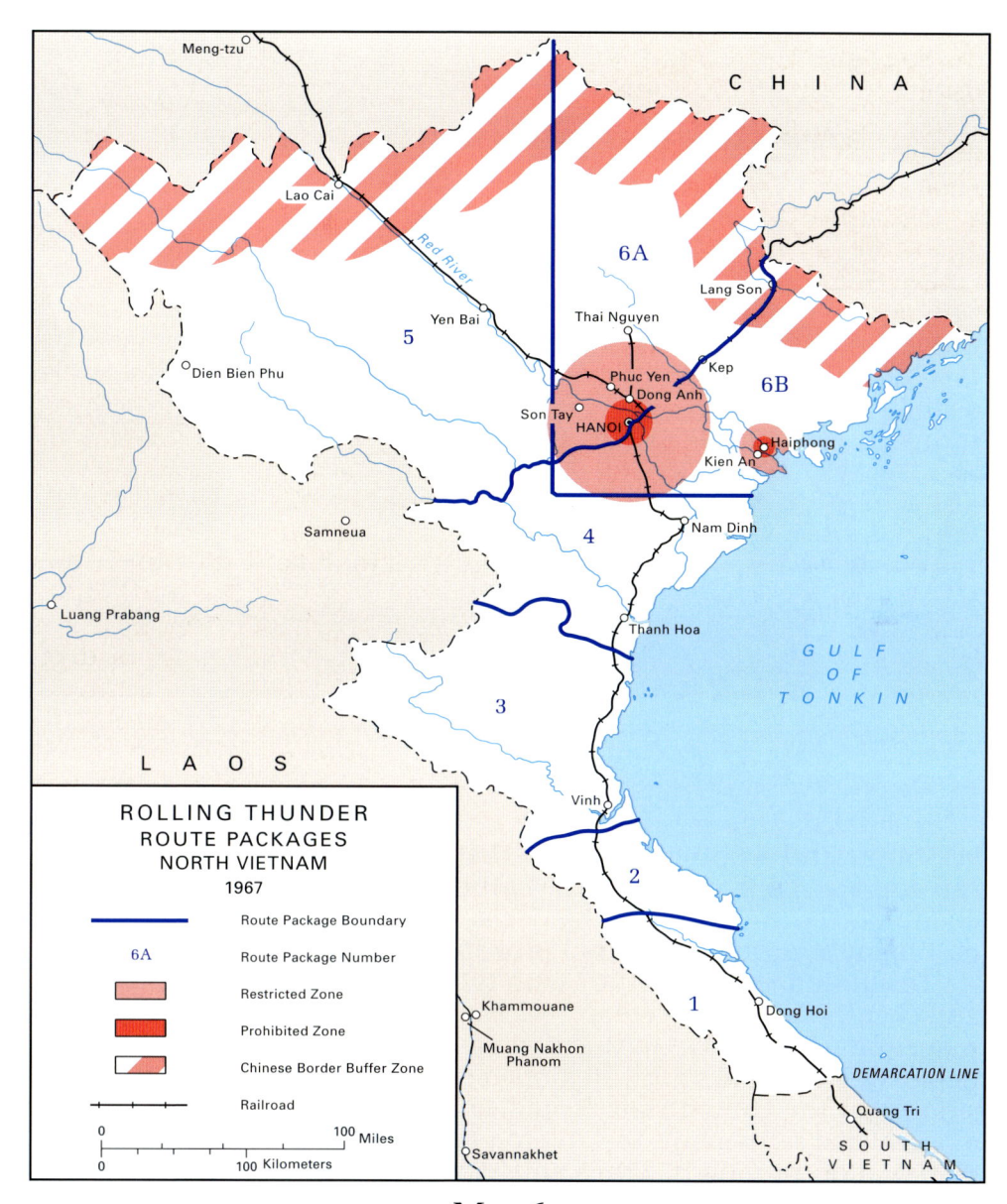

MAP 6

ROLLING THUNDER
ROUTE PACKAGES
NORTH VIETNAM
1967

ments on the air campaign with those of Sharp and Wheeler. In March, at the request of President Johnson transmitted through McNamara and Wheeler, Westmoreland held a press conference on the bombing to counter a proposal by Senator Robert F. Kennedy of New York, for an immediate suspension of attacks on North Vietnam followed by negotiations. In an on-the-record statement to reporters in Saigon,

387

MACV: The Years of Escalation, 1962–1967

Ambassador Bunker and General Westmoreland greet Secretary of Defense McNamara on his arrival in Saigon, July 1967. (NARA)

Westmoreland repeated his claim that ROLLING THUNDER "saves American and Vietnamese lives on the battlefield" by limiting the buildup of enemy forces. In that light, he declared, a cessation of bombing "will cost many additional lives and probably prolong the conflict."[38]

Disillusioned by mid-1967 with the course of the war in both North and South Vietnam, Secretary McNamara proposed a leveling off or reduction of air attacks in the north and a halt to further ground troop deployments in the south. He hoped thereby to establish a military position that the United States could sustain indefinitely while pursuing a negotiated settlement. Seeking to present a united front against these deescalation proposals, Sharp and Westmoreland worked closely with Wheeler in coordinating a response to the defense secretary. Preparing for a decisive conference with McNamara in Saigon in early July, Westmoreland and Sharp, along with General Momyer, who was drafted to defend the air war, assembled an orchestrated series of briefings for the secretary. During the Saigon conference, held from 7 to 12 July, the military leaders argued unanimously against reduction of ROLLING THUNDER, to the annoyance of McNamara, who had hoped they would provide justification for his proposals. In the end, the results of the conference, as far as the bombing campaign was concerned, were inconclusive. President Johnson held to his policy of incremental expansion of the target list but declined to give the military the authority for the heavy attacks they deemed necessary.[39]

Through the end of the year, in the face of rising debate in the United States over the war and its strategy, General Westmoreland kept up his support of the bombing campaign, always in terms of its importance in assisting allied operations and saving American lives in South Vietnam. He thus told presidential adviser Walt Rostow in November: "I believe the bombing campaign is of the greatest importance. If we are to have real impact on the enemy's lines of communication, we should bomb them throughout their entire length."[40]

A Tangled Chain of Command

In attempting to unify the air campaigns and cross-border operations in Southeast Asia in support of the war in South Vietnam, General Westmoreland faced multiple adversaries and obstacles. For reasons of both international diplomacy and U.S. interservice rivalry, the Johnson administration declined to establish a single U.S. theater command for Southeast Asia, leaving the development and execution of strategy to negotiation among a number of power centers with different interests and priorities. The administration's policy of maintaining the facade of neutrality in Laos and of avoiding confrontation with Cambodia imposed narrow limits on what MACV could do against the cross-border bases and infiltration routes that sustained the enemy in South Vietnam. Admiral Sharp's insistence on directly conducting ROLLING THUNDER operations further circumscribed Westmoreland's ability to unify the American military effort.

The Military Assistance Command's arrangements for prosecuting the cross-border wars, like those for conducting air and ground operations in South Vietnam, were a fabric of compromises that sought to reconcile military effectiveness with a multitude of contradictory diplomatic, political, and bureaucratic interests. In developing these arrangements and making them work, General Westmoreland displayed a talent for maintaining reasonably cordial personal and working relationships with colleagues, such as Ambassador Sullivan, with whom his interests conflicted. Promoting his own strategic objectives tactfully but persistently, he achieved incremental successes on many of the points that were of concern to him. But working arrangements and incremental gains on particular issues added up to much less than a coherent strategy for victory, whether in the extended battle area of Cambodia, Laos, and North Vietnam or in Westmoreland's main area of interest, South Vietnam.

MACV: The Years of Escalation, 1962–1967

Notes

¹ Quote is from Westmoreland Hist Notes, 6 Jul–3 Aug 67, tab A, Westmoreland Hist File 19 (6 Jul–3 Aug 67), CMH. Westmoreland, *A Soldier Reports*, p. 411, argues retrospectively that a Southeast Asia theater command should have been formed. General William M. Momyer, USAF (Ret.), *Airpower in Three Wars* (Washington, D.C.: Department of the Air Force, 1978), pp. 68–69; and Claude Witze, "The Case for a Unified Command: CINCSEA," *Air Force* 50, no. 1 (January 1967): 23–29, in tab C–7, Westmoreland Hist File 12 (13 Dec 66–26 Jan 67), reflect Air Force support for a theater–wide commander.

² Sharp's views are in Sharp, "Reminiscences," pp. 244, 246. MACV Staff Study, ca. Jun 65, sub: Organization of MACV, MACTHAI, USSEASIA, tab 50, Westmoreland Hist File 16 (10 May–30 Jun 65), CMH. Rosson Interv, 1981, pp. 335–38; Mrozek, *Airpower*, p. 33.

³ MACV Staff Study, ca. Jun 65, sub: Organization of MACV, MACTHAI, USSEASIA, tab 50, Westmoreland Hist File 16 (10 May–30 Jun 65), CMH.

⁴ Quote is from Msg, Westmoreland MAC 1723 to Sharp, 30 Mar 65, Westmoreland Msg Files, 1 Jan–31 Mar 65, CMH. CINCPAC Command History, 1964, pp. 19–21; MACV Command History, 1965, p. 102. Westmoreland, *A Soldier Reports*, pp. 76–77.

⁵ Msg, Wheeler JCS 1884–65 to Sharp and Westmoreland, 22 May 65, Westmoreland Msg Files, 1 Apr–30 Jun 65, CMH. MACV Command History, 1965, pp. 102–03. Quote is from MacDonald-Westmoreland Interv, 14 May 73.

⁶ MACV Command History, 1964, p. 156; ibid., 1965, pp. 156–60, 422; ibid., 1966, pp. 743–45; ibid., 1967, pp. 1021–24. Memo, Westmoreland for CINCPAC, 27 Oct 67, sub: SEATO Log TM Conference, Westmoreland Sig File, Oct 67; Msgs, Stilwell BNK 0195 to Sharp, 21 Jan 66; Westmoreland MAC 8956 to Amb Martin, 13 Oct 66. In Westmoreland Msg Files, 1 Jan–31 Mar 66 and 1 Oct–31 Dec 66, CMH. Westmoreland Hist Briefing, 5 Jun 66, tab A, Westmoreland Hist File 7 (29 May–16 Jul 66), CMH.

⁷ MACV Command History, 1967, 1:332–33, summarizes MACV's objectives in Laos. Msg, Westmoreland MAC 2015 to Sullivan, 1 Mar 67, Westmoreland Msg Files, 1 Jan–31 Mar 67, CMH, is a typical compendium of the command's knowledge of enemy infiltration.

⁸ MACV Command History, 1965, pp. 209–13, 216–17; ibid., 1966, p. 422. Westmoreland Hist Notes, 24 and 28 Nov 65, 3 and 8 Dec 65, Westmoreland Hist File 2 (25 Oct–20 Dec 65), CMH; 31 Dec 65 and 12 Jan 66, Westmoreland Hist File 3 (20 Dec 65–29 Jan 66). Both in CMH. Inception of SHINING BRASS is recounted in Interv, Senior Officers Oral History Program with Brig Gen Donald D. Blackburn, 1983, pp. 346–49, MHI. See also Msg, Westmoreland MAC 3894 to Sharp, 31 Jul 65, Westmoreland Msg Files, 1 July–30 Sep 65, CMH.

⁹ Momyer, *Airpower in Three Wars*, pp. 84–86; MACV Command History, 1965, pp. 213–14, 465; ibid., 1967, 1:439–40; Parry, *Three-War Marine*, p. 269, provides a MACV staff officer's view of the direction of operations in Laos.

¹⁰ Westmoreland, *A Soldier Reports*, pp. 107–09; Blackburn Interv, 1983, pp. 340–45, MHI; Interv, Charles B. MacDonald with Maj Gen John K. Singlaub, 18 Oct 73, Notes in CMH files; Memo, Westmoreland for Lt Gen Starbird, 17 Dec 66, sub: Barrier Plan, tab A–3, Westmoreland Hist File 12 (13 Dec 66–26 Jan 67), CMH; MACV Command History, 1966, pp. 681–83.

¹¹ Quotes are from Blackburn Interv, 1983, pp. 359–60, MHI; see also pp. 339–40, 361. MACV Command History, 1967, 1:129 and ann. G, app. 1; ibid., ann. F, pp. 1–2 and app. 1.

[12] Sullivan's role in Laos is described in Charles A. Stevenson, *The End of Nowhere: American Policy Toward Laos since 1954* (Boston: Beacon Press, 1972), pp. 208–17; quote is from p. 217. Momyer, *Airpower in Three Wars*, pp. 85–86; MACV Command History, 1965, p. 216. Blackburn Interv, 1983, p. 362, MHI. For a typical statement of Sullivan's approach to the conflict, see Memo, Sullivan for W. P. Bundy, 1 May 67, sub: Limitations on Military Actions in Laos, box 2, Warnke Papers, McNaughton Files, LBJL.

[13] Westmoreland Historical Briefing, 17 Sep 66, tab E, Westmoreland Hist File 8 (17 Jul–17 Sep 66), CMH. See also tab C, Westmoreland Hist File 3 (20 Dec 65–29 Jan 66); tab B, Westmoreland Hist File 17 (1–31 May 67); tab A, Westmoreland Hist File 19 (6 Jul–3 Aug 67); and Msg, Westmoreland MAC 3318 to Sharp, 27 Apr 66, Westmoreland Msg Files, 1 Apr–30 Jun 66. All in CMH. Air Force complaints are summarized in Momyer, *Airpower in Three Wars*, pp. 86–87; Brown Interv, 20 Oct 70, pp. 53–54; and Blood Interv, 6 Apr 70, pp. 27–34.

[14] These consultations can be followed through General Westmoreland's Message Files and Historical Files for 1965–1968. For an example of SEACOORD's activities and procedures, see Msgs, Amb Bunker Saigon 2203 to SecState and SecDef, 1 Aug 67, tab A–21, Westmoreland Hist File 19 (6 July–3 Aug 67), CMH. Rosson Interv, p. 336, MHI, comments on the slowness of SEACOORD procedures. Ltrs, Brig Gen Chaisson to Mrs Chaisson, 14 Jan and 27 May 67, box 6, Chaisson Papers, Hoover Institution, describe the Udorn meetings.

[15] MACV Command History, 1965, pp. 196–97, 213, 215–16; ibid., 1966, pp. 421, 423, 425–27; ibid., 1967, 1: 332–33, 351–52, 440–44, 453–55, and ann. G, p. G–1 and app. 4, pp. 1–2. Blackburn Interv, 1983, pp. 349–51, MHI. Memo, Sullivan for W. P. Bundy, 1 May 67, sub: Limitations on Military Actions in Laos, box 2, Warnke Papers, McNaughton Files, LBJL, summarizes Vientiane's concessions to that point. Msgs, Rosson MAC 5076 to Westmoreland, 19 Jun 66; Westmoreland MAC 6209 to Sharp and McDonald, 21 Jul 66; Wheeler JCS 1422–67 to Sharp and Westmoreland, 22 Feb 67; Westmoreland Msg Files, 1966–1967, CMH.

[16] Quotes are from Msg, Sullivan to Westmoreland and Sharp, 10 Aug 67, Westmoreland Msg Files, 1 Jul–30 Sep 67. Msg, Westmoreland MAC 7617 to Sharp, 13 Aug 67, tab A–8, Westmoreland Hist File 20 (4–20 Aug 67), CMH. The dispute can be followed through Msgs, Westmoreland MAC 7473 to Sullivan, 9 Aug 67; Westmoreland MAC 7627, MAC 8918, MAC 9415 to Sharp, 13 Aug 67; 21 Sep 67; 8 Oct 67; Gen Johnson JCS 7491 to Sharp, 23 Sep 67; Sharp to Westmoreland, 1 Oct 67; Westmoreland Msg Files, Aug–Oct 67, CMH.

[17] Early consideration of a Laos cordon by Westmoreland and Gen Johnson is described in Chapter 6 of this volume. Msg, Momyer and W. G. MacMillan MAC 3859 to Westmoreland, 23 Apr 67, Westmoreland Msg Files, 1 Apr–30 Jun 67; and Memo, MacMillan for Westmoreland, 18 Apr 67, sub: Panhandle Truck Traffic, tab A–17, Westmoreland Hist File 17 (1–31 May 67), both in CMH, reflect the conclusion that aerial interdiction could not stop enemy truck movement in Laos. For PRAIRIE FIRE's difficulties, see Msg, COMUSMACV MAC 32035 to CINCPAC, 29 Sep 67, Westmoreland Sig File, 1967, CMH.

[18] Msgs, Westmoreland MAC 0907 to Waters, 2 Feb 66; Westmoreland MAC 10627 to Sharp, 5 Dec 66; Westmoreland to McDonald, 14 Dec 66. All in Westmoreland Msg Files, 1 Jan–31 Mar 66 and 1 Oct–31 Dec 66, CMH. Westmoreland Hist Notes, 23 Jan 66, tab F, Westmoreland Hist File 3 (20 Dec 65–29 Jan 66), CMH.

[19] Westmoreland, *A Soldier Reports*, p. 272; MACV Command History, 1967, 1:333–34; Westmoreland Hist Briefing, 3 Feb 67, tab A, Westmoreland Hist File 13 (27 Jan–25 Mar 67); MFR, Rosson, 8 Apr 67, sub: CIIC Meeting, 8 Apr 67, tab A–7; Westmoreland Hist Notes, 10–30 Apr 67, tab B. Both in Westmoreland Hist File 15 (27 Mar–30 Apr 67),

CMH. Memo, Westmoreland for Secretary of Defense, sub: Laos, 10 Jul 67, tab A–19, Westmoreland Hist File 19 (6 Jul–3 Aug 67), CMH; Westmoreland Hist Notes, 19–26 Dec 67, tab A, Westmoreland Hist File 27 (19–26 Dec 67), CMH. Msg, Westmoreland MAC 00686 to Sharp and Wheeler, 15 Jan 68, tab A–28, Westmoreland Hist File 28 (27 Dec 67–31 Jan 68), CMH.

[20] "Laos: Problems, Policies, and Outlook for 1967," Approved by Ambassador and Country Team, Vientiane, 15 Jan 67, Westmoreland Hist File 14 (Baguio Conference), CMH. Memo, Sullivan for William Bundy, 1 May 67, sub: Limitations on Military Actions in Laos, box 2, Warnke Papers, McNaughton Files, LBJL. Sharp, "Reminiscences," pp. 312–13, 411–12, 562–63; Westmoreland, *A Soldier Reports*, pp. 148, 153. Palmer, *25-Year War*, pp. 187–88; and Interv, 7 and 10 Jun 68, pp. 229–32, criticizes the failure of Westmoreland and other U.S. leaders to consider the Laos cordon as an alternative to a war of attrition waged throughout South Vietnam.

[21] MACV Command History, 1965, p. 214; ibid., 1967, 1:351; Chaisson Oral History, p. 155.

[22] Msgs, Larsen NHT 0154 to Westmoreland, 21 Mar 66; Wheeler JCS 1710–66 to Sharp and Westmoreland, 1 Apr 66; Westmoreland MAC 2574 to Larsen, 1 Apr 66; Sharp to Westmoreland, 2 Apr 66. All in Westmoreland Msg Files, 1 Apr–30 Jun 66, CMH.

[23] MACV Command History, 1965, p. 209; ibid., 1966, pp. 27–28. Msg, Larsen NHT 0896 to Westmoreland, 23 Jul 67, Westmoreland Msg Files, 1 Jul–30 Sep 67, CMH. Westmoreland Hist Notes, 14 Nov 65, tab D, Westmoreland Hist File 2 (25 Oct–20 Dec 65) and 23 Dec 65, tab A, Westmoreland Hist File 3 (20 Dec 65–29 Jan 66), CMH. Memo, McChristian for Distribution, 30 Sep 66, sub: The Role of Cambodia in the NVN–VC War Effort, tab B–3, Westmoreland Hist File 9 (18 Sep–17 Oct 66), CMH. Interv, LBJL with Lt Gen Phillip Davidson, 30 Mar and 30 Jun 82, sec. 2, pp. 24–26.

[24] For administration policy, see Msgs, Westmoreland MAC 7152 to Larsen, 30 Jul 67, Westmoreland Msg Files, 1 Jul–30 Sep 67; and Bunker Saigon 13345 to SecState, 13 Dec 67, tab A–18, Westmoreland Hist File 26 (29 Nov–16 Dec 67). Both in CMH. Intelligence disagreement: Davidson Interv, 30 Mar and 30 Jun 82, sec. 2, pp. 26–35; Rpt, Ofc of ACofS for Intel, DA, "The Role of Cambodia in the NVN–VC War Effort, 1964–1970," overview, extracts in Vietnam Command File, NHC; Westmoreland, *A Soldier Reports*, pp. 180–83.

[25] Msgs, Wheeler JCS 3087–66 to Sharp, 2 Jun 66; Westmoreland MAC 4613 to Sharp, 5 Jun 66; Wheeler JCS 3307–66 to Westmoreland and Sharp, 11 Jun 66; Westmoreland MAC 5278 to Emrick, 25 Jun 66; Westmoreland MAC 10431 to Sharp, 29 Nov 66; CJCS JCS 1641–67 to Sharp and Westmoreland, 2 Mar 67. All in Westmoreland Msg Files, 1 Apr–30 Jun 66, 1 Oct–31 Dec 66, 1 Jan–31 Mar 67, CMH. MACV Command History, 1965, p. 214; ibid., 1967, 1: 444–45.

[26] MACV Command History, 1967, ann. G. app. 4, pp. 2–4.

[27] Msg, Rear Adm Ward to Vice Adms Clarey and Hyland and Rear Adm Swanson, 27 Dec 65, Rear Adm Ward's Personal Msg File, 1965, box 108, COMNAVFORV Records, NHC. Msgs, Westmoreland MAC 8213 to Sharp and Wheeler, 20 Sep 66; Wheeler JCS 5872–67 to Westmoreland, 26 Jul 67. Both in Westmoreland Msg Files, 1 Jul–30 Sep 66, 1 Jul–30 Sep 67, CMH. Westmoreland Hist Notes, 28 Dec 67–31 Jan 68, tab A–1, Westmoreland Hist File 28 (27 Dec 67–31 Jan 68), CMH. Memo, Westmoreland for Bunker, sub: Cambodia, 9 Nov 67, Westmoreland Sig File, Nov 67. All in CMH. MACV Command History, 1966, pp. 747, 750.

[28] For military planning, see tab B–4, Westmoreland Hist File 11 (30 Oct–12 Dec 66); tab A–7, Westmoreland Hist File 15 (27 Mar–30 Apr 67); tab A–11, Westmoreland Hist File 23 (1–15 Oct 67); and tab A–5, Westmoreland Hist File 26 (29 Nov–16 Dec 67).

All in CMH. Msgs, Westmoreland MAC 11702 and MAC 12208 to Sharp, 4 Dec 67, 16 Dec 67; Rosson NHT 1536 to Westmoreland, 10 Dec 67; Sharp to Wheeler, 19 Dec 67; Wheeler JCS 11097–67 to Westmoreland, 23 Dec 67; Westmoreland MAC 12674 to Wheeler, 26 Dec 67. All in Westmoreland Msg Files, 1–31 Dec 67, CMH.

[29] The official debates over ROLLING THUNDER can be followed in detail in *U.S.–Vietnam Relations*, sec. 4.C.7.(a) and (b). Development of the campaign is summarized in Sharp and Westmoreland, *Report on War*, pp. 23–43, 53–54. Admiral Sharp vigorously defends the bombing campaign in *Strategy for Defeat: Vietnam in Retrospect* (San Rafael, Calif.; Presidio Press, 1978), and in his "Reminiscences," pp. 370–72, 335–38, 511. George Herring, "'Cold Blood': LBJ's Conduct of Limited War in Vietnam," Harmon Memorial Lectures in Military History no. 33 (Colorado Springs: USAF Academy, 1990), analyzes Johnson's strategy-making by compromise.

[30] Momyer, *Airpower in Three Wars*, pp. 89–98. Sharp and Westmoreland, *Report on War*, p. 20; MACV Command History, 1965, pp. 202–06; Msgs, Westmoreland MAC 4758, MAC 5712, MAC 5937, MAC 5987 to Sharp 23 Sep, 13 Nov, 23 Nov, 26 Nov 65; Rosson MAC 4814 to Westmoreland, 27 Sep 65; Sharp to Westmoreland, 22 Nov 65. All in Westmoreland Msg Files, 1 Jul–31 Dec 65, CMH. Memo, Lt Gen Moore for Westmoreland, 26 Nov 65, sub: Procedures to Control Strikes Near the DMZ, tab E–2, Westmoreland Hist File 2 (25 Oct–20 Dec 65), CMH.

[31] The better to coordinate their operations, the Air Force and Navy divided North Vietnam into "route packages," geographical areas in which one or the other service normally flew most of the missions.

[32] MACV Command History, 1966, p. 428. Msgs, Westmoreland MAC 2165, MAC 2261, MAC 2275 to Sharp, 17, 21, 22 Mar 66, Westmoreland Msg Files, 1 Jan–31 Mar 66, CMH. Quote is from Westmoreland Hist Notes, 20 Mar 66, tab A, Westmoreland Hist File 5 (13 Mar–23 Apr 66), CMH; in same file, see tab B.

[33] Msgs, Sharp to Westmoreland, 19 and 26 Mar 66; Sharp to Wheeler, 26 Mar 66; Westmoreland MAC 2428 and MAC 3050 to Sharp, 27 Mar and 18 Apr 66. All in Westmoreland Msg Files, 1 Jan–30 Jun 66, CMH. MACV Command History, 1966, pp. 395, 428; Sharp and Westmoreland, *Report on War*, p. 24. Westmoreland Hist Notes, 3 Apr 66, tab C, Westmoreland Hist File 5 (13 Mar–23 Apr 66), CMH.

[34] Momyer, *Airpower in Three Wars*, p. 102; Westmoreland Hist Notes, 10 Jul 66, tab E, Westmoreland Hist File 7 (29 May–16 Jul 66), CMH; MACV Command History, 1966, p. 398. First quote is from Msg, Sharp to Westmoreland, 18 Jul 66; second is from Msg, Sharp to Westmoreland, 13 Jul 66; Westmoreland Msg Files, 1 Jul–30 Sep 66, CMH. In same file, see Msgs, Westmoreland MAC 6018 and MAC 6148 to Sharp, 16, 19 Jul 66.

[35] For Westmoreland's views during 1964, see Chapter 5 of this volume. Also Westmoreland Hist Notes, 8 Nov 65, tab C, Westmoreland Hist File 2 (25 Oct–20 Dec 65), CMH. Westmoreland's retrospective views on ROLLING THUNDER are in *A Soldier Reports*, pp. 112–13, 119–20, 122. Sharp quotes are from his "Reminiscences," p. 370. Westmoreland's comments on interdiction are in Msg, MAC 01297 to Sharp, 6 Feb 67, tab B–2, Westmoreland Hist File 13 (27 Jan–25 Mar 67), CMH.

[36] Msgs, Wheeler JCS 3086–66 to Sharp info Westmoreland, 2 Jun 66; Sharp to Westmoreland, 4 Jun 66; Westmoreland MAC 4613 to Sharp, 5 Jun 66. All in Westmoreland Msg Files, 1 Apr–30 Jun 66, CMH. Westmoreland Hist Notes, 5 Jun 66, tab A, Westmoreland Hist File 7 (29 May–16 Jul 66 and 17 Oct 66), tab D, Westmoreland Hist File 9 (18 Sep–17 Oct 66). Both in CMH. Quote is from latter entry.

[37] Msgs, Wheeler JCS 6339–66 to Sharp and Westmoreland, 17 Oct 66; Westmoreland (Manila) to Wheeler, 25 Oct 66; Wheeler JCS 6549–66 to Westmoreland, 25 Oct 66; Sharp to Westmoreland, 28 Oct 66. All in Westmoreland Msg Files, 1 Oct–31

Dec 66, CMH. Westmoreland Hist Notes, 21 Oct 66; Memo, Westmoreland for W. W. Rostow, 24 Oct 66, sub: COMUSMACV's Comments on Rolling Thunder, tab 4; Msg, Westmoreland to Wheeler and Sharp, 27 Oct 66, tab 3. All in Westmoreland Hist File 10 (18–29 Oct 66), CMH. Memo, McNaughton for Secretary McNamara, 26 Oct 66, sub: McNaughton in Manila . . . , box 7, Warnke Papers, McNaughton Files, LBJL.

[38] Quote is from Msg, Westmoreland MAC 2101 to Wheeler and Sharp, 3 Mar 67; Westmoreland Msg Files, 1 Jan–31 Mar 67, CMH. In same file, see Msgs, Wheeler JCS 1594–67, JCS 1613–67, JCS 1617–67 to Westmoreland, 1, 2 Mar 67; and Westmoreland MAC 2086 to Wheeler, 2 Mar 67.

[39] Msgs, Wheeler JCS 3891–67, JCS 3930–67 and JCS 3892–67, to Sharp, info Westmoreland, 25, 26 May 67; Sharp to Westmoreland, 27 May 67 and 27 Jun 67; Wheeler JCS 4200–67 to Sharp and Westmoreland, 6 Jun 67; Westmoreland MAC 5865 to Sharp, 21 Jun 67. All in Westmoreland Msg Files, 1 Apr–30 Jun 67, CMH. Westmoreland Hist Notes, 1 Jun–5 Jul 67, tab A, Westmoreland Hist File 18 (1 Jun–5 Jul 67), CMH; Sharp, "Reminiscences," pp. 463–65, 481–82. Decisions resulting from Saigon conference are summarized in *U.S.–Vietnam Relations*, sec. 4.C.7.(b), pp. 78–80.

[40] MFR, Westmoreland, 22 Nov 67, sub: Luncheon Meeting with Mr. Walter [sic] Rostow at the White House on 20 November, tab A–23, Westmoreland Hist File 25 (13–28 Nov 67), CMH.

12

An Evolving Strategy

Like everything else about the Military Assistance Command, its strategy for fighting the ground war evolved over time, in response to circumstances and to a variety of internal and external influences. Early U.S. pacification plans and operating experience; assessments of enemy capabilities and intentions; the condition of the South Vietnamese government and armed forces; the availability of American troops; and the maneuverings of individuals and agencies in Saigon, Honolulu, and Washington all influenced the way in which COMUSMACV conducted his campaign.

As senior U.S. commander in South Vietnam, General Westmoreland took the initiative in proposing ground strategy and requesting forces to carry it out. Nevertheless, his freedom of action was far from absolute. He labored under tight political restrictions, especially on operations against the enemy's Laotian and Cambodian bases; and he had to maintain the appearance, and insofar as possible the reality, of South Vietnamese sovereignty. He also had to accommodate the advice, criticism, and demands of numerous other actors. Civilian officials in Washington from the president down, the Joint Chiefs of Staff, the Department of Defense and other agencies, Admiral Sharp and his Pacific component commanders; the U.S. Mission in Saigon, the South Vietnamese government and armed forces, and the allied military contingents all sought to impose their own patterns on the conflict.

Basic Questions

By the time American ground troops entered the conflict in force, the basic allied military strategy in South Vietnam was well established. In common with most counterinsurgency struggles, the ground war effort had two elements. The first, often referred to as the "big unit war," consisted of mobile operations by regular troops to disperse or destroy the insurgents' organized military units and disrupt their logistical bases. During 1964 General Westmoreland had labeled these "search and destroy" operations. The second element comprised the complex range of military and paramilitary activities known in American parlance as "pacification" and by the Saigon government as "Revolutionary Development." The military work of pacification included small-unit patrols and ambushes to eliminate Viet Cong guerrillas in and around villages and hamlets, police operations to root out the enemy's clandestine political administration, and protection of population and economic centers and lines of communication. The most important military task in pacification and the ultimate measure of its success was the provision of round-the-clock security both to the peasants and to the government officials who provided services to them.

Even as the North Vietnamese and Viet Cong main and local forces and guerrillas operated in mutual support of one another, the two elements of allied strategy were supposed to be mutually reinforcing. Search and destroy operations would deprive the guerrillas and political infrastructure of their large-unit support and allow Saigon's police and paramilitary elements safely to carry out their work in the villages. At the same time, effective pacification would provide the allies with improved intelligence to guide their offensives while denying intelligence, supplies, and hiding places to the Viet Cong and North Vietnamese main force. Conducted simultaneously, in proper balance, search and destroy and pacification would bring every segment of the insurgent structure under constant pressure and ultimately cause the enemy to collapse.

As of late 1965, both elements of the allied campaign were in serious difficulty. By building main force regiments and divisions equipped with top-quality modern infantry weapons, the enemy was enlarging the scale of the big-unit war, intensifying its violence, and seizing the initiative in it. Mauling Saigon's regulars and driving them out of the countryside, the main force opened the way for guerrillas and local force detachments to dismantle pacification in the villages. They did not have much to dismantle. Saigon's pacification program languished as governments came and went in the capital and politico-military factions jockeyed for power. Wracked by seemingly endless political instability, Saigon could neither fight nor govern effectively.

In this context, how could the arriving American forces be best employed to halt Saigon's decline and turn the war around? Should American troops concentrate on breaking up the enemy's main force, a mission for which their mobility and firepower seemed best suited? Or should they be used in a direct relationship to the peasantry to strengthen village and hamlet security and root out the Viet Cong guerrillas and shadow government? Could pacification proceed at all while the Saigon regime lacked any semblance of stability and legitimacy? Would the introduction of massive American military power, in the air over the north and on the ground in the south, convince Hanoi and its Soviet and Chinese sponsors that their side could not win and induce them to negotiate deescalation and political accommodation? Or should the United States level off its commitment and prepare to

An Evolving Strategy

hold on through a prolonged stalemate? These questions preoccupied General Westmoreland and his civilian and uniformed superiors as they shaped military strategy during the two years following the initial commitment of American soldiers to battle in South Vietnam.

The Initial Concept

The first American combat troops who entered South Vietnam arrived before their government had formulated any real plans for their operations. President Johnson and Secretary McNamara dispatched troops to Vietnam on the assumption that they were needed to turn the tide on the battlefield and that they would attack the Viet Cong and North Vietnamese main forces and possibly help the South Vietnamese Army clear and secure the countryside. They left it to General Westmoreland, under the guidance of the JCS and CINCPAC, to produce an operational plan.[1]

The Military Assistance Command developed its ground war strategy under far from ideal conditions. The headquarters staff itself was in a state of rapid growth and organizational flux; it worked in a dispersed, barely adequate physical plant. Although MACV and its subordinate American field commands possessed a relatively sophisticated understanding of overall enemy strategy and intentions, they had little detailed current information at the outset about the opposing forces' strength and locations. Resources also were limited. In the absence of a reserve call-up, the deployment of Westmoreland's reinforcements and the establishment of the logistical base in South Vietnam to support them proceeded slowly. Most of the forces with which the MACV commander had planned to take the offensive were not in place until the last months of 1966. The South Vietnamese government was at the same time struggling to maintain its authority and establish some semblance of constitutional legitimacy. Its armed forces barely could protect the government's vital areas, and the regime could muster organization and manpower for only the most limited pacification endeavors. Fully engaged against an enemy whose main forces and guerrillas alike were increasing in numbers, aggressiveness, and effectiveness, MACV could do little at the beginning except rush American troops to the most threatened points. Westmoreland told General Wheeler on New Year's Day, 1966: "The fact is there are high security risks in almost every direction . . . and we are reacting as rapidly and forcefully as we can with the forces available to us."[2]

From MACV's perspective, strategic and operational direction of this unconventional, decentralized conflict entailed principally the establishment of general policies and objectives, the allocation of troops and combat and logistical support, and the establishment of geographical priorities for security and pacification. In South Vietnam, the corps and divisions, once deployed, remained in place and conducted operations within fixed tactical areas of responsibility. There were few opportunities for the theater headquarters to maneuver large formations. Corps areas, and regions within corps areas, differed in geography, population, and the character and disposition of enemy forces. Hence, each local commander had to work out his own mix of the search and destroy and pacification components of the overall strategy. For the most part, MACV had no choice but to allow field force and division commanders to fight their own local wars. The command's directives and campaign plans promulgated broad principles, published lists of things to be done, and established criteria—usually statistical—for measuring progress. Plans and directives often had more the character of exhortations than of specific orders, and high-level debates over the conduct of the war took on an air of abstraction.[3]

Westmoreland and his staff did not plan in a vacuum. They worked within a rough official consensus that took shape during late 1965 and early 1966. That consensus had varied origins. One was the basic spreading–oil-spot concept of pacification that had dominated American and South Vietnamese conduct of the war since Kennedy's inauguration. When the American buildup began, the South Vietnamese Army was still trying, without much success, to put into effect the latest version of that approach in the HOP TAC region around Saigon and in other national priority areas. General Westmoreland's first MACV concept of operations, issued on 1 September 1965, also centered on territorial pacification. It envisioned a three-phase campaign in which the South Vietnamese would continue their clearing and securing efforts while American forces attacked the Viet Cong's major units and base areas. The concept provided for geographical expansion of pacification in each phase until the Saigon government regained control of most of South Vietnam's population and resources.[4]

To territorial pacification, Westmoreland during late 1965 added the concept of attrition. The general predicted to the president, Secretary McNamara, Ambassador Lodge, and assorted official and unofficial visitors that the war would be prolonged and that it would be won by slowly grinding down the enemy. Typically, he told Ambassador Lodge on 29 December 1965 that "unless we escalated to the point where all weapons available to us were used . . . I foresaw an extended war of attrition." He expected to win such a war because "our troops should always be fresh because of the one year tour" and because American firepower and mobility would inflict greater losses on the Viet Cong and North Vietnamese than they could sustain in the long run. However, the MACV commander studiously avoided estimating how much time the process would take, especially in the absence of authorization to cut the Ho Chi Minh Trail and clean out the enemy's cross-border bases. On a couple of occasions, Westmoreland had his J5 Directorate examine other possible approaches to conducting the war. However, given the political limitations within which MACV had to operate, the staff could produce no workable alternative to trying to outlast the enemy in a politico-military endurance contest.[5]

As the war went on, Americans increasingly referred to attrition—meaning primarily the attack on the other side's main force—as a "strategy," contrasted with pacification. Attrition, however, was in reality more an objective and measurement of progress than a concept that shaped the deployment and maneuver of forces at theater and corps level. Particularly for American combat units, enemy casualties became the most important of the many statistical indicators that the authorities in Saigon, Honolulu, and Washington used in attempting to determine how the conflict was going. Yet the principal means of inflicting those casualties, the search and destroy operation, originated as a component of the pacification campaign and continued to be closely tied to it. Further complicating the issue, pacification was itself an attritional process of gradually wearing down the insurgent local units, guerrillas, and infrastructure. General Westmoreland deployed his American divisions more to defend important terrain objectives, notably Saigon, than to bring enemy forces to battle. Hence, the Americans would carry on attrition from a territorial security posture. In the light of these facts, the attrition versus pacification debate came down largely to an argument about the allocation of U.S. troops in particular areas between anti-main force offensives and the attack on the local Viet Cong guerrillas and political underground. In the end, the North Vietnamese and Viet Cong usually resolved that issue through their own decisions on where and when to mount a large-unit threat.

Advocates of pacification made themselves heard during the strategy deliberations of late 1965. Westmoreland, and most other American officials, appreciated that a successful pacification program could at the very least shorten the attrition process by depriving the Viet Cong of access to the food and manpower of the countryside. More positively, Ambassador Lodge and General Lansdale consistently argued that pacification—by which they meant democratic social and economic reform as well as the provision of military security—was the only road to assuring the survival of a non-Communist South Vietnam. Several high-level Washington conferences and committees produced studies and reports with the same conclusion. For example, the authors of the Army's PROVN (Program for the Pacification and Long-Term Development of South Vietnam) study, completed in March 1966 under the sponsorship of the Chief of Staff, General Johnson, declared flatly that victory in South Vietnam "can only be achieved through bringing the individual Vietnamese, typically a rural peasant, to support willingly the government." They called for radical reorganization of the U.S. Mission so that it could formulate and execute a unified civil-military program directed toward that end.[6]

This agitation of the pacification question appears to have influenced President Johnson and his senior advisers, at least to the extent

MACV: The Years of Escalation, 1962–1967

that they insisted that planning for revival of the Saigon government's rural security and development effort accompany the preparations for military escalation. General Wheeler told Westmoreland late in 1965: "We must have Vietnamese military, para-military and police actions (together with related non-security programs) compatible with the build-up of Third Country forces in order that the pacification program can move forward in step with military operations against main-force VC units. . . . A comprehensive and carefully drawn program" for these purposes, he continued, "is considered here to be the keystone of our future efforts." Emphasizing the same theme at the Honolulu conference in February 1966 President Johnson issued a ringing public call for renewed nonmilitary efforts in South Vietnam. Johnson and the South Vietnamese leaders promulgated a mixture of military and pacification goals for the allied war effort.[7]

General Westmoreland attempted to link attrition and pacification in MACV directives and in the annual Combined Campaign Plans. His concept of operations differed little in fundamentals from that which he previously had urged upon the South Vietnamese, except that American troops were taking on much of the task of fighting the enemy main force within an overall territorial-security approach to the conflict. The combined plans stated the allies' mission succinctly: "to defeat the VC and extend GVN control in the Republic of Vietnam." To accomplish this mission, the allied military forces were to defend major bases and government centers; secure key resources, such as rice and salt; open and protect important roads, railways, and waterways; conduct "sustained air and ground operations" against enemy forces and bases; assist in the expansion of government control of the countryside; and interdict enemy land and water infiltration routes. Each annual plan established national, corps, and ultimately province priority areas for pacification, very limited in the 1966 plan but gradually expanding in later years. In these areas, following the familiar sequence, government regular troops were supposed to drive out or destroy Viet Cong military units. Regional and Popular Forces, police, and pacification cadres then were to root out the insurgent infrastructure, reestablish village and hamlet administration and public services, and, it was hoped, regain the people's allegiance for the Saigon regime.[8]

The combined plans called for American and other allied contingents to concentrate on attacking North Vietnamese and Viet Cong units and base areas while the South Vietnamese regulars and the Regional and Popular Forces did most of the work of clearing and securing the villages and hamlets. Yet the distinction was never absolute. The marine and airborne battalions of Saigon's general reserve continued to perform primarily an offensive role, as did some ARVN units; and General Westmoreland left open the possibility of American participation in territorial security activities. The Combined Campaign Plan for 1967, issued late in 1966, summarized the somewhat blurry division:

RVNAF will have the primary mission of supporting Revolutionary Development [pacification] activities, with priority in and around the National Priority Areas and other areas of critical significance. . . . The primary mission of U.S. and FWMAF will be to destroy the VC/NVA main forces, base areas, and resources and/or drive the enemy into the sparsely populated and food-scarce areas. . . . Although RVNAF is assigned the primary responsibility of supporting Revolutionary Development and US/FWMAF are assigned the primary mission of destroying the main VC/NVA forces and bases, there will be no clear cut division of responsibility. RVNAF General Reserve and ARVN Corps Reserve units will conduct unilateral and participate in coordinated and combined search and destroy operations. US/FWMAF will continue to provide direct support and implicit aid to Revolutionary Development activities.[9]

In conferences with his American troop commanders, Westmoreland emphasized the attack on enemy forces. When General Larsen assumed command of U.S. troops in II Corps, Westmoreland "directed that our primary combat mission was to seek out and destroy, wherever we found them, the hard core . . . NVA and Main Force units." During his frequent visits to Larsen's headquarters, the MACV commander "emphasized one thing. 'Go out and seek the enemy and hit him wherever and whenever you can find him. Drive, drive, drive. You take the initiative and don't let him ever get back his balance.'" Westmoreland delivered similar exhortations at his periodic commanders' conferences during late 1965. However, the first MACV directive on tactics and techniques for U.S. forces in Vietnam was more cautious in tone. It emphasized the Viet Cong's skill at evading offensive sweeps and instructed American units to conduct thorough reconnaissance and establish close liaison with Vietnamese military and provincial authorities in order to locate the enemy and develop effective operations.[10]

General Westmoreland's assignment of American troops to a primarily anti-main force offensive mission reflected a widespread consensus among American and South Vietnamese officials. Secretary McNamara, the Joint Chiefs, and Admiral Sharp all assumed that American troops, with their mobility and firepower, could operate to best advantage outside the most densely populated areas and against the enemy's large units, whereas their lack of knowledge of Vietnamese language and culture would limit their usefulness in village- and hamlet-level pacification—a mission for which the South Vietnamese forces seemed best suited. The Army's PROVN study, while it emphasized the importance of pacification, also called for concentration of American troops against the enemy main force. Chief of State Thieu and other South Vietnamese officials preferred to keep American forces on the offensive outside the populated areas, both for military reasons and from reluctance to allow foreign soldiers to exercise direct police power over their citizens, as they would have to do in security activities such as searching hamlets, manning road checkpoints, or arresting suspected members of the Viet Cong underground.[11]

In Westmoreland's view, attacks on Viet Cong and North Vietnamese main forces and bases, besides being the best method of inflicting attrition on the enemy, were necessary to any revival of pacification. As Westmoreland and members of his staff interpreted it, the main lesson of the collapse of the CHIEN THANG campaign during 1964 was that forces engaged in clearing and securing had to be shielded from attacks by the enemy's concentrated large formations. The shielding could be done most effectively by allied spoiling attacks on the main force units and their assembly points. General Youngdale, McChristian's predecessor as MACV J2, declared that the command's view had changed from "if we can just get the VC infrastructure, in the hamlets, the rest of it will fall apart" to "you have got to do both, you have got to kill the main force and you have got to find the little guy. It has got to progress together."[12]

Westmoreland's plan to direct American operations primarily against enemy main forces met early on with dissent from advocates of a greater emphasis on securing people and territory. Ambassador Lodge periodically urged Westmoreland to devote more battalions to fighting guerrillas and fewer to pursuing the big units. General Taylor also questioned use of American troops in the "preponderant" offensive role, claiming that such employment would lead to U.S. assumption of an open-ended commitment to destroy the enemy throughout South Vietnam.[13]

More important operationally, the Marine command in I Corps both advocated and attempted to implement a security-oriented campaign. As the first major American ground combat element to arrive in South Vietnam, the III Marine Amphibious Force based its own independent concept of operations on its primary task—securing the large Da Nang airfield. Maj. Gen. Lewis W. Walt, the III MAF commander, quickly realized that to protect the base, he had to control the thickly populated villages that bordered it and extended southward into Quang Nam Province. Those villages were dominated by strong Viet Cong guerrilla forces and a well-entrenched clandestine administration, but they contained few enemy main force elements. Walt and his troops accordingly launched a methodical campaign emphasizing small-unit operations to drive out the guerrillas and gradually expand secure zones around Da Nang and the subsidiary Marine bases at Chu Lai in southern I Corps and Phu Bai near Hue in the north. They also took the lead in instituting a number of pacification expedients, including the Combined Action Program, under which they paired Marine rifle squads with Popular Force platoons to protect particular villages.

The marines were willing to engage big enemy units when good targets presented themselves, and they did so with considerable success on several occasions. Nevertheless, General Walt; his immediate superior at Fleet Marine Force Pacific, Lt. Gen. Victor H. Krulak; and the Marine Corps Commandant, General Greene, all believed that the struggle for the people in the hamlets and villages would decide the issue. If effective pacification denied the main forces access to the recruits, intelligence, and food of I Corps' narrow coastal plain, the Marine commanders insisted, the big units would have to choose between starving in the mountains and coming down to the plain to fight where III MAF's artillery and air power could destroy them. In this assessment, the Marine commanders left out of account the fact that the enemy large units in I Corps, operating close to their bases in Laos and North Vietnam, were less dependent than Communist forces elsewhere in South Vietnam on the populated lowlands. In addition, if the enemy came down to fight amid the villages and hamlets, the resulting destruction would wipe out whatever pacification gains the marines had made.[14]

General Krulak
(Time Life Pictures/Getty Images)

General Westmoreland criticized the marines' approach. As he saw it, by trying to occupy villages where the government was incapable of providing civil administration and territorial forces, the marines were simply bogging down their limited number of troops in what amounted to restricted beachheads, leaving the Viet Cong virtual freedom of action throughout most of I Corps. "You are already experiencing the extreme difficulty involved in pacifying an area which has long been under VC control," he told General Walt in November 1965. "The longer the VC have a free hand in the rest of the Corps, the more area they will consolidate, and the more difficult it will be for us in the long run to make significant gains." Hence, Westmoreland urged Walt to maintain a mobile force of at least two or three battalions for continuous offensive operations throughout I Corps, to destroy Viet Cong forces and keep the enemy off balance. To varying degrees, Generals Wheeler and Johnson, many other Army officers, and some civilian officials shared Westmoreland's view, deploring what they considered excessive Marine defensive-mindedness.[15]

In practice, the differences between Army and Marine strategies were less sharp than the rhetoric of partisans on both sides. The debate took form during mid- and late 1965, at a time when American forces had only just begun combat operations. Indeed, a Pentagon analyst later noted: "The Marine strategy was judged successful, at least by the Marines, long before it had even had a real test. It was applauded by many observers before the VC had begun to react to it, and . . . encouraged imitators while it was still unproven." As North Vietnamese regular divisions moved into I Corps during 1966, III MAF perforce committed more battalions to large-unit operations. General Krulak modified his descriptions of Marine strategy, pointing out to Secretary McNamara and others that it was actually a balance of pacification and offensive action; and he acknowledged that the geography of II and III Corps required a different operational approach from that adopted in I Corps.[16]

On his side, as he moved closer to taking over pacification, General Westmoreland permitted and even encouraged his Army commanders to employ battalions in clearing and securing operations with the South Vietnamese, especially when weather and lack of profitable targets prevented major offensives. At times, as in Operation FAIRFAX around Saigon, he committed brigade-size American forces to prolonged pacification campaigns in conjunction with the ARVN and territorials. He began describing MACV's strategy as "two-fisted," with one fist continually jabbing at the main forces and base areas while the other remained close to the body to secure people and territory. After three years of campaigning, General Chaisson, the Marine chief of MACV's Combat Operations Center, who previously had served as G3 of III MAF, declared that "there wasn't really a rat's ass worth of difference between the major things that [the marines]. . .were doing and the things that the Army was doing."[17]

Both MACV and III MAF were grappling with the problems inherent in contending with an enemy who combined large-unit and guerrilla military action with a highly developed system of political subversion and control. Lt. Gen. Frederick C. Weyand, who commanded successively the 25th Infantry Division and the II Field Force, summed up the problem: "There was no single element of the enemy's organization that, if attacked alone, would cause the collapse of his force structure or the reduction of his will to resist." Instead, the allies had to apply "concentrated pressure against the entire enemy system from hamlet level to Hanoi rather than against some single element" in a "strategy of all-round pressure, changing only in emphasis from time to time."[18] During most of the period from the start of the American troop buildup in mid-1965 through the end of 1967, MACV and the Saigon government lacked the military and nonmilitary resources to apply such pressure effectively against the entire enemy organization. General Westmoreland and his field commanders accordingly shifted their available resources among priorities and objectives as their own

An Evolving Strategy

views of the situation evolved and as they responded to pressures from Washington and the actions of the *PLAF* and *PAVN*.

Problems of Implementation

American and allied forces devoted late 1965 and most of 1966 to building up their troop strength and logistical base and to gradually intensifying combat operations. As U.S. Army divisions arrived, General Westmoreland deployed them to meet what seemed to be the principal enemy main force threats north of Saigon and in the Central Highlands. Not coincidentally, the other side long had viewed these areas as the decisive battlefields for large-unit combat and was building up its own main force regiments and divisions there. The two South Korean divisions and marine brigade occupied much of the coastal area of II Corps, protecting major ports and bases and controlling a portion of the agricultural region. In I Corps, III MAF deployed its two Marine divisions to protect what amounted to enclaves around Hue/Phu Bai, Da Nang, and Chu Lai. MACV initially left military operations and pacification in the Mekong Delta of IV Corps to the South Vietnamese Army, deferring to the reluctance of both the U.S. Mission and the Saigon government to place large foreign troop contingents in that thickly populated region. However, late in 1966, General Westmoreland began experimental deployments of both infantry units and riverine forces to the delta, in hopes of breaking what appeared to be a military stalemate in those rice-rich provinces.[19]

As American units established their base camps and acclimated themselves to the South Vietnamese weather and terrain, they began attempting to seek out and destroy *PLAF* and *PAVN* units in increasingly wide-ranging search and destroy operations. In III Corps, the 1st and 25th Infantry Divisions, working outward from Saigon, made their first incursions into the large enemy war zones that menaced the capital. In II Corps, the 1st Cavalry Division spent much of 1966 trying to clear strong guerrilla and main force elements out of the important coastal province of Binh Dinh; in the highlands, the 4th Division and other American units battled *PAVN* regiments, which periodically moved in from Cambodian sanctuaries to threaten Kontum and Pleiku. The marines in I Corps attempted to join their three enclaves through clearing and securing operations while occasionally lashing out, at Westmoreland's insistence, at enemy main forces. Increasingly, however, III MAF had to shift strength northward to drive back North Vietnamese divisions invading across the Demilitarized Zone, which rapidly became demilitarized in name only.[20]

In assessing the results of operations during 1966, General Westmoreland took an optimistic tone. He emphasized his command's success in blocking enemy offensives through well-timed spoiling attacks. He claimed that the Viet Cong and North Vietnamese had suffered heavy losses in men and supplies and that the allies had made limited but real progress toward all of the pacification goals set at Honolulu. Nevertheless, he also had to admit that the enemy, in spite of his casualties, had increased his troop strength during the year. While battered in many engagements, his large units remained intact and dangerous, while the allies' effort to root out the guerrillas was "just getting underway." The enemy, Westmoreland told Wheeler and Sharp early in 1967, was "hurt . . . but he is far from defeated."[21]

Overall, allied efforts to implement a combined attrition and pacification strategy had run into problems that would persist, in varying degree, for the duration of the war. The enemy's main forces proved more difficult to engage than American commanders had expected. An advocate and practitioner of attrition as MACV J3 and then commander of the 1st Infantry Division, General DePuy later admitted: "We hit more dry holes than I thought we were going to hit. They were more elusive. They controlled the battle better. They were the ones who usually decided whether or not there would be a fight." American offensives throughout 1966 and much of the following year were hampered by inadequacies in the collection, distribution, and use of intelligence, both in the field and at MACV; by a shortage of helicopters for mobility; by deficiencies in communications security; and by an insufficient number of infantry battalions. According to a later Defense Department analysis, MACV, with nearly half of its battalions normally tied up in defensive missions, much of the time barely equaled the enemy in manpower available for mobile operations. American artillery and air strikes became the equalizer in many engagements.[22]

While inefficient, the attrition campaign at the very least had hurt the enemy and effectively shut down whatever main force offensive operations he had planned. The allies' pacification effort, however, remained stalled, as the American mission struggled with issues of civil-military coordination and the Saigon government suppressed the I Corps mutiny, drafted a constitution, held elections, and completed its own "revolutionary development" organization. These actions laid essential foundations for the campaign to redeem the countryside, but in themselves they reclaimed few villages and hamlets. After a late 1966 visit to Saigon, Secretary McNamara concluded that "pacification has if anything gone backward," with enemy guerrilla forces, attacks, and terrorism increasing and no visible allied progress in controlling rice supplies, territory, and people.[23]

American air and ground combat operations created still another obstacle to pacification by inflicting a rising toll of civilian casualties, property damage, and population displacement in rural South Vietnam. As early as August 1965, Westmoreland pointed out to General Wheeler that, while he planned to keep the fighting away from inhabited areas as much as possible, nevertheless the enemy often chose to defend fortified hamlets and other populated places. His forces would have to fight

An Evolving Strategy

the enemy where they found him. In addition, since the Viet Cong's ultimate objective was "to control each and every hamlet in [South] Vietnam" and the allies' objective was "to prevent this from happening, or where it has happened, to regain control," inevitably the action was drawn "toward the people and the places where they live."[24]

As American and North Vietnamese main forces fought with increasing frequency and as guerrilla and antiguerrilla activity intensified, the toll of noncombatants caught in the crossfire steadily mounted. Many of these casualties resulted from Communist terrorism, indiscriminate rocket and mortar shellings, and road minings; but allied operations also inflicted a major share of suffering and death. American and South Vietnamese artillery fire and air strikes, necessary to defeat heavily armed guerrillas and main force units dug into populated areas, killed and injured noncombatants; there were as well occasional deliberate acts of murder and other crimes by American and allied soldiers. The war forced tens of thousands of peasants to move into refugee camps and urban shantytowns to escape bombing, shelling, and the extortion of recruits and supplies by both Vietnamese sides. In some instances, U.S. and South Vietnamese forces leveled villages and removed their inhabitants to deny food, intelligence, and concealment to the Viet Cong. The destruction of the Communist village stronghold of Ben Suc during Operation CEDAR FALLS, although militarily justifiable, received sensational critical coverage in the American news media. In the United States and around the world, the growing opposition to the Vietnam War publicized civilian death and suffering, and Communist propagandists kept up a barrage of atrocity charges.[25]

From the start of large-scale ground operations, MACV issued and attempted to enforce strict rules of engagement designed to minimize civilian casualties and property damage. The rules restricted firing in inhabited areas to positively identified enemy targets and required that commanders obtain clearance from both American and South Vietnamese authorities before employing artillery and air strikes near towns, villages, and hamlets. General Westmoreland issued directives, incorporated into the orientation of arriving American troops and printed on pocket cards for each individual soldier, calling for humane treatment of prisoners and noncombatants. The standing operating procedures of MACV's subordinate commands repeated the same principles. Given the constant rotation of personnel, lapses inevitably occurred in the enforcement of these rules, and commanders and troops had to be indoctrinated and reindoctrinated in their terms and importance. Even more thankless was Westmoreland's task of persuading his South Vietnamese and Korean allies to abide by the American standards rather than their own harsh rules of war.[26]

Too often, the desperate circumstances of combat trumped the most carefully drawn rules and the best intentions. On 12 November 1965, at the hamlet of Bau Bang, for example, the 2d Battalion, 2d Infantry,

MACV: The Years of Escalation, 1962–1967

of the U.S. 1st Infantry Division fought off a determined attack by the better part of two battalions of the Viet Cong *9th Division.* A couple of days before the battle, the American battalion had sent a civic action team into Bau Bang to distribute food, clothing, and CARE packages to the inhabitants. In the fight on the 12th, the Viet Cong used Bau Bang as a staging point for assaults, placing their supporting mortars and recoilless rifles in the hamlet itself. The Americans responded by calling in artillery and air strikes with bombs and napalm. Around 150 Viet Cong fighters and 20 American soldiers died in the action. No one counted how many people perished in Bau Bang. At the end of the fight, the hamlet "lay barren, a smoldering, lifeless ruin."[27]

The Communists met the American intervention with a counterstrategy of their own. After initial uncertainty in the face of the large-scale entry of U.S. troops into the war, an event they had not anticipated, North Vietnamese and Viet Cong leaders determined to continue and intensify both their main force and their guerrilla campaigns. One of the senior commanders of *COSVN*, which controlled enemy forces in the southern half of South Vietnam, General Tran Van Tra, recalled:

In 1965–1966, when the Americans were sending large numbers of troops into South Vietnam, a number of comrades in charge of the city of Saigon directly asked me, "The Americans are bringing in large numbers of troops and strong weapons, and are changing over to a limited war, so should we change our strategic line? Should we disperse our main force so that we can wage a protracted guerrilla war in order to defeat the enemy?" I emphatically said no. I explained the passive, fire-extinguishing role of the Americans . . . and that we would not disperse . . . to fight as guerrillas but would organize many additional divisions . . . and advance to the formation of corps. There was absolutely no question of changing the strategic line.[28]

True to the *COSVN* commander's word, the North Vietnamese and Viet Cong continued to expand their armed forces by increasing both infiltration from the north and recruiting in the south. By the end of 1966, MACV estimated that enemy troops of all categories totaled more than 280,000; the command credited them with 9 divisions, 34 regiments, and 186 combat and combat support battalions, many equipped with heavy mortars and 140-mm. and 122-mm. rockets as well as excellent Soviet- and Chinese-made infantry weapons. For practical purposes, the Communists' buildup thus matched that of the Americans. For although the allies between 1965 and the end of 1967 increased their manpower preponderance from a ratio of 3.5 to 1 to 5.9 to 1, the crucial ratio in maneuver battalions rose only from 1.25 to 1 to 1.63 to 1, a figure that helps to explain the allies' limited ability to trap and destroy the enemy's big units. The buildup included as well the village guerrillas, district companies, and provincial battalions—the key forces combating pacification. According to General Weyand, the enemy's local squads, platoons, and companies in III Corps "en toto, equated to *45* [italics in original] battalions of

General Westmoreland, center, *tours III MAF headquarters.*
(Courtesy of the Vietnam Archive at Texas Tech University)

infantry," over and above the 32 main force battalions in the corps area. Against such forces, the ARVN and territorials in many provinces simply lacked the strength to carry out their clearing and securing mission as prescribed in allied campaign plans.[29]

In a mirror image of Westmoreland's strategy, the enemy leaders, realizing that they could not defeat American forces outright, sought every opportunity to inflict casualties on U.S. units even at the cost of heavier casualties of their own. Such losses, they believed, would weaken the American people's will to continue the struggle. Seeking to retain the military initiative against superior American mobility and firepower, the *PLAF* and *PAVN* during 1966 disposed their regular units to achieve what the Military Assistance Command labeled "strategic mobility." They concentrated large numbers of battalions at several different points at once, to compel the allies to disperse their reserves and to create opportunities for major attacks that would bring significant military or psychological advantage. Thus the North Vietnamese repeatedly sent divisions through the Demilitarized Zone into northern I Corps and concentrated others nearby just above the DMZ and in Laos, compelling III MAF to shift most of the 3d Marine Division away from pacification around Da Nang to defend Quang Tri and Thua Thien Provinces. They also concentrated other forces in Cambodia for periodic incursions into II and III Corps. While these incursions cost the North Vietnamese and Viet Cong dearly whenever they resulted in engagements with American units, the Communist leaders appeared satisfied that by these tactics they were maintaining the strategic offensive.[30]

General Westmoreland understood the enemy strategy but could find no solution to it beyond trying to engage the North Vietnamese and Viet Cong at every point. In a typical assessment, he declared in October 1966: "The enemy has embarked on a war of attrition involving protracted guerrilla warfare supported by large formations of conventional troops operating from base areas and sanctuaries in difficult terrain and in neutral countries. . . . His purpose is to create a state of mind in our troop units and at home that is characterized by insecurity and futility. . . . He believes that his will and resolve are greater than ours. He expects that he will be the victor in a war of attrition in which our interest will eventually wane." The allies could foil this strategy, he concluded, only by resisting the enemy "throughout this spectrum of warfare."[31]

During 1966 Westmoreland became increasingly preoccupied with the enemy divisions massing in the DMZ and along South Vietnam's western border. He identified "containment" of these forces as a third major military mission for the allies, along with pacification support and attacks on units and bases within South Vietnam. Allied forces would, in effect, have to meet the enemy regulars and bring them to battle as soon as they crossed South Vietnam's border. To do otherwise would be to grant the enemy a psychological victory, increase his access to South Vietnam's people and resources, and allow him to infiltrate main force elements into the coastal lowlands where they could assist the guerrillas in disrupting pacification. Strategic necessity, in Westmoreland's view, was also tactical opportunity. When the enemy chose to fight in remote areas, he exposed himself to the full weight of the allies' air power and artillery, facilitating the process of attrition. Allied forces' air mobility, Westmoreland insisted, permitted rapid concentrations against emerging threats and equally rapid redeployments to the populated regions. "I can see absolutely no psychological or military advantage," he told General Wheeler, "to a strategy that would intentionally invite the war east toward the coast. It would be retrogressive, costly in casualties and refugees, and almost certainly prolong the war."[32]

Nevertheless, whatever the rationalizations Westmoreland might offer, MACV clearly was being forced to react to enemy maneuvers. As General Krulak declared during an October 1966 Marine shift northward to the DMZ, "I am deeply concerned that the enemy has played the tune, and induced us to dance to it." Early the following year, Westmoreland himself acknowledged that the enemy had developed "relatively well defined courses of action which he is still capable of implementing, under most circumstances, at times and places of his choice" and that allied concentrations against threats in some areas had resulted in "a draw down of forces in other areas and, concomitantly, a degraded capability for decisive action in these areas."[33]

An Evolving Strategy

To restore that capability while countering the Communists' initiatives, required additional allied manpower. Hence, Westmoreland sought more American troops. His reinforcement requests and the political implications of meeting them led to prolonged internal debate within the Johnson administration, and to modifications in the conduct of the war.

More Troops or a New Strategy?

Throughout 1966, American combat and support units streamed into South Vietnam under a reinforcement schedule worked out during the previous year. That schedule—which the Defense Department labeled Program Three—took final form only in mid-April, after a prolonged wrangle between Secretary McNamara and the Joint Chiefs over whether or not to mobilize the reserves. Deployments under it, however, had begun during December 1965 and were to continue well into 1967. By the end of that year, the United States would have more than 437,000 troops, including seventy-nine maneuver battalions, in South Vietnam.[34]

Secretary McNamara had hardly approved the final version of Program Three when Admiral Sharp initiated planning for its successor. Early in April 1966 the Pacific commander directed his subordinates, including General Westmoreland, to begin determining their force requirements for 1967. Sharp hoped to complete the complex process more quickly and with less confusion and disorder than had characterized the development of Program Three, soon enough in the year to give the military services the long lead times they would need to produce the additional forces. The headquarters promptly set to work, coordinating their efforts at a series of planning conferences in Saigon and Honolulu.[35]

On 18 June Admiral Sharp transmitted the results of this process to the Joint Chiefs of Staff. His request included both adjustments to Program Three and new forces for the following annual increment. It provided for rebuilding of Pacific Command's theater reserves as well as for reinforcements for MACV. The additions for Vietnam, proposed by MACV and accepted by CINCPAC, were modest compared to the dramatic force expansions of the previous year. General Westmoreland asked for what he called a "rounding out" force consisting of eleven U.S. infantry, armored cavalry, and tank battalions; a fourth rifle company for each Army infantry battalion already in Vietnam; five additional tactical air squadrons; and numerous combat and logistical support units. When deployed, they would increase total American strength in South Vietnam to more than 542,500 personnel and 90 maneuver battalions. These reinforcements, Westmoreland and Sharp declared, were required to offset the enemy's expected continuing buildup and to carry forward CINCPAC's threefold war strategy of bombing in

411

North Vietnam and attrition and pacification in South Vietnam. Westmoreland in addition requested that a "corps contingency force" of three divisions remain in readiness in the United States for dispatch to Southeast Asia in an emergency or if the administration decided on a major expansion of operations, for example a drive into Laos to cut the Ho Chi Minh Trail. That force, however, quickly disappeared from the negotiations that ensued.[36]

In contrast to his attitude of the previous year, Secretary McNamara subjected CINCPAC's new reinforcement request, which became Program Four in Pentagon terminology, to close and skeptical scrutiny. Influenced by the analyses of his civilian "whiz kids," the defense secretary during the summer of 1966 was beginning to question the prospects for success of both ROLLING THUNDER and the American ground war, and he had started to suspect that commitment of additional resources to those campaigns would bring little in the way of improved results. A visit to Honolulu early in July did nothing to resolve his doubts. As a result, when the Joint Chiefs formally presented Sharp's Program Four proposal to him on 5 August, McNamara responded with a request for a "detailed line-by-line analysis of these requirements" to determine which were "truly essential to the carrying out of our war plan." He admonished that "excessive deployments weaken our ability to win by undermining the economic structure of the RVN and by raising doubts concerning the soundness of our planning." To guide the Joint Chiefs in their review, McNamara transmitted to them a series of "issue papers" prepared by his staff that questioned the necessity for some 70,000 of the requested reinforcements.[37]

While the Joint Chiefs were conducting the analysis, prospective economic difficulties in South Vietnam and shortages of military resources in the United States emerged as obstacles to any further major reinforcement of MACV. In Saigon, Ambassador Lodge and his Economic Counselor, Roy Wehrle, became concerned that the expansion of U.S. forces, by increasing local American piaster spending, would accelerate South Vietnam's already severe inflation, with potentially devastating social, political, and economic effects. At Lodge's recommendation, Secretary McNamara set a ceiling in October of 42 billion piasters on U.S. military expenditures in Vietnam during 1967. General Westmoreland protested that under this ceiling it would be impossible to complete the Program Three deployments, let alone those proposed for Program Four. In the end, the Military Assistance Command, helped by the completion of much of its base construction, was able to reduce its troops' piaster spending per man to a level much below that assumed by the embassy, allowing further deployments within the ceiling. Nevertheless, the need to curb inflation in South Vietnam hung over the Program Four debate; if nothing else, it provided an additional argument for officials who had other reasons for wanting to limit further troop deployments.[38]

An Evolving Strategy

The Joint Chiefs of Staff drove what was perhaps the final nail into the coffin lid of Admiral Sharp's Program Four on 7 October, when they presented the secretary of defense with an analysis of the effects Program Four would have on U.S. military posture worldwide. They concluded that, to meet Program Four's requirements without dangerously weakening forces earmarked for NATO and other commitments, the services would have to call up more than 600,000 reservists, an action President Johnson considered politically out of the question. Program Four thus bumped up against what was later nicknamed the administration's "Plimsoll Line" on reinforcements for Vietnam: the point at which sending more troops would necessitate a major reserve call-up.[39]

Informed early in August that his new reinforcement package was "in trouble in the Washington arena," General Westmoreland prepared to reduce it. Throughout the spring and summer, the MACV commander received repeated warnings from General Johnson that the Army, due to lack of manpower and materiel, was straining to provide his Program Three forces on schedule as well as to replace losses in Vietnam among key personnel such as combat arms NCOs. He learned also that the Navy would have to stretch out the deployment of its riverine force in the Mekong Delta because of a McNamara-decreed cost reduction. All things considered, it seemed clear that, in the absence of a reserve call-up, the services could not furnish many additional units and might not be able adequately to support the force he already had.[40]

Late in July, Westmoreland instructed his J3 to try to establish "a possible leveling off point for our forces which might take place after the first of the year and involve no augmentation except for relatively small elements that would round out the force." The resulting structure, Westmoreland directed, should be "well-balanced," capable of "sustained combat," and "able to be supported without calling the reserves." Pursuing the same theme, early in September Westmoreland asked General Johnson for a specific estimate of "how much expansion in terms of supported maneuver battalions the Army believes it can sustain" without a reserve call-up and "without an undesirable deterioration in quality including morale." In response, the Army chief of staff sent a team to Saigon to brief MACV on the Army's likely situation in 1967. Westmoreland incorporated this information in additional guidance to his force planners.[41]

The MACV commander was thus forearmed when Secretary McNamara arrived in Saigon on 9 October to discuss additional forces for 1967, among other issues, in the light of South Vietnam's inflation problem and the Joint Chiefs' ominous posture statement. Westmoreland told the defense secretary that he agreed that the reserves should not be mobilized at that time. His headquarters, he said, was studying what size "level-off" force could be "sustained indefinitely without great degradation in quality" by "our manpower and industrial bases." He was convinced that "it is to be a long war and we should gear ourselves for it," as opposed to continuing to "build forces which might be difficult to support indefinitely, which would involve degradation in quality, and which would put increasing strains on the piaster economy." His "best estimate" put the sustainable force at between 480,000 and 500,000 men. McNamara, Westmoreland reported, "agreed with this philosophy and stated he was thinking in the same terms. He seemed to be relieved that I had thought the matter through to this extent and had taken such a position."[42]

With the field commander on record as being able to live with a ceiling on the force buildup, the decision to scale down Program Four was all but a foregone conclusion. Upon returning to Washington, McNamara on 14 October recommended that only enough troops be added in Program Four to bring U.S. strength in South Vietnam to about 470,000 men and 87 maneuver battalions by June 1968. Not coincidentally, this was the maximum force that officials then estimated could fit within the 42 billion piaster spending ceiling. About the same time, at their final CINCPAC deployment conference, Westmoreland and Sharp recommended a buildup to about 555,000 but at McNamara's direction also submitted three alternative smaller force packages based on varying piaster spending ceilings. In conversations with Assistant Secretary of Defense for International Security Affairs John McNaughton, Westmoreland suggested that 480,000 men by the end of 1967, rounded out to 500,000 during the following year, would be acceptable and sustainable. With the military commanders thus flexible, President Johnson early in November accepted McNamara's recommendation for 470,000 troops by June 1968. McNamara then informed the Joint Chiefs that he approved those strength figures for Program Four.[43]

Secretary McNamara justified his Program Four decision in terms that amounted to a major revision of his thinking about the war and to a call for reexamination of the prospects and purposes of both the air and ground campaigns. In his proposal of 14 October for a reduced Program Four, and in a draft presidential memorandum on the subject one month later, McNamara declared that he saw "no reasonable way to bring the war to an end soon." Based on studies by civilian consultants and intelligence analyses completed during the summer, he concluded that ROLLING THUNDER had not "significantly affected infiltration or cracked the morale of Hanoi" and was unlikely to do so. American ground forces in South Vietnam had inflicted heavy losses on the enemy and eliminated any chance of his winning a military victory but had not broken his morale or driven his casualties above the level he could replace. At the same time, the enemy had adopted "a strategy of keeping us busy and waiting us out (a strategy of attriting our national will)."

McNamara recommended to the president a five-point course of action aimed at girding the United States "openly, for a longer war and . . . taking actions immediately which will in 12 to 18 months give clear

An Evolving Strategy

evidence that the continuing costs and risks to the American people are acceptably limited, that the formula for success has been found, and that the end of the war is merely a matter of time"—a posture that might discourage the other side from "trying to 'wait us out.'" He proposed to "stabilize" U.S. strength in South Vietnam at 470,000 men; install a ground barrier across the Demilitarized Zone and the Laotian panhandle to reduce North Vietnamese infiltration (a possible substitute for ROLLING THUNDER); limit bombing of North Vietnam to existing sortie levels and targets; make a major effort to revive the South Vietnamese pacification campaign; and press for negotiations with Hanoi, possibly using a complete or partial cessation of ROLLING THUNDER as a bargaining chip. McNamara expressed little hope for an early diplomatic breakthrough but argued that the United States, by implementing his military recommendations and especially by improving pacification performance, could strengthen the allied position and in time perhaps bring the enemy to terms.[44]

McNamara's proposal to level off and deemphasize ROLLING THUNDER set off an acrimonious debate between himself on one side and the Joint Chiefs, Admiral Sharp, and key members of Congress on the other, one that persisted throughout the remainder of his tenure at Defense. His suggestions on ground strategy, on the other hand, produced much less confrontation because they envisioned more a shift of emphasis and rationale than a radical change of missions and tactics. McNamara did not challenge—indeed he reaffirmed—the assumption that U.S. ground forces in Vietnam should concentrate on attacking the enemy's regular units, both to "punish" them and to prevent them from interfering with pacification. But pacification itself, essential though it was, had to be performed primarily by the South Vietnamese government and armed forces. "It is known that we do not intend to stay," McNamara explained. "If our efforts worked at all, it would merely postpone the eventual confrontation of the VC and GVN infrastructures."[45]

Having made those points, McNamara asserted nonetheless that the anti-main force campaign was reaching the point of diminishing returns. Using an input-output analysis of MACV's statistics on enemy casualties and infiltration, he concluded that adding more American troops would not increase enemy losses in proportion to the cost of the reinforcement to South Vietnam in accelerated inflation and to the United States in additional casualties, government expenditures, and domestic political discontent. McNamara argued that instead of continuing in 1967 "to increase friendly forces as rapidly as possible, and without limit," and to engage in large-scale operations "to destroy the main force VC/NVA units," the United States should "follow a similarly aggressive strategy of 'seek out and destroy,' but . . . build friendly forces only to that level required to neutralize the large enemy units and prevent them from interfering with the pacification program." Not coincidentally, McNamara believed the required force level to be about

470,000 Americans, plus the 52,000 Free World allied troops and "less than half of the ARVN." The rest of the South Vietnamese Army, plus a "portion" of the U.S. force, "would give priority to improving the pacification effort." McNamara thus proposed to stop the growth of American troop strength in South Vietnam but not fundamentally to alter General Westmoreland's "two-fisted" military operations and pacification strategy, although by implication at least the defense secretary sought to tie the former element more closely to the latter.[46]

The Joint Chiefs of Staff rejected McNamara's concept of leveling off the American effort, insisting that it would prolong the war and possibly lead to allied defeat. Throughout the winter of 1966–1967, they continued to advocate a steady increase of American pressure on the enemy in both ROLLING THUNDER and the ground campaign. As part of this effort, in February General Wheeler in effect invited Westmoreland to reopen the question of Program Four force levels, claiming that President Johnson now was receptive to proposals for accelerating military operations. Reinforcing the case for reviving the issue, Admiral Sharp and General Westmoreland estimated that, as a result of economy measures, the piaster cost of the 470,000-man force would run well under the 42 billion piaster ceiling. They thereby removed one argument against expanding Program Four at least to the 550,000 men the two commanders had initially recommended.[47]

On 18 March 1967, General Westmoreland formally raised the curtain on the second act of the reinforcement drama. He dispatched to the Joint Chiefs, via Admiral Sharp, a request for additional troops over and above those in Program Four. In fact, he submitted two proposals. The first was an "optimum" reinforcement of 4 2/3 divisions (42 maneuver battalions), 10 tactical air squadrons, and a large riverine force. The second was more modest: a "minimum" augmentation of 2 1/3 divisions (21 maneuver battalions), with 4 tactical air squadrons and a smaller riverine force. The optimum plan would add more than 200,000 men to the 470,000 of Program Four, the minimum about half as many. In each case, Westmoreland wanted the additional deployments completed by 1 July 1968.

Westmoreland provided extensive justifications for both proposals. He declared that he needed additional troops both to match continuing increases in North Vietnamese and Viet Cong strength and to accelerate the allied campaign against the enemy's main forces and guerrillas. He envisioned employing most of the reinforcements in I Corps, but his maximum proposal called for augmentation of the other corps areas as well. Throughout his justifications, he talked in terms of speeding up allied success both in attrition and pacification rather than of avoiding defeat. On a public relations visit to Washington in April, he estimated for President Johnson and Secretary McNamara that with the minimum force the war might last another three years, whereas with the maximum force it might be ended in two.[48]

An Evolving Strategy

On 20 April the Joint Chiefs endorsed Westmoreland's request for the minimum package, to be deployed by mid-1968, and indicated that they would make a recommendation later on the optimum force. The chiefs declared that the additional troops were needed to "offset" growing enemy strength at the DMZ and to "improve the environment" for pacification in I and IV Corps. They also informed the secretary of defense that "considering our current worldwide commitments, a reserve call-up for a minimum of 24 months and involuntary extension of terms of service for twelve months" were "the only feasible means" of providing the minimum reinforcements within the desired period of time. Adding an additional discouraging note, they suggested that, to sustain the proposed force, it would be desirable to hold reserve units "for the duration of the emergency," an action that would require congressional authorization as would involuntary extension of terms of service. These statements once again brought reinforcements for MACV up against the administration's determination to avoid the domestic political trauma of a reserve call-up.[49]

The new reinforcement request, ultimately dubbed Program Five, set off another round of debate within the government. In general, most of the civilian participants, from the White House, the State and Defense Departments, and the CIA, opposed the military recommendation and advanced alternative strategies requiring few or no additional U.S. troops. Their arguments in the main paralleled those McNamara had made during the previous round: the need to halt the steady escalation of the human, economic, and material cost of the war to the United States; the diminishing returns of further reinforcing the main force campaign; the importance of improving South Vietnamese performance in pacification; and the desirability of adopting a military posture that would enable the United States to sustain a prolonged war of attrition while at the same time seeking a negotiated settlement. The argument became entangled with the controversy over ROLLING THUNDER, as opponents of an additional ground force increase also lined up against any further escalation of the bombing of North Vietnam.[50]

In the main, as with McNamara the previous year, the civilian critics of Program Five agreed that the principal mission of U.S. forces must be to battle the enemy's big units. They were reluctant to commit additional American troops to support of pacification, partly, no doubt, because General Westmoreland and the Joint Chiefs were using this mission as one justification for their reinforcement request. However, the civilians also appreciated that pacification in the long term depended for success primarily on South Vietnamese political and social reform, not American military force. They doubted that American troops would remain in South Vietnam long enough, and in sufficient numbers, to secure permanent control of the countryside. Preparing to take over the CORDS effort, Robert Komer observed late in April, "A major US force commitment to pacification . . . basically changes the

Dr. Enthoven (NARA)

nature of our presence in Vietnam and might force us to stay indefinitely in strength." He suggested that "an all-out effort to get more for our money" from the South Vietnamese forces promised better ultimate results. Alain Enthoven, head of the Defense Department Systems Analysis Office, concluded that American antiguerrilla and antiinfrastructure operations, such as those of the marines in I Corps and the Army in Operation FAIRFAX around Saigon, did nothing more than temporarily deny control of regions to the Viet Cong. "In the long term," he declared, "the RVNAF must assume a greater role for maintaining the security of SVN. The longer the task is delayed, the more difficult it becomes. We have made the Koreans into an effective fighting force, and we must do the same for the RVNAF. They can do the job far better and cheaper than we can, and they will remain after we leave."[51]

Writing earlier in the year, General Taylor, then serving as a special consultant on Vietnam to President Johnson, summed up the case against employing U.S. ground forces extensively in "clear-and-hold operations, static security missions, and local civil administration." Such tasks, he argued, were "inconsistent with the distinguishing attributes of our troops—mobility, fire-power, and aptitude for the offensive." Even so, Taylor expected that American soldiers probably would perform "quite well" in pacification-related operations, to the point of resolving "a lot of the short-term problems which are delaying progress in pacification." However, this short-term progress would come at the cost of creating "long-term problems resulting from substituting American initiative and leadership in areas where the Vietnamese must eventually assume responsibility." Finally, Taylor warned that an open-ended commitment of American troops to pacification support would lead to repeated requests from General Westmoreland for more forces "which it may be hard to decline." In conclusion, Taylor, like Enthoven, urged the president, in preference to enlarging American troops' role in pacification, instead to "leave no stone unturned" in expanding the South Vietnamese military contribution to the effort.[52]

As with Program Four, the availability of forces in the end determined the size of Program Five. By mid-June, Admiral Sharp and General Westmoreland had accepted that, with no reserve mobilization in prospect, the services could not provide the optimum force. Planning for a July visit of Secretary McNamara to Saigon, they prepared briefings arguing that the larger reinforcement would produce the most progress toward U.S. objectives while the minimum force would permit progress also, but more slowly. They agreed, however, not to present "too gloomy" an evaluation of the minimum force because it was the one they were likely to get. At the same time in Washington, after a detailed examination of military capabilities, Enthoven's office concluded that the services, without extending tours, calling the reserves, or diverting units earmarked for NATO, could provide the equivalent of three and two-thirds divisions for MACV by 31 December 1968—more than Westmoreland's requested minimum reinforcement. McNamara carried this study with him when he departed for Saigon on 5 July for a definitive review of both Program Five and ROLLING THUNDER.[53]

The stage thus was set for another compromise. During his stay in Saigon from 7 to 9 July, McNamara heard detailed briefings from Sharp, Westmoreland, and their staffs making the case for further expansion of ROLLING THUNDER and reviewing the effects of the optimum and minimum troop reinforcement packages. The MACV J3 briefing on the reinforcements included the familiar discussions of enemy-to-friendly battalion ratios, the question whether the "cross-over point" at which enemy casualties exceeded replacements had been or would be reached, and projections of the effects of different American troop strengths on these and other statistics. In conclusion, the J3 declared that with the smaller reinforcement, the "war of attrition" would be a "long drawn out process" that would "postpone the time when US forces could redeploy from South Vietnam."[54]

Even so, Westmoreland was prepared to settle for the lesser force. After dinner the final evening of McNamara's visit, the defense secretary and Generals Westmoreland and Abrams came to terms on an increase well within the three and two-thirds division ceiling, amounting to a bit over 50,000 more men and a final force level of 525,000. To bring the maximum number of additional combat troops under this ceiling, McNamara and the generals agreed to replace as many as 14,400 military personnel in support units with civilian contractors.

After further negotiations with MACV, the Defense Department on 14 August published the final version of Program Five. It called for a total American strength in Vietnam of 525,000 troops by 30 June 1968 and for adding 19 maneuver battalions and 5 tactical air squadrons to the forces prescribed in Program Four. General Westmoreland then set up a Force Development Section at MACV headquarters to refine the details of a "well-rounded" force within the ceiling that would accommodate the "minimum essential" numbers and types of tactical units. He also began negotiating for a speedup of deployments of all the forces scheduled for the rest of Program Four and Program Five, so as to have as many additional troops as possible in Vietnam before an expected Christmas truce that might delay the introduction of reinforcements.[55]

The exchanges over Programs Four and Five between Secretary McNamara and the military leaders never approached the level of contentiousness of the simultaneous argument over the air war against North Vietnam. Westmoreland and the Defense Department civilians all accepted the "two-fisted" ground war strategy that combined a primarily American campaign against the enemy main force with one of territorial pacification waged by the South Vietnamese with American advice and assistance. The civilians differed from MACV in doubting that the big-unit war could injure the enemy enough to break his strength or his will. Instead, they emphasized the campaign's other major objective of protecting the pacification effort, which they insisted could be done without additional forces. Both sides also implicitly acknowledged that the war, if fought within established territorial and operational limits, must be a prolonged attritional struggle. Indeed, McNamara's avowed aim in leveling off American strength was to ensure the ability of the United States to last out such a contest. General Westmoreland was aware of the limits on what the services, especially the Army, could provide in the absence of a reserve mobilization, and he was willing to accept a "level-off" force, but he pressed for a higher ceiling than McNamara initially favored. In the end, he and the defense secretary settled on the strength the services could make available without breaching the political barrier of mobilization.

Incremental Adjustments

While they produced no radical changes in strategy, the reinforcement discussions nevertheless indicated that Westmoreland's superiors desired several refinements and incremental alterations in the conduct of the war in South Vietnam. Ever sensitive to shifts in the policy consensus, Westmoreland adjusted his plans and operations accordingly. In particular, he placed greater emphasis on American forces' role in pacification, attempted to build an antiinfiltration barrier across the Demilitarized Zone and the Laotian panhandle, tried to make more efficient use of American manpower and materiel, and sought to stimulate the South Vietnamese to take a more vigorous and prominent part in combat and population security.

Westmoreland's attention to U.S. forces' role in pacification increased along with the likelihood of his being made responsible for the effort and in response to Washington pressure. In December 1966, for example, General Wheeler informed Westmoreland that the administration wanted to see new territorial security plans for South Vietnam incorporating both enhanced ARVN activity and "the participation of US troop elements in the pacification program to the degree which COMUSMACV believes desirable and feasible."[56]

Armored vehicles of the 11th Armored Cavalry Regiment advance northward during Operation JUNCTION CITY. *(AP photo)*

Beginning in late 1966, Westmoreland directed his field commanders to give "maximum weight" to support of pacification, both in their own operations and in their advice and assistance to the South Vietnamese. In their Combined Campaign Plan for 1967, besides reaffirming the ARVN's commitment to population security, MACV and the Joint General Staff declared that first priority in operations against main forces and base areas should go to those that most directly threatened the pacification zones. General Westmoreland directed his field force commanders to keep their troops busy between major offensives at hunting down guerrillas and local forces in the vicinity of their bases. As a rule, he told them, "US forces should react to hard intelligence on NVA/main force units to destroy them and their base areas. If suitable hard intelligence is lacking, US forces should conduct continuous op[eration]s directed at destroying guerrillas and VC infrastructure."⁵⁷

The exact influence of these pronouncements on the allocation of American effort is difficult to determine with any precision. During 1967 American forces, under urging from Westmoreland to "maintain the momentum of the offensive . . . on a seven-day-a-week, around-the-clock basis," continued to attack enemy base areas and hunt for their big units in operations of increasing size and duration. Early in the year, MACV and II Field Force conducted the largest American offensives of the war thus far, Operations CEDAR FALLS and JUNCTION CITY, against the enemy's Iron Triangle and War Zone C base areas north of Saigon. Yet I and II Field Forces, unilaterally and in conjunction with the South Vietnamese, also committed units to security-related missions, such as road clearing and protection of the rice harvest. The III MAF, in spite of its diversion of troops to the DMZ, continued its Combined Action Program and other pacification activities. When Army brigades deployed to southern I Corps under Task Force OREGON during the spring and summer, they operated both against guerrillas in the coastal plain and against the nearby mountain base areas.[58]

General Westmoreland claimed later that over half of his troops were employed against guerrillas and local forces during 1967. Other analysts believed that 25 to 30 percent was a more accurate estimate. The proportion varied with the season and the region of the country. Further complicating analysis was the fact that about 50 percent of American offensive operations were aimed at the enemy's provincial and district military units rather than the regiments and divisions controlled by COSVN and the other Communist regional commands. Since the province and district units conducted most of the resistance to the government's efforts to expand territorial security, and usually were more than the South Vietnamese Army could handle by itself, any enemy losses inflicted benefited pacification. General DePuy declared that advances in regaining the villages "in large measure can be equated directly to the scope and pace of US/Free World Forces operations against provincial VC forces contiguous to those areas in which Revolutionary Development activities are in progress."[59]

During 1967 enemy actions to a great degree dictated the Military Assistance Command's disposal of its forces. In particular, General Westmoreland steadily shifted strength to counter expanding PAVN pressure on the two northern provinces of I Corps. Isolated from the rest of South Vietnam by a mountain spur that runs down to the sea just above Da Nang, the region was within easy reach of the North Vietnamese logistic bases in Laos and above the DMZ; and it contained the old Vietnamese imperial city of Hue, an important political and psychological objective. Hence, General Westmoreland always had considered it the most likely target of a North Vietnamese conventional military offensive, should the enemy decide to launch one. After initial probes through the DMZ during 1966, the North Vietnamese in 1967 opened something like a regular war front in northern Quang Tri province. They attacked the marines' positions there, notably Khe Sanh and Con Thien, not only with infantry and the usual rocket and mortar barrages but also with heavy artillery emplaced in North Vietnam just beyond the demarcation line.[60]

In response Westmoreland augmented the forces under III MAF. Following a MACV contingency plan, in April 1967 he stripped brigades from I and II Field Forces to create a provisional Army division, initially designated Task Force OREGON and later renamed the Americal Division, for operations in the two southernmost provinces of I Corps. The III MAF then shifted its 1st Marine Division to the Da Nang area while the 3d Marine Division committed all its troops to the DMZ battle. During the summer and autumn, Westmoreland became increasingly convinced that the decisive engagement of the war was imminent in northern I Corps and made plans and preparations for further strengthening of the region. He arranged for expansion of ports and logistical facilities in the area and by the end of the year was preparing to move the bulk of the 1st Cavalry Division northward from II Corps to reinforce the marines. Even before transferring the air cavalry, MACV by the end of 1967 had committed 42 percent of its U.S. maneuver battalions to the northernmost corps area.[61]

Westmoreland's reinforcement of I Corps, and the intensifying combat south of the DMZ, were closely related to MACV's effort to establish an antiinfiltration barrier running across northern South Vietnam and the Laotian panhandle, an operation virtually dictated by the secretary of defense. Early in 1966 McNamara and his civilian advisers began exploring the concept of a barrier made up of mine and sensor fields supported by air and perhaps ground forces as an alternative to ROLLING THUNDER for reducing enemy vehicle and foot movement from North to South Vietnam. During the summer, an authoritative panel of government scientific consultants, set up by the Institute for Defense Analyses to review the entire northern bombing campaign, concluded that ROLLING THUNDER had done little or nothing to stop infiltration and recommended a high-technology barrier as an alternative. Influenced by a well-founded suspicion that McNamara favored the project as a way out of ROLLING THUNDER, Admiral Sharp and the Joint Chiefs expressed deep reservations about the feasibility and effectiveness of such a barrier. They warned that its creation and operation would divert American forces from other missions the Joint Chiefs considered more worthwhile.

Nevertheless, McNamara, his earlier interest strengthened by the summer study, went ahead with the project. In September he established a special Defense Department joint task force with the cover designation of Defense Communications Planning Group (DCPG), to oversee design and construction of the barrier. Indicating the importance he attached to the project, McNamara instructed its director, Lt. Gen. Alfred D. Starbird, to report directly to him and authorized Starbird to deal as necessary with the Joint Chiefs, the military services, and "subordinate organizations," including MACV.[62]

Agreeing with his military superiors, Westmoreland approached the barrier plan with much skepticism. In his initial response to McNamara's proposal, the general warned that the technologies on which the barrier was based were untried and that the project would divert MACV's resources from other endeavors, including existing, effective

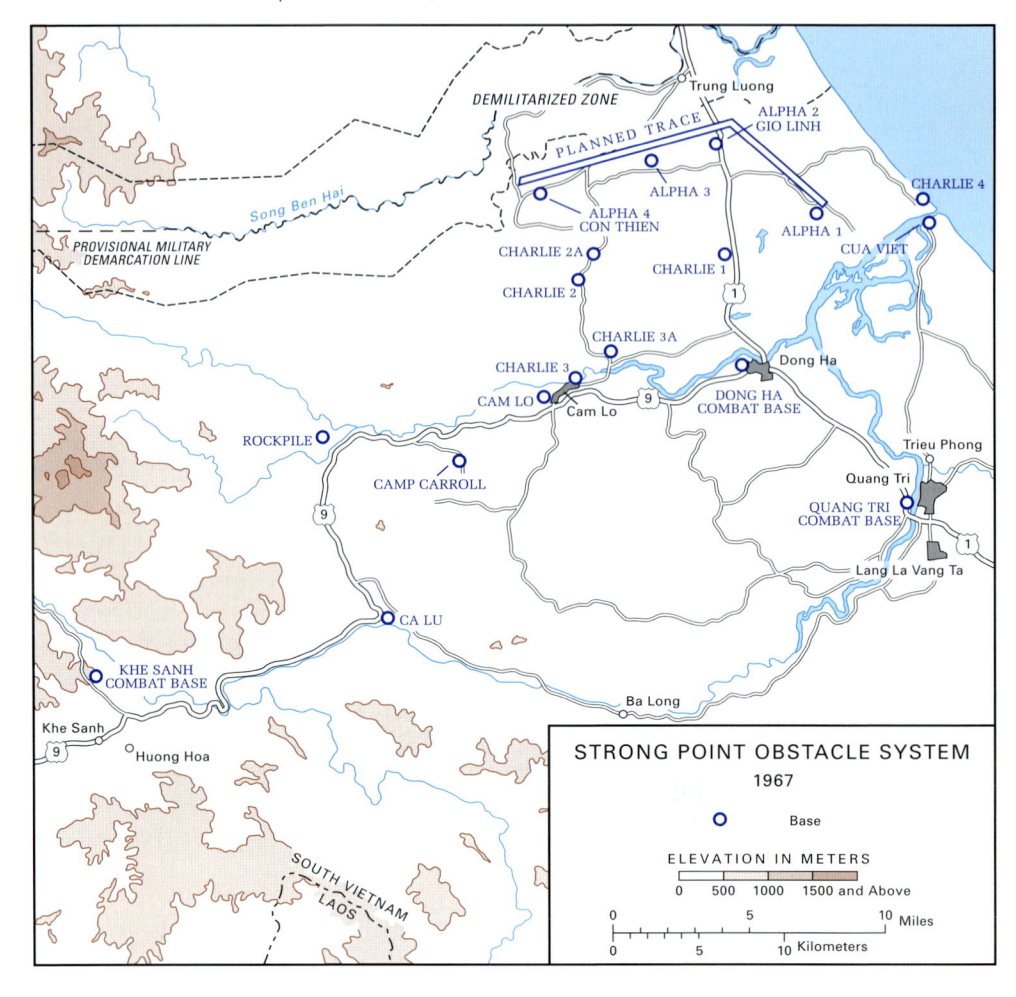

MAP 7

mobile operations below the DMZ and the various anti-infiltration activities in Laos. Above all, he sought to avoid having a detailed operational and tactical plan imposed upon him from Washington. He told General Starbird early in November that the barrier plan should be carried out "in such fashion as to preserve the commander's freedom of action and avoid jeopardizing other essential operational and logistic undertakings." As commander on the ground, Westmoreland should set the pace of development "based on his continuing assessment of the overall situation and [the] availability of resources."[63]

Westmoreland nevertheless realized that McNamara was determined to have a barrier. In prolonged discussions with Starbird and McNamara, he worked to modify the plans for both South Vietnam

An Evolving Strategy

and Laos so as to integrate them into his existing operations and to minimize the project's diversion of MACV forces and materiel. For the portion of the system within South Vietnam, he put his own staff and those of III MAF and the 3d Marine Division to work on a plan for a conventional barrier of cleared strips, barbed-wire obstacles, and minefields, backed by battalion-size outposts and artillery fire bases. This system, requiring in its final form the equivalent of two regiments—one American and one South Vietnamese—as permanent garrison, could detect, delay, and channel North Vietnamese invading forces, facilitating their destruction by mobile reserves which could move in and out of the DMZ region as required. Early in 1967 after months of discussion, McNamara essentially accepted Westmoreland's plan for the barrier in South Vietnam. He retained the air-supported sensor system for the element in Laos, modified to integrate it with PRAIRIE FIRE, TIGER HOUND, and other existing activities. However, the MACV commander was less successful in reducing the barrier's demands on his theater resources. Although he incorporated troops for the barrier in his minimum Program Five request, he was forced to employ existing forces, particularly those of III MAF, to build and man the system.[64] (*Map 7*)

During late spring of 1967, work began on the barrier, which was initially code-named PRACTICE NINE. Under the oversight of General Starbird's task force, MACV managed both programs but with a different command arrangement for each. The III Marine Amphibious Force completed the detailed planning for DYE MARKER, the segment within South Vietnam, and the 3d Marine Division carried out construction.[65] Westmoreland delegated emplacement and operation of the Laotian barrier, called MUSCLE SHOALS, to General Momyer, the Seventh Air Force commander, who already directed the air effort against the Ho Chi Minh Trail. Under Momyer, a Seventh Air Force task force headed by an Air Force brigadier general oversaw the emplacement of the sensors by aircraft and ground reconnaissance teams and the operation of the surveillance center in Thailand, which requested air strikes on the basis of sensor readouts. In setting up MUSCLE SHOALS, which required cooperation from both the Laotian and Thai governments and which had to be fitted into the extensive but publicly unacknowledged war in Laos, Westmoreland and Ambassadors Sullivan and Martin established a coordinating committee for the project. Sullivan attached an officer from his staff to MACV for MUSCLE SHOALS planning. To tie both halves of the project together, Westmoreland established a small MACV staff element under an Army brigadier general, with personnel furnished by the Defense Communications Planning Group.[66]

The MUSCLE SHOALS sensor fields in Laos went into operation in mid-December 1967, but the strong point-obstacle system fell far short of the 1 November completion date that McNamara set for it. From the start, the commanders of III MAF and the 3d Marine Division questioned the tactical soundness of establishing fixed defenses below the

DMZ, which would tie up infantry and engineers badly needed elsewhere. Supported by the entire Marine Corps chain of command, they preferred to rely on rapid temporary deployments from other areas to repel major enemy incursions. During the summer, the marines struggled to build the barrier in the midst of constant infantry and artillery battles with the North Vietnamese. In September, as casualties and equipment losses mounted and the northeast monsoon rains began, the III MAF urgently requested reduction in the scope of the project. In response, Westmoreland authorized the marines to abandon the effort to bulldoze a cleared strip along the border and to concentrate on completion of selected strongpoints and artillery positions. The year's effort ended with MACV complaining about the quality of the marines' construction work and Marine commanders denouncing the barrier as ill-conceived and unfeasible. Although General Westmoreland continued to press the barrier project into the new year, it was obvious by the end of 1967 that III MAF's part of the system, at least, had served mainly to fix many marines in exposed positions and to add one more irritant to the already contentious relationship between MACV and the Marine command.[67]

As the Military Assistance Command's demands for reinforcements increased, its operating efficiency came under close scrutiny in the Defense Department, especially by McNamara's Office of Systems Analysis. Among other things, analysts called into question the high proportion of support to combat troops in U.S. Army, Vietnam, noting that 51 percent of USARV's May 1967 Program Four strength of 322,000 officers and enlisted men were in combat and combat support units, with only 20 percent, or 66,000, in maneuver battalions. General Westmoreland and his USARV deputy responded that MACV as a whole, with about 45 percent of its troops in support units, was maintaining a combat-to-support ratio equal to that of American forces in World War II and Korea; that American support personnel in Vietnam such as engineers and artillerymen regularly exchanged fire with the enemy in this war without fronts; and that MACV furnished extensive combat and logistical assistance to South Vietnamese and Free World allies. Those rejoinders notwithstanding, McNamara wanted to pare down Westmoreland's troop requests; thus he repeatedly pressed the general to transfer noncombat functions to civilian contractors whenever possible. Westmoreland kept his command's force structure under constant review, promising to eliminate unnecessary rear-area elements; in fact he discovered few that he considered unnecessary.[68]

To save on resources and improve his command's image of managerial efficiency, during the autumn Westmoreland instituted a command-wide drive for increased economy in all aspects of operations. Dubbed Project MACONOMY, the program had as its objective "to develop a well balanced, hard hitting and efficient military force which can be sustained at a minimum cost for an indefinite period" through

An Evolving Strategy

vigorous management and attention to "cost effectiveness" by every element of the Military Assistance Command. Service components were to report monthly on the savings achieved. The reductions the commands reported were small in relation to the steadily increasing overall costs of the war, but the project did help reassure the Defense Department that the command was trying to conserve resources and probably enhanced Secretary McNamara's regard for Westmoreland's management skills.[69]

As American officials grew concerned about the war's drain on U.S. resources, they sought ways of expanding the share of the military burden borne by the South Vietnamese. As early as the discussion of the 44-battalion deployment, Admiral Sharp told General Wheeler that in addition to sending American soldiers, "we must do something positive to regenerate the ARVN as an effective force in the pacification of the country." In the months that followed, as American forces in South Vietnam expanded and casualty lists lengthened, President Johnson and his advisers reiterated the same theme during every discussion of the Military Assistance Command's reinforcement requests. During the deliberations over Program Five, General Wheeler asked Westmoreland on behalf of the president and secretary of defense whether "additional Vietnamese manpower could be recruited . . . thereby reducing the need for U.S. troops." He declared that "the subject of utilization of more Vietnamese troops rather than additional U.S. troops is very much in the forefront of people's minds here in Washington."[70]

General Westmoreland responded to his superiors' demands for additional measures to restore the South Vietnamese to the forefront of the action. As a first step, in conjunction with his assumption of responsibility for pacification, he attempted to strengthen the ARVN's role in territorial security, a project endorsed by McNamara, the U.S. Mission in Saigon, and South Vietnamese leaders. In August 1966 he told his field commanders that the South Vietnamese Army must "get more into the pacification business—do more securing, with perhaps less punching." American troop commanders and advisers "must help by teaching them saturation patrolling and proper area defense." He inserted in the 1967 Combined Campaign Plan a reiteration that pacification support was the primary, though not the only, mission of South Vietnam's regular forces. To a great extent Westmoreland was simply placing more formal emphasis on what was already a fact. Most South Vietnamese units rarely operated very far from populated areas, and the division of labor between the allies had been assumed throughout the American buildup. As he himself acknowledged, the MACV commander essentially was trying to resuscitate the CHIEN THANG plan of 1964, which had called for long-term commitment of ARVN battalions to clearing and securing particular areas. This plan, Westmoreland declared, had collapsed under attack by the enemy's expanding main forces. With U.S. and allied troops forming a shield against the big

427

units, it was time to revive it.[71]

During 1967 the South Vietnamese kept 50 to 60 of their 158 infantry battalions committed to security missions in coordination with provincial authorities. In support, the MACV advisers and special mobile training teams began systematically to instruct South Vietnamese units in the necessary tactical skills and to try to instill in them a concern for civic action and protection of the peasantry. In several areas, notably around Saigon in Operation FAIRFAX, American battalions worked with South Vietnamese units in combined territorial security campaigns, hoping to improve their allies' performance by example as well as precept.[72]

Besides attempting to revive in both word and deed the ARVN's commitment to pacification, General Westmoreland during late 1967 publicly broached the idea, for the first time since the American build-up began, of turning back to the South Vietnamese the conduct of the entire war. The concept was hardly new. American officials since John F. Kennedy's time had regularly proclaimed that the conflict was ultimately South Vietnam's to win or lose. Withdrawal also had appeared in military contingency planning. As early as September 1965 Westmoreland had directed his J5 to "begin studying how we might proceed to phase down our military effort in Vietnam." In July of the following year, MACV had made a study of the military implications of a negotiated termination or suspension of hostilities. In December 1966 Admiral Sharp had likewise directed MACV and other Pacific commands to develop contingency plans for redeploying forces from South Vietnam within six months of a cease-fire.[73]

These discussions expanded during 1967 to include the possibility of turning over the war, at least partially, to the South Vietnamese while hostilities still continued. In a June review of Vietnam strategy, the State Department Policy Planning Council recommended that "responsibility for the conduct of the war . . . be progressively turned over to the GVN as it develops the requisite competence" with American advice and assistance "on a priority basis." In November, General Wheeler informed Westmoreland that "high interest" existed in Washington in modernization of the South Vietnamese forces and in ways to make them "bear visibly a greater share of the load of combat operations." With additional American reinforcements in doubt, Wheeler added, RVNAF improvement was "one of the few remaining areas in which . . . significant increases in effectiveness and capabilities are possible." The question, he said, took on added importance "with the possibility of some kind of cease fire or negotiations hanging over our heads."[74]

General Westmoreland echoed and amplified this emerging tendency in American policy. As early as September, he suggested to Admiral Sharp that "by the 1969–70 time frame I now anticipate that the main force will be sufficiently under control to permit the withdrawal of part of the [third country allied units] if this should become necessary."

An Evolving Strategy

He included South Vietnamese units in a proposed operation in the Demilitarized Zone and secured the deployment of a regiment of the 1st ARVN Division to garrison portions of the Dye Marker strongpoint-obstacle system. Responding to General Wheeler's interest in RVNAF improvement, Westmoreland provided the chairman with a quickly drawn MACV plan that incorporated mostly existing and previously proposed measures for strengthening the South Vietnamese forces before a cease-fire.[75]

Finally, during a speech to the National Press Club in Washington on 21 November, Westmoreland made public the outlines of what later would be called Vietnamization. He told the assembled newspeople that as the military situation improved and the Saigon government became stronger, "it is conceivable to me that within two years or less, it will be possible for us to phase down our level of commitment and turn more of the burden of the war over to the Vietnamese Armed Forces, who are improving and who, I believe, will be prepared to assume this greater burden." During questioning he added that American troop withdrawals would be "token" at first but that "we're preparing our plans to make it progressive."[76]

Westmoreland tried to give his proposal some practical reality. After returning to Saigon early in December, he directed the MACV J5, in coordination with other staff agencies, to prepare a two-year plan for weakening the enemy, strengthening the South Vietnamese government, and improving the RVNAF. The main thrust would be an "orderly GVN take-over and US phasedowns in as many functional areas as possible." At the same time, he told his generals at one of his regular commanders' conferences that building up the South Vietnamese forces was now a "co-equal" objective with "grinding down the enemy" so that Saigon's army "will be able to carry more and more of its share of the load and at some future date allow us to reduce our effort here." General Abrams emphasized at the same meeting that RVNAF improvement was "everybody's job" and urged the commanders to conduct more combined operations with the South Vietnamese.[77]

As of the end of 1967, however, the accelerated drive for RVNAF improvement existed largely in plans and rhetoric rather than in fact. During the two years of the American buildup, MACV had pressed ahead with programs for modest expansion and rounding out of the South Vietnamese regular establishment and with more ambitious efforts to enlarge the Regional and Popular Forces. It had also continued trying to improve South Vietnamese combat effectiveness, logistics, military administration, and troop welfare. MACV reports from both headquarters and field advisory teams regularly recounted modest progress in these endeavors. Yet the major deficiencies of the South Vietnamese armed forces—poor leadership by a corrupt and politicized officer corps, uneven combat performance, neglect of training, and a crippling drain of manpower through desertion—persisted. MACV's campaign to get the South Vietnamese Army back into territorial security, for example, produced only meager initial results. Many ARVN leaders did not understand the mission and considered it demeaning, and disputes between division commanders and province chiefs over control of battalions engaged in pacification, among other problems, hindered operations. Most of the units committed to the campaign thus did nothing but defend static positions. Only a small percentage of their offensive operations resulted in contact with the enemy.

The American buildup itself contributed to this unhappy state of affairs. With U.S. troops pouring into their country in overwhelming numbers, the South Vietnamese perhaps inevitably responded, in the words of General Rosson, "by relaxing to some extent in their own efforts." At the same time, the MACV advisory program, lacking as it did a strong organizational focus within the headquarters, took second place to the needs of the growing American combat forces in commanders' attention and in the allocation of American leadership talent. In spite of efforts by Generals Johnson and Westmoreland to keep high-caliber officers in advisory positions and to offer "command credit" for such tours, the quality and morale of advisers suffered. Much the same story applied to materiel assistance. Due to production delays and priority for American units, for instance, issues of the M16 rifle to the South Vietnamese Army began only in late 1967—a damaging delay, considering that the army's effectiveness in its territorial security mission depended on small-scale actions in which basic infantry weapons predominated.[78]

At this stage, then, Westmoreland's increased attention to preparing the RVNAF to assume the main burden of the war was essentially a promise for the future. He publicly had committed himself and his command to that course, however, and in doing so had again responded to the shifting interests and concerns of his civilian and military superiors.

Notes

[1] Herring, "'Cold Blood,'" discusses the vagaries of Johnson's strategy-making, as does Rosson, "Involvement in Vietnam," pp. 182–92.

[2] On slowness of buildup, see Westmoreland, *A Soldier Reports*, pp. 153–54; Paper, Joel Meyerson, "Logistics in the Buildup," 1989, CMH files; Msg, Westmoreland HWA 2419 to Wheeler, 16 Aug 66, tab C–2, Westmoreland Hist File 8 (17 Jul–17 Sep 66), CMH. On the South Vietnamese, see Memo, Chester L. Cooper for Walt Rostow, 8 Apr 66, Warnke Papers, McNaughton Files, box 1, LBJL; Palmer Interv, 1975, pp. 228–29, 232–33. Quote is from Msg, Westmoreland MAC 0006 to Sharp, 1 Jan 66, Westmoreland Msg Files, 1 Jan–31 Mar 66, CMH.

[3] For an account of similar decentralization in an earlier American antiguerrilla war, see Brian M. Linn, *The U.S. Army and Counterinsurgency in the Philippine War, 1899–1902* (Chapel Hill: The University of North Carolina Press, 1989), pp. xi–xii and 163–70.

[4] For earlier RVNAF plans, see Chapters 4 and 6, of this volume. RVNAF JGS Dir AB 139, 25 Dec 64, and AB 140, 15 Dec 65; MACV, Concept of Operations in the Republic of Vietnam, 1 Sep 65. All in CMH. MACV Command History, 1965, pp. 137–40.

[5] Quote is from Westmoreland Hist Notes, 29 Dec 65, tab B, Westmoreland Hist File 3 (20 Dec 65–29 Jan 66), CMH. For other comments on same theme, see his Hist Notes, 29 Nov 65, Westmoreland Hist File 2 (25 Oct–20 Dec 65) and 25 Mar 67, tab C, Westmoreland Hist File 13 (27 Jan–25 Mar 67), CMH. Alternative strategies: Westmoreland Hist Notes, 5 and 21 Jan 66, tabs C and E, Westmoreland Hist File 3 (20 Dec 65–29 Jan 66), CMH. MACV Command History, 1966, p. 753; Westmoreland, *A Soldier Reports*, p. 153.

[6] The continued interest in pacification is summarized in *U.S.–Vietnam Relations*, sec. 4.C.8, pp. 8–27, 74–87. Sharp, "Reminiscences," pp. 286–87. Rpt, Ofc of the DCofS for Mil Ops, DA, Mar 66, sub: A Program for the Pacification and Long-Term Development of South Vietnam, copy in CMH; quote is from Summary Rpt, p. 1.

[7] Quote is from Msg, Wheeler JCS 3710–65 to Sharp and Westmoreland, 4 Oct 65, Westmoreland Msg Files, 1 Oct–31 Dec 65, CMH. See also Msg, Wheeler JCS 3499–65 to Sharp, 21 Sep 65, Westmoreland Msg Files, 1 Jul–30 Sep 65. The Honolulu conference and the military goals set there are discussed in Chapter 7 of this volume. Goals are summarized in "1966 Program to Increase the Effectiveness of Military Operations and Anticipated Results Thereof," 8 Feb 66, tab A–6, Westmoreland Hist File 4 (30 Jan–1 Mar 66), CMH.

[8] Quotes are from AB 142, JGS/MACV Combined Campaign Plan 1967, 7 Nov 66, p. 5, copy in CMH. This discussion is based also on AB 141, Campaign Plan for Military Operations in the Republic of Vietnam—1966, Dec 65; and AB 143, Combined Campaign Plan 1968, 11 Nov 67. Both in CMH files.

[9] AB 142, JGS/MACV Combined Campaign Plan 1967, 11 Nov 66, pp. 4 and 6, CMH. Westmoreland alludes to requirements for American operations in populated areas in Msg MAC 4382 to Wheeler, 28 Aug 65, Westmoreland Msg Files, 1 Jul–30 Sep 65, CMH.

[10] Quotes are from Larsen Interv, 6 Dec 68, sec. 5, pp. 22–23, and Larsen Debrief, 31 Jul 67, p. 1; see also pp. 2, 15–16, 19–20. MFR, Collins, 6 Nov 65, sub: Conference at Nha Trang on 24 Oct 65, tab H–5; MACV Dir 525–4, 17 Sep 65, sub: Tactics and Techniques for Employment of US Forces in the Republic of Vietnam, tab 7; Westmoreland Hist File 1 (29 Aug–24 Oct 65); MFR, Jones, 10 Mar 66, sub: MACV Commanders' Conference, 20 Feb 66, tab C–1, Westmoreland Hist File 4 (30 Jan–13 Mar 66). All in CMH.

[11] Memo, McNamara for the President, 20 Jul 65, sub: Recommendations of Additional Deployments to Vietnam, in NSC History, Major Forces, box 43. *U.S.–Vietnam Relations*, sec. 4.C.6, pp. 1–6, 16–17; Sharp Interv, 19 Feb 71, p. 18, AFCHO. Study, DA, n.d., "Pacification and Long Term Development," pp. 5, 23–24. MFR, DePuy, 24 Jul 65, sub: Conversation with Generals Thang and Phong, 23 July 1965, DePuy Papers, MHI; and Msg, Westmoreland MAC 5184 to Walt, 17 Oct 65, Westmoreland Msg Files, 1 Oct–31 Dec 65, CMH. Standard justifications by Westmoreland are in *A Soldier Reports*, pp. 146–47; and MacDonald-Westmoreland Interv, 28 Jan 73.

[12] This view receives systematic expression in Suplizio, "Military Support of Pacification." For other expressions of this viewpoint, see Memo, Gen Throckmorton for Taylor, 24 Oct 64, sub: Hop Tac Evaluation, tab 20, Westmoreland Hist File 9 (9 Oct–13 Nov 64); Westmoreland, Remarks for Honolulu Conf, 7 Feb 66, tab A–5, Westmoreland Hist File 4 (30 Jan–13 Mar 66), CMH. MacDonald-Westmoreland Interv, 18 June 73; Seaman, "Elements of Command," pt. 1, p. 28; and Larsen Debrief, 31 Jul 67, pp. 5–7. Youngdale quote is from Interv, 5 Jun 65, p. 17; he made these comments in June 1965.

[13] Lodge expresses his view in Memo for the President, 20 Jul 65, in NSC History, Major Forces, box 43; and Westmoreland Hist Notes, 11 Nov 66, tab B, Westmoreland Hist File 11 (30 Oct–12 Dec 66), CMH. Taylor's views are summarized in Msg, Wheeler JCS 4500–65 to Sharp and Westmoreland, 20 Nov 65, Westmoreland Msg Files, 1 Oct–31 Dec 65, CMH.

[14] Development of the Marine strategy and reasoning behind it are summarized in Shulimson and Johnson, *Marines in Vietnam, 1965*, pp. 115–16, and 133–46; and Shulimson, *Marines in Vietnam, 1966*, pp. 11–14. See also Msg, Walt to Westmoreland, 19 Nov 65, Westmoreland Msg Files, 1 Oct–31 Dec 65, CMH.

[15] Quote is from Ltr, Westmoreland to CG III MAF, 15 Nov 65, sub: Operations in I Corps, tab D–6, Westmoreland Hist File 2 (25 Oct–20 Dec 65), CMH; also, Ltr, Westmoreland to CG III MAF, sub: Letter of Instruction (LOI–4), 21 Nov 65, tab E–1 in same file. Westmoreland Hist Notes, 20 Oct 65, Westmoreland Hist File 1 (29 Aug–24 Oct 65); and 8 Dec 65, Westmoreland Hist File 2 (25 Oct–20 Dec 65). Msg, Wheeler JCS 4552–65 to Westmoreland, 23 Nov 65; Westmoreland Msg Files, 1 Oct–31 Dec 65, CMH. MFR, Gen C. W. Abrams, 25 Sep 65, 27 Sep 65, sub: JCS Meeting with Amb Johnson, Close Hold File 3; Gen H. K. Johnson, "Noteworthy Viewpoints Encountered and Observations Made on VN Trip," box 5B. Both in Johnson Papers, MHI.

[16] First quote is from *U.S.–Vietnam Relations*, sec. 4.C.8, p. 18. Krulak emphasizes balanced approach in Ltrs to McNamara, 9 May 66, and to Nitze, 17 Jul 66; he acknowledges corps area differences in Ltr to McNamara, 11 Nov 65. All in box 2, Krulak Papers, MCHC.

[17] Westmoreland makes a typical statement of his "two-fisted" strategy in MFR, Jones, 3 Oct 66 sub: MACV Commanders' Conference, 28 Aug 66, tab D–4, Westmoreland Hist File 8 (17 Jul–17 Sep 66), CMH; in same file, see Hist Notes, 10 Aug 66, tab B. Westmoreland also stresses pacification support in MFR, Jones, 10 Mar 66, sub: MACV Commanders' Conference, 20 Feb 66, tab C–1, Westmoreland Hist File 4 (30 Jan–13 Mar 66), CMH. Quote is from Chaisson Oral History, pp. 222–23, MCHC.

[18] Lt Gen Frederick C. Weyand, Senior Officer Debriefing Rpt, 15 Jul 68, pp. 3–4, CMH.

[19] Deployments and their rationale are summarized conveniently in Sharp and Westmoreland, *Report on War*, pp. 98–99 and 127–28; and Westmoreland, *A Soldier Reports*, pp. 124, 162–63. For typical considerations, see Msg, Westmoreland MAC 1450 to Wheeler, 20 Feb 66, Westmoreland Msg Files, 1 Jan–31 Mar 66, CMH. Mekong Delta: Msgs, Sharp to Westmoreland, 19 Feb 66 and 13 Dec 66; Westmoreland MAC 8211 to

Sharp, 20 Sep 66, Westmoreland Msg Files, Feb–Dec 66, CMH; MFR, Westmoreland, 10 Jun 66, sub: Meeting with Gen Vien . . ., 7 Jun 66, tab B–2, Westmoreland Hist File 7 (29 May–16 Jul 66), CMH.

[20] Convenient summaries of operations are in Sharp and Westmoreland, *Report on War*, pp. 113–14, 123–29; and *U.S.–Vietnam Relations*, sec. 4.C.6, pp. 46–48. Army operations during this period are covered in John M. Carland, *Stemming the Tide: Combat Operations, March 1965–September 1966*, United States Army in Vietnam (Washington, D.C.: Center of Military History, 2000); and George L. MacGarrigle, *Taking the Offensive: Combat Operations, October 1966–October 1967*, United States Army in Vietnam (Washington, D.C.: Center of Military History, 1998). Marine campaigns are described in Shulimson and Johnson, *Marines in Vietnam, 1965*, and Shulimson, *Marines in Vietnam, 1966*.

[21] Quotes are from Msg, Westmoreland MAC 1658 to Sharp and Wheeler, 17 Feb 67, Westmoreland Msg Files, 1 Jan–31 Mar 67, CMH. In same files, see Msgs, Westmoreland MAC 8371 and MAC 10204 to Sharp, 24 Sep 66, and 22 Nov 66, for typical claims of success. Statistics on advancement toward Honolulu goals during 1966 are summarized in MFR, Chaisson, 9 Feb 67, sub: MACV Commanders' Conference, 22 Jan 67, tab D–11, Westmoreland Hist File 12 (13 Dec 66–26 Jan 67), CMH.

[22] Quote is from DePuy, *Changing an Army*, p. 160; see also p. 161. Larsen Debrief, 31 Jul 67, pp. 1, 4; Seaman Interv, p. 40; and Palmer Interv, pp. 256–57, in MHI files, all describe combat intelligence deficiencies. Helicopter shortage: Msg, Westmoreland MAC 1658 to Sharp and Wheeler, 17 Feb 67, Westmoreland Msg Files, 1 Jan–31 Mar 67, CMH. Security: CINCPAC Operations Security Briefing, attached to Memo, Maj Gen K. G. Wickham for DA Distribution, 3 Jul 68, sub: Operations Security Briefing, CMH. Troop numbers: Thayer, "War without Fronts," pp. 837–39.

[23] The allies' struggle to organize for pacification is recounted in Chapter 9 of this volume. Slowness of the process is reviewed in Memo, Komer for Bunker, 1 Oct 67, tab A–1, Westmoreland Hist File 23 (1–15 Oct 67), CMH. McNamara quote is in *U.S.–Vietnam Relations*, sec. 4.C.6 (a), p. 82.

[24] Msg, Westmoreland MAC 4382 to Wheeler, 28 Aug 65, Westmoreland Msg Files, 1 Jul–30 Sep 65, CMH.

[25] Civilian casualty and atrocity issues can be followed in Hammond, *Military and the Media, 1962–1968*, pp. 185–93, 266–70, 274–79, 300–306. The destruction of Ben Suc is described in MacGarrigle, *Taking the Offensive*, pp. 104–11.

[26] MACV's rules of engagement are summarized in Gen William B. Rosson, "Assessment of Influence Exerted on Military Operations by Other Than Military Considerations," ch. 1, CMH; and Extracts of Remarks by General Westmoreland Relating to Noncombatant Casualties, in Westmoreland–CBS Case File Folder, MACV Collection, MHI; and Lt Gen William R. Peers, USA (Ret.), *The My Lai Inquiry* (New York: W. W. Norton, 1979), pp. 29–30. An example of enforcement efforts can be found in MACV Command History, 1967, 3: 1121–23.

[27] Carland, *Stemming the Tide*, pp. 80–84; quote is from p. 84.

[28] Quote is from Col Gen Tran Van Tra, *Vietnam: History of the Bulwark B2 Theater*, vol. 5: *Concluding the 30-Years War* (trans. by Foreign Broadcast Information Service. JPRS Southeast Asia Report no. 1247, 2 Feb 83), pp. 59–60; see also p. 58. Thomas K. Latimer, "Hanoi's Leaders and their South Vietnam Policies, 1954–1968" (Ph.D. diss., Georgetown University, 1972), ch. 8. The enemy saw large-unit and guerrilla operations as mutually supporting; see *The People's Armed Forces of the Western Highlands during the War of National Salvation against the Americans* (Hanoi: People's Army Publishing House, 1980), pp. 69ff; translated excerpt in CMH files.

[29] MACV strength estimate is from Msg, Westmoreland MAC 0610 to Sharp and

MACV: The Years of Escalation, 1962–1967

Wheeler, 2 Jan 67, in *U.S.–Vietnam Relations*, sec. 4.C.6 (b), pp. 26–28. Enemy weaponry is described in Sharp and Westmoreland, *Report on War*, pp. 114–15, 146. Battalion ratios are compared in Paper, n.d., sub: Analysis of Strategies, Folder 42, Thayer Papers, CMH. Quote on local forces is from Weyand Debrief, 15 Jul 68, pp. 1–3.

[30] Gen Tran Van Tra affirms the *PAVN/PLAF* commitment to attrition in Interv, John M. Carland, CMH, with Tra, 23 Nov 90, transcript, pp. 7–8, CMH files. A convenient U.S. summary of the enemy strategy is in MACV Command History, 1966, pp. 19–22. Westmoreland gives his view in Assessment of the Situation in South Vietnam, drafted during the Manila Conference, 23 Oct 66, encl. 15, Westmoreland Hist File 10 (18–29 Oct 66), CMH. For an enemy commander's assertion that they have the initiative, see translation of speech by "9 Vinh" attached to Memo, Lt Col Henry Ajina, 7 May 67, sub: Translation Report, tab A–4, Westmoreland Hist File 17 (1–31 May 67), CMH.

[31] Assessment of the Situation in South Vietnam, Drafted during Manila Conference, 23 Oct 66, encl. 15, Westmoreland Hist File 10 (18–29 Oct 66), CMH.

[32] Quote is from Msg, Westmoreland MAC 11956 to Wheeler, 10 Dec 67, Westmoreland Msg Files, 1–31 Dec 67, CMH; in same file see Msg, Sharp BNK 2388 to Gen Johnson, 11 Dec 67. MacDonald-Westmoreland Interv, 5 Feb 73. Westmoreland Hist Notes, 17 Sep 66, tab E; MFR, Rosson, 17 Sep 66, sub: CIIC Meeting, 17 Sep 66, tab E–6. Both in Westmoreland Hist File 8 (17 Jul–17 Sep 66), CMH. Msg, Westmoreland MAC 8212 to Sharp, 20 Sep 66, tab A–2; Mission Council Action Memo no. 123, 22 Sep 66, tab A–8. Both in Westmoreland Hist File 9 (18 Sep–17 Oct 66), CMH. Chaisson Oral History, pp. 119–20.

[33] Krulak quote is from Msg to Walt, 7 Oct 66, box 2, Krulak Papers, MCHC. Westmoreland quote is from Msg, MAC 01928 to Sharp, 26 Feb 67, Westmoreland Msg Files, 1 Jan–31 Mar 67, CMH.

[34] For development of Program 3, see Chapter 7 of this volume. Force levels are summarized in *U.S.–Vietnam Relations*, sec. 4C.6(a), pp. 52–53; and Memo, Col A. C. Edmunds, USAF, for Westmoreland, 16 Nov 67, sub: Force Requirements, tab A–7, Westmoreland Hist File 25 (13–28 Nov 67), CMH.

[35] Msgs, Sharp to Westmoreland and Stilwell, 5 Apr 66, and to Westmoreland, 10 Jun 66; Stilwell BNK 0847 to Sharp, 7 Apr 66; Westmoreland MAC 2810 to Sharp, 9 Apr 66; Tillson HWA 1781 to Westmoreland, 7 Jun 66. All in Westmoreland Msg Files, 1 Apr–30 Jun 66, CMH.

[36] *U.S.–Vietnam Relations*, sec. 4.C.6(a), pp. 52–53; Rosson, "Involvement in Vietnam," p. 215. Memo, Col A. C. Edmunds, USAF, for Westmoreland, 16 Nov 67, sub: Force Requirements, tab A–7, Westmoreland Hist File 25 (13–28 Nov 67), CMH. On corps contingency force, see Msgs, Sharp to Westmoreland, 30 May 66, and Westmoreland MAC 4437 to Sharp, 31 May 66. Both in Westmoreland Msg Files, 1 Apr–30 Jun 66, CMH.

[37] *U.S.–Vietnam Relations*, sec. 4.C.6(a), pp. 53–54; McNamara quotes are from this source. For McNamara's growing disillusionment with ROLLING THUNDER, see ibid., sec. 4.C.7(a), pp. 138–45. On his July visit to Saigon, see Msg, Sharp to Westmoreland, 6 Jul 66, Westmoreland Msg Files, 1 Jul–30 Sep 66, CMH. Rosson, "Involvement in Vietnam," pp. 214–15, sees McNamara's request as the formal opening of the civilian-military confrontation over reinforcements.

[38] *U.S.–Vietnam Relations*, sec. 4.C.6(a), pp. 69–79; Msg, Gen Johnson WDC 12415 to Westmoreland, 19 Oct 66, Westmoreland Msg Files, 1 Oct–31 Dec 66, CMH. Mac-Donald-Westmoreland Interv, 17 Jun 73; Westmoreland, *A Soldier Reports*, pp. 248–49.

[39] *U.S.–Vietnam Relations*, sec. 4.C.6(a), pp. 79–81. Palmer, *25-Year War*, pp. 44, 175. The Plimsoll line is the mark on a vessel's side that indicates when the vessel is loaded beyond safe limits.

An Evolving Strategy

⁴⁰ Quote is from Msg, Emrick to Westmoreland, 3 Aug 66, Westmoreland Msg Files, 1 Jul–30 Sep 66, CMH. In same file, see Msgs, Abrams WDC 8561 to Engler, 21 Jul 66; Engler MAC 6480 to Abrams, 28 Jul 66; Gen Johnson WDC 9860 to Engler, Waters, Westmoreland, and Eifler, 20 Aug 66; and Gen Johnson WDC 10849 to Westmoreland, 13 Sep 66. Msgs, Polk WDC 4023 to Engler, 1 Apr 66; Westmoreland MAC 4787 and MAC 4848 to Sharp, 10 and 12 Jun 66; Sharp to Westmoreland, 14 Jun 66; Westmoreland Msg Files, 1 Apr–30 Jun 66; Msg, Gen Johnson WDC 11776 to Westmoreland, 5 Oct 66, Westmoreland Msg Files, 1 Oct–31 Dec 66. All in CMH.

⁴¹ First quote is from Westmoreland Hist Notes, 24 Jul 66; see also Hist Notes, 17 Sep 66; tabs A and E, Westmoreland Hist File 8 (17 Jul–17 Sep 66), CMH; Msgs, Westmoreland MAC 7720 and MAC 8085 to Gen Johnson, 5 and 16 Sep 66; Msg, Gen Johnson WDC 10846 to Westmoreland, 13 Sep 66. All in Westmoreland Msg Files, 1 Jul–30 Sep 66, CMH. MacDonald-Westmoreland Intervs, 12 Mar 73, and n.d., Strategy and Policy Section, CMH files. Rosson, "Involvement in Vietnam," p. 217.

⁴² Westmoreland describes this conference in his Hist Notes, 17 Oct 66, tab D, Westmoreland Hist File 9 (18 Sep–17 Oct 66), CMH. See also Westmoreland, *A Soldier Reports*, pp. 193–94.

⁴³ *U.S.–Vietnam Relations*, sec. 4.C.6(a), pp. 81–119. Westmoreland Hist Notes, 17 Oct 66, tab D, Westmoreland Hist File 9 (18 Sep–17 Oct 66); see also Hist Notes, 25 Nov 66, tab C, Westmoreland Hist File 11 (30 Oct–12 Dec 66). Both in CMH. Memo, McNaughton for McNamara, 26 Oct 66, sub: McNaughton in Manila . . . , box 7, Warnke Papers, McNaughton Files, LBJL.

⁴⁴ McNamara's memorandums are reproduced in *U.S.–Vietnam Relations*, sec. 4.C.6(a), pp. 81–91 and 105–19.

⁴⁵ Quote is from *U.S.–Vietnam Relations*, sec. 4.C.6(a), p. 85.

⁴⁶ McNamara develops this argument most fully in his 17 Nov 66 draft Memo for the President, reproduced in *U.S.–Vietnam Relations*, sec. 4.C.6(a), pp. 105–19; quotes are from pp. 108–11.

⁴⁷ *U.S.–Vietnam Relations*, sec. 4.C.6(b), pp. 22–24. Msgs, Wheeler JCS 1284–67 to Sharp and Westmoreland, 17 Feb 67; Westmoreland MAC 1658 to Wheeler and Sharp, 17 Feb 67; Sharp to Westmoreland, 21 Feb 67 and 15 Mar 67; Westmoreland MAC 1928 to Sharp, 26 Feb 67. All in Westmoreland Msg Files, 1 Jan–31 Mar 67, CMH.

⁴⁸ *U.S.–Vietnam Relations*, sec. 4.C.6(b), pp. 61–67, 83. Msgs, COMUSMACV MAC 09101 to CINCPAC, 18 Mar 67; COMUSMACV MAC 10311 to JCS, 28 Mar 67; tab A–8, Westmoreland Hist File 15 (27 Mar–30 Apr 67); Msg, Sharp to Westmoreland, 28 Mar 67, Westmoreland Msg Files, 1 Jan–31 Mar 67. All in CMH. For the detailed MACV justification of this request, see Ltr, Westmoreland to CINCPAC, 5 Apr 67, sub: FY 68 Force Requirements, with appendixes and annexes, in CMH files.

⁴⁹ Memo, Wheeler JCSM–218–57 for Secretary of Defense, 20 Apr 67, sub: Force Requirements—Southeast Asia FY 1968, box 6, Warnke Papers, McNaughton Files, LBJL. *U.S.–Vietnam Relations*, sec. 4.C.6(b), pp. 73–77.

⁵⁰ These arguments are recounted in detail in *U.S.–Vietnam Relations*, sec. 4.C.6(b), pp. 77–82, 85–89, 93–100, 105–92. Rosson, "Involvement in Vietnam," pp. 219–20.

⁵¹ Komer quote is from *U.S.–Vietnam Relations*, sec. 4.C.6(b), p. 80; Enthoven remarks are in ibid., pp. 108–09. In late 1966, in a speech at Manila, President Johnson promised to withdraw American combat forces within six months if the North Vietnamese would do the same. Gelb and Betts, *Irony of Vietnam*, p. 150.

⁵² Taylor, "Comments on Vietnam," 1 Jan 67, in U.S. Department of State, *Foreign Relations of the U.S., 1964–1968*, vol. 5, *Vietnam, 1967* (Washington, D.C.: Government Printing Office, 2002), pp. 1–2.

⁵³ Msgs, Sharp to Westmoreland, 13 Jun 67; Westmoreland MAC 5601 to Sharp,

435

13 Jun 67; Westmoreland Msg Files, 1 Jan–30 Sep 67, CMH. Memo, Maj Gen Walter T. Kerwin, Jr., for Westmoreland, 6 Jul 67 sub: SecDef Briefing, tab A–1, Westmoreland Hist File 19 (6 Jul–3 Aug 67), CMH. Enthoven paper is summarized in *U.S.–Vietnam Relations*, sec. 4.C.6(b), pp. 195–96.

[54] Saigon briefings are described in *U.S.–Vietnam Relations*, sec. 4.C.6(b), pp. 197–208; J3 quotes are from p. 208. Westmoreland's view of the conference is in his Hist Notes, 6 Jul–3 Aug 67, tab A, Westmoreland Hist File 19 (6 Jul–3 Aug 67), CMH.

[55] Final negotiations are summarized in *U.S.–Vietnam Relations*, sec. 4.C.6(b), pp. 209–22. Westmoreland Hist Notes, 6 Jul–3 Aug 67, tab A, Westmoreland Hist File 19 (6 Jul–3 Aug 67), and 6–18 Aug 67, tab A, Westmoreland Hist File 20 (4–20 Aug 67). Both in CMH. Msg, Westmoreland to Abrams via CG Ft. Jackson, SC, 11 Jul 67, Tab A–8, Westmoreland Hist File 19 (6 Jul–3 Aug 67), CMH. Negotiations for accelerated deployment can be followed in Westmoreland Msg Files, 1 Jul–31 Oct 67, CMH; see also Chapter 3, above.

[56] Quote is from Msg, Wheeler JCS 7420–66 to Sharp and Westmoreland, 3 Dec 66, Westmoreland Msg Files, 1 Oct–31 Dec 66, CMH; in same file, see Msgs, Wheeler JCS 7859–66 to Sharp and Westmoreland, 21 Dec 66; and Westmoreland MAC 10608 to Wheeler and Sharp, 4 Dec 66.

[57] First quote is from MFR, Jones, 3 Oct 66, sub: MACV Commanders' Conference, 28 Aug 66, tab D–4, Westmoreland Hist File 8 (17 Jul–17 Sep 66); see also tab C–3, Westmoreland Hist File 11 (30 Oct–12 Dec 66); and tab A–11, Westmoreland Hist File 18 (1 Jun–5 Jul 67). All in CMH. RVNAF/MACV Combined Campaign Plan 1967, AB 142, 7 Nov 66, p. 13, CMH. Final quote is from Msg, CG I FFORCEV to COMUSMACV, 2 Jan 67, tab B–3, Westmoreland Hist File 12 (13 Dec 66–26 Jan 67), CMH; in same file, see Draft Msg, Westmoreland to Sharp and Wheeler, Jan 67, tab B–9.

[58] Westmoreland quote is in *U.S.–Vietnam Relations*, sec. 4.C.6(b), p. 24. For the course of operations, see MacGarrigle, *Taking the Offensive*, and Maj Gary L. Telfer, USMC; Lt Col Lane Rogers, USMC; and V. Keith Fleming, Jr., *U.S. Marines in Vietnam: Fighting the North Vietnamese, 1967* (Washington: History and Museums Division, Headquarters, U.S. Marine Corps, 1984). For pacification efforts, see: MFR Maj Gen J. R. Chaisson, USMC, 24 Jun 67, sub: MACV Commanders' Conference, 11 Jun 67, tab A–11, Westmoreland Hist File 18 (1 Jun–5 Jul 67); Msg, CG II FFORCEV to COMUSMACV, 21 Sep 67, tab A–17, Westmoreland Hist File 22 (10–30 Sep 67). All in CMH. Rosson Interv, pp. 367–69, MHI.

[59] Westmoreland's estimate is in his and Sharp's *Report on War*, pp. 131–32. Thirty percent figure comes from *U.S.–Vietnam Relations*, sec. 4.C.6(b), p. 35. DePuy quote and analysis are in his paper, "Revolutionary Development," sec. 1, 20 Apr 67; see also Memo, W. W. Rostow for the President, 20 May 67. Both in NSC Country Files, Vietnam, boxes 74 and 75, LBJL.

[60] The fighting in northern I Corps is detailed in Telfer et al., *Marines in Vietnam, 1967*, chs. 1–4, 7, 8, and 10. Typical expressions of Westmoreland's concern about the area are in MFR, Rosson, 17 Sep 66, sub: CIIC Meeting, 17 Sep 66, tab E–6, and Westmoreland Hist Notes, 17 Sep 66, tab E, both in Westmoreland Hist File 8 (17 Jul–17 Aug 66), CMH. See also Hist Notes, 6 Oct 66, tab A, Westmoreland Hist File 9 (18 Sep–17 Oct 66); 1 Jan 67, tab B, Westmoreland Hist File 12 (13 Dec 66–26 Jan 67); and 28 Dec 67–31 Jan 68, tab A–1, Westmoreland Hist File 28 (27 Dec 67–31 Jan 68). All in CMH.

[61] Sharp and Westmoreland, *Report on War*, pp. 137–38, 143–44. Formation and operations of Task Force OREGON are covered in MacGarrigle, *Taking the Offensive*, chs. 12, 14, and 17. Westmoreland Hist Notes, 1–13 Oct 67, tab A, Westmoreland Hist File 23 (1–15 Oct 67); 29 Nov–16 Dec 67, tab A, Westmoreland Hist File 26 (29 Nov–16 Dec 67); 28 Dec 67–31 Jan 68, tab A–1, Westmoreland Hist File 28 (27 Dec 67–31 Jan 68).

An Evolving Strategy

All in CMH. On additional reinforcements, Msgs, COMUSMACV MAC 31448 to CG, III MAF, 23 Sep 67, Westmoreland Sig File, 1967, CMH. Battalion distribution is from Paper, Analysis of Strategies, Folder. 42, Thayer Papers, CMH.

[62] *U.S.–Vietnam Relations*, sec. 4.C.7(a), pp. 145–62, summarizes the genesis of the barrier scheme. Memo, McNamara for Lt Gen A. D. Starbird, 15 Sep 66, sub: Infiltration Interdiction System for Vietnam, tab E–4, Westmoreland Hist File 8 (17 Jul–17 Sep 66); Msgs, Wheeler JCS 5586–66 and JCS 7590–66 to Sharp, 17 Sep 66 and 10 Dec 66. All in Westmoreland Msg Files, Sep 66–31 Jan 67, CMH.

[63] Quote is from Memo, Westmoreland for Director, DCPG, 5 Nov 66, sub: Barrier Concepts, tab A–2, Westmoreland Hist File 11 (30 Oct–12 Dec 66), CMH. See also Memo, Westmoreland for Starbird, 17 Dec 66, sub: Barrier Plan, tab A–3, Westmoreland Hist File 12 (13 Dec 66–26 Jan 67); and Hist Notes, 6 Oct 66, tab A, Westmoreland Hist File 9 (18 Sep–17 Oct 66), CMH. See also Msg, Westmoreland MAC 10295 to Sharp, 24 Nov 66, Westmoreland Msg Files, 1 Oct–31 Dec 66, CMH; and MacDonald-Westmoreland Intervs, 11 Feb 73 and 17 Jun 73.

[64] The course of barrier planning is traced in detail in Shulimson, *Marines in Vietnam, 1966*, pp. 314–318; and Telfer et al., *Marines in Vietnam, 1967*, pp. 86–90. *U.S.–Vietnam Relations*, sec. 4.C.6(b), pp. 39–41, 43–44. Westmoreland Hist Notes, 17 Oct 66, tab D, Westmoreland Hist File 9 (18 Sep–17 Oct 66); 6 Nov 66, tab A, Westmoreland Hist File 11 (30 Oct–12 Dec 66); MFR, Rosson, 3 Dec 66, sub: CIIC Meeting, 3 Dec 66, tab D–7, ibid.; Msgs, Starbird to Westmoreland, 18 Dec 66; Wheeler JCS 2752–67 to Westmoreland, 14 Apr 67; Westmoreland MAC 3600 to Wheeler, 15 Apr 67; Westmoreland Msg Files, Dec 66–Apr 67. All in CMH.

[65] The code-name PRACTICE NINE was discontinued in June 1967 because officials believed it had been compromised. MACV temporarily renamed the project ILLINOIS CITY. On 14 July the separate names for the two portions of the barrier came into effect. See Telfer et al., *Marines in Vietnam*, p. 91.

[66] Msgs, Westmoreland MAC 4866, MAC 7600, MAC 7616, MAC 7718, MAC 9963, to Sharp, 24 May 67, 13 Aug 67, 17 Aug 67, 22 Oct 67; Westmoreland MAC 5793 to Wheeler and Sharp, 19 Jun 67; Wheeler JCS 6127–67 and JCS 6812–67 to Westmoreland, 2 Aug 67 and 21 Aug 67; Sharp to Westmoreland, 8 Aug 67; Westmoreland MAC 7432 to Wheeler, 8 Aug 67; Westmoreland MAC 7472 to Starbird, 9 Aug 67; Dr John W. Foster, DDR&E 9034 to Westmoreland, 24 Oct 67; Westmoreland MAC 10256 to Foster, 28 Oct 67; Westmoreland Msg Files, 1 Apr–31 Oct 67. All in CMH.

[67] Shulimson, *Marines in Vietnam, 1966*, pp. 317–19, documents Marine Corps opposition to the project. Msgs, COMUSMACV MAC 27375 and MAC 34760 to CG III MAF, 17 Aug 67 and 22 Oct 67; COMUSMACV MAC 32676 to CINCPAC, 5 Oct 67. All in Westmoreland Sig File, 1967, CMH. Msg, Westmoreland MAC 9056 to Johnson and Sharp, 27 Sep 67, tab A–33, Westmoreland Hist File 22 (10–30 Sep 67), CMH. Criticism of marines: Msg, CG III MAF to COMUSMACV, 13 Oct 67, tab A–20, Westmoreland Hist File 23 (1–15 Oct 67); Westmoreland Hist Notes, 19–26 Dec 67, Westmoreland Hist File 27 (19–26 Dec 67). All in CMH.

[68] Analysts' estimates are in *U.S.–Vietnam Relations*, sec. 4.C.6(b), p. 132. Msg, Westmoreland MAC 1550 to Sharp, 14 Feb 67, Westmoreland Msg Files, 1 Jan–31 Mar 67; Ltr, Westmoreland to W. W. Rostow, 9 Dec 67, Westmoreland Sig File, 1967. Both in CMH. Palmer Interv, 7 and 10 Jun 68, pp. 250–52, 266–68. Sharp and Westmoreland, *Report on War*, pp. 147–48, 253.

[69] MACV Command History, 1967, pp. 1195–97. Msg, COMUSMACV MAC 35612 to CINCPAC, 29 Oct 67, Westmoreland Sig File, 1967, CMH.

[70] First quote is from Msg, Sharp to Wheeler info Westmoreland, 25 Jun 65; second is from Msg, Wheeler JCS 3332–67 to Westmoreland and Sharp, 5 May 67; third is from

Msg, Wheeler JCS 4495–67 to Sharp info Westmoreland, 15 Jun 67. All in Westmoreland Msg Files, 1 Apr–30 Jun 65 and 1 Apr–30 Jun 67, CMH.

[71] Quotes are from MFR, Jones, 3 Oct 66, sub: MACV Commanders' Conference, 28 Aug 66, tab D–4, Westmoreland Hist File 8 (17 Jul–17 Sep 66), CMH. The evolution of the reemphasis on RVNAF's pacification mission is traced in Clarke, *Final Years*, pp. 173–83.

[72] Clarke, *Final Years*, pp. 184–87, 249–50. Sharp and Westmoreland, *Report on War*, pp. 129, 216–17. MFR, Rosson, 17 Dec 66, sub: CIIC Meeting, 17 Dec 66, tab A–4, Westmoreland Hist File 12 (13 Dec 66–26 Jan 67), CMH.

[73] Westmoreland Hist Notes, 12 Sep 65, Westmoreland Hist File 1 (29 Aug–24 Oct 65). COMUSMACV Policy Points, Notes for Discussing with Amb Lodge, 13 Oct 66, tab D–7, Westmoreland Hist File 9 (18 Sep–17 Oct 66), CMH. MACV Command History, 1966, p. 748. Msg, Sharp to Wheeler, 15 Dec 66, Westmoreland Msg Files, 1 Oct–31 Dec 66, CMH.

[74] First quote is from Paper, Dept of State, Policy Planning Council, 15 Jun 67, sub: Possible Alternatives to the Present Conduct of the War in Vietnam, tab A–13, Westmoreland Hist File 18 (1 Jun–5 Jul 67), CMH. Second and third are from Msgs, Wheeler JCS 9449–67 and JCS 9680–67 to Westmoreland, 3 Nov and 10 Nov 67, Westmoreland Msg Files, 1–30 Nov 67, CMH.

[75] Quote is from Msg, Westmoreland MAC 8908 to Sharp, 21 Sep 67, Westmoreland Msg Files, 1 Jul–30 Sep 67. Msgs, Westmoreland MAC 10451 to Sharp, 3 Nov 67; Westmoreland MAC 10556 and MAC 10817 to Wheeler, 6 Nov and 12 Nov 67, Westmoreland Msg Files, 1–30 Nov 67. All in CMH. Clarke, *Final Years*, pp. 279–80.

[76] Address by General W. C. Westmoreland . . . to National Press Club, Washington, D.C., 21 November 1967, copy in CMH files.

[77] First quote is from MFR, Bryan, 2 Dec 67, sub: CIIB Meeting, 2 Dec 67, tab A–5, Westmoreland Hist File 26 (29 Nov–16 Dec 67), CMH. Remaining quotes are from Clarke, *Final Years*, pp. 281–82; see also pp. 280 and 283. Memo, Westmoreland for Bunker, 20 Dec 67, sub: Address to National Press Club . . . , Westmoreland Sig File, 1967, CMH. MacDonald-Westmoreland Interv, 11 Feb 73, CMH.

[78] Discussion of RVNAF improvement efforts and results is drawn from Clarke, *Final Years*, chs. 8–15, passim. Rosson quote is from his Interv, 1981, pp. 331–32; see also Rosson, "Involvement in Vietnam," pp. 208–09, 243–44. Detrimental effects of the delay in rearming ARVN are noted in Weyand Debrief, 15 Jul 68, p. 7.

13

An Autumn of Uncertainty

As 1967 wore on, General Westmoreland and his field commanders expressed growing confidence that they were achieving their goal of grinding down all elements of the enemy's interlocked military and political systems. While still hampered by what the military leaders thought were excessive political restrictions, ROLLING THUNDER was nevertheless battering North Vietnam's economy and society and increasing the cost and difficulty of that country's prosecution of the war in the south. Meanwhile in South Vietnam, American and allied troops were inflicting heavy casualties on the enemy's big units in every engagement, pushing them away from the population and agricultural centers, and invading and disrupting their base areas. Gradually improving South Vietnamese regular and territorial forces, with growing allied help, were whittling away at the Viet Cong guerrillas and their political infrastructure. Evidence was mounting of declining enemy strength and morale. Communist forces were encountering difficulties in attracting recruits within South Vietnam, the flow of reinforcements from North Vietnam was slowing. Most of all, North Vietnamese and Viet Cong military offensives seemed regularly to end in bloody failure.

Rural pacification continued to progress slowly, if at all; but the future seemed to hold promise. A series of orderly, reasonably honest elections during 1967 produced, for the first time since the fall of Ngo Dinh Diem, a stable Saigon government with a degree of constitutional legitimacy and popular support. With the new CORDS organization unifying American backing for pacification, the elements finally seemed to be coming together for an effective allied political and paramilitary offensive in the countryside.[1]

General Westmoreland's civilian counterparts in Saigon for the most part shared his belief that the allies were moving forward. Barry Zorthian, the U.S. Mission's chief of public relations, recalled that "the senior people in the U.S. Mission" genuinely "felt we were making progress in the war, although newspaper headlines usually overstated the degree of that feeling." In July Ambassador Komer, the new CORDS chief, told President Johnson that "at long last we are slowly but surely winning [the] war of attrition in [the] South." The Viet Cong, he

MACV: The Years of Escalation, 1962–1967

General Westmoreland with Barry Zorthian (Time Life Pictures/Getty Images)

declared, were "visibly declining." "Wasteful and painful though it is," he assured Johnson, "our massive investment out here is finally beginning to pay off."[2]

Even as officials in the embassy and commanders at MACV made plans to continue their campaign along the lines they believed were gradually producing success, events in the United States and North Vietnam were shifting the sand under their feet. In the United States, a growing number of Americans in the executive branch and Congress, in the news media, and among the general public did not share the optimism. To the dissenters, the incremental progress regularly reported from Saigon appeared more like stalemate, especially when weighed against the apparently limitless duration and steadily increasing cost of the conflict. Doubts about the success of the war, as well as its wisdom and morality, continued to spread in the United States. In an effort to counter this pessimism, the Johnson administration during 1967 mobilized all its forces, including the Saigon embassy and the Military Assistance Command, to convince the nation that the war was being won. Privately, however, the president himself was concerned about the increasing cost and inconclusive results of the American military effort. He was beginning to search for a way out of the war.

An Autumn of Uncertainty

Unknown to the Americans, North Vietnam's leaders also were reevaluating their strategy during the last half of 1967. Like many of their adversaries the Communists believed that, as then being conducted, the war had reached a stalemate. As they saw it, the Americans, for all their numbers and firepower, could not defeat the North Vietnamese and Viet Cong decisively, but neither could the Communist forces defeat the Americans. Still committed to ultimate victory and more confident than the Americans of their ability to achieve it, officials in Hanoi began making plans to force the conflict off dead center and to shift the balance of forces conclusively in their favor.

The Public Relations War

From the time President Johnson committed the United States to large-scale ground and air combat in Southeast Asia in 1965, he and his senior advisers were preoccupied with what they perceived to be the fragility of American domestic support for their policies. They had reason for concern. Public questioning of and opposition to the war mounted even as combat expanded and casualties increased. By mid-1967, outright antiwar protest had spread beyond the campuses and left-wing fringe groups and was drawing in major political, religious, labor, and civil rights leaders. Even more ominous, belief in victory was declining among politically moderate, patriotic Americans. Members of Congress who initially had supported the war began moving away from the administration's position, mainly on the grounds that the war was costing too much and making too little progress. In the news media, important journals, reporters, and columnists were beginning to reflect official and popular doubts, although the bulk of news coverage of the conflict still was neutral or favorable to the administration's position. President Johnson's performance ratings in the polls steadily declined, and an ever larger percentage of respondents to the same polls agreed with the proposition that U.S. intervention in Vietnam had been a mistake. Arguing against further expansion of American forces in Vietnam, Assistant Secretary of Defense for International Security Affairs John McNaughton summarized the general unease: "A feeling is widely and strongly held that 'the Establishment' is out of its mind. The feeling is that we are trying to impose some US image on distant peoples we cannot understand (anymore than we can the younger generation here at home), and that we are carrying the thing to absurd lengths."[3]

General Wheeler repeatedly communicated the administration's worries about public opinion to General Westmoreland and Admiral Sharp. As early as the I Corps troubles in spring 1966, he warned his subordinates that the upheaval had cost "irretrievably and for all time some of the support which until now we have received from the American people," many of whom "will never again believe that the effort

Antiwar protesters at the Pentagon, October 1967 (NARA)

and the sacrifices are worthwhile." A little more than a year later, he told field commanders that "there is deep concern here in Washington because of the eroding support for our war effort," with particular distress over "the allegations of 'stalemate.'" Sharp and Westmoreland shared Wheeler's apprehensive reading of the popular mood. The Pacific commander concluded late in 1966 that "The American people can become aroused either for or against this war. At the moment, with no end in sight, they are more apt to become aroused against it."[4]

At the administration's urging, transmitted through Wheeler, General Westmoreland redoubled his command's efforts to inform the press and public about the war and, in Sharp's words, "to convince our people and Hanoi that there is an end in sight and that it is clearly defeat for Hanoi." From his assumption of command in mid-1964, Westmoreland, who appreciated the importance of the news media as a channel of communication to the American public, had labored diligently to repair MACV's relations with the Saigon reporters. Westmoreland enlarged the MACV Office of Information and secured able officers to head it. In cooperation with the embassy's Joint U.S. Public Affairs Office, which oversaw all mission information efforts, and in consultation with the correspondents, MACV public affairs officers developed voluntary guidelines for news reporting which adequately protected sensitive military information without imposing outright censorship. Insofar as they could, MACV information officers at Westmoreland's direction maintained a policy of openness and candor, albeit with constant accent on the positive aspects of events. Faithfully adhering to his own policy, Westmoreland held frequent on-and off-the-record sessions with reporters, both individuals and in groups. He routinely took correspondents along with him on field trips, especially those he expected would generate favorable stories.[5]

In discussions with correspondents and civilian visitors, as well as in his official reports, Westmoreland tried to avoid the extremes of optimism that had destroyed the credibility of his predecessor, General Harkins. In December 1965 he enjoined officers of the 1st Infantry Division and the 173d Airborne Brigade to curb the "inclination toward optimism concerning the course of the war," be "realistic" in their reporting, and concentrate on "hard facts and capabilities." Nevertheless, Westmoreland persistently expressed confidence in progress and victory. Before McNamara's visit to Saigon in July 1967, he directed his subordinates to emphasize to the secretary of defense that "though the enemy is tough and elusive he can and is being licked. It will just take time and resourcefulness to do it." He justified his positive stance in terms reminiscent of those used by Harkins: "Even slight pessimism will pervade the ranks. A commander is the weathervane and must be positive. When I appeared before the press and public, I had to reflect confidence. I really was confident. . . . It was no act on my part, but I was sharply cognizant of the need to avoid any impression of pessimism or defeatism. I tried consciously to reflect this image."[6]

During 1967 General Westmoreland and his public affairs officers became deeply engaged in the Johnson administration's effort to convince the American public that the allies were making progress in the war. To counter persistent press claims that the South Vietnamese armed forces were incompetent and ineffective, they fed both reporters and officials a steady stream of reports of ARVN organizational improvement and battlefield success. They also tried, with at best limited results, to improve their allies' public relations techniques. As part of an administration-wide campaign to counter allegations that the war was a stalemate, Westmoreland kept up a barrage of news conferences and official reports detailing slow but steady improvement in every aspect of the struggle against the Viet Cong. He also tried to exploit distinguished visitors to promote optimism and neutralize war critics. When retired General James M. Gavin, who had questioned administration war strategy, planned a visit to South Vietnam, the MACV commander and General Wheeler sought to trump him in the headlines with an overlapping tour by the Korean war hero, General Matthew B.

MACV: The Years of Escalation, 1962–1967

General Westmoreland addresses a joint session of Congress, April 1967.
(© Bettmann/CORBIS)

Ridgway, whom they considered more friendly to their side. Ridgeway, however, declined Westmoreland's invitation.[7]

Twice during 1967 General Westmoreland journeyed to the United States to report in person to various audiences on the state of the war. The MACV commander had declined previous invitations to speak to groups in America, arguing that such activities were inappropriate for a field general during hostilities. However, in April 1967, at President Johnson's insistence, he agreed to address the annual luncheon of Associated Press executives in New York. The trip quickly expanded to include several other public appearances, culminating in an address to a joint session of Congress, probably the first ever delivered to that body by a theater commander during a war. Although antiwar senators and representatives criticized Johnson's use of an active duty general as the administration's political spokesman, Westmoreland's remarks drew a generally respectful and heavily favorable public response. Hence, Johnson in November brought Westmoreland and Ambassador Bunker back to the United States for another round of appearances intermingled with private consultations. During this trip Westmoreland suggested in a speech to the National Press Club that it might be possible to begin withdrawing U.S. troops from Vietnam within a couple of years. At a White House breakfast the day after the Press Club speech, the president, Secretaries Rusk and McNamara, Bunker, Westmoreland,

An Autumn of Uncertainty

and other senior officials planned still further expansion of the public relations offensive, with emphasis once again on offsetting "the common belief that the South Vietnamese won't fight."[8]

The administration's optimism campaign had mixed results. President Johnson in late January 1968 told his National Security Council that he detected "improvement" in media reporting from South Vietnam, a circumstance he attributed to the administration's and MACV's efforts. Nevertheless, large segments of the press and public remained unconvinced by the barrage of official reassurance. By emphasizing only progress and good news, the administration risked severe public reaction if a setback occurred or if the enemy displayed unexpected aggressiveness and vigor. MACV faced the same danger. In the view of the Saigon correspondents, General Westmoreland's ventures into the political arena had imbued all information and assessments released by his headquarters with a taint of administration propaganda. Westmoreland and his command thus lost rather than gained credibility with the news media.[9]

Giving credence to media suspicions, under the pressure of the optimism campaign Westmoreland allowed public relations considerations to influence his command's official military reports and assessments. In March 1967, for example, the MACV commander reported to General Wheeler that the monthly rate of enemy battalion-size attacks had increased during 1966, resulting in a total of 174 for the year instead of the 45 published in preliminary estimates. In response, Wheeler asked Westmoreland to keep this information closely held, even within the government. The chairman explained that he and the Joint Chiefs had used the lower total of large-scale enemy attacks in arguing to the president, the Congress, and the news media that the allies had seized the military initiative in the ground war. Having taken this position, Wheeler declared, he could not go back to the president and tell him that in fact "the situation is such that we are not sure who has the initiative in South Vietnam." Westmoreland defended the procedures his staff had used to derive the larger number. Nevertheless, after a special team from Washington reviewed MACV's methods for counting enemy large-scale attacks, the general reduced the estimate for 1966 back to 45.[10]

As was true of many statistical controversies in this war, the issue of enemy attacks turned heavily on definitions and counting methods. In addition, as was frequently the case, the meaning of the numbers was ambiguous. An increase in enemy attacks could indeed be interpreted as showing that the Viet Cong and North Vietnamese held the tactical initiative. The same increase, however, could be explained as an effort by the enemy to retrieve a losing situation, creating opportunities for American forces to destroy him with firepower. Westmoreland and the administration he served risked the total loss of public faith by using such questionable estimates to support claims of military success.

The Order of Battle Controversy

During the summer and fall of 1967, as the progress campaign reached its climax, the Military Assistance Command and the Central Intelligence Agency engaged in a lengthy, often bitter argument over the size and composition of the enemy's forces. That argument brought MACV into unresolved conflict with the majority of the U.S. intelligence community. It also left the command at odds with much of its own intelligence staff. The sources of the dispute lay in part in the substance of complex issues and in part in a tangle of personality and bureaucratic conflicts. Pervading the entire controversy was the Johnson administration's obsession with convincing the American people that the war was going well.

Measurement of the enemy's order of battle, both current and retrospective, was essential to determining whether the allies were making progress in attrition and pacification. It was a complex, often frustrating task. Most of the enemy's military units made only infrequent contact with allied forces. The enemy's irregulars and political infrastructure, which lacked standardized organization and hid among the people most of the time, were even more difficult to count. Adding to the complexity, many Communist organizations performed both civilian and military functions, a circumstance that gave rise to arguments among the Americans over which categories belonged in the "military" order of battle and which did not. Most of the numbers used in making strength estimates, whether of enemy casualties and deserters or of monthly rates of recruitment and infiltration, were difficult to obtain and prone to over- or underestimation. Hence, calculations of trends based on them had to be employed with great caution. However, officials trying to validate their policy positions or to demonstrate progress often treated approximations as firm figures and drew from them unwarrantedly positive conclusions. When personal and institutional reputations became tied to such conclusions, acrimonious interagency disputes were certain to follow.[11]

Every major U.S. intelligence organization—the Central Intelligence Agency, the Defense Intelligence Agency (DIA), the National Security Agency (NSA), and the State Department's Bureau of Intelligence and Research (INR), as well as the MACV and Pacific Command J2 sections—took part in the collection and analysis of information on the enemy. While these agencies exchanged considerable amounts of data among themselves, they operated, in both Washington and the field, without any overarching authority to coordinate their efforts. Early in his tenure, General McChristian, invoking an established organizational principle that in wartime CIA stations should come under operational control of the theater military headquarters, attempted to bring the CIA station in South Vietnam under the authority of MACV. The agency blocked this effort. Its Saigon station continued to work directly for the ambassador while also transmitting analyses to agency headquarters in Langley, Virginia. Similarly, the NSA installations in Vietnam, which were not under MACV's operational control, sent their highly classified product back to the United States for distribution. In Washington, the Office of National Estimates presided over attempts to reach unified interagency positions on major issues but possessed no directing authority over the intelligence community as a whole. Agencies developed stubbornly held institutional positions that often seemed impervious to contrary facts, as typified by the running MACV-CIA argument over whether or not the Communists were bringing weapons into South Vietnam through the Cambodian port of Sihanoukville.[12]

While the resulting system was inefficient and filled with contention, it did afford senior administration officials a broad base of reports and raw data from which to develop their own assessments of the war's progress. For example, besides receiving the entire product of military intelligence, Secretary of Defense McNamara also arranged late in 1965 for weekly briefings by the CIA director's deputy for Southeast Asia affairs. Thus President Johnson and his top advisers were aware of the intelligence community's disagreement over the enemy order of battle. They imposed their own policy concerns upon its resolution.[13]

The president and his advisers were particularly concerned about the impact of enemy strength figures on American public opinion. As the U.S. intelligence establishment in South Vietnam expanded in size and capabilities, its estimates of the size of the enemy expanded as well. The increase reflected in part a real buildup of Communist forces, but it also resulted in large measure from belated American confirmation of the existence of enemies long present. As early as July 1964, Ambassador Taylor explained a substantial jump in mission estimates of Viet Cong strength as "not a sudden or dramatic increase but rather the acceptance of the existence of units suspected for two or three years for which confirmatory evidence has become available only in the last few months." Similar enlargements of the VC/NVA order of battle continued even as American troops entered combat and began inflicting heavy enemy casualties. Critics of the war were quick to seize on the seeming contradiction between administration claims of progress and reports of steadily growing North Vietnamese and Viet Cong numbers. The administration in turn pressed its military and civilian intelligence agencies to develop consistent order of battle procedures and to agree on a single common set of strength estimates for both internal government and external public affairs use.[14]

At General Wheeler's direction, delegations from Pacific Command, the Military Assistance Command, and all the military and civilian intelligence agencies met at Honolulu from 6 to 11 February 1967 to standardize their methods for developing and presenting enemy order of battle and infiltration statistics. The conference essentially endorsed a methodology already developed by General McChristian, who headed the MACV contingent. It established four categories of enemy forces—combat units, administrative service units, irregulars, and political cadre—and defined the enemy's total strength as the sum of those four elements. The conferees adopted McChristian's criteria for accepting new combat units into the order of battle and for counting North Vietnamese infiltrators, and they called for more work on estimating the strength of the less formally organized categories. They also adopted relatively conservative rules for estimating enemy losses from death, wounds, desertion, and other causes.[15]

The Honolulu conference acknowledged the necessity for revision of American estimates of the number of enemy irregulars. Those forces, as defined at Honolulu, consisted of three Viet Cong military and paramilitary elements subordinate to village and hamlet VC political authorities: the guerrillas, the self-defense forces, and the secret self-defense forces. The guerrillas were village platoon and hamlet squads of armed, full-time fighters who regularly engaged in combat operations. The self-defense forces were made up of elderly men, women, youths, and children in Viet Cong-controlled areas who occasionally performed—either willingly or under duress—a variety of tasks in defense of their immediate localities, for example, gathering intelligence, planting booby traps and punji stakes, and constructing fortifications. The secret self-defense forces were similar, but lived in government-dominated rural communities and in towns and cities, where they engaged in espionage, propaganda, and sabotage.[16]

Since they possessed only rudimentary military organization and lacked uniforms and often weapons, these elements—except the guerrillas to some degree—could not be counted by MACV's normal method of identifying units and assigning strengths to them. Instead, intelligence analysts tried to extrapolate their numbers from whatever fragmentary returns and reports they could find in captured documents. This frequently meant simply taking figures, of unknown accuracy, for one province or a few villages and multiplying them by the number of provinces and villages in South Vietnam, then making various adjustments for casualties, desertions, and other factors to arrive at an approximate total. Overall, the process could produce widely varying results, depending on the documents, formulas, and assumptions used.[17]

The MACV Intelligence Directorate began trying to count the irregulars and the Viet Cong political cadres in mid-1966. Up to that time, the Military Assistance Command had published figures for these categories provided by the South Vietnamese, which everyone, including the Vietnamese, conceded were probably too low. During the buildup of his directorate, General McChristian gave first priority to creating an order of battle for the enemy's regular units, which constituted the most urgent threat to the Saigon government. With this task in hand

An Autumn of Uncertainty

and with the volume of captured documents and other source material rapidly increasing, the intelligence chief sought to complete MACV's picture of the opposing forces. Thus he instituted new collection programs that targeted the irregulars and the political elements. By the time of the Honolulu conference in February 1967, McChristian's analysts had confirmed that the existing irregular and political strength estimates needed to be raised. The conference attendees directed MACV to continue its studies in this field and cautioned that the result likely would be a "book increase" in enemy strength. The command, therefore, was to consider means to "reflect these figures in the order of battle in a manner which will help prevent consumers of intelligence from viewing the increases as indicative of a sudden growth in the enemy force structure." Instead, "consumers should view such changes as an increase of our knowledge of enemy strength already in being."[18]

Following the Honolulu meeting, the MACV Combined Intelligence Center (CICV), after extensive consultation with ARVN intelligence officers and American province advisers, completed its studies and refined its analyses. On 18 May General McChristian signed the completed irregular forces study, which MACV was to issue with the Joint General Staff as a combined estimate. Using the categories defined at Honolulu, he numbered the enemy guerrilla force at 60,750, the self-defense forces at 101,150, and the secret self-defense forces at 23,400—a grand total of 185,300 irregulars, in contrast to the old South Vietnamese aggregate of about 112,000. McChristian noted that captured enemy documents contained much higher strength figures for the irregulars than those he was presenting. However, the age and accuracy of those numbers were uncertain, and CICV had discounted them on the basis of field reports and also of evidence in the documents themselves of the enemy's inability to achieve recruiting goals. McChristian also declared that in the unanimous view of the province intelligence officers, among the irregulars only the guerrillas represented "a real military threat," since they were normally well armed, fought as units, and conducted offensive operations. The self-defense and secret self-defense components, which lacked both weapons and training, should be included in the MACV order of battle "in order to present a complete picture of enemy strength, but with the notation that as a combat force they are only marginally effective." McChristian announced plans to incorporate the new categories and estimates in the monthly MACV order of battle for June with retroactive adjustments "to preclude inference of a sudden increase" in the number of irregulars.[19]

The new figures did not appear in the June summary. Early one evening in mid-May, McChristian met privately with Westmoreland in the latter's office. McChristian presented for Westmoreland's signature a cable to Admiral Sharp and the Joint Chiefs that transmitted both the revised irregular total and an increase in political cadre strength from the previous estimate of about 40,000 to 88,000. Between them, the new figures would raise the Military Assistance Command's total enemy strength holdings from about 300,000 to nearly 420,000. Only recently returned from the first of his public relations trips to the United States, Westmoreland seemed dismayed at the size of the numbers confronting him. He protested, according to McChristian, that the cable would "create a political bombshell" in Washington. The MACV commander refused to sign the cable or to allow McChristian, then about to leave Vietnam at the end of his tour, to hand carry the document to Honolulu and Washington. Instead, he instructed McChristian to leave it with him for further study.[20]

Westmoreland retained the revised estimates in his headquarters for the ensuing month, although information as to their contents seems gradually to have leaked out to other intelligence agencies. At his regular staff meeting on 19 May, he directed the J2, with representatives from the J3 and, significantly, from public information, "to analyze this study in depth and to determine how this information should be presented both officially and publicly." He also "requested specifically that those irregular forces that are armed be identified." Westmoreland directed a similar study of the new political order of battle estimate. The studies continued through the next month, although the MACV commander was sure enough of the figures by the end of May to have the Joint Public Affairs Office and the Mission Council briefed on them. Nevertheless, he continued to delay wider dissemination of the estimates, even when pressed for them by the DIA through Admiral Sharp.[21]

It became clear during this period that Westmoreland, for both substantive and public relations reasons, wanted to find some way to avoid reporting a 100,000-man increase in enemy strength, especially an increase based entirely upon a retrospective enlargement of the irregulars. He appears to have questioned the validity of counting the self-defense forces as the equivalent of regular soldiers, a position in which he was not alone. A DIA team that reviewed MACV's new estimates in April 1967 had recommended excluding both the self-defense elements and the political cadre from the military order of battle, and McChristian's 18 May report had indicated that only the guerrillas were a significant combat force. In addition, Westmoreland was all too aware that the press and public would juxtapose reports of increased enemy strength with his statements about progress in the war, to his and the administration's embarrassment. The newly arrived CORDS chief, Robert Komer, shared this awareness. As a result, Westmoreland adopted a strategy of removing the self-defense forces and political cadre from the military order of battle. By this means, MACV could keep total Communist strength around 300,000 even while accepting higher figures for some of the military categories.[22]

The Military Assistance Command's slowness in releasing its revised estimates created increasing impatience and suspicion in the Central Intelligence Agency. Agency analysts in both Saigon and Langley during 1966 had begun producing estimates independent of the military but using the military's sources for all elements of the Communist order of battle. Relying heavily on extrapolation and multiplication from limited evidence, they arrived at what they considered more up-to-date and useful, and usually higher, estimates of enemy combat power than those MACV was producing. The CIA analysts also defined enemy forces more broadly than did MACV. They preferred to talk of an "insurgency base" that included paramilitary and political as well as military elements in contrast to MACV's more conventional "order of battle," which was limited to organized armed formations. Following this approach, CIA analysts, notably the articulate and aggressive Sam Adams, were estimating the enemy's irregular strength by late 1966 at more than 300,000 and the entire Communist order of battle at perhaps 600,000. They continued to circulate figures of this magnitude during and after the February 1967 Honolulu conference.[23]

CIA Director Helms
(© Bettmann/CORBIS)

The issue came to a head in mid-1967, when CIA Director Richard Helms, responding to a presidential request, instructed the Board of National Estimates to prepare a new assessment of Communist strength and capabilities in South Vietnam. The estimate, drafted initially by CIA representatives, was to reflect a consensus of the entire intelligence community on the basic issue of the enemy's ability to continue the war. Entitled Special National Intelligence Estimate (SNIE) 14.3–67, this document became the focal point of the order of battle controversy.[24]

On 23 June, the first interagency meeting to review the CIA draft of the special estimate ended in deadlock. The document estimated total enemy strength at around 500,000 personnel of all categories, including substantially larger numbers than previously used for the administrative services, irregulars, and political cadre. All sides concurred in their estimates of enemy combat troops. However, spokesmen for the Defense Intelligence Agency, representing MACV at the meeting, rejected the CIA's totals for the other categories and insisted on using MACV's old figures, which would keep overall enemy strength around 300,000. The meeting ended without a decision on which numbers to use in the SNIE, but with the State Department and National Security Agency delegations generally supporting the CIA position.[25]

In spite of this unpromising beginning, Director Helms' deputy in charge of Vietnam War intelligence, George Carver, soon developed the outlines of a compromise.[26] Carver appreciated the Military Assistance Command's public relations problem with the higher estimates. He, and most other CIA analysts, also recognized that lumping the self-defense elements and political cadre with the more definitely military enemy components gave a distorted and exaggerated picture of the armed Communist threat. Carver also regarded the numbers for the nonmilitary categories as extremely "soft," little more than general approximations. Hence, he was willing to separate the self-defense forces and political cadre from the military order of battle, provided that the paramilitary groups continued to be counted as part of the total enemy manpower base and that it was recognized that those elements contributed a share of battlefield casualties, deserters, and prisoners. Carver assistant George Allen early in July summarized the emerging CIA position. He proposed to divide enemy forces into "two principal groupings—military and non-military. The military would include combat, administrative support, and guerrilla, while the non-military would include the self-defense (militia) and political. The totals for the military grouping would approximate the current listing (295,000), and this is the figure MACV could use in discussing—officially and unofficially—the enemy's military potential. The non-military grouping would not—and should not—be used in assessing military matters, but would be considered in computations on input and loss . . . , particularly with reference to Chieu Hoi figures."[27]

By the time Carver and Allen developed this position, a change of Military Assistance Command chiefs of intelligence had complicated matters. At the end of May, under an arrangement made by Generals Westmoreland and Johnson in March, General McChristian, who had completed his regular two-year tour of duty, left Vietnam to take command of the 2d Armored Division at Fort Hood, Texas. His replacement, Maj. Gen. Phillip B. Davidson, was an experienced Army intelligence officer and like McChristian had served as the chief of intelligence of U.S. Army, Pacific, before coming to MACV."[28]

Davidson, however, was also a long-time professional rival of his predecessor. Considering McChristian's method of operation ponderous and pedantic, the new chief lost no time in imposing his own stamp on the MACV Intelligence Directorate, with abrasive effect. To staff the senior positions in his directorate, Davidson brought in his own men from USARPAC and the United States. Relations between Davidson's people and the McChristian-era holdovers who staffed many J2 offices and the Combined Intelligence Center were often contentious. In particular, Col. Daniel O. Graham, the new chief of indications and estimates, seemed to many to be overbearing and opinionated, rigid in

General Davidson, left, and Colonel Graham (shown as a brigadier general)

holding to his established preconceptions, and inclined to browbeat analysts who did not substantiate his positions.[29]

General Davidson and Colonel Graham took up their duties already convinced that their predecessors had been overestimating enemy numbers. They claimed that McChristian had inflated the size of the enemy main force and also doubted the validity of McChristian's enlarged estimates of guerrilla and political strength. They could not reconcile the intelligence section's regular claims of a larger enemy with operational reports of a low level of Communist offensive activity and with the evidence their own office was accumulating of heavy enemy casualties, an apparent leveling-off of North Vietnamese infiltration, and recruiting difficulties and high desertion rates among the Viet Cong. To Davidson and Graham, logic and evidence indicated that enemy strength must be decreasing, and they were less than receptive to analyses that maintained the contrary position. Early in his tenure Graham prepared an extensive briefing which claimed that in fact the "cross-over point," at which the enemy was losing more men in the south than he could replace, already had been reached.[30]

Besides Davidson and his assistants, other American officials questioned McChristian's steady enlargement of the enemy order of battle. Walt Rostow, Deputy Secretary of Defense Paul Nitze, and Ambassador Robert Komer all suspected that MACV had been overcounting the enemy, both out of understandable military caution and in order to support requests for still more American troops. Komer, who had become involved in order of battle discussions as the president's special assistant for counterinsurgency, weighed heavily into the question as the new chief of CORDS. He dismissed an early draft of SNIE 14.3–67 as a "rather superficial" document that did not "take into account the interaction of our capabilities with those of the enemy" and portrayed an "inflated" estimate of Communist strength. He also praised Davidson's endeavors to bring the Intelligence Directorate's enemy strength estimates into line with what Komer thought was reality. He strongly endorsed proposals to stop counting the self-defense forces and political cadre as part of the military order of battle.[31]

Unfortunately, the Intelligence Directorate's working order-of-battle analysts disagreed with their superiors' views. Trained by McChristian and loyal to him, they stuck by the results of their own examination of documents and prisoner interrogation reports, which they contended did not support claims of an enemy decline and might in fact indicate increases in some categories. Yet they felt themselves under pressure to adjust downward their estimates of both regular and irregular forces and found it difficult if not impossible to gain a hearing for their claims that the enemy was being undercounted. Colonel Graham himself admitted that he kept "pounding on" the analysts to reduce their guerrilla strength estimates. In the view of many of the young intelligence officers, who usually were on their first tours in their specialty, this amounted to a demand that they lie. Faced with this pressure, Col. Gains Hawkins, head of the Combined Intelligence Center's Order of Battle Branch, which published MACV's monthly estimates of enemy forces, later admitted that he had arbitrarily reduced his subordinates' estimates of guerrilla, self-defense, and political cadre strength. He declared that he never received a "direct order" to do this, but "I had a distinct understanding . . . that these figures were going to have to go down."[32]

The divisions within MACV intelligence notwithstanding, it seemed initially as though the command and the CIA would reach a quick agreement. Early in July, George Carver traveled to Saigon with Secretary McNamara, who had come for final discussions with Westmoreland on the Program Five reinforcement. Carver took the opportunity to present to Komer and Davidson the CIA plan for resolving the "political and presentational" problem of the larger enemy numbers by separating military from nonmilitary elements. Komer and Davidson appeared "very receptive" to Carver's proposal and also to the idea, favored by the CIA, of using ranges of figures for all categories but the regular troops. At a final amicable meeting on 9 July, the principals agreed that Davidson would secure Westmoreland's approval of a revised estimate; then Hawkins would bring it to Washington for presentation to the interagency board working on the special intelligence estimate. Reporting to Director Helms on the meeting, Carver expected the estimate to "slide through . . . without dissent" and form the basis

An Autumn of Uncertainty

of a "solid piece of agreed national intelligence which all participants can support."[33]

Carver's optimism was premature. By the time the next round of discussions on SNIE 14.3–67 opened at CIA headquarters at Langley in mid-August, whatever understanding he had achieved with MACV had broken down. The conference, which Carver did not attend, turned into an acrimonious, confusing interagency wrangle with the military representatives from MACV, Pacific Command, and the DIA arrayed against the CIA and State Department. While all concerned agreed on estimates of the Communist regular combat forces, the CIA held out for higher numbers than MACV would accept for the administrative support troops, guerrillas, and political cadre and also insisted on including large numbers of self-defense and secret self-defense forces in the total enemy strength.[34]

The military delegations refused to count the self-defense categories and maneuvered to keep the total number of enemy in the estimate below what all believed was an arbitrary, command-established ceiling of 300,000. General Westmoreland denied then and later ever setting such a ceiling, and no documentation has been found of a direct order from him to do so. Nevertheless, his intelligence officers clearly believed that their commander wanted to keep enemy strength estimates within the set maximum. During the conference, General Davidson told the MACV delegation head, Brig. Gen. George Godding, "I am sure that this headquarters will not accept a figure in excess of the current strength . . . carried by the press." "Let me make it clear," he continued, "that this is my view of General Westmoreland's sentiments. I have not discussed this directly with him but I am 100 per cent sure of his reaction."[35]

Privately, the military delegates at Langley were divided among themselves. Lower-ranking officers from MACV and from the other military agencies, who were under orders to support the MACV position, confided to their CIA colleagues that the command figures they were compelled to defend were lower than their own best estimates. As for the conference sessions, according to one MACV participant, they "more closely resembled a labor negotiation than an intelligence operation." Col. George Hamscher of Pacific Command recalled: "we haggled and bargained, even blustered. It progressed from unprofessional to wrongful; and it amounted to falsification of intelligence." In the end, trying to stay under the 300,000 ceiling while making concessions to the CIA on some categories, Colonels Hawkins and Graham, both of whom took part in the discussions, resorted to arbitrary reduction of their own estimates.[36]

In the midst of the sessions the press published an apparently leaked version of the CIA's estimates, which included a total enemy strength of 420,000. This development provoked a barrage of cables to the White House and Defense Department from Westmoreland, Abrams, Bunker, and Komer. All declared emphatically that the self-defense and secret self-defense forces did not belong in the military order of battle because they lacked significant combat capability, and they warned that their inclusion would result in a 100,000-man increase in apparent enemy strength that would falsely undercut valid claims of progress. General Abrams succinctly summed up the MACV and embassy position:

> We have been projecting an image of success over the recent months, and properly so. Now, when we release the figure of 420,000–431,000, the newsmen will immediately seize on the point that the enemy force has increased about 120,000–130,000. All available caveats and explanations will not prevent the press from drawing an erroneous and gloomy conclusion as to the meaning of the increase. All those who hold an incorrect view of the war will be reenforced and the task will become more difficult.
>
> In our view, the strength figures for the [self-defense] and [secret self-defense forces] should be omitted entirely from enemy strength tables in the forthcoming NIE. This will prevent the possibility that they can be added to the valid figures, and an erroneous conclusion drawn as to an enemy strength increase.[37]

The Saigon officials may have misunderstood the Central Intelligence Agency's position. Headquarters at Langley cabled the Saigon station at the end of the conference that the agency "does not repeat not" advocate including the irregulars in the "full-time military force figure" and still adhered essentially to Carver's July proposal. Indeed, the final draft estimate that emerged from the Langley meeting came close to MACV's figures for all categories of the enemy and did not add together the military and paramilitary/political elements. Westmoreland, Bunker, and Komer nevertheless continued their protests to Washington, joined by Admiral Sharp and the Pacific Command chief of intelligence, General Peterson.[38]

As General Abrams indicated, the substance of the special estimate had come to be less important than its public relations effects in the view of MACV and the Saigon embassy and indeed throughout the Johnson administration. As Komer declared at one point, publication of estimates showing increased Communist numbers would undercut the administration's claims of progress and "give the American public a misleading picture." Komer concluded, "The intelligence aspects have ceased to be important, it is the press relations which are crucial now." The Joint Chiefs of Staff, according to General Godding, also viewed the "public release problem" as "the major problem." The figures themselves the chiefs considered "of lesser importance."[39]

On 25 August, with discussion of the intelligence estimate seemingly deadlocked, General Westmoreland with Ambassador Bunker's concurrence recommended to General Wheeler that "a team from the Washington intelligence agencies concerned with this NIE visit this command as soon as possible to develop a common and valid set of enemy strength statistics." Agreeing that the self-defense elements should be omitted from total enemy strength but willing to compromise on fig-

An Autumn of Uncertainty

ures for the guerrillas and administrative services, Wheeler granted the request. After the Joint Chiefs heard a report by General Godding on the Langley talks, Wheeler asked CIA Director Helms, in his capacity as head of the intelligence community, to send a personal representative to Saigon to try to resolve the dispute with MACV. Helms dispatched George Carver, along with a team of CIA analysts. The other military and civilian intelligence agencies and—betokening the true nature of higher level concerns—the assistant secretary of defense for public affairs also sent delegates. Informing Westmoreland of arrangements for the meeting, Wheeler left little doubt that more than technical intelligence issues were at stake. It was "imperative," he told the MACV commander, "that we use comparable figures both in Saigon and Washington" because "in addition to the intelligence estimative problem, there is involved here an important public affairs problem."[40]

The Saigon conference opened on 9 September and promptly fell into deadlock. The MACV delegation, headed by Davidson himself, remained intransigent. It insisted on a strength of 119,000 for the combat forces, 29,000 for the administrative services, 65,000 for the guerrillas, and 85,000 for the political cadre, with no quantification of the self-defense and secret self-defense forces. The CIA figures were essentially those of the final Langley SNIE draft: 121,000 combat, 40,000–60,000 administrative, 60,000–100,000 guerrillas, and 90,000 political cadre, plus 120,000 for the self-defense and secret self-defense elements. Mutual frustration and irritation increased as the contending sides juggled figures. The other delegations, both civilian and military, concluded that MACV was defending a position based purely on public relations considerations in total disregard of both logic and evidence. Outbursts of profanity and aspersions on personal and professional integrity punctuated the discussions.[41]

Carver had come out with instructions from CIA Director Helms to take all reasonable steps to secure interagency agreement on a set of figures. He had hoped to meet with Westmoreland and Komer in advance of the working sessions to secure a lifting of the presumed MACV ceiling on enemy strength before trying to negotiate numbers for specific force categories. Westmoreland and Komer, however, had just finished shepherding the South Vietnamese through their presidential election, and both had left Saigon for short vacations. Fortunately, both Westmoreland and Komer returned to Saigon on 11 September. After a meeting with Komer the following day, Carver assembled the Washington delegations to prepare a final offer for MACV. In six hours of intense discussion they hammered out a compromise set of figures and a method for dealing with the irregulars, which Carver presented to General Westmoreland in a meeting on the 13th. Westmoreland promptly approved the proposal while denying that he ever had set an arbitrary "ceiling" on MACV's estimates of enemy strength. Subsequently, Ambassador Bunker also endorsed the agreement.[42]

In the accord, the concerned agencies set enemy strength at 119,000 for the combat forces, 35,000–40,000 for the administrative services, and 70,000–90,000 for the guerrillas, and agreed that only those elements would be counted in the military order of battle. Higher figures for the political cadre would be published but not added to the military forces on grounds that "such an aggregate total is inherently meaningless and misleading." The conferees omitted the self-defense and secret self-defense forces from the estimate's strength tables. Instead, they used the narrative portion of the estimate to insert a paragraph, drafted by the Washington representatives, that described the composition and role of those forces and suggested that they might number as many as 150,000. These adjustments were a logical evolution from the terms of the final Langley draft, which had avoided any totaling of military, paramilitary, and political strengths. The CIA secured acceptable higher figures for the administrative services, guerrillas, and political cadre and at least acknowledgment of the existence of the self-defense elements. MACV could continue to publish an enemy military strength of under 300,000 and could keep the partially armed militia from artificially inflating the size of the opposing army. General Westmoreland declared himself "satisfied that this is a good estimate and the best that can be derived from available intelligence."[43]

The final version of Special National Intelligence Estimate 14.3–67, published on 13 November 1967 with the concurrence of the CIA, the State Department, the DIA, and the NSA, incorporated the compromises reached in Saigon. It was a far from optimistic document. SNIE 14.3–67 declared that, in spite of heavy casualties and growing desertion and recruiting difficulties among the Viet Cong, the enemy could carry on his existing strategy of attrition in South Vietnam for "at least another year." In support of this judgment, the estimate declared that although sustaining losses to ROLLING THUNDER, North Vietnam still had sufficient manpower reserves to sustain indefinitely its forces in the south and to compensate at least partially for what the estimate considered to be a decline in Viet Cong strength.

The estimate reiterated that the increases in Communist force categories outside the regular forces resulted primarily from more sophisticated analysis and asserted that the strength of those elements actually was less than it had probably been earlier. The estimate declared that any attempt to add together the military, paramilitary, and political components of enemy strength "would be misleading since it would involve adding components that have widely different missions and degrees of skill or dedication." Nevertheless, the SNIE noted that the military force of 223,000–248,000 "constitutes but one component of the total Communist organization" and warned that "any comprehensive judgment of Communist capabilities in South Vietnam must embrace the effectiveness of all the elements which comprise that organization, the total size of which is of course considerably greater than the figure given for the military force."[44]

Reaction to SNIE 14.3–67 within the intelligence community was mixed. CIA Director Helms, George Carver, the senior military officers, and some uniformed and civilian analysts accepted the estimate as a reasonably accurate picture of enemy strength. Other CIA analysts denounced Helms and Carver for "caving in" to MACV by marching the self-defense elements out of the order of battle and accepting overly low estimates for the other components. A substantial faction of military intelligence officers at MACV and other headquarters echoed CIA criticism of the estimate and continued to resent the command positions they had been forced to support and the order of battle methods they were compelled to follow. Some, increasingly disillusioned and cynical, became convinced they were participating in a deliberate falsification of intelligence. An officer from the Army staff who followed the issue reflected the extreme view: "I came to believe that General Westmoreland had authorized his MACV intelligence staff to intentionally falsify intelligence information about enemy strength . . . to give the erroneous impression that we were winning the war. I viewed this as a conscious effort or conspiracy on MACV's part to distort crucial intelligence on the enemy we faced in Vietnam."[45]

Tensions between the Military Assistance Command and the Central Intelligence Agency were further exacerbated during preparation of the official statement presenting SNIE 14.3–67 to the news media. Although the release was issued by MACV in Saigon, the Office of the Assistant Secretary of Defense for Public Affairs in Washington prepared the draft, which underwent intensive review by the White House and other interested agencies. Early versions of the statement all but omitted mention of the self-defense forces and political cadre or dismissed them as of no military importance. They also stressed the decline of enemy forces rather than the intelligence estimate's conclusion that the other side was far from collapse. A senior CIA officer called the first draft of the statement "one of the greatest snow jobs since Potemkin constructed his village." The final version, issued by Brig. Gen. Winant Sidle, the MACV chief of information, on 24 November, gave due treatment to the self-defense forces and political cadre as significant elements of the enemy's manpower, although not of his military strength. Nevertheless, the statement reiterated that any increases in enemy numbers resulted solely from improved analysis and that the opposing forces actually were decreasing in size. While mollified, the CIA still refused to associate itself with the briefing on the grounds that it drew unsupportable conclusions at variance with the letter of SNIE 14.3–67 and the spirit of the Saigon agreements.[46]

The order of battle dispute consumed a great deal of time and energy and created considerable ill will, with no satisfactory resolution, among the agencies involved. Since the dispute involved recalculation of the size of the enemy force already in the field rather than sudden discovery of a new buildup, its impact on policy and strategy was minimal. Although aware of the issue, departmental and White House policymakers considered it at best peripheral to their own judgments of the state of the war. William P. Bundy, Assistant Secretary of State for East Asian and Pacific Affairs, recalled: "We attached far more weight to action evidence of enemy capabilities and performance than estimates of size and tended to view all size estimates with considerable scepticism." Secretary McNamara, even more emphatically, declared that, however the argument over the size of the enemy had come out, it "would not have influenced my thinking because I already felt there was no way to win the war militarily."[47]

Which side was right in the argument over the number of enemy irregulars remains impossible to determine. Probably, the Communists themselves did not know for certain the strength of their guerrillas, self-defense personnel, and political cadre. All of the intelligence agencies conceded the desirability of dividing the purely military elements of the order of battle from the paramilitary and political. The sticking point was MACV's insistence, largely for public relations reasons, that the self-defense elements should not be quantified and that SNIE 14.3-67 should not contain any numbers for the paramilitary and political forces that the press could add to the military strength to enlarge the Communist order of battle. That insistence, and what many CIA and military intelligence officers considered MACV's unprofessional, even dishonest manipulation of figures to stay within an arbitrary enemy strength ceiling, prolonged and embittered the controversy. In the end, the Saigon agreement proved only a temporary compromise that left the CIA analysts, in particular, angry, frustrated, and spoiling for an opportunity to revive the dispute. The Military Assistance Command had permitted public relations to invade the intelligence process, to the detriment of the process itself and of the command's reputation within the intelligence community.[48]

MACV's strenuous campaign to maintain an image of progress in the war reflected more than the excessive salesmanship of an administration hypersensitive to the pronouncements of news commentators and the fluctuations of public opinion polls. The command and its Washington overseers understood, though probably less well than their adversaries, that the unconventional war in Vietnam would turn on appearances as much as on realities.[49] Since the military struggle would inevitably be prolonged and indecisive, victory might well go to whichever side could persuade enough people, officials and ordinary citizens alike, both within its own ranks and among the enemy, that its cause was just, its methods honorable, and its victory inevitable. What peoples and governments believed about the situation in Vietnam in the end would determine their political actions and the outcome of the war. Hence, the allies and the Communists strove to shape the perceptions of various audiences in Southeast Asia and the rest of the world even as they tried to destroy each other's forces on the battlefield. By late 1967, the Johnson administration probably was already beginning to lose the battle of perceptions even as its combat fortunes may have been improving.

President Johnson Moves to Level Off the War

If the American administration was losing the external battle of perceptions, it also was losing the same battle within its own ranks. Officials who took an optimistic line in public often expressed growing doubts in private about the rightness and sustainability of the government's course. After a trip to South Vietnam in late October to represent the United States at President Thieu's inauguration, Vice President Hubert Humphrey, for example, cabled to President Johnson from Saigon that he had observed "evident progress" and declared that he was certain that "what we are doing here is right and that we have no choice but to persevere and see it through to success." At the same time, he confided to a close friend who accompanied him, "I think we're in real trouble. America is throwing lives and money down a corrupt rat hole." Humphrey's visit to South Vietnam left him convinced, as he later recalled, that "the American people would not stand for this involvement much longer."[50]

Even as Humphrey was expressing his misgivings, Secretary McNamara reiterated his long-standing opposition to further American military escalation and proposed an alternative course of action. In a 1 November memorandum to President Johnson, McNamara repeated more emphatically his earlier assertion that heavier bombing of North Vietnam and the dispatch of additional U.S. troops to South Vietnam would not cause the enemy to give up. Instead, this course, besides increasing America's war costs and casualties, would lead simultaneously to military demands for still more escalation and to intensified congressional and public calls for U.S. withdrawal. Under such circumstances, McNamara doubted that the United States could maintain its efforts in South Vietnam "for the time necessary to accomplish our objective there."

McNamara went on to elaborate on his proposals for stabilizing both U.S. ground operations in the south and bombing in the north, so as to reduce domestic opposition to the war and to create an incentive for Hanoi to negotiate and/or cut back its military activities in South Vietnam. He urged the administration to top off the American troop commitment at the approved Program Five level of 525,000 and to rule out a mobilization of reserves and an expansion of ground actions into North Vietnam, Laos, and Cambodia. Instead, the United States should "endeavor to maintain our current rates of progress but with lesser U.S. casualties and lesser destruction in South Vietnam" while gradually transferring the "major burden of the fighting" to Saigon's forces.

Regarding North Vietnam, McNamara argued against any intensification of ROLLING THUNDER and opposed any blockade of the enemy's seaports. He strongly advocated a complete cessation of the bombing in the belief that in response Hanoi would open negotiations and possibly halt or reduce its attacks across the Demilitarized Zone. Even if these results did not occur, he insisted, the United States at least would have established in the eyes of domestic and foreign public opinion that its bombing campaign was not the main obstacle to a peaceful settlement of the war. In conclusion, McNamara urged Johnson publicly to announce a stabilization policy; to halt ROLLING THUNDER before the end of the year; and to conduct an intensive review of U.S. operations in South Vietnam with a view to reducing American casualties, lessening the destruction of the south's people and wealth, and progressively increasing Saigon's combat role.[51]

The most immediately tangible effect of McNamara's memorandum was to convince President Johnson that his secretary of defense could no longer be relied upon to support the war. Unwilling to fire McNamara, for whom he still had high respect, and desiring to avoid a politically embarrassing resignation by so prominent a member of his cabinet, Johnson resorted to indirection to rid himself of his wavering defense secretary. He arranged for McNamara's nomination for the presidency of the World Bank, a position in which McNamara had previously expressed interest. After the bank's member governments approved the nomination, McNamara accepted the job. On 29 November he announced at a Pentagon news conference that he would be leaving the post that he had held for nearly seven years, but that he would remain in office through February 1968 to prepare the next defense budget. To the disappointment of Robert Kennedy and other antiwar Democrats, McNamara made no public mention of his disillusionment with existing policy on Vietnam when announcing his departure and throughout his remaining months in the Pentagon. He explained later that despite his growing differences with Johnson over the war, he did not resign in protest because he remained "loyal to the presidency and loyal to him" and believed that he could still influence the president's decisions. "I therefore felt I had a responsibility to stay at my post."[52]

Although Johnson eased McNamara out as secretary of defense, his principal advisers were moving toward a consensus in favor of leveling off if not deescalating the American effort. Commenting at the president's request on McNamara's 1 November memorandum, Secretary of State Rusk, Undersecretary of State Nicholas DeB. Katzenbach, McGeorge Bundy, Walt Rostow, Ambassador Bunker, and unofficial presidential counselors Justice Abe Fortas and Clark Clifford all opposed an immediate halt to the bombing of North Vietnam and any publicly announced stabilization or deescalation of operations in South Vietnam. At the same time, however, they all rejected further escalation—whether by heavier bombing or a naval blockade of the north, deployment of additional U.S. troops to the south, or ground offensives in Laos and Cambodia—as unlikely to result in decisive success and certain to raise the human, economic, and political costs of the war to an unsustainable level. To maintain American public support and gird the country for a prolonged struggle, all advocated keeping ROLLING THUNDER at about its current intensity, holding MACV's forces at 525,000, and gradually shifting the burden of combat and pacification to the South Vietnamese.[53]

General Westmoreland's views fitted in with this emerging consensus. He had discussed leveling off American troop strength with McNamara the previous year and realized that Johnson's decision not to mobilize the reserves established a ceiling on the forces he could expect to receive. Commenting along with Bunker on McNamara's 1 November memorandum, Westmoreland rejected a bombing halt but declined to recommend blockading or mining North Vietnam's ports. He declared that it would be "foolish" for the United States to announce publicly a 525,000-man limit to its troop strength in South Vietnam, although he expressed the hope that no greater numbers would be needed. Despite his continuing concern with reducing casualties and destruction in South Vietnam, the MACV commander insisted that those considerations should not be allowed to dictate the conduct of his tactical operations. Recognizing the political problems that inhibited ground attacks in North Vietnam, Laos, and Cambodia, he nevertheless favored maintaining the capability for those incursions and keeping the options open. Finally, Westmoreland declared that over the next two years he would have as his "central purpose" the transfer of military functions to the South Vietnamese, although he acknowledged that a "mature operational program" for doing so had yet to be developed. He declared, nevertheless, that he was "extremely conscious" that the United States, beyond achieving its "immediate purpose" in Vietnam, must "leave behind a military establishment capable of looking after itself increasingly."[54]

The allies' Combined Campaign Plan for 1968, issued by MACV and the Joint General Staff on 11 November, contained no program for transferring functions to the South Vietnamese. It called for the allies to continue military offensives to drive the North Vietnamese and Viet Cong main forces away from major population centers and food-producing areas and to conduct pacification operations that would provide "territorial security at a level adequate to permit the destruction of VC infrastructure" and facilitate "the uninterrupted and accelerated progress of political, economic, sociological and pyschological programs" of the Saigon government. Maintaining the existing military division of labor, American and other allied forces would operate primarily against enemy units and bases, and the South Vietnamese would concentrate on territorial security. Without mentioning any turnover of responsibilities, the plan provided for continued improvement of the South Vietnamese armed forces with emphasis on the Regional and Popular Forces and for an increase in combined U.S.-Vietnamese training and operations.[55]

In contrast to his campaign plan, Westmoreland's public pronouncements reflected and amplified the inclination of the administration to stabilize the war effort. The MACV commander sounded many of these themes in his speech to the National Press Club on 21 November. Besides suggesting that the United States could begin turning over military operations to the South Vietnamese within the next two years, Westmoreland predicted that in 1968 the war would enter a new phase characterized by American efforts to ready Saigon's forces for their assumption of "an ever-increasing share of the war." At the same time, the allies would work harder to "isolate the guerrilla from the people," destroy the Viet Cong shadow government, help the Saigon regime eliminate corruption and "respond to popular aspirations," and improve the South Vietnamese economy and standard of living. This phase would be followed by a final one during which the United States would progressively withdraw its military forces while the enlarged, modernized South Vietnamese armed forces took charge of "the final mopping up of the Viet Cong," a process that probably would take several years. Westmoreland did not address the question of who, if anyone, would mop up the North Vietnamese. Asked whether he had enough American troops to achieve his objective, Westmoreland declared that Program Five would provide him with "a well-balanced, hard-hitting military force that our country is capable of sustaining as long as required." With it, he could continue "indefinitely" to maintain and accelerate his pressure on the enemy.[56]

Shortly after the speech, Westmoreland explained to General Abrams that he made these statements "on my own initiative," after "considerable thought," and with several considerations in mind:

I believe the concept and objective plan . . . is feasible and as such it should serve as an incentive. The concept is compatible with the evolution of the war since our initial commitment and portrays to the American people 'some light at the end of the tunnel.' The concept justifies the augmentation of troops I've asked for based on the principle of reinforcing success and also supports an increase in the strength of the Vietnamese forces and their modernization. The concept straddles the presidential election of November 1968, implying that the election is not a bench mark from a military point of view. Finally, it puts emphasis on the essential role of the Vietnamese in carrying a major burden of their war against the Communists but also suggests that we must be prepared for a protracted commitment.[57]

Westmoreland's motives in making his pronouncements were clearly mixed. He seemed as concerned with ensuring American public support for further U.S. troop deployments and a prolonged conflict as with strengthening the South Vietnamese. Nevertheless, the MACV commander had obviously assimilated the themes that had emerged during nearly two years of exchanges with Washington over Programs Four and Five and that were coming to dominate administration thinking. He acknowledged implicitly that the struggle would be long; that the American buildup was nearing the limits of resources and political feasibility; that the South Vietnamese must be made to carry more of the load; and that, as McNamara had suggested, the American people required reassurance that their government knew how to end the conflict or at minimum how to control the costs of U.S. engagement in it.

The final word belonged to Lyndon Johnson, who gave it in a "memorandum for the file" dated 18 December. Johnson declared that he had studied McNamara's proposals of 1 November and consulted about them with his Washington advisers as well as with Ambassador Bunker and General Westmoreland. He had, he said, reached certain conclusions. On ROLLING THUNDER, he had decided to continue the bombing at about the existing level of intensity and range of targets, while trying at the same time to reduce the "drama and public attention" that the air strikes received in the United States. "Under present circumstances," the president ruled out a unilateral bombing halt because it would be interpreted in both North Vietnam and the United States as "a sign of weakening will." In the United States, a bombing cessation would "decrease support from our most steady friends" and gain support from "only a small group of moderate doves." The United States should play its "bombing card" only when "there is reason for confidence that it would move us toward peace." In Johnson's judgment, that time had not yet come.

Regarding operations in South Vietnam, the president considered that the announcement of a "so-called policy of stabilization" would be another indication of American lack of determination. However, he endorsed stabilization in fact. He declared that "at the moment" he saw "no basis" for increasing U.S. forces above the Program Five level. In considering proposals for American ground offensives outside South Vietnam, he was "inclined to be extremely reserved unless a powerful case can be made" because such operations entailed political risks and would divert forces from "pressure on the VC" and pacification. Nevertheless, he deemed it unwise to announce a policy that would deny the United States these options. Johnson agreed with McNamara's recommendation that the administration review the conduct of military operations in the south with a view to reducing the toll of American dead and wounded, "accelerating" the turnover of combat to Saigon's forces, and "working toward less destruction and fewer casualties in South Vietnam."[58]

By the close of 1967, the Johnson administration had reached a consensus on ending the expansion of the American military effort in Vietnam and had abandoned its hope, which had never been very strong, for a clear-cut battlefield victory. Instead, the administration would try to hold the line in Southeast Asia and at home until diplomacy or improvements in the Saigon government and its armed forces opened an honorable way out of the war. Although this approach had yet to be embodied in formal operational plans and directives, key elements of it were in effect as the result of earlier decisions. By his repeated refusal to breach the political "Plimsoll line" of a reserve call-up, for example, Johnson for practical purposes had already imposed a ceiling on U.S. troop strength in South Vietnam.

The Enemy Plans an Offensive

Even as President Johnson and his advisers tentatively decided to level off the American war effort in Vietnam, their adversaries in Hanoi completed preparations to do the opposite. Undeterred by the increasing American pressure, the northern and southern revolutionary leaders held unwaveringly to their maximum goal: a unified Communist Vietnam. Like the Americans, the Communist leaders believed that the conflict had reached a stalemate, but for them a stalemate represented only a temporary equilibrium of forces, a stage on their march to inevitable victory. Instead of a way out of the conflict, they sought a means to shift the balance in their favor.[59]

By the spring of 1967, the Vietnamese Communists believed that they had passed through the first two stages of revolutionary people's war—those of organization and base building and of guerrilla warfare—and had entered the third and final stage. In that stage, large combat-seasoned guerrilla and main forces, backed by a strong political infrastructure and mass popular following, were in position to launch what the Communists called the General Offensive–General Uprising. In this revolutionary climax, North Vietnamese and Viet Cong military units would launch attacks to destroy the South Vietnamese Army and pin down American forces. As these actions went on, urban and rural popular uprisings, spearheaded by commando assaults on South Vietnamese military headquarters, administrative facilities, and communications centers, would sweep away the puppet regime and install National Liberation Front governments at every level from the hamlets to Saigon. Since the early 1960s, the North Vietnamese Communist party had identified the General Offensive–General Uprising as the culminating point of its politico-military campaign in the south. For the Saigon area, the *Central Office for South Vietnam (COSVN)*, the senior enemy headquarters for the southern half of South Vietnam, had prepared detailed plans for such an operation. Since 1965 *COSVN* had been compelled to divert its resources to the growing battle against the Americans, but its plans remained in the files ready to be brought up to date and executed.

More than the diversion of resources may have held back the offensive. In response to the massive intervention of American combat forces, factions among the North Vietnamese leaders engaged in a two-year debate over war strategy. Masking their differences in Marxist-Leninist jargon, the contending groups promoted their views through polemics published in the official Communist press and broadcast on North Vietnam's state radio. They argued over the proper relationship between large-unit and guerrilla operations, the relative roles of political and military struggle and of fighting and diplomacy, and the merits of protracted conflict versus an all-out drive for victory in the shortest possible time. By mid-1967, they had reached a consensus that would blend most of the contending elements of their strategy in the context of the General Offensive–General Uprising.[60]

In a mirror image of General Westmoreland's view of the conflict, the Communist leaders believed that they were making slow but steady progress in their struggle. Maj. Gen. Tran Van Tra, the *COSVN* military commander, for example, acknowledged in retrospect that his forces had encountered "difficulties and weaknesses" in replacing casualties, building political strength, and "conducting mass movements in urban areas." Nevertheless, he argued, these problems existed "in the context of a favorable situation" in which the revolutionary army held the initiative and the Americans were "bewildered by the new battlefield" and by the Communists' "new form of war."[61]

Although the North Vietnamese and Viet Cong were taking heavy losses and winning few victories on the battlefield and the U.S. bombing was placing severe pressure on the north's society and economy, the political situation held much promise. The leaders in Hanoi knew that antiwar sentiment was mounting in the United States and among "progressive" forces around the world. Still better, during 1968, a presidential election year, the American administration would be under additional strain that likely would inhibit its response to new Communist initiatives. Even more promising, South Vietnam appeared to be extremely vulnerable. The majority of South Vietnamese soldiers and people, the Communists assumed, in their hearts hated the Saigon regime and its American "imperialist" sponsors. Viewed from Hanoi, the I Corps revolt of 1966, periodic antigovernment demonstrations by Buddhists and other groups, the relatively small proportion of the popular vote received by the Thieu-Ky ticket in the September 1967 presidential election, and the presence of tens of thousands of impoverished, displaced peasants in city slums were harbingers of incipient revolution in the urban centers of Saigon's power. Only a spark, a catalytic event, was needed to set South Vietnam's cities aflame, inspire Saigon's troops to defect, and sweep away the puppet regime.

Around May 1967 the collective leadership of the North Vietnamese Communist (Lao Dong) Party initiated planning for the General Offensive–General Uprising. At that time, the Politburo, the party's inner executive directorate, instructed the Central Party Military Affairs Committee, in coordination with the major theater commands in the south, to prepare an overall plan for the assault. During June, the party's Central Committee unanimously endorsed the Politburo's strategic decision to "prepare a decisive victory in 1968." In July the Politburo approved the Military Affairs Committee's plan and set a tentative date for the offensive. At the end of October, on the basis of reports from the south, the leaders in Hanoi pushed the date forward to 30–31 January 1968, the beginning of Vietnam's Tet lunar new year holiday. The change left local commanders in the south with a very short time for preparation, but the Communist leaders believed that an offensive during the festivities would catch Saigon's forces off guard and have maximum military and political impact. The Politburo then developed a policy resolution and a detailed operational plan based on the earlier work of the Military Affairs Committee.

In December the Politburo presented the resolution to the Fourteenth Plenum, or general meeting, of the Lao Dong Party Central Committee. Approved by the delegates and formally issued on 1 January 1968 as Central Resolution Fourteen, the document defined the enemy's "crucial mission" during the winter–spring 1967–1968 campaigning season as "to mobilize the greatest efforts of the entire Party, the entire army, and the entire people in both regions [north and south] to carry our revolutionary war to the highest level of development and use the general offensive and general uprising to secure a decisive victory in a relatively short time."

By the time the Central Committee adopted Resolution Fourteen, preparations for the campaign were well under way. During the summer and fall, North Vietnam concluded new military and economic aid agreements with the Soviet Union and China, ensuring itself of the wherewithal to fight the coming battles. The North Vietnamese increased the flow of men and materiel down the Ho Chi Minh Trail. According to a later Communist account, more than 31,700 personnel entered South Vietnam during 1967, more than twice the number infiltrated during the previous year, along with over 6,500 tons of weapons and supplies. The weaponry included thousands of automatic rifles, machine guns, and rocket-propelled antitank grenade launchers. Viet Cong military units clandestinely assembled supplies near South Vietnam's cities and prepared for their urban attack missions. Party cadres assembled lists of government officials and supporters to be killed or kidnapped, as well as lists of members of the prospective NLF town and province administrations. To wear down American forces and divert their attention from the offensive preparations, North Vietnamese and Viet Cong main forces launched heavy attacks on allied positions near South Vietnam's borders in I, II, and III Corps. General Westmoreland interpreted these engagements, all of which ended in Communist defeats, as desperate enemy efforts to gain limited successes for political and psychological purposes that had backfired by exposing their troops to slaughter by American firepower.[62]

As 1967 ended, the two sides in Vietnam were moving in opposite directions. Believing that its escalation during the previous two years had resulted only in stalemate, the Johnson administration was set on stabilizing the American effort in the hope of holding on long enough to negotiate an acceptable compromise with the Communists or, failing that, to prepare the South Vietnamese to take over the fighting. By contrast, the North Vietnamese and Viet Cong, equally aware that the war seemed to be on dead center but still committed to their maximum objectives, were preparing for a major escalation of violence that they believed would bring them closer to final victory. Largely ignorant of each other's intentions, the antagonists marched toward a climactic collision.

MACV: The Years of Escalation, 1962–1967

Notes

¹ This and the preceding paragraph are based on Msg, Westmoreland MAC 5310 to Sharp, 4 Jun 67, and Memo, Westmoreland for Bunker, 21 Jun 67, tabs A–7 and A–17, Westmoreland Hist File 19 (1 Jun–5 Jul 67); Westmoreland Notes for Talk with the President, Nov 67, tab A–13, Westmoreland Hist File 25 (13–28 Nov 67). Msgs, Westmoreland MAC 8073 and MAC 10295 to Wheeler, 25 Aug and 30 Oct 67; Lt Gen Bruce Palmer to Westmoreland, 11 Dec 67. All in Westmoreland Msg Files, Aug–Dec 67, CMH.

² First quote is from Affidavit, Barry Zorthian, 15 Dec 83, in U.S. District Court, Southern District of New York, *General William C. Westmoreland, Plaintiff, v. CBS, Inc., et al., Defendants. 82 Civ. 7913 (PNL). Plaintiff General William C. Westmoreland's Memorandum of Law in Opposition to Defendant CBS's Motion to Dismiss and for Summary Judgment. Appendix A—Affidavits Cited in Support of Plaintiff's Opposition to Defendant's Motion*, p. 406. Second is from Msg, Komer to President via CIA Channel, 9 Jul 67, Montague Papers, copy in CMH; in same collection, see Draft Ltr, Komer to President, 20 Aug 67. Memo, Roy Wehrle for Ambassador Bunker, 6 Jul 67, sub: Stalemate?, tab A–3, Westmoreland Hist File 19 (6 Jul–7 Aug 67), CMH.

³ McNaughton quote is from *U.S.–Vietnam Relations*, sec. 4.C.6(b), p. 147. For accounts of trends in public opinion, see: Hammond, *Military and the Media, 1962–1968*, pp. 263–64, 338–40; and Don Oberdorfer, *Tet!* (New York: DaCapo Press, 1984), ch. 3, passim.

⁴ First quote is from Msg, Wheeler CJCS 2837–66 to Westmoreland info Sharp, 20 May 66. Second quote is from Msg, Wheeler JCS 7126–67 to Westmoreland, 30 Aug 67. Third is from Msg, Sharp to Wheeler, 24 Dec 66. See also Msg, Gen Johnson WDC 13029 to Westmoreland, 2 Oct 67. All in Westmoreland Msg Files, 1966–1967, CMH. Memo, Westmoreland for Bunker, 16 May 67, sub: Mobilization of the Republic of Vietnam, Westmoreland Sig File, May 67, CMH. Affidavit, Maj Gen Winant Sidle, 20 Apr 84, in U.S. District Court, *Westmoreland Law Memorandum, app. A*, p. A–369.

⁵ The evolution of mission and MACV information policy is traced in detail in Hammond, *Military and the Media, 1962–1968*, chs. 3–10, passim. Examples of Westmoreland's approach to the media are in Westmoreland Hist Notes, 20 Nov 65, tab D, Westmoreland Hist File 2 (25 Oct– 20 Dec 65), CMH; in same file, see "Speech Delivered by General Westmoreland at the Closing of the MACV Information Officers' Conference," 8 Nov 65, tab D–2; and Westmoreland Hist Notes, 1 Dec 65, tab F.

⁶ First quote is from MFR, Maj K. W. Accousti, 25 Dec 65, sub: COMUSMACV Visit to 1st Inf Div and 173d Airborne Bde, 24 Dec 65, tab A–2, Westmoreland Hist File 3 (20 Dec 65–29 Jan 66), CMH. Second quote is from Msg, Westmoreland MAC 5693 to Component and Field Force Cmdrs, 16 Jun 67, Westmoreland Msg Files, 1 Apr–30 Jun 67, CMH. Third is from MacDonald-Westmoreland Interv, 28 Jan 73, CMH files.

⁷ Hammond, *Military and the Media, 1962–1968*, pp. 292–300, 328–31. MACV Command History, 1967, p. 1200. Memo, Westmoreland for Bunker, 8 Aug 67, sub: Recent Improvement in RVNAF Combat Effectiveness, Westmoreland Sig File, Aug 67, CMH; Msgs, Wheeler JCS 6105–67 to Westmoreland and Gen Johnson, 1 Aug 67; Westmoreland MAC 7180 to Wheeler, Johnson and Sharp, 2 Aug 67; Westmoreland MAC 7189 and MAC 7430 to Sharp, 3 Aug and 8 Aug 67. All in Westmoreland Msg Files, Jul–Sep 67, CMH. For Ridgway visit, see same files for Oct 67.

⁸ Hammond, *Military and the Media, 1962–1968*, pp. 287–90, 330–40. Westmoreland tells his own story of the trips in *A Soldier Reports*, pp. 224–34, 276. Senate criticisms of Westmoreland's speech are in Summary of Senate Remarks on Westmoreland

Visit, 28 Apr 67, tab B–20, Westmoreland Hist File 15 (3 Mar–30 Apr 67), CMH. Final quote is from MFR, Westmoreland, 22 Nov 67, sub: Breakfast Meeting at White House on 22 November, tab A–31, Westmoreland Hist File 25 (13–28 Nov 67), CMH.

[9] Msg, Wheeler JCS 00920 to Westmoreland info Sharp, 27 Jan 68, Westmoreland Msg Files, Jan 68, CMH, describes the president's hopefulness. Hammond, *Military and the Media, 1962–1968*, pp. 289–90, notes correspondents' growing skepticism after Westmoreland's first Washington trip. Brig Gen Winant Sidle, the MACV chief of public affairs, warns of the danger of overselling progress in MFR, Chaisson, 12 Oct 67, sub: MACV Commanders' Conference, 24 Sep 67, encl. 3, tab A–22, Westmoreland Hist File 22 (10–30 Sep 67), CMH.

[10] This issue is recounted in Hammond, *Military and the Media, 1962–1968*, pp. 280–82.

[11] Thayer, *War Without Fronts*, pp. 785–88; Deposition, George Carver, pp. 15, 299–300, in *Vietnam: A Documentary Collection—Westmoreland v. CBS* (Microfiche), (Broomfield, Colo.: Clearwater Publishing Co., Inc., 1985), cards 167 and 170; U.S. District Court, *Westmoreland v. CBS, Memorandum of Law*, app. A, pp. 135–38; Memo, J. A. Norkin for Dr. Heyman through Mr. Thayer, 24 Jan 67, sub: VC/NVA Offensive Capability—Battalions with No Positive Contact, Folder 123, Thayer Papers, CMH. Lt Gen Phillip B. Davidson, *Secrets of the Vietnam War* (Novato, Calif.: Presidio Press, 1990), pp. 74–75, 80–81.

[12] Gen Bruce Palmer, Jr., "US Intelligence in Vietnam," *Studies in Intelligence*, Special Issue, 28 (1984):10–14; Palmer, *25-Year War*, p. 30; Westmoreland, *A Soldier Reports*, pp. 415–16; U.S. District Court, *Westmoreland v. CBS, Memorandum of Law*, p. 14. Ibid., app. A, pp. 39–40, 221, 228; Carver Deposition, pp. 22–23, *Vietnam: A Documentary Collection*, card 167. Intervs, LBJL with Lt Gen Phillip B. Davidson, 30 Mar and 30 Jun 82, Interv 1, pp. 22–25; Interv 2, pp. 27–32.

[13] U.S. District Court, *Westmoreland v. CBS, Memorandum of Law*, app. A, pp. 17–18, 25–26, 327–29, 331–32, 357–58; Carver Deposition, pp. 75–77, *Vietnam: A Documentary Collection*, card 167; Memo, Rostow for the President, Friday, 20 Jan 67, 3:05 p.m., LBJL, copy in CMH.

[14] Quote is from Msg, Taylor Saigon 108 to SecState, 15 Jul 64; see also Taylor Saigon 107 to SecState, 15 Jul 64; and Msg, State 234 to AmEmb Saigon, 24 Jul 64. All in NSC Country File, Vietnam, box 6, LBJL. Msg, Wheeler CJCS 7859–66 to Westmoreland and Sharp, 21 Dec 66, Westmoreland Msg Files, Oct–Dec 66, CMH. U.S. District Court, *Westmoreland Memorandum of Law*, app. A, p. 328. Interv, CMH with George Allen (tape), 4 May 92, emphasizes general agreement that the enemy force was declining, but from a higher starting point than earlier estimated.

[15] Msg, Wheeler CJCS 0547–67 to Westmoreland and Sharp, 20 Jan 67, in U.S. District Court, Southern District of New York, *General William C. Westmoreland, Plaintiff, v. CBS, Inc., et al., Defendants. 82 Civ. 7913 (PNL). Plaintiff's Counter–Statement of Undisputed Material Facts Pursuant to Local Rule 3(g) and Appendix B—Important Documents Cited in Support of Plaintiff's Opposition to Defendant's Motion*, pp. 363–67; Rpt, Intelligence Conference, CINCPAC, Camp H. M. Smith, Hawaii, 6–11 Feb 67, JX 227, *Vietnam: A Documentary Collection*, card 615; 6–11 Feb 67; McChristian, *Military Intelligence*, pp. 128–29.

[16] CINCPAC Intel Conf, 6–11 Feb 67, ann. B, pp. 1–2.

[17] For an early discussion of the problem of counting irregulars, see Msg, COMUSMACV to DIA, 21 May 64, CMH files. Affidavit, Col Edward H. Caton, USAF, 16 Mar 84, in U.S. District Court, *Westmoreland v. CBS: Memorandum of Law*, app. A, pp. 42–43; Davidson, *Vietnam Secrets*, pp. 33–34; and CINCPAC Intel Conf Rpt, 6–11 Feb 67, pp. 9–10, are additional typical statements of the problem.

MACV: The Years of Escalation, 1962–1967

[18] Quotes are from CINCPAC Intel Conf Rpt, 6–11 Feb 67, p. 8; see also pp. 9–11. Davidson, *Vietnam Secrets*, pp. 32, 34–35; U.S. District Court, *Westmoreland v. CBS, Memorandum of Law*, pp. 12–13, 33–38; and *app. A*, pp. 197, 223–26, 310–11.

[19] Memo, McChristian for Komer, 21 May 67, sub: Strength of VC Irregular Forces, with attachment: USMACV–JGS RVNAF Estimate of the Strength of Viet Cong Irregular Forces in SVN, 18 May 67, U.S. District Court, *Westmoreland v. CBS, Memorandum of Law, app. B*, pp. 441–43; all quotes are from latter document. Memo, McChristian for Louis W. Sandine, 12 Mar 67, sub: Request for Comment on Captured Notebooks and Possible Impact on Order of Battle Holdings, in ibid., pp. 446–47.

[20] McChristian gives two slightly different versions of this meeting in his Affidavit, 21 Dec 83, in U.S. District Court, *Westmoreland v. CBS, Memorandum of Law, app. A*, pp. 222–24; and Affidavit, 20 Apr 84, in U.S. District Court, Southern District of New York, *General William C. Westmoreland, Plaintiff, v. CBS, Inc., et al., Defendants. 82 Civ. 7913 (PNL). Memorandum in Support of Defendant CBS's Motion to Dismiss and for Summary Judgment*, pp. 47–48. See also Davidson, *Vietnam Secrets*, pp. 36–41.

[21] Quotes are from MFR, Hendry, USAF, 20 May 67, sub: CIIC Meeting, 19 May 67, tab A–20, Westmoreland Hist File 17 (1–31 May 67), CMH; in same file, see tab B–6. U.S. District Court, *Westmoreland v. CBS, Memorandum of Law*, pp. 16–18; Affidavit, Kelly Robinson, 25 Jul 83, ibid., *app. A*, p. 311. Ltr, Col Gains B. Hawkins to Mrs Hawkins, 30 May 67, U.S. District Court, *Westmoreland v. CBS, Memorandum of Law, app. B*, p. 147. Msgs, Sharp to Westmoreland, 10 Jun 67; Westmoreland MAC 5616 and MAC 6117 to Sharp, 14 Jun 67 and 29 Jun 67. All in Westmoreland Msg Files, 1 Apr–30 Jun 67, CMH.

[22] The public relations element in Westmoreland's approach is acknowledged in Davidson, *Vietnam Secrets*, pp. 41–42; and Palmer, *Intelligence in Vietnam*, pp. 49–50. For views on military importance of the self-defense and secret self-defense forces, see: Memo, Col R. M. Montague for Komer, 29 Sep 66, sub: Guerrilla Strength, LBJL, copy in CMH; and U.S. District Court, *Westmoreland v. CBS, Counter-Statement, app. B*, pp. 310, 365, 377–78, 397–411, 446–47. Komer emphasizes the public relations aspect in Memo for Westmoreland, 19 Jun 67, sub: How to Get Our Case across to McNamara, in Westmoreland Memos, RWK (1967–68), DEPCORDS Files, CMH.

[23] Davidson, *Vietnam Secrets*, pp. 34–36; Palmer, *Intelligence in Vietnam*, pp. 34–35, 40–41, 52–54; U.S. District Court, *Westmoreland v. CBS, CBS Memorandum*, pp. 64–65. U.S. District Court, *Westmoreland v. CBS, Memorandum of Law*, pp. 31–33, 46, 194 and *app. A*, pp. 25, 219, 266–67, 399; MFR, Allen, 5 Jul 67, in U.S. District Court, *Westmoreland v. CBS, Counter-Statement, app. B*, pp. 309–11; Carver Deposition, pp. 446–52, in *Vietnam: A Documentary Collection*, card 171; Paper, 28 Jun 68, sub: Uncertainties about VC/NVA Force Levels, Folder 42, Thayer Papers, CMH.

[24] U.S. District Court, *Westmoreland v. CBS, Memorandum of Law*, p. 47. Carver Deposition, pp. 56–57, 66–67, in *Vietnam: A Documentary Collection*, card 167.

[25] *CBS Memorandum*, p. 65. Draft MFR, Sam Adams, 23 Jun 67, sub: NIE 14.3–67—The USIB Representatives Meeting, 23 Jun 67, in U.S. District Court, *Westmoreland v. CBS, Memorandum of Law, app. B*, pp. 336–40.

[26] Director Helms, and Carver as his deputy and alter ego on Vietnam matters, played a dual role in preparation of the intelligence estimate, in that the CIA director acted both as chairman of the Board of National Estimates and as head of the CIA. In the former role, he was supposed to preside impartially over the interagency debate and try to secure consensus; in the latter, he was expected, at least by his CIA subordinates, to fight hard for the agency position. For comment on these points, see Carver Deposition, pp. 9–10, 54–55, 413–14, 417–18, 421, in *Vietnam: A Documentary Collection*, cards 167 and 171.

[27] Quote is from MFR, Allen, 5 Jul 67, U.S. District Court, *Westmoreland v. CBS, Counter-Statement*, app. B, pp. 309–11. U.S. District Court, *Westmoreland v. CBS, Memorandum of Law*, app. A, pp. 213–16, 269–71, 309–10, 317–18, 396. Carver's views are in his Deposition, pp. 299–300, 454, 463–64, 635–37, *Vietnam: A Documentary Collection*, cards 170, 171, 173.

[28] Msgs, Westmoreland MAC 2014 and MAC 2311 to Gen Johnson, 1 Mar 67 and 10 Mar 67, Westmoreland Msg Files, 1 Jan–31 Mar 67; Westmoreland Hist Notes, 23–31 May 67, tab B, Westmoreland Hist File 17 (1–31 May 67). All in CMH. McChristian Affidavit, 21 Dec 83, in U.S. District Court, *Westmoreland v. CBS, Memorandum of Law*, app. A, p. 222. Davidson Interv, 30 Mar and 30 Jun 82, sess. 1, pp. 1–2, 4–5, 21–22; Davidson, *Vietnam Secrets*, pp. 1–2, 6–7.

[29] This discussion is based on depositions and affidavits in U.S. District Court, *Westmoreland v. CBS, Memorandum of Law*, app. A, pp. 46, 137, 254–55, 263–64, 281–82, 300–301, 383; U.S. District Court, *Westmoreland v. CBS, CBS Memorandum*, pp. 149–53; and *Vietnam: A Documentary Collection*, cards 251, 269, 275, 345, 346, 358. See also Davidson, *Vietnam Secrets*, pp. 10–14, 108; Davidson Intervs, 30 Mar and 30 Jun 82, sess.1, pp. 6–8; Intervs, LBJL with Daniel O. Graham, 24 May and 8 Nov 82, sess. 1, pp. 1–3, 33–34; sess. 2, pp. 10–13, 18–19.

[30] Davidson, *Vietnam Secrets*, pp. 69–70. Graham Intervs, 24 May and 8 Nov 82, sess. 1, pp. 6–10, 31–33; sess. 2, pp. 1–6, 22–23. U.S. District Court, *Westmoreland Memorandum of Law*, app. A, p. 134. Msg, Scorberg to Director, CIA, 11 Jul 67, in U.S. District Court, *Westmoreland v. CBS, Memorandum of Law, App. B*, pp. 332–34. Memo, Thomas Thayer for Mr. Glass, [1967], sub: VC/NVA Order of Battle, etc., Folder 123, Thayer Papers, CMH. Depositions, Michael D. Hankins, p. 63; Charles Morris (no. 2), pp. 427–29; in *Vietnam: A Documentary Collection*, cards 269 and 351.

[31] Komer quote is from Memo for Davidson, 7 Sep 67, copy in CMH. Memos, Walt Rostow for the President, 3 Jan 67, 6:10 pm., and 31 Jul 67, 1:55 pm., LBJL, copies in CMH. *Westmoreland Memorandum of Law*, app. A, pp. 197–98, 228, 261. Westmoreland Hist Notes, 17 Jul 66, tab F, Westmoreland Hist File 7 (29 May–16 Jul 66), CMH. Msg, Robert Komer to President via CIA Channel, 9 Jul 67; Draft Ltr, Komer to the President, 20 Aug 67. Both in Robert Montague Papers, Historians files, CMH.

[32] Graham quote is from LBJL Intervs, 24 May and 8 Nov 82, sess. 2, pp. 3–4. U.S. District Court, *Westmoreland v. CBS, Memorandum of Law*, app. A, pp. 96, 239. U.S. District Court, *Westmoreland v. CBS, CBS Memorandum*, pp. 18–32, 57–58, 123–26; Jones, *War Without Windows*, pp. 63–65, 72. Affidavits, Howard A. Daniel III; Michael Fraboni; George Hamscher; Kelly Robinson; cards 444 and 445. Quote is from Hawkins Deposition, p. 356; see also pp. 58–62, 160, 189, 443–45, 506–09, cards 271–76. All in *Vietnam: A Documentary Collection*.

[33] Quotes and most details of this meeting are from U.S. District Court, *Westmoreland v. CBS, Memorandum of Law*, app. B, pp. 168–71; see also pp. 311, 332–33. Komer Affidavit, 19 Apr 84, ibid., app. A, p. 202. Carver Deposition, pp. 466–67, *Vietnam: A Documentary Collection*, card 171. U.S. District Court, *Westmoreland v. CBS, CBS Memorandum*, pp. 65–66.

[34] Davidson, *Vietnam Secrets*, pp. 42–45, 53–54. Copy of MACV Vu–Graph Slide, Aug 67; Msg, Brig Gen George Godding DB–2CI 050 to Maj Gen C. G. Peterson info Davidson, 19 Aug 67. Both in U.S. District Court, *Westmoreland v. CBS, Memorandum of Law*, app. B, pp. 183, 414–15. U.S. District Court, *Westmoreland v. CBS, CBS Memorandum*, p. 66; Deposition, George Godding, pp. 5–6, 262–66, *Vietnam: A Documentary Collection*, cards 250 and 252.

[35] Quote is from Msg, Davidson to Godding, 19 Aug 67, U.S. District Court, *Westmoreland v. CBS, Memorandum of Law*, app. B, p. 198. Westmoreland defends his actions

MACV: The Years of Escalation, 1962–1967

in *A Soldier Reports*, p. 416. For other testimony that MACV intelligence officers believed there was a ceiling, see U.S. District Court, *Westmoreland v. CBS, CBS Memorandum*, pp. 72–78.

[36] Hawkins Deposition, see also pp. 244–45, 527. First Quote is from Kelly Robinson, Affidavit, 28 Oct 83, paras. 22–26; second is from Hamscher Affidavit, Question 9, see also Question 1; Carver Deposition, p. 322; Godding Deposition, pp. 85, 196, 198–99. All in *Vietnam: A Documentary Collection*, cards 250–52, 273, 276, 322, 444, 445. U.S. District Court, *Westmoreland v. CBS, Memorandum of Law*, app. A, pp. 312–15. U.S. District Court, *Westmoreland v. CBS, CBS Memorandum*, pp. 67–68, 70–72, 81.

[37] Msg, Abrams MAC 7840 to Wheeler, Sharp, and Westmoreland, 20 Aug 67, Westmoreland Msg Files, 1 Jul–30 Sep 67, CMH; in same file, see Msgs, Abrams MAC 7841 to Westmoreland, 20 Aug 67, and Westmoreland MAC 7859 to Wheeler and Sharp, 20 Aug 67. Msgs, Komer to Carver, 19 Aug 67; Bunker to Rostow, 29 Aug 67, in U.S. District Court, *Westmoreland v. CBS, Memorandum of Law*, app. B, pp. 195–96, 449–50. Affidavits, Ellsworth Bunker 22 Dec 83; Robert Komer 19 Apr 84. Both in U.S. District Court, *Westmoreland v. CBS*, app. A, pp. 26, 202–04.

[38] U.S. District Court, *Westmoreland v. CBS, Memorandum of Law*, app. B, pp. 346, 417–18, 424–25. Msg, Godding to Peterson and Davidson, 25 Aug 67, Historians Files, CMH. Msg, Sharp to Wheeler, 26 Aug 67, Westmoreland Msg Files, 1 Jul–30 Sep 67, CMH.

[39] First two quotes are from Draft Cable, Westmoreland to Wheeler, att. to Memo, Davidson for Komer, [Aug 67], CMH. While nominally drafted by Davidson, the key points in the message seem to have been provided by Komer. Third quote is from Msg, Godding to Peterson and Davidson, 25 Aug 67, CMH. U.S. District Court, *Westmoreland v. CBS, Memorandum of Law*, app. A, pp. 18–20, 27, 205–06, 329–30, 406–08. Davidson, *Vietnam Secrets*, pp. 44, 66–67.

[40] Quotes are from Msgs, Westmoreland MAC 8068 to Wheeler and Sharp, 25 Aug 67; and Wheeler JCS 7143–67 to Sharp and Westmoreland, 30 Aug 67; see also Msg, Wheeler JCS 6483–67 to Westmoreland, 11 Aug 67. All in Westmoreland Msg Files, 1 Jul–30 Sep 67, CMH. Msgs, Godding DB–2C1050 to Peterson info Davidson, 19 Aug 67; CIA Washington to Saigon Station. Both in U.S. District Court, *Westmoreland v. CBS, Memorandum of Law*, app. B, pp. 343–47, 413. Godding Deposition, p. 318; Hawkins Deposition, pp. 434–35. Both in *Vietnam: A Documentary Collection*, cards 253, 275.

[41] U.S. District Court, *Westmoreland v. CBS, Memorandum of Law*, app. B, pp. 205–35, 393–94. U.S. District Court, *Westmoreland v. CBS, Memorandum of Law*, app. A, pp. 120–23, 204–05, 368. U.S. District Court, *Westmoreland v. CBS, CBS Memorandum*, pp. 112, 121–22; Davidson, *Vietnam Secrets*, pp. 45–47, 71. Carver Deposition, pp. 417, 459–60, 481–83; Davidson Deposition 2, pp. 74–75. Both in *Vietnam: A Documentary Collection*, cards 171, 172, 231; Graham Intervs, 24 May and 8 Nov 1982, sess. 2, pp. 13–15.

[42] Msgs, Carver to Helms, in U.S. District Court, *Westmoreland v. CBS, Memorandum of Law*, app. B, pp. 211–35, 237–39; Bunker, Affidavit 22 Dec 83, in ibid., *app. A*, p. 27. Carver Deposition, pp. 423–24, 509–11, 540–41, 552–55, 632–35, 641–42, 662–64; Davidson Deposition 1, pp. 149–50. Both in *Vietnam: A Documentary Collection*, cards 171–73, 228. Davidson, *Vietnam Secrets*, pp. 47–50, 68–69. Westmoreland Hist Notes, 21 Aug–9 Sep 67, Westmoreland Hist File 21 (21 Aug–9 Sep 67), and Hist Notes, 10–29 Sep 67, tab A, Westmoreland Hist File 22 (10–30 Sep 67), CMH.

[43] First quote, and text of the compromise, is in Msg, Carver to Helms, *Westmoreland v. CBS, Memorandum of Law, App. B*, pp. 221–28. Second quote is from Msg, Westmoreland MAC 8703 to McConnell and Sharp, 14 Sep 67, Westmoreland Msg Files, 1 Jul–30 Sep 67, CMH. Paper, CIA Directorate of Intelligence, 15 Sep 67, sub: Communist Strength in South Vietnam, no. 1269/67, copy in CMH. For comparison

of final figures with earlier CIA and MACV versions, see Davidson, *Vietnam Secrets*, pp. 50–51.

[44] Special National Intelligence Estimate (SNIE). Submitted by Richard Helms, Director of Central Intelligence. Concurred in by the United States Intelligence Board . . . 13 Nov 67, reproduced in U.S. District Court, *Westmoreland v. CBS, Memorandum of Law*, app. B, pp. 243–72; Quote is from p. 262 (p. 16 of original). In ibid., pp. 385–89, see Memo, CIA, 15 Nov 67.

[45] MFR, Adams, 9 Nov 67; quote is from Affidavit, Col Elmer Martin, paras. 1 and 15. Both in U.S. District Court, *Westmoreland v. CBS, CBS Memorandum*, pp. 33n and 130; see also pp. 114–25, 131. Jones, *War Without Windows*, pp. 106–10. For defenses of the estimate, see U.S. District Court, *Westmoreland v. CBS, Memorandum of Law*, app. A, pp. 49–52, 120, 122, 215–16, 395–98; Davidson, *Vietnam Secrets*, p. 51; and Carver Deposition, pp. 396–97, 596–98, in *Vietnam: A Documentary Collection*, cards 171, 173.

[46] Quote is from U.S. District Court, *CBS Memorandum*, pp. 133–34; see also pp. 135–42. U.S. District Court, *Westmoreland v. CBS, Memorandum of Law*, pp. 89–90; and app. A, pp. 127–28, 369, 398–99, 405–06. MACV Briefing on Enemy Order of Battle, Released in Saigon at 0400 hrs EST, 24 Nov 67, in U.S. District Court, *Westmoreland v. CBS, Memorandum of Law*, app. B, pp. 273–82; see also p. 241. Carver Deposition, pp. 229–30, 250–52, 809–10, in *Vietnam: A Documentary Collection*, cards 169, 175. White House involvement with the press release is recounted in Hammond, *Military and the Media, 1962–1968*, p. 327.

[47] First quote is from Affidavit, William P. Bundy, 19 Dec 83; second is from Affidavit, Robert S. McNamara, 1 Dec 83. Both in U.S. District Court, *Westmoreland v. CBS, Memorandum of Law*, app. A, pp. 20, 231–32. In same collection, see Affidavits, John P. Roche, 20 Apr 84, pp. 322–23; and John L. Hart, 21 Feb 84, pp. 116–18. Davidson, *Vietnam Secrets*, pp. 63–66.

[48] For comments on the uncertainty of numbers, see Lung, *Intelligence*, p. 86. Allen Interv eloquently expresses a CIA officer's frustration at "unprofessional" MACV intelligence behavior. A retrospective CIA history alleges that Carver caved in in Saigon; see Harold P. Ford, *CIA and the Vietnam Policymakers: Three Episodes, 1962–1968* (Washington, D.C.: History Staff, Center for the Study of Intelligence, Central Intelligence Agency, 1998), pp. 95–104.

[49] North Vietnamese emphasis on molding perceptions of the struggle and thereby shaping the result is summarized in Douglas Pike, *PAVN: People's Army of Vietnam* (Novato, Calif.: Presidio Press, 1986), pp. 247–49.

[50] U.S. Congress, Senate, Committee on Foreign Relations, *The U.S. Government and the Vietnam War: Executive and Legislative Roles and Relationships, Part IV: July 1965–January 1968* (Washington, D.C.: Government Printing Office, 1994), pp. 894–95. Hereafter cited as U.S. Congress, Senate, *Government and the Vietnam War 4*.

[51] U.S. Department of State, *Foreign Relations of the United States, 1964–1968*. vol. 5, *Vietnam 1967* (Washington, D.C.: Government Printing Office, 2002), hereafter cited as *FRUS Vietnam, 1967*, pp. 943–50.

[52] Quotes are from Robert S. McNamara with Brian VanDeMark, *In Retrospect: The Tragedy and Lessons of Vietnam* (New York: Random House, 1995), pp. 311–14. See also Deborah Shapley, *Promise and Power: The Life and Times of Robert McNamara* (Boston: Little, Brown, and Company, 1993), pp. 436–41.

[53] U.S. Congress, Senate, *Government and the Vietnam War 4*, pp. 884–91.

[54] *FRUS Vietnam, 1967*, pp. 1040–42.

[55] HQMACV, Combined Campaign Plan, 1968, AB 143, 11 Nov 67, pp. 1–12. Historians Files, CMH.

[56] Gen William C. Westmoreland, Address to National Press Club, Washington, D.C., 21 Nov 67, Historians Files, CMH. Westmoreland also made the "well balanced hard–

hitting force" comment in a meeting with President Johnson and his advisers on 20 November; see *FRUS Vietnam, 1967*, p. 1058.

[57] Quotes are from Msg, Westmoreland HWA 3445 to Abrams, 25 Nov 67, Westmoreland Msg Files, 1–30 Nov 67, CMH. Westmoreland, *A Soldier Reports*, pp. 221–22, 234–35, 255, gives his version of the origins and rationale of his remarks. He comments in a similar vein in Sharp and Westmoreland, *Report on War*, pp. 136, 219.

[58] Full text is in *FRUS Vietnam, 1967*, pp. 1118–20. See also U.S. Congress, Senate, *Government and the Vietnam War 4*, pp. 892–93, 924–28.

[59] Unless otherwise noted, this section is based on John M. Carland, "The Tet Offensive of 1968: Desperate Gamble or Calculated Risk?" (Unpublished paper, U.S. Army Center of Military History, 2001) and William M. Hammond, "Preparations Begin" (Unpublished Paper, U.S. Army Center of Military History, 2002).

[60] Thomas K. Latimer, "Hanoi's Leaders and their South Vietnam Policies, 1954–1968" (Ph.D. diss., Georgetown University, 1972), chs. 8 and 9, summarizes the controversies.

[61] Quotes are from Carland, "Tet Offensive," pp. 4–5.

[62] Westmoreland gives his view of the purpose of the border battles in Msg, MAC 10547 to Wheeler, 6 Nov 67, Westmoreland Msg Files, Nov 67, CMH.

14

Conclusion: The Years of Escalation

The first five years of the existence of the Military Assistance Command, Vietnam, were years of expansion amid an escalating war. Established in 1962 as a small, temporary command to provide advice and support to the South Vietnamese government in antiguerrilla operations and pacification, MACV had grown by the end of 1967 into a large permanent headquarters that controlled half a million U.S. military personnel engaged in combat against formidable enemy guerrilla and light infantry forces. At the same time, it remained responsible for assisting the South Vietnamese in building up their armed forces and had become the principal U.S. agency supporting pacification. The command played a substantial role in American efforts to develop a stable, constitutional government in Saigon.

At its activation, the Military Assistance Command confronted a well-established rural guerrilla insurgency in South Vietnam. Supporting and directing the insurgency as an integral part of a unified Vietnamese nationalist movement, the North Vietnamese Communist government countered each incremental increase of American aid to Saigon with an increase of its own support to the revolutionary forces. Beginning with political and military cadres, this aid grew to comprise a growing volume of arms and supplies and eventually regiments and divisions of the North Vietnamese regular army. The enemy had the capacity to move as he chose along the spectrum of people's revolutionary war, opportunistically combining guerrilla and large-unit military operations with campaigns of political subversion. He had access to substantial military and economic assistance from the Soviet Union and the People's Republic of China. North Vietnamese and Viet Cong pressure, along with the military and political disarray of successive South Vietnamese regimes, elicited a succession of improvised American responses that expanded the size and proliferated the tasks of MACV.

The war developed through three stages. In the first, during 1962 and 1963, the Military Assistance Command directed an enlarged advisery contingent engaged in training and equipping South Vietnam's armed forces while commanding American helicopter and other specialized military units supporting President Ngo Dinh Diem's strategic hamlet pacification campaign. In this stage, the long-standing U.S. Military Assistance Advisory Group (MAAG) remained in operation under the supervision of the small MACV headquarters, which was supposed to complete its task and go out of business by mid-1965. After apparent early gains, the counterinsurgency effort foundered. The Viet Cong learned to counter the ARVN's American-advised tactics and American-supplied weapons, and President Diem stumbled into a fatal conflict with South Vietnam's Buddhists and ultimately with his own generals. The overthrow and murder of Diem in November 1963 ended the first phase of MACV's war and discredited the first MACV commander, General Paul D. Harkins, who had defended to the end the policy of supporting the fallen president.

During the second stage, which lasted through all of 1964 and into early 1965, the United States followed a two-track strategy in Vietnam. The first track was more of the same in South Vietnam—more advisers and more American support units for a revived antiguerrilla pacification campaign. On the second track, the administration of President Lyndon B. Johnson initiated planning and preparation for direct pressure on North Vietnam to cease its support of the Viet Cong. Initially, this pressure took the form of small-scale commando raids on the north combined with equally limited American air operations in Laos. In August 1964 the Tonkin Gulf incident brought one-time U.S. air attacks on North Vietnam and provided the occasion for Johnson to secure congressional authorization for expanded military action in Southeast Asia. By the end of 1964 an American air buildup was under way in the western Pacific, and troop deployments to South Vietnam were under discussion.

During this period MACV, under a new commander, General William C. Westmoreland, absorbed the MAAG and prepared for long–term participation in a growing struggle. Attempting to press ahead with the counterinsurgency campaign, the command's efforts were frustrated by persistent South Vietnamese governmental instability and by an equally persistent increase in Viet Cong numbers and military effectiveness. Unknown to the Americans until the very end of the period, the Communists had decided to move from purely guerrilla warfare to large-unit operations aimed at demoralizing or destroying Saigon's army, the only remaining pillar of the South Vietnamese state. To this end, the enemy began sending North Vietnamese regular army units into the south. As 1965 began, with success in the south nowhere in sight, American officials in Washington and Saigon prepared to implement their plans for an air offensive against North Vietnam.

With the start of ROLLING THUNDER in March 1965, followed by the dispatch to South Vietnam of U.S. combat units, the war entered its third stage. At this point, the Johnson administration attempted to secure success in Vietnam through a massive commitment of U.S. military forces on the ground in the south and in the air over the north.

Conclusion: The Years of Escalation

While continuing its assistance and advisory mission, the Military Assistance Command deployed an American and allied expeditionary force of more than half a million troops to fight the North Vietnamese and Viet Cong. After much controversy within the American government, the Military Assistance Command through the Office of Civil Operations and Revolutionary Development Support assumed the principal responsibility for U.S. support to the South Vietnamese pacification campaign. At ever-growing cost in money and blood, this stage of the war continued through the end of 1967 with American claims of progress but with no end in sight.

The evolution of MACV as a U.S. military organization was itself a complex process driven by American interservice and bureaucratic politics as well as by the requirements of the Southeast Asian conflict. At every point, service interests affected MACV's structure and command relationships. In the initial planning, the Navy insisted upon the insertion of the Pacific Command into the chain between the headquarters in Vietnam and the secretary of defense. In a process that at times resembled a nineteenth-century political fight over patronage spoils, the services battled each other for key positions in the expanding MACV staff. Formation of MACV's component commands also required negotiation with the services, whose leaders occasionally tried to intervene in operational matters that were properly the prerogative of the joint commander.

Control of air power was especially controversial because the resolution of disputes in Vietnam would set precedents of wider application. During MACV's early days, General Harkins and his Air Force commanders took opposing positions on the control of helicopters and fixed-wing tactical aircraft. Within the Air Force, MACV's air component commander contended with the Strategic Air Command for control of the B–52s. After the Johnson-McConnell agreement settled Army–Air Force differences over helicopters, Generals Westmoreland and Momyer united against the Marine Corps in repeated skirmishes over central management of fixed-wing tactical aircraft.

By the end of 1967, most of these command disputes had been resolved by compromises in which General Westmoreland usually played the role of honest broker among the services while at the same time trying to maintain effective control over his forces. By informal means, Westmoreland, Admiral Sharp, and General Wheeler maintained harmony along the Saigon-Honolulu-Washington chain of command. They formed a united front in dealing with Secretary of Defense Robert S. McNamara, the president's principal civilian deputy for conducting the war. By late 1967 MACV's field force and component commands had taken mature form, and their relationships with the joint headquarters had stabilized. However, MACV and the III Marine Amphibious Force were still in contention over arrangements for directing the increasingly large and complicated battle for I Corps. Although the

479

basic doctrinal disputes over control of air power persisted, Westmoreland and his service components put into effect working compromises that allowed the MACV commander to wield his fixed- and rotary-wing aircraft as a unified weapon in support of the ground campaign.

Organizational weaknesses persisted in the Military Assistance Command throughout the years of escalation. After MACV absorbed the advisory group, the headquarters lacked a strong staff agency to give focus and force to the Army advisory effort. Creation of an assistant chief of staff for military assistance came late and was at best a partial remedy. Intelligence was an even more significant deficiency. MACV's expansion in this area ran well behind the buildup of its combat forces. Not until late 1966 did the command's J2 Directorate and its Joint Intelligence Centers reach a point where they could provide a full and accurate picture of the enemy threat. Even then, public relations distorted the directorate's product at times, most notably in MACV's order of battle dispute with the Central Intelligence Agency. If knowledge is power, MACV was for too long a ninety-pound weakling in its contest with the Communist enemy.

The MACV commander and the U.S. ambassador to South Vietnam were supposed to cooperate as equals, referring unresolved disputes to Washington through their respective chains of command. In practice, harmony did not always prevail between the military and civilian heads of the American effort. General Harkins and Ambassador Frederick Nolting worked smoothly together at the start, but Harkins fell out with Henry Cabot Lodge over the American role in Diem's overthrow. Westmoreland restored MACV's cooperation with Lodge, then acted as a virtual military deputy to Ambassador Maxwell Taylor, to whom President Johnson had granted full authority over military as well as civilian activities. In spite of differences over the organization of pacification support, which President Johnson ultimately resolved by establishing CORDS, the general maintained cooperation with Lodge during that ambassador's second tour of duty. From Ellsworth Bunker's arrival in Saigon in May 1967 onward, the embassy and MACV acted as one on most policy issues. At any event, by the time Bunker took over, the sheer weight of manpower and resources had shifted the embassy-MACV balance decisively in favor of the latter, as exemplified by the placement of CORDS within the military headquarters.

Where operations outside South Vietnam were concerned, General Westmoreland had to deal with Admiral Sharp and the Ambassador to Laos, William Sullivan. Both men jealously guarded their jurisdictions over their respective pieces of the Southeast Asian war, and both had Washington's support in doing so. In this area also, compromise prevailed. Under close Washington supervision, Sharp directed the ROLLING THUNDER air attacks on North Vietnam. Even so, he delegated control of operations in the southernmost route package to Westmoreland. Similarly, Sullivan protected his role as "field marshal" of the unacknowl-

Conclusion: The Years of Escalation

edged American war in Laos and restricted MACV's operations against the Ho Chi Minh Trail so as to protect the facade of Laotian neutrality. Westmoreland nevertheless gradually negotiated the expansion of his cross-border ground and air attacks on the enemy's infiltration routes. In each case, he maintained cordial working relations with his military superior and civilian colleague while securing a substantial degree of influence over the operations that most directly affected the war in South Vietnam.

Political considerations dominated the Military Assistance Command's relationships with allied forces. Until the introduction of major American combat units, MACV's role was one of advice and support to a host government; a combined U.S.–South Vietnamese command never was contemplated. As U.S. troops prepared to enter the battle, General Westmoreland initially favored a combined command, or at least a U.S.–South Vietnamese central military staff. He quickly abandoned this concept, however, in deference to South Vietnamese nationalist sensitivities and to an American official policy of maintaining at least the appearance and as much as possible the reality of Saigon's sovereignty. Instead, MACV and its American forces worked with the South Vietnamese on the basis of cooperation and coordination. General Westmoreland attempted to shape South Vietnamese operations by means of his advisory network, regular high-level contacts with the Joint General Staff and South Vietnamese political leaders, the promotion of combined campaign plans and other cooperative staff work, and the provision or threatened withholding of military assistance. His influence, however, was limited, especially when it came to inducing the Saigon government to correct its forces' deficiencies in leadership, administration, and operations. Due to the vast difference in capabilities between the American and Vietnamese armies, cooperation between them in the field was usually a matter of form rather than substance. In the end, the Americans made do by concentrating primarily on attacking the enemy's large units while the South Vietnamese regulars and territorials conducted clearing and securing operations in support of pacification.

With the other allies, notably the South Koreans, political considerations also prevailed. Given Washington's eagerness to obtain "more flags" in Vietnam, the allies could set their own terms for their presence. The Koreans in particular did so in a restrictive manner, insisting upon and obtaining what amounted to their own independent area of operations. Westmoreland employed persuasion and the provision of U.S. combat and logistical support to influence their activities, largely to limited effect. Other allies, such as the Australians and New Zealanders, were more cooperative; but they, too, kept some political strings on their contingents.

At full development, the structure that resulted from all these compromises was complex and fell far short of the military ideal of unity of command. Nevertheless, every alternative seemed to pose insuperable political and military problems. Making MACV independent of Pacific Command, for example, would still have left the forces in Vietnam dependent on PACOM for their line of communications and would have raised issues of control of the naval task forces supporting MACV's operations. By the same token, if the MACV commander had been given control of U.S. forces throughout mainland Southeast Asia, the arrangement would have created diplomatic difficulties with allies such as Thailand and would have forced MACV to deal with many problems unrelated to the war in South Vietnam. A combined allied command in South Vietnam might have increased General Westmoreland's leverage over Saigon's forces, but at the cost of allowing the Communists to portray the American effort as colonialist aggression and possibly of demoralizing South Vietnamese officers and troops. In addition, a combined military command would have required an allied civilian authority to oversee it and lend it political legitimacy, but no such authority was readily available. Overall, the U.S. command structure in Southeast Asia was dictated by the complexities and contradictions of American policy toward the region's conflicts.

In practice, General Westmoreland exercised effective control over the military operations of principal concern to him in South Vietnam and its neighboring countries. He had full command of the American military effort within South Vietnam and by late 1967 was in charge of the pacification program as well. Insofar as he could within restrictions imposed by the embassy in Vientiane and by President Johnson's policy of limiting the war, he conducted ground and air operations against the Ho Chi Minh Trail in Laos. Although Admiral Sharp directed the air war against North Vietnam, that campaign, particularly in the route packages that covered the Hanoi-Haiphong area and the Tonkin delta, was more closely related to President Johnson's diplomacy than to the fighting in South Vietnam. Westmoreland controlled strikes in the route package where air interdiction most directly influenced the course of combat in the south.

Disputes among the American armed services and civilian agencies, along with interallied diplomacy, were a constant source of friction for Harkins and Westmoreland. They and their staffs had to devote many hours to these issues, but the extent to which these controversies hampered actual military and pacification operations remains difficult to determine. Similar policy disputes, personal and institutional rivalries, and organizational inefficiencies have characterized America's conduct of even its most successful wars. Often, as in Vietnam, leaders resolved the problems through compromises that appeared illogical but made sense in the context of the time. The MACV commander possessed, in the main, sufficient authority over the operations for which he was responsible. In the field, American soldiers, sailors, airmen, and marines made even the most convoluted arrangements work well enough to accomplish their missions. Coordination between American and allied forces was adequate for the relatively static territorial struggle being waged, especially when the inherent differences in capability among the forces are taken into account. In summary, it seems clear that policy and strategy on both sides, rather than the American and allied command structure, were decisive in shaping the course of the Vietnam War.

Under the Truman, Eisenhower, Kennedy, and Johnson administrations, the strategic objective of the United States in Vietnam remained the same: preventing a Communist takeover of the country as part of the general containment policy. After the Geneva Agreement in 1954, the objective was reduced to saving South Vietnam but otherwise held firm. Equally consistent was the method for achieving this goal: providing military and other assistance to an anti-Communist Vietnamese nationalist government. At the time of MACV's activation, the United States, as it had since the mid-1950s, pinned its hopes to Ngo Dinh Diem. After Diem's overthrow, as one successor regime after another proved ineffective and as enemy pressure increased, the Johnson administration incrementally enlarged the American commitment, ultimately to the point of large-scale, although still limited, war.

In South Vietnam, the pattern of the allies' campaign against the Viet Cong was set well before MACV's activation. It comprised on the one hand attacks by regular forces against the enemy's organized military units and logistical bases and on the other efforts to protect the villages, to uproot the Communist underground, and to reestablish the peasants' allegiance to the Saigon government. The two elements often were described by the shorthand labels of attrition and pacification. In 1965 the Johnson administration added to the mixture a campaign to interdict the flow of enemy troops and supplies through Laos and one of air attacks on North Vietnam. Begun as an exercise in diplomatic coercion, when the raids on the north failed to bring Hanoi to terms, they came to be explained and justified as contributing to interdiction.

The Military Assistance Command played the dominant role in carrying out attrition and pacification within South Vietnam, was a significant participant in interdiction in Laos, and took a secondary part in the bombing of the north. Its commanders as a result sought all possible resources for the effort in South Vietnam and Laos. They viewed the attack on North Vietnam as at best a secondary campaign and urged the administration to delay undertaking it until the situation in the south was stabilized. Once ROLLING THUNDER began, General Westmoreland, supported by Secretary McNamara, consistently fought to ensure first priority for the south in the allocation of American air power.

The two successive commanders of MACV faced different situations and had varying degrees of success in performing their jobs and influencing U.S. policy. Although General Harkins lacked experience in antiguerrilla warfare, his background in working with allies and in administering military assistance, along with his knowledge of the Southeast Asia theater gained during his service at U.S. Army, Pacific, made him a sensible selection for what was expected to be primarily a high-level diplomatic and managerial assignment. Rather than leading troops in combat, Harkins was supposed to direct the expansion of American military aid and advice and to work with the ambassador in persuading Diem to adopt and carry out effective policies.

Harkins performed his military administrative and planning tasks with competence, and he cooperated harmoniously with Ambassador Nolting in the thankless chore of trying to influence Diem. He fell out of step with Nolting's successor, Henry Cabot Lodge, and with his Washington superiors, however, when President Kennedy, dismayed at Diem's handling of the Buddhist crisis, changed American policy first to confrontation with the South Vietnamese president and then to support for his overthrow. In increasingly acrimonious conflict with Ambassador Lodge, who enthusiastically endorsed and did much to shape the anti-Diem policy, Harkins remained stubbornly loyal to Diem. In retrospect, Harkins' assessment that the generals who deposed and murdered the president would do little to improve South Vietnamese performance proved to be correct; but that fact did not save the MACV commander. Diem's fall discredited Harkins in the view of the administration, the American press, and the American public, and his tour of duty in Vietnam soon came to a bitter end.

Perhaps the most persistent legacy of Harkins' command was the pattern of optimism that he established in MACV's reporting of the situation in Vietnam. From the beginning of his tenure in Saigon, Harkins emphasized progress in his classified communications to Honolulu and Washington and in his public statements to the news media. Although fully aware of the many deficiencies of Diem's regime and its armed forces and while working to change them, Harkins persistently put the best face on even the most disastrous events, to the point of suppressing reports from field advisers that contradicted his optimism. He did this in the belief that the American programs were doing as well overall as could be expected and in the conviction that he had to maintain a positive tone to sustain the morale of the Vietnamese. Harkins' upbeat assessments nonetheless increasingly were challenged by other U.S. officials and by the Saigon news correspondents, whom the general accused of undermining the war effort.

When he succeeded Harkins, General Westmoreland initially announced a policy of objective reporting and had considerable success at the outset in restoring his command's credibility with the newsmen. Westmoreland, however, soon fell into much the same pattern of optimism. He couched his reports in terms of progress, accentuated the positive, and rarely if ever admitted setbacks. He did so for the same reasons Harkins had—a conviction that the allies were in fact moving forward and that he had to keep up South Vietnamese spirits. In addi-

Conclusion: The Years of Escalation

tion, as the conflict became controversial, President Johnson pressed him for good news to counter allegations that the war was a stalemate. During 1965 and 1966, the years of the American buildup, Westmoreland portrayed his command as seizing the initiative from the enemy when in fact his operations were mostly spoiling attacks to cover the U.S. deployment and to keep the Viet Cong and North Vietnamese off balance. He thereby left the American public and many government officials unaware of the actual difficulties he was facing and raised unwarranted expectations of early success. On issues such as the number of enemy battalion-size attacks and the question of enemy strength, Westmoreland permitted public relations to influence MACV's reports and analyses, causing other agencies to lose confidence in the command's integrity. Westmoreland's emergence in 1967 as a spokesman for and advocate of Johnson's war policy further weakened his credibility.

In Westmoreland's defense, it should be noted that the general attempted to balance his overall optimistic tone with acknowledgment of the enemy's strength and tenacity and warnings that the war would be long and difficult. When he asked for troops in mid-1965, for example, he promised in return a prolonged struggle, not a quick victory. He was also candid in stating that the war would be one of attrition. In his November 1967 speech at the National Press Club, moreover, if he presented a generally hopeful picture of progress, he still declared that any substantial American turnover of the burden to the South Vietnamese was at least two more years away. These caveats notwithstanding, the dominant note sounded by the Military Assistance Command was positive. As a result, by the end of 1967 the command's assurances of progress were beginning to ring hollow in the ears of government officials and of an increasingly skeptical American press and public.

General Westmoreland assumed command of MACV with a reputation as one of the U.S. Army's most promising general officers and with a stronger background than Harkins in the theory of counterinsurgency warfare. He grasped the unconventional dimensions of the conflict in Vietnam and began with a firm commitment to a pacification-oriented approach. After his first year in command, three factors shaped his operational priorities: the military and political disarray of the Saigon regime, the growing North Vietnamese and Viet Cong main force threat, and Johnson's decision to respond to those problems by committing American combat troops on a large scale. Westmoreland continued the twofold strategy of attrition and pacification, but with more emphasis on attrition, especially as the mission of his expanding U.S. contingent. Advice and support to the South Vietnamese took second place to the completion of the American buildup and the organization of American forces. Pacification remained in the doldrums while MACV and the embassy struggled to reestablish a stable Saigon government and provincial administration and tried to resolve the U.S. interagency conflict over organization for pacification support.

Throughout this period, Westmoreland, in contrast to Harkins, retained the confidence of his civilian and military superiors, even those like McNamara who came to have doubts about the correctness of U.S. policy. A team player by temperament, Westmoreland sought to lead by consensus and compromise. He carefully tailored his advice and recommendations to conform to administration desires as he perceived them. He probed constantly by every available means to discover the trend of Washington thinking and continually sought to embody in his recommendations the official policy consensus as he saw it developing in conferences and exchanges of messages between himself and his superiors in Honolulu and Washington. As a result, his recommendations usually met with acceptance. On issues where he knew he could not prevail, such as offensive operations in Laos, he tactfully advocated his position but never to the point of irrevocably antagonizing his superiors. Westmoreland exercised great apparent influence on the course of operations in South Vietnam, but he did so by ascertaining at each step which way most of the crowd was already moving and then going in that direction himself.

Westmoreland's method of operation is illustrated by his role in deciding two of the most important policy issues of the period—the commitment of large American combat forces to South Vietnam and the evolution of U.S. strategy in the ground war. President Johnson took the fateful step of sending in combat forces for reasons that were a combination of "push" from within the administration and "pull" from the developing crisis in South Vietnam. At the start, the "push" factor predominated, as the president and his advisers searched for a means other than bombing the north to reinvigorate the allied war effort. To this end, Johnson in late December 1964 urged a reluctant ambassador and the MACV commander to propose increased use of American combat troops within South Vietnam. Administration prodding and encouragement continued with General Harold K. Johnson's March 1965 visit to Saigon and with further presidential imperatives in April. At this stage, however, politically motivated presidential caution, disagreements among his advisers over whether American soldiers could fight effectively under South Vietnamese conditions, and Ambassador Taylor's resistance limited actual troop commitments.

At mid-year, the "pull" element came into play. The absence of political results from ROLLING THUNDER, combined with MACV and U.S. Mission reports of South Vietnamese military and governmental deterioration and possible imminent collapse, prompted a major troop commitment in late July. Yet the "push" side was also still present. Far from sending the minimum force required to stabilize the situation, the president and his associates, once committed to a large American reinforcement, initiated planning for the insertion of enough U.S. troops to overwhelm the enemy with numbers and firepower and to reestablish Saigon's authority throughout the country. They accepted

Conclusion: The Years of Escalation

almost without question Westmoreland's steadily increasing estimates of the force required to accomplish those objectives. Indeed, at Honolulu in February 1966 President Johnson confirmed the American commitment to ambitious military and pacification goals and assured his field commander that all the troops he requested would be sent.

Throughout this sequence of decisions, General Westmoreland and his headquarters played an influential but largely reactive role. Rather than creating it, MACV headquarters responded to and amplified the emerging policy consensus. Westmoreland furnished the ambassador and the president with much of the information they used to form their understanding of the situation in South Vietnam. And certainly his and Ambassador Taylor's declaration in June that South Vietnam probably would fall if not shored up by American divisions decisively affected the timing and nature of administration actions. To that extent, he influenced political as well as military decisions.

Yet at the same time Westmoreland, in recommending military courses of action, tempered his advice with a view to what would be acceptable higher up the chain of command. Although the general and key members of his staff became convinced early in 1965 that substantial American ground forces would be necessary to counter the Viet Cong's main force buildup, the MACV commander held back from requesting those forces, in part in deference to Taylor's reluctance to bring in American troops. His first major request, aside from limited ones for air base defense, came only after General Johnson indicated in March that the authorities in Washington were receptive. Westmoreland continued to move cautiously during April and May, seeming to follow rather than lead the administration's experimental initiatives. He took a more forceful position in June, but even then he acted only after Taylor changed his stand on the issue and after General Wheeler indicated that the Joint Chiefs were going to reopen the question of committing division-size forces. He made his initial Phase II proposals at the direction of Secretary McNamara.

On questions of troop employment and campaign strategy, Westmoreland also tried to stay within a policy consensus. While early persuaded that American units should concentrate on pursuing and attacking the enemy's main forces, he readily modified the wording of his concepts of operation to accommodate the interest of Admiral Sharp and other officials in the systematic securing of the populated coastal areas. His campaign plans and troop dispositions were derived in large part from earlier MACV and Pacific Command contingency plans and incorporated concepts from Sharp and the Joint Chiefs.

During the two years of combat that followed the initial deployments, General Westmoreland modified his strategy in response to the situation and to his perception of official concerns. He advocated the buildup when it was administration policy but shifted emphasis to a "level-off" force when administration interest and his own appreciation of service capabilities pointed in that direction. He pursued the anti-main force campaign but also paid increasing attention to pacification in response to presidential urging and as responsibility for conduct of the program fell into MACV's hands. Westmoreland chafed at civilian-imposed restrictions on his freedom of action in Laos and Cambodia and, like Admiral Sharp, deplored what he considered the administration's excessive caution in striking at North Vietnam. Unlike Sharp, he never pressed his recommendations for more aggressive action to the point of direct conflict with Secretary McNamara or other high officials. Although annoyed at the interventions into military matters of embassy civilians, Defense Department analysts, and other outsiders, Westmoreland endured them with outward equanimity. At times, as in the barrier episode, he adjusted his operations to accommodate their views. In many aspects of the campaign, he repeatedly accepted less in terms of forces and actions than what his best military judgment indicated would bring the most expeditious and favorable result. He did so, he claimed later, out of confidence that he could win within the limits imposed upon him, which he saw "not as leading to failure but only as delaying success."[1] He was convinced that he was making progress within the constraints and always hoped that he could obtain additional reinforcements and wider freedom of action in the future.

Westmoreland's decision to employ his American troops primarily against the North Vietnamese and Viet Cong big units was perhaps his most controversial one. U.S. Marine commanders and other military and civilian officials at the time, echoed subsequently by historians and analysts, argued that this approach diverted to a secondary objective forces that could have been more profitably employed in clearing and securing the villages, the true road to victory. In addition, they claimed that the accompanying military division of labor, which left pacification support mainly to the South Vietnamese Army, demoralized the South Vietnamese and excessively "Americanized" the conduct of the war.

Westmoreland's defenders rest their case on both political and military grounds. On the political side, Westmoreland was following a consensus among both American and South Vietnamese policymakers. His decision conformed to the Johnson administration's preoccupation with limiting the extent and duration of the U.S. military commitment. If the Americans concentrated on fighting the North Vietnamese while the South Vietnamese focused on territorial security, a negotiated de-escalation of the conflict or mutual withdrawal of outside forces would leave Saigon in a relatively favorable position against the indigenous Viet Cong. On the other hand, if territorial security depended on American troops, a mutual U.S.–North Vietnamese withdrawal would doom Saigon. McNamara, Komer, and the Defense Department's systems analysts all considered pacification the key to success, but all insisted that it must be done with South Vietnamese forces to have lasting effect. American troops could at most provide a shield while the Saigon government pulled itself and its army together. Even though McNamara ultimately concluded that military escalation in Vietnam had reached a point of diminishing returns, he never challenged Westmoreland's allocation of the American troops under MACV's command.

Militarily, Westmoreland's approach made the best use of the mobility and firepower of his American soldiers while minimizing the adverse effects of their ignorance of local language and culture. In addition, the American infantry battalions available to MACV, especially in the critical period of late 1965 and early 1966, were too few to clear and secure any significant portion of the South Vietnamese countryside while helping ARVN forces to ward off the enemy regiments and divisions. The III Marine Amphibious Force tried to overcome this deficiency by pairing some of its rifle squads with Vietnamese Popular Force platoons to defend hamlets in the Combined Action Program. There were far more hamlets than Marine rifle squads, however; and III MAF had to keep most of its infantry battalions concentrated against the North Vietnamese regulars who began moving into I Corps. Inevitably, then, most of the manpower for clearing and securing operations had to be Vietnamese.

Retrospective commentaries from the other side affirm the importance of the main force threat and the effectiveness of Westmoreland's deployment of American troops to counter it. In North Vietnamese revolutionary theory, a "general offensive" by massed regular forces to smash the south's "puppet" army was the essential precondition for the "general uprising" or insurrection of the masses that would overthrow the counterrevolutionary regime. According to North Vietnamese accounts, during the years after 1963 when the Saigon government was in disarray and the revolution was advancing throughout the countryside, only Communist organizational weakness in the cities and the lack of a strong enough main force "fist" stood between the party and victory. By early 1965, the party was building up its main force and beginning to conduct offensive campaigns, only to be blocked by the "savagery" and "guile" of U.S. units. As a result, a former *COSVN* commander declared in a postwar analysis, "the conditions for a general insurrection at that time never became ripe and disappeared."[2]

During the period of the American buildup, General Westmoreland's disposition of his forces and conduct of operations were sound within the strategic limitations under which he had to work. Given the administration's determination to restrict the conflict as much as possible to South Vietnam, Westmoreland had no alternative to waging what amounted to a defensive war of attrition while trying to rebuild the Saigon government and restart pacification. By late 1967, he had achieved the administration's minimum goal of preventing a South Vietnamese collapse and had laid the foundations for progress in pacifying the countryside. However, nothing that he could do in the south would affect the will and capacity of the North Vietnamese to continue the war. Hence, he was unable to bring the conflict to an end.

Were there alternative ways of fighting the war? The Johnson administration ruled out one—an invasion of North Vietnam—due to well-grounded concern that it would provoke Communist Chinese intervention as had happened in Korea.[3] In addition, the Hanoi government had organized its people for guerrilla warfare in anticipation of a U.S. invasion; hence this course of action would simply have extended to North Vietnam the pacification problems with which the Americans and South Vietnamese were already contending in the south. By conducting limited amphibious attacks just north of the Demilitarized Zone, the United States could have inflicted heavy losses on the enemy fighting the marines in northern I Corps, but this would have been a tactical success rather than a war-deciding stroke and was not worth the risk of hostilities with China it would have entailed.

Similar objections applied to the solution favored by Admiral Sharp and many U.S. Air Force leaders: heavier bombing and a naval blockade of North Vietnam. That course of action also ran the risk, in Johnson's view, of provoking the Russians and Chinese while offering in return no certain prospect of a military decision. At a later point in the war, President Richard Nixon would bomb and blockade North Vietnam with no Chinese intervention and with apparent success in securing a peace agreement, but he would do so in international circumstances much different from those Johnson faced.[4]

A more politically acceptable and militarily feasible alternative would have been the establishment of a cordon of American, South Vietnamese, and possibly Thai and Laotian troops across the Laos panhandle from the western end of the Demilitarized Zone in Vietnam to the Mekong River. Since the cordon could be established without invading North Vietnam, this strategy entailed minimal risk of Chinese intervention. Especially if supplemented by a naval blockade or quarantine of Sihanoukville, the move would have prevented the infiltration of large North Vietnamese units and heavy tonnages of supplies into South Vietnam and would thus have limited the escalation of the fighting there. With American advisers and air support, the South Vietnamese could then have handled the struggle against the Viet Cong and whatever small Communist reinforcements managed to slip through from the north. Standing on the defense, the U.S. divisions would have had a simply defined protective mission and probably would have suffered fewer casualties, making the troop commitment more acceptable to the American public. While not directly knocking North Vietnam out of the war, the cordon would have prevented Hanoi's leaders from expanding the battle in the south, making it possible for Saigon, if it could achieve a measure of reform, to eliminate the Viet Cong as a serious threat to the regime.

Conclusion: The Years of Escalation

At various times, the Joint Chiefs of Staff, General Westmoreland, and the Chief of the Joint General Staff, General Cao Van Vien, all acknowledged the potential value of this course of action. General Bruce Palmer, a former deputy commander of U.S. Army, Vietnam, and commander of II Field Force, argued in retrospect that the divisions sent to Westmoreland in 1965 and 1966 should have been used for this purpose instead of being spread all over South Vietnam on missions that the South Vietnamese Army should have been performing.[5] Even with these endorsements, however, the Johnson administration never seriously considered adopting the cordon strategy. The embassy in Vientiane adamantly opposed such a policy, along with Westmoreland's proposals for limited attacks on the Ho Chi Minh Trail, on the familiar grounds that it would wreck Laotian neutrality, lead to the overthrow of Souvanna Phouma's government, and perhaps result in the North Vietnamese overrunning northern Laos. Admiral Sharp and the Joint Chiefs, for their parts, were more interested in expanding ROLLING THUNDER than in establishing a line across Laos. McNamara saw possibilities in a barrier, but not one manned by ground troops. In his commander's estimate of March 1965, moreover, Westmoreland himself emphasized the diplomatic and logistical difficulties of establishing a cordon and declared that it would not help him solve the immediate military crisis in South Vietnam. He later proposed operations in Laos, but only as a supplement to his campaign in South Vietnam, a campaign that he believed he was slowly winning. Above all, President Johnson was determined to minimize enlargement of the war beyond South Vietnam's borders. In summary, whatever its merits, the cordon concept had powerful enemies and no determined individual or institutional sponsor.

A final alternative would have been to minimize escalation during and after 1965 and go for a stalemate at the lowest possible cost in lives, money, and political controversy. In this approach, the administration would have conducted ROLLING THUNDER at a level of intensity sufficient only to inflict limited pain on the North Vietnamese and to keep up the morale of the South Vietnamese. It would have avoided committing U.S. ground troops or sent in only enough to provide a last–ditch reserve to back up the ARVN. The United States would have relied on the South Vietnamese, reinforced by American advisers and tactical air power, to contain the enemy main force offensive. At the same time, MACV would have made a maximum effort to expand the RVNAF and improve its training and armament. The objective would have been to keep the Saigon government and armed forces in being and in control of the cities and at least a portion of the countryside during a struggle that would continue indefinitely. This policy would have minimized the diplomatic and political cost to the United States of the northern bombing campaign and at the same time have prevented the steadily rising toll of American battle casualties that more than any other factor undermined domestic support for the war. It also, of course, entailed the risk of defeat if the South Vietnamese could not hold out.

In mid-1965 President Johnson and his advisers rejected this course of action because of the continuing ineffectiveness of their Saigon ally. Less from overconfidence than from a conviction that there was nothing else to be done, they inserted American air and ground forces into the war on a large scale. In late 1967, when that commitment appeared to to have reached the limit of political and economic feasibility without producing decisive results, Johnson set his course toward the lower cost alternative. He leveled off both ROLLING THUNDER and MACV's troop strength and initiated an effort to turn the fighting in the south over to Saigon's forces. By that time, however, the size of the American military presence in South Vietnam had become so great that cutting back would be a prolonged and difficult process. Considering the toll that escalation had already taken in American lives, treasure, and political capital, it was uncertain whether even under the most favorable circumstances the government could retain public support for the Southeast Asia struggle long enough to carry the low-cost strategy through to a successful conclusion.

As 1967 came to an end, the Vietnam War was thus in an uneasy balance. In South Vietnam, the American forces had completed their buildup and inflicted heavy combat losses on the North Vietnamese and Viet Cong. MACV and the U.S. embassy had restored stability and a semblance of constitutional legitimacy to the Saigon government and had put in place an organization to support another try at pacification. On the other side, the Communist leaders in Hanoi and in the south believed that they had survived the worst that the United States could throw at them and had achieved an equilibrium of forces. They were making plans and preparations for a major offensive to tilt that equilibrium in their favor. In Washington, President Johnson and his advisers proclaimed that the war was going well in their public statements. Privately, they were none too certain and had decided to level off the American effort and seek a way out of the conflict, either by turning over combat to the South Vietnamese or through negotiation with the Communists. For the Military Assistance Command, as for the rest of the U.S. government, the years of escalation had come to an end.

Conclusion: The Years of Escalation

Notes

[1] Quotation is from Westmoreland, *A Soldier Reports*, p. 261; see also pp. 230, 262, and 410–11. Westmoreland enumerates the restraints under which he had to operate in Ltr to CINCPAC, 30 Jun 68, in Sharp and Westmoreland, *Report on War*, p. 292.

[2] See for example Senior General Hoang Van Thai, "A Few Strategic Issues in the Spring 1968 Tet Offensive and Uprising," *Military History Magazine*, Published by the Ministry of Defense's Military Institute of Vietnam, Issue 2 (26), 1988. Translated by Merle Pribbenow. Copy in Historians files, CMH; quote is from p. 6 of the translation. General Van Thai was military commander of *COSVN* at the time of the Tet offensive.

[3] Accounts based on Chinese sources indicate that Johnson's concerns were well founded. See for example Xiaoming Zhang, "The Vietnam War: A Chinese Perspective, 1964–1969," *Journal of Military History* 60 (October 1996): 731–62.

[4] Mark Clodfelter, *The Limits of Air power: The American Bombing of North Vietnam* (New York: The Free Press, 1989), compares the circumstances and objectives of Johnson's and Nixon's bombing campaigns.

[5] Palmer, J., *25-Year War*, pp. 187–88.

Bibliographical Note

This account of a joint headquarters engaged in the making of theater-level policy and strategy, the conduct of joint and combined military operations, and the provision of advice and support to the South Vietnamese government and armed forces of necessity draws on a wide range of sources. The work is based primarily on the message traffic and other papers of successive MACV commanders, principally those of General William C. Westmoreland. These materials are supplemented by documents from the MACV records in the National Archives; the national security files of Presidents John F. Kennedy and Lyndon B. Johnson; and the records of the Department of State, the Central Intelligence Agency, the Joint Chiefs of Staff, and the American armed services.

Unpublished Sources

National Archives and Records Administration

Major record groups bearing on the Military Assistance Command are located in the National Archives and Records Administration facility at College Park, Maryland. Record Group (RG) 472 (Records of the United States Forces in Southeast Asia, 1950–1975) now contains the main body of MACV headquarters material. This record group also includes the records of the Military Assistance Advisory Group, Vietnam, and those of many agencies subordinate or related to MACV. These include Headquarters U.S. Army, Vietnam; Army corps, divisions, brigades, and support organizations; Army and Air Force advisory groups; the regional assistance commands; the U.S. Military Assistance Command, Thailand; the Defense Attaché Office, Saigon; the Military Equipment Delivery Team to Cambodia; and the U.S. Delegation to the Four-Party Joint Military Commission. Also useful are records of the Army Staff (RG 319), U.S. Army commands (RG 338), and Interservice Agencies (RG 334). Since citations in this volume may retain the former record group designation, researchers should seek the assistance of NARA archivists in locating documents.

MACV: The Years of Escalation, 1962–1967

U.S. Army Center of Military History

The U.S. Army Center of Military History (CMH) in Washington, D.C., holds a large and varied mass of documents collected by the historians preparing the Center's multivolume history of the Army's role in Southeast Asia. Many of these are copies or duplicates of material in other repositories. The Center will transfer these materials to the National Archives upon completion of the U.S. Army in Vietnam series.

Most important of these for the historian of the Military Assistance Command, Vietnam, are the papers of General Westmoreland. The Westmoreland Papers are photocopies of those held by the Lyndon Baines Johnson Library in Austin, Texas. They consist of two main collections. The first is a historical diary that the general dictated at intervals to members of his staff, describing his day-to-day activities and decisions and supported by copies of messages, memorandums, reports, staff studies, and other documents. The second is a chronological file of messages between Westmoreland and other senior commanders in Vietnam and between him and his superiors in Hawaii and Washington. Through these messages, the historian can follow the policy dialogue between the theater commander and higher authorities. Unfortunately, a comparable collection does not exist for Westmoreland's predecessor, General Paul D. Harkins, although the Center's files contain scattered messages and other documents for his period in command.

Besides the Westmoreland Papers, the Center's holdings include more than 100 linear feet of documents provided by Ambassador Robert Komer on the CORDS effort. These messages, memorandums, and reports detail the pacification effort under both Ambassador Komer and Ambassador William E. Colby. Other Vietnam holdings include an extensive body of province pacification reports; a complete set of the annual combined campaign plans; manuals for MACV's automated data processing systems; message files of U.S. Army, Vietnam, deputy commanders; and numerous unit operational reports.

U.S. Army Military History Institute

The U.S. Army Military History Institute (MHI) at Carlisle Barracks, Pennsylvania, holds important collections on the history of the Military Assistance Command. These include numerous MACV Periodical Intelligence Reports and officer end-of-tour debriefings. Besides these paper documents, the institute possesses a microfilm collection of documents used to support the annual MACV command histories with a printout of a computer-generated finding aid.

Other personal papers collections at MHI bear on MACV's history. Most important is the large body of papers of General Harold K. Johnson. Smaller but quite useful for the 1962–1967 period are the papers of Arthur S. Collins, William E. DePuy, Joseph H. McChristian, Francis Fox Parry,

Bibliographical Note

William R. Peers, and John P. Vann. The institute also holds a duplicate set of the Westmoreland historical and message files.

Air Force, Navy, and Marine Corps Documents

This volume draws from materials held by the other service historical offices in the Washington, D.C., area. The Office of Air Force History contains copies of documents and oral histories held at the Air University at Maxwell Air Force Base, Alabama. The Naval Historical Center at the Washington Navy Yard possesses the records of the commander, U.S. Naval Forces, Vietnam. Among the collections of the Marine Corps Historical Center, also at the Washington Navy Yard, the III Marine Amphibious Force message files, the Marine Corps headquarters file on single management, the Victor H. Krulak Papers, and the Keith B. McCutcheon Papers were of special value for this study.

Other Manuscript Collections

The Lyndon Baines Johnson Library holds the national security files of the Johnson administration. They include National Security Council histories, compilations of key documents on particular topics. The histories of Presidential Decisions on the Gulf of Tonkin Attacks; the Honolulu Conference, 1966; and the Deployment of Major U.S. Forces to Vietnam, 1965, were used extensively in this volume.

In Washington, D.C., the National Defense University holds the papers of Maxwell D. Taylor. This collection documents Taylor's successive roles as special military assistant to President Kennedy, chairman of the Joint Chiefs of Staff, and ambassador to South Vietnam; it also includes important documents on the creation of the Military Assistance Command and command relations in Southeast Asia.

The Hoover Institution on War, Revolution, and Peace at Stanford University, Palo Alto, California, contains the papers of Maj. Gen. John R. Chaisson, USMC, the officer who headed the MACV Combat Operations Center from late 1966 until well into 1968. Chaisson's letters to his wife and the notebooks he used during his travels and meetings with Westmoreland provide a rare glimpse of the personalities and inner workings of MACV headquarters during a critical period of the war. They are especially useful when read in conjunction with Westmoreland's history and message files. Also in the Hoover Institution are the papers of Lt. Gen. Samuel T. Williams, a chief of the Military Assistance Advisory Group.

Oral History Interviews

Most of the principal figures in this study—the successive Pacific Command and MACV commanders and the ambassadors to South

Vietnam—were interviewed at different times by various institutions. While uneven in coverage and candor, these materials are an indispensable supplement to the documentary record, especially for the details they provide concerning official and personal relationships among the senior leaders. The Naval Historical Center holds the transcript of a lengthy reminiscence by Admiral Ulysses S. G. Sharp. This interview formed the basis of Sharp's published memoir, *Strategy for Defeat*, but the transcript contains blunt comments on events and personalities that do not appear in the book. A briefer interview with Sharp by the Air Force's Project CORONA HARVEST is available at the Office of Air Force History in Washington, D.C.

Of the MACV commanders, the Military History Institute holds a transcript of an interview of General Paul D. Harkins, conducted for the Army War College's Senior Officer Debriefing Program, that covers his entire career including his tenure as MACV commander. Harkins also gave an interview to Project CORONA HARVEST, which can be consulted at the Office of Air Force History. The Lyndon B. Johnson Library conducted an interview with General Westmoreland, which is available at the library. An extensive interview with Westmoreland, done for the Senior Officer Debriefing Program, is available at the Military History Institute. The Center of Military History possesses a copy of the MHI interview and also the notes which Army historian Charles B. MacDonald took while assisting Westmoreland in the writing of his memoirs. As with Admiral Sharp's reminiscences, these notes include revealing material that did not appear in the published volume.

As to the ambassadors, Frederick C. Nolting was interviewed for Project CORONA HARVEST; a transcript is at the Office of Air Force History. The Military History Institute possesses a career interview of General Maxwell Taylor and one of Ambassador Ellsworth Bunker, although the Bunker interview is more useful for the period after that covered in this volume.

Military History Institute files also contain career and topical interviews with Army officers who played significant roles in MACV's history. They include Donald D. Blackburn, William E. DePuy, Jean E. Engler, John A. Heintges, Harold K. Johnson, Walter T. Kerwin, Stanley R. Larsen, Glenn Muggleberg, Spurgeon H. Neel, Bruce Palmer, William R. Peers, William B. Rosson, and John L. Throckmorton. Copies of transcripts of many of these interviews are available at the Center of Military History, which also possesses a transcript of an interview of John P. Vann, conducted by a CMH historian immediately after Vann's return from Vietnam in July 1963. The Center also possesses a copy of an interview of Ambassador Robert Komer by the RAND Corporation on pacification organization and management, as well as tapes and transcripts of interviews the author conducted with George Allen, James M. Loome, and Paul E. Suplizio bearing on aspects of intelligence, pacification, and military operations.

Interviews of value to this study are contained in other service historical collections. The Office of Air Force History possesses transcripts of interviews of key officers of Seventh Air Force and other air commands involved in Southeast Asia, including Generals Rollen Anthis, Gordon Blood, Hunter Harris, John McConnell, and Gilbert Myers. The Naval Historical Center's holdings include the aforementioned reminiscences of Admiral Sharp. The Marine Corps Historical Center contains interviews with almost all the important Marine commanders of the period, as well as numerous lower-ranking Marine officers. Most useful for this study were those of John Chaisson, William K. Jones, Victor H. Krulak, Keith B. McCutcheon, and Carl Youngdale.

In the Lyndon B. Johnson Library, the interviews of Philip Davidson and Daniel Graham are of value on the 1967 order of battle controversy. For insights into the interaction of State Department officials with MACV and the military in Southeast Asia, at every level from the embassy to CORDS district offices, researchers should consult the growing collections of the Foreign Affairs Oral History Program, Association for Diplomatic Studies and Training, located at the National Foreign Affairs Training Center, Arlington, Virginia. Nearly 900 transcripts of these interviews have been published on CD-ROM.

Published Primary Sources

Heading the list of published primary sources are the so-called Pentagon Papers. Initially classified histories of Defense Department policy-making on Vietnam from 1945 through early 1968, prepared at Secretary McNamara's direction, they were leaked to the press in 1971 by Daniel Ellsberg. The narrative in these volumes is supplemented by extracts and complete reproductions of many high-level official documents. Throughout, this study cites the original Defense Department version of the papers, which was published as U.S. Congress, House Committee on Armed Services. *United States–Vietnam Relations, 1945–1967: Study Prepared by the Department of Defense.* 12 vols. Washington, D.C.: Government Printing Office, 1971.

Second in importance for the story of the Military Assistance Command are its own annual histories, comprehensive, highly detailed multivolume studies prepared by the headquarters' Military History Branch. Although these histories generally conform in their interpretation to the progress-oriented MACV view of the war, they contain occasional candid observations and large quantities of raw historical data. They are indispensable sources for study of the Military Assistance Command's many functions. Most of them include a special annex, which was published and distributed separately, covering activities of the Studies and Observations Group (SOG). Complete citations for the histories used in this volume are:

Military History Branch, Headquarters, United States Military Assistance Command, Vietnam. Command History, 1964. Saigon, 1965.

———. Command History, 1965. Saigon, 1966.

———. *Command History, 1966*. Saigon, 1967.
———. *Command History, 1967*. 3 vols. Saigon, 1968.

For the period 1964–1968, Admiral Sharp and General Westmoreland directed the preparation of an overview of their stewardship. See U.S. Pacific Command, *Report on the War in Vietnam (as of 30 June 1968)*. Washington, D.C.: Government Printing Office, 1969. While it contains useful information, this report is very much a defense of its authors' conduct of the war and should be read as such.

The Office of the Joint Chiefs of Staff prepared its own official histories of the JCS role in the Southeast Asia conflict. Now in the process of being published in declassified and updated form, these histories illuminate the higher-level policy context within which the Military Assistance Command operated and record the Saigon command's exchanges with its overseers in Washington. The critical volume for the period covered in this volume is:

Historical Division, Joint Secretariat, U.S. Joint Chiefs of Staff. "The Joint Chiefs of Staff and the War in Vietnam, 1960–1968." Pts. 1–3. The History of the Joint Chiefs of Staff. Washington, D.C., 1970.

The Pacific Command also issued annual official histories of the Vietnam War period. These volumes are less useful than the MACV and JCS histories for study of the Military Assistance Command since they concentrate heavily on PACOM's responsibilities outside the Southeast Asian theater of war and largely duplicate the MACV histories in coverage of the conflict itself.

In 1984 General Westmoreland sued the Columbia Broadcasting System (CBS) for libel in response to a CBS documentary, "The Uncounted Enemy," which aired on *CBS Reports* and which charged Westmoreland with falsification of intelligence during the 1967 order of battle controversy. The trial, which ended inconclusively, resulted in the declassification and publication of a large mass of documents, affidavits, and testimony concerning not only the immediate issue of enemy numbers but also the inner workings and personal feuds of the MACV intelligence staff. The Center of Military History possesses copies of the memorandums of law and affidavits assembled by both sides. These are:

U.S. District Court, Southern District of New York. *William C. Westmoreland, Plaintiff, v. CBS, Inc., et al., Defendants. 82 Civ. 7913 (PNL). Plaintiff General William C. Westmoreland's Memorandum of Law in Opposition to Defendant CBS's Motion to Dismiss and for Summary Judgment.*
———.*William C. Westmoreland, Plaintiff, v. CBS Inc., et al., Defendants. 82 Civ. 7913 (PNL). Memorandum in Support of Defendant CBS's Motion to Dismiss and for Summary Judgment.*
———. *William C. Westmoreland, Plaintiff, v. CBS Inc., et al., Defendants. 82 Civ. 7913 (PNL). Plaintiff's Counter-Statement of Undisputed Material Facts Pursuant to Local Rule 3(g) and Appendix B—Important Documents Cited in Support of Plaintiff's Opposition to Defendant's Motion.*

Bibliographical Note

In addition, the testimony and documents of the trial are available on microfiche as *Vietnam: A Documentary Collection—Westmoreland v. CBS*. Broomfield, Colo.: Clearwater Publishing Company, Inc., 1985. Copies of this collection exist, among other places, in the Library of Congress and the Military History Institute. The original documents are in the National Archives.

Two sets of studies prepared under Department of the Army auspices contain primary elements. The first series, the Vietnam Studies, consists of monographs by active and retired Army officers who served in Southeast Asia on subjects of which they had special knowledge. While authored in some instances by subordinates instead of the principals, these studies provide information on many aspects of the war. The monographs of most use in this study were:

Eckhardt, George S. *Command and Control, 1950–1969*. Washington, D.C.: Department of the Army, 1974.

Kelley, Francis J. *U.S. Army Special Forces, 1961–1971*. Washington, D.C.: Department of the Army, 1973.

Larsen, Stanley R., and Collins, James L., Jr., *Allied Participation in Vietnam*. Washington, D.C.: Department of the Army, 1975.

McChristian, Joseph A. *The Role of Military Intelligence, 1965–1967*. Washington, D.C.: Department of the Army, 1974.

Rienzi, Thomas M. *Communications-Electronics, 1962–1970*. Washington, D.C.: Department of the Army, 1972.

Tolson, John J. *Airmobility, 1961–1971*. Washington, D.C.: Department of the Army, 1973.

The second set of studies, the Indochina Monographs, helps to fill in the South Vietnamese side of the history of the war. A series of twenty narratives prepared by former South Vietnamese, Cambodian, and Laotian military leaders under the supervision of Lt. Gen. William E. Potts, USA (Ret.) and the staff of the General Research Corporation, the monographs are based on records available to the authors but also include much personal comment and experience, thereby acquiring to some extent the character of primary documents. The Center of Military History published these studies for limited distribution and retains copies of them. For this volume, the following monographs were the most useful:

Truong, Ngo Quang. *RVNAF and U.S. Operational Cooperation and Coordination*. Washington, D.C.: U.S. Army Center of Military History, 1976.

Vien, Cao Van, et. al. *The U.S. Advisor*. Washington, D.C.: U.S. Army Center of Military History, 1980.

Since the end of the Cold War, published source documents on the North Vietnamese and Viet Cong conduct of the Vietnam conflict are gradually becoming available. The Center of Military History is accumulating a growing body of translated official *People's Army of Vietnam* operational histories. While highly propagandistic in some respects, especially their handling of statistics, these histories contain valuable information on enemy plans, order of battle, and combat operations. Of more direct use in preparing this history of MACV were translations of two other accounts from the revolutionary side which treat high level policy and strategy. They are:

Tra, Tran Van. *History of the Bulwark B2 Theater*. Vol 5. *Concluding the Thirty-Years War*. Ho Chi Minh City, Vietnam, 1982. Trans. by Foreign Broadcast Information Service. Joint Publications Research Service, Southeast Asia Report no. 1247, 1983.

War Experiences Recapitulation Committee of the High-Level Military Institute. *Vietnam: The Anti-U.S. Resistance War for National Salvation, 1954–1975: Military Events*. Hanoi: People's Army Publishing House, 1980. Trans. by Joint Publications Research Service. Doc no. 80968, 1982.

Published Official Histories

U.S. Army

The Center of Military History's U.S. Army in Vietnam series currently consists of eight published works, including a pictorial volume, with additional volumes in progress. The following have been published:

Bergen, John D. *Military Communications: A Test for Technology*. Washington, D.C.: U.S. Army Center of Military History, 1986.

Carland, John M. *Combat Operations: Stemming the Tide, May 1965 to October 1966*. Washington, D.C.: U.S. Army Center of Military History, 2000.

Clarke, Jeffrey J. *Advice and Support: The Final Years*. Washington, D.C.: U.S. Army Center of Military History, 1988.

Hammond, William M. *Public Affairs: The Military and the Media, 1962–1968*. Washington, D.C.: U.S. Army Center of Military History, 1988.

———. *Public Affairs: The Military and the Media, 1968–1973*. Washington, D.C.: U.S. Army Center of Military History, 1996.

MacGarrigle, George L. *Combat Operations: Taking the Offensive, October 1966 to October 1967*. Washington, D.C.: U.S. Army Center of Military History, 1998.

Meyerson, Joel D. *Images of a Lengthy War*. Washington, D.C.: U.S. Army Center of Military History, 1986.

Spector, Ronald H. *Advice and Support: The Early Years, 1941–1961*. Washington, D.C.: U.S. Army Center of Military History, 1983.

U.S. Air Force

The Office of Air Force History is publishing its own series, The United States Air Force in Southeast Asia, three volumes of which were drawn upon:

Bowers, Ray L. *Tactical Airlift*. Washington, D.C.: Office of Air Force History, 1983.

Futrell, Robert F. *The Advisory Years to 1965*. Washington, D.C.: Office of Air Force History, 1981.

Schlight, John. *The War in South Vietnam: The Years of the Offensive, 1965–1968*. Washington, D.C.: Office of Air Force History, 1988.

In addition, the author had access to an unpublished study, Wayne Thompson's "From Rolling Thunder to Linebacker: The Air War over North Vietnam, 1966–1973." This study has now been published as *To Hanoi and Back: The U.S. Air Force and North Vietnam, 1966–1973*. Washington, D.C.: Smithsonian Institution Press, 2000.

U.S. Navy

Two volumes of the Naval Historical Center's series, The United States Navy and the Vietnam Conflict, have been published. The volume bearing on Military Assistance Command, Vietnam, is:

Marolda, Edward J. and Fitzgerald, Oscar P. *From Military Assistance to Combat, 1959–1965*. Washington, D.C.: Naval Historical Center, 1986.

The Naval Historical Center also has published an illustrated overview of the Navy's role in Southeast Asia:

Marolda, Edward J. *By Sea, Air, and Land: An Illustrated History of the U.S. Navy and the War in Southeast Asia*. Washington, D.C.: Naval Historical Center, 1994.

U.S. Marine Corps

The Marine Corps History and Museums Division has completed publication of its chronological series on U.S. Marines in Vietnam. The following volumes were consulted in the preparation of this study:

Shulimson, Jack and Johnson, Charles M. *The Landing and the Buildup, 1965*. Washington, D.C.: History and Museums Division, Headquarters, U.S. Marine Corps, 1978.

Shulimson, Jack. *An Expanding War, 1966*. Washington, D.C.: History and Museums Division, Headquarters, U.S. Marine Corps, 1982.

Telfer, Gary L.; Rogers, Lane; and Fleming, V. Keith. *Fighting the North Vietnamese, 1967*. Washington, D.C.: History and Museums Division, Headquarters, U.S. Marine Corps, 1984.

Whitlow, Robert H. *The Advisory and Combat Assistance Era, 1954–1964*. Washington, D.C.: History and Museums Division, Headquarters, U.S. Marine Corps, 1977.

Largely superceded by the chronological volumes but still useful is:

The Marines in Vietnam, 1954–1973: An Anthology and Annotated Bibliography. Washington, D.C.: History and Museums Division, Headquarters, U.S. Marine Corps, 1974.

MACV: The Years of Escalation, 1962–1967

Joint History Office

Cole, Ronald H.; Poole, Walter S.; Schnabel, James F.; Watson, Robert J.; and Webb, Willard J. *The History of the Unified Command Plan, 1946–1993*. Washington, D.C.: Joint History Office, Office of the Chairman of the Joint Chiefs of Staff, 1995.

Secondary Works

Books and Articles

Adams, Sam. *War of Numbers: An Intelligence Memoir*. South Royalton, Vt.: Steerforth Press, 1994.

Berman, Larry. *Planning a Tragedy: The Americanization of the War in Vietnam*. New York: W. W. Norton and Company, 1982.

Blaufarb, Douglas S. *The Counterinsurgency Era: U.S. Doctrine and Performance, 1950 to the Present*. New York: The Free Press, 1977.

Borklund, C. W. *The Department of Defense*. New York: Frederick A. Praeger, 1968.

Brownlee, Romie L. and Mullen, William J., III. *Changing an Army: An Oral History of General William E. DePuy, USA Retired*. Washington, D.C.: U.S. Army Military History Institute and U.S. Army Center of Military History, 1988.

Cardwell, Thomas A. *Command Structure for Theater Warfare: The Quest for Unity of Command*. Maxwell AFB, Ala.: Air University Press, 1984.

Davidson, Phillip B. *Secrets of the Vietnam War*. Novato, Calif.: Presidio Press, 1990.

———. *Vietnam at War: The History, 1946–1975*. New York: Oxford University Press, 1988.

Duiker, William J. *The Communist Road to Power in Vietnam*. Boulder, Colo.: The Westview Press, Inc., 1981.

Ford, Harold P. *CIA and the Vietnam Policymakers: Three Episodes, 1962–1968*. Washington, D.C.: Center for the Study of Intelligence, Central Intelligence Agency, 1998.

Furgerson, Ernest B. *Westmoreland: The Inevitable General*. Boston: Little, Brown and Company, 1968.

Gelb, Leslie H. and Betts, Richard K. *The Irony of Vietnam: The System Worked*. Washington, D.C.: Brookings Institution, 1979.

Halberstam, David. *The Best and the Brightest*. New York: Random House, 1972.

———. *The Making of a Quagmire*. New York: Random House, 1972.

Hammer, Ellen J. *A Death in November: America in Vietnam, 1963*. New York: E. P. Dutton, 1987.

Hannah, Norman B. *The Key to Failure: Laos and the Vietnam War*. New York: Madison Books, 1987.

Herring, George C. *America's Longest War: The United States and Vietnam, 1950–1975*. New York: Wiley, 1979.

———. "'Peoples Quite Apart': Americans, South Vietnamese, and the War in Vietnam." *Diplomatic History* 14 (Winter 1990): 1–23.

———. *"Cold Blood": LBJ's Conduct of Limited War in Vietnam*. The Harmon Memorial Lectures in Military History, Number Thirty-Three. Colorado Springs, Colo.: U.S. Air Force Academy, 1990.

Hilsman, Roger. *To Move a Nation: The Politics of Foreign Policy in the Administration of John F. Kennedy*. Garden City, N.Y.: Doubleday and Company, Inc., 1967.

Hunt, Richard A. *Pacification: The American Struggle for Vietnam's Hearts and Minds*. Boulder, Colo.: Westview Press, 1995.

Jones, Bruce. *War Without Windows: A True Account by a Young Army Officer Trapped in an Intelligence Cover-Up in Vietnam*. New York: Vanguard Press, 1987.

Kahin, George McT. *Intervention: How America Became Involved in Vietnam*. New York: Alfred A. Knopf, 1986.

Kinnard, Douglas. *The War Managers*. Hanover, N.H.: The University Press of New England, 1977.

Komer, Robert W. *Bureaucracy Does Its Thing: Institutional Constraints on U.S.-GVN Performance in Vietnam*. Santa Monica, Calif.: The Rand Corporation, 1973.

McMaster, H. R. *Dereliction of Duty: Lyndon Johnson, Robert McNamara, the Joint Chiefs of Staff, and the Lies That Led to Vietnam*. New York: Harper Collins, 1997.

McNamara, Robert S. with Brian VanDeMark. *In Retrospect: The Tragedy and Lessons of Vietnam*. New York: Times Books, 1995.

Momyer, William M. *Airpower in Three Wars*. Washington, D.C.: Department of the Air Force, 1978.

Nolting, Frederick. *From Trust to Tragedy: The Political Memoirs of Frederick Nolting, Kennedy's Ambassador to Diem's Vietnam*. New York: Praeger Publishers, 1988.

Oberdorfer, Don. *Tet!* Da Capo Edition. New York: Da Capo Press, Inc., 1984.

Palmer, Bruce. *The 25-Year War: America's Military Role in Vietnam*. Lexington: The University Press of Kentucky, 1984.

Pike, Douglas. "The Other Side." *The Wilson Quarterly* (Summer 1983): 114–124.

———. *PAVN: People's Army of Vietnam*. Novato, Calif.: Presidio Press, 1986.

———. *Viet Cong: The Organization and Techniques of the National Liberation Front of South Vietnam*. Cambridge, Mass.: The M.I.T. Press, 1966.

———. *Vietnam and the Soviet Union: Anatomy of an Alliance*. Boulder, Colo.: Westview Press, 1987.

Porter, Gareth, ed. *Vietnam: The Definitive Documentation of Human Decisions*. 2 vols. Stanfordville, N.Y.: Earl M. Coleman Enterprises, Inc., 1979.

Rostow, Walt W. *The Diffusion of Power: An Essay in Recent History*. New York: The Macmillan Company, 1972.
Rust, William J. and the Editors of *U.S. News* Books. *Kennedy in Vietnam*. New York: Charles Scribner's Sons, 1985.
Schlight, John, ed. *Second Indochina War Symposium: Papers and Commentary*. Washington, D.C.: U.S. Army Center of Military History, 1986.
Scoville, Thomas W. *Reorganizing for Pacification Support*. Washington, D.C.: U.S. Army Center of Military History, 1982.
Shapley, Deborah. *Promise and Power: The Life and Times of Robert McNamara*. Boston: Little, Brown, and Company, 1993.
Sharp, Ulysses S. G. *Strategy for Defeat: Vietnam in Retrospect*. San Rafael, Calif.: Presidio Press, 1978.
Sheehan, Neil. *A Bright Shining Lie: John Paul Vann and America in Vietnam*. New York: Random House, 1988.
Smith, Ralph B. *An International History of the Vietnam War*. Vol. 1. *Revolution versus Containment, 1955–1961*. New York: St. Martin's Press, 1983.
———. *An International History of the Vietnam War*. Vol. 2. *The Kennedy Strategy*. New York: St. Martin's Press, 1985.
Sorley, Lewis. *Thunderbolt: General Creighton Abrams and the Army of His Times*. New York: Simon and Schuster, 1992.
Stevenson, Charles A. *The End of Nowhere: American Policy Toward Laos Since 1954*. Boston: Beacon Press, 1972.
Taylor, Maxwell D. *Swords and Ploughshares*. New York: W. W. Norton and Co., Inc., 1972.
Thayer, Thomas C. *How To Analyze a War Without Fronts: Vietnam 1965–1972. Journal of Defense Research*. Series B, Tactical Warfare Analysis of Vietnam Data, 7B, no. 3, Fall 1975.
Thies, Wallace J. *When Governments Collide: Coercion and Diplomacy in the Vietnam Conflict, 1964–1968*. Berkeley and Los Angeles: University of California Press, 1980.
Turley, William S. *The Second Indochina War: A Short Political and Military History, 1954–1975*. New York: New American Library, 1987.
Westmoreland, William C. *A Soldier Reports*. Garden City, N.Y.: Doubleday and Company, 1976.
Zaffiri, Samuel. *Westmoreland: A Biography of General William C. Westmoreland*. New York: William Morrow and Company, Inc., 1994.

Unpublished Secondary Works

Barlow, Jeffrey G. "President John F. Kennedy and His Joint Chiefs of Staff." PhD Dissertation. University of South Carolina, 1981.
Dietrich, Steve E. "Corps-Level Command-and-Control in an Unconventional Conflict: U.S. Army Field Forces in Vietnam."

Bibliographical Note

Unpublished MS. Military Studies Branch, U.S. Army Center of Military History, 1989.

Hermes, Walter. "Department of the Army: The Buildup." Unpublished MS. Washington, D.C.: U.S. Army Center of Military History, n.d.

Latimer, Thomas K. "Hanoi's Leaders and their South Vietnam Policies, 1954–1968." PhD Dissertation. Georgetown University, 1972.

Lewis, Thomas J. "Year of the Hare: Bureaucratic Distortion in the U.S. Military View of the Vietnam War in 1963." MA Thesis. George Washington University, 1972.

Meyerson, Joel. "Logistics in the Buildup" and "Logistics of an Open-Ended War." Unpublished Papers. U.S. Army Center of Military History, 1989.

Rosson, Gen William B. "Four Periods of American Involvement in Vietnam: Development and Implementation of Policy, Strategy and Programs, Described and Analyzed on the Basis of Service Experience at Progressively Senior Levels." PhD Thesis. New College, Oxford University, England, 1979.

Suplizio, Maj. Paul E. "A Study of the Military Support of Pacification in South Vietnam, April 1964–April 1965." Thesis. U.S. Army Command and General Staff College, 1966.

Von Luttichau, Charles. "The U.S. Army Role in the Conflict in Vietnam." MS. U.S. Army Center of Military History, 1964.

Glossary

ACTIV	Army Concept Team in Vietnam
ADVON	Advance Echelon
AID	Agency for International Development (U.S.)
ARPA	Advanced Research Projects Agency
ARVN	Army of the Republic of Vietnam
BLT	Battalion landing team
CDTC	Combat Development and Test Center
CIA	Central Intelligence Agency
CICV	Combined Intelligence Center, Vietnam
CIDG	Civilian Irregular Defense Group
CINCPAC	Commander in Chief, Pacific (U.S.)
COC	Combat Operations Center
COMUSMACV	Commander, U.S. Military Assistance Command, Vietnam
CORDS	Civil Operations and Revolutionary Development Support
COSVN	*Central Office for South Vietnam*
DCA	Defense Communications Agency
DCPG	Defense Communications Planning Group
DIA	Defense Intelligence Agency
DRV	Democratic Republic of Vietnam (North Vietnam)
FMFPAC	Fleet Marine Force, Pacific
HAWK	Homing All the Way Killer
HES	Hamlet Evaluation System
HSAS	Headquarters Support Activity, Saigon
IMAO	International Military Assistance Office
JAOC	Joint Air Operations Center
JGS	Joint General Staff (South Vietnamese)
JOEG-V	Joint Operational Evaluation Group–Vietnam

MACV: The Years of Escalation, 1962–1967

JTD	Joint Table of Distribution
JTF	Joint Task Force
JUSMAG	Joint U.S. Military Assistance Group
JUSPAO	Joint U.S. Public Affairs Office
KANZUS	Korea, Australia, New Zealand, United States forces
LAAM	Light Antiaircraft Missile
MAAG	Military Assistance Advisory Group (U.S.)
MACEVAL	MACV Operations Research/Systems Analysis Office
MACOI	MACV Office of Information
MACV	Military Assistance Command, Vietnam
MAF	Marine Amphibious Force
MAG	Marine aircraft group
MAP	Military Assistance Program
MEB	Marine Expeditionary Brigade
MEF	Marine Expeditionary Force
NAVFORV	(U.S.) Naval Forces, Vietnam
NCO	Noncommissioned officer
NLF	National Liberation Front
NSAM	National Security Action Memorandum
OCO	Office of Civil Operations
PACAF	(U.S.) Pacific Air Forces
PACOM	Pacific Command (U.S.)
PAVN	*People's Army of Vietnam*
PERINTREP	Periodic Intelligence Report
PLAF	*People's Liberation Armed Forces*
PROVN	Program for the Pacification and Long-Term Development of South Vietnam
PRP	People's Revolutionary Party
R&R	Rest and recuperation
ROKFORV	Republic of Korea Forces, Vietnam
RVNAF	Republic of Vietnam Armed Forces
SAC	Strategic Air Command
SEACOORD	Coordinating Committee for U.S. Missions in Southeast Asia
SEATO	Southeast Asia Treaty Organization
SITREP	Situation Report
SLF	Special Landing Force

Glossary

SNIE	Special National Intelligence Estimate
SOG	Studies and Observations Group
TACS	Tactical air control system
TAOR	Tactical area of responsibility
TASE	Tactical air support element
TF	Task Force
USAID	U.S. Agency for International Development
USARPAC	United States Army, Pacific
USARYIS	U.S. Army, Ryukyu Islands
USASCV	U.S. Army Support Command, Vietnam
USASGV	U.S. Army Support Group, Vietnam
USFV	United States Forces, Vietnam
USIA	United States Information Agency
USIS	United States Information Service
USMACTHAI	U.S. Military Assistance Command, Thailand
USOM	United States Operations Mission
VNAF	(South) Vietnamese Air Force
VNSF	(South) Vietnamese Special Forces

Military Map Symbols

Function

Airborne Infantry	⊠
Airmobile Infantry	⊠
Armored Cavalry	⊘
Infantry	⊠
Marine Infantry	⊠

Size

Regiment	I I I
Brigade	X
Division	X X
Corps	X X X

Examples

1st Brigade, 101st Airborne Division   1 ⊠ 101

Headquarters, 1st Cavalry Division (Airmobile)   ⊠ 1 CAV

Index

Abrams, General Creighton W., Jr., 277–78, 289, 326, 362, 456
Accelerated Model Plan, 81
Adams, Maj. Gen. Milton B., 57, 174
Administrative control
  defined, 63*n*
Advance Echelon (ADVON), 326–27
Advanced Research Projects Agency (ARPA), 46, 50–52, 66*n*, 127, 293
Agency for International Development (AID), 21, 172, 363
Air defense missiles, 169, 170–71, 176–77, 183*n*
Air Force, Eighth
  command of, 325–26
Air Force, Seventh
  command of, 320–23
Air Force Test Unit, 127
Air offensive
  command of, 323–30
  increased campaign in South Vietnam, 230–32
  against North Vietnam in 1965, 172–80
Air Support Operations Centers (ASOC), 59
Airborne Brigade, 173d, 218, 234, 236, 249
Airborne Division, 101st, 234, 236, 245
Aircraft
  B–52 heavy bombers, 231–32, 325–27
  B–26 light bomber, 58
  duplication of services, 56, 68*n*
  F–4B Phantom II, 199
  Stratofortresses, 231
  T–28 fighter-bombers, South Vietnamese, 58
Airmobility controversy, 56–60, 68*n*
Allen, George, 452
Allies. *See also* specific country by name.
  counterinsurgency strategy, 75–85
  operations coordination, 343–48
Anderson, Admiral George W., Jr., 37–38, 53

Anthis, Brig. Gen. Rollen H., 55–59, 134
Antiaircraft missiles, 169, 170–71, 176–77, 183*n*
Antiwar protests, 441–45
Ap Bac battle, 86, 91
Armed Forces Council, 144
Armed Forces of the Republic of Vietnam. *See* Republic of Vietnam Armed Forces (RVNAF).
Armed Forces Radio station, 129
Army Concept Team in Vietnam (ACTIV), 50, 56–57, 127
Army-Navy Mobile Riverine Force, 312–13
Army of the Republic of Vietnam (ARVN), 11, 82–83, 86–87, 190–92, 420–22
Army Special Forces, 15, 16, 18, 78
Associated States of Indochina, 7
Australia
  allied force troops, 343
  KANZUS force, 164
  Westmoreland's operational control over forces, 248, 344

Back Porch, 282–83
Ball, George, 237–38, 244
Bankson, Col. Roger, 129
Bao Dai, Emperor, 6–10
Battalion landing teams (BLT), 178
Bien Hoa Air Base, 159, 172
Binh Gia ambush, 194
Binh Xuyen, 9, 10
Blackburn, Col. Donald D., 375–76
Bonesteel, General Charles, 348
Brink Hotel bombing, 172
British Advisory Mission, 76
Brown, Dr. Harold, 51
Brownfield, Brig. Gen. Albert R., 289
Buddhists
  conflict with Diem, 88, 93, 97
  riots against U.S. in 1965, 144
  self-immolation, 89
Buddhists' General Association, 88

Bundy, McGeorge, 122, 173–74, 189, 210, 237
Bunker, Ellsworth, 354, 356, 360, 388
Bureau of Intelligence and Research (INR), 446

Cam Ranh Bay complex, 245–47
Cambodia
  command relationships, 379–82
  enemy-controlled areas, 373–74
Cao Dai, 9, 10, 12, 121
Carver, George, 452, 454–57, 472*n*
Cavalry Division, 1st, 240, 245–46, 249
Central Committee of the Vietnam Workers' Party, 121
Central Intelligence Agency (CIA), 15, 21, 78–79, 103, 160, 375, 446–61
Central Office for South Vietnam (COSVN), 14, 71, 72, 74, 87, 408, 466–67
Central Pacification Committee, 141
Central Party Military Affairs Committee, 467–68
Chae Myung Shin, General, 248–49, 345–46
Chaisson, Brig. Gen. John R., 279
Chapman, General Leonard D., 334
CHIEN THANG plan, 139, 141, 190–95, 427
Civil Guard, 16, 86, 135
Civil Operations and Revolutionary Development Support (CORDS), 361–64
Civilian Irregular Defense Groups (CIDGs), 78–79, 80, 136, 145–46
Collins, Brig. Gen. James L., 289
Collins, General James F., 54, 214–15
Collins, Maj. Gen. William R., 310
Combat Development and Test Center (CDTC), 50, 51
Combat Operations Center (COC), 127, 278–79, 297–98
Combined Action Program, 402
Combined Campaign Plans, 351, 400, 463
Combined Document Exploitation Center, 287
Combined Intelligence Center, Vietnam (CICV), 287, 325, 449
Combined Materiel Exploitation Center, 287
Combined Military Interrogation Center, 286
Combined Planning Section, 165–66
Comintern, 5
Commander, Military Assistance Command, Vietnam (COMUSMACV), 24, 27, 39

Commander, Republic of Korea Forces, Vietnam, 248
Commander in Chief, Pacific Fleet (CINCPACFLT), 53
Commander in Chief, U.S. Forces, Pacific (CINCPAC), 11, 27, 37–38, 167
Commander, U.S. Military Assistance Command, Thailand (COMUSMACTHAI), 39–40, 372
Commander, U.S. Military Assistance Command, Vietnam/Thailand (COMUSMAC, Vietnam/Thailand), 40
Communications system, 282–83
Communist International, 5
Communist Party. *See* Vietnam Workers' Party.
Communist Party Central Committee, 13, 14
Comprehensive Plan for South Vietnam, 80–81, 99, 100
Computerized data management, 292
"Concept of Operations in the Republic of Vietnam," 249–50
Construction Directorate, 282
Construction program, 281–82
Cook, Col. Robert M., 284
Coordinating authority defined, 339*n*
Coordinating Committee for U.S. Missions in Southeast Asia (SEACOORD), 163–64, 376–77, 382
CORDS, 357–64. *See also* Pacification.
Counterinsurgency Plan, 16, 75
Counterintelligence Advisory Committee, 128
Current Intelligence and Indications Center, 128
Cushman, Lt. Gen. Robert E., 334

Da Nang, dispatch of Marine Expeditionary Brigade to, 177–80
Data Management Agency, 292
Davidson, Maj. Gen. Phillip B., 452–55
De Gaulle, Charles, 118
De Saussure, Brig. Gen. Edward H., 346
Decker, General George W., 47
Defense Communications Agency (DCA), 283
Defense Communications Planning Group (CDPG), 423, 425
Defense Communications System, 283
Defense Intelligence Agency (DIA), 72, 446
Defense Research and Engineering, Deputy for (DDR&E), 66*n*

Index

Democratic Republic of Vietnam (DRV)
    establishment of, 6, 8
DePuy, Brig. Gen. William E., 138, 146, 190, 242, 252–54, 276, 279, 330
Detachment 7, 55
Diem, Ngo Dinh
    acceptance of British counterinsurgency plan, 76–77
    conflict with Buddhist movement, 88, 93, 97
    death of, 104
    establishment of ground forces chain of command, 82–83
    Harkins support of, 90–91
    impact of U.S. command creation, 21, 24, 26–28
    increased U.S. assistance during 1960s, 15–16, 18–19
    Kennedy's expectations, 20
    leadership style, 86–88
    military coup against, 95–106
    National Internal Security Council, 75
    presidential election, 10
    Presidential Survey Office, 78
    as Prime Minister, 9
    strategic hamlet plan, 78
    uprisings against regime, 13–15
    U.S. advisory group actions, 10–12
Dien Huong pacification plan, 139
Directorate of Intelligence, 129
Disosway, Lt. Gen. Gabriel P., 68*n*
DMZ Front Command, 280
Don, Maj. Gen. Tran Van, 95, 99–100, 102–05
"DOVE" unit, 343, 345
Dulles, John Foster, 8
Dunn, Lt. Col. John M., 151*n*
Dunn, Maj. Gen. Carroll H., 281–82, 298
Durbrow, Elbridge, 21, 95

Easterbrook, Maj. Gen. Ernest F., 372
Eighth Air Force, command of, 325–26
Eisenhower, Dwight D., 8, 9–10, 187, 316
Engineer's Office, 281
Engler, Lt. Gen. Jean E., 315, 318
Enthoven, Alain, 418
Explosion Plan, 82

5th Special Forces Group (Airborne), 136
Far East Command, 37
Farm Gate unit, 55, 56, 58, 89, 134, 162, 165, 167
Felt, Admiral Harry D.
    mediation of air power control debate, 59

Felt, Admiral Harry D.—*Continued*
    objection to McNamara's MACV headquarters plan, 37–38
    opposition to eliminating the MAAG, 125–26
    as PACOM commander, 21, 27, 35, 41–42, 50–51, 55
    proposal for COMUSMAC, Thailand/Vietnam formation, 39–40
    reorganization of MAAG headquarters, 43–44
    Research and Evaluation Division proposal, 52
Field Force Vietnam, 247, 248, 331–34
Fleet Marine Force Pacific (FMFPAC), 312
Flexible Response strategy, 36
Forrestal, Michael, 96, 123, 124
Forsythe, Maj. Gen. George, 362
Foster, Dr. John W., 293
France
    beginnings of antagonism in Vietnam, 5
    cease-fire agreement with Viet Minh, 8
    mutual assistance pact with U.S. in Indochina, 7
    war with Viet Minh beginning in 1946, 6–7
Free World Military Assistance Office, 344
Freund, Brig. Gen. John F., 289, 352

Gavin, General James M., 443
General Offensive Campaign Plan, 83, 85
General Offensive–General Uprising, 466–67
Geneva Conference, 7–8
Geographically Phased National Level Operation Plan for Counterinsurgency, 75
Giap, Vo Nguyen, 71
Godding, Brig. Gen. George, 455, 457
Graham, Col. Daniel O., 452–53
Green Berets, 136
Greene, General Wallace M., Jr., 207, 312, 333
Ground troop commitment
    collapse of the Chien Thang plan, 190–95
    command questions, 212–19
    concept of operations questions, 212–19
    decisions from 1966 Honolulu conference, 256–59
    implementing Phase I, 245–51

515

Ground troop commitment—*Continued*
  increase in reinforcements, 232–45
  limited response, 195–200
  movement into ground war, 206–12
  Phase I Add-ons, 251
  Phase II planning, 252–56
  plans and proposals, 1954–1964, 187–90
  proposals for sending troops, 200–206
Group 559, 73
Group 759, 73

Halberstam, David, 94
Hamlet Evaluation System (HES), 291, 292
Hamscher, Col. George, 455
Harkins, Gen. Paul Donal
  acceptance of Khanh's coup, 119
  air power control debate, 56–59
  assumption of duties as MACV commander, 3
  career background, 3, 38–39
  component commands, 53–56, 483–84
  Comprehensive Plan for South Vietnam, 80–81
  concerns related to the strategic hamlet project, 77
  conflict with Lodge, 100–103, 122–23
  criticism of U.S. action in overthrow of Diem, 105–06
  McNamara's nomination as MACV commander, 24
  National Campaign Plan, 81–82
  opposition to eliminating the MAAG, 125
  opposition to escalation of war, 158
  optimism concerning progress of the war, 91–92
  recommendations for MACV staff, 46–49
  reorganization of MAAG headquarters, 43–44
  Research and Evaluation Division proposal, 52
  responsibilities as MACV commander, 26–28, 35, 39–42, 45, 50–52
  retirement of, 123
  support of Diem regime, 90–91, 101–02
  support of pressure to remove Nhu from Diem's regime, 97–98, 100
Harriman, W. Averell, 96
Harris, General Hunter, 321
HAWK battalions, 169, 170–71, 176–77, 183n
Hawkins, Col. Gains, 454

Headquarters Area Command, 312
Headquarters Support Activity, Saigon (HSAS), 53, 170, 312
Heintges, Lt. Gen. John A., 277, 296, 302n
Helms, Richard, 451, 457, 472n
High National Council, 144
Hilsman, Roger, 96
Ho Chi Minh
  beginnings of antagonism with France, 5–6
  establishment of Democratic Republic of Vietnam, 6
Ho Chi Minh Trail, 13–14, 18, 73, 373–79
Hoa Hao, 9, 10, 12, 121
Honolulu conference
  order of battle determination, 447–48
  Phase II planning decisions, 256–59
Howze, Lt. Gen. Hamilton H., 68n
Humphrey, Hubert, 461
Huong, Tran Van, 144
Hyland, Vice Admiral John J., 314

Indochina Military Assistance Advisory Group, 7, 9–10
Infantry Division, 1st, 234, 245, 249
Information and Reports Working Group, 130
Integrated Wideband Communications System, 282
Intelligence agencies, 127–29
Intelligence Collection Plan, 128
Intelligence Directorate, 284, 286, 290, 454
Intelligence system, 284–88
Interagency Committee on Province Rehabilitation, 77
International Military Assistance Office (IMAO), 127, 344

Johnson, Capt. William R., 93
Johnson, General Harold K., 200–202, 205, 207, 244, 315, 320
Johnson, Lyndon B.
  authorization of ground troop commitment, 208, 212
  authorization of ground troop reinforcement, 240, 243–44
  commitment to pacification, 353, 360
  conference with McNamara and Taylor, 166
  consideration of ground troop commitment, 189

Index

Johnson, Lyndon B.—*Continued*
consideration of Westmoreland's request for increase in ground troops, 237–39
decision against mobilization of reserves, 244–45, 253
efforts to level off the war, 461–66
escalation of war in 1964, 157–58
Honolulu Conference, 1966, 256–58
implementing Phase I of ground troop reinforcement, 245–51
Khanh regime support, 119
order for removal of dependents from South Vietnam, 176
public relations aspect of war, 441–45
relationship with Westmoreland, 308–09
Johnson, U. Alexis, 141, 233
Joint Air-Ground Operations System, 328
Joint Air Operations Center (JAOC), 57, 58, 59
Joint Airlift Allocation Board, 57
Joint Chiefs of Staff (JCS), 22–24, 135, 169–70, 206–07, 209, 233–34, 307–10
Joint General Staff, South Vietnamese (JGS), 11, 50, 82–83, 85, 100, 129, 268, 351–52
Joint Operational Evaluation Group, 46, 60
Joint Operational Evaluation Group–Vietnam (JOEG-V), 50, 51, 127
Joint Operations Center, 83, 104
Joint Personnel Recovery Center, 375
Joint Research and Testing Agency, 127, 293
Joint Table of Distribution (JTD), 46, 132, 150*n*, 268, 296
Joint Task Force 116 (JTF 116), 39–40
Joint U.S. Military Assistance Group (JUSMAG), 39
Joint U.S. Public Affairs Office (JUSPAO), 363
Jones, Brig. Gen. William K., 278, 279, 298

KANZUS force, 164
Kennedy, John F.
assasination of, 106
civilian-military command creation in South Vietnam, 21–29
consideration of ground troop commitment, 187–88
counterinsurgency plan for South Vietnam, 16–20
creation of USMACTHAI, 39

Kennedy, John F.—*Continued*
differences among administration concerning coup against Diem, 96–99
reneutralization plan in Laos, 17–18
support of military coup against Diem, 99–100, 103
Kerwin, Maj. Gen. Walter T., 277, 362
Khan, Lt. Gen. Le Nghen, 350
Khanh, Maj. Gen. Nguyen, 118–19, 139, 141–42, 144–45, 167, 174, 190
Khiem, Maj. Gen. Tran Thien, 119
Khruschev, Nikita S., 122
Knowlton, Brig. Gen. William A., 359
Komer, Robert W., 357, 358, 360–63, 439–40, 453–56
Korea
KANZUS force, 164
Westmoreland's operational control over forces, 248–49
Korean Capital Division, 245
Krulak, Lt. Gen. Victor H., 330, 333, 403–04
Ky, Marshal Nguyen Cao, 145, 212, 229–30, 237, 242, 256–57, 353–57

Lansdale, Brig. Gen. Edward G., 357
Lao Dong Central Committee and Politburo, 71–72
Lao Dong (Communist) Party of North Vietnam, 71, 73, 467
Laos
air war planning, 164–67
enemy-controlled areas, 373–74
U.S. air and ground operations, 161–64
U.S. air campaign, 374–76
U.S. reneutralization plan, 17–18
Larsen, Maj. Gen. Stanley R., 248, 333, 345–46, 380
Lathram, L. Wade, 361
LeMay, General Curtis E., 47–48, 55, 135
Lemnitzer, General Lyman W., 24–25, 28
Light Antiaircraft Missile Battalion (LAAM), 171, 177
Loc, General Vinh, 248
Lodge, Henry Cabot, 95–103, 122–24, 141–42, 151*n*, 242, 353–54, 357–58
Logistical Command, 1st, 246, 273, 312
Logistics Directorate, 282
Loi, Col. Ho Van, 286
Long Binh headquarters, 317
Lotz, Brig. Gen. Walter E., Jr., 283, 297

517

MacArthur, General Douglas, 316
McChristian, Maj. Gen. Joseph A., 284–86, 296, 448–50, 452–54
McCone, John A., 79
McConnell, General John P., 207, 236–37, 255, 321–23
McCutcheon, Brig. Gen. Keith B., 328
McGarr, Lt. Gen. Lionel C.
   as chief of MAAG, 21, 23
   counterinsurgency recommendation in War Zone D, 77
   opposition to command structure, 24–25, 45
   replacement by Maj. Gen. Timmes, 43
McGown, Maj. Gen. Hal D., 347
McMillan, Dr. William G., 293–94
McNamara, Robert S.
   conference with Johnson and Taylor, 166
   as director of Kennedy's Vietnam program, 20–26, 29
   dissatisfaction with MACV staff qualifications, 137
   ground troop commitment recommendations, 211–12
   Honolulu Conference, 1966, 258
   Khanh regime support, 118
   MACV command structure proposal, 37–38, 40, 47
   management style controversy, 36
   opposition to military escalation, 461–62
   plan to phase out MACV, 79–80
   presidency of the World Bank, 462
   recommendation to deemphasize ROLLING THUNDER campaign, 414–16
   recommendation for full implementation of Phase II plan, 254
   rejection of Comprehensive Plan for South Vietnam, 80–81
   rejection of McGarr's counterinsurgency recommendation in War Zone D, 77
   request for estimate of required troop reinforcements, 241–43, 411–12
   support of increase in ground troop reinforcement, 240–41
   support of plan to eliminate the MAAG, 125
   support for single pacification manager, 357
   transfer of Civilian Irregular Defense Program to MACV, 79
McNaughton, John, 179, 441

MACV Office of Information (MACCOI), 129, 132
MACV Operations Research/Systems Analysis Office (MACEVAL), 292–93
Mao Tse Tung, 71
Marine aircraft group (MAG), 186*n*
Marine Amphibious Force (MAF), III, 214, 218, 245–47, 310–12, 329, 331–34, 425–26
Marine Divisions
   3d, 234
   7th, 245, 249
Marine Expeditionary Brigade (MEB), 169–70, 177–80, 186*n*, 213, 217
Marine Expeditionary Force (MEF), 213–14
Martin, Graham, 347, 372
Massive Retaliation strategy, 36
Military Assistance Advisory Group, Vietnam, 10–11
Military Assistance Advisory Groups (MAAGs)
   Geographically Phased National Level Operation Plan for Counterinsurgency, 75
   Indochina, 7, 9–10
   relationship with Military Assistance Command, Vietnam, 42–44
   South Vietnam, 11–12, 15–16, 20–21
Military Assistance Command, Thailand (MACTHAI), 373
Military Assistance Command, Vietnam (MACV). *See also* Harkins, Gen. Paul Donal; Westmoreland, Lt. Gen. William C.
   advisory mission, 288–90, 481
   air power control debate, 56–60
   amenities for staff, 272
   campaign progress during 1962 and 1963, 85–86
   command structure, 60–62, 307–10, 479–83
   commander's responsibilities, 35
   component commands, 53–56
   Comprehensive Plan for South Vietnam, 80–81
   creation of, 24, 26–27, 29
   Executive Council, 138
   function of, 3, 35, 477
   headquarters expansion, 1965–1967, 267–75
   headquarters formation, 44–53
   headquarters reorganization and expansion, 125–39

Index

Military Assistance Command, Vietnam (MACV)—*Continued*
  initial strategy concept, 397–405
  intelligence system, 284–88
  joint command, 295–99
  operations planning and control, 275–84
  OPLAN 34A, 159–61, 164–67
  order of battle controversy, 446–61
  pacification role, 139–43, 478, 483
  place in Pacific chain of command, 36–41
  reinforcement of South Vietnam after Tonkin Gulf attacks, 167–72
  relationship with Military Assistance Advisory Groups, 42–44
  reporting, research, and analysis, 290–95
  Research and Evaluation Division proposal, 52
  Rolling Thunder campaign, 382–89, 478
  staff organization, 44–53, 133, 276
  strategy implementation problems, 405–11
  strategy questions, 395–97
  strength adjustments, 420–30
  support of military coup against Diem, 95–106
  troop strength strategy, 411–20
Military Assistance Program (MAP), 42–44, 78, 80–81, 126
Military Assistance Program Directorate, 288, 290
Military operations. *See* Operations, military.
Military Police, 172, 176
Military Revolutionary Council, 104, 119
Military Working Arrangement, 248–49
Minh, Maj. Gen. Duong Van, 82–83, 95–96, 98, 100, 104, 118–19
Ministry of Defense, 11
Ministry of Revolutionary Development, 353
Mission Council, 141
Mission Intelligence Committee, 233
Mobilization Directorate, 190
Model M plan, 81
Momyer, Lt. Gen. William W., 323, 326–27, 330, 339*n*
Montagnards, 12, 145–47
Montague, Maj. Robert, 143
Moore, Maj. Gen. Joseph H., 132, 134–35, 166–68, 296, 322, 329–30
Movement of MACV dependents out of Saigon, 272–73

National Campaign Plan, 81–82, 87, 92
National Front for the Liberation of South Vietnam (NLF), 14, 71, 72, 74, 118, 121
National Internal Security Council, 75
National Pacification Program, 345
National Police Force, 81, 192
National Security Action Memorandum (NSAM) 18, 52, 119–20, 157, 288
National Security Agency (NSA), 446
National Security Council, 141, 244
Nationalist Chinese, occupation of northern Indochina in 1945, 6
Naval Advisory Group, 310
Naval Forces, Vietnam (NAVFORV)
  command of, 310–14
New Life Hamlets, 139
New Zealand
  allied force troops, 343
  KANZUS force, 164
  Westmoreland's operational control of forces, 344
News media
  reports concerning U.S. role in war, 94
  Westmoreland's reorganization of the Public Information Office, 129–30
Nhu, Ngo Dinh, 76, 77, 87, 88, 95–97, 104
Nitze, Paul, 453
Nolting, Frederick E., 23–29, 55, 90, 93–94, 95
North Atlantic Treaty, 6
Norton, Brig. Gen. John, 315–16

O'Daniel, Lt. Gen. John W. ("Iron Mike"), 11
Office of Assistant Chief of Staff for Military Assistance, 290
Office of Civil Operations and Revolutionary Development Support (OCORDS), 361–64
Office of Civil Operations (OCO), 358–61
Office of the Inspector General, 283–84
Office of the Scientific Adviser, 294
Office of Special Assistant for Counterinsurgency and Special Activities (SACSA), 16
Operation Plan 37–64, 165, 168
Operation Plan 32 (OPLAN 32), 188
Operation Plan 34A (OPLAN 34A), 159–61, 164–67, 375
Operational control defined, 63*n*

519

Operations, military
- ARC LIGHT, 231–32, 325–27
- BARREL ROLL, 163, 374–75
- CEDAR FALLS, 407, 422
- DANIEL BOONE, 381
- DE SOTO, 167
- DORSAL FIN, 381
- DYE MARKER, 425
- FAIRFAX/RAND DONG, 352–53
- FLAMING DART, 172, 174
- FULL CRY, 378
- HIGH PORT, 378–79
- HOP TAC, 142–44, 191–92, 194, 197, 358
- ILLINOIS CITY, 437n
- JACKSTAY, 314
- JUNCTION CITY, 422
- LEAPING LENA, 161
- MARKET TIME, 310
- MOOSE, 272–273
- MUSCLE SHOALS, 425
- PRACTICE NINE, 425, 437n
- ROLLING THUNDER, 173, 175, 177, 205, 227, 243, 323, 382–89, 414–16, 423
- SHINING BRASS, 374, 377
- SLAM, 330
- SOUTHPAW, 378–79
- STARLITE, 249
- STEAM BATH, 382
- SUNRISE, 77
- SWITCHBACK, 79
- YANKEE TEAM, 162–63

Operations Analysis Section, 127
Operations Directorate, 290
Operations Research/Systems Analysis Office, 292–93
Osmanski, Brig. Gen. Frank A., 49, 170
Oum, Prince Boun, 17

Pacific Air Forces (PACAF), 55, 57, 321–23
Pacific Command, U.S. (PACOM)
  command relationships, 1967, 319
  contingency plans for Southeast Asia during the late 1950s, 15
  MACV command structure, 36–41
  Phase II planning conference, 253
  unified command structure, 22, 307–10
Pacific Fleet, 311–13
Pacification. *See also* CORDS.
  CHIEN THANG plan, 139, 141, 190–95, 427
  defined, 17
  DIEN HUONG pacification plan, 139

Pacification—*Continued*
  MACV's role in, 139–43
  Saigon politics and, 353–57
  U.S. policy after overthrow of Diem, 117–20
Pacification Committee, 140
Pacification Planning and Operations Branch, 127, 131
Pagoda raids, 88, 97
Palmer, General Bruce, 124, 289, 317, 318
Parry, Col. Francis F., 278–79
Pathet Lao, 8, 17–18, 73, 162
People's Army of Vietnam (PAVN), 122, 197, 405, 409
People's Liberation Armed Forces (PLAF), 14, 72, 74, 121, 249, 405, 409
People's Revolutionary Committees, 6
People's Revolutionary Party, 71
Periodic Intelligence Report (PERINTREP), 285
Philippines
  allied force troops, 343
  Westmoreland's operational control of forces, 344
Phoumi Nosavan, General, 17
Plain of Jars, 373–79
Plan 37, 165
Policy Planning Council, 428
Political Warfare Advisory Directorate, 288
Pomeroy, Col. Philip S., Jr., 49
Popular Forces, 191–92
Porter, William, 358–59
PRAIRIE FIRE zone, 377–79
Preparedness Investigating Subcommittee, 134
Press Relations Division, 129
Program Four, 412–14
Program Five, 417–19, 427
Program for the Pacification and Long-Term Development of South Vietnam (PROVN), 399, 401
Programs Evaluation Office, 17
Project 640, 290
Project MACONOMY, 426
Province Reports Center, 131
Province Studies Working Group, 130
Public Information Office, 127, 129
Public relations, 441–45, 484–85

Quat, Dr. Phan Huy, 144, 178, 206, 214, 229–30

Raborn, William, 237
Rasmussen, Maj. Gen. Henry A., 281

Index

Raymond, Morrison-Knudsen, Brown and Root, and J.A. Jones (RMK-BRJ), 268, 281
Reedy, George F., 239
Regional Communications Group, 283
Regional Forces, 191–92
Republic of Korea
  allied force troops, 343
  command of troops, 345–47
Republic of Korea Forces, Vietnam (ROKFORV), 345–46
Republic of Vietnam Armed Forces (RVNAF), 3, 11, 16, 80–81, 429–30
Republic of Vietnam Statistical Data Base, 130
Research Development Test and Evaluation, 51
Resolution Fourteen, 468
Revolutionary Development. *See* Pacification.
Revolutionary Development Support Directorate, 359, 361
Rhade Montagnard tribe, 146
Richardson, John, 93–94, 99
Ridgway, General Matthew B., 443–44
Rifles, AK–47, 193
Rosson, Maj. Gen. William B., 215, 243, 280
Rostow, Walt W., 16, 18–19, 389, 453
Rowney, Maj. Gen. Edward L., 56–57
Royal Laotian Air Force, 162
Royal Laotian Army, 17
Rusk, Dean, 20, 23–26, 29, 122, 237, 240, 257
Ryan, General John D., 231

2d Advance Echelon, Thirteenth Air Force (2d ADVON), 55
2d Air Division, 55–56
Seventh Air Force, command of, 320–27
Sackton, Maj. Gen. Frank J., 253
Second Indochina War, beginning of, 14
Self-Defense Corps, 86, 135
Senior Adviser's Monthly Report, 131
Sharp, Admiral Ulysses S. Grant
  air campaign command, 166–67, 328–30, 383–89
  clarification of Westmoreland's authority, 239–40
  disagreement with Westmoreland concerning air campaign, 174–75
  ground troop strategy, 178–79, 216–17, 411
  opposition to establishment of deputy COMUSMACV, 134, 135

Sharp, Admiral Ulysses S. Grant—*Continued*
  supervision of MACV activities, 307–09
Sides, Admiral John H., 53
SIGMA I–64, 165
Sihanouk, Prince Norodom, 379–82
Situation Reports (SITREPs), 279
Smart, General Jacob E., 321
Smith, Brig. Gen. Paul, 359
South Vietnam
  decline in Army's combat strength, 228
  MACV's advisory mission, 288–90
  Military Assistance Advisory Group, 11–12, 15–16, 20–21
  operations coordination, 348–53
  U.S. civilian-military command creation, 21–29
  U.S. counterinsurgency plan, 16–20
South Vietnamese Central Training Command, 288
South Vietnamese Joint General Staff, 43–44, 46, 54
South Vietnamese Special Forces, 136, 153*n*, 161–62
Southeast Asia Airlift System, 57, 58, 59
Southeast Asia Treaty Organization (SEATO), 10, 37, 40
Souvanna Phouma, Prince, 17–18, 161, 162–63, 376–77
Spears, Col. John H., 146
Special Assistant for Counterinsurgency and Special Activities, Office of (SACSA), 16
Special Forces, 15, 16, 18, 136, 146–47
Special Landing Force (SLF), 313–14
Special Liaison Officer, 357
Special National Intelligence Estimate (SNIE), 451–52, 454, 457–59
Special Operations Group, 160
Special Projects and Liaison, 129–30
Special Warfare Branch, 79
Stalin, Joseph, 7
Starbird, Gen. Alfred D., 423–24
STEEL TIGER zone, 374
Stennis, John, 134
Stilwell, Maj. Gen. Richard G., 103, 131–32, 138, 140–41, 347
Strategic Air Command (SAC), 231, 325–27
Strategic Communications Command, 283
Strategic hamlets, 76–78, 87, 93, 120. *See also* New Life Hamlets.
Studies and Observations Group (SOG), 127, 160, 374–75

521

Sullivan, William L., 163, 375–78
Suu, Phan Khac, 144, 229–30
Systems Analysis Division, 292
Systems Analysis Office, 292–93, 418, 426

Tactical air control system (TACS), 57, 59
Tactical Air Support Element (TASE), 324
Tactical area of responsibility (TAOR), 179, 218
Tam, General Tran Ngoc, 142–43
Tan Son Nhut facility, 270, 273
Target Research and Analysis Center, 128
Task Forces (TFs)
   115, 310
   116, 310
   117, 312–13
   Alpha, 247, 331
Taylor, General Maxwell D.
   acceptance of British counterinsurgency plan, 76
   approval of Harkin's appointment, 38
   as chairman of the Joint Chiefs of Staff, 41
   command creation proposals, 23, 25
   conference with Johnson and McNamara, 166
   counterinsurgency plan recommendations, 19–20
   ground troop commitment opposition, 189–90
   ground troop operations proposal, 216
   Khanh regime support, 118
   MACV reorganization support, 126
   Mission Council establishment, 141
   opposition to Phase II plan, 255
   opposition to Young Turks movement, 144–45
   recommendation for larger air campaign, 227
   recommendation for slow commitment of ground troops, 207–08, 210–11
   replacement of Lodge as ambassador in South Vietnam, 124
   support of increase in ground troops, 237
   support of Kennedy administration's counterinsurgency plan, 18–19
   support of marine landing in Da Nang, 178–79
Terrorism, 273

Thailand
   allied force troops, 343
   Military Assistance Command, Thailand (MACTHAI), 373
   Westmoreland's operational control of forces, 344
Thang, Col. Nguyen Duc, 190
Thi, Maj. Gen. Nguyen Chanh, 179, 355
Thich Tri Quang, 88
Thieu, General Nguyen Van, 212, 229–30, 237, 242, 256–57, 350, 353–57
Tho, Nguyen Ngoc, 96, 104
Thompson, Sir Robert G.K., 76–77
Throckmorton, Lt. Gen. John L., 131, 137, 177, 214, 277, 296, 302n
TIGER HOUND zone, 374, 377
Timmes, Maj. Gen. Charles, 28, 43
Tonkin Gulf engagements, 158, 166–67
Tra, General Tran Van, 408, 467
Training Directorate, 288
Troop Information division, 129
Trueheart, William, 103
Truman, Harry S.
   mutual assistance pact with France, 7
   policy of containment in Indochina, 6–7

Unger, Leonard, 161, 163
United States
   civilian-military command creation in South Vietnam, 21–29
   collective security pact for Southeast Asia, 10
   KANZUS force, 164
   Military Assistance Advisory Groups, 10–12
   mutual assistance pact with France in Indochina, 7
   policy after overthrow of Diem, 117–20
   response to Viet Cong insurgency during late 1950s and early 1960s, 15–20
United States Forces, Vietnam (USFV), 22–24
U.S. Agency for International Development (USAID), 21, 172, 363
U.S. Air Force, air power control debate, 56–60
U.S. Army
   air power control debate, 56–60
   field force command, 331–34
U.S. Army, Pacific (USARPAC), 38, 316
U.S. Army, Ryukyu Islands (USARYIS), 54
U.S. Army, Vietnam (USARV), 273, 289, 314–20

Index

U.S. Army Support Command, Vietnam (USASCV), 169, 183*n*, 314–15
U.S. Army Support Group, Vietnam (USASGV), 54
U.S. Department of Defense and Civilian Irregular Defense Groups, 79
U.S. Information Agency (USIA), 21, 128, 141
U.S. Military Assistance Command, Thailand (USMACTHAI), 39
U.S. Mission, 77–78, 139
U.S. Naval Forces Vietnam (NAVFORV), 312
U.S. Operations Mission (USOM), 15–16, 78, 128, 141
USS *Card*, 171
USS *Maddox*, 183*n*

Vance, Cyrus, 243
Vann, Lt. Col. John P., 93, 94
Vien, General Cao Van, 289, 345, 350–51
Viet Cong. *See* Vietnamese Communists.
Viet Minh
    beginnings of antagonism with France, 5–6
    breakdown of Diem's authority, 14
    cease-fire agreement with France, 8
    Diem's denunciation campaigns, 10
    establishment of Democratic Republic of Vietnam, 8
    war with France beginning in 1946, 6–7
Vietnam Coordinating Committee, 353
Vietnam Workers' Party, 14, 121
Vietnamese Advisory Division, 288
Vietnamese Air Force (VNAF), 56, 58, 89, 173, 174–75
Vietnamese Communists
    Diem's naming of, 14
    ground troop strength buildup, 228
    insurgency organization, 71–75
    offensive uprising, 466–69
    preparation for escalation of the war, 120–22
    terrorism aimed at MACV personnel and installations, 273
    U.S. response to insurgency during late 1950s and early 1960s, 15–20
Vietnamese Independence League. *See* Viet Minh.
Vietnamese National Army, 7
Vietnamese Special Forces (VNSF), 82, 99, 100, 162

Walt, Maj. Gen. Lewis W., 310, 312, 333, 402
War Room, 127

Ward, Rear Adm. Norvell G., 311
Waters, General John K., 315, 318
Weede, Maj. Gen. Richard G., 46–49, 81, 131
Westmoreland, Lt. Gen. William C.
    advisory team expansion, 136
    air offensive command, 323–26, 374–78
    career background, 123
    command coordination with Cambodia, 379–82
    command coordination with South Vietnamese, 348–53
    command fragmentation, 371–73, 389, 481–82
    comprehensive campaign plan, 249–50
    confidence in military progress in 1967, 439–40
    coordination of air and ground operations in Laos, 162–64, 166
    creation of deputy commander for air operations position, 135
    efforts toward pacification, 354–64
    ground troop command proposal, 214–15
    ground troop operations proposal, 216–19
    ground troop strategy, 395–410, 487–89
    Honolulu Conference, 1966, 258
    implementing Phase I of ground troop reinforcement, 245–51
    increased air campaign in South Vietnam, 230–32
    as intermediary for political stability, 145
    interpretation of Viet Cong strategy, 196–98
    involvement in air offensive against North Vietnam in 1965, 173–75
    joint command of MACV, 295–99
    joint command of U.S. troops, 307–10, 314–18, 320, 331–34
    leadership style, 137–38, 275–76, 485–87
    operational control over allied forces, 248–49, 344–45
    opposition of ground troop commitment, 189–90
    order of battle controversy, 449–50
    public relations concerns, 441–45, 484–85
    reaction to escalation of war, 158–59
    recommendations for ground troop commitment, 203–05, 209–12

Westmoreland, Lt. Gen. William C.—
Continued
  reinforcement of South Vietnam after Tonkin Gulf attacks, 167–72
  reorganization of the Public Information Office, 129–30
  replacement of Harkin's as MACV commander, 123–25
  request for increase in ground troops, 233–34, 236, 238–41
  request of troops for Phase II, 252–55
  role in pacification plan, 140–43
  ROLLING THUNDER campaign, 382–89
  staff rotation policies, 271–72
  support of Johnson's efforts to level off the war, 463–65, 490–92
  support of marine landing in Da Nang, 178–79

Westmoreland, Lt. Gen. William C.—
Continued
  support of plan to eliminate the MAAG, 125
Weyand, Lt. Gen. Frederick, 271, 404
Wheeler, General Earle G., 126, 135, 207, 233, 298, 309, 360, 386–87
Williams, Lt. Gen. Samuel T. ("Hanging Sam"), 11–12, 21
Wilson, Col. Jasper, 142
Wilton, Lt. Gen. John, 344
World Bank, McNamara's presidency of, 462

Yarborough, Maj. Gen. William P., 187
York, Brig. Gen. Robert H., 51, 60, 93
Young Turks, 144, 179
Youngdale, Brig. Gen. Carl A., 128–29, 296

Zorthian, Barry, 129, 439–40